NUMERICAL ANALYSIS

A PROGRAMMING APPROACH

VINAY VACHHARAJANI

BPB PUBLICATIONS

FIRST EDITION 2017

Copyright © BPB Publications, INDIA

ISBN :978-81-8333-551-5

Distributors:

BPB PUBLICATIONS
20, Ansari Road, Darya Ganj
New Delhi-110002
Ph: 23254990/23254991

BPB BOOK CENTRE
376 Old Lajpat Rai Market,
Delhi-110006
Ph: 23861747

COMPUTER BOOK CENTRE
12, Shrungar Shopping Centre,
M.G.Road, BENGALURU–560001
Ph: 25587923/25584641

DECCAN AGENCIES
4-3-329, Bank Street,
Hyderabad-500195
Ph: 24756967/24756400

MICRO MEDIA
Shop No. 5, Mahendra Chambers, 150
DN Rd. Next to Capital Cinema, V.T.
(C.S.T.) Station, MUMBAI-400 001 Ph:
22078296/22078297

Published by Manish Jain for BPB Publications, 20, Ansari Road, Darya Ganj, New Delhi-110002 and Printed him at Balaji Printer, New Delhi

PREFACE

In the present scenario where the knowledge of computer has become an absolute necessity, there has been an increasing desire for numerical answers to any applied problems. This has led to high demand for courses in numerical analysis. Many real world problems are solved first by converting them into mathematical models and then applying analytical methods to solve that model. In several cases, where ordinary analytical methods fail, numerical methods can give the result.

This book is divided into twelve chapters. Chapter 1 describes the concept of computer arithmetic. Chapter 2 explains the concept of errors and propagation of errors in numerical computation. Chapter 3 discusses the iterative methods for finding the roots of transcendental and algebraic equations. In chapter 4, the direct and iterative methods for the solution of a system of linear algebraic equations and the convergence of these methods are given. Chapter 5 explains finite differences, which includes different finite difference operators, factorial notation and summation of given series. In Chapter 6, the interpolation methods for approximating the polynomial are discussed. Chapter 7 deals with curve fitting for a given set of data. Chapter 8 and 9 discusses numerical differentiation and integration respectively. Chapter 10 gives the solution of various difference equations while Chapter 11 provides numerical solution of ordinary differential equations and chapter 12 discusses the numerical methods for the solution of elliptic, parabolic and hyperbolic partial differential equations.

This book is intended to cover the syllabi of Undergraduate (B.A., B.Sc. (Mathematics and Computer Science), BCA, B.E. / B.Tech., PGDCA), Post – graduate (M.A., MCA, M.Sc. IT, M.Sc. Mathematics and Computer Science) and Engineering students of different Indian Universities and has been designed to serve as a text book for these courses. After reviewing the syllabi of many Indian Universities I have decided to write this book which covers almost all required and important topics of syllabi. Throughout the book, the major emphasis is given on numerous solved and unsolved examples. Many topics in this book such as process graph, cubic spline method, Taylor series, Legendre's and Chebyshev polynomials, Gauss – Chebyshev integration method and boundary value problems make this book unique.

Other salient features of this book are concise but lucid and student friendly presentation of derivation of formulas used in various numerical methods; objectives and outcomes of each chapter; multiple choice questions; problems given as exercises followed by answers given at the end of every exercise and C programs for various numerical methods.

First and foremost I am grateful to God for his blessings. I wish to thank my family members for their inspiration and moral support in every situation.

I also express my gratitude to Shri Bipin V. Mehta, Associate Dean, School of Computer Studies, Ahmedabad University for encouraging me to write this book. I would also like to thank all my colleagues for their constant encouragement and support.

Finally, I am thankful to the publisher, BPB Publication, New Delhi for their co-operation and efforts in publishing this book in a short span of time.

I am sure that students and faculty members will find this book useful. Critical suggestions for the improvement of the book will be highly appreciated and gratefully acknowledged.

Vinay Vachharajani

ABOUT THE AUTHOR

Vinay Vachharajani is a senior faculty member in School of Computer Studies at Ahmedabad University, Gujarat. He received his Bachelor of Science and first Master degree in Mathematics from Gujarat University and the second Master degree in Computer Applications (MCA) from Gujarat University. He has more than 12 years of teaching experience at UG and PG level.

His research interests include e-learning, Natural Language Processing, Technology for Education and Business Analytics. He has published/ presented several research papers in prestigious national and international journals/conferences. He is a life member of Computer Society of India (CSI) and Operation Research Society of India (ORSI).

TABLE OF CONTENTS

Preface

Chapter 1   Computer Arithmetic

Objectives

- To understand the concept of significant digits
- To understand the concept of accuracy and precision
- To understand the concept of floating point representation and normalization
- To identify binay and decimal numbers
- To convert from binary to decimal and decimal to binary number system

Learning Outcomes

After reading this lesson students should be able to

- Define and use floating point representation
- Understand the number of significant digits, accuracy and precision
- Understand number systems, mainly binary and decimal number systems
- Efficiently convert from binary to decimal and decimal to binary number system
- Know the limitations of floating point representation

1.1   INTRODUCTION

The foundation of modern numerical analysis was built during the late 40's and 50's. Numerical analysis involves design, analysis and implementation of numerical algorithms for finding scientific and engineering problems. It always gives an approximate solution and not exact solution to these problems. Computers have drastically changed the field of numerical analysis. The aim of numerical analysis is to provide suitable methods, known as numerical methods, for solving the problems effectively. Numerical methods are techniques by which mathematical problems are formulated so that they can be solved with arithmetic operations like addition, subtraction, multiplication and division. There are in general very few analytical methods for solving large number of engineering problems. Due to limitations of analytical methods in real life applications and the advancements in digital computers and calculators numerical methods have gained popularity. Numerical analysis has been strongly linked to mathematics, applications and the computer.

In this chapter, we discuss the basic and fundamental concepts like significant digits, approximate numbers, floating point representation and their limitations, number system particulary decimal and binary number systems, conversion from binary to decimal and vice versa, storage of real numbers in computer memory and arithmetic operations on normalized floating point numbers.

1.2   NUMBERS AND THEIR ACCURACY

There are mainly two kind of numbers: exact and approximate numbers. The numbers like 5, 7, 3/7. 2.35 are *exact numbers* because there is no uncertainty. Other examples of exact numbers are numbers of tires on a bicycle (exactly 2) or the number of students in a class of MCA. Exact numbers can be derived by counting (for ex. Summation of two digit number), mathematical relatioships(for ex. Cos 30^0, area of square etc.) or definition (for ex. Number of litre in a kilolitre) and decision (for ex. Marriage age). The numbers like $\sqrt{2}, \sqrt{5}$, e, π ...etc. do have uncertainty. They are exact numbers but cannot be expressed exactly by finite number of digits. They are very close to exact numbers. These numbers are known as *approximate numbers*. These numbers are obtained due to the measurement procedure (for ex. Distance between two cities is 109 km – here 109 is an approximate number) or rounding of a number (for ex. π is approximated to 3.1415) .

Number	Actual Number	Approximate number
$\sqrt{2}$	1.41421356237...	1.4142
e	2.71828182845...	2.7183
π	3.14159265359...	3.1415

1.2.1   Significant Digits

Generally numerical methods yield approximate results so we need to specify how confident we are in our approximate result in terms of significant figures. A significant number is any of the meaningful number 1, 2, 3,...., 9 and 0 with one exception when it is used just to locate the decimal point or to fill the places of unknown or discarded digits . For example,

Number	Significant Digits	Total Significant Digits
34.9	3, 4, 9	3
0.000456	4, 5, 6	3 (here three leading zeros are used to fix the position of the decimal point)
20.067	2, 0, 6,7	5
23, 400	2, 3, 4	3 or 4 or 5 (the last two zeros might indicate precision of measurement or be there simply as place holders)
0.2300	2, 3, 0	4
2300.0	2, 3, 0	5

In the large numbers like 23,400 it is not always clear that how many zeros are significant. For example, 23,400 may have 3, 4 or 5 significant digits depending on whether the zeros are known with confidence. These numbers can be converted into 2.34×10^4 , 2.340×10^4, 2.3400×10^4 indicates that the number is known to three, four and five significant figures respectively. To resolve this issue, convert the given number into scientific notation where the first digit after the decimal point being non zero and before decimal point being zero. So, the numbers given in the above table can be converted into 0.349×10^2, 0.456×10^{-3}, 0.20067×10^2, 0.23400×10^5, 0.2300, 0.23000×10^4. Now it is cearly observed that the numbers given in the table have 3, 3, 5, 5, 4 and 5 significant digits respectivly.

1.2.2   Accuracy and Precision

In numerical analysis, the *accuracy* of an approximate number is decided by the number of significant digits in it. For example, 7.63, 0.00763 and 763000 numbers have an accuracy of three significant numbers and 5.78 is more accurate than 5.7. In general, we can say that accuaracy means how our measured value is closed to the true value. If the measured value is very far from the standard value then it is not accurate. For example, if the weight of a particular item is 4.3 kg. but the original weight of that item is 10 kg. then the measurement is not accurate. In numerical analysis, the *precision* of an approximate number is given by the position of the rightmost significant digit. For example, 32.987 has a precision of 0.001, 0.00234 has a precision of 0.00001 and 0.2300 has a precision of 0.01. In general, we can say that precision is the closeness within individual values. For example, if we weigh an item four times and get 4.3 kg. each time then our measurement is very precise.

In real life, measurement can be accurate but not precise, precise but not accurate, neither accurate nor precise or accurate as well as precise. The below Figure 1.1 clarify this concept.

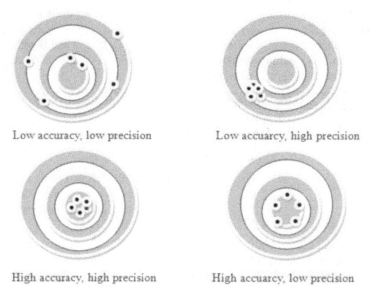

Low accuracy, low precision   Low accuarcy, high precision

High accuracy, high precision   High accuarcy, low precision

Figure 1.1 Concept of accuracy and precision

The example of accuary and precision of different numbers is given in the below table.

Number	Accuracy	Precision
34.9	3 significant digits	0.1
0.000456	3 significant digits	0.000001
20.067	5 significant digits	0.001
$23,400$	3, 4 or 5 significant digits	Precision of hundreds (Assuming right most two zeros are not significant)
0.2300	4 significant digits	0.01
$234,000,000$	3 significant digits (Assuming all trailing zeros are not significant)	Precision of millions

Remarks: If the right most significant digit is to the right of the decimal point, we state the position as so many decimal places. If that position is to the left of the decimal point, it is more common to state the precision using words like "tens," "hundreds," "thousands," " millions," etc.

1.2.3   Rounding – off and Chopping a Number

There are some large numbers like $\pi = 3.142857143$ and $e = 2.718281828$. In computation we generally don't use this orginal value but we limit these numbers to certain manageable number of digits like 3.14 and 2.71 respectively.

Here it comes the concept of rounding and chopping (or truncation). Rounding and chopping is a process of dropping unwanted digits as per the requirements.

If we ignore (discard) all digits after n^{th} digit then it is called *chopping* a number to n significant digits. This concept is used by many early computers. It is not preferable as it introduces an error that can be larger than the error in rounding – off.

To *rounding - off* a number to n significant digits, discard all digits to the right of the nth digit. Rounding is more common and better procedure compare to chopping. The general rules for rounding – off a number to n – significant figures are

(i)   if the discarded number is less than half a unit in the nth place, leave the nth digit unchanged.

(ii)   If the discarded number is greater than half a unit in the nth place, increase the nth digit by one.

(iii)   If the discarded digit is exactly half a unit in the nth digit, leaving the nth digit unaltered if it is an even number, but increase it by one if is an odd number. Due to this step the errors in computation will be minimized as even numbers are exactly divisible by more numbers compare to odd numbers.

Remark: The rounding – off process described in (i) and (ii) above is known as *symmetric rounding – off*.

If a given number has been rounded – off to n – digits according to above rules, it is said to be *correct up to n significant figures*. The example of chopping and rounding – off different numbers is given in the below table.

Number	Chopping to significant digits				Rounded to significant digits			
	Two	Three	Four	Five	Two	Three	Four	Five
23.765489	23	23.7	23.76	23.765	24	23.8	23.76	23.765
0.00985796	0.0098	0.00985	0.009857	0.0098579	0.0098	0.00986	0.009858	0.0098580
5.67890	5.6	5.67	5.678	5.6789	5.7	5.68	5.679	5.6789
40.09876	40	40.0	40.09	40.098	40	40.1	40.10	40.099
0.35575	0.35	0.355	0.3557	0.35575	0.36	0.356	0.3558	0.35575

1.3   CLASSIC THEOREMS OF NUMERICAL METHODS

There are certain classical theorems in numerical analysis which will be used in error analysis and derivation of some of the numerical methods. Rolle's theorem (Generalized version) will be used in error analysis of Lagrange's interpolation, Mean value theorem will be used in finding the roots of a given equation and Taylor's theorems are frequently used in approximations in numerical methods.

Theorem 1.1 (Rolle's Theorem) Let $f(x)$ be a funtion such that
(i) $f(x)$ is continuous on $[a, b]$
(ii) $f(x)$ is differentiable on (a, b)
(iii) $f(a) = f(b)$
then there is some $c \in (a, b)$ such that $f(c) = 0$.

Theorem 1.2 (Generalized Rolle's Theorem)
Let $f(x)$ be a function. Assume that $f \in C[a,b]$ and that $f'(x), f''(x), f'''(x), ..., f^n(x)$ exist over (a, b) and $x_0, x_1, x_2, ..., x_n \in [a, b]$. If $f(x_j) = 0$ for $j = 0, 1, 2, ..., n$, then there exists a number c, with $c \in (a, b)$ such that $f^n(c) = 0$.
It derives from Theorem 1.2 that between any two zeros of a polynomial $f(x)$ of degree ≥ 2, there lies at least one zero of the polynomial $f'(x)$.

Theorem 1.3 (Intermediate Value Theorem)
Let $[a, b] \in R$ and let $f(x)$ be a continuous on $[a, b]$. If k is a number between $f(a)$ and $f(b)$, $f(a) < k < f(b)$ (or $f(a) > k > f(b)$). Then there exists at least one number $c \in (a, b)$ such that $f(c) = k$.

(i.e. If a continuous function takes on two values $f(a)$ and $f(b)$ at points a and b, it also takes on every value between $f(a)$ and $f(b)$ at some point between a and b.)
The specialization of this theorem stated if a continuous function has values of

opposite sign inside an interval, then it has a root in that interval which will be used in Bisection's theorem to locate the root of given equation.

The following theorem (Mean value theorem) is one of the most important theorem in matehmatical analysis.

Theorem 1.4 (Mean Value Theorem) Let $f(x)$ be a function such that
(i) $f(x)$ is continuous on $[a , b]$
(ii) $f(x)$ is differentiable on (a, b)
then there is at least one number $c \in (a, b)$ such that $f'(c) = \frac{f(b)-f(a)}{b-a}$.

Remark: The special case when $f(a) = f(b)$ is Rolle's theorem.

Theorem 1.5 (Taylor's Theorem for a Function of One Variable)

Let $f(x)$ be a continuous function and posseses continuous derivatives of order n in $[a, b]$. If $x_0 \in [a , b]$, then for every $x \in [a , b]$, there exists a number $x_0 < \xi < x$ such that

$$f(x) = f(x_0) + (x - x_0)f'(x_0) + \frac{(x-x_0)^2}{2!}f''(x_0) + \cdots + \frac{(x-x_0)^{(n-1)}}{(n-1)!}f^{(n-1)}(x_0) + R_n(x)$$

$$........ (1.3.1)$$

where,

$$R_n(x) = \frac{(x - x_0)^n}{n!}f^{(n)}(\xi), x_0 < \xi < x.$$

If $x = x_0 + h$, then we get

$$f(x_0 + h) = f(x_0) + hf'(x_0) + \frac{h^2}{2!}f''(x_0) + \cdots + \frac{h^{(n-1)}}{(n-1)!}f^{(n-1)}(x_0) + \frac{h^n}{n!}f^{(n)}(\xi)$$

$$........ (1.3.2)$$

Maclaurin's Series for Function of One Variable

A Maclaurin's series is a special case of Taylor's series or we can say a Maclaurin's series is a Taylor's series expansion of a function about 0. Substitute $x_0 = 0$ in Eq. (1.3.1) we get a Maclaurin's series,

$$f(x) = f(0) + x f'(0) + \frac{x^2}{2!}f''(0) + \frac{x^3}{3!}f'''(0) + \cdots + \frac{x^n}{n!}f^{(n)}(0)$$
$$+ \ldots\ldots$$

$$\ldots\ldots\ldots (1.3.3)$$

Theorem 1.6 (Taylor's Theorem for Function of Several Variables)

If $f(x, y)$ and all its partial derivatives of order n are finite and continuous for all points (x, y) in the domain $a \le x \le a + h, b \le y \le b + k$, then

$$f(a + h, b + k) = f(a, b) + df(a, b) + \frac{1}{2!}d^2 f(a, b) + \ldots + \frac{1}{(n-1)!}d^{n-1} f(a, b) + R_n$$

$$........ (1.3.4)$$

where,
$$d = h\frac{\partial}{\partial x} + k\frac{\partial}{\partial y}$$

and
$$R_n = \frac{1}{n!}d^n f(a + \theta h, b + \theta k), \ 0 < \theta < 1$$

Maclaurin's Series for Function of Several Variables

Substituting $a = b = 0$, $h = x$ and $k = y$ in Eq. (1.3.4), we get

$$f(x,y) = f(0,0) + df(0,0) + \frac{1}{2!}d^2 f(0,0) + \ ... + \frac{1}{(n-1)!}d^{n-1} f(0,0) + R_n$$

$$........ (1.3.5)$$

where,

$$R_n = \frac{1}{n!}d^n f(\theta x, \theta y), 0 < \theta < 1$$

which is known as Maclaurin's Series for function of Several Variables.

1.4   NUMBER SYSTEM

We found numbers all around us in various form. This is the reason we need to understand how the number system works, the relation between numbers and how we can convert from one number system to another.

A value of each digit in a particular number can be determined using
- The digit itself
- The position of the digit in a given number
- The radix (base) of the number system

The *base* is defined as the total number of digits available in the number system. The general form is described as:

$$(Number)_{base} = d_n \times R^{n-1} + d_{n-1} \times R^{n-2} + \ ...... + d_2 \times R + d_1$$

where, n is the position of digit in the given number, d_i is the digit in the ith position in the number and R is the base of the number.

The basic concepts of decimal and binary number systems and how to convert from one system to another system are explained as under.

1.4.1   Decimal Number System

Decimal number system is the oldest number system which is used in our day-to-day life. It uses the numbers from 0 to 9, total 10 numbers and hence its base is considered to be 10. For example, decimal number 5678 is represented as $(5678)_{10}$. Each position represents a specific power of 10 and each successive position to the left of the decimal point represents units, tens, hundreds, thousands and so on. In fractional decimal number (for ex. 12.456) each successive position to the right of the decimal point represents tenth, hundredth, thousandth and so on.

For example, a decimal number $(1234.567)_{10}$ can be expressed as

$(1234.567)_{10} = 1 \times 10^3 + 2 \times 10^2 + 3 \times 10^1 + 4 \times 10^0 + 5 \times 10^{-1} + 6 \times 10^{-2} + 7 \times 10^{-3}$

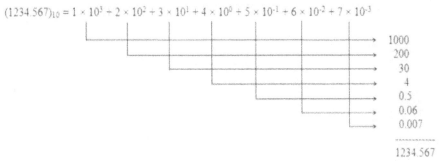

The general form of decimal number system is:

$(Number)_{10} = d_n\ 10^{n-1} + d_{n-1}\ 10^{n-2} + \ldots\ldots + d_2\ 10 + d_1$

1.4.2   Binary Number System

Computers understand the language of 0 and 1, called binary numbers. A system deals with these binary numbers is called binary number system. It uses only two digits 0 and 1 and hence its base is considered to be 2. For example, 101010 is a binary number and represented as $(101010)_2$. Each position represents a specific power of 2 and each successive position in the integral part of the binary number has a value two times greater than the position to its right.

For example, a binary number 10111.01 can be expressed as

$(10111.01)_2 = 1 \times 2^4 + 0 \times 2^3 + 1 \times 2^2 + 1 \times 2^1 + 1 \times 2^0 + 0 \times 2^{-1} + 1 \times 2^{-2}$

The general form of binary number system is:

$(Number)_2 = d_n\ d_{n-1}\ d_{n-2}\ \ldots..d_1d_0d_{-1}\ldots\ldots.d_{-k}$ where, $d_n, d_{n-1,\ldots\ldots}\ d_{-k}$ are binary values 0 or 1.

1.4.3   Conversion of Decimal to Binary Number

The steps to convert from decimal to binary number are as follows:

1. Divide the given decimal number by 2. It is clear that when the number is even the remainder will be zero and the number is odd the binary remainder will be one.
2. Write the quotient below the number which will be the new number.
3. Continue downwards, dividing each new quotient by two and writing the remainders to the right of each number.
4. Continue the same process till the quotient becomes 0.

Finally, the answer would be all remainders from bottom to top.

The steps to convert fractional decimal number to fractional binary number are given below:

1. Start with the decimal fraction and multiply it by 2. The result contains an integral part and fractional part.
2. The integer part of the result is the first binary digit to the right of the decimal point.

3. Multiply again the fractional part of the previous result by 2. The integer part of this new reault is the second binary digit to the right of the decimal point.
4. Continue the same procedure until we get 0 as a decimal part or until an infinite repeating pattern is recognized.
5. The whole numbers (integer part) starting from top to bottom will be the required fractional part of binary number.

Finally, the combination of integer and fractional part is the required binary number.

Example 1.1 Convert decimal number 123 to corresponding binary number.
Solution:

Divion	Quotient	Remainder	
123/2	61	1	← Least significant bit in the solution
61/2	30	1	
30/2	15	0	
15/2	7	1	
7/2	3	1	
3/2	1	1	
1/2	0	1	← Most significant bit in the solution

$$(123)_{10} = (1111011)_2$$

Example 1.2 Convert decimal number 0.1250 to corresponding binary number.
Solution:

Multiplication	Result	Fraction Part	Integer Part
0.1250×2	0.25	0.25	0
0.25×2	0.50	0.50	0
0.50×2	1.00	0	1

$$(0.1250)_{10} = (0.001)_2$$

Example 1.3 Convert decimal number 0.8 to corresponding binary number.
Solution:

Multiplication	Result	Fraction Part	Integer Part
0.8×2	1.60	0.6	1
0.6×2	1.20	0.20	1
0.20×2	0.40	0.40	0
0.40×2	0.80	0.80	0
0.80×2	1.60	0.60	1
......	....	....	......

$$(0.8)_{10} = (0.11001100......)_2$$

Example 1.4 Convert decimal number 119.59375 to corresponding binary number.

Solution: Conversion of integer part to its binary equivalent

Divion	Quotient		Remainder
119/2	59	1	← —— Least significant bit in the solution
59/2	29	1	
29/2	14	1	
14/2	7	0	
7/2	3	1	
3/2	1	1	
1/2	0	1	← —— Most significant bit in the solution

$$(119)_{10} = (1110111)_2$$

Conversion of fractional part to its binary equivalent

Multiplication	Result	Fraction Part	Integer Part
0.59375×2	1.1875	0.1875	1
0.1875×2	0.375	0.375	0
0.375×2	0.75	0.75	0
0.75×2	1.5	0.5	1
0.5×2	1.0	0	1

$$(0.59375)_{10} = (0.10011)_2$$

Therefore, $(119.59375)_{10} = (1110111.10011)_2$

1.4.4   Conversion of Binary to Decimal Number

Conversion from binary to decimal number is performed using following formula:

$(Binary\ Number)_2 = d_n \times 2^{n-1} + d_{n-1} \times 2^{n-2} + ... + d_2 \times 2 + d_1 + \cdots$ up to possible terms

Example 1.5   Convert binary number $(10011100)_2$ to corresponding decimal number.

Solution:

$$\begin{aligned}
(10011100)_2 &= 1 \times 2^7 + 0 \times 2^6 + 0 \times 2^5 + 1 \times 2^4 + 1 \times 2^3 + 1 \times \\
&\quad 2^2 + 0 \times 2^1 + 0 \times 2^0 \\
&= 1 \times 128 + 0 \times 64 + 0 \times 32 + 1 \times 16 + 1 \times 8 + \\
&\quad 1 \times 4 + 0 \times 2 + 0 \times 1 \\
&= 128 + 16 + + 8 + 4 \\
&= 156
\end{aligned}$$

$$\therefore \quad (10011100)_2 = (156)_{10}$$

Example 1.6   Convert binary number $(1001.001)_2$ to corresponding decimal number.

Solution:

$$(1001.001)_2 = 1 \times 2^3 + 0 \times 2^2 + 0 \times 2^1 + 1 \times 2^0 + 0 \times 2^{-1} + 0 \times 2^{-2} + 1 \times 2^{-3}$$

$$= 1 \times 8 + 0 \times 4 + 0 \times 2 + 1 \times 1 + 0 \times \frac{1}{2} + 0 \times \frac{1}{4} + 1 \times \frac{1}{8}$$

$$= 8 + 1 + 0.125$$

$$= 9.125$$

$$\therefore \quad (1001.001)_2 = (9.125)_{10}$$

1.5   FLOATING POINT REPRESENTATION

The real numbers can be represented in two number formats.
(i)   Fixed point
(ii)   Floating point

In fixed point format, the place of decimal point is fixed or we can say it has a fixed number of digits after the decimal point. The bits to the left of the decimal point are called integer bits and right of the decimal point are called the fractional bits. For example, 18.625, 98.765 etc. are fixed point numbers. This representation is used when we don't require a very precised value for eg. money, height, weight, percentage etc.

A floating point format represents arbitrary precision. Like fixed point representation, the number of bits (digits) in the integer part or the number of bits in the fractional part are not fixed. This representation is same as scientific notation where the number is multiplied by a base number raised to some power. That number is known as *mantissa* or *significand* and power is known as *exponent*.

For example, 12.5841 can be expressed as 1.25841×10^1 (or 1.25841 E1) or 0.125841×10^2 (or 0.125841E2) as per the requirement of the precision.

The general form of floating point representation is

$$\text{Real Number} = M \times 10^E$$

Where, M = Mantissa (approx. equal to the required number of significant digits)
        E = Exponent

According to the need of the precision the decimal point can be moved freely to the left or to the right in floating point format. The shifting of the decimal point to the left of the first non zero digit or most significant digit is called *normalization*. The numbers represented in this form are known as *normalized floating point numbers*. The objective of normalization is to represent real numbers with maximum possible precision in computer memory.

The range of mantissa in this representation is:

For positive numbers: $0.1 \leq \text{mantissa} < 1.0$
For negative numbers: $-1.0 < \text{mantissa} \leq -0.1$
Therefore, $0.1 \leq |mantissa| < 1.0$

Example 1.7   Convert the following numbers into normalized floating point representation.

(a)   23.6758   (b)   0.0003450   (c)   -112.768 × 10³   (d) 96.0023 × 10⁻²

Solution:

(a) 0.236758×10^2 (b) 0.3450×10^{-3} (c) -0.112768×10^6 (d) 0.960023

1.6   STORAGE OF REAL NUMBER IN COMPUTER MEMORY

Computer uses a fixed number of bits like 8 bits, 16 bits, 32 bits, 64 bits etc. to represent any information.   Computer memory location only stores a binary pattern. The floating point numbers are represented in computer memory as normalized binary floating point numbers.IEEE standardizes floating – point representation. According to its standard, floating point numbers are represented using three parts: the sign bit, the exponent and the mantissa. The mantissa is represented using last 23 bits, exponent in the next 8 bits and sign bit in the most significant bit .

| Sign | Biased Exponent | Mantissa |

Figure 1.2 Storage of 32 – bit single precision floating point number

The first bit is sign bit which is either 0 or 1. Based on that the number (mantissa) is considered to be positive or negative respectively.

The exponent, occupies 8 – bits, can be either positive or negative. In this scheme one bit of the byte is reserved for the sign of the exponent. It ranges from -126 to +127. But it is not used very often, instead the exponent can be biased by adding 127 (The bias is $2^{k-1} - 1$ where k = number of bits in the exponent field. Here, k = 8 so, $2^{8-1} - 1 = 127$) to the desired exponent. Then the modified exponent is stored, which now ranges from 0 to 255 ($1 \leq$ Exponent ≤ 254). All these are positive values, so the use of sign bit is eliminated.

The mantissa is the normalized binary representation to be multiplied by 2 raised to the power defined by the exponent. The steps to convert a decimal number to floating point number are given below.

Steps to convert decimal number to floating point number

1.   Convert the decimal number into an equivalent binary number
2.   Convert the obtained binary number into normalized binary floating point number (where the base is 2)
3.   The mantissa is represented using 23 bits. So, extend the given mantissa upto 23 bits by adding 0's on its right

4. Modify the given exponent by addding 127 to it. Convert the modified exponent into its binary equivalent.
5. Set the most significant bit (sign bit) as 0 or 1. If the mantissa is positive it is 0 and 1 if the mantissa is negative.
6. Combining the above value of exponent and mantissa give the final result.

Remark: If the decimal number is negative then we have to take absolute value of that number and then follow the above steps. The only difference is that after representing the mantissa using 23 bits by adding 0's on its right, we have to take 2's complement of that number. All other steps are same as described above.

Example 1.8   Convert 19.250 into 32 – bit single precision floating point format.

Solution:
1. The equivalent binary number of 19.250 is 10011.01.
2. The normalized binary floating point number of 10011.01 is 0.1001101×2^5.
3. The mantissa of the normalized floating point number is 1001101. The extended mantissa to 23 bits is 10011010000000000000000.
4. The exponent of the number is 5. So, the modified exponent (by adding 127 to it) is 132. The binary equivalent of 132 is 10000100.
5. Set the sign bit as 0 because the given number is positive.
6. Combining the value of mantissa and exponent we get

Mantissa: 10011010000000000000000, Exponent: 10000100, Sign bit: 0.

So, 19.250 is

0	10000100	10011010000000000000000

Example 1.9   Convert -19.250 into 32 – bit single precision floating point format.

Solution:
1. The absolute value of -19.825 is 19.250. The equivalent binary number of 19.250 is 10011.01.
2. The normalized binary floating point number of 10011.01 is 0.1001101×2^5.
3. The mantissa of the normalized floating point number is 1001101. The extended mantissa to 23 bits is 10011010000000000000000.
4. 2's complement of the extended mantissa is 11001100000000000000000.
5. The binary equivalent of the modified exponent is 10000100.
6. Set the sign bit as 1 because the given number is negative.
7. Combining the value of mantissa and exponent we get

Mantissa: 11001100000000000000000, Exponent: 10000100, Sign bit: 1.

So, 19.250 is

1	10000100	11001100000000000000000

1.7   ARITHMETIC OPERATIONS ON NORMALIZED FLOATING POINT NUMBERS

To explain the concept of arithmetic operations on normalized floating point numbers we assume that first four digits are used to store mantissa and last two for exponent in our computer. The mantissa and exponent can be either positive or negative. So, they have their own sign. For example, the number 0.5678E-02 is stored in memory location as shown in Figure 1.3.

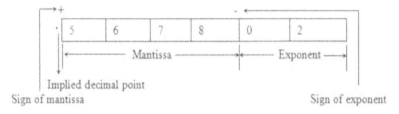

Figure 1.3 Storage of floating point number in memory location

In our hypothetical computer the range of mantissa is -0.9999 to 0.9999 and the range of exponent is -99 to 99. During the arithmetic operation of normalized floating point numbers, because of normalization process, the exponent of sum may become greater than +99, which is greater than the largest number that the hypothetical computer can store. This condition is called *overflow*. If the exponent is less than -99, which is less than the smallest number that the hypothetical computer can store. This condition is called *underflow*. In both situations, the system will signal the error.

1.7.1   Addition

Rule:
➢ If the exponents of two given normalized floating point numbers are equal then we can perform addition operation.
➢ If the exponents of two given normalized floating point numbers are not equal then the exponent of the number with smaller exponent is made equal to the larger exponent using the following steps.
• Subtract the smaller exponent from the larger exponent. Let's $K = |e_1 - e_2|$.
• Shift the decimal point to the left by the value of K.

Now add two mantissa. It may happen that the value of mantissa of the final result is not in normalized form then convert it into normalized form.

Example 1.10   Add 0.3476E6 and 0.2315E6

Solution: Since the exponents of both numbers are equal, so, mantissa are added without shifting the decimal point.

$$0.3476E6$$
$$+\,0.2315E6$$
$$\overline{}$$
$$0.5791E6$$

Example 1.11   Add 0.2679E8 and 0.1342E6

Solution: The exponents of both the numbers are not same. So, the number with larger exponent (i.e.0.2679) kept as it is and shift the decimal point of the second mantissa to the left by the value = | first exponent – second exponent | = | 8 – 6 | = 2. After shifting the decimal point the second mantissa becomes 0.0013E8 and the digits 4 and 2 are truncated. The modified numbers can be added as follows.

$$0.2679E8$$
$$+\,0.0013E8$$
$$\overline{}$$
$$0.2692E8$$

Example 1.12   Add 0.9287E99 and 0.5846E99

Solution: The exponents of both the numbers are same, therefore , mantissa are added directly as follows.

$$0.9287E99$$
$$+\,0.5846E99$$
$$\overline{}$$
$$1.5133E99$$

Mantissa is not in normalized form, therefore, the decimal point is shifted one place left and the exponent is increased by 1. So, the exponent becomes 100. According to our hypothetical computer, exponent can store only two digits. This condition is called an *overflow* and the system will signal error message.

1.7.2   Subtraction

Rule:
> ➤   The rule for subtraction of two normalized floating point numbers is similar to the addition in the cases when exponents are equal or unequal.

Let's clarify this concept with the following examples.

Example 1.13   Subtract 0.1432E8 from 0.4378E8.

Solution: The exponents of both the numbers are equal, therefore, mantissa are subtracted directly as follows.

$$0.4378E8$$
$$-\,0.1432E8$$
$$\overline{}$$
$$0.2946E8$$

Example 1.14   Subtract 0.7537E5 from 0.5291E7.

Solution: The exponents of both the numbers are not same. So, the number with larger exponent (i.e. 0.5291) kept as it is and shift the decimal point of the other mantissa to the left by the value = | first exponent – second exponent | = | 5 – 7 | = 2. After shifting the decimal point the other mantissa becomes 0.0075E7 and the digits 3 and 7 are truncated. The modified numbers can be subtracted as follows.

$$0.5291E7$$
$$- 0.0075E7$$
$$\overline{}$$
$$0.5216E7$$

Example 1.15   Subtract 0.7322E-99 from 0.7346E-99

Solution: The exponents of both the numbers are same, therefore , mantissa are subtracted directly as follows.

$$0.7346E\text{-}99$$
$$- 0.7322E\text{-}99$$
$$\overline{}$$
$$0.0024E\text{-}99$$

In this case, mantissa of the final result is not in normalized form, therefore, the decimal point is shifted two place right and the exponent is decreased by 2. So, the exponent becomes -101. According to our hypothetical computer, exponent can store only two digits. This condition is called an *underflow* and the system will signal error message.

1.7.3   Multiplication

Rule:
> ➢   The mantissa of two normalized floating point numbers are multiplied and exponents are added.

The mantissa of the product may not be in normalized form, so, it needs to be converted into normalized form consisting four digits.

Example 1.16   Multiply 0.3698E10 by 0.4976E10

Solution:

$$0.3698E10$$
$$\times\quad 0.4976E10$$
$$\overline{}$$
$$0.18401248E20$$

After truncating the mantissa of the product into four digits, we obtain 0.1840E20.

Example 1.17   Multiply 0.7254E-24 by 0.2314E45

Solution:

$$0.7254E\text{-}24$$
$$\times\ 0.2314E\ 45$$
_____

$$0.16785756E21$$

After truncating the mantissa of the product into four digits, we obtain
0.1678E21.

Example 1.18   Multiply 0.9145E56 by 0.3214E45

Solution:

$$0.9145E56$$
$$\times\ 0.3214E45$$
_____

$$0.2939203E101$$

After truncating the mantissa of the product into four digits, we obtain
0.2939E101. But our   hypothetical computer can store only two digits in
exponent. This condition is called an *overflow* condition. The system will signal
an error message.

Example 1.19   Multiply 0.1145E-62 by 0.2140E-45

Solution:

$$0.1145E\text{-}62$$
$$\times\ 0.2140E\text{-}45$$
_____

$$0.024503E\text{-}107$$

Here, mantissa of the final result is not in normalized form, therefore, the decimal
point is shifted one place right and the exponent is decreased by 1. So, the
exponent becomes -108. According to our hypothetical computer, exponent can
store only two digits. This condition is called an *underflow* and the system will
signal error message.

1.7.4   Division

Rule:
> ➤   The mantissa of numerator is divided by the mantissa of denominator
>   and the exponent of numerator is subtracted from the exponent of
>   denominator.

The mantissa of the division may not be in normalized form, so, it needs to be
converted into normalized form consisting four digits.

Example 1.20   Divide 0.4783E17 by 0.1956E10

Solution: $0.4783E17 \div 0.1956E10$
$= (0.4783 \div 0.1956)\ E\ (17-10)$
$= 2.445296....E7$

After truncating and converting into normalized form the final result is 0.2445E7.

Example 1.21   Divide 0.3278E24 by 0.1111E24

Solution: 0.3278E24 ÷ 0.1111E24
     = (0.3278 ÷ 0.1111) E(24 – 24)
     = 2.95049504.....E0

After truncating and converting into normalized form the final result is 0.2950.

Example 1.22   Divide 0.9145E56 by 0.5000E-45

Solution: 0.9145E56 ÷ 0.5000E-45
     = (0.9145 ÷ 0.5000) E(56 – (-45))
     = 1.829 E101

After truncating and converting into normalized form the final result is 0.1829
E101. Since exponent is greater than 99, this is *overflow* condition.

Example 1.23   Divide 0.1242E-62 by 0.2000E45

Solution: 0.1242E-62 ÷ 0.2000E45
     = (0.1242 ÷ 0.2000) E(-62 – 45)
     = 0.621 E-107

Since exponent is less than -99, this is *underflow* condition.

1.8   LIMITATIONS OF FLOATING POINT REPRESENTATION

Due to our hypothetical computer, mantissa can store only four digits in
normalized floating point representation. The mantissa has to be truncated to four
digits to satisfy the need of this format. This truncation process leads to some
unexpected results. Some familiar laws of arithmetic are not necessarily true for
floating point numbers.

(1)   Associative laws are always not true in floating point representation.

   i.e $(x + y) + z \neq x + (y + z)$ (Associative law for addition)
     $(x \times y) \times z \neq x \times (y \times z)$ (Associative law for multiplication)

   To prove $(x + y) + z \neq x + (y + z)$
   Let x = 0.3426E-2, y = 0.5934, z = - 0.5959
      $(x + y)$ = 0.3426E-2 + 0.5934
           = 0.0034E0 + 0.5934E0
           = 0.5968E0
      $(x + y) + z$ = 0.5968E0 - 0.5959E0
              = 0.0009E0
           = 0.9000E-3
         $(y + z)$ = 0.5934 - 0.5959
              = - 0.0025
           = - 0.2500E-2
      $x + (y + z)$ = (0.3426 - 0.2500) E-2

$$= 0.0926\text{E-2}$$
$$= 0.9260\text{E-3}$$

Thus, it is proved that $(x + y) + z \neq x + (y + z)$. Similarly, we can prove associative law for multiplication. i.e. $(x \times y) \times z \neq x \times (y \times z)$.

(2)   Distributive law is always not true in floating point representation.

i.e $x\,(y - z) \neq (x\,y - x\,z)$

Let $x = 0.5632\text{E-1}$, $y = 0.2300\text{E0}$, $z = 0.1100\text{E0}$

$(y - z) = 0.2300\text{E0} - 0.1100\text{E0}$
$\qquad = 0.1200\text{E0}$

$x\,(y - z) = 0.5632\text{E-1} \times 0.1200\text{E0}$
$\qquad\qquad = 0.067584\text{E-1}$
$\qquad\qquad = 0.6758\text{E-2}$

$x \times y = 0.5632\text{E-1} \times 0.2300\text{E0} = 0.129536\text{E-1} = 0.1295\text{E-1}$
$x \times z = 0.5632\text{E-1} \times 0.1100\text{E0} = 0.061952\text{E-1} = 0.0619\text{E-1}$
$(x\,y - x\,z) = 0.1295\text{E-1} - 0.0619\text{E-1} = 0.0676\text{E-1} = 0.6760\text{E-2}$

Thus, it is proved that $x\,(y - z) \neq (x\,y - x\,z)$

(3)   There is some limitation in the computation of numbers in the case of normalized floating point representation.

It is known that $4\,x = x + x + x + x \neq (x + x) + (x + x)$ in the case of normalized floating point representation of numbers due to truncating or rounding – off .

Let $x = 0.7778\text{E0}$

LHS $= 4\,x = x + x + x + x = 0.7778\text{E0} + 0.7778\text{E0} + 0.7778\text{E0} + 0.7778\text{E0} = 0.3111\text{E1}$

RHS $= (x + x) + (x + x)$
$\qquad = (0.7778\text{E0} + 0.7778\text{E0}) + (0.7778\text{E0} + 0.7778\text{E0})$
$\qquad = 0.1555\text{E1} + 0.1555\text{E1}$
$\qquad = 0.3110\text{E1}$

(4)   The equality of an equation to zero can never be guaranteed in arithmetic operations of normalized floating point numbers.

For example, the root of equation $x^2 - 5 = 0$ is $\pm\sqrt{5}$. After converting the root into normalized floating point format and truncating it into 4 digit mantissa we get 0.2236E1 and -0.2236E1.

Now, substitute $x = 0.2236\text{E1}$ in the equation $x^2 - 5 = 0$ we get

$x^2 - 5 = 0 = (0.2236\text{E1} \times 0.2236\text{E1}) - 0.5000\text{E1}$
$\qquad\qquad = 0.04999696\text{E2} - 0.5000\text{E1}$
$\qquad\qquad = 0.4999\text{E1} - 0.5000\text{E1}$
$\qquad\qquad = -0.1000\text{E-2}$

Since $\sqrt{5}$ is the root of the equation $x^2 - 5 = 0$, we should get exact zero, but in this case it may not be true.

1.9   PROGRAMS IN C

1.9.1   Menu driven program for converting decimal to binary number system and binary to decimal number system

```c
#include<stdio.h>
#include<math.h>
#include<stdlib.h>
#include<conio.h>
void main()
{
    int decimal=0,binary=0,choice,rem,temp_number,i,number;
    while(1)
    {
        clrscr();
        printf("\n\t\t\tBinary To Decimal And Decimal To Binary");
        printf("\n\t\t\t-------------------------------------");
        printf("\n1) Binary  to decimal");
        printf("\n2) Decimal to binary");
        printf("\n3) Exit");
        printf("\nEnter your Choice");
        scanf("%d",&choice);
        switch(choice)
        {
                case 1:
                {

                        i=0;
                        printf("\nEnter the binary number :- ");
                        scanf("%d",&binary);
                        number=binary;
                        while(number!=0)
                        {
                                rem=number%10;
                                number=number/10;
                                if(!(rem == 1 || rem == 0))
                                {

                                        printf("\nInvalid data");
                                        goto z;
                                }
                        }
                        rem=0;
                        temp_number=binary;
```

```
                    while(temp_number!=0)
                    {

                              rem=temp_number%10;
                              temp_number/=10;
                              decimal+=rem*pow(2,i);
                              i++;
                    }
                     printf("\nThe Binary number is :- %d \nThe
                     Decimal number is :- %d",binary,decimal);
                     break;
            }
            case 2:
            {

                    i=1;
                    printf("\nEnter the decimal number :- ");
                    scanf("%d",&decimal);
                    rem=0;
                    temp_number=decimal;
                    while(temp_number!=0)
                    {

                              rem=temp_number%2;
                              temp_number/=2;
                              binary+=rem*i;
                              i*=10;
                    }
                    printf("\nThe Decimal number is :- %d \nThe    Binary
                    number is :- %d",decimal,binary);
                    break;
            }
            case 3:
            {

                    exit(0);
            }
            default:
            {

                    printf("\nEnter the proper choice");
            }
      }
      z:
      decimal=binary=temp_number=0;
      getch();
 } }
```

1.9.2   Program to convert a given number into normalized floating point number

```
// Program to input a number and convert it into normalised number.
#include<stdio.h>
#include<conio.h>
void main()
{
        int e, i;
        float m;
        clrscr();
        printf(" Enter mantissa:");
        scanf("%f",&m);
        printf(" Enter exponent:");
        scanf("%d",&e);
        if(m>=1)
        {
                while(m>=1)
                {
                        m/=10;
                        e++;
                }
        }
        else if(m<=-1)
        {
                while(m<=-1)
                {
                        m/=10;
                        e++;
                }
        }
        else if(m<0.1 && m>=0)
        {
                while(m<0.1)
                {
                        m*=10;
                        e--;
                }
        }
        else if(m>=-0.1 && m<0)
        {
                while(m>=-0.1)
                {
                        m*=10;
```

```
                                    e--;
                         }
              }
              printf(" \n\n Normailsed number is %0.4fE%2d", m,e);
              getch();  }
```

1.9.3   Menu driven program to add, subtract, multiply and divide two floating point numbers

```
#include<stdio.h>
#include<stdib.h>
#include<conio.h>
void normalize(float *,int *);
void ufof(float,int);
void main()
{
        clrscr();
           float x,x1,x2;
           int e,e1,e2,k,choice;
           printf("\n1) add");
           printf("\n2) sub");
           printf("\n3) mul");
           printf("\n4) div");
           printf("\nenter ur choice");
           scanf("%d",&choice);
           printf("\nenter the 1st mantissa");
           scanf("%f",&x1);
           printf("\nenter the 1nd exponent");
           scanf("%d",&e1);
           printf("\nenter the 2nd mantissa");
           scanf("%f",&x2);
           printf("\nenter the 2nd exponent");
           scanf("%d",&e2);
           switch (choice)
           {
                   case 1:
                              {
                                      k=e1-e2;
                                      if(e1>e2)
                                      {
                                              x2=x2/pow(10,k);
                                              e=e1;
                                      }
                                      else
                                      {
```

```
                                        x1=x1/pow(10,k);
                                        e=e2;
                        }
                        x=x1+x2;
                        normalize(&x,&e);
                        ufof(x,e);
                        break;
                }
        case 2:
                {
                        k=e1-e2;
                        if(e1>e2)
                        {
                                x2=x2/pow(10,k);
                                e=e1;
                        }
                        else
                        {
                                x1=x1/pow(10,k);
                                e=e2;
                        }
                        x=x1-x2;
                        normalize(&x,&e);
                        ufof(x,e);
                        break;
                }
        case 3:
                {
                        x=x1*x2;
                        e=e1+e2;
                        normalize(&x,&e);
                        ufof(x,e);
                        break;
                }
        case 4:
                {
                        x=x1/x2;
                        e=e1-e2;
                        normalize(&x,&e);
                        ufof(x,e);
                        break;
                }
        default:
```

```
                            {
                                        printf("\nenter the proper choice");
                                        break;
                            }
                }
            getch();
}
void normalize(float *x,int *e)
{
            while(*x<0.1)
            {
                        *x*=10;
                        *e-=1;
            }
            while(*x>=1.0)
            {
                        *x/=10;
                        *e+=1;
            }
}
void ufof(float x,int e)
{
                    if(e>99)
                    {
                                printf("\nThe ans is mantissa=%.4f,
                                exponent=%d",x,e);
                                printf("\nover flow error");
                    }
                    else if(e<-99)
                    {
                                printf("\nThe ans is mantissa =%.4f,
                                exponent=%d",x,e);
                                printf("\nunder flow error");
                    }
                    else
                    {
                                printf("\nThe  ans is mantissa=%.4f,
                                exponent=%d",x,e);
                    }
}
```

EXERCISES

1. Multiple Choice Questions

(1)   How many significant digits are there in the number 0.000234?
      (a)   3   (b)   4   (c)   5   (d)   6   (e)   None of these

(2)   How much precision is there in the number 0.0002345×10^3 ?
      (a) 10^{-3} (b)   0.0001 (c) 10^{-7} (d)   0.001   (e)   None of these

(3)   What is the range of mantissa for the normalized floating point
      representation for positive numbers?
      (a) $0.1 \leq$ mantissa < 1.0 (b) $1.0 \leq$ mantissa < 0.1
      (c) $-1.0 \leq$ mantissa < -0.1 (d) $-1.0 <$ mantissa ≤ -0.1
      (e)   None of these

(4)   What do you understand by underflow condition?
      (a)   If the mantissa of the result is larger than the maximum capacity of 99.
      (b)   If the exponent of the result is larger than the maximum capacity of 99.
      (c)   If the mantissa of the result is lesser than the minimum capacity of -99.
      (d)   If the exponent of the result is lesser than the minimum capacity of -99.
      (e)   None of these

(5)   What is normalized floating point representation of 0.00527865 ?
      (a) 0.527865×10^{-1} (b)   0.527865   (c) 0.527865×10^{-2}
      (d) 0.527865×10^2 (e)   None of these

(6)   Which of the following formats belong to any real number?
      (a) Fixed – point (b) Floating – point   (c) All of these

(7)   Fixed point format means any real number without exponent.
      (a)   True   (b)   False

(8)   Which of the following rule is followed in addition of two floating point
      numbers?
      (a)   Addition operation can be performed if the exponents are equal,
            otherwise the larger exponent is kept as it is and the number with
            smaller exponent is made equal to the larger exponent and according
            to that mantissa is changed.

      (b)   Addition operation can be performed if the exponents are equal,
            otherwise the smaller exponent is kept as it is and the number with
            larger exponent is made equal to the smaller exponent and according
            to that mantissa is changed.
      (c)   Mantissas and exponents are added.
      (d)   Only mantissas are added without seeing the exponents.
      (e)   None of these

(9)   What is the binary representation of 95?
      (a)   1011111   (b)   1111101   (c)   1110111   (d)   1111101
      (e)   None of these

(10) What is the decimal representation of 110001?
      (a)   47   (b)   48   (c)   49   (d)   50   (e)   None of these

Answers: (1) (a) (2)   (b) (3)   (a) (4) (d)   (5) (c) (6) (c) (7) (a) (8) (a)
(9) (a) (10) (c)

2.   Problems

(1)   Find the number of significant digits in each of the following numbers :
      (a)   12.4653   (b)   0.2090   (c)   7896.0   (d) 10.00050
      (e)   1879   (f) 0.000013×10^4 (g)   0.00008

(2)   Find the precision and accuracy of the following numbers :
      (a)   123.9   (b)   938   (c)   0.00034   (d) - 23.9846
      (e)   0.20010   (f) 911.3040×10^{-3}

(3)   Round – off the following numbers correct upto 4 – significant figures :
      (a)   5.937654   (b) 0.0093745 (c)   384.539   (d) 26.0000123

(4)   Round – off the following numbers correct upto 3 – decimal places :
      (a)   0.300089   (b) 497.6678   (c)   30.00862   (d) 0.00368

(5)   Convert the following decimal numbers into equivalent binary numbers:
      (a)   324.0   (b)   768   (c)   400.76   (d) 98.125

(6)   Convert the following binary numbers into equivalent decimal numbers:
      (a)   10101010   (b) 1000.01   (c)   1111.110   (d) 110100.101

(7)   Express the following numbers in the normalized floating point
      representation.
      (a)   - 100.293   (b) 0.0006078 (c)   1234   (d)   12.00935
      (e)   579.009   (f) 0.001030×10^4 (g) 386.125×10^3

(8)   Represent each of the following numbers into 32 – bit single precision
      floating point format.
      (a)   58.125   (b)   -72.250   (c)   38.25   (d)   -200.25

(9)   Calculate $\frac{(p+q)}{2}$ for numbers $a = 6.326$ and $b = 4.185$ using four digit
      arithmetic and compare the result by taking $r = p + \frac{(q-p)}{2}$. Comment on
      the result.

(10)   Apply rounding and chopping on each of the following numbers and
       determine the results using the floating – point arithmetic operations.
       Assume that our computer is hypothetical.

       (Note: first apply normalization process and then floating point arithmetic
       operations)
       (a)   72.4278 + 0.01426   (b)   -0.0123 + 0.000157
       (c)   15.6 – 0.0329   (d)   -745 + 74.5

(11)   Using floating point arithmetic operations, determine the value of each of
       the following and comment on the result.
       (a)   0.9714E57 × 0.1592E80   (b)   0.6217E-80 × 0.1256E-35
       (c)   0.1111E-1 ÷ 0.8265E101   (d)   0.9999E12 ÷ 0.1234E-132

Chapter 2   Error Analysis

Objectives

- To understand the concept of errors
- To develop the concept of errors
- To analyze and predict errors in numerical analysis
- To identify the types of errors
- To develop the concept of propagation of errors in numerical computation

Learning Outcomes

After reading this lesson students should be able to

- Identify the sources of errors in computation
- Apply the concept of errors and efficiently analyze different problems
- Identify absolute and relative errors
- Distinguish between truncation and round – off errors
- Identify the propagation of errors in numerical computation and try to minimize it

2.1   INTRODUCTION

Error analysis is one of the important aspects in numerical analysis. To solve any practical applications in the field of science and engineering, one would require a result in numerical form. Numerical methods serve this purpose but these methods generally provide approximate values which are subject to certain errors. The data, involved in computation, are not accurate but are true up to certain significant digits. This is the reason, it is important to identify the sources of errors and observe their growth during numerical computation. However, our ultimate goal is to reduce the amount of error.

Any measurement is based on some pre defined standard. This standards are considered as accurate, while others are derived from these. The derived observations are generally not so accurate. This causes the error.

In this chapter, we discuss the basic types of errors, the computation of errors, their sources , their propogation in operations, errors in series approximation, their propagation through process graph etc.

2.2   ERRORS

It is well known that computers can not represent real or complex numbers exactly. It has a finite word length. Due to this limitation, only a fixed number of digits is stored and operations can be performed on these numbers only. Hence, while storing any exact decimal number in its converted form according to computer memory, an error is introduced. This error is machine dependent and is known as *machine epsilon*.

Basically, an *error* is the difference between actual and approximate value obtained from numerical computation, any experiment, observations or measurements. Based on this, errors are classified in following three categories:

Data Error (Inherent Error):

These type of errors occur due to approximation of the given data or limitations of measuring devices like volt meter, ammeter, multimeter, thermometer, vernier calliper etc. or limitations of computing aids like calculator, computer etc. Due to their limitations, they can measure values upto cetain accuracy. These errors are caused by mistake in using instruments, recording data and calculating measurement results.

Human blunders or mistakes in reading, recording or calculating data also come under this category. For example, a student may read 36 instead of 63 and perform calculation based on this or a person may read his/her weight as 60.5 instead of 61.This may cause error in data.

Many transcendental or irrational numbers like π, e, $\sqrt{2}$ etc. cannot have exact decimal re-presentation. For example, π = 3.14 or 3.1415, e = 2.71 or 2.7182, $\sqrt{2}$ = 1.41 or 1.4142. When using these numbers in computation only required number of significant digits can be used, which causes data error.

The following actions should be taken to minimize data errors.

- One should check the work of another.
- A proper care should be taken in reading, recording or calculating the data.
- Calculation of error should be done accurately.
- One should increase the number of experiments and then take an average of those readings.

Truncation Error (Discretization Error):

Many mathematical series (for eg. any Taylor's series) are infinite which in practice very difficult to accommodate. It is practically not feasible to involve all the terms in the calculation. Therefore, approximations are used to estimate the value. It results into an error, known as *truncation error* or *discretization error*.

We often use only finite number of terms of the series.For example if we want to calculate the value of sine series

$$sin\ x = x - \frac{x^3}{3!} + \frac{x^5}{5!} - \frac{x^7}{7!} + \cdots$$

then it is very difficult to use all the terms in the calculation of series, therefore, the process is terminated after some finite number of terms. The omitted terms will generate a truncation error in the final result.

We know that the computer can accommodate only few digits in mantissa during normalized floating point representation. For example, 12.167534 is converted into 0.1216E2 in our hypothetical computer in normalized floating point representation. The digits 7,5,3 and 4 are truncated, which results in error.

If a number is converted from one number system to another it may have repeated fraction. Therefore, such numbers have been discarded after some digits which causes an error.

For example, $(0.8)_{10}$ = $(0.11001100......)_2$. In this conversion 1100 fraction is repreated so it has been discarded after some digits.

Many algorithms use infinite series in the processing or calculating so this error is of great importance. The study of this type of error is generally associated with the problem of convergence.

Round – off Error (Quantization Error):

To represent any real number in its exact form is not possible due to limitation of digital computers. Rounding is introduced to handle such situations. The error occurs due to this is known as *round- off error* or *quantization error*. A round – off error represents the difference between the actual value and its closest real number value depending on how the rounding is applied.

For example, 9.3678 is rounded to 9.368 introduces this kind of error.

The following actions should be taken to minimize round – off errors.

• Change the calculation procedure to avoid subtraction of nearly equal numbers or division by a small number.

• At each step of calculation, at least one more significant digit should be retained than that given in the data, then perform the last operation and then round – off.

If the hypothetical computer allowed four digits in the mantissa and if we add two numbers, we get a sum as x = 0.13429×10^1. It can be expressed as

x = (0.1342 + 0.00009) × 10^1
  = $0.1342 \times 10^1 + 0.9 \times 10^{-3}$ = $0.1342 \times 10^1 + 0.9 \times 10^{-4+1}$

In our hypothetical case it is always the case that the exponent of the second term is four less than the exponent of the first term.

Similarly, if t digits are allowed in the mantissa the result of any mathematical number is written as

True value x = $f_x \cdot 10^e + g_x \cdot 10^{e-t}$
      = Approximate x + Error

Where, t = number of digits in mantissa, e = exponent

$$\frac{1}{10} \le |f_x| < 1 \implies 1 < \left|\frac{1}{f_x}\right| \le 0.1$$

and $0 \le g_x < 1$

(1)   **Chopping**   When we chop off the number the maximum bound on the absolute value of the relative error is

$$E_r = \left|\frac{e_x}{x}\right| = \left|\frac{g_x \cdot 10^{e-t}}{f_x \cdot 10^e}\right| \le \left|\frac{1 \cdot 10^{e-t}}{0.1 \cdot 10^e}\right| = 10^{-t+1} \qquad \text{........ (2.2.1)}$$

where, $e_x = x - \bar{x} = Absolute\ Error$

(2)   **Symmetric Round – off**   When symmetric rounding off is done we have the following two cases.

$$\text{Approximate value } \bar{x} = \begin{cases} |f_x| \cdot 10^e & if\ |g_x| < \frac{1}{2} \\ f_x \cdot 10^e + 10^{e-t} & if\ |g_x| \ge \frac{1}{2} \end{cases}$$

Where $\bar{x}$ has the same sign as f_x. The addition of 10^{e-t} in the second line of the equation corresponds to adding 1 in the last digit retained if the first digit dropped is 5 or greater.

If $|g_x| < \frac{1}{2}$, the absolute error $|e_x| = |g_x| \cdot 10^{e-t}$

If $|g_x| \ge \frac{1}{2}$, the absolute error $|e_x| = |1 - g_x| \cdot 10^{e-t}$

Therefore, $|e_x| \le \frac{1}{2} 10^{e-t}$ (we combine both cases)

The maximum bound of the relative error in the case of symmetric rounding off is

$$\left|\frac{e_x}{x}\right| \le \left|\frac{\frac{1}{2} 10^{e-t}}{|f_x| \cdot 10^e}\right| \le \left|\frac{\frac{1}{2} 10^{e-t}}{0.1 \cdot 10^e}\right| = 5 \cdot 10^{-t} = 0.5 \cdot 10^{-t+1} \qquad \text{........ (2.2.2)}$$

2.2.1   Absolute Error, Relative Error and Percentage Error

Absolute Error: If x_t is the true value of a quantity and x_a is the approximate value of a quantity then the absolute error (E_a) is defined by

$$\text{Absolute Error} = |\text{True value} - \text{Approximate value}|$$

i.e. $E_a = |x_t - x_a|$

The important thing in error calculation is the magnitude of error, not the sign as it may be positive or negative. Therefore the concept of absolute error comes into the picture. But sometimes absolute error may not give its correct impact as it does not take into account the order of magnitude of value under study. For example, absolute error of 1.6 has more relavance in the actual voltage of 2.5786 than in the voltage of 2500. Due to this the concept of relative error comes into the picture.

Relative Error: If x_t is the true value of a quantity and x_a is the approximate value of a quantity then the relative error (E_r) is defined by

$$\text{Relative Error} = \frac{\text{Absolute Error}}{|True\ Value\ |}$$

i.e.
$$E_r = \frac{|x_t - x_a|}{|x_t|}$$

Percentage Error: If x_t is the true value of a quantity and x_a is the approximate value of a quantity then the percentage error (E_p) is defined by

$$\text{Percentage Error} = \text{Relative Error} \times 100$$

i.e.
$$E_p = \frac{|x_t - x_a|}{|x_t|} \times 100$$

Remarks: Let x be any number expressed as $0.d1d2d3 \ldots \times 10^n$ where, $d1, d2, d3\ldots$ are decimal digits, then

1.   If x_a is the approximate value of true value x_t after truncating to p digits, the value of upper bound of absolute error because of truncation becomes

$$E_a = |x_t - x_a| < 10^{\,n-p}$$

and the value of relative error because of truncation becomes

$$E_r = \frac{|x_t - x_a|}{|x_t|} < 10^{-p+1}$$

2.   If x_a is the approximate value of true value x_t after rounding – off to p digits, the value of upper bound of absolute error because of rounding – off becomes

$$E_a = |x_t - x_a| < 0.5 \times 10^{\,n-p}$$

and the value of relative error because of rounding – off becomes

$$E_r = \frac{|x_t - x_a|}{|x_t|} < 0.5 \times 10^{-p+1}$$

3.   If a number is rounded to p decimal places, then the absolute error Ea $= 0.5 \times 10^{-p}$

4.   If ϵ is a small positive quantity such that $|x_t - x_a| \le \epsilon$, then ϵ is called error tolerance or limit in estimating the true value of x.

5.   The relative and relative percentage errors are independent of units while absolute error is expressed in terms of units.

6.   Here we discuss only the statement of the theorem which describes the relation between the relative error and the number of correct significant digits.

Theorem: If a number is correct to n significant digits and if the first significant digit of the number is k then the relative error

$$E_r < \frac{1}{k \times 10^{n-1}} \cdot (n \neq 1)$$

The converse of the above theorem is also true. The statement is given below.

Theorem: Let E_r be the relative error in rounding – off x_t to x_a and $E_r <$ $\frac{1}{2(k+1)10^{n-1}}$ where k is the first significant digit in x_a then x_a is correct to n significant digits.

Example 2.1   If $x_t = 2.34569$ then find the value of absolute and relative error if x is truncated to three decimal places.

Solution: Given, $x_t = 2.34569$

After converting it into normalized floating point form, $x_t = 0.234569E1$
After truncating to three decimal places, $x_a = 0.234E1$

Therefore, Absolute Error $= E_a = |x_t - x_a| = |0.234569E1 - 0.234E1|$

$$= 0.000569E1 = 0.5690E-2$$

Relative Error $= E_r = \frac{|x_t - x_a|}{|x_t|} = \frac{0.000569\,E1}{0.234569\,E1} = 0.00242572 = 0.242572E-2$

Remark: Here, value of $E_a < 10^{1-3} = 10^{-2}$. So, $E_a = |x_t - x_a| < 10^{n-p}$ is verified and value of $E_r < 10^{-3+1} = 10^{-2}$. So, $E_r = \frac{|x_t - x_a|}{|x_t|} < 10^{-p+1}$ is verified.

Example 2.2   If $x_t = 0.00893487$ then find the value of absolute, relative and relative percentage error if x is rounded – off to four decimal places.

Solution: Given, $x_t = 0.00893487$

After converting it into normalized floating point form, $x_t = 0.893487E-2$
After rounded – off to four decimal places, $x_a = 0.8935E-2$

Therefore, Absolute Error $= E_a = |x_t - x_a| = |0.893487E-2 - 0.8935E-2|$
$$= |-0.000013\ E-2|$$
$$= 0.1300E-2$$

Relative Error $= E_r = \frac{|x_t - x_a|}{|x_t|} = \frac{0.000013\ E-2}{0.893487\ E-2} = 1.454973E-5 = 0.1454E-4$

Relative Percentage Error $= E_r \times 100 = 0.00001454 \times 100 = 0.001454\ \%$

Remark: Here, value of $E_a < 0.5 \times 10^{-2-4} = 10^{-6}$. So, $E_a = |x_t - x_a| < 0.5 \times 10^{n-p}$ is verified. and value of $E_r < 0.5 \times 10^{-4+1} = 10^{-3}$. So, $E_r = \frac{|x_t - x_a|}{|x_t|} < 0.5 \times 10^{-p+1}$ is verified.

Example 2.3   If true value of x is 13.1497 and approximate value is 13.14, then find absolute, relative and relative percentage error.

Solution: Given, $x_t = 13.1497$

Approximate value, $x_a = 13.14$

Therefore, Absolute Error $= E_a = |x_t - x_a| = |13.1497 - 13.14| = 0.0097$
$$= 0.9700E-2$$

Relative Error $= E_r = \frac{|x_t - x_a|}{|x_t|} = \frac{0.0097}{13.14} = 7.3820\text{E-4} = 0.7382\text{E-3}$

Relative Percentage Error $= E_r \times 100 = 0.0007382 \times 100 = 0.07382 \%$

Example 2.4 The solution of a problem is given as 56.423. with the absolute error in the solution is less than 1%. Find the range of values within which the exact value of the solution must lie.

Solution: Here, $x_a = 56.423$ and maximum absolute error is 1%

$$\text{Therefore,} \quad |x_t - x_a| < 0.01$$

$\therefore$
$$-0.01 < x_t - x_a < 0.01$$

$\therefore$
$$-0.01 < x_t - 56.423 < 0.01$$

$\therefore$
$$56.423 - 0.01 < x_t < 56.423 + 0.01$$

$\therefore$
$$56.413 < x_t < 56.433$$

Therefore, the exact value of the solution must lie in the interval (56.413 , 56.433).

Example 2.5 The solution of a problem is given as $x_a = 13.45$. with the relative error in the solution is less than 2%. Find the range of values within which the exact value of the solution must lie.

Solution: Here, maximum relative error is 2% = 0.02

Therefore,
$$\left| \frac{x_t - x_a}{x_t} \right| < 0.02$$

$\therefore$
$$-0.02 < \frac{x_t - x_a}{x_t} < 0.02$$

Taking
$$\frac{x_t - x_a}{x_t} < 0.02$$

$\therefore$
$$(x_t - x_a) < 0.02 \, x_t$$

$\therefore$
$$0.98 \, x_t < x_a$$

$\therefore$
$$x_t < \frac{x_a}{0.98} = \frac{13.45}{0.98} = 13.7244....$$

Now, taking
$$-0.02 < \frac{x_t - x_a}{x_t} \Rightarrow x_t - x_a > -0.02 x_t$$

$\therefore$
$$1.02 \, x_t > x_a$$

$\therefore$
$$x_t > \frac{x_a}{1.02} = \frac{13.45}{1.02} = 13.1863...$$

Therefore, true value of x lies between 13.1863 and 13.7244.

Example 2.6   Given the series

$$Sinx = x - \frac{x^3}{3!} + \frac{x^5}{5!} - \frac{x^7}{7!} + \cdots, -\infty < x < \infty$$

Calculate the truncation error in computation of $Sinx$ if only three terms are considered for $x = 0.5$.

Solution: Actual value of $Sin\ 0.5 = 0.47942553$

Now, considering only first three terms and substituting $x = 0.5$ in the above series we get,

$$\text{Truncated series of } Sinx = x - \frac{x^3}{3!} + \frac{x^5}{5!}$$

Therefore,   truncated value of $Sin\ 0.5 = 0.5 - \frac{0.5^3}{3!} + \frac{0.5^5}{5!}$

$$= 0.5 - 0.02083 + 0.0002604167$$

$$= 0.47943042$$

$$\text{Truncation error} = |\text{ Actual value} - \text{Truncated value }|$$

$$= |\ 0.47942553 - 0.47943042|$$

$$= 0.00000489$$

Example 2.7 Evaluate the sum $\sqrt{2} + \sqrt{3} + \sqrt{5}$ to 4 significant digits and find its absolute, relative and percentage error.

Solution: Given, $\sqrt{2} = 1.414$, $\sqrt{3} = 1.732$, $\sqrt{5} = 2.236$

Hence, Sum = S = 5.382. Therefore, $E_a = 0.0005 + 0.0005 + 0.0005 = 0.0015$
($\because$ If a number is rounded or correct to p decimal places, then the absolute error Ea $= 0.5 \times 10^{-p}$. So, in this case, number is correct to 3 decimal places and hence Ea $= 0.5 \times 10^{-3} = 0.0005$)

The total absolute error shows that the sum is correct to 3 significant figures only. Therefore, we take S = 5.38

Hence, $E_r = \frac{Total\ Absolute\ Error}{Sum\ of\ true\ value} = \frac{E_a}{S} = \frac{0.0015}{5.38} = 0.0002788$

Percentage Error $= E_p = E_r \times 100 = 0.0002788 \times 100 = 0.02788\%$

2.3 GENERAL FORMULA FOR ESTIMATION OF ERRORS

Let $y = f(x_1, x_2, x_3, \ldots x_n)$ .... (2.3.1)
be a function of n variables $x_1, x_2, x_3, \ldots x_n$. Let $\Delta x_1, \Delta x_2, \ldots, \Delta x_n$ be the errors in $x_1, x_2, x_3, \ldots x_n$. Then the error Δy in y is given by

$$y + \Delta y = f(x_1 + \Delta x_1, x_2 + \Delta x_2, x_3 + \Delta x_3 \ldots x_n + \Delta x_n) \ldots\ldots (2.3.2)$$

Expanding the right-hand side of eq. (1.6) by Taylor's theorem for a function of several variables, we have

$$y + \Delta y = f(x_1, x_2, \dots x_n) + \left(\Delta x_1 \frac{\partial}{\partial x_1} + \dots + \Delta x_n \frac{\partial}{\partial x_n}\right) f + \frac{1}{2}\left(\Delta x_1 \frac{\partial}{\partial x_1} + \dots + \Delta x_n \frac{\partial}{\partial x_n}\right)^2 f + \dots$$

Since the errors Δx_1, Δx_2 ... are relatively small, so their squares and higher powers can be neglected, then we have

$$y + \Delta y = f(x_1, x_2, \dots x_n) + \left(\Delta x_1 \frac{\partial}{\partial x_1} + \dots + \Delta x_n \frac{\partial}{\partial x_n}\right) f \qquad \dots\dots (2.3.3)$$

Subtracting Eq. (2.3.1) from Eq.(2.3.3), we have

$$\Delta y = \Delta x_1 \frac{\partial f}{\partial x_1} + \Delta x_2 \frac{\partial f}{\partial x_2} + \dots + \Delta x_n \frac{\partial f}{\partial x_n}$$

Or
$$\Delta y = \frac{\partial y}{\partial x_1}\Delta x_1 + \frac{\partial y}{\partial x_2}\Delta x_2 + \dots + \frac{\partial y}{\partial x_n}\Delta x_n$$

Which is known as general formula for error. Here, the right hand side is the total derivative of the function y.

For the computation of relative error E_r of the function y, we have

$$E_r = \frac{\Delta y}{y} = \frac{\partial y}{\partial x_1}\frac{\Delta x_1}{y} + \frac{\partial y}{\partial x_2}\frac{\Delta x_2}{y} + \dots + \frac{\partial y}{\partial x_n}\frac{\Delta x_n}{y}$$

Example 2.8   If $u = \frac{6 x y^4}{z^3}$ and errors in x, y , z be 0.001, compute the relative maximum error in u when x = y = z = 1.

Solution: We have $u = \frac{6 x y^4}{z^3}$.

$$\frac{\partial u}{\partial x} = \frac{6 y^4}{z^3}, \quad \frac{\partial u}{\partial y} = \frac{24 x y^3}{z^3}, \quad \frac{\partial u}{\partial z} = -\frac{18 x y^4}{z^4}$$

Therefore, $\Delta u = \frac{\partial u}{\partial x}\Delta x + \frac{\partial u}{\partial y}\Delta y + \frac{\partial u}{\partial z}\Delta z$

$$= \frac{6 y^4}{z^3}\Delta x + \frac{24 x y^3}{z^3}\Delta y - \frac{18 x y^4}{z^4}\Delta z$$

But it is given that $\Delta x = \Delta y = \Delta z = 0.001$ and x = y = z = 1. Also, errors may be positive or negative and so, we take the absolute values of terms on the right side.

So, $(\Delta u)_{max} \approx \left|\frac{6 y^4}{z^3}\Delta x\right| + \left|\frac{24 x y^3}{z^3}\Delta y\right| + \left|\frac{18 x y^4}{z^4}\Delta z\right| = 6(0.001) + 24(0.001) +$

$18(0.001) = 0.048$

Hence, the relative maximum error $(E_r)_{max} = \frac{(\Delta u)max}{u} = \frac{0.048}{6} = 0.008$

Example 2.9   If $u = 4v^6 - 5v$, find the percentage error in u at v = 1, if the error in v = 0.05.

Solution:

$$\Delta u = \frac{\partial u}{\partial v}\Delta v = (24 v^5 - 5) \times 0.05$$

Therefore, at v = 1, $\quad\quad \Delta u = (24(1)^5 - 5) \times 0.05 = 0.95$

Also, at v = 1 $\Rightarrow$ u = -1

Now, percentage error = $\left|\frac{\Delta u}{u}\right| \times 100 = \frac{0.95}{1} \times 100 = 95\%$

2.4 ERRORS ON FUNDAMENTAL OPERATIONS OF ARITHMETIC

A series of computational steps are required to solve any expression numerically. If error occurs in any step then it propagates with progressive computations. Hence, it is important to understand the way of error propagation. To understand this concept let x_a and y_a be the approximate values of x and y respectively. Then,

$$E_{ax} = x_t - x_a \text{ and } E_{ay} = y_t - y_a$$

where E_{ax} and E_{ay} denotes the absolute errors in x_t and y_t respectively and

$E_{rx} = \frac{x_t - x_a}{x_t}$ and $E_{ry} = \frac{y_t - y_a}{y_t}$ denotes the relative errors in x_t and y_t respectively.

Here, we take errors on different operations of two numbers, but similar concept can be generalized for *n* numbers.

2.4.1 Errors on Addition Operation

$x_t + y_t = (x_a + E_{ax}) + (y_a + E_{ay}) = x_a + y_a + E_{ax} + E_{ay}$

$(x_t + y_t) - (x_a + y_a) = E_{ax} + E_{ay}$

Therefore, the absolute error is $|(x_t + y_t) - (x_a + y_a)| = |E_{ax} + E_{ay}|$

Hence, $E_{x+y} \leq |E_{ax}| + |E_{ay}|$ ($\because$ Triangular Inequality) .... (2.4.1)

Thus, the absolute error of a sum of approximate numbers is less than or equal to the sum of the absolute errors of the numbers.

Remark: The following rules should be followed for addition of several floating point numbers with different absolute accuracies.

(1) The numbers with greatest absolute errors (i.e. least accurate) should be kept isolated and unchanged.

(2) All other numbers should be rounded off to one more decimal places than isolated numbers.

(3) Then the numbers so obtained be added

(4) Rounded off the sum by discarding one digit.

2.4.2 Errors on Subtraction Operation

$x_t - y_t = (x_a + E_{ax}) - (y_a + E_{ay}) = x_a - y_a + E_{ax} - E_{ay}$

$(x_t - y_t) - (x_a - y_a) = E_{ax} - E_{ay}$

Therefore, the absolute error is $|(x_t - y_t) - (x_a - y_a)| = |E_{ax} - E_{ay}|$

Hence, $E_{x-y} \leq |E_{ax}| + |E_{ay}|$ ($\because$ Triangular Inequality)   .... (2.4.2)

Thus, the upper bound of absolute error of a difference of approximate numbers is less than or equal to the sum of absolute errors of the numbers.

In multiplication and division operation we use relative error instead of absolute error.

2.4.3   Errors on Multiplication Operation

$\frac{x_t - x_a}{x_t} = E_{rx}$ $\Rightarrow$ $x_t - x_a = x_t . E_{rx}$ $\Rightarrow$ $x_a = x_t - x_t . E_{rx} = x_t (1 - E_{rx})$

Since the relative error can be negative, therefore we can write

$x_a = x_t (1 + E_{rx})$

Similarly, we can write, $y_a = y_t (1 + E_{ry})$

Now, $x_a \times y_a = \{x_t (1 + E_{rx})\} \{y_t (1 + E_{ry})\}$

$$= x_t . y_t (1 + E_{rx}) (1 + E_{ry})$$
$$= x_t . y_t (1 + E_{rx} + E_{ry} + E_{rx} . E_{ry})$$

Since E_{rx} and E_{ry} are errors, so their values are small and therefore, $E_{rx} . E_{ry}$ is such a small value that it can be ignored.

$x_a \times y_a = x_t . y_t (1 + E_{rx} + E_{ry}) = x_t . y_t (1 + E_r) = x_t . y_t + (x_t . y_t) E_r$

So, $\frac{(x_a y_a - x_t y_t)}{x_t y_t} = E_r$, which gives us relative error in multiplication on x and y.

Where, $E_r = E_{rx} + E_{ry}$

Therefore, $|E_r| = |E_{rx} + E_{ry}| \leq |E_{rx}| + |E_{ry}|$ .... (2.4.3)

Thus, the relative error of the product of approximate numbers is less than or equal to the sum of the relative errors of the approximate numbers.

Therefore, Absolute error $E_a = E_r \times x_t$

2.4.4   Errors on Division Operation

$\frac{x_a}{y_a} = \frac{x_t(1+E_{rx})}{y_t(1+E_{ry})}$ $= \frac{x_t}{y_t}(1 + E_{rx})(1 + E_{ry})^{-1}$

$$= \frac{x_t}{y_t}(1 + E_{rx})(1 - E_{ry} + E_{ry}^2 - .....)$$

$$= \frac{x_t}{y_t}(1 + E_{rx} - E_{ry} - E_{rx} . E_{ry} + E_{ry}^2 - .....)$$

Since E_{rx} and E_{ry} are errors, so their values are small and therefore, $E_{rx} . E_{ry}$ and E_{ry}^2 are such a small value that they can be ignored.

$\frac{x_a}{y_a} = \frac{x_t}{y_t}(1 + E_{rx} - E_{ry}) = \frac{x_t}{y_t}(1 + E_r) = \frac{x_t}{y_t} . \frac{x_t}{y_t} E_r$

So, $\dfrac{(\frac{x_t}{y_t} - \frac{x_a}{y_a})}{\frac{x_t}{y_t}} = E_r$ which gives us relative error in division on x and y.

where, $E_r = E_{rx} - E_{ry}$

Therefore, $|E_r| = |E_{rx} - E_{ry}| \le |E_{rx}| + |E_{ry}|$ .... (2.4.4)

Thus, the relative error of the quotient of approximate numbers is less than or equal to the sum of the relative errors of the approximate numbers.

Example 2.10   Find the sum of the following approximate numbers:

0.1267, 13.49, 0.000238, 309.2, 7.16, 150.4, 0.0214 and 0.1896

Where in each of which all the given digits are correct.

Solution: In our case we have two numbers 309.2 and 150.4 which have the greatest absolute error which is 0.05. Therefore, other numbers are rounded – off to two decimal digits.
Hence, the numbers are:

0.13, 13.49, 0.00, 309.2, 7.16, 150. 4, 0.02, and 0.19

Sum S = 0.13 + 13.49 + 0.00 + 309.2 + 7.16 + 150. 4 + 0.02 + 0.19
        = 480.59
        = 480.6

To determine the absolute error, we note that the numbers 309.2 and 150.4 have each an absolute error of 0.05 and rest of the six numbers have each an absolute error of 0.005. So, the absolute error in all the 8 numbers is = 2 (0.05) + 6 (0.005)

$$= 0.1 + 0.03$$
$$= 0.13$$

Apart from absolute error, the rounding error in above numbers is 0.01. Therefore, the total error in S = 0.13 + 0.01 = 0.14

Thus,   S = 480.6 ± 0.14

Example 2.11   Given that
$$a = 10.00 \pm 0.05$$
$$b = 0.0356 \pm 0.0002$$
$$c = 15300 \pm 100$$
$$d = 62000 \pm 500$$

Find the maximum value of the absolute error in (i) a + b + c + d
(ii) a + 5c – d (iii) c^3
Solution:

(i)   Let a_t, b_t, c_t and d_t are true values of a, b, c and d respectively, the

$|(a_t + b_t + c_t + d_t) - (a + b + c + d)| = |(a_t - a) + (b_t - b) + (c_t - c) + (d_t - d)|$

$$\leq |(a_t - a)| + |(b_t - b)| + |(c_t - c)| + |(d_t - d)|$$

$$= |0.05| + |0.0002| + |100| + |500|$$

$$= 600.0502$$

Which is the required maximum value of the absolute error in a + b + c + d.

(ii)   Let a_t, c_t and d_t are true values of a, c and d respectively, then

$$| (a_t + 5c_t - d_t) - (a + 5c - d) | = | (a_t - a) + 5(c_t - c) + (d - d_t) |$$

$$\leq |(a_t - a)| + 5|(c_t - c)| + |(d_t - d)|$$

$$= |0.05| + 5|100| + |500|$$

$$= 1000.05$$

(iii)   If Δ is the error in c, then

$$| (c + \Delta)^3 - c^3 | = | \Delta^3 + 3c\Delta^2 + 3c^2\Delta |$$

$$\leq | 100^3 | + |3 \ (15300)(100)^2 | + |3 \ (15300)^2 \ (100)|$$

$$= \ 10^6 + 459 \ (10^4) + 3(153)^2 \ (10^6)$$

$$= \ 10^6 + 459 \ (10^4) + 70227(10^6)$$

$$= \ 10^{10}(0.0001 + 0.000459 + 7.0227)$$

$$= \ 10^{10} \ (7.023259)$$

Which is the required maximum absolute error.

2.5 ERROR IN A SERIES APPROXIMATION

The remainder term of Taylor's series is generally used to evaluate the error in a series approximation. Taylor's series for $f(x)$ at $x = a$ is given by

$$f(x) = f(a) + (x - a)f'(a) + \frac{(x - a)^2}{2!}f''(a) + \cdots$$

$$+ \frac{(x - a)^{(n-1)}}{(n - 1)!}f^{(n-1)}(a) + R_n(x)$$

Where $R_n(x)$ is the remainder term, which can be expressed in the form

$$R_n(x) = \frac{(x-a)^n}{n!}f^{(n)}(\xi), \quad a < \xi < x$$

For a convergent series, $R_n(x) \to 0$ as $n \to \infty$. If we approximate $f(x)$ by the first n terms of a series, then the maximum error will be given by the remainder term. On the other hand, if the required accuracy is specified in advance, then it would be possible to find n, the number of terms which would yield the desired accuracy.

Example 2.12   Find the number of terms of the exponential series

$$e^x = 1 + \frac{x}{1!} + \frac{x^2}{2!} + \frac{x^3}{3!} + \cdots$$

such that their sum gives the value of e^x correct to five decimal places for $x = 1$.

Solution: The exponential series can be written as

$$e^x = 1 + \frac{x}{1!} + \frac{x^2}{2!} + \frac{x^3}{3!} + \cdots + \frac{x^{(n-1)}}{(n-1)!} + R_n(x)$$

where $R_n(x) = \frac{x^n}{n!}e^\xi$, $0 < \xi < x$.

At $\xi = x$, maximum absolute error $= \frac{x^n}{n!}e^x$.

and maximum relative error $= \dfrac{Absolute\ Error}{True\ value} = \dfrac{\frac{x^n}{n!}e^x}{e^x} = \dfrac{x^n}{n!} = \dfrac{1}{n!}$ at $x = 1$.

For five – decimal accuracy at x = 1, we have $\frac{1}{n!} < \frac{1}{2}10^{-5}$ i.e. $n! > 2 \times 10^5$

which gives n = 9. Thus, we need 9 terms of the exponential series to ensure that its sum is correct to 5 decimal places.

Example 2.13 The Maclaurin's expansion for $\cos x$ is given by

$$\cos(x) = 1 - \frac{x^2}{2!} + \frac{x^4}{4!} - \frac{x^6}{6!} + \cdots$$

Find the number of terms required to estimate $\cos\left(\frac{\pi}{3}\right)$ so that the result is correct to at least 4 significant digits.

Solution: Given that $\cos(x) = 1 - \frac{x^2}{2!} + \frac{x^4}{4!} - \frac{x^6}{6!} + \cdots + R_n(x)$

where $R_n(x) = (-1)^n \frac{x^{2n}}{(2n)!}\cos(\xi)$, $0 < \xi < x$,

At $\xi = x$, maximum absolute error $= \left|(-1)^n \frac{x^{2n}}{(2n)!}\cos(x)\right| = \frac{x^{2n}}{(2n)!}\cos(x)$

and maximum relative error $= \dfrac{Absolute\ Error}{True\ value} = \dfrac{\frac{x^{2n}}{(2n)!}\cos(x)}{\cos(x)} = \dfrac{x^{2n}}{(2n)!}$

At $x = \frac{\pi}{3}$, maximum relative error $= \dfrac{\left(\frac{\pi}{3}\right)^{2n}}{(2n)!}$

For four significant digit accuracy, $\dfrac{\left(\frac{\pi}{3}\right)^{2n}}{(2n)!} \leq \frac{1}{2} \times 10^{-4}$

i.e. $\dfrac{(2n)!}{\left(\frac{\pi}{3}\right)^{2n}} \geq 20{,}000$

Therefore, n = 4 satisfies it. Thus, 4 terms are required to estimate $\cos\left(\frac{\pi}{3}\right)$ so that the result is correct to at least 4 significant digits.

2.6 PROCESS GRAPH

The concept of error propagation can be described in a more convenient way using a process graph. A process graph is a pictorial representation of the sequence in which the arithmetic operations in a calculation are carried out. Using this scheme we can easily find the total error of the final result and the bound on relative and absolute error at the end of any given process and also at the subsequent stages.

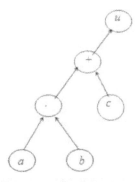

Figure 2.1 Process graph of the expression $u = a.b + c$

In the process graph, circles are known as nodes and arrows are known as branches. It is read from the bottom up with an arrow indicating the direction of flow. All operations at lowest level are performed first then all operations at the second last level, then at the next higher level and so on.

For example, in the Figure 2.1, first a and b are multiplied, then the result is added to c.

Each branch of the graph carrries two values, one is the value of a variable or an operation and second is the relative error in that variable or operation. For example, in the Figure 2.1, the branch leaving the node $'a'$ carries the value of $'a'$ and the relative error in $'a'$. The branch leaving the $'.'$ node carries the value of the multiplication $a.b$ and the value of the relative error in that multiplication. The error at any particular stage is the sum of three terms, two of these terms are the error values entering the nodes multiplying with the corresponding branch labels. The third term is the round off error created by the operation in the given node. We find the branch labels as follows.

(1)   **Addition:**

Let the branches leading to the + node carry the values of the variables x and the y. The branch, where the variable is x, is labeled as $\frac{x}{x+y}$, and for y it is labeled as $\frac{y}{x+y}$.

(2)   **Subtraction:**

The branches corresponding to x is labeled as $\frac{x}{x-y}$ and corresponding to y is labeled as $\frac{-y}{x+y}$.

(3)   **Multiplication:**

If x and y lead to the $'.'$ node, the branch label for both of them will be +1.

(4)   **Division:**

If x is divided by y then +1 corresponds with x and -1 corresponds with y.
Let's take some examples to understand this concept.

Example 2.14 Find the relative error bound of the arithmetic operation $u = (x + y) \cdot z$

Solution: The process graph with the branches labeled to show the propagation of errors is given below.

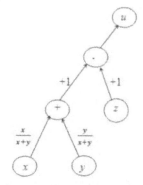

Figure 2.2 Process graph of the expression $u = (x + y) \cdot z$

Relative error upto $'+' = (\frac{e_x}{x})(\frac{x}{x+y}) + (\frac{e_y}{y})(\frac{y}{x+y}) + r_a$

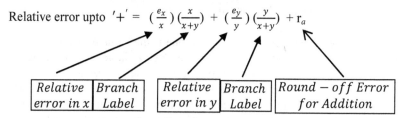

Relative error in x	Branch Label		Relative error in y	Branch Label		Round − off Error for Addition

where, $(\frac{e_x}{x})$ = relative error entering in the node x

$(\frac{e_y}{y})$ = relative error entering in the node y

r_a = relative round – off error for addition

Now, relative error upto $'.' = ((\frac{e_x}{x})(\frac{x}{x+y}) + (\frac{e_y}{y})(\frac{y}{x+y}) + r_a) \cdot 1 + (\frac{e_z}{z}) \cdot 1 + r_m$

where, $(\frac{e_z}{z})$ = relative error entering in the node z

r_m = relative round – off error for multiplication

Therefore, $|\frac{e_u}{u}| \le [|\frac{x}{x+y}| + |\frac{y}{x+y}| + 3] \times 5 \times 10^{-t}$ (from 2.2.2)

$\le [1 + 3] \times 5 \times 10^{-t}$

$= 20 \times 10^{-t} = 2 \times 10^{-t+1}$

Example 2.15 Assume that a is a positive, properly rounded number, and that the number 2 can be represented in a computer exactly (i.e. don't have any inherent error). Draw process graphs and derive bounds on maximum relative errors to show that the bounds are the same for $u = a + a$ and $v = 2a$.

Solution: We have to find the relative error for both $u = a + a$ and $v = 2a$. Process graph of $u = a + a$

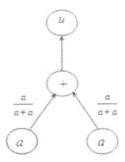

Figure 2.3 Process graph of the expression $u = a + a$

$$\frac{e_u}{u} = \left(\frac{a}{a+a}\right) \quad r_a + \left(\frac{a}{a+a}\right) r_a + r$$

where, r_a = relative error for a

r = relative round – off error for addition

Therefore, $\left| \frac{e_u}{u} \right| \leq r_a + r \quad = \quad 2 \times 5 \times 10^{-t} \quad = \quad 10^{-t+1}$

Process graph of $v = 2a$

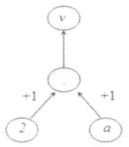

Figure 2.4 Process graph of the expression $v = 2a$

$$\frac{e_v}{v} = 1.(i_2) + 1.(i_a) + i_m$$

where, i_2 = relative error for $2 = 0$ (as it is given that 2 can be represented in a computer exactly i.e. there is no inherent error in 2)

i_a = relative error for a

r = relative round – off error for addition

Therefore, $\left| \frac{e_v}{v} \right| \leq i_a + i_m$

$$= 2 \times 5 \times 10^{-t} \quad = \quad 10^{-t+1}$$

Thus, the error bounds are the same for $u = a + a$ and $v = 2a$.

2.7 PROGRAM IN C

2.7.1 Menu driven program for finding absolute or relative error after truncating or rounding – off to given decimal digits

```c
#include <stdio.h>
#include <stdlib.h>
#include <math.h>
#include<conio.h>

float absoulte(float x,float xa,int e,int t);
float approximation(int choice,float x);
void normalizexa(float *xa);
void normalize(float *num,int *e);
void exitProgram(void);
void main(void)
{
        int opt,choice;
        char ans;
        do
        {
                float x=0,xa=0;
                int e=0;
                float absoluteError=0,relativeError=0;
                clrscr();
                printf("Enter Mantissa:- ");
                scanf("%f",&x);
                printf("Enter Exponent:- ");
                scanf("%d",&e);
                normalize(&x,&e);
                clrscr();
                printf("\n\t\t\t-------------");
                printf("\n\t\t\t| MAIN MENU |");
                printf("\n\t\t\t-------------\n\n");
                printf("\n\t1. Absolute Error");
                printf("\n\t2. Relative Error");
                printf("\n\t3. Exit");
                printf("\n\nEnter Option:- ");
                scanf("%d",&opt);
                printf("\n\t\t\t-------------");
                printf("\n\t\t\t| SUB MENU |");
                printf("\n\t\t\t------------\n\n");
                printf("\n\t1. Truncate");
                printf("\n\t2. Round-off");
                printf("\nEnter Option:- ");
```

```
            scanf("%d",&choice);
            xa=approximation(choice,x);
            switch(opt)
            {
                case 1:
                {
                        absoluteError=fabs(x-xa);
                        normalize(&absoluteError,&e);
                    printf("\nAbsolute Error = %.4f 10^%d.",absoluteError,e);
                        getch();
                        break;
                }
                case 2:
                {
                        absoluteError=fabs(x-xa);
                        relativeError=fabs((absoluteError/x)*(e=e/e));
                        normalize(&relativeError,&e);
                    printf("\nRelative Error = %.4f 10^%d.",relativeError,e-1);
                        getch();
                        break;
                }
                case 3:
                {
                        exitProgram();
                }
            }
            printf("\nContinue (y/n): ");
            ans=getch();
            printf("%c",ans);
        }while(ans=='y');
        return (0);
}
float approximation(int choice,float xa)
{
            int t=0,r=0,x1,swap;
            int i;
            float tempxa;
            if(choice==1)
            {
                    printf("Enter Truncation for X:- ");
                    scanf("%d",&t);
                    for (i=1;i<=t;i++)
                    {
```

```
                                xa*=10;
                        }
                        xa=(int) xa;
                        normalizexa(&xa);
                        return (xa);
                }
                else if(choice==2)
                {
                        printf("Enter Round-off for X:- ");
                        scanf("%d",&r);
                        tempxa=xa;
                        for (i=1;i<=r+1;i++)
                        {
                                xa*=10;
                        }
                        for (i=1;i<=r;i++)
                        {
                                tempxa*=10;
                        }
                        xa=(int) xa;
                        tempxa = (int)tempxa;
                        x1= (int)xa % 10;
                        if(x1>=5)
                        {
                                tempxa+=1;
                        }
                        normalizexa(&tempxa);
                        return (tempxa);
                }
                else
                {
                        printf("Enter Valid Option.");
                        main();
                }
        }
        void normalizexa(float *xa)
        {
                while(*xa<0.1)
                {
                        *xa*=10;
                }
                while(*xa>=1.0)
                {
```

```
                        *xa/=10;
                }
        }
        void normalize(float *num,int *e)
        {
                while(*num<0.1)
                {
                        *num*=10;
                        *e-=1;
                }
        while(*num>=1.0)
        {
                *num/=10;
                *e+=1;
        }
}
void exitProgram(void)
{
  clrscr();;
  printf("\n\n\n\n\n\t\t\tPress Any Key to Exit.....");
  getch();
  exit(0);
}
```

EXERCISES

1.   Multiple Choice Questions

(1)   If we consider only few terms of any infinite series in the computation then it is an example of

(a)   Round-off Error   (b) Data Error   (c) Relative Error
(d)   Truncation Error   (e) None of these

(2)   Which are two most commonly used measures of accuracy?
(a)   Absolute Error & Relative Error
(b)   Data error & Absolute error
(c)   Data Error & Relative Error
(d)   Truncation Error & Round–off Error
(e)   None of these

(3)   If the number 9.8696041 is approximated by 9.870 then what is the value of absolute error?
(a)   0.40113   (b) 0.40113×10^{-3} (c) 0.0003959
(d) 0.3959×10^3 (e) None of the these

(4)   The approximate value of a true value of a variable is 1.246. If the upper limit of the absolute error is 0.005 what is the interval within which true value lies?
(a)   (1.241 , 1.251) (b)   (1.251 , 1.241)   (c)   (1.247 , 1.257)
(d)   (1.257 , 1.247) (e)   None of these

(5)   If the function $f(x) = 1 + 2x + 3x^2 + 4x^3 + 5x^4 + 6x^5$ is approximated by the first four terms what is the value of relative error for $x = 1$?
(a)   11   (b) 0.5238   (c) 10
(d)   0.5536   (e) None of these

(6)   Which type of error occurred during the conversion from one number system to another?
(a)   Data Error   (b) Absolute Error   (c) Round-off Error
(d)   Truncation Error (e) None of these

(7) π is an example of
(a)   Round – off Error (b) Truncation Error   (c) Inherent Error
(d)   Absolute Error   (e) None of these

(8)   The positive difference between the true value and the approximate value of a variable is known as
(a)   Relative Error   (b) Absolute Error   (c) Data Error
(d)   Truncation Error (e) None of these

(9)   The ratio of an absolute error to the true value of a variable is known as
(a)   Absolute Error   (b) Relative Error   (c) Data Error
(d)   Truncation Error (e) None of these

(10)   Which type of error occurred due to limitations of physical measurement, human blunder etc.?
(a)   Data Error   (b) Absolute Error   (c) Round-off Error
(d)   Truncation Error (e) None of these

Answers: (1) (d)   (2) (a)   (3) (c)   (4) (a)   (5) (b)   (6) (d)
            (7) (c)   (8) (b)   (9) (b)   (10) (a)

2.   Problems

(1)   Find the sum of the numbers 98.7, 37.25, 7.86, 0.1234, 379.8, 0.000376, 0.0189 and 12.29, where each number is correct to the digits given. Estimate the absolute error in the obtained sum.

(2)   Calculate the value of $\frac{x-y}{x+y}$, where $x = 0.9978$ and $y = 0.3607$, using normalized floating point arithmetic. Find the relative error in the result.

(3)   If $x = 0.007389$, find the absolute, relative and percentage error if x is rounded to three decimal places.

(4)   Given $x = 27.8935$, find the absolute, relative and percentage error if x is truncated to three decimal palces.

(5)   If an approximate solution of a given problem is 52.124. It is found that there is an absolute error in the solution, which is less than 1%. Find the interval within which the exact value of the solution lie.

(6)   Given an approximate solution of a problem is 79.2567. The relative error in the solution is less than 2%. Find the range within which the exact value of the solution lie.

(7)   Given the series
$$\cos x = 1 - \frac{x^2}{2!} + \frac{x^4}{4!} - \frac{x^6}{6!} + \cdots, -\infty < x < \infty$$
Calculate the truncation error in computation of $\cos x$ if only three terms are considered for $x = 0.9$.

(8)   If $u = 9x^2\, y\, z^3$ and errors in x, y , z be 0.01, 0.02 and 0.03 respectively, compute the relative maximum error in u when $x = y = z = 1$.

(9)   Compute the percentage error in the time period $T = 2\pi \sqrt{\dfrac{l}{g}}$ for $l = 1$ m if the error in the measurement of l is 0.01.

(10)   If $R = \frac{1}{2}\left(\frac{r^2}{h} + h\right)$ and the error in R is at the most 0.4%, find the percentage error allowable in r and h when $r = 5.1\ cm$ and $h = 5.8\ cm$.

(11)   If $f(x) = 5\tan x - 7x$, find the percentage error in $f(x)$ for x = 1, if the error in x = 0.003.

(12)   Current flows through a 10-ohm resistance that is accurate within 10%. The current is measured as 2.0 amp., within $\pm$ 0.1 amp. From Ohm's law, the voltage drop across the resistance is the product of the resistance and the current. What are the absolute and relative errors in the computed voltage? Neglect roundoff errors.

(13)   The reactance of a capacitor is given by
$$X_c = \frac{1}{2\pi f C}$$
where X_c = capacitive reactance, Ω
        f = frequency, hertz
        C = capacitance, farads
What are the bounds on X_c for $f = 400 \pm 1$ hertz and C = 10^{-7} farads $\pm$ 10%?

(14)   The position S of a body falling freely in a vacuum is given by
$$S = \frac{1}{2}\, g t^2$$
where g = acceleration of gravity, ft/ sec^2, t = time since release, sec. Assume that g = 32.2 ft / sec^2, exactly, but that t can be measured to only $\pm$ 0.1 sec. Show that, the relative error decreases.

(15)   Consider the polynomial $P(x) = a + bx + cx^2$ for some value of x_0 such that $|x_0| \leq 1$. Let m_1, m_2, m_3 are the relative round off errors in the multiplications. α_1, α_2 are the relative round off errors in addition. Δ is the relative inherent error in x_0 and $\delta_a, \delta_b, \delta_c$ are the relative inherent errors in a, b ,c respectively. Find the error in $P(x_0)$ by the process graph.

(16)   Assume that a is a positive properly rounded number and that the number 3 can be represented in the computer exactly. (i.e. 3 don't have any inherent error). Draw process graph and show that the bound on the maximum relative error for $u = a + a + a$ is greater than that of $v = 3a$.

(17)   Assume that x is a properly rounded number. Draw process graph and derive error bound expressions to show that $u = x.(x.(x.x))$ and $v = (x^2)^2$ have the same error bounds.

(18)   Assume that a, b and x are positive and exact. Draw process graphs and derive error – bound expressions to show that the relative round – off error bounds for $u = ax + bx^2$ and $v = x(a + bx)$ are the same.

Answers

(1)   Sum = 536.0, AE = 0.13, Total Error S = 0.14
(2)   0.4688E0, Relative Error = 0.4264E-3
(3)   AE = 0.1 E-5, RE = 0.1353E-3, PE = 0.01353%
(4)   AE = 0.9350E-1, RE = 0.3352E-2, PE = 0.3352%
(5)   (52.114, 52.134)   (6)   (77.7026, 80.8742)
(7)   Truncation Error = 0.7275E-3
(8)   0.13   (9) 0.5%   (10) 0.3%
(14) $|e_p| \leq (6|c| + 5|b| + 3|a|) \times 5 \times 10^{-t}$
(15) $\left|\frac{e_u}{u}\right| \leq \left(\frac{8}{3}\right) \times 5 \times 10^{-t}, \left|\frac{e_v}{v}\right| \leq 2 \times 5 \times 10^{-t}$
(16) $\left|\frac{e_u}{u}\right| \leq 7 \times 5 \times 10^{-t}, \left|\frac{e_v}{v}\right| \leq 7 \times 5 \times 10^{-t}$
(17) $\left|\frac{e_u}{u}\right| \leq 5 \times 10^{-t} + \left|\frac{bx}{a+bx}\right| \times 5 \times 10^{-t} + 5 \times 10^{-t}, \left|\frac{e_v}{v}\right| \leq 5 \times 10^{-t} +$ $\left|\frac{bx}{a+bx}\right| \times 5 \times 10^{-t} + 5 \times 10^{-t}$

Chapter 3   Solution of Algebraic and Transcendental Equations

Objectives

- To understand the difference between algebraic and transcendental equation
- To understand the importance of iterative methods
- To understand the difference between bracketing and open end methods
- To analyze the problem and apply appropriate iterative algorithm

Learning Outcomes

After reading this lesson students should be able to

- Identify the difference between algebraic and transcendental equation
- Identify the difference between bracketing and open end methods
- Solve the equations by using appropriate bracketing method
- Solve the equations by using appropriate open end method
- Choose appropriate iterative algorithm and solve the problem

3.1   INTRODUCTION

In this chpater, we use different numerical methods for solving the roots of an equation of the form $\quad f(x) = 0 \qquad \qquad$ .... (3.1.1)
where $f(x)$ may be in polynomial form of degree n in variable x given by

$$f(x) = a_n x^n + a_{n-1} x^{n-1} + \dots + a_1 x + a_0 \qquad \qquad \text{........ (3.1.2)}$$

or may be in transcendental form. The roots may be real and diffferent, real and repeated or complex numbers. The function $f(x)$ which involves some other functions namely logarithmic (eg. $log_{10}x - 1.2$), trigonometric (eg. $sinx + cosx$, $2x - cosx - 5$), exponential (eg. $e^{-x} - x$), arithmetic (eg. $2^x - cosx - 5$) etc. is called transcendental equation. This category of equations may have a finite or an infinite number of real roots or may not have real root at all.

If $f(x)$ is a cubic, quadratic or biquadratic equation, algebraic methods like Cardon's Method, Euler's Method, Ferrari's Method are avaliable for finding the roots. But if the equation is of higher degree polynomial (greater than four) or transcendental, algebraic methods are not available. Therefore, we take help of numerical methods to solve such type of equations.

In this chapter, first we discuss numerical methods for obtaining solution of equation of the form (3.1.1) to find the single real root involving single variable. This equation $f(x)$ is algebraic or transcendental or a combination of both. Later, we would discuss the methods to find the solution of a system of equations involving two real variables x and y, given by

$$f(x, y) = 0, \ g(x, y) = 0 \qquad \text{............ (3.1.3)}$$

Let $f(x)$ be a continuous and continuously differentiable function. The real number p is called the *root* or *zero* of an equation $f(x) = 0$ if and only if $f(p) = 0$. Geometrically, the real root of an equation $f(x) = 0$ is the value of x where the graph of $y = f(x)$ intersects the x – axis.

Every numerical methods divided into two parts. In the first part, we find the approximation to the actual root called the location of the root and next using an iterative procedure we find a better value of the root to get desired accuracy.

3.2   IMPORTANT PROPERTIES OF EQUATION

1.   If a given equation is of degree n then it has only n roots (real or complex).

     Converse: If $a_1, a_2, a_3, \ldots, a_n$ be the roots of the nth degree equation $f(x) = 0$ then

     $f(x) = P(x - a_1)(x - a_2)(x - a_3)\ldots(x - a_n)$ where P is a constant.

2.   If $f(x)$ is exactly divisible by $x - a$, then a is a root of $f(x) = 0$.

3.   Every equation of the odd degree has at least one real root whose sign is opposite to that of the constant term.

4.   If an equation $f(x) = 0$ is of even degree and the constant term is negative, then the equation has at least one positive and one negative root.

5.   Imaginary roots occur in conjugate pairs, for an equation with real co-efficients. i.e. if $a + ib$ is a root of the equation $f(x) = 0$ then $a - ib$ must also be its root.

6.   If a polynomial equation $f(x) = 0$ has a multiple root a of multiplicity p, then $f'(x) = 0$ has a multiple root a of multiplicity $(p - 1)$.

7.   The largest root of the polynomial $f(x) = a_n x^n + a_{n-1} x^{n-1} + \ldots + a_1 x + a_0 = 0$ may be approximated by solving $a_n \, x + a_{n-1} = 0$, or by the root of quadratic equation $a_{n-2} x^{n-2} + a_{n-1} x^{n-1} + a_n = 0$ whichever is greater in absolute value. This value can be taken as the initial approximation when we can't obtain any other value.

8.   The smallest root of the polynomial can be approximated by the root of the equation $a_1 x + a_0 = 0$ or by the zeros of the quadratic equation $a_2 x^2 + a_1 x + a_0 = 0$,   whichever is smaller in absolute value.

9. If $f(x) = a_n x^n + a_{n-1} x^{n-1} + \dots + a_1 x + a_0 = 0$ is a polynomial then solution lies between $(-|x^*_{max}|, |x^*_{max}|)$

where, $|x^*_{max}| = \sqrt{(\frac{a_{n-1}}{a_n})^2 - 2(\frac{a_{n-2}}{a_n})}$

Let's understand properties 7 to 9 with the help of example.

e.g. consider the polynomial equation $f(x) = 3x^3 - 12x^2 + 9x + 18 = 0$

Property - 7

Then the largest root is $-\frac{a_{n-1}}{a_n} = -\frac{-12}{3} = 4$

i.e. no root of this polynomial equation can be larger than the value 4.

Property - 8

Similarly, the smallest root is $-\frac{a_0}{a_1} = -\frac{18}{9} = -2$

i.e. no root of this polynomial equation can be smaller than the value -2.

Property – 9

Compare the given polynomial with the general form of polynomial we get $a_n = 3$, $a_{n-1} = -12$, $a_{n-2} = 9$

$|x^*_{max}| = \sqrt{(\frac{a_{n-1}}{a_n})^2 - 2(\frac{a_{n-2}}{a_n})} = \sqrt{(\frac{12}{3})^2 - 2(\frac{9}{3})} = 10$

Therefore, solution lies within the interval $(-\sqrt{10}, \sqrt{10})$
= (-3.1623, 3.1623)

3.2.1 Descarte's Rule of Sign

If $f(x)$ is a polynomial of degree n (i.e. $f(x) = a_n x^n + a_{n-1} x^{n-1} + \dots + a_1 x + a_0$) then the number of positive roots of $f(x)$ is equal to the number of changes in sign of the co-efficients of $f(x)$ taken in order or less than that quantity by a multiple of two.

Result: The number of negative roots of $f(x)$ is same as the number of positive roots of $f(-x)$.

Example 3.1 Find the number of positive and negative roots of the equation

$$f(x) = x^6 + 5x^4 - 3x^3 - 3x^2 + x - 11$$

Solution: Consider the equation

$$f(x) = x^6 + 5x^4 - 3x^3 - 3x^2 + x - 11$$

Sign of co-efficients of f(x) are   +   + $\overline{-}$ $-$ + $-$

$f(x)$ has 3 changes of sign + to −, − to + and + to −.
Therefore, number of positive roots = 3 or 1.

Now, $f(-x) = (-x)^6 + 5(-x)^4 - 3(-x)^3 - 3(-x)^2 + (-x) - 11$

$= x^6 + 5x^4 + 3x^3 - 3x^2 - x - 11$

Sign of co-efficients of $f(-x)$ are $+$ $+$ $+$ $-$ $-$ $-$

$f(-x)$ has 1 change of sign $+$ to $-$. Therefore, number of positive roots of $f(-x) = 1$. Hence, the number of negative roots of $f(x) = 1$.

Result: If an equation of nth degree has at the most p positive roots and at the most q negative roots, then it follows that the equation has at least $n - (p + q)$ imaginary roots.

For eg. above is an equation of 6th degree and it has 3 positive and 1 negative roots then it has at least $6 - (3 + 1) = 2$ imaginary roots.

3.3   METHODS OF SOLUTION

There are mainly four types of methods used to find the root of non linear equations.
1.   Direct method
2.   Graphical method
3.   Trial and error method
4.   Iterative method

3.3.1   Direct Method

Direct methods are used to find the roots of some of polynomials. Consider a quadratic equation

$$ax^2 + bx + c = 0 \qquad\qquad \text{........ (3.3.1)}$$

The roots of the Eq. (3.3.1) are given by

$$x_1 = \frac{-b+\sqrt{b^2-4ac}}{2a}, \qquad x_2 = \frac{-b-\sqrt{b^2-4ac}}{2a}$$

Similarly, cubic and bi quadratic polynomial equations can be solved using same types of formulae.

Limitations:

• The higher order polynomial equations can not be solved by direct method.
• Transcendental equations can not be solved using this method.

3.3.2   Graphical Method

In this method we draw the graph of the function $y = f(x)$ with respect to rectangular axes. Then the points at which the graph intersects the $x -$ axis are the location of the roots of the equation $f(x) = 0$. If $f(x)$ is complicated in form then we re $-$ write the equation $f(x) = 0$ as $g(x) = h(x)$ where $g(x)$ and $h(x)$ are simple functions such that we can draw the graphs of $y = g(x)$ and $y = h(x)$ with respect to rectangular axes. Then the point of intersection of two curves give the rough approximation or location of the real roots of the equation $f(x) = 0$. For eg. $sinx + 5x - 1$ can be re – written as $sinx = 5x - 1$ and the graphs of $y = sinx$ and $y = 5x - 1$ are drawn.

Limitation:

- Provide approximate result
- Cumbersome and time consuming
- Accuracy of the results are inadequate for the requirements of many engineering and scientific applications.

3.3.3 Trial and Error Method

This method of finding the roots involves several guesses for x. Each time we substitute the value of x in the function and evaluating to see whether it is close to zero. The value of x which satisfies the function is one of the approximate roots of the equation. This situation can be avoided with the advent of computer by developing an algorithm.

Limitation:

- Provide approximate result
- Cumbersome and time consuming
- Accuracy of the results are inadequate for the requirements of many engineering and scientific applications.

3.3.4 Iterative Method

This method starts with an initial guess, which is then successively corrected by the number of iterations. The process is continued untill we get the desired level of accuracy. With the advent of computers it becomes very easy to calculate large number of iterations and obtain the final result.

Based on the number of initial guesses they use to solve equation, iterative methods can be divided into two major categories.

1. Bracketing methods (Close end methods)

These methods, also known as interpolation methods, start with two initial guesses that 'bracket' the root and then the width of the bracket is reduced systematically until solution is reached. These methods require to find sign changes in the function during every iteration. In these, it is required that the values of two functions are of opposite signs.

Bisection and False position are bracketing methods.

2. Open end methods

Open end methods, also known as extrapolation methods, start with one or two initial guesses that do not necessarily bracket the root. These methods do not require to find sign changes in the function during every iteration. In these methods, it is not required that the values of two functions are of opposite signs.

Secant method, Newton-Raphson method, Fixed point method, Muller's method and Lin – Bairstow's method are open end methods.

3.4   TERMINATION CRITERION

As we have discussed that iterative methods start with initial guess, which is then successively corrected by the number of iterations. The important question is when to stop this procedure? The process is continued untill we get the desired level of accuracy in the final result. Depending on the behaviour of the function one of the following criteria can be used to terminate the procedure.

1. $|x_{i+1} - x_i| \leq \epsilon$ i.e. Absolute error in x is less than or equal to prescribed tolerance

2. $\left|\frac{x_{i+1} - x_i}{x_{i+1}}\right| \leq \epsilon$ i.e. Relative error in x is less than or equal to prescribed tolerance $x_{i+1} \neq 0$

3. $|f(x_{i+1})| \leq \epsilon$ i.e. Value of function at root is less than or equal to prescribed tolerance

4. $|f(x_{i+1}) - f(x_i)| \leq \epsilon$ i.e. Difference in function values is less than or equal to prescribed tolerance

where x_i is the approximation of the root at i^{th} iteration and $f(x_i)$ is the value of the function at x_i.

x_{i+1} is the approximation of the root at $(i+1)^{th}$ iteration and $f(x_{i+1})$ is the value of function at x_{i+1}. The single termination criteria or the combination of criterion can be used to stop the iterative procedure. If the convergence of the process is not guaranteed we must have a limit on the number of iterations.

3.5   BISECTION METHOD (BOLZANO METHOD)

This method is based on the repeated application of intermediate value theorem which states that if a real valued function $f(x)$ be continous in a closed interval $[a, b]$ and $f(a).f(b) < 0$, then there exists at least one real root of the equation $f(x) = 0$ between a and b. If $f'(x)$ exists and keeps the same sign in $[a, b]$, then there is a unique real root of $f(x) = 0$ in $[a, b]$.

It is the most simplest and reliable bracketing method. This method is also known as *Bolzano method* or *Interval halving method*.

This method starts with two initial guesses say x_1 and x_2 between which the root p exists. The root p lies between x_1 and x_2 based on the fact that $f(x_1).(x_2) < 0$. Then the first approximation to the root is

$$x_3 = \frac{x_1 + x_2}{2}$$ .... (3.5.1)

There are three posibilities for $f(x_3)$.

1. If $f(x_3) = 0$ then x_3 is a root of $f(x) = 0$.
2. If $f(x_1).f(x_3) < 0$ then the root lies between x_1 and x_3, so replace x_2 by x_3.
3. If $f(x_1).f(x_3) > 0$ then the root lies between x_3 and x_2, so replace x_1 by x_3.

Then we bisect the interval as before and continue the same procedure. This process is repeated until we get the interval within which the root lies as small as we desired. If *epsilon* (ϵ) is the prescibed tolerance in the requred root p then the iterative procedure terminates when the absolute error becomes less than or equal to *epsilon* . i.e. $|x_2 - x_1| \leq \epsilon$.

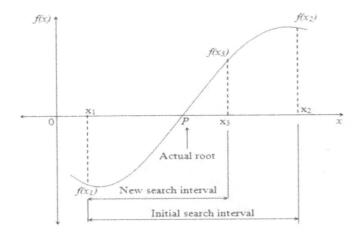

Figure 3.1 Bisection method

In the Figure 3.1, $f(x_1)$ is negative and $f(x_2)$ is positive, so that the root lies between x_1 and x_3. Then the second approximation to the root is $x_4 = \frac{x_1 + x_3}{2}$. If $f(x_4)$ is negative, the root lies between x_4 and x_3 and so on.

3.5.1 Convergence of Bisection Method

In the bisection method, every time the new interval containing the root is reduced by a factor of 2 than the previous interval. The same procedure is repeated for the new interval. If the procedure is repeated n times, then the search interval containing the root is reduced to the size $\frac{x_2 - x_1}{2^n}$.

If we repeat this process then the last interval is as small as given tolerance (ϵ), then

$$\frac{x_2 - x_1}{2^n} \leq \epsilon \qquad \qquad \dots\dots\dots (3.5.2)$$

i.e. the error bound at n^{th} iteration is $\frac{x_2 - x_1}{2^n} = E_b$

Similarly, error bound at $(n+1)^{th}$ iteration is $E_{b+1} = \frac{x_2 - x_1}{2^{n+1}} = \frac{E_b}{2}$ $\qquad \dots\dots (3.5.3)$

From Eq. (3.5.3) we can say that the error decreases linearly with each step by a factor of 0.5. Therefore, the bisection method is linearly convergent and convergence rate is 0.5. Because the convergence is slow to attain a high degree of accuracy, a large number of iterations may be needed. However, this method is guaranteed to converge.

Now, we derive the equation by which we can find the number of iterations required for obtaining an accuracy of ϵ.

From Eq. (3.5.2),

$$log(x_2 - x_1) - nlog2 \leq log\,\epsilon$$
$$\Rightarrow log(x_2 - x_1) - log\,\epsilon \leq nlog2$$
$$\Rightarrow n \geq \frac{log\,(x_2 - x_1) - log\,\epsilon}{log\,2}$$

For example, the minimum number of iterations required for converging to a root in the interval (2, 3) for a given tolerance (ϵ) is shown in Table 3.1.

Table 3.1 Number of Iterations for a Given Tolerance

Tolerance (ϵ)	10^{-2}	10^{-3}	10^{-4}	10^{-5}	10^{-6}
No. of iterations required (n)	7	10	14	17	20

This table also proves that a large number of iterations require to obtain a reasonable degree of accuracy for the desired root.

Remark: Let's understand some basic terminologies which will be useful further.

1. **Convergence of a sequence**

A sequence $x_0, x_1, x_2, ..., x_n$ of successive approximations of a root $x = p$ of the equation $f(x) = 0$ is said to converge to $x = p$ with order $q \geq 1$ if and only if

$$|x_{n+1} - p| \leq c\,|x_n - p|^q,\; n \geq 0$$

c is some constant greater than zero.

For eg. Let $x_0, x_1, x_2, ..., x_n$ be a sequence of successive approximations of an actual root $x = 2.7065$ of some equation $f(x) = 0$. The values of this root calculated by three different methods, are as given in below table:

Approximation	x_0	x_1	x_2	x_3	x_4	x_5	x_6
1st method	4	4.6	5.9	6.3	8.5	9.3	10.7
2nd method	4	3.5659	2.7785	2.7088	2.70669	2.70654	2.70652
3rd method	4	3.4536	2.7769	2.70662	2.70653		

The first method do not converge to the root 2.7065 while the 2nd and 3rd methods converge to the root after the 6th and 4th interations respectively.

2. If $q = 1$ and $0 < c < 1$ then convergence is called **linear or of first order**. Constant c is called the **rate of linear convergence**.

3. **Order of convergence:** An iterative process is said to have k^{th} order

convergence, if k is the largest positive real number, such that

$$\lim_{n \to \infty} \left| \frac{e_{n+1}}{e_n^k} \right| \leq M$$

where M is a non zero finite number. e_n and e_{n+1} are the errors in successive approximations. k^{th} order convergence gives us the idea that in each iteration, the number of significant digits in each approximation increases k times. The error in any iteration is proportional to the kth power of the error in the previous iteration.

Example 3.2   Find the root of the equation $x^3 - 9x + 1 = 0$ using bisection method, correct to 3 – significant figures.

Solution: The first step is to guess two initial values that would bracket a root. According to 9th property of equations the maximum possible

solution is $\sqrt{(\frac{a_{n-1}}{a_n})^2 - - 2(\frac{a_{n-2}}{a_n})}$.

Therefore, $x_{max} = \sqrt{\left(\frac{-9}{1}\right)^2 - 2\left(\frac{1}{1}\right)}$ = 8.888. Therefore, we have both the roots in the interval (-8.88, 8.88). From the below table we can say that there is a root in the interval (-4, -3), (0,1) and in (2, 3).

x	-9	-8	-7	- 6	-5	-4	-3	-2	-1	0	1	2
$f(x)$	-647	-439	-279	-161	-79	-27	1	11	9	1	-7	-9

3	4	5	6	7	8	9
1	29	81	163	281	441	649

Iteration 1:   Let us take $x_1 = 2$ and $x_2 = 3$

$f(x_1) = -9$, $f(x_2) = 1$

Let $x_3 = \frac{1}{2}(x_1 + x_2) = \frac{1}{2}(2+3) = 2.5$

$f(x_3) = f(2.5) = (2.5)^3 - 9(2.5) +1 = -5.875$

$f(x_1) \times f(x_3) = -9 \times -5.875 > 0$

Therefore, replace x_1 by x_3. The new search interval is (2.5, 3)

Iteration 2:   Now, $x_1 = 2.5$ and $x_2 = 3$

$f(x_1) = -5.875$, $f(x_2) = 1$

Let $x_3 = \frac{1}{2}(x_1 + x_2) = \frac{1}{2}(2.5 + 3) = 2.75$

$f(x_3) = f(2.75) = (2.75)^3 - 9(2.75) +1 = -2.9531$

$f(x_1) \times f(x_3) = -5.875 \times -2.9531 > 0$

Therefore, replace x_1 by x_3. The new search interval is (2.75, 3)
The remaining iterations are given in the Table 3.2.

Table 3.2 Remaining Iterations for the Bisection Method

n	x_1	$f(x_1)$	x_2	$f(x_2)$	x_3	$f(x_3)$
3	2.75	-2.9531	3	1	2.88	-1.0321
4	2.88	-1.0321	3	1	2.94	-0.0478
5	2.94	-0.0478	3	1	2.97	0.4681
6	2.94	-0.0478	2.97	0.4681	2.955	0.2081
7	2.94	-0.0478	2.955	0.2081	2.9475	0.07966
8	2.94	-0.0478	2.9475	0.07966	2.9438	0.0166
9	2.94	-0.0478	2.9438	0.0166	2.9419	-0.016

In the 9th iteration, x_1 and x_2 are equal upto 3 significant figures.
Therefore, the root of the given equation, upto 3 significant figures, is $\boxed{2.94}$.

Example 3.3   Find the positive root of the equation $2x - cosx - 3 = 0$ using bisection method, correct to 3 – decimal places.

Solution: First we find the initial approximations. One can also find initial guesses by the method described in Ex. 3.2 . Here we find it directly based on the fact that the values of two functions should be opposite in signs. Here, root lies between 1 and 2, more specifically between 1.5 and 1.75.

x	0	1	2	1.5	1.75
$f(x)$	- 4	-1.5403	1.4161	- 0.07073	0.6782

Iteration 1:   Let us take $x_1 = 1.5$ and $x_2 = 1.75$

$f(x_1) = -0.07073$, $f(x_2) = 0.6782$

Let $x_3 = \frac{1}{2}(x_1 + x_2) = \frac{1}{2}(1.5 + 1.75) = 1.6250$

$f(x_3) = f(1.6250) = 2 \times 1.6250 - \cos(1.6250) - 3 = 0.3042$

$f(x_1) \times f(x_3) = - 0.07073 \times 0.3042 < 0$

Therefore, replace x_2 by x_3. The new search interval is (1.5, 1.6250)

Iteration 2:   Now, $x_1 = 1.5$ and $x_2 = 1.6250$

$f(x_1) = -0.07073$, $f(x_2) = 0.3042$

Let $x_3 = \frac{1}{2}(x_1 + x_2) = \frac{1}{2}(1.5 + 1.6250) = 1.5625$

$f(x_3) = f(1.5625) = 2 \times 1.5625 - \cos(1.5625) - 3 = 0.1167$

$f(x_1) \times f(x_3) = -0.07073 \times 0.1167 < 0$

Therefore, replace x_2 by x_3. The new search interval is (1.5, 1.5625)
The remaining iterations are given in the Table 3.3.

In the 11th iteration, x_1 and x_2 are equal upto 3 decimal figures.
Therefore, the root of the given equation, upto 3 decimal figures, is $\boxed{1.5236}$

Table 3.3 Remaining Iterations for the Bisection Method

n	x_1	$f(x_1)$	x_2	$f(x_2)$	x_3	$f(x_3)$
4	1.5	-0.07073	1.5313	0.0230	1.5156	-0.0239
5	1.5156	-0.0239	1.5313	0.0230	1.5234	-0.0005
6	1.5234	-0.0005	1.5313	0.0230	1.5273	0.0112
7	1.5234	-0.0005	1.5273	0.0112	1.5254	0.0054
8	1.5234	-0.0005	1.5254	0.0054	1.5244	0.0025
9	1.5234	-0.0005	1.5244	0.0025	1.5239	0.0010
10	1.5234	-0.0005	1.5239	0.0010	1.5237	0.0003
11	1.5234	-0.0005	1.5237	0.0003	1.5236	-0.0001

Merits

1. Bisection method is very simple and easy to understand.
2. One function calculation per iteration.
3. It always guarantees convergence.
4. The error bound decreases by 0.5 with each iteration.

Demerits

1. It is very time consuming method.
2. It is very slow compared with other iterative methods.
3. If a function touches the x – axis (eg. $f(x) = x^2 = 0$) then it will be unable to find two approximations x_1 and x_2 such that $f(x_1).f(x_2) < 0$.
4. It can not be used to find multiple roots.
5. This method fails to determine complex roots.

3.6   REGULA – FALSI METHOD (FALSE POSITION METHOD, LINEAR INTERPOLATION METHOD)

False position is the oldest method for finding the real roots of an equation f(x) = 0. In bisection method, we start with two initial approximations x_1 and x_2 and then the interval between x_1 and x_2 is divided into two equal halves, irrespective of location of the root. It is possible that the root is closer to one value than the other. It is better to join the points x_1 and x_2 by a straight line. The line intersects the point with the x – axis gives an improved estimate of the root and is known as the *false position* of the root. Since this method uses the false position of the root repeatedly, it is called the *false position method*. It is also known as *regula – falsi* or *linear interpolation method*.

Method of false position is similar to bisection method but it is faster compare to the bisection method. As in bisection method, we start with two initial approximations x_1 and x_2 within which the root p lies such that $f(x_1).(x_2) < 0$.

As given in Figure 3.2, Draw a straight line joining the points $(x_1, f(x_1))$ and $(x_2, f(x_2))$. The point at which the straight line intersects the x – axis gives the next approximation x_3.

There are three posibilities for $f(x_3)$.
1. If $f(x_3) = 0$ then x_3 is a root of $f(x) = 0$.
2. If $f(x_1).f(x_3) < 0$ then the root lies between x_1 and x_3, so replace x_2 by x_3 and the procedure is repeated.
3. If $f(x_1).f(x_3) > 0$ then the root lies between x_3 and x_2, so replace x_1 by x_3 and the procedure is repeated.

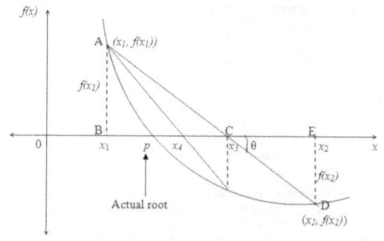

Figure 3.2 False position method

We know that the equation of the line joining the points $(x_1, f(x_1))$ and $(x_2, f(x_2))$ is given by

$$\frac{y - f(x_1)}{x - x_1} = \frac{f(x_2) - f(x_1)}{x_2 - x_1} \qquad \dots\dots(3.6.1)$$

(The equation of the line joining the points (x_1, y_1) and (x_2, y_2) is $\frac{y - y_1}{x - x_1} = \frac{y_2 - y_1}{x_2 - x_1}$)

Since the line intersects the x – axis at x_3. Therefore, substitute $x = x_3$ and $y = 0$ in Eq. (3.6.1) we have

$$\frac{- f(x_1)}{x_3 - x_1} = \frac{f(x_2) - f(x_1)}{x_2 - x_1}$$

After solving this we have,

$$x_3 = \frac{x_1\ f(x_2) - x_2\ f(x_1)}{f(x_2) - f(x_1)} \qquad \dots\dots(3.6.2)$$

In general, the formula can be written as

$$x_{n+1} = \frac{x_{n-1}\ f(x_n) - x_n\ f(x_{n-1})}{f(x_n) - f(x_{n-1})}$$

The procedure will terminate when either the search interval is less than the prescribed tolerance or the value of the function vanishes at a particular approximation. i.e. either $|\frac{x_{n+1} - x_n}{x_n}| < \epsilon$ or $|f(x_{n+1}) - f(x_n)| < \epsilon$

Remark: There is an another way also, by which we can find the formula of new approximation.
From two similar triangles ABC and CED (Figure 3.2), we have

$$\frac{BC}{BA} = \frac{CE}{ED} \qquad \text{or} \qquad BC = \frac{BA}{ED} CE = |\frac{f(x_1)}{f(x_2)}| \ .(BE - BC)$$

Therefore, $\quad BC \left[1 + |\frac{f(x_1)}{f(x_2)}|\right] = |\frac{f(x_1)}{f(x_2)}| \quad BE = |\frac{f(x_1)}{f(x_2)}| \ (x_2 - x_1)$

Hence, $\ BC = x_3 - x_1 = \frac{|f(x_1)|}{|f(x_1)|+|f(x_2)|} (x_2 - x_1)$

Therefore, $x_3 = x_1 + \frac{|f(x_1)|}{|f(x_1)|+|f(x_2)|} (x_2 - x_1)$. Which is the formula for False position method.

3.6.1 Convergence of False Position Method

If the function $f(x)$ in the equation $f(x) = 0$ is not convex than one of the starting points is fixed while the other moves towards the solution. Let x_1 and x_2 be the initial approximations within which the root lies and suppose x_2 is fixed and x_1 moves towards the solution. Let p be the actual root.

Therefore, $\quad e_1 = p - x_1$
$$e_2 = p - x_2$$
$$\vdots$$
$$e_i = p - x_i$$

We can easily derive that

$$e_{i+1} = p - \frac{(p-x_2)f''(a)}{f'(a)} \qquad \qquad \text{........ (3.6.3)}$$

where a is some point and $a \ \varepsilon \ [x_i, x_2]$. This indicates that the process converges linearly. The rate of convergence is one.

Example 3.4 Find the root of the equation $2x - log_{10}x - 7 = 0$, by False position method, correct to four decimal places.

Solution: First we find the initial approximations.

x	1	2	3	4
$f(x)$	-5	-3.3010	-1.4771	0.3979

Here, root lies between 3 and 4. Since f(3) = -1.4771 and f(4) = 0.3979.

Iteration 1: Let us take $x_1 = 3$ and $x_2 = 4$

$$f(x_1) = -1.4771, f(x_2) = 0.3979$$

Let $x_3 = \frac{x1 \ f(x2) - x2 \ f(x1)}{f(x2) - f(x1)} = \frac{(3)(0.3979) - (4)(-1.4771)}{(0.3979) - (-1.4771)} = 3.7878$

$f(x_3) = f(3.7878) = 2 \times 3.7878 - log_{10}(3.7878) - 7 = -0.002839$

$$f(x_1) \times f(x_3) = -1.4771 \times -0.002839 > 0$$

Therefore, replace x_1 by x_3. The new search interval is (3.7878, 4)

Iteration 2: Now, $x_1 = 3.7878$ and $x_2 = 4$

$$f(x_1) = -0.002839, f(x_2) = 0.3979$$

Let $x_3 = \dfrac{x1\ f(x2) - x2\ f(x1)}{f(x2) - f(x1)} = \dfrac{(3.7878)(0.3979) - (4)(-0.002839)}{(0.3979) - (-0.002839)} = 3.7893$

$f(x_3) = f(3.7893) = 2 \times 3.7893 - \log_{10}(3.7893) - 7 = -0.000004$

$$f(x_1) \times f(x_3) = -0.002839 \times -0.000004 > 0$$

Therefore, replace x_1 by x_3. The new search interval is (3.7893, 4)

Iteration 3: $x_1 = 3.7893$ and $x_2 = 4$.

$$f(x_1) = -0.000004\ ,\ f(x_2) = 0.3979$$

Let $x_3 = \dfrac{x1\ f(x2) - x2\ f(x1)}{f(x2) - f(x1)} = \dfrac{(3.7893)(0.3979) - (4)(-0.000004)}{(0.3979) - (-0.000004)} = 3.7893$

$f(x_3) = f(3.7893) = 2 \times 3.7893 - \log_{10}(3.7893) - 7 = -0.000004$

In the 3rd iteration, the values of previous x_3 and new x_3 are equal upto 4 decimal figures.

Therefore, the root of the given equation, upto 4 decimal figures, is $\boxed{3.7893}$.

Example 3.5 Use false position method to find the value of $\sqrt{30}$ correct to four decimal places.

Solution: Let $f(x) = x^2 - 30$

x	0	3	4	5	6
$f(x)$	-30	-21	-14	-5	6

Here, root lies between 5 and 6, since $f(5) = -5 < 0$ and $f(6) = 6 > 0$

Table 3.4 Iterations of False Position Method

n	x1	fx1	x2	fx2	x3	fx3
1	5	-5	6	6	5.4545	-0.2479
2	5.4545	-0.2479	6	6	5.4762	-0.0113
3	5.4762	-0.0113	6	6	5.4772	-0.0005
4	5.4772	-0.0005	6	6	5.477223	-0.000025

Since, in the 3rd and 4th iterations the values of x_3 are same upto 4 decimal places. Therefore, the square root of 30, correct upto 4 decimal places is $\boxed{5.4772}$.

Merits

1. One function calculation per iteration.
2. It always guarantees convergence with the assumption that the function f(x) is continuous and changes sign on [a , b].
3. The error bound decreases with each successive iteration.
4. We can get an accurate error estimate

Demerits

1. The function calculation is very time consuming.
2. Although the convergence rate of false position is greater than bisection method, in some cases, the bisection method will converge faster and generate better results.

3.7 FIXED POINT METHOD (SUCCESSIVE APPROXIMATION METHOD, METHOD OF ITERATION, METHOD OF DIRECT SUBSTITUTION)

To find the root of the equation

$$f(x) = 0 \qquad\qquad \text{........ (3.7.1)}$$

Let the equation (3.7.1) can be manipulated as

$$x = g(x) \qquad\qquad \text{........ (3.7.2)}$$

Both the equations Eq.(3.7.1) and Eq.(3.7.2) are equivalent. Therefore, the root of the equation $f(x) = 0$ is same as the point of intersection of the curve $y = x$ and the curve $y = g(x)$. This point of intersection is known as the fixed point of $g(x)$ as shown in the Figure 3.3. If these two curves intersect at the point p means both the equations are satisfied at this point and the x – coordinate of this point gives the root.

Let x_0 be the initial approximation to the actual root p. Substituting $x = x_0$ in the right hand side of Eq. (3.7.2), we get the first approximation $x_1 = g(x_0)$.
Then the second approximation is $x_2 = g(x_1)$
Similarly, next approximation is $x_3 = g(x_2)$
$$\vdots$$

In general, $\boxed{x_{n+1} = g(x_n)}$ n = 0,1,2.......

Which is called the fixed point formula.

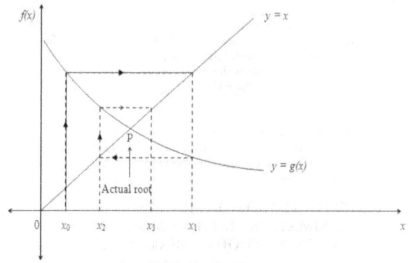

Figure 3.3 Fixed point method

3.7.1   Criterion of Convergence

It is not sure that the iteration process of fixed point method always converges to the root of
$f(x) = 0$. It depends on the nature of $g(x)$. If we choose proper initial approximation then the successive approximations converges to the root p. The following theorem helps to choose appropriate initial guess.

Theorem 3.1

1.   If p is the root of $f(x) = 0$ which is equivalent to $x = g(x)$
2.   I, be any interval containing the root $x = p$
3. $|g'(x)| < 1$ for all x in I.

then the sequence of approximations $x_0, x_1, x_2,....,x_n$ will converge to the root p provided the initial approximation x_0 is chosen in I.

3.7.2   Different Cases of Convergence

As we know that the iteration process of fixed point method always not converges to the root of $f(x) = 0$. It depends on the nature of $g(x)$. Diagrammatic representation of different cases of convergence of fixed point method are given below.

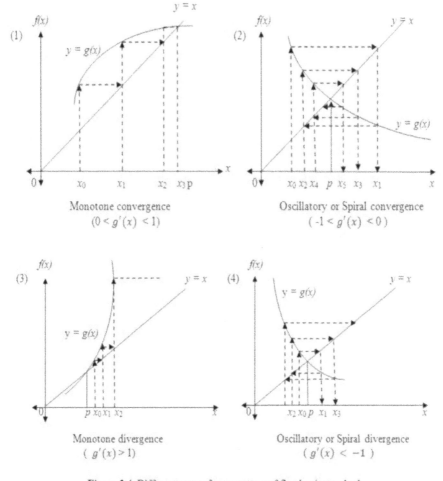

Figure 3.4 Different cases of convergence of fixed point method

3.7.3   Convergence of Fixed Point Method

If p is the exact value of the root of the equation $f(x) = 0$, then
let
$$x_n = p + e_n$$
$$x_{n+1} = p + e_{n+1}$$
where e_n and e_{n+1} are the errors involved in n^{th} and $(n+1)^{th}$ approximations, respectively. Substitute the values of x_n and x_{n+1} in the formula of fixed point $x_{n+1} = g(x_n)$ we get,

$$p + e_{n+1} = g(p + e_n)$$
$$= g(p) + e_n g'(p) + \frac{e_n^2}{2!} g''(p) + \dots$$

Therefore, $e_{n+1} = e_n g'(p) + (g(p) - p) + o(e_n^2)$ (neglacting higher power of

e_n^2)   If we assume that $p = g(p)$, we have

$$\lim_{n \to \infty} \left| \frac{e_{n+1}}{e_n} \right| = \text{constant} = g'(p)$$

Above equation indicates that the fixed point method is linearly convergent and the order of convergence is 1.

3.7.4   Aitken's Δ^2 Method

The slow rate of fixed point method can be improved using Aitken's Δ^2 Method. If p is a root of $x = g(x)$ then we have $p = g(p)$. If x_{n-1} and x_n be two successive approximations to p, we have

$$x_n = g(x_{n-1})$$

Therefore, $x_n - p = g(x_{n-1}) - g(p)$ .... (3.7.3)

By mean value theorem,

$$g(x_{n-1}) - g(p) = (x_{n-1} - p)g'(\alpha), \ x_{n-1} < \alpha < p$$

Hence, Eq. (3.7.3) becomes $x_n - p = (x_{n-1} - p) \, g'(\alpha)$

As per our convergence criterion, if $|g'(x_i)| \leq k < 1$ for all i, then

$$|x_n - p| \leq k \, |(x_{n-1} - p)|$$ .... (3.7.4)

Let x_{n-1}, x_n and x_{n+1} be three successive approximations to the desired root p of the equation $x = g(x)$. Then from Eq. (3.7.4) we have,

$$p - x_n = k \, (p - x_{n-1}) \quad ....(1)$$
$$p - x_{n+1} = k \, (p - x_n) \quad ....(2)$$

Dividing (1) by (2) we get,

$$\frac{p - x_n}{p - x_{n+1}} = \frac{p - x_{n-1}}{p - x_n}$$

Hence, $$p = x_{n+1} - \frac{(x_{n+1} - x_n)^2}{x_{n+1} - 2x_n + x_{n-1}}$$ .... (3.7.5)

But in the sequence of successive approximations, we have

$$\Delta x_n = x_{n+1} - x_n$$

$$\begin{aligned}
\Delta^2 x_n = \Delta \, (\Delta x_n) &= \Delta(x_{n+1} - x_n) \\
&= \Delta x_{n+1} - \Delta x_n \\
&= x_{n+2} - x_{n+1} - (x_{n+1} - x_n) \\
&= x_{n+2} - 2x_{n+1} + x_n
\end{aligned}$$

Therefore, $\Delta^2 x_{n-1} = x_{n+1} - 2x_n + x_{n-1}$

Hence, Eq. (3.7.5) can be written as

$$p = x_{n+1} - \frac{(\Delta x_n)^2}{\Delta^2 x_{n-1}}$$ .... (3.7.6)

which gives the new approximate value of the root in terms of three previously successive approximations. This modified iterative method is known as the Aitken's Δ^2 method or the Aitken extrapolation method.

Example 3.6   Find the root of $e^x - 3x = 0$, by the iteration method, upto three significant figures.

Solution: Let $f(x) = e^x - 3x$

x	0	0.6	0.8
$f(x)$	1	0.02211	- 0.1745

Here, $f(0.6) = 0.02211 > 0$ and $f(0.8) = - 0.1745 < 0$.

Therefore, one root of the equation lies between 0.6 and 0.8.

Now, convert the given function into $x = g(x)$ form. Therefore, $x = \dfrac{e^x}{3}$

Where, $g(x) = \dfrac{e^x}{3}$ and hence, $g'(x) = \dfrac{e^x}{3}$

$$|g'(0.6)| = \left|\frac{e^{0.6}}{3}\right| = |0.6074| < 1$$

$$|g'(0.8)| = \left|\frac{e^{0.8}}{3}\right| = |0.7418| < 1$$

Thus, for $x \in [0.6, 0.8]$, $|g'(x)| < 1$

Iteration 1:   Take $x_0 = 0.6$ as initial approximation.

$$x_1 = \frac{e^{0.6}}{3} = 0.6074$$

Iteration 2:

$$x_2 = \frac{e^{0.6074}}{3} = 0.6119$$

Iteration 3:

$$x_3 = \frac{e^{0.6119}}{3} = 0.6146$$

Iteration 4:

$$x_4 = \frac{e^{0.6146}}{3} = 0.6163$$

Iteration 5:

$$x_5 = \frac{e^{0.6163}}{3} = 0.6174$$

Iteration 6:

$$x_6 = \frac{e^{0.6174}}{3} = 0.6180$$

Iteration 7:

$$x_7 = \frac{e^{0.6180}}{3} = 0.6184$$

Therefore, the root of the given equation, upto three significant figures, is

$\boxed{0.618}$

Example 3.7   Find the positive root of $x^3 + x - 1 = 0$, by fixed point method, corret to three decimal places.

Solution: Let $f(x) = x^3 + x - 1$

x	0	1	0.5	0.8
$f(x)$	-1	1	-0.375	0.312

Here, f(0.5) < 0 and f(0.8) > 0. Therefore, one root of the equation lies between 0.5 and 0.8. The possible forms of the equation are as follows:

1. $x = \dfrac{1}{x^2+1}$ $= g_1(x)$

2. $x = 1 - x^3$ $= g_2(x)$

3. $x = (1-x)^{1/3}$ $= g_3(x)$

4. $x = (\dfrac{1}{x} - 1)^{1/2}$ $= g_4(x)$

In case 1. $g'_1(x) = -\dfrac{2x}{(x^2+1)^2}$, for $x \in [0.5, 0.8]$, $|g'(x)| < 1$

In case 2. $g'_2(x) = -3x^2$, for $x \in [0.5, 0.8]$, $|g'(x)| > 1$

In case 3. $g'_3(x) = -\dfrac{1}{3(1-x)^{2/3}}$, for $x \in [0.5, 0.8]$, $|g'(x)| < 1$

In case 4. $g'_4(x) = \dfrac{1}{2x^2(1-x)^{1/2}}$, for $x \in [0.5, 0.8]$, $|g'(x)| > 1$

Thus, $g_1(x)$ and $g_3(x)$ both give us convergent sequence. Let's take $g(x) = (1-x)^{1/3}$ and $x_0 = 0.5$

$$x_1 = g(x_1) = (1-0.5)^{1/3} = 0.794$$

$$x_2 = g(x_2) = (1-0.794)^{1/3} = 0.591$$

$$x_3 = g(x_3) = (1-0.591)^{1/3} = 0.742$$

$$x_4 = g(x_4) = (1-0.742)^{1/3} = 0.637$$

Table 3.5   Remaining Iterations of Fixed Point Method

n	x_n	$g(x_n)$	n	x_n	$g(x_n)$
5	0.637	0.713	12	0.686	0.680
6	0.713	0.660	13	0.680	0.684
7	0.660	0.698	14	0.684	0.681
8	0.698	0.671	15	0.681	0.683
9	0.671	0.690	16	0.683	0.682
10	0.690	0.677	17	0.682	0.6825
11	0.677	0.686			

The root of the given equation, upto three decimal places, is $\boxed{0.682}$.

Example 3.8   Find a real root of the equation $3x - \cos x - 1 = 0$ correct to four decimal places using
1.   Fixed point method
2.   Aitken's Δ^2 method

Solution:
1.   Let $f(x) = 3x - \cos x - 1$

x	0	1	0.5
$f(x)$	-2	1.4597	-0.3776

Here, $f(0.5) = -0.3776 < 0$ and $f(1) = 1.4597 > 0$.

Therefore, one root of the equation lies between 0.5 and 1.

Now, convert the given function into $x = g(x)$ form. Therefore, $x = \frac{\cos x + 1}{3}$

Where, $g(x) = \frac{\cos x + 1}{3}$ and hence, $g'(x) = \frac{-\sin x}{3}$

$$|g'(0.5)| = \left|\frac{-\sin (0.5)}{3}\right| = |-0.1598| < 1$$

$$|g'(1)| = \left|\frac{-\sin (1)}{3}\right| = |-0.2805| < 1$$

Thus, for $x \in [0.5, 1]$, $|g'(x)| < 1$

Take $x_0 = 0.5$ as initial approximation.

$$x_1 = \frac{\cos (0.5)+1}{3} = 0.6259$$

$$x_2 = \frac{\cos (0.6259)+1}{3} = 0.6035$$

$$x_3 = \frac{\cos (0.6035)+1}{3} = 0.6078$$

$$x_4 = \frac{\cos (0.6078)+1}{3} = 0.6070$$

$$x_5 = \frac{\cos (0.6070)+1}{3} = 0.6071$$

$$x_6 = \frac{\cos (0.6071)+1}{3} = 0.6071$$

Therefore, the root of the given equation, upto four decimal places, is $\boxed{0.6071}$

2.   From the above we know that $x_1 = 0.6259$, $x_2 = 0.6035$, $x_3 = 0.6078$. In Aitken's Δ^2 method

we have to find the value of Δ^2. So, we have

x	Δx	$\Delta^2 x$
$x_1 = 0.6259$		
	-0.0224	
$x_2 = 0.6035$		0.0267
	0.0043	
$x_3 = 0.6078$		

Now, $x_4 = x_3 - \frac{(\Delta x_2)^2}{\Delta^2 x_1} = 0.6078 - \frac{(0.0043)^2}{0.0267} = 0.60711$

which corresponds to 6th iteration in normal fixed point method.

Thus, the required root is $\boxed{0.6071}$.

Example 3.9   Find the smallest root of the equation

$$1 - x + \frac{x^2}{(2!)^2} - \frac{x^3}{(3!)^2} + \frac{x^4}{(4!)^2} - \frac{x^5}{(5!)^2} + \dots = 0$$

using fixed point method.

Solution: Writing the given equation in the form of $x = g(x)$ as

$$x = 1 + \frac{x^2}{(2!)^2} - \frac{x^3}{(3!)^2} + \frac{x^4}{(4!)^2} - \frac{x^5}{(5!)^2} + \dots = g(x)$$

Omitting x^2 and higher powers of x, we get $x = 1$ approximately.
Taking $x_0 = 1$ we get,

$$x_1 = g(x_0) = 1 + \frac{1}{(2!)^2} - \frac{1}{(3!)^2} + \frac{1}{(4!)^2} - \frac{1}{(5!)^2} + \dots = 1.2239$$

$$x_2 = g(x_1) = 1 + \frac{(1.2239)^2}{(2!)^2} - \frac{(1.2239)^3}{(3!)^2} + \frac{(1.2239)^4}{(4!)^2} - \frac{(1.2239)^5}{(5!)^2} + \dots = 1.3263$$

Similarly, $x_3 = 1.38$, $x_4 = 1.409$, $x_5 = 1.425$, $x_6 = 1.434$, $x_7 = 1.439$, $x_8 = 1.442$

The values of x_7 and x_8 indicate that the root is $\boxed{1.44}$ correct to two decimal places.

3.7.5 Finding a Square Root of a Number Using Fixed Point Method

If we want to find a square root of a number say, N then we have $x = \sqrt{N} = (N)^{1/2}$
Therefore, $x^2 = N$ i.e. $x = \frac{N}{x}$

It can be written as $x + x = \frac{N}{x} + x$.

Therefore, $x = \frac{\frac{N}{x} + x}{2}$

If x_0 is the initial approximation to the square root, then

$$x_{i+1} = \frac{\frac{N}{x_i} + x_i}{2}, \quad i = 0,1,2 \dots \dots \qquad \dots\dots\dots (3.7.7)$$

Example 3.10   Evaluate the value of $\sqrt{11}$ by the fixed point algorithm.

Solution: Given, N = 11. The equation is $x^2 - 11 = 0$. To find the initial approximations.

x	0	1	2	3	4
f(x)	-11	-10	-7	-2	5

Here, $f(3) = -2 < 0$ and $f(4) = 5 > 0$. Therefore, the root lies between 3 and 4.
Let $x_0 = 3$

$$x_1 = \frac{\frac{11}{3} + 3}{2} = 3.3333 , \qquad x_2 = \frac{\frac{11}{3.3333} + 3.3333}{2} = 3.316667,$$

$$x_3 = \frac{\frac{11}{3.316667} + 3.316667}{2} = 3.316625, \quad x_4 = \frac{\frac{11}{3.316625} + 3.316625}{2} = 3.316625$$

Therefore, the value of $\sqrt{11}$, correct to six decimal places is, $\boxed{3.316625}$

Merit

1.   If we take smaller value of $g'(x)$ then the equation converges more rapidly.

Demerits

1.   It does not gurantee convergence and converges only if $|g'(x)| < 1$.
2.   If the equation has more than one root and $f(x)$ is continuous then this method may miss one or two roots.
3.   When we try to rearrange the function $f(x)$ to make x the subject, not all rearrangements will work

3.8   NEWTON RAPHSON METHOD (TANGENT METHOD)

Newton – Raphson method is a widely used numerical method for finding a root of an equation $f(x) = 0$. It is generally used to improve the result obtained by one of the previous methods. This method is the fastest method compare to other root finding methods. It approximates the curve of function f(x) by tangents. Hence, it is also known as *tangent method*.

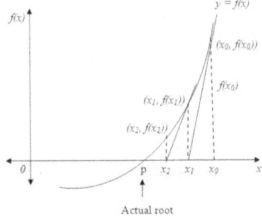

Figure 3.5 Newton – Raphson method

Let x_0 be the initial approximation. Draw a tangent from the point $(x_0, f(x_0))$ to the x – axis. This tangent will intersect x – axis at some point say x_1.

In the next iteration x_1 will be taken as the initial approximation and a tangent is drawn from the point $(x_1, f(x_1))$. The point at which it intersects the x- axis gives the next approximattion x_2. The process is repreated till the difference between two successive approximation is less than the prescribed tolerance.   From the Figure 3.5, the slope of the tangent is given by

$$\tan \theta = \frac{f(x_0)}{x_0 - x_1} = f'(x_0)$$

where, $f'(x_0)$ is the slope of $f(x)$ at $x = x_0$.

Therefore,
$$x_0 - x_1 = \frac{f(x_0)}{f'(x_0)}$$

Hence,
$$x_1 = x_0 - \frac{f(x_0)}{f'(x_0)}$$

The next approximation would be
$$x_2 = x_1 - \frac{f(x_1)}{f'(x_1)}$$

In general, the formula can be written as

$$\boxed{x_{n+1} = x_n - \frac{f(x_n)}{f'(x_n)}}$$ .... (3.8.1)

This is called the Newton – Raphson formula.

3.8.1   Analytical Derivation of Newton Raphson Formula

Let x_0 be the initial approximation of the function $f(x) = 0$ and h be a small correction to the root so   that $f(x_0 + h) = 0$.

Expanding $f(x_0 + h)$ by Taylor's series we get,

$$f(x_0 + h) = f(x_0) + hf'(x_0) + \frac{h^2}{2!}f''(x_0) + \cdots + \frac{h^n}{n!}f^{(n)}(x_0) = 0$$
.... (3.8.2)

Assuming h to be very small, neglecting h^2 and other higher power of h, we get
$$f(x_0) + hf'(x_0) = 0$$

or
$$h = -\frac{f(x_0)}{f'(x_0)}$$ .... (3.8.3)

Substituting the value of h in the equation $x_1 = x_0 + h$ we get the next approximation to the root as,
$$x_1 = x_0 - \frac{f(x_0)}{f'(x_0)}$$

Similarly, taking x_1 as initial approximation, a next approximation x_2 can be written as
$$x_2 = x_1 - \frac{f(x_1)}{f'(x_1)}$$

In general,
$$x_{n+1} = x_n - \frac{f(x_n)}{f'(x_n)}$$ .... (3.8.4)

This general formula is called Newton – Raphson formula.

3.8.2   Criterion of Convergence

Comparing Eq. (3.8.4) with the formula of fixed point method $x_{n+1} = g(x_n)$, we get
$$g(x_n) = x_n - \frac{f(x_n)}{f'(x_n)}$$

In general, $$g(x) = x - \frac{f(x)}{f'(x)}$$

Therefore, $$g'(x) = 1 - \left[\frac{f'(x)f'(x) - f(x)f''(x)}{(f'(x))^2}\right] = \frac{f(x)f''(x)}{(f'(x))^2}$$

We know that fixed point method converges if $|g'(x)| < 1$

Hence, Newton Raphson method converges if $|\frac{f(x)f''(x)}{(f'(x))^2}| < 1$ $\Rightarrow$
$|f'(x).f''(x)| < |f'(x)|^2$ in the pre-decided interval. Assuming $f(x)$, $f'(x)$ and $f''(x)$ to be continuous, we can select a small interval in the neighbourhood of the root p, in which the above condition is satisfied. Newton Raphson formula converges rapidly if the initial approximation x_0 is chosen sufficiently close to the root p. If multiple roots exist then this method converges slowly.

3.8.3   Different Cases of Divergence

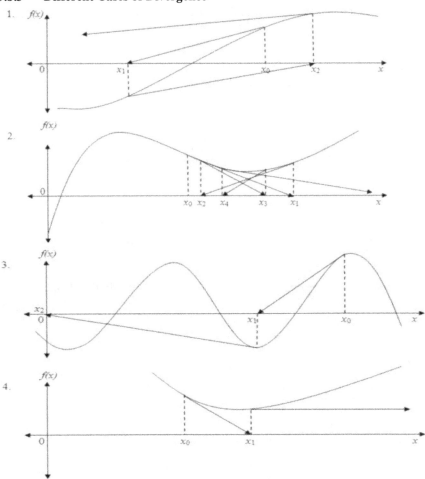

Figure 3.6 Different cases of divergence of Newton - Raphson method

In the case 1, it starts with the initial approximation x_0 and then slowly diverges. It is important to note that here an inflection point (i.e. $f''(x) = 0$) occurs in the neighbourhood of a root.

In the case 2, the method oscillates around a local maximum or minimum or we obtain a solution very far from the area of interest. Case 3 shows how an initial approximation x_0 that is very close to one root can jump to a location x_2 which is very far from other roots. This happens due to the value of slope which is nearly equal to zero (i.e. $f'(x) \approx 0$). It causes division by zero situation in the Newton Raphson method.

In case 4, the solution never hits the x – axis. So, ultimately it diverges from the root.

3.8.4   Convergence of Newton Raphson Method

If p is the exact value of the root of the equation $f(x) = 0$, then
let
$$x_n = p + e_n$$
$$x_{n+1} = p + e_{n+1}$$

where e_n and e_{n+1} are the errors involved in n^{th} and $(n+1)^{th}$ approximations, respectively. Therefore, Eq. (3.8.4) becomes

$$p + e_{n+1} = p + e_n - \frac{f(p + e_n)}{f'(p + e_n)}$$

$$e_{n+1} = e_n - \frac{f(p + e_n)}{f'(p + e_n)}$$

Expanding this using Taylor's theorem for one variable (Eq. 1.3.2) we get,

$$= e_n - \frac{\left[f(p) + e_n f'(p) + \frac{e_n^2}{2!} f''(p) + \dots \right]}{[f'(p) + e_n f''(p) + \dots]}$$

$$= e_n - \frac{\left[e_n f'(p) + \frac{e_n^2}{2!} f''(p) + \dots \right]}{[f'(p) + e_n f''(p) + \dots]} \quad (\because f(p) = 0 \text{ as } p \text{ is a root})$$

$$= \frac{e_n f'(p) + e_n^2 f''(p) - e_n f'(p) - \frac{1}{2} e_n^2 f''(p)}{f'(p) + e_n f''(p)} \quad (\because \text{ neglecting third and higher}$$

powers of e_n)   .... (3.8.5)

$$\therefore e_{n+1} = \frac{e_n^2 f''(p)}{2 [f'(p) + e_n f''(p)]} = \frac{e_n^2}{2} \frac{f''(p)}{f'(p) \{1 + e_n \frac{f''(p)}{f'(p)}\}} = \frac{e_n^2}{2} \frac{f''(p)}{f'(p)} \left\{ 1 + \right.$$

$$e_n f''p f'p \, -1$$

$$= \frac{e_n^2}{2} \frac{f''(p)}{f'(p)} \left\{ 1 - e_n \frac{f''(p)}{f'(p)} + \dots \right\} = \frac{e_n^2}{2} \frac{f''(p)}{f'(p)} - \frac{e_n^3}{2} \left\{ \frac{f''(p)}{f'(p)} \right\}^2 + \dots \dots$$

$$\therefore \frac{e_{n+1}}{e_n^2} = \frac{1}{2} \frac{f''(p)}{f'(p)} - \frac{e_n}{2} \left\{ \frac{f''(p)}{f'(p)} \right\}^2 + \dots \dots$$

Therefore, $e_{n+1} \approx \frac{1}{2} e_n^2 \frac{f''(p)}{f'(p)}$ (Neglecting terms containing powers of e_n)

.... (3.8.6)

Thus, $e_{n+1} = k\,e_n^2$, where k is a constant.

This shows that the error is approximately proportional to the square of the error in the previous iteration. Therefore, Newton Raphson method is said to have quadratic convergence. It means that if the answer of the first iteration is correct to one decimal place, then it should be correct to two decimal places at the second iteration, four decimal places at third iteration and so on. Hence, by the definition, the order of convergence is 2 and the Newton Raphson formula is known as second order formula.

Example 3.11   Find the real root of $x^3 - 4x - 9 = 0$ by Newton Raphson method, correct to four decimal places.

Solution: Let $f(x) = x^3 - 4x - 9$ and $f'(x) = 3x^2 - 4$

x	1	2	3
$f(x)$	-12	-9	6

Here, $f(2) = -9 < 0$ and $f(3) = 6 > 0$.
Therefore, one root of the equation lies between 2 and 3.
Take initial approximation as $x_0 = 3$.

Iteration 1 $x_1 = x_0 - \dfrac{f(x_0)}{f'(x_0)}$

$\qquad = 3 - \dfrac{3^3 - 4(3) - 9}{3(3)^2 - 4}$

$\qquad = 3 - \dfrac{6}{23}$

$\qquad = 2.7391$

Iteration 2 $x_2 = x_1 - \dfrac{f(x_1)}{f'(x_1)}$

$\qquad = 2.7391 - \dfrac{(2.7391)^3 - 4(2.7391) - 9}{3(2.7391)^2 - 4}$

$\qquad = 2.7391 - \dfrac{0.5962}{18.5080}$

$\qquad = 2.7070$

Iteration 3 $x_3 = x_2 - \dfrac{f(x_2)}{f'(x_2)}$

$\qquad = 2.7070 - \dfrac{(2.7070)^3 - 4(2.7070) - 9}{3(2.7070)^2 - 4}$

$\qquad = 2.7070 - \dfrac{0.0085}{17.9835}$

$\qquad = 2.7065$

Iteration 4 $x_4 = x_3 - \dfrac{f(x_3)}{f'(x_3)}$

$\qquad = 2.7065 - \dfrac{(2.7065)^3 - 4(2.7065) - 9}{3(2.7065)^2 - 4}$

$$= 2.7065 - \frac{-0.0005025}{17.9754}$$

$$= 2.7065$$

The root of the given equation, upto four decimal places, is $\boxed{2.7065}$

Example 3.12   Find the real root of $x\tan x - 1 = 0$ by Newton Raphson method, correct to four decimal places.

Solution: Let $f(x) = x\tan x - 1$ and $f'(x) = x\sec^2 x + \tan x = \frac{x}{\cos^2 x} + \tan x$

x	0	1	0.5
$f(x)$	-1	0.5574	-0.7268

Here, $f(0.5) = -0.7268 < 0$ and $f(1) = 0.5574 > 0$.

Therefore, one root of the equation lies between 0.5 and 1.

Take initial approximation as $x_0 = 1$

Iteration 1: $x_1 = x_0 - \dfrac{f(x_0)}{f'(x_0)}$

$$= 1 - \frac{(1)\tan(1)-1}{\frac{(1)}{\cos^2(1)} + \tan(1)}$$

$$= 1 - \frac{0.5574}{4.9829}$$

$$= 0.8881$$

Iteration 2: $x_2 = x_1 - \dfrac{f(x_1)}{f'(x_1)}$

$$= 0.8881 - \frac{(0.8881)\tan(0.8881)-1}{\frac{(0.8881)}{\cos^2(0.8881)} + \tan(0.8881)}$$

$$= 0.8881 - \frac{0.0923}{3.4615}$$

$$= 0.8615$$

Iteration 3: $x_3 = x_2 - \dfrac{f(x_2)}{f'(x_2)}$

$$= 0.8615 - \frac{(0.8615)\tan(0.8615)-1}{\frac{(0.8615)}{\cos^2(0.8615)} + \tan(0.8615)}$$

$$= 0.8615 - \frac{0.0036}{3.1957}$$

$$= 0.8603$$

Iteration 4: $x_4 = x_3 - \dfrac{f(x_3)}{f'(x_3)}$

$$= 0.8603 - \frac{(0.8603)\tan(0.8603)-1}{\frac{(0.8603)}{\cos^2(0.8603)}+\tan(0.8603)}$$

$$= 0.8603 - \frac{0.000006}{3.1850}$$

$$= 0.8603$$

The root of the given equation, upto four decimal places, is $\boxed{0.8603}$

3.8.5   Finding pth Root Using Newton Raphson Formula

We first derive generalized formula for finding p^{th} root of a given number N. Then from that we deduce particular formulas of square root, cube root, inverse etc. We want to derive the formula for finding p^{th} root of a given number N.

Let $x = N^{1/p}$ Therefore, $x^p = N$

$$\Rightarrow x^p - N = 0. \quad \text{Let} \quad f(x) = x^p - N$$

$$\Rightarrow f'(x) = px^{p-1}$$

We know that the Newton Raphson formula is $x_{n+1} = x_n - \dfrac{f(x_n)}{f'(x_n)}$

$$\Rightarrow \quad x_{n+1} = x_n - \frac{x_n^p - N}{px_n^{p-1}}$$

$$= \frac{px_n^p - x_n^p + N}{px_n^{p-1}}$$

$$= \frac{1}{p}\left[\frac{(p-1)x_n^p}{x_n^{p-1}} + \frac{N}{x_n^{p-1}}\right]$$

$$\Rightarrow \quad x_{n+1} = \frac{1}{p}\left[(p-1)x_n + \frac{N}{x_n^{p-1}}\right] \qquad \text{....... (3.8.7)}$$

1.   Finding Square Root

Substitute $p = 2$ in the Eq. (3.8.7) we get,

$$x_{n+1} = \frac{1}{p}\left[(p-1)x_n + \frac{N}{x_n^{p-1}}\right]$$

Therefore,

$$x_{n+1} = \frac{1}{2}\left[(2-1)x_n + \frac{N}{x_n^{2-1}}\right]$$

$$x_{n+1} = \frac{1}{2}\left[x_n + \frac{N}{x_n}\right] \qquad \text{....... (3.8.8)}$$

Eq. (3.8.8) is known as Hero's formula for finding square root of a given number N using Newton Raphson formula.

Example 3.13   Find $\sqrt{6}$ correct up to four decimal places using Newton – Raphson formula.

Solution: $x = \quad \sqrt{6}$ Therefore, $x^2 - 6 = 0$.   Let $f(x) = x^2 - 6$

x	2	3
$f(x)$	-2	3

Since f(2) = -2 < 0 and f(3) = 3 > 0

Therefore, the root of the equation lies between 2 and 3.

Let $x_0 = 2$. Using Eq. (3.8.8) we get,

$$x_1 = \frac{1}{2}\left[x_0 + \frac{6}{x_0}\right] = \frac{1}{2}\left[2 + \frac{6}{2}\right] = 2.5$$

$$x_2 = \frac{1}{2}\left[x_1 + \frac{6}{x_1}\right] = \frac{1}{2}\left[2.5 + \frac{6}{2.5}\right] = 2.45$$

$$x_3 = \frac{1}{2}\left[x_2 + \frac{6}{x_2}\right] = \frac{1}{2}\left[2.45 + \frac{6}{2.45}\right] = 2.4495$$

$$x_4 = \frac{1}{2}\left[x_3 + \frac{6}{x_3}\right] = \frac{1}{2}\left[2.4495 + \frac{6}{2.4495}\right] = 2.4495$$

Therefore, $\sqrt{6} = 2.4495$ correct up to four decimal places

2.   Finding Cube Root

Substitute $p = 3$ in the Eq. (3.8.7) we get,

$$x_{n+1} = \frac{1}{p}\left[(p-1)x_n + \frac{N}{x_n{}^{p-1}}\right]$$

Therefore, $$x_{n+1} = \frac{1}{3}\left[(3-1)x_n + \frac{N}{x_n{}^{3-1}}\right]$$

$$x_{n+1} = \frac{1}{3}\left[2x_n + \frac{N}{x_n{}^2}\right] \qquad .... (3.8.9)$$

Eq. (3.8.9) is the formula for finding cube root of a given number N using Newton Raphson formula.

Example 3.14   Find $\sqrt[3]{12}$ correct up to four decimal places.

Solution: $x = \sqrt[3]{12}$ Therefore, $x^3 - 12 = 0$.   Let $f(x) = x^3 - 12$

x	2	3	2.5
$f(x)$	-4	15	3.625

Since f(2) = -4 < 0 and f(2.5) = 3.625 > 0

Therefore, the root of the equation lies between 2 and 2.5.

Let $x_0 = 2$. Using Eq. (3.8.9) we get,

$$x_1 = \frac{1}{3}\left[2x_0 + \frac{12}{x_0{}^2}\right] = \frac{1}{3}\left[2(2) + \frac{12}{2^2}\right] = 2.3333$$

$$x_2 = \frac{1}{3}\left[2x_1 + \frac{12}{x_1{}^2}\right] = \frac{1}{3}\left[2(2.3333) + \frac{12}{(2.3333)^2}\right] = 2.2902$$

$$x_3 = \frac{1}{3}\left[2x_2 + \frac{12}{x_2{}^2}\right] = \frac{1}{3}\left[2(2.2902) + \frac{12}{(2.2902)^2}\right] = 2.2894$$

$$x_4 = \frac{1}{3}\left[2x_3 + \frac{12}{x_3{}^2}\right] = \frac{1}{3}\left[2(2.2894) + \frac{12}{(2.2894)^2}\right] = 2.2894$$

Therefore, $\sqrt[3]{12} = 2.2894$ correct up to four decimal places

3. Finding Reciprocal or Inverse

Substitute $p = -1$ in the Eq. (3.8.7) we get,

$$x_{n+1} = \frac{1}{p}\left[(p-1)x_n + \frac{N}{x_n^{p-1}}\right]$$

Therefore,

$$x_{n+1} = \frac{1}{-1}\left[(-1-1)x_n + \frac{N}{x_n^{-1-1}}\right]$$

$$x_{n+1} = -\left[-2x_n + \frac{N}{x_n^{-2}}\right] = 2x_n - N x_n^2$$

or

$$x_{n+1} = x_n(2 - Nx_n) \qquad \text{........ (3.8.10)}$$

Eq. (3.8.10) is the formula for finding reciprocal of a given number N using Newton Raphson formula.

Example 3.15   Find e^{-1} using the initial approximation $x_0 = 0.2$ correct up to six decimal places.

Solution: Here, $N = e = 2.718282$ and $x_0 = 0.2$

Using Eq. (3.8.10) we get,

$x_1 = 2x_0 - e\, x_0^2 = 2(0.2) - (2.718282)(0.2)^2 = 0.291269$

$x_2 = 2x_1 - e\, x_1^2 = 2(0.291269) - (2.718282)(0.291269)^2 = 0.351925$

$x_3 = 2x_2 - e\, x_2^2 = 2(0.351925) - (2.718282)(0.351925)^2 = 0.367187$

$x_4 = 2x_3 - e\, x_3^2 = 2(0.367187) - (2.718282)(0.367187)^2 = 0.367878$

$x_5 = 2x_4 - e\, x_4^2 = 2(0.367878) - (2.718282)(0.367878)^2 = 0.367879$

$x_6 = 2x_5 - e\, x_5^2 = 2(0.367879) - (2.718282)(0.367879)^2 = 0.367879$

Therefore, $e^{-1} = 0.367879$ correct up to six decimal places

4. Finding Inverse Square Root

Substitute $p = -2$ in the Eq. (3.8.7) we get,

$$x_{n+1} = \frac{1}{p}\left[(p-1)x_n + \frac{N}{x_n^{p-1}}\right]$$

Therefore, $x_{n+1} = \frac{1}{-2}\left[(-2-1)x_n + \frac{N}{x_n^{-2-1}}\right]$

$$x_{n+1} = -\frac{1}{2}\left[-3x_n + \frac{N}{x_n^{-3}}\right] = \frac{1}{2}[3x_n - N x_n^3]$$

or

$$x_{n+1} = \frac{1}{2}x_n(3 - Nx_n^2) \qquad \text{........ (3.8.11)}$$

Eq. (3.8.11) is the formula for finding inverse square root of a given number N using Newton Raphson formula.

Example 3.16   Evaluate $1/\sqrt{10}$ using the initial approximation $x_0 = 0.2$ correct up to six decimal places by Newton – Raphson formula.

Solution: Here, $N = 10$ and $x_0 = 0.2$

Using Eq. (3.8.11) we get,

$$x_1 = \frac{1}{2}[3x_0 - 10\,x_0{}^3] = \frac{1}{2}[3(0.2) - 10\,(0.2)^3] = 0.26$$

$$x_2 = \frac{1}{2}[3x_1 - 10\,x_1{}^3] = \frac{1}{2}[3(0.26) - 10\,(0.26)^3] = 0.30212$$

$$x_3 = \frac{1}{2}[3x_2 - 10\,x_2{}^3] = \frac{1}{2}[3(0.30212) - 10\,(0.30212)^3] = 0.315298$$

$$x_4 = \frac{1}{2}[3x_3 - 10\,x_3{}^3] = \frac{1}{2}[3(0.315298) - 10\,(0.315298)^3] = 0.316224$$

$$x_5 = \frac{1}{2}[3x_4 - 10\,x_4{}^3] = \frac{1}{2}[3(0.316224) - 10\,(0.316224)^3] = 0.316228$$

$$x_6 = \frac{1}{2}[3x_5 - 10\,x_5{}^3] = \frac{1}{2}[3(0.316228) - 10\,(0.316228)^3] = 0.316228$$

Therefore, $1/\sqrt{10} = 0.316228$ correct up to six decimal places.

3.8.6   Generalized Newton's Method for Multiple Roots

If p is a root of the equation $f(x) = 0$ with multiplicity m, then the iteration formula of Newton Raphson is taken as

$$x_{n+1} = x_n - m\frac{f(x_n)}{f'(x_n)} \qquad\qquad \text{........ (3.8.12)}$$

Which is known as *generalized Newton's formula*. In Eq. (3.8.12) $\left(\frac{1}{m}\right)f'(x_n)$ is the slope of the straight line passing through (x_n, y_n) and intersecting the x- axis at the point $(x_{n+1}, 0)$. If $m = 1$ then it is converted into Newton Raphson formula. If p is a root of the equation $f(x) = 0$ with multiplicity m, then p is also a root of $f'(x) = 0$ with multiplicity $(m-1)$, $f''(x) = 0$ with multiplicity $(m-2)$ and so on. Hence, if initial approximation x_0 is sufficiently close to the root, then the expressions

$$x_0 - m\frac{f(x_0)}{f'(x_0)}, \quad x_0 - (m-1)\frac{f'(x_0)}{f''(x_0)}, \quad x_0 - (m-2)\frac{f''(x_0)}{f'''(x_0)}, \quad \text{..........} \text{ will have}$$

the same value as if there is a root with multiplicity m.

Remark:
If we can write the equation $f(x) = 0$ as $f(x) = (x - p)^m\, g(x) = 0$ where $g(x)$ is bounded and $g(p) \neq 0$ then p is called a *multiple root* of multiplicity m. In this case, $f(p) = f'(p) = \cdots = f^{m-1}(p) = 0, f^m(p) \neq 0$
For $m = 1$, p is called the simple root.

Example 3.17   Find a double root of the equation $f(x) = x^3 - 5x^2 + 8x - 4 = 0$ by taking initial approximation $x_0 = 1.8$.

Solution: It is given that $f(x) = x^3 - 5x^2 + 8x - 4$, therefore, $f'(x) = 3x^2 - 10x + 8$ and $f''(x) = 6x - 10$.

Using the generalized Newton's formula, we have

$$x_0 - m\frac{f(x_0)}{f'(x_0)} = 1.8 - 2\frac{(1.8)^3 - 5(1.8)^2 + 8(1.8) - 4}{3(1.8)^2 - 10(1.8) + 8} = 1.8 - 2\frac{0.032}{-0.28} = 2.02857$$

$$x_0 - (m-1)\frac{f'(x_0)}{f''(x_0)} = 1.8 - (2-1)\frac{3(1.8)^2 - 10(1.8) + 8}{6(1.8) - 10} = 1.8 - \frac{-0.28}{0.8} = 2.15$$

Both the obtained values suggest that a double root is close to 2. Let the next approximation $x_1 = 2.02$. Then,

$$x_1 - m\frac{f(x_1)}{f'(x_1)} = 2.02 - 2\frac{(2.02)^3 - 5(2.02)^2 + 8(2.02) - 4}{3(2.02)^2 - 10(2.02) + 8} = 2.02 - 2\frac{0.000408}{0.0412} = 2.0001$$

$$x_1 - (m-1)\frac{f'(x_1)}{f''(x_1)} = 2.02 - (2-1)\frac{3(2.02)^2 - 10(2.02) + 8}{6(2.02) - 10} = 2.02 - \frac{0.0412}{2.12} = 2.0005$$

Therefore, there is a double root at x = 2.0001 which is very close to the actual double root 2.

Let's compare generalized Newton method with the Newton Raphson method.

$$x_0 = 1.8 \quad \text{and} \quad x_1 = x_0 - \frac{f(x_0)}{f'(x_0)} = 1.8 - \frac{f(1.8)}{f'(1.8)} = 1.8 - \frac{0.032}{-0.28} = 1.9143$$

$$x_2 = x_1 - \frac{f(x_1)}{f'(x_1)} = 1.9143 - \frac{f(1.9143)}{f'(1.9143)} = 1.9143 - \frac{0.0307}{-0.1494} = 2.1198$$

$$x_3 = x_2 - \frac{f(x_2)}{f'(x_2)} = 2.1198 - \frac{f(2.1198)}{f'(2.1198)} = 2.1198 - \frac{0.01607}{0.2827} = 2.0630$$

$$x_4 = x_3 - \frac{f(x_3)}{f'(x_3)} = 2.0630 - \frac{f(2.0630)}{f'(2.0630)} = 2.0630 - \frac{0.0042}{0.1379} = 2.0325$$

$$x_5 = x_4 - \frac{f(x_4)}{f'(x_4)} = 2.0325 - \frac{f(2.0325)}{f'(2.0325)} = 2.0325 - \frac{0.0011}{0.0682} = 2.0164$$

$x_6 = 2.0084$, $x_7 = 2.0043$, $x_8 = 2.0031$

The comparative study of the two methods shows that the generalized Newton method converges faster than the Newton Raphson method.

Merits

1. This method is generally used to improve the result obtained by other methods.
2. It can be used when the roots are complex. i.e. we can find complex roots using this method.
3. The order of convergence is 2. So, it is a fast converging method in most cases.
4. It is the excellent method provided the initial guess is near the root.

Demerits

1. It needs to calculate two functions $f(x)$ and $f'(x)$ per iteration.
2. It does not guarantee convergence.
3. The approximation to the root oscillate for quite large, before it converge to the root.
4. At any point if $|f'(x)|$ is zero or very near to zero, divergence may occur. Then we will have to take a new initial guess and start the process again.

5.   If a curve has multiple roots then after reaching close to the roots the method may become very slow.
6.   If the initial guess is too far from the required root, the process may converge to some other root.

3.9   SECANT METHOD (CHORD METHOD)

Newton Raphson method requires the evaluation of $f(x)$ and $f'(x)$ per iteration. In some cases it becomes difficult to derive the formula for $f'(x)$ from $f(x)$. Therefore, we need a method which does not require the derivative of a function and the convergence rate is almost similar to Newton's method. To satisfy this requirement we introduce a new method known as secant. Secant method is similar to the false position method as it uses two initial approximations but does not require that they must enclose the root. Also it is not required that the condition $f(x_1).f(x_2) < 0$ is satisfied. It is known as secant method as the graph of the function $y = f(x)$ is approximated by a secant line.

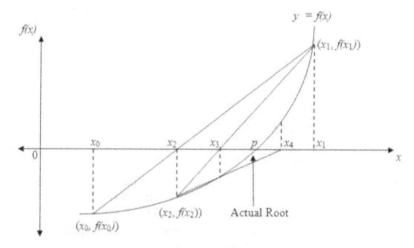

Figure 3.7 Secant method

Let x_0 and x_1 be two initial approximations as shown in Figure 3.7 although they do not bracket the root. Join the points $(x_0, f(x_0))$ and $(x_1, f(x_1))$ by means of a straight line. The next approximation is the point where this line intersect the x – axis. Let this point be x_2. Now, x_1 and x_2 will become our new approximations for the next iteration. Now, again join the points $(x_1, f(x_1))$ and $(x_2, f(x_2))$ by a straight line. The next approximation is the point where this line intersects the x – axis, say x_4.

Using slope formula of the secant line passing through x_0 and x_1, we have

$$\frac{f(x_1) - f(x_0)}{(x_1 - x_0)} = \frac{f(x_1)}{x_1 - x_2}$$

Solving for x_2 we get,

$$x_2 = \frac{x_0 \, f(x_1) - x_1 \, f(x_0)}{f(x_1) - f(x_0)}$$

Using x_1 and x_2 repeat this process. The method will terminate when we get the root with required accuracy. In general the formula is given by,

$$x_{i+1} = \frac{x_{i-1} \, f(x_i) - x_i \, f(x_{i-1})}{f(x_i) - f(x_{i-1})} \qquad \ldots\ldots (3.9.1)$$

Eq. (3.9.1) is known as secant formula.

3.9.1   Convergence of Secant Method

If $\{x_n\}$ is the sequence of approximations obtained from

$$x_{n+1} = x_n - \frac{(x_n - x_{n-1})}{f(x_n) - f(x_{n-1})} f(x_n) \qquad \ldots\ldots (3.9.2)$$

and if p is the exact value of the root of the equation $f(x) = 0$, then

let
$$x_n = p + e_n$$
$$x_{n+1} = p + e_{n+1}$$

where e_n and e_{n+1} are the errors involved in n^{th} and $(n+1)^{th}$ approximations, respectively. But $f(p) = 0$. Therefore, Eq. (3.9.2) becomes

$$p + e_{n+1} = p + e_n - \frac{(p + e_n - p + e_{n-1})}{f(p + e_n) - f(p + e_{n-1})} f(p + e_n)$$

$$\therefore \qquad e_{n+1} = \frac{e_{n-1} f(p + e_n) - e_n f(p + e_{n-1})}{f(p + e_n) - f(p + e_{n-1})}$$

Expanding this using Taylor's theorem for one variable (Eq. 1.3.2) we get,

$$= \frac{e_{n-1}\left[f(p) + e_n f'(p) + \frac{e_n^2}{2!}f''(p) + \ldots\right] - e_n\left[f(p) + e_{n-1}f'(p) + \frac{e_{n-1}^2}{2!}f''(p) + \ldots\right]}{\left[f(p) + e_n f'(p) + \frac{e_n^2}{2!}f''(p) + \ldots\right] - \left[f(p) + e_{n-1}f'(p) + \frac{e_{n-1}^2}{2!}f''(p) + \ldots\right]}$$

$$= \frac{(e_{n-1} - e_n) f(p) + \frac{e_{n-1} e_n}{2!}(e_n - e_{n-1})f''(p) + \ldots\ldots}{(e_n - e_{n-1})f'(p) + \frac{(e_n - e_{n-1})(e_n + e_{n-1})}{2!}f''(p) + \ldots\ldots}$$

$$= \frac{\frac{e_{n-1} e_n}{2!}f''(p) + \ldots\ldots}{f'(p) + \frac{(e_n + e_{n-1})}{2!}f''(p) + \ldots\ldots} \qquad (\because f(a) = 0 \text{ and taking } (e_n - e_{n-1})$$

outside from numerator and denomiator)

$$\therefore \quad e_{n+1} \approx \frac{e_{n-1} e_n}{2!} \frac{f''(p)}{f'(p)} \qquad (\because \text{ neglecting high powers of } e_n, e_{n-1})$$

$$\ldots\ldots (3.9.3)$$

Let $e_{n+1} = c \, e_n^k$, where c is a constant and k > 0.

$$\therefore \quad e_n = c \, e_{n-1}^k \qquad \text{or} \qquad e_{n-1} = c^{-1/k} e_n^{1/k}$$

$\therefore$ From Eq. 3.9.3, $c\,e_n^k \approx \dfrac{e_n\,c^{-1/k}\,e_n^{1/k}}{2!}\dfrac{f''(p)}{f'(p)} = \dfrac{c^{-1/k}}{2!}e_n^{1+1/k}\dfrac{f''(p)}{f'(p)}$

Comparing two sides we get $k = 1 + \dfrac{1}{k}$ and $c = \dfrac{c^{-1/k}}{2!}\dfrac{f''(p)}{f'(p)}$

Now, $k = 1 + \dfrac{1}{k}$ $\Rightarrow k^2 - k - 1 = 0$ $\Rightarrow k = 1.618$

Also, $c = \dfrac{c^{-1/k}}{2!}\dfrac{f''(p)}{f'(p)}$ $\therefore c^{1+1/k} = c^{1.618} = \dfrac{1}{2}\dfrac{f''(p)}{f'(p)}$ or $c = \left[\dfrac{f''(p)}{2f'(p)}\right]^{0.618}$

This gives the rate of convergence and k = 1.618 (the Golden Ratio) gives the order of convergence of secant method. It shows that the convergence is super linear.

3.9.2   Difference Between False Position Method and Secant Method

False Position Method	Secant Method
• It is a bracketing method	• It is an open end method
• It guarantees convergence	• It does not guarantee convergence.
• If x_0 and x_1 are two initial approximations then the next approximation x_2 is based on the sign of $f(x_0) \times f(x_2)$.	• If x_0 and x_1 are two initial approximations then x_2 replaces x_1 and x_1 replaces x_0 without depending on the sign of $f(x_0) \times f(x_2)$.
• If the function $f(x)$ in the equation $f(x) = 0$ is not convex than one of the starting points is fixed while the other moves towards the solution.	• Both the approximations vary to obtain the desired root.
• While choosing initial approximations it is necessary that the functions value are of opposite sign. (i.e. $f(x_0) \times f(x_1) < 0$)	• While choosing initial approximations it is not necessary that the functions value are of opposite sign.

Example 3.18   Find the real root of $cosx - xe^x = 0$ by secant method, correct to four decimal places.

Solution: Let $f(x) = cosx - xe^x$

x	0	1	0.5	0.75
$f(x)$	1	-2.1780	0.05322	-0.8561

Here, $f(0.75) = -0.8561 < 0$ and $f(0.5) = 0.05322 > 0$

Therefore, one root of the equation lies between 0.5 and 0.75.

Iteration 1:   Let us take $x_0 = 0.75$ and $x_1 = 0.5$

$$f(x_0) = -0.8561, f(x_1) = 0.05322$$

Let $x_2 = \dfrac{x0\ f(x1) - x1\ f(x0)}{f(x1) - f(x0)} = \dfrac{(0.75)(0.05322) - (0.5)(-0.8561)}{(0.05322) - (-0.8561)} = 0.5146$

$f(x_2) = f(0.5146) = \cos(0.5146) - (0.5146)e^{(0.5146)} = 0.009580$

Therefore, replace x_0 by x_1 and x_1 by x_2. The new search interval is (0.5, 0.5146)

Iteration 2:   Now, $x_0 = 0.5$ and $x_1 = 0.5146$

$$f(x_0) = 0.05322, f(x_1) = 0.009580$$

Let $x_2 = \dfrac{x0\ f(x1) - x1\ f(x0)}{f(x1) - f(x0)} = \dfrac{(0.5)(0.009580) - (0.5146)(0.05322)}{(0.009580) - (0.05322)} = 0.5178$

$f(x_2) = f(0.5178) = \cos(0.5178) - (0.5178)e^{(0.5178)} = -0.0001297$

Therefore, replace x_0 by x_1 and x_1 by x_2. The new search interval is (0.5146, 0.5178)

Iteration 3: $x_0 = 0.5146$ and $x_1 = 0.5178$

$$f(x_0) = 0.009580 , f(x_1) = -0.0001297$$

Let $x_2 = \dfrac{x0\ f(x1) - x1\ f(x0)}{f(x1) - f(x0)} = \dfrac{(0.5146)(-0.0001297) - (0.5178)(0.009580)}{(-0.0001297) - (0.009580)}$

$\qquad = 0.5178$

$f(x_2) = f(0.5178) = \cos(0.5178) - (0.5178)e^{(0.5178)} = -0.0001297$

Therefore, replace x_0 by x_1 and x_1 by x_2. The new search interval is (0.5178, 0.5178)

In the 3rd iteration, the values of previous x_2 and new x_2 are equal upto 4 decimal figures.

Therefore, the root of the given equation, upto 4 decimal figures, is $\boxed{0.5178}$.

Merits

1. The convergence of secant method is super linear. So, once it converges, it is more faster than the false position method.
2. This method is considered as most economical compare to other root finding methods as it gives rapid convergence at a low cost.
3. There is no need to find derivative of the function.
4. It requires one function evaluation per iteration as compared with Newton's method,

Demerits

1.   As it is not a bracketing method, it may not converge.
2.   If at any stage $f(x_n) - f(x_{n-1}) = 0$, this method fails to converge.
3.   In this method the previous two iterates are required for estimating the new one.
4.   There is no guaranteed error bound for the computed iterates.

3.10 SOLUTION OF POLYNOMIAL EQUATIONS

3.10.1 Birge – Vieta Method

Birge – Vieta method is used to find the root of polynomial equations only. We use the Newton – Raphson formula.

$$x_n = x_{n-1} - \frac{F(x_{n-1})}{F'(x_{n-1})} \qquad \text{........ (3.10.1)}$$

Consider a polynomial $F(x) = a_0 + a_1 x + a_2 x^2 + a_3 x^3 + \ ... + a_m x^m$ of degree m. $\qquad$ .... (3.10.2)

We want to evaluate F(x) at different values of x which can be $x_0, x_1, x_2, \ ...\ ...$

Divide the polynomial F(x) by $(x - \bar{x})$ where $\bar{x}$ is some value at which we want to evaluate F(x).

$$\therefore \ \frac{F(x)}{x - \bar{x}} = b_1 + b_2 x + b_3 x^2 + \ ... + b_m x^{m-1} + \frac{b_0}{x - \bar{x}}$$

Therefore, $F(x) = (x - \bar{x})(b_1 + b_2 x + b_3 x^2 + \ ... + b_m x^{m-1}) + b_0$
$\qquad\qquad$ .... (3.10.3)

Hence, $F(\bar{x}) = (\bar{x} - \bar{x})(b_1 + b_2 \bar{x} + b_3 \bar{x}^2 + \ ... + b_m \bar{x}^{m-1}) + b_0 = b_0$

Comparing co-efficients of different powers of x of right hand side of Eq. (3.10.2) and (3.10.3), we get

$$a_m = b_m$$
$$a_{m-1} = b_{m-1} - \bar{x} \, b_m$$
$$a_{m-2} = b_{m-2} - \bar{x} \, b_{m-1}$$
$$\vdots \qquad \vdots \qquad \vdots$$
$$a_j = b_j - \bar{x} \, b_{j+1}$$

Hence, $\qquad \boxed{b_j = a_j + \bar{x} \, b_{j+1}}$

Thus, $\qquad\qquad\qquad$
$$b_0 = a_0 + \bar{x} \, b_1$$
$$b_1 = a_1 + \bar{x} \, b_2$$
$$b_2 = a_2 + \bar{x} \, b_3$$
$$\vdots \qquad \vdots \qquad \vdots$$
$$b_{m-1} = a_{m-1} + \bar{x} \, b_m$$

Therefore , $b_0 = a_0 + \bar{x}(a_1 + \bar{x} \, (\, a_2 + \bar{x} + \ ...\ ... + \bar{x}\,(a_{m-1} + \bar{x} \, a_m)))$ and
$F(\bar{x}) = b_0$ $\qquad\qquad\qquad\qquad$ .... (3.10.4)

This is called Horner's Method or Nesting Procedure of evaluating polynomial

$F(x)$. Now, we want to evaluate $F'(\bar{x})$.

$$F(x) = (x - \bar{x})G(x) + b_0$$

where, $G(x) = b_1 + b_2 x + b_3 x^2 + ... + b_m x^{m-1}$

Therefore,

$$F'(x) = (x - \bar{x})G'(x) + G(x)$$

Hence,

$$F'(\bar{x}) = G(\bar{x})$$

We evaluate $G(\bar{x})$ by the Horner's Rule.

Thus, $\boxed{c_j = b_j + \bar{x}\,c_{j+1}}$ where, $j = m\text{-}1, m\text{-}2, ...2, 1$

$F'(\bar{x}) = G(\bar{x}) = c_1$ .... (3.10.5)

From Eqs. (3.10.1), (3.10.4) and (3.10.5) we can derive that,

$$\boxed{x_n = x_{n-1} - \frac{b_0}{c_1}}$$ .... (3.10.6)

where, $b_j = a_j + \bar{x}\,b_{j+1}$

$\qquad\qquad c_j = b_j + \bar{x}\,c_{j+1}$ where, $j = m\text{-}1, m\text{-}2, ...2, 1, 0$

and $a_m = b_m = c_m$

The method will terminate when the difference between two approximations is less than the prescribed tolerance.

Example 3.19   Find the root of the polynomial equation $x^4 - 9x^3 - 2x^2 + 120x - 130 = 0$ using Birge – Vieta method.

Solution: Let $f(x) = x^4 - 9x^3 - 2x^2 + 120x - 130$

x	3	4
$f(x)$	50	-2

Iteration 1: Let $x_0 = 4$

i	a_i	b_i	c_i
4	1	1	1
3	-9	-5	-1
2	-2	-22	-26
1	120	32	-72
0	-130	-2	

where, $a_4 = b_4 = c_4$ $a_i = coefficients\ of\ x^i$

$b_3 = a_3 + \bar{x}b_4 = (-9) + (4)(1) = -5$ $c_3 = b_3 + \bar{x}c_4 = (-5) + (4)(1) = -1$

$b_2 = a_2 + \bar{x}b_3 = (-2) + (4)(-5) = -22$ $c_2 = b_2 + \bar{x}c_3 = (-22) + (4)(-1) = -26$

$b_1 = a_1 + \bar{x}b_2 = 120 + (4)(-22) = 32$ $c_1 = b_1 + \bar{x}c_2 = (32) + (4)(-26) = -72$

$b_0 = a_0 + \bar{x}b_1 = (-130) + (4)(32) = -2$

Now,

$$x_1 = x_0 - \frac{b_0}{c_1} = 4 - \frac{(-2)}{(-72)} = 3.9722$$

Iteration 2: $x_1 = 3.9722$

i	a_i	b_i	c_i
4	1	1	1
3	-9	-5.0278	-1.0556
2	-2	-21.9714	-26.1645
1	120	32.7252	-71.2052
0	-130	-0.009	

$$x_2 = x_1 - \frac{b_0}{c_1} = 3.9722 - \frac{(-0.009)}{(-71.2052)} = 3.9721$$

Iteration 3: $x_2 = 3.9721$

i	a_i	b_i	c_i
4	1	1	1
3	-9	-5.0279	-1.0558
2	-2	-21.9713	-26.16504
1	120	32.7278	-71.2029
0	-130	-0.0019	

$$x_3 = x_2 - \frac{b_0}{c_1} = 3.9721 - \frac{(-0.0019)}{(-71.2029)} = 3.9721$$

Therefore, root of the given polynomial equation is $\boxed{3.9721}$.

Remark: While using the Birge – Vieta method, we are using the Horner's Rule (Nesting Procedure) to find out $f(x)$ and $f'(x)$.

i.e. we use $f(x) = a_0 + \bar{x}(a_1 + \bar{x}(a_2 + \bar{x} + \ldots\ldots + \bar{x}(a_{m-1} + \bar{x}\, a_m)))$. This will require m additions and m multiplications. So, this is the most efficient way of evaluating the polynomial as it requires fewer and simpler arithmetic computations. Hence, in the case of finding roots of polynomial equations by computer algorithms Birge – Vieta method is preferred to Newton – Raphson method.

3.10.2 Graeffe's Root Squaring Method

This method is used to find the roots of polynomial equations only. It is one of the direct root finding method as it does not require any initial guesses for roots. It is capable of giving all the roots. It was invented independently by Graeffe Dandelin and Lobachevsky. This was the most popular method for finding roots of polynomials in the 19th and 20th centuries.

Principle: Let $f(x)$ be a polynomial of degree n. Graeffe's root squaring method consists of transforming $f(x)$ into a polynomial $g(z)$ of the same degree but whose roots are the squares of the roots of the original polynomial. The process is repeated so that the roots of the new polynomial are distributed more speciously.

The roots are then evaluated directly from the coefficients.

The basic idea behind this method is to seperate the roots of the equations by squaring the roots. This can be done by seperating even and odd powers of x in the polynomial equation

$$x^n + a_1 x^{n-1} + a_2 x^{n-2} + \dots \dots + a_{n-1} x + a_n = 0 \qquad \dots\dots (3.10.7)$$

and squaring on both sides. We get

$$(x^n + a_2 x^{n-2} + a_4 x^{n-4} + \dots)^2 = (a_1 x^{n-1} + a_3 x^{n-3} + \dots)^2$$

Therefore, $(x^{2n} - (a_1{}^2 - 2a_2)x^{2n-2} + (a_1{}^2 - 2a_1 a_3 + 2a_4)x^{2n-4} + \dots + (-1)^n a_n{}^2 = 0$

Putting $-x^2 = y$ and simplifying the new equation becomes,

$$y^n + b_1 y^{n-1} + b_2 y^{n-2} + \dots \dots + b_{n-1} y + b_n = 0 \qquad \dots\dots (3.10.8)$$

where,

$$\begin{aligned} b_1 &= a_1{}^2 - 2a_2 \\ b_2 &= a_2{}^2 - 2a_1 a_3 + 2a_4 \end{aligned} \qquad \dots\dots (3.10.9)$$

$$\vdots \qquad \vdots$$
$$\vdots \qquad \vdots$$

$$b_n = a_n{}^2$$

Thus all $b_i{}'s$ ($i = 1,2,\dots n$) are known in terms of $a_i{}'s$. The roots of the Eq. (3.10.8) are $-\alpha_1{}^2, -\alpha_2{}^2, \dots, -\alpha_n{}^2$ where $\alpha_1, \alpha_2, \dots, \alpha_n$ are the roots of Eq. (3.10.7). A coefficient b_k of b_i, $i = 1, 2, \dots n$ is obtained by following.

The first term is the square of the coefficient a_k The second term is $-$ve of twice the product of the nearest neighbouring coefficients a_{i-1} and a_{i+1}. The third is $-$ve of twice the product of the next neighbouring coefficients a_{i-2} and a_{i+2}. This procedure is continued until there are no available coefficients to form the cross products.

This procedure is repeated m times. Let the new transformed equation be

$$z^n + c_1 z^{n-1} + c_2 z^{n-2} + \dots \dots + c_{n-1} z + c_n = 0 \qquad \dots\dots (3.10.10)$$

whose roots $\beta_1, \beta_2, \dots, \beta_n$ are such that $\beta_i = -\alpha_i{}^{2^m}, i = 1,2, \dots \dots n$.

If we assume $|\alpha_1| > |\alpha_2| > \dots \dots > |\alpha_n|$ then $|\beta_1| \gg |\beta_2| \gg \dots \gg |\beta_n|$

that is the roots β_i are much greater than α_i.

Thus, $\dfrac{|\beta_2|}{|\beta_1|} = \dfrac{\beta_2}{\beta_1}, \dots\dots\dots\dots, \dfrac{|\beta_n|}{|\beta_{n-1}|} = \dfrac{\beta_n}{\beta_{n-1}}$ are negligible as compared to unity.

$$\dots\dots (3.10.11)$$

From the Eq. (3.10.10), we have

$$\sum \beta_1 = -c_1 \quad \text{i.e.} \quad c_1 = -\beta_1 \left(1 + \frac{\beta_2}{\beta_1} + \frac{\beta_3}{\beta_1} + \dots\right)$$

$$\sum \beta_1 \beta_2 = c_2 \quad \text{i.e.} \quad c_2 = \beta_1 \beta_2 \left(1 + \frac{\beta_3}{\beta_1} + \dots\right)$$

$$\sum \beta_1 \beta_2 \beta_3 = -c_3 \quad \text{i.e.} \quad c_3 = -\beta_1 \beta_2 \beta_3 \left(1 + \frac{\beta_4}{\beta_1} + \dots\right)$$

$$\cdots \quad \cdots \quad \cdots \quad \cdots \quad \cdots \quad \cdots \quad \cdots \quad \cdots$$

$$\beta_1 \beta_2 \beta_3 \cdots \beta_n = (-1)^n c_n$$
$$\text{i.e. } c_n = (-1)^n \beta_1 \beta_2 \beta_3 \cdots \beta_n$$

By Eq. (3.10.11) we get $c_1 \approx -\beta_1, c_2 \approx \beta_1 \beta_2, c_3 \approx -\beta_1 \beta_2 \beta_3, \ldots\ldots\ldots$

i.e. $\beta_1 \approx -c_1, \beta_2 \approx -\dfrac{c_2}{c_1}, \beta_3 \approx -\dfrac{c_3}{c_2}, \ldots\ldots, \beta_n \approx -\dfrac{c_n}{c_{n-1}}$

Since $\beta_i = -\alpha_i^{2^m}$, therefore, $\alpha_i = (-\beta_i)^{\frac{1}{2m}} = \left|\dfrac{c_i}{c_{i-1}}\right|^{\frac{1}{2m}}$ .... (3.10.12)

This determines the values of the roots $\alpha_1, \alpha_2, \ldots, \alpha_n$ of the original polynomial given in Eq. (3.10.7). The sign of α_i can be determined by actual substitution in the given equation. Thus, the root squaring process is terminated after n iterations from which the desired roots can be found easily.

Remarks:

- If the magnitude of c_i is half the square of the magnitude of the corresponding coefficient in the previous equation after a few squarings, then it shows that α_i is a double root of the polynomial given in the Eq. (3.10.7). It is given by $\alpha_k^{2^m} = \beta_k^2 = \left|\dfrac{c_{k+1}}{c_{k-1}}\right|$

- The whole root squaring process can be performed as given below:

a_0	a_1	a_2	a_3	a_4	a_5		a_n
						...	
a_0^2	a_1^2	a_2^2	a_3^2	a_4^2	a_5^2	...	a_n^2
	$-2a_0 a_2$	$-2a_1 a_3$	$-2a_2 a_4$	$-2a_3 a_5$	$-2a_4 a_6$	...	
		$2a_0 a_4$	$2a_1 a_5$	$2a_2 a_6$	$2a_3 a_7$		
						...	
			$2a_0 a_6$				
c_0	c_1	c_2	c_3	c_4	c_5	...	c_n

Example 3.20 Find all the roots of polynomial equation $x^3 - 6x^2 + 11x - 6 = 0$ using Graeffe's method by squaring three times.

Solution:

m	2^m				
0	1	1	-6	11	-6
	(Squaring)	1	36	121	36
			-22	-72	
1	2	1	14	49	36
	(Squaring)	1	196	2401	1296
			-98	-1008	
2	4	1	98	1393	1296
	(Squaring)	1	9604	1940449	1679616
			-2786	-254016	
3	8	$C_0 = 1$	$C_1 = 6818$	$C_2 = 1686433$	$C_3 = 1679616$

Here, m = 3. We know that $\alpha_i = \left|\frac{c_i}{c_{i-1}}\right|^{\frac{1}{2^m}}$ $i = 1, 2, 3$

We have,

$$\alpha_1 = \left|\frac{c_1}{c_0}\right|^{\frac{1}{8}} = \left(\frac{1679616}{1686433}\right)^{1/8} = 0.999 \approx 1$$

$$\alpha_2 = \left|\frac{c_2}{c_1}\right|^{\frac{1}{8}} = \left(\frac{1686433}{6818}\right)^{1/8} = 1.9919 \approx 2$$

$$\alpha_3 = \left|\frac{c_3}{c_2}\right|^{\frac{1}{8}} = \left(\frac{6818}{1}\right)^{1/8} = 3.0144 \approx 3$$

By actual substitution we find that all $\alpha_i's$ are positive.
Thus, the required roots of the given equation are 1, 2, 3.

Example 3.21 Solve the equation $x^3 + 3x^2 - 4 = 0$ using Graeffe's root squaring method.

Solution:

m	2^m				
0	1	1	3	0	-4
	(Squaring)	1	9	0	16
			0	24	
1	2	1	9	24	16
	(Squaring)	1	81	576	256
			-48	-288	
2	4	1	33	288	256
	(Squaring)	1	1089	82944	65536
			-576	-16896	
3	8	$C_0 = 1$	$C_1 = 513$	$C_2 = 66048$	$C_3 = 65536$

In this case, C_1 is almost half of the corresponding value in the previous squaring. This suggests the possibility of a double root based on C_0, C_1 and C_2.

Here, m = 3. By the formula, $\alpha_i = \left|\frac{c_i}{c_{i-1}}\right|^{\frac{1}{2^m}}$ $i = 1, 2, 3$

We have,

$$\alpha_1 = \left|\frac{c_1}{c_0}\right|^{\frac{1}{8}} = \left(\frac{65536}{66048}\right)^{1/8} = 0.999 \approx 1$$

$$\alpha_2 = \left|\frac{c_2}{c_1}\right|^{\frac{1}{8}} = \left(\frac{66048}{573}\right)^{1/8} = 1.8353 \approx 2$$

$$\alpha_3 = \left|\frac{c_3}{c_2}\right|^{\frac{1}{8}} = \left(\frac{513}{1}\right)^{1/8} = 2.1815 \approx 2$$

Substituting α_2 and α_3 in the given equation, it is clear that α_2, α_3 should be negative. Thus, the required roots of the given equation are 1, -2, -2.

3.11 BUDAN'S THEOREM

Let $f(x) = a_0 + a_1x + a_2 x^2 + a_3x^3 + ... + a_mx^m$ be a polynomial of degree m. Let $f^k(L)$ be the kth derivative of $f(x)$ evaluated at the point L. Let V_L be the changes in sign in the sequence of numbers $f(L), f'(L), f''(L), ..., f^m(L)$. The number of roots in the interval $L < x < U$ is the quantity $|V_L - V_U|$ or less than that by a multiple of two.

Remark: Descarte's rule gives only number of roots that are possible for a given equation. Whereas Budan's theorem not only gives number of roots but also specifies in which interval one will get how many roots. This way Budan's theorem is better than Descarte's rule.

Example 3.22 Apply Budan's theorem to estimate the number of roots of the polynomial equation $1 + 3x - 3x^2 - 4x^3 + x^4 + x^5$ in each of the interval (-2, -1), (-1, 0), (0,1), (1, 2).

Solution: Let $f(x) = 1 + 3x - 3x^2 - 4x^3 + x^4 + x^5$

$$f(x) = 1 + 3x - 3x^2 - 4x^3 + x^4 + x^5$$
$$f'(x) = 3 - 6x - 12x^2 + 4x^3 + 5x^4$$
$$f''(x) = -6 - 24x + 12x^2 + 20x^3$$
$$f'''(x) = -24 + 24x + 60x^2$$
$$f^{iv}(x) = 24 + 120x$$
$$f^{v}(x) = 120$$

The sign of coefficients in the sequence of numbers $f(x), f'(x), f''(x)$, $f'''(x), f^{iv}(x), f^{v}(x)$ are given in the below table and V_L be the changes in sign of these numbers.

x	$f(x)$	$f'(x)$	$f''(x)$	$f'''(x)$	$f^{iv}(x)$	$f^{v}(x)$	V_L
-2	–	+	–	+	–	+	5
-1	–	–	+	+	–	+	3
0	+	+	–	–	+	+	2
1	–	–	+	+	+	+	1
2	+	+	+	+	+	+	0

Interval wise number of roots are given below.

Interval	Changes in sign	Number of roots
$-2 < x < -1$	$|V_L - V_U| = |5 - 3|$	2 or 0
$-1 < x < 0$	$|V_L - V_U| = |3 - 2|$	1
$0 < x < 1$	$|V_L - V_U| = |2 - 1|$	1
$1 < x < 2$	$|V_L - V_U| = |1 - 0|$	1

3.12   RAMANUJAN METHOD

Srinivasa Ramanujan described this method for evaluating the smallest root of the equation $f(x) = 0$ where $f(x) = 1 - (a_1x + a_2 x^2 + a_3x^3 + a_4x^4 + \ldots)$.
For smaller values of x, we write

$$[1 - (a_1x + a_2 x^2 + a_3x^3 + a_4x^4 + \ldots)]^{-1} = b_1 + b_2x + b_3 x^2 + \ldots$$
$$\ldots\ldots (3.12.1)$$

Expanding the left hand side of (3.12.1) by binomial theorem, we get

$$1 + (a_1x + a_2 x^2 + a_3x^3 + a_4x^4 + \ldots)$$
$$+ (a_1x + a_2 x^2 + a_3x^3 + a_4x^4 + \ldots)^2 + \ldots$$
$$= b_1 + b_2x + b_3 x^2 + \ldots \qquad\qquad \ldots\ldots (3.12.2)$$

Comparing the coefficient of like powers of x on both the sides of Eq. (3.12.2) we get,

$$b_1 = 1$$
$$b_2 = a_1 = a_1 b_1$$
$$b_3 = a_1{}^2 + a_2 = a_1 b_2 + a_2 b_1$$
$$\ldots\ldots\ldots\ldots\ldots\ldots\ldots\ldots\ldots$$
$$b_n = a_1 b_{n-1} + a_2 b_{n-2} + \ldots\ldots + a_{n-1} b_1 \quad n = 2,3,\ldots\ldots$$

Without proof, Ramanujan states that b_n/b_{n+1} approach a root of the equation $f(x) = 0$.

Remark: The binomial theorem is:

$$(1 + x)^n = 1 + nx + \frac{n(n-1)}{1 \cdot 2} x^2 + \ldots + \frac{n(n-1) \ldots (n - (r-1))}{1 \cdot 2 \cdot 3 \cdot \ldots\ldots \cdot r} x^r + \ldots$$

In particular, $(1 + x)^{-1} = 1 - x + x^2 - x^3 \ldots + (-1)^n x^n$
and $\qquad\qquad (1 - x)^{-1} = 1 + x + x^2 + x^3 \ldots + x^n + \cdots$

Example 3.23   Find the smallest root of the equation

$$f(x) = x^3 - 7x^2 + 13x - 7 = 0.$$

Solution: The given equation can be re - written as

$$f(x) = 1 - \frac{13x - 7x^2 + x^3}{7}$$

Therefore, we have

$$\left[1 - \frac{13x - 7x^2 + x^3}{7}\right]^{-1} = b_1 + b_2x + b_3x^2 + \ldots$$

Comparing we have,

$$a_1 = \frac{13}{7}, \; a_2 = -1, a_3 = \frac{1}{7}, a_4 = a_5 = \cdots = 0$$

Hence, $\qquad\qquad b_1 = 1$
$$b_2 = a_1 = \frac{13}{7}$$

$$b_3 = a_1 b_2 + a_2 b_1 = \frac{169}{49} - 1 = \frac{120}{49}$$

$$b_4 = a_1 b_3 + a_2 b_2 + a_3 b_1 = \frac{1560}{343} - \frac{13}{7} + \frac{1}{7} = \frac{972}{343}$$

$$b_5 = a_1 b_4 + a_2 b_3 + a_3 b_2 + a_4 b_1 = \frac{12636}{2401} - \frac{120}{49} + \frac{13}{49} = \frac{7393}{2401}$$

$$b_6 = a_1 b_5 + a_2 b_4 + a_3 b_3 + a_4 b_2 + a_5 b_1 = \frac{96109}{16807} - \frac{972}{343} + \frac{120}{343} = \frac{54361}{16807}$$

Therefore,

$$\frac{b_1}{b_2} = \frac{7}{13} = 0.5385 \qquad\qquad \frac{b_2}{b_3} = \frac{91}{120} = 0.7583$$

$$\frac{b_3}{b_4} = \frac{840}{972} = 0.8642 \qquad\qquad \frac{b_4}{b_5} = \frac{6804}{7393} = 0.9203$$

$$\frac{b_5}{b_6} = \frac{51751}{54361} = 0.9520$$

By inspection, the smallest root of the given equation is unity.

Example 3.24   Find the real root of the equation

$$1 - x + \frac{x^2}{(2!)^2} - \frac{x^3}{(3!)^2} + \frac{x^4}{(4!)^2} - \ldots = 0.$$

Solution: The given equation can be re - written as

$$f(x) = 1 - \left[x - \frac{x^2}{(2!)^2} + \frac{x^3}{(3!)^2} - \frac{x^4}{(4!)^2} + \ldots \right] = 0$$

Therefore, we have

$$\left\{ 1 - \left[x - \frac{x^2}{(2!)^2} + \frac{x^3}{(3!)^2} - \frac{x^4}{(4!)^2} + \ldots \right] \right\}^{-1} = b_1 + b_2 x + b_3 x^2 + \ldots$$

Comparing we have,

$$a_1 = 1, \; a_2 = -\frac{1}{(2!)^2}, \; a_3 = \frac{1}{(3!)^2}, \; a_4 = -\frac{1}{(4!)^2}$$

Hence,

$$b_1 = 1$$
$$b_2 = a_1 = 1$$
$$b_3 = a_1 b_2 + a_2 b_1 = 1 - \frac{1}{(2!)^2} = \frac{3}{4}$$
$$b_4 = a_1 b_3 + a_2 b_2 + a_3 b_1 = \frac{3}{4} - \frac{1}{(2!)^2} + \frac{1}{(3!)^2} = \frac{3}{4} - \frac{1}{4} + \frac{1}{36} = \frac{19}{36}$$
$$b_5 = a_1 b_4 + a_2 b_3 + a_3 b_2 + a_4 b_1 = \frac{19}{36} - \left(\frac{1}{4}\right)\left(\frac{3}{4}\right) + \left(\frac{1}{36}\right)(1) - \frac{1}{576} = \frac{211}{576}$$

Therefore,

$$\frac{b_1}{b_2} = 1; \quad \frac{b_2}{b_3} = \frac{4}{3} = 1.33 \ldots; \quad \frac{b_3}{b_4} = \frac{3}{4} \times \frac{36}{19} = \frac{27}{19} = 1.4210.. ; \quad \frac{b_4}{b_5} = \frac{19}{36} \times$$

$$\frac{576}{211} = 1.4408 \ldots;$$

By inspection, the real root of the given equation upto three significant figures is 1.440.

3.13   METHODS OF FINDING COMPLEX ROOTS

The following two methods are used to find the complex roots of the given polynomial.

3.13.1   Muller's Method

Muller method is a generalization of the secant method. It is used to find real or complex roots of a polynomial or transcendental equation. This method is iterative in nature and converges quadratically. Instead of starting with two initial values and then joining them with a straight line as secant method, Muller's method starts with three initial approximations to the root and then join them with a second degree polynomial. Thus, the function $f(x)$, in this method, is approximated by a second degree curve in the neighbourhood of the root. Then the roots of the quadratic polynomial are taken as approximate values of the root of the equation $f(x) = 0$.

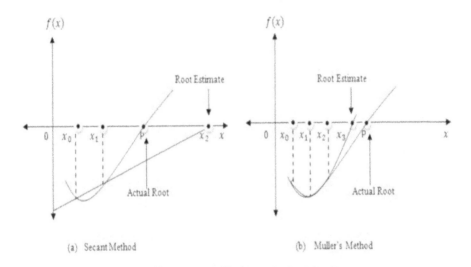

Figure 3.8 Comparison between Secant and Muller's method

Let x_0, x_1, x_2 be the three distinct approximations to a root of $f(x) = 0$, and $f(x_0)$, $f(x_1), f(x_2)$ be the corresponding values of $y = f(x)$. Consider that parabola

$$y = A(x - x_2)^2 + B(x - x_2) + C \qquad .... (3.13.1)$$

passes through $(x_0, f(x_0))$, $(x_1, f(x_1))$ and $(x_2, f(x_2))$.

Therefore, we have

$$f(x_0) = A(x_0 - x_2)^2 + B(x_0 - x_2) + C \qquad .... (3.13.2)$$
$$f(x_1) = A(x_1 - x_2)^2 + B(x_1 - x_2) + C \qquad .... (3.13.3)$$
$$f(x_2) = A(x_2 - x_2)^2 + B(x_2 - x_2) + C = A.\,0^2 + B.0 + C$$
$$C = f(x_2)$$

Solving Eqs. (3.13.2) and (3.13.3) for A and B, we get

$$A = \frac{(x_1-x_2)[f(x_0)-f(x_2)]-(x_0-x_2)[f(x_1)-f(x_2)]}{(x_0-x_2)(x_1-x_2)(x_0-x_1)}$$

$$B = \frac{(x_0-x_2)^2[f(x_1)-f(x_2)]-(x_1-x_2)^2[f(x_0)-f(x_2)]}{(x_0-x_2)(x_1-x_2)(x_0-x_1)}$$

With the values of A and B, the quadratic Eq. (3.13.1) gives the next approximation x_3 as

$$x_3 - x_2 = -\frac{B \pm \sqrt{B^2-4AC}}{2A} \qquad \text{........ (3.13.4)}$$

A solution from Eq. (3.13.4) leads to inaccurate results and is usually written in the following form:

$$x_3 = x_2 - \frac{2C}{B+sign\,(B)\,\sqrt{B^2-4AC}} \qquad \text{........ (3.13.5)}$$

To obtain the smallest root of the equation $f(x) = 0$ select the sign of the denominator which corresponds to the largest magnitude. Once x_3 is determined, let $x_0 = x_1$, $x_1 = x_2$, $x_2 = x_3$ and repeat the whole process.

Example 3.25   Apply Muller's method to find a root of the equation $x^3 - 4x - 9 = 0$ which lie between 2 and 3.

Solution: We have $f(x) = x^3 - 4x - 9 = 0$

Let $x_0 = 2.5$, $x_1 = 2.6$ and $x_2 = 2.7$

Then $f(x_0) = -3.375$, $f(x_1) = -1.824$ and $f(x_2) = -0.117$

Therefore,

$$A = \frac{(x_1-x_2)[f(x_0)-f(x_2)]-(x_0-x_2)[f(x_1)-f(x_2)]}{(x_0-x_2)(x_1-x_2)(x_0-x_1)}$$

$$= \frac{(-0.1)(-3.258)-(-0.2)(-1.707)}{(-0.2)(-0.1)(-0.1)} = \frac{(-0.0156)}{(-0.002)} = 7.8$$

$$B = \frac{(x_0-x_2)^2[f(x_1)-f(x_2)]-(x_1-x_2)^2[f(x_0)-f(x_2)]}{(x_0-x_2)(x_1-x_2)(x_0-x_1)}$$

$$= \frac{(-0.2)^2(-1.707)-(-0.1)^2(-3.258)}{(-0.2)(-0.1)(-0.1)} = \frac{(-0.0357)}{(-0.002)} = 17.85$$

The approximating quadratic equation is $7.8\,(x - 2.7)^2 + 17.85(x - 2.7) - 0.117 = 0$

Then, the next approximation is

$$x_3 = x_2 - \frac{2C}{B + sign(B)\,\sqrt{B^2 - 4AC}}$$

$$= 2.7 - \frac{2(-0.117)}{17.85+\sqrt{318.6225}+3.6504}$$

$$= 2.7 - \frac{-0.234}{17.85+17.9520} \quad \text{(Taking +ve sign in denominator)}$$

$$= 2.7 + 0.006536 = 2.706536$$

Now the procedure is repeated with the three approximations as 2.6, 2.7 and 2.706536

$$x_0 = 2.6, \quad x_1 = 2.7 \quad \text{and} \quad x_2 = 2.706536$$

Then $f(x_0) = -1.824$, $f(x_1) = -0.117$ and $f(x_2) = 0.000145$

Therefore,

$$A = \frac{(x_1 - x_2)[f(x_0) - f(x_2)] - (x_0 - x_2)[f(x_1) - f(x_2)]}{(x_0 - x_2)(x_1 - x_2)(x_0 - x_1)}$$

$$= \frac{(-0.006536)(-1.8241) - (-0.106536)(-0.1171)}{(-0.106536)(-0.006536)(-0.1)} = \frac{-0.00056}{(-0.00007)} = 8$$

$$B = \frac{(x_0 - x_2)^2 [f(x_1) - f(x_2)] - (x_1 - x_2)^2 [f(x_0) - f(x_2)]}{(x_0 - x_2)(x_1 - x_2)(x_0 - x_1)}$$

$$= \frac{(-0.106536)^2 (-0.1171) - (-0.006536)^2 (-1.8241)}{(-0.106536)(-0.006536)(-0.1)} = \frac{(-0.001251)}{(-0.00007)} = 17.8714$$

Then, the next approximation is

$$x_3 = x_2 - \frac{2C}{B + sign\,(B)\,\sqrt{B^2 - 4AC}}$$

$$= 2.706536 - \frac{2(0.000145)}{17.8714 + \sqrt{319.3869 - 0.00464}}$$

$$= 2.706536 - \frac{0.00029}{17.8714 + 17.8713} = 2.706536 - 0.0000081 = 2.706528$$

Hence, the approximate value of the root correct to four decimal places is 2.7065.

Example 3.26   Apply Muller's method to find a root of the equation $e^x - 3x = 0$ which lie between 1 and 2.

Solution: We have $f(x) = e^x - 3x = 0$

Let $x_0 = 1.3, \quad x_1 = 1.4 \quad \text{and} \quad x_2 = 1.5$

Then $f(x_0) = -0.2307$, $f(x_1) = -0.1448$ and $f(x_2) = -0.0183$

Therefore,

$$A = \frac{(x_1 - x_2)[f(x_0) - f(x_2)] - (x_0 - x_2)[f(x_1) - f(x_2)]}{(x_0 - x_2)(x_1 - x_2)(x_0 - x_1)}$$

$$= \frac{(-0.1)(-0.2124) - (-0.2)(-0.1265)}{(-0.2)(-0.1)(-0.1)} = \frac{(-0.00406)}{(-0.002)} = 2.03$$

$$B = \frac{(x_0 - x_2)^2 [f(x_1) - f(x_2)] - (x_1 - x_2)^2 [f(x_0) - f(x_2)]}{(x_0 - x_2)(x_1 - x_2)(x_0 - x_1)}$$

$$= \frac{(-0.2)^2 (-0.1265) - (-0.1)^2 (-0.2124)}{(-0.2)(-0.1)(-0.1)} = \frac{(-0.002936)}{(-0.002)} = 1.468$$

The approximating quadratic equation is

$$2.03(x - 1.5) + 1.468(x - 1.5) - 0.0183 = 0$$

Then, the next approximation is

$$x_3 = x_2 - \frac{2C}{B + sign\,(B)\,\sqrt{B^2 - 4AC}}$$

$$= 1.5 - \frac{2(-0.0183)}{1.468 + \sqrt{2.155024 + 0.148596}}$$

$$= 1.5 - \frac{-0.0366}{1.468 + 1.616596} \qquad \text{(Taking +ve sign in denominator)}$$

$$= 1.5 + 0.01187 = 1.51187$$

Now the procedure is repeated with the three approximations as 1.4, 1.5 and 1.51187. $x_0 = 1.4$, $x_1 = 1.5$ and $x_2 = 1.51187$

Then $f(x_0) = -0.1448$, $f(x_1) = -0.0183$ and $f(x_2) = -0.00041$

Therefore,

$$A = \frac{(x_1 - x_2)[f(x_0) - f(x_2)] - (x_0 - x_2)[f(x_1) - f(x_2)]}{(x_0 - x_2)(x_1 - x_2)(x_0 - x_1)}$$

$$= \frac{(-0.01187)(-0.14439) - (-0.11187)(-0.01789)}{(-0.11187)(-0.01187)(-0.1)} = \frac{-0.000287}{(-0.00013)} = 2.2077$$

$$B = \frac{(x_0 - x_2)^2[f(x_1) - f(x_2)] - (x_1 - x_2)^2[f(x_0) - f(x_2)]}{(x_0 - x_2)(x_1 - x_2)(x_0 - x_1)}$$

$$= \frac{(-0.11187)^2(-0.01789) - (-0.01187)^2(-0.14439)}{(-0.11187)(-0.01187)(-0.1)} = \frac{(-0.0002037)}{(-0.00013)} = 1.5669$$

Then, the next approximation is

$$x_3 = x_2 - \frac{2C}{B + sign\,(B)\,\sqrt{B^2 - 4AC}} = 1.51187 - \frac{2(-0.00041)}{1.5669 + \sqrt{2.4552 + 0.003620}}$$

$$= 1.51187 - \frac{-0.00082}{1.5669 + 1.5705} \qquad \text{(Taking +ve sign in denominator)}$$

$$= 1.51187 + 0.000261 = 1.512131$$

Hence, the approximate value of the root correct to four significant places is 1.512.

3.13.2   Lin – Bairstow's Method

Bairstow's method is valid for polynomials with real coefficients only. This method is used to obtain the real and complex roots of polynomial equations. Let the polynomial be,

$$f(x) = a_0 x^n + a_1 x^{n-1} + a_2 x^{n-2} + \ldots + a_n = 0 \qquad \ldots\ldots\ldots (3.13.6)$$

As we know that complex roots of $f(x)$ occur as complex conjugate pairs $a \pm ib$, and so $f(x)$ has real quadratic factor

$$\{x - (a + ib)\}\{x - (a - ib)\} = x^2 - 2ax + a^2 + b^2 = x^2 + px + q$$

where coefficients p and q are real.

If we divide $f(x)$ by $x^2 + px + q$, then

$$f(x) = (x^2 + px + q)g(x) + Rx + S$$

where $g(x)$ is a polynomial of degree $(n-2)$.

Therefore,

$$g(x) = x^{n-2} + b_1 x^{n-3} + \dots + b_{n-2}$$

and a remainder $\qquad R_n = Rx + S$

Thus, $f(x) = (x^2 + px + q)(x^{n-2} + b_1 x^{n-3} + \dots + b_{n-2}) + Rx + S$

$$\dots\dots (3.13.7)$$

If $(x^2 + px + q)$ divides $f(x)$ completely, the remainder $Rx + S = 0$. It implies that both $R = S = 0$, such that

$$R(p, q) = 0 \text{ and } S(p, q) = 0 \qquad\qquad \dots\dots (3.13.8)$$

Let $p + \Delta p, q + \Delta q$ be the actual values of p and q which satisfy Eq. (3.11.8) then

$$R(p + \Delta p, q + \Delta q) = 0 \text{ and } S(p + \Delta p, q + \Delta q) = 0 \qquad \dots\dots(3.13.9)$$

To obtain the values of Δp and Δq, expand Eq. (3.13.9) by Taylor's series and neglecting the second and higher degree terms, we get

$$R(p,q) + \frac{\partial R}{\partial p}\,\Delta p + \frac{\partial R}{\partial q}\,\Delta q = 0$$

$$S(p,q) + \frac{\partial S}{\partial p}\,\Delta p + \frac{\partial S}{\partial q}\,\Delta q = 0 \qquad\qquad \dots\dots (3.13.10)$$

Now, to find the coefficients b_i, R and S, compare the coefficients of Eqs. (3.13.6) and (3.13.7), we get

$$b_0 = 1$$
$$b_1 = a_1 - p$$
$$b_2 = a_2 - pb_1 - q$$
$$b_3 = a_3 - pb_2 - qb_1$$
$$\vdots \qquad \vdots \qquad \vdots$$
$$b_i = a_i - pb_{i-1} - qb_{i-2} \qquad\qquad \dots\dots (3.13.11)$$
$$\vdots \qquad \vdots \qquad \vdots$$
$$b_n = a_n - pb_{n-1} - qb_{n-2}$$
$$R = a_{n-1} - pb_{n-2} - qb_{n-3}$$
$$S = a_n - qb_{n-2}$$

Therefore,

$$b_{n-1} = a_{n-1} - pb_{n-2} - qb_{n-3} = R$$
$$b_n = a_n - pb_{n-1} - qb_{n-2} = S - pb_{n-1}$$

So, we have $\qquad R = b_{n-1} \text{ and } S = b_n + pb_{n-1} \qquad \dots\dots (3.13.12)$

Substitute values of R and S in Eq. (3.13.10) we get,

$$b_{n-1} + \frac{\partial b_{n-1}}{\partial p}\,\Delta p + \frac{\partial b_{n-1}}{\partial q}\,\Delta q = 0$$

$$(b_n + pb_{n-1}) + \left[\frac{\partial b_n}{\partial p} + p\frac{\partial b_{n-1}}{\partial p} + b_{n-1}\right]\Delta p + \left[\frac{\partial b_n}{\partial q} + p\frac{\partial b_{n-1}}{\partial p}\right]\Delta q = 0$$

Multiplying the first equation by p and subtracting from the second equation, we get

$$\frac{\partial b_{n-1}}{\partial p} \Delta p + \frac{\partial b_{n-1}}{\partial q} \Delta q + b_{n-1} = 0$$

$$\left[\frac{\partial b_n}{\partial p} + b_{n-1} \right] \Delta p + \frac{\partial b_n}{\partial q} \Delta q + b_n = 0 \qquad \text{........ (3.13.13)}$$

Keeping in the mind that all $a_i's$ are constants and all $b_i's$ are functions of p and q, taking partial derivatives of the expressions of Eq. (3.13.11) with respect to p and defining them in terms of c's, we have

$$\frac{\partial b_0}{\partial p} = 0$$

$$\frac{\partial b_1}{\partial p} = -1 = -c_0 \qquad\qquad\qquad \therefore c_0 = 1$$

$$\frac{\partial b_2}{\partial p} = -b_1 - p\frac{\partial b_1}{\partial p} = -b_1 + p = -c_1 \qquad\qquad \therefore c_1 = b_1 - p$$

$$\frac{\partial b_3}{\partial p} = -b_2 - p\frac{\partial b_2}{\partial p} - q\frac{\partial b_1}{\partial p} = -b_2 + pc_1 + q = -c_2 \therefore c_2 = b_2 - pc_1 - q$$

$$\frac{\partial b_4}{\partial p} = -b_3 + pc_2 + qc_1 = -c_3 \qquad\qquad \therefore c_3 = b_3 - pc_2 - qc_1$$

$$\vdots$$

$$\frac{\partial b_n}{\partial p} = -b_{n-1} + pc_{n-2} + qc_{n-3} = -c_{n-1} \therefore c_{n-1} = b_{n-1} - pc_{n-2} - qc_{n-3}$$

Similarly, taking partial derivatives of the expressions of Eq. (3.13.11) with respect to q, we have

$$\frac{\partial b_0}{\partial q} = 0$$

$$\frac{\partial b_1}{\partial q} = -1 = -c_0 \qquad\qquad\qquad \therefore c_0 = 1$$

$$\frac{\partial b_2}{\partial q} = -b_1 - p\frac{\partial b_1}{\partial q} = -b_1 + p = -c_1 \qquad\qquad \therefore c_1 = b_1 - p$$

$$\frac{\partial b_3}{\partial q} = -b_2 - p\frac{\partial b_2}{\partial q} - q\frac{\partial b_1}{\partial q} = -b_2 + pc_1 + q = -c_2$$

$$\therefore c_2 = b_2 - pc_1 - q$$

$$\frac{\partial b_4}{\partial q} = -b_3 + pc_2 + qc_1 = -c_3 \qquad \therefore c_3 = b_3 - pc_2 - qc_1$$

$$\vdots$$

$$\frac{\partial b_n}{\partial q} = -b_{n-1} + pc_{n-2} + qc_{n-3} = -c_{n-1}$$

$$\therefore c_{n-1} = b_{n-1} - pc_{n-2} - qc_{n-3}$$

The final values of all $c_i's$ are given as

$$c_0 = 1$$
$$c_1 = b_1 - p$$

$$c_2 = b_2 - pc_1 - q$$
$$c_3 = b_3 - pc_2 - qc_1$$
$$\vdots \qquad \vdots$$
$$c_i = b_i - pc_{i-1} - qc_{i-2} \quad \text{for } i = 2,3,4,....,\ n\text{-}1$$

Therefore, from Eq. (3.13.13) it is derived that,

$$b_{n-1} = C_{n-2}\,\Delta p + C_{n-3}\,\Delta q$$
$$b_n = (C_{n-1} - b_{n-1})\,\Delta p + C_{n-2}\,\Delta q \qquad .... \ (3.13.14)$$

After finding the values of b_i's and c_i's and Eq. (3.13.14) we can find the approximate values of Δp and Δq. If p_0 and q_0 be the initial approximations then their improved values are $p_1 = p_0 + \Delta p$ and $q_1 = q_0 + \Delta q$. Now, taking p_1 and q_1 as initial values and repeating the above procedure, we obtain better approximations of p and q.

Example 3.27   Find the complex roots of the following polynomial equation using Lin – Bairstow's method

$$x^4 - 2x^3 + 4x^2 - 4x + 4 = 0$$

Solution: Let $f(x) = x^4 - 2x^3 + 4x^2 - 4x + 4$

Comparing given equation with $f(x) = a_0x^4 + a_1x^3 + a_2x^2 + a_3x + a_4$

We get, $a_0 = 1,\ a_1 = -2,\ a_2 = 4,\ a_3 = -4,\ a_4 = 4$

Let

$$f(x) = (x^2 + px + q)(b_0x^2 + b_1x + b_2) + Rx + S$$

Putting the values of a_i's in Eq. (3.13.11), we get

$b_0 = 1$

$b_1 = a_1 - p = -2 - p$

$b_2 = a_2 - pb_1 - q = 4 - p(-2 - p) - q = p^2 + 2p - q + 4$

$R = a_3 - pb_2 - qb_1 = -4 - p(p^2 + 2p - q + 4) - q(-2 - p)$

$\qquad = -4 - 4p - 2p^2 - p^3 + 2pq + 2q$

$S = a_4 - qb_2 = 4 - q(p^2 + 2p - q + 4) \quad = 4 - 4q - 2pq - p^2q + q^2$

$$\frac{\partial R}{\partial P} = -4 - 4p - 3p^2 + 2q \qquad\qquad \frac{\partial R}{\partial q} = 2p + 2$$

$$\frac{\partial S}{\partial P} = -2q - 2pq \qquad\qquad \frac{\partial S}{\partial q} = -4 - 2p - p^2 + 2q$$

$$D = \left(\frac{\partial R}{\partial P}\right)\left(\frac{\partial S}{\partial q}\right) - \left(\frac{\partial S}{\partial P}\right)\left(\frac{\partial R}{\partial q}\right)$$

and $\qquad \Delta p = \dfrac{\begin{vmatrix} -R & \frac{\partial R}{\partial q} \\ -S & \frac{\partial S}{\partial q} \end{vmatrix}}{D} \qquad \Delta q = \dfrac{\begin{vmatrix} \frac{\partial R}{\partial P} & -R \\ \frac{\partial S}{\partial P} & -S \end{vmatrix}}{D}$

p	0	1	-2
q	0	1	1
R	-4	-7	2
S	4	-2	1

Iteration 1:   Let $(p, q) = (-2, 1)$

p	q	R	S	$\frac{\partial R}{\partial P}$	$\frac{\partial R}{\partial q}$	$\frac{\partial S}{\partial P}$	$\frac{\partial S}{\partial q}$	D
-2	1	2	1	-6	-2	2	-2	16

and $\Delta p = 0.125$ and $\Delta q = 0.625$

Therefore, $p = p + \Delta p = -2 + 0.125 = -1.875$

$q = q + \Delta q = 1 + 0.625 = 1.625$

Iteration 2:

p	q	R	S	$\frac{\partial R}{\partial P}$	$\frac{\partial R}{\partial q}$	$\frac{\partial S}{\partial P}$	$\frac{\partial S}{\partial q}$	D
-1.875	1.625	0.2168	0.5215	-3.7969	-1.75	2.84375	-0.5156	6.9342

and $\Delta p = -0.1155$ and $\Delta q = 0.3745$

Therefore, $p = p + \Delta p = -1.875 - 0.1155 = -1.9905$

$q = q + \Delta q = 1.625 + 0.3745 = 1.9995$

Iteration 3:

p	q	R	S	$\frac{\partial R}{\partial P}$	$\frac{\partial R}{\partial q}$	$\frac{\partial S}{\partial P}$	$\frac{\partial S}{\partial q}$	D
-1.9905	1.9995	-0.0366	0.0378					7.7764

and $\Delta p = -0.0095$ and $\Delta q = 0.004$

Therefore, $p = p + \Delta p = -1.9905 - 0.0095 = -2$

$q = q + \Delta q = 1.9995 + 0.0004 = 2$

Now, values of R and S becomes 0.

Therefore, $f(x) = (x^2 + px + q)(b_0 x^2 + b_1 x + b_2)$

Putting final values of p and q we get,

$$b_0 = 1$$
$$b_1 = a_1 - p = -2 + 2$$
$$b_2 = a_2 - pb_1 - q = 4 + 2(-2 + 2) - 2 = 2$$

Hence,

$$f(x) = (x^2 - 2x + 2)(x^2 + 2)$$

By solving $(x^2 - 2x + 2) = 0$ using direct method, the roots are $1 \pm i$.

By solving $(x^2 + 2) = 0$ using direct method, the roots are $\pm \sqrt{2}i$.

The roots of the given polynomial equation are $1 + i, 1 - i, \sqrt{2}i$ and $-\sqrt{2}i$.

3.14   SYSTEM OF NON – LINEAR EQUATIONS

A system of equations is a set of more than one equation. If maximum power of any term of equation is one then the system is said to be linear. On the other hand, if any term involves with power more than one then the system is said to be nonlinear. In this section, we discuss Newton – Raphson method and fixed point method for solving such equations. We consider the case of two equations in two variables. However, the process can be extended to n number of equations in n unknowns. The solution of system of non – linear equations is the intersection points of the curves represented by these equations.

3.14.1   Newton – Raphson Method

Consider two polynomial equations in variables x and y which are
$f_1(x,y) = 0$ and $f_2(x,y) = 0$.
If x_0 and y_0 are the approximations and h and k are the corrections respectively then $x = x_0 + h$ and $y = y_0 + k$.

Therefore, $f_1(x_0 + h, y_0 + k) = 0$ .... (3.14.1)
$f_2(x_0 + h, y_0 + k) = 0$ .... (3.14.2)

Using the Taylor's series expansion for Eq. (3.14.1) and Eq. (3.14.2) for a function of two variables we get

$$f_1(x_0 + h, y_0 + k) = f_1(x_0, y_0) + h \left.\frac{\partial f_1}{\partial x}\right|_{(x_0,y_0)} + k \left.\frac{\partial f_1}{\partial y}\right|_{(x_0,y_0)} = 0$$

$$f_2(x_0 + h, y_0 + k) = f_2(x_0, y_0) + h \left.\frac{\partial f_2}{\partial x}\right|_{(x_0,y_0)} + k \left.\frac{\partial f_2}{\partial y}\right|_{(x_0,y_0)} = 0$$

Since h and k are relatively small, their squares, products and higher powers can be neglected.
From Eqs. (3.14.1) and (3.14.2) the above equations can be re – written as

$$h \left.\frac{\partial f_1}{\partial x}\right|_{(x_0,y_0)} + k \left.\frac{\partial f_1}{\partial y}\right|_{(x_0,y_0)} = -f_1(x_0, y_0) \qquad .... (3.14.3)$$

$$h \left.\frac{\partial f_2}{\partial x}\right|_{(x_0,y_0)} + k \left.\frac{\partial f_2}{\partial y}\right|_{(x_0,y_0)} = -f_2(x_0, y_0) \qquad .... (3.14.4)$$

Solving Eqs. (3.14.3) and (3.14.4) for h and k using Cramer's rule we get,

$$h = \frac{\begin{vmatrix} -f_1(x_0,y_0) & \left.\frac{\partial f_1}{\partial y}\right|_{(x_0,y_0)} \\ -f_2(x_0,y_0) & \left.\frac{\partial f_2}{\partial y}\right|_{(x_0,y_0)} \end{vmatrix}}{D} \qquad k = \frac{\begin{vmatrix} \left.\frac{\partial f_1}{\partial x}\right|_{(x_0,y_0)} & -f_1(x_0,y_0) \\ \left.\frac{\partial f_2}{\partial x}\right|_{(x_0,y_0)} & -f_2(x_0,y_0) \end{vmatrix}}{D}$$

$$\text{where } D = \begin{vmatrix} \left.\frac{\partial f_1}{\partial x}\right|_{(x_0,y_0)} & \left.\frac{\partial f_1}{\partial y}\right|_{(x_0,y_0)} \\ \left.\frac{\partial f_2}{\partial x}\right|_{(x_0,y_0)} & \left.\frac{\partial f_2}{\partial y}\right|_{(x_0,y_0)} \end{vmatrix}$$

Therefore, $D = \dfrac{\partial f_1}{\partial x} \cdot \dfrac{\partial f_2}{\partial y} - \dfrac{\partial f_1}{\partial y} \cdot \dfrac{\partial f_2}{\partial x}$ at point (x_0, y_0).

Additional corrections can be made by taking repeated approximations of x and y till the roots with desired accuracy are obtained. That means the process will terminate when the new approximations to x and y are within the prescribed tolerance.

Example 3.28   Solve the following simultaneous non – linear equations

$$3x^2 - 2y^2 - 1 = 0$$
$$x^2 - 2x + y^2 + 2y - 8 = 0$$

using Newton – Raphson method correct to four significant places.

Solution: Let $f_1(x,y) = 3x^2 - 2y^2 - 1$ and

$$f_2(x,y) = x^2 - 2x + y^2 + 2y - 8$$

$\dfrac{\partial f_1}{\partial x} = 6x$ $\dfrac{\partial f_1}{\partial y} = -4y$ $\dfrac{\partial f_2}{\partial x} = 2x - 2$ $\dfrac{\partial f_2}{\partial y} = 2y + 2$

> **Remark:** Take initial values of x and y in such a way that the values of f_1 and f_2 are near to zero.

x	0	2
y	0	2
f_1	-1	3
f_2	-8	0

Iteration 1: $(x_0, y_0) = (2, 2)$

$$f_1 = 3(2)^2 - 2(2)^2 - 1 = 3$$
$$f_2 = (2)^2 - 2(2) + (2)^2 + 2(2) - 8 = 0$$

$\dfrac{\partial f_1}{\partial x} = 12$, $\dfrac{\partial f_1}{\partial y} = -8$

$\dfrac{\partial f_2}{\partial x} = 2$, $\dfrac{\partial f_2}{\partial y} = 6$

$\therefore\ D = (12).(6) - (2)(-8) = 88$

$$h = \frac{\begin{vmatrix} -3 & -8 \\ 0 & 6 \end{vmatrix}}{88} = -0.2045 \ , \quad k = \frac{\begin{vmatrix} 12 & -3 \\ 2 & 0 \end{vmatrix}}{88} = 0.0682$$

$x_1 = x_0 + h = 2 - 0.2045 = 1.7955$
$y_1 = y_0 + k = 2 + 0.0682 = 2.0682$

Iteration 2: $(x_1, y_1) = (1.7955, 2.0682)$

$f_1 = 3(1.7955)^2 - 2(2.0682)^2 - 1 = 0.1166$
$f_2 = (1.7955)^2 - 2(1.7955) + (2.0682)^2 + 2(2.0682) - 8 = 0.04667$

$\dfrac{\partial f_1}{\partial x} = 10.773$, $\dfrac{\partial f_1}{\partial y} = -8.2728$

$\dfrac{\partial f_2}{\partial x} = 1.591$, $\dfrac{\partial f_2}{\partial y} = 6.1364$

$\therefore\ D = (10.773).(6.1364) - (1.591)(-8.2728) = 79.2694$

$$h = \frac{\begin{vmatrix} -0.1166 & -8.2728 \\ -0.04667 & 6.1364 \end{vmatrix}}{79.2694} = -0.0139 \, , \quad k = \frac{\begin{vmatrix} 10.773 & -0.1166 \\ 1.591 & -0.04667 \end{vmatrix}}{79.2694} = -0.004$$

$$x_2 = x_1 + h = 1.7955 - 0.0139 \ = 1.7817$$
$$y_2 = y_1 + k = 2.0682 - 0.004 \ = 2.0642$$

Iteration 3: $(x_2, y_2) = (1.7817, 2.0642)$

$$f_1 = 3(1.7817)^2 - 2(2.0642)^2 - 1 = 0.0015$$
$$f_2 = (1.7817)^2 - 2(1.7817) + (2.0642)^2 + 2(2.0642) - 8 = 0.0004$$

$$\frac{\partial f_1}{\partial x} = 10.6902 \, , \qquad \frac{\partial f_1}{\partial y} = -8.2568$$

$$\frac{\partial f_2}{\partial x} = 1.5634 \, , \qquad \frac{\partial f_2}{\partial y} = 6.1284$$

$$\therefore \ D = (10.6902).(6.1284) - (1.5634)(-8.2568) = 78.4225$$

$$h = \frac{\begin{vmatrix} -0.0015 & -8.2568 \\ -0.0004 & 6.1284 \end{vmatrix}}{78.4225} = 0.00016 \, , \quad k = \frac{\begin{vmatrix} 10.6902 & -0.0015 \\ 1.5634 & -0.0004 \end{vmatrix}}{78.4225} = -0.00002$$

$$x_3 = x_2 + h = 1.7817 - 0.00016 \ = 1.7819$$
$$y_3 = y_2 + k = 2.0642 - 0.00002 \ = 2.0642$$

In the second and third iterations the values of x and y are same upto three decimal places. Therefore, the solution is $(x , y) = (1.781, 2.064)$.

3.14.2   Fixed Point Method

Let's consider two non linear equations
$$f(x,y) = 0$$
$$g(x,y) = 0 \qquad \text{........ (3.14.5)}$$
whose real roots are required to be found within a specified accuracy. As described in section 3.7, we write
$$x = F(x,y)$$
$$y = G(x,y) \qquad \text{........ (3.14.6)}$$

Let (x_0 , y_0) be the initial approximation to a root of Eq. (3.14.5). If (x_0 , y_0) is chosen sufficiently close to the root and if F and G satisfy the conditions

$$\left| \frac{\partial F}{\partial x} \right| + \left| \frac{\partial F}{\partial y} \right| < 1$$

$$\left| \frac{\partial G}{\partial x} \right| + \left| \frac{\partial G}{\partial y} \right| < 1 \qquad \text{........ (3.14.7)}$$

then the iterations converges to the root.

Here, we assume that the functions in Eq. (3.14.6) and their first partial derivatives are continous on a region that contains the fixed point (x, y).

The next approximations are computed successively as

$$\left. \begin{array}{l} x_1 = F(x_0 , \ y_0) \\ y_1 = G(x_0 , \ y_0) \end{array} \right\} \ 1^{st} \text{ approximations}$$

$$\left. \begin{array}{l} x_2 = F(x_1, y_1) \\ y_2 = G(x_1, y_1) \end{array} \right\} \text{ 2}^{\text{nd}} \text{ approximations}$$

$$\left. \begin{array}{l} x_3 = F(x_2, y_2) \\ y_3 = G(x_2, y_2) \end{array} \right\} \text{ 3}^{\text{rd}} \text{ approximations}$$

$$\vdots$$

$$\left. \begin{array}{l} x_{n+1} = F(x_n, y_n) \\ y_{n+1} = G(x_n, y_n) \end{array} \right\} \text{ (n+1)}^{\text{th}} \text{ approximations}$$

till we obtain the required root within the prescribed tolerance.

Example 3.29   Find a real root of the non-linear equations
$$x = 0.2 \, x^2 + 0.8$$
$$y = 0.3 \, xy^2 + 0.7$$
using fixed – point method correct to four decimal places.

Solution: We have
$$F(x, y) = 0.2 \, x^2 + 0.8, \qquad G(x, y) = 0.3 \, xy^2 + 0.7$$
Therefore,
$$\frac{\partial F}{\partial x} = 0.4x, \quad \frac{\partial F}{\partial y} = 0, \quad \frac{\partial G}{\partial x} = 0.3y^2, \quad \frac{\partial G}{\partial y} = 0.6xy$$

Consider the initial approximations $(x_0, y_0) = (0.5, 0.5)$ then
$$\left| \frac{\partial F}{\partial x} \right|_{(x_0, y_0)} + \left| \frac{\partial F}{\partial y} \right|_{(x_0, y_0)} = 0.2 < 1, \quad \left| \frac{\partial G}{\partial x} \right|_{(x_0, y_0)} + \left| \frac{\partial G}{\partial y} \right|_{(x_0, y_0)} = 0.225 < 1$$

Therefore, conditions are satisfied. Hence,
$$x_1 = F(x_0, y_0) = (0.2)(0.5)^2 + 0.8 = 0.85$$
$$y_1 = G(x_0, y_0) = (0.3)(0.5)(0.5)^2 + 0.7 = 0.74$$
For next approximation,
$$x_2 = F(x_1, y_1) = (0.2)(0.85)^2 + 0.8 = 0.9445$$
$$y_2 = G(x_1, y_1) = (0.3)(0.85)(0.74)^2 + 0.7 = 0.81$$
Similarly,

$(x_3, y_3) = (0.9784, 0.8859)$	$(x_4, y_4) = (0.9915, 0.9304)$
$(x_5, y_5) = (0.9966, 0.9575)$	$(x_6, y_6) = (0.9986, 0.9741)$
$(x_7, y_7) = (0.9994, 0.9843)$	$(x_8, y_8) = (0.9998, 0.9905)$
$(x_9, y_9) = (0.9999, 0.9943)$	$(x_{10}, y_{10}) = (1.0000, 0.9966)$
$(x_{11}, y_{11}) = (1.0000, 0.998)$	$(x_{12}, y_{12}) = (1.0000, 0.999)$
$(x_{13}, y_{13}) = (1.0000, 0.9994)$	$(x_{14}, y_{14}) = (1.0000, 1.000)$

The solution of a given system of non – linear equations is $x = 1.000$ and $y = 1.000$ correct upto three decimal places.

3.15   PROGRAMS IN C
3.15.1   Program for Bisection Method

```c
//Program to implement Bisection method to find the root of given equation
#include<stdio.h>
#include<math.h>
#include<conio.h>
#define f(x) 2*(x) - cos(x) - 3
void main()
{
        int i, n=1;
        float x1, x2, x3, fx1, fx2, fx3, epsilon;
        clrscr();
        printf("\n\t\t\tBisection method for Transcendental Equation");
        printf("\n\t\t\t----------------------------------------------------------");
        fx1=fx2=fx3=x1=x2=x3=0;
        printf("\nEnter the first approximation");
        scanf("%f",&x1);
        printf("\nEnter the second approximation");
        scanf("%f",&x2);
        printf("\nEnter prescribed tolerance");
        scanf("%f",&epsilon);
        printf("\nIteration     x1\t    |    x2\t  |    x3\t    |
        f(x3)\n");
    printf("----------------------------------------------------------------------");
        fx1 = f(x1);
        fx2 = f(x2);
        if((fx1>0 && fx2<0)|| (fx1 < 0 && fx2>0))
        {
                do
                {
                        x3=(x1+x2)/2;
                        fx3 = f(x3);
                        printf("\n %d) \t %f  |%f  |    %f |
                        %f\n",n,x1,x2,x3,fx3);
                            if(fx1 * fx3>0)
                            {
                                    x1=x3;
                                    fx1=fx3;
                            }
                            else if(fx3 == 0.00)
                            {
                                    printf("\n %d) \t %f  |        %f  |
                                    %f  |%f\n",n,x1,x2,x3,fx3);
```

```
                                        printf("\n\n\t\t\t Answer : %f",x3);
                                        break;
                            }
                            else
                            {
                                    x2=x3;
                                    fx2=fx3;
                            }
                            n++;
                    }while(fabs(x1-x2)> epsilon);
                    printf("\n\n\t\t\t Answer : %f",x3);
        }
        else
        {       printf("\nEntert valid range");
        }
        getch(); }
```

3.15.2   Program for False Position Method

```
//Program to implement False Position method to find the root of given equation
#include<stdio.h>
#include<math.h>
#include<conio.h>
#define f(x)  2*(x) - log10(x) - 7
void main()
{
        int i,n=1;
        float x1,x2,x3,fx1,fx2,fx3,temp,tempx1,tempx2,tempx3,epsilon;
        clrscr();
        printf("\n\t\t\tFalse Position method");
        printf("\n\t\t\t----------------------");

        fx1=fx2=fx3=x1=x2=x3=0;
        printf("\nEnter the first approximation");
        scanf("%f",&x1);
        printf("\nEnter the second approximation");
        scanf("%f",&x2);
        printf("\nEnter prescribed tolerance");
        scanf("%f",&epsilon);
    printf("\nIteration     x1\t    |    x2\t    |    x3\t    |  f(x3)\n");
    printf("----------------------------------------------------------------------------------");
        fx1 = f(x1);
        fx2 = f(x2);
```

```
if((fx1>0 && fx2<0)|| (fx1 < 0 && fx2>0))
{
               do
               {
                   temp = x3;
                       x3=((x1*fx2) - (x2*fx1))/(fx2 - fx1);
                       fx3 = f(x3);
                       printf("\n %d) \t %f  |%f  |      %f  |
                       %f\n",n,x1,x2,x3,fx3);
                       if(fx1 * fx3>0)
                       {
                                   x1=x3;
                                   fx1=fx3;
                       }
                       else if(fx3 == 0.00)
                       {
                                   printf("\n %d) \t %f  |  %f  | %f  |
                                   %f\n",n,x1,x2,x3,fx3);
                                   printf("\n\n\t\t\t Answer : %f",x3);
                                   break;
                       }
                       else
                       {
                                   x2=x3;
                                   fx2=fx3;
                       }
                       n++;
               }while(fabs(temp-x3)> epsilon || fabs(fx3) > epsilon);
               printf("\n\n\t\t\t Answer : %f",x3);
}
else
{        printf("\nEnter valid range");
}
getch();  }
```

3.15.3   Program for Fixed Point Method

```
//Program to implement Fixed point method to find the root of given equation
#include<stdio.h>
#include<math.h>
#include<conio.h>
#define g(x) exp(x)/3
void main()
{
```

```
int n = 1;
float x1,x2,x,temp=0,epsilon;
clrscr();
printf(" \t\t\tFixed Point Method \n");
printf("\t\t\t----------------------------\n");
printf("enter approximation");
scanf("%f",&x1);
printf("enter the value of epsilon");
scanf("%f",&epsilon);
x2=0;
printf("\nIteration |   x1\t  \n");
printf(" ------------------------------\n");
do
{
        temp = x2;
        x2=g(x1);
        printf("\n %d\t %f\n", n, x2);
        x1=x2;
        n++;
} while(fabs(temp-x2) > epsilon);
printf("answer: %f",x1);
getch(); }
```

3.15.4   Program for Newton – Raphson Method

```
//Program to implement Newton Raphson method to find the root of given
equation
#include<stdio.h>
#include<math.h>
#include<conio.h>
#define f(x) pow(x,3) - 4*(x) - 9
#define fd(x) 3*pow(x,2) - 4
void main()
{
        int i,n=1;
        float x0,x1,fx0,fdx0,temp,epsilon;
        clrscr();
        printf("\n\t\t\tNewton Raphson method");
        printf("\n\t\t\t----------------------");
        fx0=fdx0=x0=x1=0;
        printf("\nEnter the first approximation");
        scanf("%f",&x0);
        printf("\nEnter prescribed tolerance");
```

```
scanf("%f",&epsilon);
printf("\nIteration  x1\t   |   fx1\t   |   fdx1\t  | x2\n");
printf("---------------------------------------------------------------");
fx0 = f(x0);
fdx0 = fd(x0);
do
{
                temp = x1;
                x1= x0 - (fx0/fdx0);
                x0 = x1;
                fx0 = f(x0);
            fdx0 = fd(x0);
                printf("\n %d) \t %f  |    %f  |    %f  |
                %f\n",n,x0,fx0,fdx0,x1);
                n++;
}while(fabs(temp - x1)>= epsilon);
printf("\n\n\t\t\t Answer : %f",x1);
getch();  }
```

3.15.5 Program for Secant Method

```
//Program to implement Secant method to find the root of given equation
#include<stdio.h>
#include<math.h>
#include<conio.h>
#define f(x) cos(x) - (x)*exp(x)
void main()
{
        int i,n=1;
        float x1,x2,x3,fx1,fx2,fx3,temp,tempx1,tempx2,tempx3,epsilon;
        clrscr();
        printf("\n\t\t\tSecant Method");
        printf("\n\t\t\t----------------------");
        fx1=fx2=fx3=x1=x2=x3=0;
        printf("\nEnter the first approximation");
        scanf("%f",&x1);
        printf("\nEnter the second approximation");
        scanf("%f",&x2);
        printf("\nEnter prescribed tolerance");
        scanf("%f",&epsilon);
        printf("\nIteration  x1\t   |    x2\t   |    x3\t  | f(x3)\n");
        printf("---------------------------------------------------------------");
        fx1 = f(x1);
        fx2 = f(x2);
```

```
        do
        {               temp = x3;
                        x3=((x1*fx2) - (x2*fx1))/(fx2 - fx1);
                        fx3 = f(x3);
                        printf("\n %d) \t %f  |   %f  |    %f
        %f\n",n,x1,x2,x3,fx3);                                              |
                        x1 = x2;
                        fx1 = fx2;
                        x2 = x3;
                        fx2 = fx3;
                        n++;
        }while(fabs(temp-x3)> epsilon || fabs(fx3) > epsilon);
        printf("\n\n\t\t\t Answer : %f",x3);
 getch();  }
```

3.15.6   Program for Birge Vieta Method

```
//Program to implement Birge Vieta Method to find the root of given polynomial
equation
#include<stdio.h>
#include<conio.h>
#include<math.h>
#define t 10
void main()
{
        int i,j,n[t],count;
        float x,fx,tempfx,k,l,x1,bi[t],ci[t];
        char ch;
        clrscr();

        fx=tempfx = 0.00;
        printf("\t\t:: BIRGE-VIETA METHOD ::\n");
        printf("\t\t\t----------------------\n");
        printf("Enter the max degree ==>");
        scanf("%d",&j);

        for(i=j;i>=0;i--)
        {
                printf("Enter the value of x^%d ==> ",i);
                scanf("%d",&n[i]);
        }
        printf("\n\tThe equation is ==> ");
        for(i=j;i>=0;i--)
        {
```

```
                if(i == j)
                {
                                printf("%dx^%d",n[i],i);
                }
                else if(n[i] < 0)
                {
                                printf("%dx^%d",n[i],i);
                }
                else
                {
                                printf("+%dx^%d",n[i],i);
                }
}
start:
count=1;
fx=tempfx=0.00;
printf("\n\n\tEnter the range ==>");
scanf("%f",&x);
x1=x;
for(i=j;i>=0;i--)
{
                tempfx=n[i]*pow(x,i);
                fx=fx+tempfx;
}
printf("\n\t fx = %.2f\n",fx);
printf("\nDo you want to enter nearest range?(Y/N) ==>");
scanf("%s",&ch);
if(ch == 'y' || ch == 'Y')
{
                goto start;
}
loop:
x=x1;
printf("\n\t\t\tITERATION %d ::\n",count);
printf("\n    |-------------------------------------------|\n");
printf("\t i  |  ai   |   bi    |   ci\n");
printf("    |-------------------------------------------|\n");
for(i=j;i>=0;i--)
{
                if(i == j)
                {
                                bi[i]=ci[i]=n[i];
                                k=bi[i];
```

```
                                        l=ci[i];
                }
                else
                {

                                bi[i]=n[i]+(x*k);
                                k=bi[i];
                                ci[i]=k+(x*l);
                                l=ci[i];
                }
                printf("\t %d  |   %d\t|  %.4f \t|   %.4f \n",i,n[i],bi[i],ci[i]);
        }
        x1=x-(bi[0]/ci[1]);
        printf("\n x%d = %.4f \n",count,x1);
        printf("\n press enter for continue....");
        getch();
        printf("\n\n");
        if(fabs(bi[0])<0.0001)
        {
                        printf("\t\tTotal iteration are ==> %d",count);
                        printf("\n\n\t\t ---------------------");
                        printf("\n\t\t |  Answer ==> %.4f |\n",x1);
                        printf("\t\t ---------------------");
        }
        else
        {
                        count++;
                        goto loop;
        }
        getch();
}
```

3.15.7   Program for Ramanujan Method

```
//Program to implement Ramanujan Method to find the root of given polynomial
equation
#include<stdio.h>
#include<stdlib.h>
#include<math.h>
#include<conio.h>
void main()
{
        int md,i,j,k,n,z;   //cons variable of div
        float a[10]={0},b[15]={0},arr[20]={0},Cons,temp[15]={0};
        clrscr();
```

```
printf("\n\t\t\tRamanujan Method");
printf("\n\t\t\t---------------");
printf("\n\nEnter the maximum degree of x : ");
scanf("%d",&md);

//Data enter
for(i=md;i>=0;i--)
{
            if(i==0)
            {
                        printf("\nEnter the coefficent of x^%d : ",i);
                        scanf("%f",&Cons);
                        Cons=fabs(Cons);
            }
            else
            {
                        printf("\nEnter the coefficent of x^%d : ",i);
                        scanf("%f",&arr[i]);
            }
}
printf("\nEnter total number of iterations you want to perform");
scanf("%d",&n);
//count a1,a2,a3,...,an
for(i=1;i<=md;i++)
{
            a[i]=arr[i]/Cons;
}

//logic of b1,b2,b3,...,bn and b1/b2,b2/b3,....,bn-1/bn
j=3;
b[1]=1;
b[2]=a[1];
temp[1]=b[1]/b[2];
printf("\nb[1]/b[2] = %.4f",temp[1]);
for(z=0;z<n-1;z++)
{
            k=j-1;
            for(i=1;i<j;i++)
            {
                        b[j]+=(a[i]*b[k]);
                        k--;
            }
            i--;
            temp[i]=(b[i]/b[j]);
```

```
                printf("\nb[%d]/b[%d] = %.4f",i,j,templ[i]);
                j++;


        }
        getch();  }
```

3.15.8   Program for Muller's Method

```
//Program to implement Muller's Method to find the root of given polynomial
equation
#include<stdio.h>
#include<math.h>
#include<stdlib.h>
#include<conio.h>
#define EBS 0.0001
void main()
{
        int i,md;
        float A=0,B=0,C=0,temp=0,x[3],arr[i];
        float fx0=0.0,fx1=0.0,fx2=0.0,tempx0=0,tempx1=0,tempx2=0;
        clrscr();
        printf("\n\t\t\tMuller's Method");
        printf("\n\t\t\t---------------");
        printf("\n\nEnter the maximum degree of x : ");
        scanf("%d",&md);

        for(i=md;i>=0;i--)
        {
                printf("\nEnter the coefficent of x^%d : ",i);
                scanf("%f",&arr[i]);
        }

        for(i=0;i<3;i++)
        {
                printf("\nEnter the %d approximation : ",i+1);
                scanf("%f",&x[i]);
        }
        while(1)
        {
                for(i=md,fx1=0,fx2=0,fx0=0;i>=0;i--)//loop to find fx of each x
                {
                        tempx0=pow(x[0],i)*arr[i];
                        fx0+=tempx0;
                        tempx1=pow(x[1],i)*arr[i];
```

```
                                    fx1+=tempx1;
                                    tempx2=pow(x[2],i)*arr[i];
                                    fx2+=tempx2;
                    }
                    C=fx2;
A=(((x[1]-x[2])*(fx0-fx2))-((x[0]-x[2])*(fx1-fx2)))/((x[0]-x[2])*(x[1]-x[2])*(x[0]-
x[1]));
B=(((x[0]-x[2])*(x[0]-x[2])*(fx1-fx2))-((x[1]-x[2])*(x[1]-x[2])*(fx0-fx2)))/((x[0]-
x[2])*(x[1]-x[2])*(x[0]-x[1]));
printf("\n x1\t x2\t x3\t A\t B");
printf("\n%.4f\t%.4f\t%.4f\t%.4f\t%.4f",x[0],x[1],x[2],A,B);//printing table
                    if(B<0)
                    {           temp=x[2]-((2*C)/(B-sqrt((B*B)-(4*A*C))));
                    }
                    else
                    {           temp=x[2]-((2*C)/(B+sqrt((B*B)-(4*A*C))));
                    }

                    if(fabs(x[2]-temp) < EBS)
                    {
                                    printf("\n\t\tAnswer is :- %.4f",temp);
                                    break;
                    }
                    x[0]=x[1];
                    x[1]=x[2];
                    x[2]=temp;
                    //initalization
                    temp=0,A=B=0;
            }
            getch();
}
```

EXERCISES

1.   Multiple Choice Questions

(1)   Which of the following is a linear equation?
    (a) $x^2 - 5x + 6 = 0$ (b) $x^4 - 3x^2 + 5x - 6 = 0$ (c) $xy + x - 8 = 0$
    (d) $x + y - 6 = 0$ (e)   None of these

(2)   The equation $x^4 - 3x^3 + 11x - 12 = 0$ has _____ number of roots.
    (a)   1   (b)   2   (c)   3
    (d)   4   (e)   None of these

(3)   Which of the following is a close end method?
    (a)   False Position   (b)   Secant method   (c)   N – R method
    (d)   Fixed Point method   (e)   None of these

(4)   Which of the following is a transcendental equation?
    (a) $x^3 - 2x^2 + 5x - 9 = 0$ (b) $x^2 - 5x + 6 = 0$ (c) $2^x - x - 3 = 0$
    (d) $x^2 - 5 = 0$ (e)   None of these

(5)   Which method is known as the most economical method?
    (a)   False Position   (b)   Secant method   (c)   Newton Raphson
    (d)   Bisection   (e)   Method of iteration

(6)   Which is the fastest method to solve non – linear equations?
    (a)   Bisection method (b)   Regula Falsi method   (c)   Secant method
    (d)   N – R method   (e)   Fixed point method

(7)   What is the convergence rate of Successive Approximation method?
    (a)   0.5   (b)   1   (c)   1.618
    (d)   2   (e)   None of the above

(8)   Which of the following is a direct method?
    (a)   Bisection method   (b)   Secant method   (c)   N – R method
    (d)   Fixed point method (e)   Graffe's root Squaring method

(9)   What is the convergence criterion for Method of iteration?
    (a) $x = g(x)$ (b) $|g'(x)| > 1$ (c) $g'(x) < 1$
    (d) $|g'(x)| = 1$ (e) $|g'(x)| < 1$

(10)   What do you mean by the root of equation geometrically?
    (a)   The value of x where the graph of $y = f(x)$ meets the x – axis in rectangular co-ordinate system.
    (b)   The value of y where the graph of $y = f(x)$ meets the x – axis in rectangular co- ordinate system.
    (c)   The value of x where the graph of $y = f(x)$ meets the y – axis in rectangular co-ordinate system.
    (d)   The value of y where the graph of $y = f(x)$ meets the y – axis in rectangular co-ordinate system.
    (e)   None of these

(11)   The equation $x^4 + 3x^3 - 5x^2 + 11x - 12 = 0$ has _____ number of positive roots.

(a)   1   (b) 2 or 0   (c) 3 or 1
(d)   4 or 2 or 0   (e)   5 or 3 or 1

Answers: (1) (d) (2) (d) (3) (a)   (4) (c)   (5) (b) (6) (d)   (7) (b)
(8) (e) (9) (e) (10) (a) (11) (c)

2.   Problems

(1)   Find a root, correct to three decimal places, for each of the following
equations, by bisection method
(a) $x^3 - 4x - 9 = 0$ (b) $2x - 3sinx - 5 = 0$ (c) $xe^x - 1 = 0$
(d) $3x = \sqrt{1 + sinx}$ (e) $x \log_{10} x - 1.2 = 0$
(f) $10^x = -(2x + sinx)$

(2)   Find a real root, correct to four decimal places, for each of the following
equations, by false position method.
(a) $\log_{10} x - cosx = 0$ (b) $4x^3 - 2x - 6 = 0$ (c) $x = e^{-x}$
(d) $x^3 - x - 1 = 0$ (e) $\sqrt{13}$ (f) $3x = 1 + cosx$

(3)   Solve each of the following examples by iteration method, correct upto
three decimal places.
(a) $x^2 = 2 - lnx$ (between 1 and 2) (b) $x^3 - x - 0.1 = 0$
(c) $x = (5 - x)^{1/3}$ (d) $\sqrt{5}$ (e) $x^3 + x^2 - 100 = 0$
(f) $5x - sinx - 2 = 0$

(4)   Using Newton – Raphson method, compute the real root of the following
equations correct to four decimal places.
(a) $x^4 + 2x^2 - 16x + 5 = 0$ (b) $2x - \log_{10} x - 7 = 0$
(c) $x = 4 - x^x$ (d) $x^3 - sinx + 1 = 0$ (e) $x^3 - 9x + 1 = 0$
(f) $x^4 - x - 10 = 0$

(5)   Compute the value of $\sqrt{17}$, correct upto six decimal palces, using Newton
Raphson method.

(6)   Compute the value of $\sqrt[3]{14}$, correct upto six decimal places, using Newton
– Raphson method

(7)   Find the reciprocal of 31 correct upto six decimal places, using Newton-
Raphson method.

(8)   Find, by secant method, a root of the following equations correct to four
significant figures.
(a) $x^3 - 4x + 1 = 0$ (b) $sinx + cosx = 1$ (c) $xlnx - 1 = 0$
(d) $x^3 + 2x - 2 = 0$ (e) $sinx = x - 2$ (f) $10^x = 4 - x$

(9)   Using Birge Vieta method, find the root of the following equations :
(a) $x^4 + x^3 - 4x^2 - 16 = 0$
(b) $x^4 - 8x^3 + 14.91x^2 + 9.54x - 25.92 = 0$
(c) $x^4 - 4x^3 + 3x^2 + 8x - 10 = 0$ (Take initial value of x = 1.45)
(d) $x^3 - 2x^2 + 5x + 10 = 0$
(e) $x^4 + 0.5x^3 - 8.5x^2 + 0.5x + 7.5 = 0$
(f) $x^4 - 7x^3 + 12x^2 + 4x - 6 = 0$

(10) Apply Graeffe's root squaring method, correct to four significant figures, to determine the approximate roots of each of the following equations :
(a) $x^3 - 2x^2 - x + 2 = 0$ (b) $2x^3 + x^2 - 2x - 1 = 0$
(c) $x^3 - 8x^2 + 17x - 10 = 0$ (d) $x^3 - 5x^2 - 17x + 20 = 0$
(e) $2x^3 - 7x^2 + 7x - 2 = 0$
(f) $x^4 - 4x^3 - 2x^2 - 12x - 15 = 0$

(11) Apply Budan's theorem to estimate the given polynomials for the given intervals :
(a) $x^4 - 3x^3 + 5x^2 - 7x + 1 = 0$ for (-1, 0), (0,1), (1,2)
(b) $3x^4 - 5x^3 + 3x^2 - 5x - 1 = 0$ for (-1, 0), (0,1)
(c) $x^4 - 4x^3 + 3x^2 - 5x + 2 = 0$ for (0,1), (3,4)
(d) $x^5 - 3x^4 - 2x^3 + x^2 + 10x + 9 = 0$
                     for (-2, -1), (-1,0), (0,1), (1,2)

(12) Using Ramanujan's method, obtain the root of each of the following equations :
(a) $xe^x - 1 = 0$ (b) $sinx = 1 - x$ (c) $x^3 + x^2 + x = 1$
(only first eight convergent)   (d) $x^2 + x = 1$ (only
first eight convergent)

(13) Using Muller's method, correct to four significant figures, find the root of the following equations :
(a) $cosx - xe^x = 0$ (Take $x_1 = -1, x_2 = 0, x_3 = 1$)
(b) $x^3 + 3x - 3 = 0$ (Take $x_1 = 0.6, x_2 = 0.7, x_3 = 0.8$)
(c) $x^3 - 2x - 5 = 0$ (Take $x_1 = 1.8, x_2 = 1.9, x_3 = 2.0$)

(14) Find all posible roots of each of the following equations using Bairstow's method :
(a) $x^3 - 6x^2 + 11x - 6 = 0$ (b) $x^4 + 4x^3 - 7x^2 - 22x + 24 = 0$
(c) $x^4 - 8x^3 + 39x^2 - 62x + 50 = 0$
(d) $x^4 - 5x^3 + 10x^2 - 10x + 4 = 0$
(e) $x^3 - 2x^2 + x - 2 = 0$

(15) Find the following system of non – linear equations using Newton – Raphson method.
(a) $4x^2 + 2xy + y^2 = 30$ and $2x^2 + 3xy + y^2 = 3$
(b) $x^2 + y^2 = 16$ and $x^2 + y^2 - 4x - 2y = 4$
(Take $x_0 = 1, y_0 = 4$)
(c) $x^2 - y^2 - 4 = 0$ and $x^2 + y^2 - 16 = 0$ (Upto 2 decimal places)

(16) Find the following system of non – linear equations using fixed – point method.
(a) $1 + y^2 - 4x^2 = 0$ and $3 + 2x - x^2 - y^2 = 0$
(b) $x^2 - y = 3$ and $xy - 3 = 0$
(c) $x^2 - 2x - y + 0.5 = 0$ and $x^2 + 4y^2 - y = 0$

Answers

(1) (a) 2.706 (b) 2.883 (c) 0.567 (d) 0.392 (e) 2.741 (f) -0.207

(2) (a) 1.4184 (b) 1.2896 (c) 0.5671 (d) 1.323 (e) 3.605551 (f) 0.6071

(3) (a) 1.3141 (b) 1.0467 (c) 1.5160 (d) 2.236 (e) 4.3311 (f) 0.4951

(4) (a) 0.3265 (b) 3.7893 (c) 1.6646 (d) -1.24905 (e) 2.943 (or 0.11113)
(f) -1.6975 (or 1.8556)

(5) 4.123106

(6) 2.410142

(7) 0.032258

(8) (a) 1.861 (b) 1.571 (c) 1.763 (d) 0.7709 (e) 2.554 (f) 0.5392

(9) (a) -2.9640 (b) 1.5 (c) 1.4142 (d) -1.1562 (e) 1.0905 (f) 0.6562

(10) (a) 1,1,2 (b) 0.4995, 0.9176, 1.0908 (c) 5, 2, 1 (d) 7.0175,
2.9744, 0.9582 (e) 0.4998, 1, 2, (f) -1, 5, $\pm 1.732i$

(11) (a) (-1,0) = 1, (0,1) = 3 or 1, (1,2) = 0 (b) (-1,0) = 1, (0,1) = 2 or 0
(c) (3,4) =1, (0,1) = 3 or 1 (d) (-2,-1) = 0, (-1,0) = 3 or 1, (0,1) = 0,
(1,2) = 0

(12) (a) 0.5671 (b) 0.5110 (c) 0.5437 (d) 0.6180

(13) (a) 0.5177 (b) 0.8177 (c) 2.094

(14)(a) 0.9822, 1.942, 3.147 (b) 1,2,-3,-4 (c) $1 \pm i, 1 \ 3 \pm 4i$
(d) $1 \pm i, 1, 2$ (e) $i, -i, 2$

(15) (a) $x = -3.131, y = 2.362$ (b) 1.07, 3.86 (c) 3.16, 2.45

(16) (a) $x = 1.116, y = 1.997$ (b) $x = 2.104, y = 1.426$ (c) $x = -0.222, y = 0.994$

Chapter 4   Solution of System of Linear Equations and Eigenvalue Problems

Objectives

- To understand the basic concepts and operations of matrices
- To understand the difference between direct methods and iterative methods for solving system of simultaneous linear algebraic equations
- To understand the concept of eigenvalue and eigenvector
- To find numerically largest and smallest eigenvalues

Learning Outcomes

After reading this lesson students should be able to

- Perform basic operations of matrices
- Identify the difference between direct and iterative methods for solving system of simultaneous linear algebraic equations
- Solve the equations by using appropriate direct method
- Solve the equations by using appropriate iterative method
- Effectively find numerically largest and smallest eigenvalues

4.1   INTRODUCTION

A linear equation is an equation in which the maximum power of any term is one. A linear equation having n variables is of the form $a_1 x_1 + a_2 x_2 + a_3 x_3 + \ldots \ldots + a_n x_n = b$ where $a_i \in R$ and at least one $a_i \neq 0$ $(i = 1, 2, 3, \ldots , n)$. In this equation, the number of variables are more than the number of equations and hence there is no unique solution. To obtain a unique solution of the equation having n variables it requires a set of n independent equations. This set of equations is known as system of linear equations.

The system of linear equations has many applications in various branches of applied mathematics, computer science, engineering and science such as analysis of electrical circuits, networking (particularly in network security for solving encryption and decryption algorithm), computer graphics, nuclear physics, aerodynamics etc. In this aspect, the analysis of system of linear equations is very important to study.

4.2   MATRICES

Matrices play an important role in solving system of linear equations. In this section, we will recall some basic information about matrices like special types of matrices, operations on matrices, inverse of matrix etc. which are required in the later sections of this chapter. Our assumption is that the concept of determinant and its properties are known to the reader.

Definition 4.1 A system of mn numbers arranged in a rectangular form having m rows and n columns written in a [ ] is called *m* by *n matrix* or $m \times n$ matrix.

4.2.1   Special Types of Matrices

1.   *Row and Column Matrices:* A matrix having a single row is called a *row matrix*, also known as a *row vector* eg. [2   5   7   9]
while a matrix having a single column is called a *column matrix*, also known as a

column vector eg. $\begin{bmatrix} 1 \\ 3 \\ 6 \\ 8 \end{bmatrix}$

2.   *Square Matrix:* A matrix having same number of rows and columns is
called a *square matrix* eg. $\begin{bmatrix} a_{11} & a_{12} & a_{13} \\ a_{21} & a_{22} & a_{23} \\ a_{31} & a_{32} & a_{33} \end{bmatrix}$ is a square matrix of order 3.

3.   *Null Matrix:* If all the elements of a matrix are zero (i.e. $a_{ij} = 0 \ for \ i,j =$
1,2,3, ... , n) then it is called a *null matrix* or *zero matrix* eg. $\begin{bmatrix} 0 & 0 & 0 \\ 0 & 0 & 0 \\ 0 & 0 & 0 \end{bmatrix}$

4.   *Singular and Non singular Matrices:* If the determinant of a square matrix A is zero,
i.e. $| \ A \ | = 0$ then A is said to be *singular* otherwise (i.e. $| \ A \ | \neq 0$), A is called *non – singular*.

Eg.   If $A = \begin{bmatrix} 1 & 1 & 2 \\ 0 & 2 & 2 \\ 0 & 2 & 2 \end{bmatrix}$ then $|A| = 0$ and hence, it is singular. If $A = \begin{bmatrix} 1 & 2 & 2 \\ 1 & 3 & 2 \\ 1 & 2 & 3 \end{bmatrix}$
then $|A| = 1$ therefore it is non – singular.

5.   *Diagonal Matrix:* The elements a_{ii} in a square matrix is called *leading or principal diagonal*. The sum of the diagonal elements $a_{11} + a_{22} + a_{33} +$
...... + a_{nn} of a square matrix A is called *trace of A*. If all the elements except leading diagonal elements are zero (i.e. $a_{ii} \neq 0, i = 1,2, ... , n$ and $a_{ij} =$
$0 \ for \ i \neq j$) then the square matrix is said to be a *diagonal matrix*.

eg. A = $\begin{bmatrix} a_{11} & 0 & 0 \\ 0 & a_{22} & 0 \\ 0 & 0 & a_{33} \end{bmatrix}$ is diagonal matrix. a_{11}, a_{22}, a_{33} is called the leading or
principal diagonal and trace of A = $a_{11} + a_{22} + a_{33}$

6.   *Unit Matrix or Identity Matrix:* A diagonal matrix of order n in which all

the elements on leading diagonal are equal to 1 (i.e. $a_{ii} = 1, i = 1,2,...,n$), is called a *unit matrix* or *identity matrix* and is denoted by I_n.

eg. $\begin{bmatrix} 1 & 0 & 0 \\ 0 & 1 & 0 \\ 0 & 0 & 1 \end{bmatrix} = I_3$ is an identity matrix of order 3.

7. *Symmetric and Skew – symmetric Matrix:* A square matrix A in which $a_{ij} = a_{ji}$ for all i's and j's or $A = A^T$ is said to be *symmetric* and $a_{ij} = -a_{ji}$ for all i's and j's or $A = -A^T$ so that all the leading diagonal elements are zero is said to be *skew – symmetric*.

Remark: The matrix obtained from any given matrix A, by interchanging rows and columns is called the *transpose of a matrix* A and denoted by A^T or A'.

---

eg. $A = \begin{bmatrix} a_{11} & a_{21} & a_{31} \\ a_{21} & a_{22} & a_{23} \\ a_{31} & a_{23} & a_{33} \end{bmatrix}$ is symmetric and $B = \begin{bmatrix} 0 & -a_{21} & a_{31} \\ a_{21} & 0 & -a_{32} \\ -a_{31} & a_{32} & 0 \end{bmatrix}$ is

skew – symmetric.

8. *Triangular Matrix:* A square matrix is called an *upper triangular matrix* if all the elements below the leading diagonal are zero (i.e. $a_{ij} = 0 \ for \ all \ i > j$) and *lower triangular matrix* if all the elements above the leading diagonal are zero (i.e. $a_{ij} = 0 \ for \ all \ i < j$).

eg. $\begin{bmatrix} a_{11} & a_{12} & a_{13} \\ 0 & a_{22} & a_{23} \\ 0 & 0 & a_{33} \end{bmatrix}$ and $\begin{bmatrix} a_{11} & 0 & 0 \\ a_{21} & a_{22} & 0 \\ a_{31} & a_{32} & a_{33} \end{bmatrix}$ are examples of upper and

lower triangular matrices respectively.

A *band matrix* has all the elements equal to zero except a band centered on the leading diagonal particularly matrices of the type $\begin{bmatrix} a_{11} & a_{12} & 0 & 0 \\ a_{21} & a_{22} & a_{23} & 0 \\ 0 & a_{32} & a_{33} & a_{34} \\ 0 & 0 & a_{43} & a_{44} \end{bmatrix}$ (i.e.

$a_{ij} = 0 \ for \ |i - j| > 1$) is called *tridiagonal matrices*.

9. *Diagonally Dominant Matrix:* A matrix A is said to be diagonally dominant

if $|a_{ii}| \geq \sum_{\substack{j=1 \\ i \neq j}}^{n} |a_{ij}|, i = 1,2,3,...,n.$ eg. $\begin{bmatrix} 7 & 1 & 2 \\ 3 & 3 & 0 \\ 2 & 1 & 2 \end{bmatrix}$

10. *Hermitian Matrix:* A square matrix A is known as hermitian matrix, denoted by A^* or A^H if $A = (\bar{A})^T$ where $\bar{A}$ is the complex conjugate of A.

eg.
$$\begin{bmatrix} 5 & 3-2i & -4+7i \\ 3+2i & -2 & 5-i \\ -4-7i & 5+i & 4 \end{bmatrix}$$ is a Hermitian matrix.

Remarks:
- If the elements of a matrix A are complex numbers $\alpha_{ij} + i\,\beta_{ij}$, α_{ij} and β_{ij} being real, then the matrix $\bar{A} = [\alpha_{ij} - i\,\beta_{ij}]$ is called the conjugate matrix of A.
- The elements of the main diagonal of a Hermitian matrix are real, while every other element is the complex conjugate of the element in the transposed position.
- A square matrix A is known as *Skew - Hermitian matrix* if $A = (\overline{-A})^T$ where $\bar{A}$ is the complex conjugate of A.

11. *Orthogonal Matrix:* A square matrix A is said to be orthogonal if $A^{-1} = A^T$ or $AA^T = A^TA = I$

eg. $\begin{bmatrix} 1 & 2 & 2 \\ 2 & 1 & -2 \\ 2 & -2 & 1 \end{bmatrix}$ is the orthogonal matrix.

12. *Unitary Matrix:* A square matrix A is said to be unitary if $A^{-1} = (\bar{A})^T$.

eg. $\begin{bmatrix} (1+i)/2 & (-1+i)/2 \\ (1+i)/2 & (1-i)/2 \end{bmatrix}$ is a unitary matrix.

13. *Normal Matrix:* A square matrix A is said to be normal if $AA^H = A^H A$.

14. *Permutation Matrix:* Matrix A is known as permutation matrix if it has exactly one 1 in each row and column and all other entries are 0.

15. *Reducible Matrix :* Matrix A is said to be reducible if there exists a permutation matrix P such that
$$P\,AP^T = \begin{bmatrix} A_{11} & A_{12} \\ 0 & A_{22} \end{bmatrix}$$ where A_{11}, A_{22} are square sub matrices.

16. *Positive Definite Matrix:* A square matrix A is said to be positive definite, if $x^H A\,x \geq 0$ for any vector $x \neq 0$ and $x^H = (\bar{x})^T$ and $x^H A\,x = 0$ if $x = 0$.

Remark: if $x^H A\,x > 0$ for any vector $x \neq 0$ then it is strictly positive definite matrix and a square matrix is a negative definite matrix if $x^H A\,x \leq 0$ and strictly negative definite matrix if $x^H A\,x < 0$ for any vector $x \neq 0$.

4.2.2 Matrix Operations

We have discussed what we mean by a matrix and their types in the previous section. After giving this overview we can discuss the basic operations on matrices like addition, subtraction and multiplication.

1. *Equality of Two Matrices:* Two m by n matrices are said to be equal if they

are of the same order and their corresponding elements are equal. i.e. [A] = [B] if and only if $a_{ij} = b_{ij}$ for all i and j.

2. *Addition and Subtraction of Matrices:* If A and B are two square matrices then the adddition A + B is defined as the matrix whose elements are the sum of the corresponding elements of A and B. i.e. $C_{ij} = a_{ij} + b_{ij}$, for all i, j

Similarly, the subtraction of matrix A – B is defined as the matrix whose elements are obtained by the subtracting the elements of B from the corresponding elements of A.

i.e. $C_{ij} = a_{ij} - b_{ij}$, for all i, j

For eg. $A = \begin{bmatrix} 1 & 2 \\ 3 & 4 \end{bmatrix}$ and $B = \begin{bmatrix} 2 & -3 \\ 7 & 9 \end{bmatrix}$ then

$$A + B = \begin{bmatrix} 1+2 & 2-3 \\ 3+7 & 4+9 \end{bmatrix} = \begin{bmatrix} 3 & -1 \\ 10 & 13 \end{bmatrix}$$

$$A - B = \begin{bmatrix} 1-2 & 2-(-3) \\ 3-7 & 4-9 \end{bmatrix} = \begin{bmatrix} -1 & 5 \\ -4 & -5 \end{bmatrix}$$

3. *Scalar Multiplication:* The multiplication of a matrix A by a scalar k is a matrix whose each element is k times the corresponding elements of A. i.e. k [A] = k. a_{ij} , for all i , j.

For eg. $A = \begin{bmatrix} 3 & -5 & 2 \\ 1 & 8 & 9 \end{bmatrix}$ then $2A = \begin{bmatrix} 2 \times 3 & 2 \times -5 & 2 \times 2 \\ 2 \times 1 & 2 \times 8 & 2 \times 9 \end{bmatrix} =$

$\begin{bmatrix} 6 & -10 & 4 \\ 2 & 16 & 18 \end{bmatrix}$

4. *Multiplication of Matrices:* If A and B are two matrices then the multiplication AB is possible if the number of columns of matrix A is equal to the number of rows of the matix B.

i.e. If A = m × n and B = n × p then multiplication AB is possible which will be m × p type.

Thus, matrix multiplication AB is defined as the sum of products of corresponding elements of the ith row of A with those of the jth column of B.

i.e. $c_{ij} = \sum_{k=1}^{n} a_{ik} b_{kj}$ for i = 1,2,3, ..., m , for j = 1,2,3 ..... p for each value of i. For eg.

If $A = \begin{bmatrix} a_{11} & a_{12} & a_{13} \\ a_{21} & a_{22} & a_{23} \\ a_{31} & a_{32} & a_{33} \end{bmatrix}$ and $B = \begin{bmatrix} b_{11} & b_{12} \\ b_{21} & b_{22} \\ b_{31} & b_{32} \end{bmatrix}$ then A is 3×3 matrix, B is

3×2 matrix. Therefore, number of columns in A is 3, number of rows in B is 3 and hence, AB is possible which will be 3×2 matrix and

$$A \times B = \begin{bmatrix} a_{11}b_{11} + a_{12}b_{21} + a_{13}b_{31} & a_{11}b_{12} + a_{12}b_{22} + a_{13}b_{32} \\ a_{21}b_{11} + a_{22}b_{21} + a_{23}b_{31} & a_{21}b_{12} + a_{22}b_{22} + a_{23}b_{32} \\ a_{31}b_{11} + a_{32}b_{21} + a_{33}b_{31} & a_{31}b_{12} + a_{32}b_{22} + a_{33}b_{32} \end{bmatrix}$$

$A = \begin{bmatrix} -1 & 4 & 9 \\ 0 & 6 & 5 \\ 3 & 2 & 1 \end{bmatrix}$ and $B = \begin{bmatrix} 1 & 7 \\ 2 & 5 \\ 3 & 4 \end{bmatrix}$ then

$$AB = \begin{bmatrix} (-1 \times 1) + (4 \times 2) + (9 \times 3) & (-1 \times 7) + (4 \times 5) + (9 \times 4) \\ (0 \times 1) + (6 \times 2) + (5 \times 3) & (0 \times 7) + (6 \times 5) + (5 \times 4) \\ (3 \times 1) + (2 \times 2) + (1 \times 3) & (3 \times 7) + (-2 \times 5) + (1 \times 4) \end{bmatrix} = \begin{bmatrix} 34 & 49 \\ 27 & 50 \\ 10 & 15 \end{bmatrix}$$

• The following properties can be easily seen from the definitions:

(i) $A + B = B + A$ (i.e. Addition of two square matrices is commutative)

(ii) $A + (B + C) = (A + B) + C$ (i.e. Addition of two square matrices are associative)

(iii) $k(A + B) = kA + kB$ where, k is a scalar

(iv) $(k_1 + k_2)A = k_1 A + k_2 A$ where, k_1 and k_2 are scalars

(v) $AB \neq BA$, if A and B both exist. (i.e. Multiplication of two matrices may not be commutative)

(vi) If A is a square matrix then $A . A = A^2$, $A.A^2 = A^3$ and so on.

4.2.3 Inverse of a Matrix

Finding the inverse of a matrix is very important in many areas of computer science like decrypting a coded message uses the inverse of a matrix. Before we find the inverse of a matrix, some of the terminologies are important to know.

1. *Determinant of a matrix*: Associated quantity with every matrix A, is known as determinant of A and denoted by *det(A)* or *|A|*.

If $A = \begin{bmatrix} a_{11} & a_{12} & a_{13} \\ a_{21} & a_{22} & a_{23} \\ a_{31} & a_{32} & a_{33} \end{bmatrix}$ then $|A| = \begin{vmatrix} a_{11} & a_{12} & a_{13} \\ a_{21} & a_{22} & a_{23} \\ a_{31} & a_{32} & a_{33} \end{vmatrix}$

2. *Minor:* An element a_{ij} of a given determinant, obtained by deleting the row *i* and the column *j* in the matrix is called a minor.

For eg. $|A| = \begin{vmatrix} a_{11} & a_{12} & a_{13} \\ a_{21} & a_{22} & a_{23} \\ a_{31} & a_{32} & a_{33} \end{vmatrix}$ then minor of $a_{22} = \begin{vmatrix} a_{11} & a_{13} \\ a_{31} & a_{31} \end{vmatrix}$

3. *Co-factor*: The co – factor of the element a_{ij} of the determinant is its minor with a proper sign attached to it.

Co-factor of $a_{ij} = (-1)^{i+j} |A_{ij}|$ Where, A_{ij} is the minor of a_{ij}.

For eg. Co – factor of $a_{22} = A_{22} = (-1)^{2+2} \begin{vmatrix} a_{11} & a_{13} \\ a_{31} & a_{31} \end{vmatrix} = \begin{vmatrix} a_{11} & a_{13} \\ a_{31} & a_{31} \end{vmatrix}$

4. *Value of a determinant:* The value of a determinant is equal to the sum of the products of the elements of any row or column by its corresponding co-factors.

eg. $\begin{vmatrix} 1 & 2 & 1 \\ 0 & 3 & 0 \\ 2 & 5 & 2 \end{vmatrix} = 1 \begin{vmatrix} 3 & 0 \\ 5 & 2 \end{vmatrix} - 2 \begin{vmatrix} 0 & 0 \\ 2 & 2 \end{vmatrix} + 1 \begin{vmatrix} 0 & 3 \\ 2 & 5 \end{vmatrix} = 1(6 - 0) - 2(0-0) + 1(0 - 6) = 0$

5. *Adjoint of a square matrix:* Transpose matrix of co-factors of square matrix A is known as adjoint of a square matrix A and denoted by adjA.

6. *Inverse of a matrix:* Let A be a non singular square matrix (i.e. $|A| \neq 0$) of order n then there exists a matrix A^{-1} of the same order which is called the inverse of A such that $A.A^{-1} = A^{-1}. A = I$ where, I is the identity matrix. Also, inverse can be obtained by $A^{-1} = \frac{adj\ (A)}{|A|}$.

Properties of inverse of a square matrix

1. Inverse of A exists if and only if A is non singular (i.e. $|A| \neq 0$). If $|A| = 0$ then A is called singular matrix.
2. If A^{-1} exists, it is unique.
3. $(A^{-1})^{-1} = A$
4. $(A')^{-1} = (A^{-1})'$
5. If A^{-1} exists, $|A^{-1}| = |A|^{-1} = \frac{1}{|A|}$
6. $(AB)^{-1} = B^{-1}A^{-1}$
7. If $A = \begin{bmatrix} a_{11} & 0 & 0 \\ 0 & a_{22} & 0 \\ 0 & 0 & a_{33} \end{bmatrix}$ then $A^{-1} = \begin{bmatrix} \dfrac{1}{a_{11}} & 0 & 0 \\ 0 & \dfrac{1}{a_{22}} & 0 \\ 0 & 0 & \dfrac{1}{a_{33}} \end{bmatrix}$ with $a_{ii} \neq 0$.
8. The inverse of an identity matrix is also an identity matrix. i.e. $I^{-1} = I$
9. The inverse of an upper triangular matrix is also an upper triangular matrix and the inverse of a lower triangular matrix is also a lower triangular matrix.

Remark: The inverse of 2×2 matrix $A = \begin{bmatrix} a & b \\ c & d \end{bmatrix}$ where, a, b, c, d are numbers, can be obtained by $A^{-1} = \frac{1}{ad-bc} \begin{bmatrix} d & -b \\ -c & a \end{bmatrix}$ provided that $|A| = \begin{vmatrix} a & b \\ c & d \end{vmatrix} = ad - bc \neq 0$.

Example 4.1   Find the inverse of $A = \begin{bmatrix} 3 & -2 \\ 4 & -5 \end{bmatrix}$.

Solution: $|A| = \begin{vmatrix} 3 & -2 \\ 4 & -5 \end{vmatrix} = (3)(-5) - (-2)(4) = -7 \neq 0$

Therefore, A is non – singular and hence, A^{-1} exists.

$$A^{-1} = \frac{1}{ad-bc} \begin{bmatrix} d & -b \\ -c & a \end{bmatrix} = \frac{1}{-7} \begin{bmatrix} -5 & 2 \\ 4 & 3 \end{bmatrix}$$

Example 4.2   Find the inverse of $A = \begin{bmatrix} 1 & 3 & 7 \\ 2 & -1 & 5 \\ 1 & 0 & 1 \end{bmatrix}$

Solution: $|A| = \begin{vmatrix} 1 & 3 & 7 \\ 2 & -1 & 5 \\ 1 & 0 & 1 \end{vmatrix} = 1(-1) - 3(2-5) + 7(1) = 15 \neq 0$

Therefore, A^{-1} exists.

Computation of adj A:

Co-factor of $1 = a_{11} = (-1)^{1+1} \begin{vmatrix} -1 & 5 \\ 0 & 1 \end{vmatrix} = -1$ Co-factor of $5 = a_{23} = (-1)^{2+3}$ $\begin{vmatrix} 1 & 3 \\ 1 & 0 \end{vmatrix} = 3$

Co-factor of 3 $= a_{12} = (-1)^{1+2} \begin{vmatrix} 2 & 5 \\ 1 & 1 \end{vmatrix} = 3$ Co-factor of 1 $= a_{31} = (-1)^{3+1}$

$\begin{vmatrix} 3 & 7 \\ -1 & 5 \end{vmatrix} = 8$

Co-factor of 7 $= a_{13} = (-1)^{1+3} \begin{vmatrix} 2 & -1 \\ 1 & 0 \end{vmatrix} = 1$ Co-factor of 0 $= a_{32} = (-1)^{3+2}$

$\begin{vmatrix} 1 & 7 \\ 2 & 5 \end{vmatrix} = -9$

Co-factor of 2 $= a_{21} = (-1)^{2+1} \begin{vmatrix} 3 & 7 \\ 0 & 1 \end{vmatrix} = -3$ Co-factor of 1 $= a_{33} = (-1)^{3+3}$

$\begin{vmatrix} 1 & 3 \\ 2 & -1 \end{vmatrix} = -7$ Co-factor of -1 $= a_{22} = (-1)^{2+2} \begin{vmatrix} 1 & 7 \\ 1 & 1 \end{vmatrix} = -6$

$$\text{adj}(A) = \begin{bmatrix} -1 & -3 & 8 \\ 3 & -6 & -9 \\ 1 & 3 & -7 \end{bmatrix}$$

Hence, $A^{-1} = \dfrac{adj\ (A)}{|A|} = \dfrac{1}{15} \begin{bmatrix} -1 & -3 & 8 \\ 3 & -6 & -9 \\ 1 & 3 & -7 \end{bmatrix}$

4.3 SOLUTION OF SIMULTANEOUS LINEAR ALGEBRAIC EQUATIONS

As we have discussed, simultaneous linear algebraic equations has importance in various field of engineering and science. Earlier such equations can be solved by Cramer's rule but this method involves large amount of calculations for the systems involve more than four equations. On the other hand, there are some numerical methods which require less amount of calculations and very well suited for computer operations. There are two types of such numerical methods (i) Direct methods (ii) Iterative methods.

4.3.1 Direct Methods

In this section, we shall focus on matrix inversion method, Gauss elimination method, Gauss Jordan method and triangularization methods.

Matrix Inversion Method

Consider the system of n linear equations in n unknowns

$$\begin{aligned}
a_{11}x_1 + a_{12}x_2 + \dots + a_{1n}x_n &= b_1 \\
a_{21}x_1 + a_{22}x_2 + \dots + a_{2n}x_n &= b_2 \\
a_{31}x_1 + a_{32}x_2 + \dots + a_{3n}x_n &= b_3 \\
\vdots \qquad \vdots \qquad\quad \vdots \qquad \vdots & \\
a_{n1}x_1 + a_{n2}x_2 + \dots + a_{nn}x_n &= b_n
\end{aligned} \qquad \dots\dots (4.3.1)$$

If we denote

$$A = \begin{bmatrix} a_{11} & a_{12} & a_{13} & \cdots & \cdots & a_{1n} \\ a_{21} & a_{22} & a_{23} & \cdots & \cdots & a_{2n} \\ \cdots & \cdots & \cdots & \cdots & \cdots & \cdots \\ \cdots & \cdots & \cdots & \cdots & \cdots & \cdots \\ a_{n1} & a_{n2} & a_{n3} & \cdots & \cdots & a_{nn} \end{bmatrix}, \quad x = \begin{bmatrix} x_1 \\ x_2 \\ \cdots \\ x_n \end{bmatrix} \quad \text{and} \quad b = \begin{bmatrix} b_1 \\ b_2 \\ \cdots \\ b_n \end{bmatrix}$$

Then Eq. (4.3.1) can be written as $A x = b$ .... (4.3.2)

Where A is an $n \times n$ matrix, known as co-efficient metrix, a_{ij} $(i, j = 1,2,3,....n)$, and b_i $(i = 1,2,....n)$ are known constants and x is a vector of n unknowns.

If b_i $(i = 1,2,....n) = 0$ then the system of linear equations given in Eq. (4.3.1) is said to be *homogeneous*. On the other hand, if at least one b_i $(i = 1,2,....n) \neq 0$, the system is said to be *non – homogeneous*.

If det (A) $= \begin{vmatrix} a_{11} & a_{12} & a_{13} & \cdots & \cdots & a_{1n} \\ a_{21} & a_{22} & a_{23} & \cdots & \cdots & a_{2n} \\ \cdots & \cdots & \cdots & \cdots & \cdots & \cdots \\ \cdots & \cdots & \cdots & \cdots & \cdots & \cdots \\ a_{n1} & a_{n2} & a_{n3} & \cdots & \cdots & a_{nn} \end{vmatrix} \neq 0$ i.e. A is non – singular then

A^{-1} exists such that $A A^{-1} = A^{-1}A = I$, where I is an identity matrix. By premultiplying Eq. (4.3.2) we get,

$$A^{-1} (A x) = A^{-1}b$$
$$\therefore \quad (A^{-1}A) x = A^{-1}b$$
$$\therefore \quad x = A^{-1}b$$

Hence, we get a unique solution of Eq. (4.3.1) as $x = A^{-1}b$.

Example 4.3   Solve the following equations using matrix inversion method
$$x - y + 5z = 2$$
$$3x + y + 2z = 1$$
$$-2x - 3y + z = -3$$

Solution: We have,

$$A = \begin{bmatrix} 1 & -1 & 5 \\ 3 & 1 & 2 \\ -2 & -3 & 1 \end{bmatrix}, \quad x = \begin{bmatrix} x \\ y \\ z \end{bmatrix}, \quad b = \begin{bmatrix} 2 \\ 1 \\ -3 \end{bmatrix}$$

$$|A| = \begin{vmatrix} 1 & -1 & 5 \\ 3 & 1 & 2 \\ -2 & -3 & 1 \end{vmatrix} = -21 \neq 0$$

Therefore, $A^{-1} = \dfrac{1}{21} \begin{bmatrix} -7 & 14 & 7 \\ 7 & -11 & -13 \\ 7 & -5 & -4 \end{bmatrix}$

Hence, $x = \begin{bmatrix} x \\ y \\ z \end{bmatrix} = A^{-1}b = \dfrac{1}{21} \begin{bmatrix} -7 & 14 & 7 \\ 7 & -11 & -13 \\ 7 & -5 & -4 \end{bmatrix} \begin{bmatrix} 2 \\ 1 \\ -3 \end{bmatrix} = \dfrac{1}{21} \begin{bmatrix} 21 \\ 42 \\ 21 \end{bmatrix} = \begin{bmatrix} 1 \\ 2 \\ 1 \end{bmatrix}$

Thus, $x = 1, y = 2, z = 1$

Gauss Elimination Method

This is one of the most widely used and the simplest method. In this method, the solution is obtained in two stages: i. Triagularization ii. Back substitution. In triagularization, the given system of equations is reduced to an equivalent upper triangular form using elementary transformations. Back substitution is used to get actual solution. Consider the system of n – equations with n – unknowns as:

$$
\begin{aligned}
a_{11}x_1 + a_{12}x_2 + \ldots + a_{1n}x_n &= b_1 \\
a_{21}x_1 + a_{22}x_2 + \ldots + a_{2n}x_n &= b_2 \\
a_{31}x_1 + a_{32}x_2 + \ldots + a_{3n}x_n &= b_3 \\
\vdots \qquad \vdots \qquad\qquad \vdots \qquad\quad \vdots \\
a_{n1}x_1 + a_{n2}x_2 + \ldots + a_{nn}x_n &= b_n
\end{aligned}
$$

.... (4.3.3)

We use a_{ii} element of position (i, i) in the equations to eliminate x_i from the rows $i + 1, i + 2, \ldots, n$ is called the ith pivotal element and the row is called the pivotal row. The details of the algorithm are described as follows:

1. To eliminate x_1 from the second, third, ...n^{th} equation, we multiply the first equation by $\frac{a_{21}}{a_{11}}$ and then subtract it from the second equation, multiply the first equation by $\frac{a_{31}}{a_{11}}$ and then subtract it from the third equation and so on . In this step, a_{11} is the pivotal element and first row is the pivotal row and we have also assumed that $a_{11} \neq 0$. At the end of this step, the resulting system of equations is

$$
\begin{aligned}
a_{11}x_1 + a_{12}x_2 + a_{13}x_3 \ldots + a_{1n}x_n &= b_1 \\
a'_{22}x_2 + a'_{23}x_3 \ldots + a'_{2n}x_n &= b'_2 \\
a'_{32}x_2 + a'_{33}x_3 \ldots + a'_{3n}x_n &= b'_3 \\
\vdots \qquad \vdots \qquad\quad \vdots \qquad\quad \vdots \\
a'_{n2}x_2 + a'_{n3}x_3 \ldots + a'_{nn}x_n &= b'_n
\end{aligned}
$$

.... (4.3.4)

Where $a'_{22}, \ldots \ldots \ldots, a'_{nn}$ are all new elements. Now, a'_{22} is the new pivot element and second row becomes the pivot row.

2. To eliminate x_2 from the third, fourth, ...n^{th} equations of (4.3.4), we multiply the second equation by $\frac{a'_{32}}{a'_{22}}$ and then subtract it from the third equation, multiply the second equation by $\frac{a'_{33}}{a'_{22}}$ and then subtract it from the third equation and so on . We have also assumed that $a'_{22} \neq 0$.

3. Continue the same procedure of eliminating one variable at a time. At the nth step, we have the following modified system of linear equations:

$$
\begin{aligned}
a_{11}x_1 + a_{12}x_2 + a_{13}x_3 \ldots + a_{1n}x_n &= b_1 \\
a_{22}x_2 + a_{23}x_3 \ldots + a_{2n}x_n &= b_2 \\
a_{33}x_3 \ldots + a_{3n}x_n &= b_3 \\
\ldots \qquad \ldots \qquad \ldots \\
a_{nn}^{n-1}x_n &= b_n^{n-1}
\end{aligned}
$$

.... (4.3.5)

This process is known as *triangularization*.

It is clear that if at least one of the pivot elements $a_{11}, a'_{22}, \ldots$ vanishes then the method will fail. In such situation, we can modified the method by rearranging the row so that the pivot element will be non zero.

In the new system of equations, the value of x_n is obtained from the nth equation as $\frac{b_n^{n-1}}{a_{nn}^{n-1}}$. Putting this value of x_n in the preceding equation, the value of x_{n-1} can be found. If we continue the same procedure, putting the value of $x_n, x_{n-1}, \ldots \ldots, x_3, x_2$ in the first equation we get the value of x_1. This process is called *back substitution*.

Example 4.4   Solve the following system of linear equations by Gauss elimination method:

$2x_1 + 6x_2 + 2x_3 = 14, x_1 + 5x_2 + 7x_3 = 18, x_1 + x_2 + 2x_3 = 3$

Solution: The given system of linear equations is

$$2x_1 + 6x_2 + 2x_3 = 14$$
$$x_1 + 5x_2 + 7x_3 = 18$$
$$x_1 + x_2 + 2x_3 = 3$$

In this step, 2 is the pivot element and first row is the pivotal row. To eliminate x_1 from the second and third equations first apply $R_2 - \frac{a_{21}}{a_{11}} R_1 = R_2 - \frac{1}{2} R_1$.

The coefficients of the second equation are

$a_{21} = a_{21} - \frac{1}{2} a_{11} = 1 - \frac{1}{2}(2) = 0, a_{22} = a_{22} - \frac{1}{2} a_{12} = 5 - \frac{1}{2}(6) = 2$

$a_{23} = a_{23} - \frac{1}{2} a_{13} = 7 - \frac{1}{2}(2) = 6, b_2 = b_2 - \frac{1}{2} b_1 = 18 - \frac{1}{2}(14) = 11$

Now, $R_3 - \frac{a_{31}}{a_{11}} R_1 = R_3 - \frac{1}{2} R_1$

The coefficients of the third equation are

$a_{31} = a_{31} - \frac{1}{2} a_{11} = 1 - \frac{1}{2}(2) = 0, a_{32} = a_{32} - \frac{1}{2} a_{12} = 1 - \frac{1}{2}(6) = -2$

$a_{33} = a_{33} - \frac{1}{2} a_{13} = 2 - \frac{1}{2}(2) = 1, b_3 = b_3 - \frac{1}{2} b_1 = 3 - \frac{1}{2}(14) = -4$

After this stage the new system of equations is

$$2x_1 + 6x_2 + 2x_3 = 14$$
$$2x_2 + 6x_3 = 11$$
$$-2x_2 + x_3 = -4$$

To eliminate x_2 from the third equation apply

$R_3 - \frac{a_{32}}{a_{22}} R_2 = R_3 + \frac{2}{2} R_2 = R_3 + R_2$

The coefficients of the third equation are

$a_{32} = a_{32} + a_{22} = -2 + 2 = 0, a_{33} = a_{33} + a_{23} = 1 + 6 = 7$
$b_3 = b_3 + b_2 = -4 + 11 = 7$

The final system of equations is

$$2x_1 + 6x_2 + 2x_3 = 14$$
$$2x_2 + 6x_3 = 11$$
$$7x_3 = 7$$

Using back substitution we get

$$x_3 = 1, x_2 = \frac{11 - 6(1)}{2} = 2.5, x_1 = \frac{14 - 6(2.5) - 2(1)}{2} = -1.5$$

Example 4.5   Solve the following system of linear equations by Gauss elimination method:

$$2x_1 + x_2 - x_3 + 2x_4 = 5$$
$$4x_1 + 5x_2 - 3x_3 + 6x_4 = 9$$
$$-2x_1 + 5x_2 - 2x_3 + 6x_4 = 4$$
$$4x_1 + 11x_2 - 4x_3 + 8x_4 = 2$$

Solution: The given system of linear equations is

$$2x_1 + x_2 - x_3 + 2x_4 = 5$$
$$4x_1 + 5x_2 - 3x_3 + 6x_4 = 9$$
$$-2x_1 + 5x_2 - 2x_3 + 6x_4 = 4$$
$$4x_1 + 11x_2 - 4x_3 + 8x_4 = 2$$

In this step, 2 is the pivot element and first row is the pivotal row. To eliminate x_1 from the second, third and fourth equations apply $R_2 - \frac{a_{21}}{a_{11}} R_1 = R_2 - \frac{4}{2} R_1 = R_2 - 2 R_1$, $R_3 - \frac{a_{31}}{a_{11}} R_1 = R_3 - \frac{-2}{2} R_1 = R_3 + R_1$ and $R_4 - \frac{a_{41}}{a_{11}} R_1 = R_4 - \frac{4}{2} R_1 = R_4 - 2R_1$

After this stage the new system of equations is

$$2x_1 + x_2 - x_3 + 2x_4 = 5$$
$$3x_2 - x_3 + 2x_4 = -1$$
$$6x_2 - 3x_3 + 8x_4 = 9$$
$$9x_2 - 2x_3 + 4x_4 = -8$$

To eliminate x_2 from the third and fourth equations apply $R_3 - \frac{a_{32}}{a_{22}} R_2 = R_3 - \frac{6}{3} R_2 = R_3 - 2 R_2$, $R_4 - \frac{a_{42}}{a_{22}} R_2 = R_4 - \frac{9}{3} R_2 = R_4 - 3 R_2$,

The new system of equations is

$$2x_1 + x_2 - x_3 + 2x_4 = 5$$
$$3x_2 - x_3 + 2x_4 = -1$$
$$-1x_3 + 4x_4 = 11$$
$$1x_3 - 2x_4 = -5$$

To eliminate x_3 from the fourth equation apply

$$R_4 - \frac{a_{43}}{a_{33}} R_3 = R_4 - \frac{1}{-1} R_3 = R_4 + R_3$$

The final system of equations is

$$2x_1 + x_2 - x_3 + 2x_4 = 5$$
$$3x_2 - x_3 + 2x_4 = -1$$
$$-1x_3 + 4x_4 = 11$$
$$2x_4 = 6$$

Using back substitution we get $x_4 = 3$, $x_3 = 1, x_2 = -2$, $x_1 = 1$

Gauss Elimination with Pivoting

As we have discussed, in each step of Gauss elimination method, the leading coefficient a_{ij} where i = j (i.e. the coefficient of the first unknown in the first equation) is called *pivot element*. We have also discussed that if at least one of the pivot elements becomes zero then the method will fail. In such situation, we can modified the method by rearranging the row so that the pivot element will be non zero. This arrangement of equations is called *pivoting*.

For large systems of linear equations, Gauss elimination can involve hundreds of arithmetic computation, each of which can produce rounding error and that error will be propagated to such an extent that the final solution will become highly inaccurate. If the pivot element a_{kk} of the row happens to be zero or near to zero then there may be more than one non − zero values in the kth column below the element a_{kk} . Our aim is to reduce the rounding error. This is happened only when we choose the pivot element whose absolute value is large. We can interchange the row having zero pivot element with the row having the largest absolute value.

$$\text{i.e. } a_{kk} > \left| a_{jk} \right| where, j = 1,2,3,....,j \neq k$$

This procedure is continued till *(n-1)* unknowns are eliminated. This process is known as *partial pivoting*. We can further reduce the rounding error propagation by performing complete or full or total pivoting. In *complete pivoting*, one searches for the largest absolute value not only in the current column but in any of the remaining rows. The pivoting involves not merely interchange of rows , but also of columns. Partial pivoting is prefered over complete pivoting as complete pivoting involves a lot of overhead and is more complicated compare to partial pivoting.

Remark: Even if the diagonal element (pivot element) is non zero, the rearranging of equations is done to improve the accuracy and to reduce the round − off error in the final answer.

Example 4.6   Solve the following equations by Gauss elimination method
$$x + y + z = 4 , 2x + y + 3z = 7 , 3x + y + 6z = 2$$

Solution: The given system of linear equations is
Pivot element $\longrightarrow$ $\quad \textcircled{x} + y + z = 4$
$\quad 2x + y + 3z = 7$
Largest absolute value $\longrightarrow$ $\textcircled{3} x + y + 6z = 2$

Here we found that the element of largest magnitude is found in row 3. Therefore, partial pivoting is applied to interchange rows 1 and 3. The modified system is
$$3x + y + 6z = 2$$
$$2x + y + 3z = 7$$
$$x + y + z = 4$$

To eliminate x from the second and third equations apply $R_2 - \frac{a_{21}}{a_{11}} R_1 = R_2 - \frac{2}{3} R_1$ and $R_3 - \frac{a_{31}}{a_{11}} R_1 = R_3 - \frac{1}{3} R_1$

After this stage the new system of equations is

$$3x + y + 6z = 2$$

Pivot element $\longrightarrow$ $\boxed{1/3}y - z = 17/3$

Largest absolute value $\longrightarrow$ $\boxed{2/3}y - z = 10/3$

Here also the absolute value of $2/3$ is greater than the absolute value of $1/3$. Therefore interchange rows 2 and 3. The modified system is

$$3x + y + 6z = 2$$
$$2/3\,y - z = 10/3$$
$$1/3\,y - z = 17/3$$

To eliminate y from the third equation apply $R_3 - \dfrac{a_{32}}{a_{22}} R_2 = R_3 - \dfrac{1/3}{2/3} R_2 =$

$R_3 - \dfrac{1}{2}R_2$

The final system of equations is

$$3x + y + 6z = 2$$
$$2/3\,y - z = 10/3$$
$$-\,1/2\,z = 4$$

Using back substitution we get

$$z = -8, \qquad y = \frac{\dfrac{10}{3} - 8}{2/3} = -7, \qquad x = \frac{2 - 6(-8) - (-7)}{3} = 19$$

Gauss – Jordan Method

This is a modification of the Gauss elimination method. In this method, the elimination of unknowns is done not only in the equations below pivot equation but in the equations above. As a result, only one unknown is left in each equation and at the end we get a diagonal matrix. Therefore, we directly get the value of unknowns from these equations which eliminates the requirement of back substitution.

Practically Gauss- Jordan method is rarely used as it requires more computational effort compare to Gauss elimination method.

Example 4.7 Solve the following system of equations by Gauss – Jordan method. $\quad x + y + z = 5 , 2x + 3y + 5z = 8 , 4x + 5z = 2$

Solution: The given system of equations is

$$x + y + z = 5$$
$$2x + 3y + 5z = 8$$
$$4x + 5z = 2$$

To eliminate x from the second and third equations apply

$$R_2 - \frac{a_{21}}{a_{11}} R_1 = R_2 - \frac{2}{1} R_1 = R_2 - 2R_1 \quad R_3 - \frac{a_{31}}{a_{11}} R_1 = R_3 - 4R_1$$

After this stage the new system of equations is

$$x + y + z = 5$$
$$y + 3z = -2$$
$$-4y + z = -18$$

To eliminate y from the first and third equation apply $R_1 - \frac{a_{12}}{a_{22}} R_2 = R_1 - R_2$,

$R_3 - \frac{a_{32}}{a_{22}} R_2 = R_3 - \frac{-4}{1} R_2 = R_3 + 4R_2$

The new system of equations is

$$x - 2z = 7$$
$$y + 3z = -2$$
$$13z = -26$$

To eliminate z from the first two equations apply $R_1 - \frac{a_{13}}{a_{33}} R_3 = R_1 + \frac{2}{13} R_3$,

$R_2 - \frac{a_{23}}{a_{33}} R_3 = R_2 - \frac{3}{13} R_3$

We get $x = 3, \ y = 4, \ 13z = -26$

Therefore, the solution of the equations is $x = 3, y = 4$ and $z = -2$

Triangularization (Triangular Factorization) Method

We express the coefficient matrix A of a system of linear equations in the form of LU where L is a lower triangular and U is an upper triangular matrix. Thus, a non singular matrix A is said to have a triangular factorization if it can be expressed as a product of a lower triangular matrix L and an upper triangular matrix U.

Let $\hspace{3cm}$ A = LU $\hspace{3cm}$ .... (4.3.6)

In three dimensions we write,

$$\begin{bmatrix} a_{11} & a_{12} & a_{13} \\ a_{21} & a_{22} & a_{23} \\ a_{31} & a_{32} & a_{33} \end{bmatrix} = \begin{bmatrix} l_{11} & 0 & 0 \\ l_{21} & l_{22} & 0 \\ l_{31} & l_{32} & l_{33} \end{bmatrix} \begin{bmatrix} u_{11} & u_{12} & u_{13} \\ 0 & u_{22} & u_{23} \\ 0 & 0 & u_{33} \end{bmatrix}$$

Therefore, the system of equations $Ax = B$ can be written as

$$(LU) x = B$$

or $\hspace{3cm}$ L(Ux) = B $\hspace{3cm}$ .... (4.3.7)

Let us assume that $\hspace{2cm}$ U x = Y $\hspace{3cm}$ .... (4.3.8)

where Y is an unknown vector. From the Eq. (4.3.8) and Eq. (4.3.7) we get,

$$LY = B \hspace{3cm} .... (4.3.9)$$

Now the system given in Eq. (4.3.9) can be solved for Y by forward substitution and the system given in Eq. (4.3.8) can be solved for x using Y by back substitution.

In this procedure, the elements of L and U can be determined by comparing the elements of the product of L and U with the corresponding elements of A. Here we get a system of 9 equations with 12 unknowns and hence L and U are not unique. In order to get unique L and U we should reduce the number of unknowns by 3 which we get by assuming the diagonal elements of L and U to be unity.

In the algorithm if the decomposition with L having diagonal values 1 is formally known as *Dolittle LU decomposition* while the decomposition with U having diagonal values 1 is known as the *Crout LU decomposition*.

Dolittle LU Decomposition Method

In this method, we express the coefficient matrix A in the form of LU where L is the lower triangular and U is the upper triangular matrix
i.e. A = LU, provided that all the principal minors of A are non – singular.

i.e. $a_{11} \neq 0, \begin{vmatrix} a_{11} & a_{12} \\ a_{21} & a_{22} \end{vmatrix} \neq 0, \begin{vmatrix} a_{11} & a_{12} & a_{13} \\ a_{21} & a_{22} & a_{23} \\ a_{31} & a_{32} & a_{33} \end{vmatrix} \neq 0, etc.$ If such factorization

exists, it is unique.

Here, we take three variables to explain the procedure for a system of linear equations easily but we can extend it to a system of n linear equations in n variables without any difficulty.

Let's consider the system of linear equations

$$a_{11}x_1 + a_{12}x_2 + a_{13}x_3 = b_1$$
$$a_{21}x_1 + a_{22}x_2 + a_{23}x_3 = b_2$$
$$a_{31}x_1 + a_{32}x_2 + a_{33}x_3 = b_3$$

which can be written as   AX = B   .... (4.3.10)

where $A = \begin{bmatrix} a_{11} & a_{12} & a_{13} \\ a_{21} & a_{22} & a_{23} \\ a_{31} & a_{32} & a_{33} \end{bmatrix}, X = \begin{bmatrix} x_1 \\ x_2 \\ x_3 \end{bmatrix}$ and $B = \begin{bmatrix} b_1 \\ b_2 \\ b_3 \end{bmatrix}$

Let   A = LU   .... (4.3.11)

where $L = \begin{bmatrix} 1 & 0 & 0 \\ l_{21} & 1 & 0 \\ l_{31} & l_{32} & 1 \end{bmatrix}$ and $U = \begin{bmatrix} u_{11} & u_{12} & u_{13} \\ 0 & u_{22} & u_{23} \\ 0 & 0 & u_{33} \end{bmatrix}$

Therefore, from Eq. (4.3.11) we have   LUX = B   .... (4.3.12)
By substituting   UX = Y, ... (4.3.13)
Eq. (4.3.12) becomes

$$LY = B$$ .... (4.3.14)

where $Y = \begin{bmatrix} y_1 \\ y_2 \\ y_3 \end{bmatrix}$. which is equivalent to the equations,

$$y_1 = b_1$$
$$l_{21}y_1 + y_2 = b_2$$ .... (4.3.15)
$$l_{31}y_1 + l_{32}y_2 + l_{33}y_3 = b_3$$

Solving these equations for y_1, y_2, y_3 by the forward substitution we get the value of Y. The system (4.3.13) becomes,

$$u_{11}x_1 + u_{12}x_2 + u_{13}x_3 = y_1$$
$$u_{22}x_2 + u_{23}x_3 = y_2$$ .... (4.3.16)
$$u_{33}x_3 = y_3$$

which can be solved for x_1, x_2, x_3 by back substitution.
From Eq. (4.3.11)

$$LU = A$$

$$\begin{bmatrix} 1 & 0 & 0 \\ l_{21} & 1 & 0 \\ l_{31} & l_{32} & 1 \end{bmatrix} \begin{bmatrix} u_{11} & u_{12} & u_{13} \\ 0 & u_{22} & u_{23} \\ 0 & 0 & u_{33} \end{bmatrix} = \begin{bmatrix} a_{11} & a_{12} & a_{13} \\ a_{21} & a_{22} & a_{23} \\ a_{31} & a_{32} & a_{33} \end{bmatrix}$$

After applying matrix multiplication and equating on both the sides we get,

$$\begin{bmatrix} u_{11} & u_{12} & u_{13} \\ l_{21}u_{11} & l_{21}u_{12} + u_{22} & l_{21}u_{13} + u_{23} \\ l_{31}u_{11} & l_{31}u_{12} + l_{32}u_{22} & l_{31}u_{13} + l_{32}u_{23} + u_{33} \end{bmatrix} = \begin{bmatrix} a_{11} & a_{12} & a_{13} \\ a_{21} & a_{22} & a_{23} \\ a_{31} & a_{32} & a_{33} \end{bmatrix}$$

$$u_{11} = a_{11}, \qquad u_{12} = a_{12}, \qquad u_{13} = a_{13}$$

$$l_{21}u_{11} = a_{21} \;\rightarrow\; l_{21}a_{11} = a_{21} \;\rightarrow\; l_{21} = \frac{a_{21}}{a_{11}},$$

$$l_{21}u_{12} + u_{22} = a_{22} \;\rightarrow\; u_{22} = a_{22} - \frac{a_{21}}{a_{11}}a_{12}$$

$$l_{21}u_{13} + u_{23} = a_{23} \;\rightarrow\; u_{23} = a_{23} - \frac{a_{21}}{a_{11}}a_{13}$$

$$l_{31}u_{11} = a_{31} \;\rightarrow\; l_{31} = \frac{a_{31}}{a_{11}}, \quad l_{31}u_{12} + l_{32}u_{22} = a_{32} \;\rightarrow\; l_{32} = \frac{a_{32} - \frac{a_{31}}{a_{11}}a_{12}}{u_{22}}$$

and u_{33} can be obtained from $l_{31}u_{13} + l_{32}u_{23} + u_{33} = a_{33}$.

Remark: It is important to note that, not every non singular matrix A can be factored as A = LU

For eg. Let $A = \begin{bmatrix} 1 & 0 & 0 \\ 0 & 0 & 2 \\ 0 & 1 & -1 \end{bmatrix}$

then $\begin{bmatrix} 1 & 0 & 0 \\ l_{21} & 1 & 0 \\ l_{31} & l_{32} & 1 \end{bmatrix} \begin{bmatrix} u_{11} & u_{12} & u_{13} \\ 0 & u_{22} & u_{23} \\ 0 & 0 & u_{33} \end{bmatrix} = \begin{bmatrix} 1 & 0 & 0 \\ 0 & 0 & 2 \\ 0 & 1 & -1 \end{bmatrix}$

$u_{11} = a_{11} = 1, u_{12} = a_{12} = 0, u_{13} = a_{13} = 0$, $l_{21} = \frac{a_{21}}{a_{11}} = 0, u_{22} = a_{22} - \frac{a_{21}}{a_{11}}a_{12} = 0$

$u_{23} = a_{23} - \frac{a_{21}}{a_{11}}a_{13} = 2, l_{31} = \frac{a_{31}}{a_{11}} = 0, l_{32} = \frac{a_{32} - \frac{a_{31}}{a_{11}}a_{12}}{u_{22}} = \frac{1}{0}$ is not possible.

Example 4.8 Using Dolittle LU decomposition method, decompose the matrix

$$A = \begin{bmatrix} 5 & -2 & 1 \\ 7 & 1 & -5 \\ 3 & 7 & 4 \end{bmatrix}$$

into LU form and hence solve the system of equations

$$5x - 2y + z = 4$$
$$7x + y - 5z = 8$$
$$3x + 7y + 4z = 10$$

Solution: Let $\begin{bmatrix} 1 & 0 & 0 \\ l_{21} & 1 & 0 \\ l_{31} & l_{32} & 1 \end{bmatrix} \begin{bmatrix} u_{11} & u_{12} & u_{13} \\ 0 & u_{22} & u_{23} \\ 0 & 0 & u_{33} \end{bmatrix} = \begin{bmatrix} 5 & -2 & 1 \\ 7 & 1 & -5 \\ 3 & 7 & 4 \end{bmatrix}$

$$u_{11} = 5, \qquad u_{12} = -2, \qquad u_{13} = 1$$

$l_{21}u_{11} = 7$ therefore, $l_{21} = \frac{7}{5}$, $l_{31}u_{11} = 3$ therefore, $l_{31} = \frac{3}{5}$

$l_{21}u_{12} + u_{22} = 1$ therefore, $u_{22} = \frac{19}{5}$, $l_{21}u_{13} + u_{23} = -5$ therefore, $u_{23} = -\frac{32}{5}$, $l_{31}u_{12} + l_{32}u_{22} = 7$ therefore, $l_{32} = \frac{41}{19}$,

$l_{31}u_{13} + l_{32}u_{23} + u_{33} = 4$ therefore, $u_{33} = \frac{327}{19}$

Therefore,

$$L = \begin{bmatrix} 1 & 0 & 0 \\ \frac{7}{5} & 1 & 0 \\ \frac{3}{5} & \frac{41}{19} & 1 \end{bmatrix} \quad \text{and} \quad U = \begin{bmatrix} 5 & -2 & 1 \\ 0 & \frac{19}{5} & -\frac{32}{5} \\ 0 & 0 & \frac{327}{19} \end{bmatrix}$$

Thus, from Eq. (4.3.14), we have

$$y_1 = 4$$
$$\frac{7}{5}y_1 + y_2 = 8$$
$$\frac{3}{5}y_1 + \frac{41}{19}y_2 + y_3 = 10$$

and hence, by forward substitution $y_1 = 4$, $y_2 = 2.4$, $y_3 = 2.42$
Now, from Eq. (4.3.15) we obtain

$$5x - 2y + z = 4$$
$$3.8y - 6.4z = 2.4$$
$$17.21z = 2.42$$

Solving these equations by back substitution method we get $x = 1.119$, $y = 0.869$ and $z = 0.141$

Example 4.9   Solve the equations

$$2x - 1y - 2z = -1$$
$$-4x + 6y + 3z = 13$$
$$-4x - 2y + 8z = -6$$

by the factorization method.

Solution: We have $A = \begin{bmatrix} 2 & -1 & -2 \\ -4 & 6 & 3 \\ -4 & -2 & 8 \end{bmatrix}$

We have to factorize A into L and U, where L is lower triangular and U is upper triangular matrices as discussed above.

$$\text{Let } \begin{bmatrix} 1 & 0 & 0 \\ l_{21} & 1 & 0 \\ l_{31} & l_{32} & 1 \end{bmatrix} \begin{bmatrix} u_{11} & u_{12} & u_{13} \\ 0 & u_{22} & u_{23} \\ 0 & 0 & u_{33} \end{bmatrix} = \begin{bmatrix} 2 & -1 & -2 \\ -4 & 6 & 3 \\ -4 & -2 & 8 \end{bmatrix}$$

$$u_{11} = 2, \qquad u_{12} = -1, \qquad u_{13} = -2$$

$l_{21}u_{11} = -4$ therefore, $l_{21} = -2$, $l_{31}u_{11} = -4$ therefore, $l_{31} = -2$

$l_{21}u_{12} + u_{22} = 6$ therefore, $u_{22} = 4$, $l_{21}u_{13} + u_{23} = 3$ therefore, $u_{23} = -1$

$l_{31}u_{12} + l_{32}u_{22} = -2$ therefore, $l_{32} = -1$, $l_{31}u_{13} + l_{32}u_{23} + u_{33} = 8$ therefore, $u_{33} = 3$

Therefore,

$$L = \begin{bmatrix} 1 & 0 & 0 \\ -2 & 1 & 0 \\ -2 & -1 & 1 \end{bmatrix} \quad \text{and} \quad U = \begin{bmatrix} 2 & -1 & -2 \\ 0 & 4 & -1 \\ 0 & 0 & 3 \end{bmatrix}$$

Thus, from Eq. (4.3.10), we have

$$y_1 = -1$$
$$-2y_1 + y_2 = 13$$
$$-2y_1 - y_2 + y_3 = -6$$

and hence, by forward substitution $y_1 = -1$, $y_2 = 11$, $y_3 = 3$

Now, from Eq. (4.3.11) we obtain

$$2x - y - 2z = -1$$
$$4y - z = 11$$
$$3z = 3$$

Solving these equations by back substitution method we get $x = 2$, $y = 3$ and $z = 1$

Crout's LU Decomposition Method (Crout's Reduction Method)

As discussed earlier, coefficient matrix A can be expressed as product of L and U where L is a lower triangular and U is an upper triangular matrix. In order to get unique L and U we assume unit diagonal elements of L and U. In Crout's decomposition algorithm we assume unit values of diagonal.

Therefore, if we take LU = A then in Crout's algorithm we have,

$$\begin{bmatrix} l_{11} & 0 & 0 \\ l_{21} & l_{22} & 0 \\ l_{31} & l_{32} & l_{23} \end{bmatrix} \begin{bmatrix} 1 & u_{12} & u_{13} \\ 0 & 1 & u_{23} \\ 0 & 0 & 1 \end{bmatrix} = \begin{bmatrix} a_{11} & a_{12} & a_{13} \\ a_{21} & a_{22} & a_{23} \\ a_{31} & a_{32} & a_{33} \end{bmatrix}$$

Using the same approach that we have used in Dolittle decomposition algorithm we can calculate the elements of L and U and thus obtain the solution of the system of linear equations.

It is left for the readers to check that the coefficients of matrices L and U are given by

$$l_{11} = a_{11}, \qquad l_{21} = a_{21}, \qquad l_{31} = a_{31}$$

$$u_{12} = \frac{a_{12}}{l_{11}} = \frac{a_{12}}{a_{11}}, \qquad u_{13} = \frac{a_{13}}{l_{11}} = \frac{a_{13}}{a_{11}}$$

$$l_{22} = a_{22} - l_{21}u_{12} = a_{22} - a_{21}\frac{a_{12}}{a_{11}}, \quad l_{32} = a_{32} - l_{31}u_{12} = a_{32} - a_{31}\frac{a_{12}}{a_{11}}$$

$$l_{21}u_{13} + l_{22}u_{23} = a_{23} \quad \rightarrow \quad u_{23} = \frac{a_{23} - l_{21}u_{13}}{l_{22}}$$

$$l_{31}u_{13} + l_{32}u_{23} + l_{33} = a_{33} \quad \rightarrow \quad l_{33} = a_{33} - l_{31}u_{13} - l_{32}u_{23}$$

Example 4.10 Solve the equations

$$2x - 1y - 2z = -1$$
$$-4x + 6y + 3z = 13$$
$$-4x - 2y + 8z = -6$$

by the Crout's decomposition method.

Solution: Let the coefficient matrix A = LU.
Thus,

$$\begin{bmatrix} l_{11} & 0 & 0 \\ l_{21} & l_{22} & 0 \\ l_{31} & l_{32} & l_{33} \end{bmatrix} \begin{bmatrix} 1 & u_{12} & u_{13} \\ 0 & 1 & u_{23} \\ 0 & 0 & 1 \end{bmatrix} = \begin{bmatrix} 2 & -1 & -2 \\ -4 & 6 & 3 \\ -4 & -2 & 8 \end{bmatrix}$$

$$l_{11} = a_{11} = 2, \qquad l_{21} = a_{21} = -4, \qquad l_{31} = a_{31} = -4$$

$$u_{12} = \frac{a_{12}}{l_{11}} = \frac{a_{12}}{a_{11}} = \frac{-1}{2}, \qquad u_{13} = \frac{a_{13}}{l_{11}} = \frac{a_{13}}{a_{11}} = \frac{-2}{2} = -1$$

$$l_{22} = a_{22} - l_{21}u_{12} = a_{22} - a_{21}\frac{a_{12}}{a_{11}} = 6 - (-4)\frac{-1}{2} = 4$$

$$l_{32} = a_{32} - l_{31}u_{12} = a_{32} - a_{31}\frac{a_{12}}{a_{11}} = -2 - (-4)\frac{-1}{2} = -4$$

$$l_{21}u_{13} + l_{22}u_{23} = a_{23} \quad \rightarrow \quad u_{23} = \frac{a_{23} - l_{21}u_{13}}{l_{22}} = \frac{3 - (-4)(-1)}{4} = \frac{-1}{4}$$

$$l_{33} = a_{33} - l_{31}u_{13} - l_{32}u_{23} = 8 - (-4)(-1) - (-4)\frac{-1}{4} = 3$$

Thus, $\quad L = \begin{bmatrix} 2 & 0 & 0 \\ -4 & 4 & 0 \\ -4 & -4 & 3 \end{bmatrix}$ and $\quad U = \begin{bmatrix} 1 & -0.5 & -1 \\ 0 & 1 & -0.25 \\ 0 & 0 & 1 \end{bmatrix}$

Hence, we have

$$\begin{aligned} l_{11}y_1 &= b_1 \\ l_{21}y_1 + l_{22}y_2 &= b_2 \\ l_{31}y_1 + l_{32}y_2 + l_{33}y_3 &= b_3 \end{aligned} \Rightarrow \qquad \begin{aligned} 2y_1 &= -1 \\ -4y_1 + 4y_2 &= 13 \\ -4y_1 - 4y_2 + 3y_3 &= -6 \end{aligned}$$

and hence, by forward substitution $y_1 = -0.5$, $y_2 = 2.75$, $y_3 = 1$
Now,

$$\begin{aligned} x + u_{12}y + u_{13}z &= y_1 \\ y + u_{23}z &= y_2 \\ z &= y_3 \end{aligned} \Rightarrow \qquad \begin{aligned} x - 0.5y - z &= -0.5 \\ y - 0.25z &= 2.75 \\ z &= 1 \end{aligned}$$

Solving these equations by back substitution method we get $x = 2$, $y = 3$ and $z = 1$

Crout's Method for Finding the Inverse of Matrix

We know that, $A = LU$ where, L is a lower triangular matrix and U is an upper triangular matrix.

Therefore, inverse can be obtained by $A^{-1} = (LU)^{-1} = U^{-1} L^{-1}$. Once we have obtained L and U by the above discussed method, we can easily find L^{-1} and U^{-1} as $L L^{-1} = U U^{-1} = I$. It can be easily seen that if L is a lower triangular matrix, L^{-1} is also lower triangular and if U is an upper triangular matrix, U^{-1} is also upper triangular.

Example 4.11   Find the inverse of

$$A = \begin{bmatrix} 1 & 1 & 2 \\ 1 & 2 & 4 \\ 2 & 4 & 7 \end{bmatrix}$$

using Crout's method.

Solution: Let $A = LU$

$$\begin{bmatrix} l_{11} & 0 & 0 \\ l_{21} & l_{22} & 0 \\ l_{31} & l_{32} & l_{33} \end{bmatrix} \begin{bmatrix} 1 & u_{12} & u_{13} \\ 0 & 1 & u_{23} \\ 0 & 0 & 1 \end{bmatrix} = \begin{bmatrix} 1 & 1 & 2 \\ 1 & 2 & 4 \\ 2 & 4 & 7 \end{bmatrix}$$

Then,

$$l_{11} = a_{11} = 1, \qquad l_{21} = a_{21} = 1, \qquad l_{31} = a_{31} = 2$$

$$u_{12} = \frac{a_{12}}{l_{11}} = \frac{a_{12}}{a_{11}} = 1, \qquad u_{13} = \frac{a_{13}}{l_{11}} = \frac{a_{13}}{a_{11}} = \frac{2}{1} = 2$$

$$l_{22} = a_{22} - l_{21}u_{12} = a_{22} - a_{21}\frac{a_{12}}{a_{11}} = 2 - (1)\frac{1}{1} = 1$$

$$l_{32} = a_{32} - l_{31}u_{12} = a_{32} - a_{31}\frac{a_{12}}{a_{11}} = 4 - (2)\frac{1}{1} = 2$$

$$l_{21}u_{13} + l_{22}u_{23} = a_{23} \rightarrow u_{23} = \frac{a_{23} - l_{21}u_{13}}{l_{22}} = \frac{4 - (1)(2)}{1} = 2$$

$$l_{33} = a_{33} - l_{31}u_{13} - l_{32}u_{23} = 7 - (2)(2) - (2)(2) = -1$$

Therefore,

$$L = \begin{bmatrix} 1 & 0 & 0 \\ 1 & 1 & 0 \\ 2 & 2 & -1 \end{bmatrix} \quad \text{and} \quad U = \begin{bmatrix} 1 & 1 & 2 \\ 0 & 1 & 2 \\ 0 & 0 & 1 \end{bmatrix}$$

To find L^{-1}, we have $L L^{-1} = I$. Hence,

$$\begin{bmatrix} 1 & 0 & 0 \\ 1 & 1 & 0 \\ 2 & 2 & -1 \end{bmatrix} \begin{bmatrix} x_{11} & 0 & 0 \\ x_{21} & x_{22} & 0 \\ x_{31} & x_{32} & x_{33} \end{bmatrix} = \begin{bmatrix} 1 & 0 & 0 \\ 0 & 1 & 0 \\ 0 & 0 & 1 \end{bmatrix}$$

From this we get, $x_{11} = 1$, $x_{11} + x_{21} = 0$, $x_{22} = 1$, $2x_{11} + 2x_{21} - x_{31} = 0$, $2x_{22} - x_{32} = 0$, $-x_{33} = 1$

Therefore, $x_{11} = 1$, $x_{21} = -1$, $x_{22} = 1$, $x_{33} = -1$, $x_{31} = 0$, $x_{32} = 2$

Therefore, $\quad L^{-1} = \begin{bmatrix} 1 & 0 & 0 \\ -1 & 1 & 0 \\ 0 & 2 & -1 \end{bmatrix}$

Now, we compute U^{-1} from the relation $U\,U^{-1} = I$. We have,

$$\begin{bmatrix} 1 & 1 & 2 \\ 0 & 1 & 2 \\ 0 & 0 & 1 \end{bmatrix} \begin{bmatrix} 1 & y_{12} & y_{13} \\ 0 & 1 & y_{23} \\ 0 & 0 & 1 \end{bmatrix} = \begin{bmatrix} 1 & 0 & 0 \\ 0 & 1 & 0 \\ 0 & 0 & 1 \end{bmatrix}$$

So, we have $y_{12} + 1 = 0$, $y_{13} + y_{23} + 2 = 0$, $y_{23} + 2 = 0$

Hence, $y_{12} = -1, y_{23} = -2, y_{13} = 0$

Therefore, $\quad U^{-1} = \begin{bmatrix} 1 & -1 & 0 \\ 0 & 1 & -2 \\ 0 & 0 & 1 \end{bmatrix}$

Thus, $A^{-1} = (LU)^{-1} = U^{-1}.\,L^{-1}$

$$= \begin{bmatrix} 1 & -1 & 0 \\ 0 & 1 & -2 \\ 0 & 0 & 1 \end{bmatrix} . \begin{bmatrix} 1 & 0 & 0 \\ -1 & 1 & 0 \\ 0 & 2 & -1 \end{bmatrix} = \begin{bmatrix} 2 & -1 & 0 \\ -1 & -3 & 2 \\ 0 & 2 & -1 \end{bmatrix}$$

Triangularization of Symmetric Matrix (Cholesky Reduction Method)

The cholesky factorization is defined only if A is symmetric or Hermitian positive definite matrix. In such cases, LU decomposition can be modified so that $U = L^T$ or $L = U^T$. Cholesky Factorization theorem says that "Givan a symmetric positive definite matrix A there exists a lower triangular matrix L such that $A = L.L^T$ or $A = U^T.U$. Here L is called the Cholesky factor of A and can be interpreted as square root of a positive definite matrix.

Let us take 3×3 matrix, we have

$$A = \begin{bmatrix} a_{11} & a_{12} & a_{13} \\ a_{21} & a_{22} & a_{23} \\ a_{31} & a_{32} & a_{33} \end{bmatrix} = \begin{bmatrix} l_{11} & 0 & 0 \\ l_{21} & l_{22} & 0 \\ l_{31} & l_{32} & l_{33} \end{bmatrix} \begin{bmatrix} l_{11} & l_{21} & l_{31} \\ 0 & l_{22} & l_{32} \\ 0 & 0 & l_{33} \end{bmatrix} = L\,L^T$$

$$= \begin{bmatrix} l^2_{11} & l_{21}l_{11} & l_{31}l_{11} \\ l_{21}l_{11} & l^2_{21} + l^2_{22} & l_{31}l_{21} + l_{32}l_{22} \\ l_{31}l_{11} & l_{31}l_{21} + l_{32}l_{22} & l^2_{31} + l^2_{32} + l^2_{33} \end{bmatrix}$$

There is a calculation pattern for the diagonal elements (l_{kk}) of L,

$l_{11} = \sqrt{a_{11}}$, $l_{22} = \sqrt{a_{22} - l^2_{21}}$, $l_{33} = \sqrt{a_{33} - (l^2_{31} + l^2_{32})}$

In general, $l_{kk} = \sqrt{a_{kk} - \sum_{j=1}^{k-1} l^2_{kj}}$

There is also a calculation pattern for the elements below the diagonal (l_{ik} where $i > k$) $l_{21} = \dfrac{1}{l_{11}} a_{21}$, $l_{31} = \dfrac{1}{l_{11}} a_{31}$, $l_{32} = \dfrac{1}{l_{22}} (a_{32} - l_{31}l_{21})$

In general, $l_{ik} = \dfrac{1}{l_{kk}} (a_{ik} - \sum_{j=1}^{k-1} l_{ij} l_{kj})$

Comparing the elements of the product of L and L^T with the corresponding elements of A we get,

$l^2{}_{11} = a_{11}$, $l_{21}l_{11} = a_{12}$, $l_{31}l_{11} = a_{13}$, $l_{21}l_{11} = a_{21}$, $l^2{}_{21} + l^2{}_{22} = a_{22}$,

$l_{31}l_{21} + l_{32}l_{22} = a_{23}$, $l_{31}l_{11} = a_{31}$, $l_{31}l_{21} + l_{32}l_{22} = a_{32}$,

$l^2{}_{31} + l^2{}_{32} + l^2{}_{33} = a_{33}$

It may happen that some terms are purely imaginary but it does not create any special complication.

The matrix equation A.X = B convets to $L.L^T$. X = B or L.Y = B and L^T. X = Y. This method of solving the system of linear equations is known as Cholesky reduction method or square root method.

Example 4.12   Solve by Cholesky reduction method

$$25x_1 + 15x_2 - 5x_3 = 10$$
$$15x_1 + 18x_2 = 12$$
$$-5x_1 + 11x_3 = 45$$

Solution: The matrix form of the given system is AX = B

$$A = \begin{bmatrix} 25 & 15 & -5 \\ 15 & 18 & 0 \\ -5 & 0 & 11 \end{bmatrix}, \quad X = \begin{bmatrix} x_1 \\ x_2 \\ x_3 \end{bmatrix}, \quad B = \begin{bmatrix} 10 \\ 12 \\ 45 \end{bmatrix}$$

Here, A is symmetric. Therefore, Cholesky method is possible. Let $A = LL^T$
Hence, we have

$$\begin{bmatrix} 25 & 15 & -5 \\ 15 & 18 & 0 \\ -5 & 0 & 11 \end{bmatrix} = \begin{bmatrix} l_{11} & 0 & 0 \\ l_{21} & l_{22} & 0 \\ l_{31} & l_{32} & l_{33} \end{bmatrix} \begin{bmatrix} l_{11} & l_{21} & l_{31} \\ 0 & l_{22} & l_{32} \\ 0 & 0 & l_{33} \end{bmatrix}$$

$$= \begin{bmatrix} l^2{}_{11} & l_{21}l_{11} & l_{31}l_{11} \\ l_{21}l_{11} & l^2{}_{21}+l^2{}_{22} & l_{31}l_{21} + l_{32}l_{22} \\ l_{31}l_{11} & l_{31}l_{21} + l_{32}l_{22} & l^2{}_{31} + l^2{}_{32} + l^2{}_{33} \end{bmatrix}$$

$l^2{}_{11} = 25$ therefore, $l_{11} = 5$, $l_{21}l_{11} = 15$ therefore, $l_{21} = 3$, $l_{31}l_{11} = -5$ therefore, $l_{31} = -1$

$l^2{}_{21} + l^2{}_{22} = 18$ therefore, $l_{22} = 3$, $l_{31}l_{21} + l_{32}l_{22} = 0$ therefore, $l_{32} = 1$

$l^2{}_{31} + l^2{}_{32} + l^2{}_{33} = 11$ therefore, $l_{33} = 3$

Thus,

$$L = \begin{bmatrix} 5 & 0 & 0 \\ 3 & 3 & 0 \\ -1 & 1 & 3 \end{bmatrix}$$

Therefore, LY = B gives,

$$\begin{bmatrix} 5 & 0 & 0 \\ 3 & 3 & 0 \\ -1 & 1 & 3 \end{bmatrix} \begin{bmatrix} y_1 \\ y_2 \\ y_3 \end{bmatrix} = \begin{bmatrix} 10 \\ 12 \\ 45 \end{bmatrix}$$

So, we get $y_1 = 2$, $3y_1 + 3y_2 = 12$ therefore, $y_2 = 2$, $-y_1 + y_2 + 3y_3 = 45$

therefore, $y_3 = 15$. Now, $L^T . X = Y$ gives

$$\begin{bmatrix} 5 & 3 & -1 \\ 0 & 3 & 1 \\ 0 & 0 & 3 \end{bmatrix} \begin{bmatrix} x_1 \\ x_2 \\ x_3 \end{bmatrix} = \begin{bmatrix} 2 \\ 2 \\ 15 \end{bmatrix}$$

Hence, $x_3 = 5$, $3x_2 + x_3 = 2$ therefore, $x_2 = -1$, $5x_1 + 3x_2 - x_3 = 2$ therefore, $x_1 = 2$

Thus, the solution is $x_1 = 2, x_2 = -1$ and $x_3 = 5$.

4.3.2 Iterative Methods

In the previous section, we have seen different direct methods. These methods are known as direct methods in the sense that they yield exact solutions in a fixed number of computations. On the other hand, in iterative methods we provide initial value for the unknown which is improved and refined in the successive iterations using iteration formulae. We continue our computation cycle until we get the desired accuracy. Hence, in an iterative method, the number of iterations depend upon the level of desired accuracy. Iterative methods are unreliable compare to direct methods as in some cases it converges very slow or it may not converge at all but in a certain situations where the matrix is large and sparse they are much faster than direct methods.

In this section, we will discuss three iterative methods for solving system of linear equations.

(a)   Jacobi Iteration method
(b)   Gauss Seidel Method
(c)   Relaxation method

Convergence Criteria for Iterative Methods

The sufficient condition for iterative methods to be converged is the system of equations are strictly diagonally dominant. i.e. the iteration converges if

$$\sum_{j=1, j \neq i}^{n} |a_{ij}| < |a_{ii}| , \text{for } i = 1,2,3, \dots , n$$

or an alternative sufficient condition is

$$\sum_{i=1, j \neq i}^{n} |a_{ij}| < |a_{jj}| , \text{for } j = 1,2,3, \dots , n$$

Jacobi Iteration Method

Consider the system of equations in n unknowns

$$\begin{aligned}
a_{11}x_1 + a_{12}x_2 + \dots + a_{1n}x_n &= b_1 \\
a_{21}x_1 + a_{22}x_2 + \dots + a_{2n}x_n &= b_2 \\
a_{31}x_1 + a_{32}x_2 + \dots + a_{3n}x_n &= b_3 \\
\vdots \qquad \vdots \qquad\quad \vdots \qquad \vdots & \\
a_{n1}x_1 + a_{n2}x_2 + \dots + a_{nn}x_n &= b_n
\end{aligned}$$

.... (4.3.17)

This method assumes that the system given in Eq. (4.3.17) has a unique solution and the coefficient matrix A has no zeros on its main diagonal. If this is not the case, the equations should be rearranged so that this condition is satisfied. Now, the system of equations (4.3.17) can be rewritten as:

$$x_1 = \frac{1}{a_{11}}(b_1 - a_{12}x_2 - \dots - a_{1n}x_n)$$
$$x_2 = \frac{1}{a_{22}}(b_2 - a_{21}x_1 - \dots - a_{2n}x_n) \qquad \dots\dots (4.3.18)$$
$$\dots \quad \dots \quad \dots \quad \dots \quad \dots$$
$$x_n = \frac{1}{a_{nn}}(b_n - a_{n1}x_1 - \dots - a_{n(n-1)}x_{n-1})$$

Suppose $x_1', x_2', \dots, x_n'$ are the initial approximations to the unknowns $x_1, x_2, \dots, x_n$. Substituting these values in RHS of (4.3.18) we get a system of second approximations.

$$x_1'' = \frac{1}{a_{11}}(b_1 - a_{12}x_2' - \dots - a_{1n}x_n')$$
$$x_2'' = \frac{1}{a_{22}}(b_2 - a_{21}x_1' - \dots - a_{2n}x_n') \qquad \dots\dots (4.3.19)$$
$$\dots \quad \dots \quad \dots \quad \dots \quad \dots$$
$$x_n'' = \frac{1}{a_{nn}}(b_n - a_{n1}x_1' - \dots - a_{n(n-1)}x_{n-1}')$$

Continue the same procedure untill you get the desired accuracy in the solution of the system of linear equations. i.e. the difference between two consecutive approximations is negligible.

In general, if $x_1^{(n)}, x_2^{(n)}, \dots, x_n^{(n)}$ are the nth approximations then the next approximation is given by

$$x_1^{(n+1)} = \frac{1}{a_{11}}(b_1 - a_{12}x_2^{(n)} - \dots - a_{1n}x_n^{(n)})$$
$$x_2^{(n+1)} = \frac{1}{a_{22}}(b_2 - a_{21}x_1^{(n)} - \dots - a_{2n}x_n^{(n)}) \qquad \dots\dots (4.3.20)$$
$$\dots \quad \dots \quad \dots \quad \dots \quad \dots$$
$$x_n^{(n+1)} = \frac{1}{a_{nn}}(b_n - a_{n1}x_1^{(n)} - \dots - a_{n(n-1)}x_{n-1}^{(n)})$$

This method is called Jacobi method, after Carl Gustav Jacob Jacobi (1804-1851).

Example 4.13   Solve the following system of equations
$$5x - 2y + 3z = -1$$
$$-3x + 9y + z = 2$$
$$2x - y - 7z = 3$$
by Jacobi Iteration method correct to three significant digits.

Solution: We write the given system in the form,
$$x = -\frac{1}{5} + \frac{2}{5}y - \frac{3}{5}z$$
$$y = \frac{2}{9} + \frac{3}{9}x - \frac{1}{9}z \qquad \dots\dots (1)$$
$$z = -\frac{3}{7} + \frac{2}{7}x - \frac{1}{7}y$$

Let the initial approximation be $x = y = z = 0$

Iteration 1: Substituting these on the right hand side of the equations (i), we get

$$x = -\frac{1}{5} + \frac{2}{5}(0) - \frac{3}{5}(0) \approx -0.20$$

$$y = \frac{2}{9} + \frac{3}{9}(0) - \frac{1}{9}(0) \approx 0.222$$

$$z = -\frac{3}{7} + \frac{2}{7}(0) - \frac{1}{7}(0) \approx -0.429$$

Iteration 2: Substituting these values in the right hand side of the equations (i) we get,

$$x = -\frac{1}{5} + \frac{2}{5}(0.222) - \frac{3}{5}(-0.429) \approx 0.146$$

$$y = \frac{2}{9} + \frac{3}{9}(-0.200) - \frac{1}{9}(-0.429) \approx 0.203$$

$$z = -\frac{3}{7} + \frac{2}{7}(-0.200) - \frac{1}{7}(0.222) \approx -0.517$$

Iteration 3: Substituting the values obtained in the second iteration in the right hand side of the equations (i) we get,

$$x = -\frac{1}{5} + \frac{2}{5}(0.203) - \frac{3}{5}(-0.517) \approx 0.192$$

$$y = \frac{2}{9} + \frac{3}{9}(0.146) - \frac{1}{9}(-0.517) \approx 0.328$$

$$z = -\frac{3}{7} + \frac{2}{7}(0.146) - \frac{1}{7}(0.203) \approx -0.416$$

Iteration 4: Substituting the values obtained in the third iteration in the right hand side of the equations (i) we get,

$$x = -\frac{1}{5} + \frac{2}{5}(0.328) - \frac{3}{5}(-0.416) \approx 0.181$$

$$y = \frac{2}{9} + \frac{3}{9}(0.192) - \frac{1}{9}(-0.416) \approx 0.332$$

$$z = -\frac{3}{7} + \frac{2}{7}(0.192) - \frac{1}{7}(0.328) \approx -0.421$$

Iteration 5: Substituting the values obtained in the fourth iteration in the right hand side of the equations (i) we get,

$$x = -\frac{1}{5} + \frac{2}{5}(0.332) - \frac{3}{5}(-0.421) \approx 0.185$$

$$y = \frac{2}{9} + \frac{3}{9}(0.181) - \frac{1}{9}(-0.421) \approx 0.329$$

$$z = -\frac{3}{7} + \frac{2}{7}(0.181) - \frac{1}{7}(0.332) \approx -0.424$$

Iteration 6: Substituting the values obtained in the fifth iteration in the right hand side of the equations (i) we get,

$$x = -\frac{1}{5} + \frac{2}{5}(0.329) - \frac{3}{5}(-0.424) \approx 0.186$$

$$y = \frac{2}{9} + \frac{3}{9}(0.185) - \frac{1}{9}(-0.424) \approx 0.331$$

$$z = -\frac{3}{7} + \frac{2}{7}(0.185) - \frac{1}{7}(0.329) \approx -0.423$$

Iteration 7: Substituting the values obtained in the sixth iteration in the right hand side of the equations (i) we get,

$$x = -\frac{1}{5} + \frac{2}{5}(0.331) - \frac{3}{5}(-0.423) \approx 0.186$$

$$y = -\frac{2}{9} + \frac{3}{9}(0.186) - \frac{1}{9}(-0.423) \approx 0.331$$

$$z = -\frac{3}{7} + \frac{2}{7}(0.186) - \frac{1}{7}(0.331) \approx -0.423$$

Since the values of x , y and z in the sixth and seventh iterations are same upto three significant figures. Threfore, the solution is $x = 0.186, y = 0.331$ and $z = -0.423$.

Gauss – Seidel Method

This is a simple and improved version of the Jacobi method. In this method, it requires fewer iterations to produce the same degree of accuracy than Jacobi method as in each iteration it uses improved values of the unknowns for computing unknowns of the subsequent iterations. That means when x_1 is determined from the first equation its value is then used in the second equation to obtain the new x_2. Similarly, the new x_1 and x_2 are used in the third equation to obtain the new x_3 and so on. Consider the system of equations in n unknowns

$$
\begin{aligned}
a_{11}x_1 + a_{12}x_2 + \ldots + a_{1n}x_n &= b_1 \\
a_{21}x_1 + a_{22}x_2 + \ldots + a_{2n}x_n &= b_2 \\
a_{31}x_1 + a_{32}x_2 + \ldots + a_{3n}x_n &= b_3 \\
\vdots \qquad \vdots \qquad\qquad \vdots \qquad \vdots & \\
a_{n1}x_1 + a_{n2}x_2 + \ldots + a_{nn}x_n &= b_n
\end{aligned}
\qquad \ldots\ldots (4.3.21)
$$

After verifying the convergent conditions, the system of equations given in (4.3.21) can be rewritten as:

$$x_1 = \frac{1}{a_{11}}(b_1 - a_{12}x_2 - \ldots - a_{1n}x_n)$$

$$x_2 = \frac{1}{a_{22}}(b_2 - a_{21}x_1 - \ldots - a_{2n}x_n) \qquad \ldots\ldots (4.3.22)$$

$$\ldots \quad \ldots \quad \ldots \quad \ldots \quad \ldots$$

$$x_n = \frac{1}{a_{nn}}(b_n - a_{n1}x_1 - \ldots - a_{n(n-1)}x_{n-1})$$

Let the initial approximations of the unkowns $x_1, x_2, \ldots, x_n$ are $x_1^{(0)}, x_2^{(0)}, \ldots, x_n^{(0)}$ respectively. Using these values the Eq. (4.3.22) becomes,

$$x_1^{(1)} = \frac{1}{a_{11}}(b_1 - a_{12}x_2^{(0)} - \ldots - a_{1n}x_n^{(0)})$$

$$x_2^{(1)} = \frac{1}{a_{22}}(b_2 - a_{21}x_1^{(1)} - \ldots - a_{2n}x_n^{(0)}) \qquad \ldots\ldots (4.3.23)$$

$$\ldots \quad \ldots \quad \ldots \quad \ldots \quad \ldots \quad \ldots \quad \ldots \quad \ldots$$

$$x_n^{(1)} = \frac{1}{a_{nn}}(b_n - a_{n1}x_1^{(1)} - \ldots - a_{n(n-1)}x_{n-1}^{(1)})$$

Thus, the new values of the unknowns are used immediately in the following equation. Similarly, we can proceed for other iterations. In general,

$$x_1^{(n+1)} = \frac{1}{a_{11}}(b_1 - a_{12}x_2^{(n)} - \dots - a_{1n}x_n^{(n)})$$

$$x_2^{(n+1)} = \frac{1}{a_{22}}(b_2 - a_{21}x_1^{(n+1)} - \dots - a_{2n}x_n^{(n)}) \dots\dots(4.3.24)$$

$$\dots \quad \dots \quad \dots \quad \dots \quad \dots \quad \dots \quad \dots \quad \dots$$

$$x_n^{(n+1)} = \frac{1}{a_{nn}}(b_n - a_{n1}x_1^{(n+1)} - \dots - a_{n(n-1)}x_{n-1}^{(n+1)})$$

The procedure is repeated till the values of $x_1, x_2, \dots, x_n$ are same in two consecutive iterations. This method is called successive displacements or Gauss – Seidel method, after Carl Friedrich Gauss (1777 - 1855) and Philipp L. Seidel (1821 – 1896).

Example 4.14 Apply Gauss – Seidel method to solve the following equations

$$5x - 2y + 3z = -1$$
$$-3x + 9y + z = 2$$
$$2x - y - 7z = 3$$

Solution: The sufficient condition for convergence is satisfied as equations are diagonally dominant. We write the given system of equations in the form,

$$x = -\frac{1}{5} + \frac{2}{5}y - \frac{3}{5}z \qquad \dots\dots \text{ (i)}$$

$$y = \frac{2}{9} + \frac{3}{9}x - \frac{1}{9}z \qquad \dots\dots \text{ (ii)}$$

$$z = -\frac{3}{7} + \frac{2}{7}x - \frac{1}{7}y \qquad \dots\dots \text{ (iii)}$$

Let the initial approximations be $x_0 = y_0 = z_0 = 0$.

Iteration 1: Putting $y = y_0$ and $z = z_0$ in (i) we get,

$$x_1 = -\frac{1}{5} + \frac{2}{5}y_0 - \frac{3}{5}z_0 = -0.2$$

Putting $x = x_1, z = z_0$ in (ii) we get,

$$y_1 = \frac{2}{9} + \frac{3}{9}x_1 - \frac{1}{9}z_0 = 0.156$$

Putting $x = x_1, y = y_1$ in (iii) we get,

$$z_1 = -\frac{3}{7} + \frac{2}{7}x_1 - \frac{1}{7}y_1 = -0.508$$

Iteration 2:

$$x_2 = -\frac{1}{5} + \frac{2}{5}y_1 - \frac{3}{5}z_1 = 0.167$$

$$y_2 = \frac{2}{9} + \frac{3}{9}x_2 - \frac{1}{9}z_1 = 0.334$$

$$z_2 = -\frac{3}{7} + \frac{2}{7}x_2 - \frac{1}{7}y_2 = -0.429$$

Iteration 3:

$$x_3 = -\frac{1}{5} + \frac{2}{5}y_2 - \frac{3}{5}z_2 = 0.191$$

$$y_3 = \frac{2}{9} + \frac{3}{9}x_3 - \frac{1}{9}z_2 = 0.333$$

$$z_3 = -\frac{3}{7} + \frac{2}{7}x_3 - \frac{1}{7}y_3 = -0.422$$

Iteration 4:

$$x_4 = -\frac{1}{5} + \frac{2}{5}y_3 - \frac{3}{5}z_3 = 0.186$$

$$y_4 = \frac{2}{9} + \frac{3}{9}x_4 - \frac{1}{9}z_3 = 0.331$$

$$z_4 = -\frac{3}{7} + \frac{2}{7}x_4 - \frac{1}{7}y_4 = -0.423$$

Iteration 5:

$$x_5 = -\frac{1}{5} + \frac{2}{5}y_4 - \frac{3}{5}z_4 = 0.186$$

$$y_5 = \frac{2}{9} + \frac{3}{9}x_5 - \frac{1}{9}z_4 = 0.331$$

$$z_5 = -\frac{3}{7} + \frac{2}{7}x_5 - \frac{1}{7}y_5 = -0.423$$

The values in fourth and fifth iterations are same. Hence, the solution of given system of linear equations is $x = 0.186$, $y = 0.331$, $z = -0.423$.

Remark: In Gauss – Jacobi method, although the new value of x_1 is computed from the first iteration but it is not used in the current iteration. The new value of x_1 is obviously better than the old one. In Gauss Seidel method, x_1 is determined from the first equation its value is then used in the second equation to obtain the new x_2 i.e. in the current iteration itself. Therefore, it is faster to produce the same degree of accuracy and hence, preferred over Gauss – Jacobi method. In some cases it may happen that Jacobi method will converge even though Gauss Seidel method does not but convergence is faster in Gauss – Seidel method compare to Gauss – Jacobi method.

Relaxation Method (Southwell Relaxation Method)

Consider the system of equations

$$a_1x + b_1y + c_1z = d_1$$
$$a_2x + b_2y + c_2z = d_2$$
$$a_3x + b_3y + c_3z = d_3$$

We take three equations in three variables to explain the procedure for a system of linear equations easily but we can extend it to a system of n linear equations in n variables without any difficulty. We define the residuals R_1, R_2 and R_3 corresponding to above equations by the relations

$$R_1 = a_1x + b_1y + c_1z - d_1$$
$$R_2 = a_2x + b_2y + c_2z - d_2$$
$$R_3 = a_3x + b_3y + c_3z - d_3$$

Our purpose is to obtain the solution by reducing the value of residuals step by step by incrementing the variables. We start the procedure with assumption $x = y = z = 0$ and calculate the initial residuals. We go on relaxing (increamenting) the value of variables till all the residuals become zero or very near to zero.

For this purpose we construct the following operation table:

Operation	Δx	Δy	Δz	ΔR_1	ΔR_2	ΔR_3
0_1	1	0	0	a_1	a_2	a_3
0_2	0	1	0	b_1	b_2	b_3
0_3	0	0	1	c_1	c_2	c_3

This table shows the effect on residuals R_1, R_2 and R_3 when x is increased by 1, keeping y and z constant, calling this operator by 0_1 and similarly for y and z.

Remark: $R_1 = a_1x + b_1y + c_1z - d_1$ and let $R_1' = a_1(x + 1) + b_1y + c_1z - d_1$. Therefore, $\Delta R_1 = R_1' - R_1 = a_1$. For change in x we get $\Delta R_2 = a_2, \Delta R_3 = a_3$. Similarly, if the value of y alone is increased by 1 then changes in residuals are given by $\Delta R_1 = b_1, \Delta R_2 = b_2, \Delta R_3 = b_3$ and if z alone is increased by 1 then changes in residuals are $\Delta R_1 = c_1, \Delta R_2 = c_2, \Delta R_3 = c_3$

We can see that the above operational table consist of unit matrix I and the transpose matrix A^T of the matrix A of the coefficients of the given system of equations. The numerically largest residual is reduced to zero or near to zero at each step. To reduce a particular residual, the value of corresponding variable is changed. The convergence criteria of this method is same as iterative methods for solving system of simultaneous linear equations. i.e. The relaxation method converges if the coefficient matrix is diagonally dominant. i.e.

$$|a_1| \geq |b_1| + |c_1|$$
$$|b_2| \geq |a_2| + |c_2|$$
$$|c_3| \geq |a_3| + |b_3|$$

where, $>$ sign should be valid for at least one row.

We explain the procedure of this method by taking suitable example.

Example 4.15 Solve the following system of equations, by relaxation method.

$$10x - 2y - 3z = 205, -2x + 10y - 2z = 154, -2x - y + 10z = 120$$

Solution:

Step 1: Check the convergence criteria. If system does not satisfy the convergence criteria then rearrange the equations such that convergence criteria is satisfied. In our case,

$$|10| \geq |-2| + |-3|$$
$$|10| \geq |-2| + |-2|$$
$$|10| \geq |-2| + |-1|$$

The system of equations is diagonally dominant. Hence, convergence criteria is satisfied.

Step 2:   Let the residuals R_1, R_2 and R_3 be defined as

$$R_1 = a_1 x + b_1 y + c_1 z - d_1$$
$$R_2 = a_2 x + b_2 y + c_2 z - d_2$$
$$R_3 = a_3 x + b_3 y + c_3 z - d_3$$

In our case, let

$$R_1 = 10x - 2y - 3z - 205$$
$$R_2 = -2x + 10y - 2z - 154$$
$$R_3 = -2x - y + 10z - 120$$

Step 3:   Prepare following initial operation table.

Operation	Δx	Δy	Δz	ΔR_1	ΔR_2	ΔR_3
O_1	1	0	0	a_1	a_2	a_3
O_2	0	1	0	b_1	b_2	b_3
O_3	0	0	1	c_1	c_2	c_3

This table shows the effect on residuals R_1, R_2 and R_3 when x is increased by 1, keeping y and z constant, calling this operator by O_1 and similarly for y and z. In our case,

Operation	Δx	Δy	Δz	ΔR_1	ΔR_2	ΔR_3
O_1	1	0	0	10	-2	-2
O_2	0	1	0	-2	10	-1
O_3	0	0	1	-3	-2	10

Step 4:   We first start with initial values $x = y = z = 0$ and find the corresponding values of residuals.

In our case, if we take $x = y = z = 0$ then $R_1 = -205, R_2 = -154, R_3 = -120$

Step 5:   Choose the absolute maximum residue and try to relax it by applying suitable increment.It is clear that at any stage we should neither over relax nor under relax.

Step 6:   The increment is given by taking the ratio of highest residue and the highest diagonal element circled in the operation table. If the values of highest residue and highest diagonal element are of the same sign, we give a negative sign for the increment and if both values are of opposite sign, we give a positive sign for the increment.

For example in the first row of table 4.1, the absolute highest residue R_1 is -205 (-ve sign) and in operation table corresponding entry is 10 (+ve sign) so the increment is $\frac{205}{10} = 21$.

Step 7:   Using the increment obtained in step 6, we get the new values of R_1, R_2 and R_3. At the end of stage 1,the increments of x, y ,z are added to the initial approximations.

For example, in table 4.1, we have seen that the increment is 21. So, multiply 21 by the first row of operation table we get

Operation	Δx	Δy	Δz	ΔR_1	ΔR_2	ΔR_3
21 O_1	21	0	0	(210)	-42	-42

Add these values to the corresponding values of x, y, z, R_1, R_2 and R_3 of table 4.1.

Step 8: Repeat the above steps to minimize the value of residuals. If the ratio obtained in step 6 will be less than 0.5 then we have to give fractional increments to x, y, z which will be tedious. To improve the solution, we multiply the approximations of x, y, z and corresponding residues by 10, so that, the units represent the first decimal place.

Continue the same steps from step 5 till the solution to the desired accuracy is obtained. Now, from step 5 onwards the example is explained in table 4.1.

Table 4.1 Remaining Steps of the Method

Initial Stage	x	y	z	R_1	R_2	R_3
	0	0	0	-205	-154	-120
21 O_1	21	0	0	5	-196	-162
20 O_2	0	20	0	-35	4	-182
18 O_3	0	0	18	-89	-32	-2
9 O_1	9	0	0	1	-50	-20
5 O_2	0	5	0	-9	0	-25
3 O_3	0	0	3	-18	-6	5
1 O_1	1	0	0	-8	-8	3
1 O_1	1	0	0	8	-10	1
1 O_2	0	1	0	6	0	0
End of Stage 1	32	26	21	6	0	0

Hence, the solution is $x = 32$, $y = 26$ and $z = 21$

Example 4.16 Solve the following system of equations by relaxation method, correct to one place of decimal.

$$8x - 7y + 4z = 32, \quad 2x + 5y - 2z = 17, \quad -2x + 3y + 7z = 19$$

Remark: In such type of example, where coefficients are nearly equal, ordinary relaxation method is not suitable. In such cases, group relaxation method is applied. Using the ordinary operation table, the group operation table will be constructed, in which combinations of increments will be chosen.

Solution: The system is diagonally dominant. Therefore, convergence criteria is satisfied. The residuals are given by

$$R_1 = 8x - 7y + 4z - 32$$
$$R_2 = 2x + 5y - 2z - 17$$
$$R_3 = -2x + 3y + 7z - 19$$

The operation table is

Operation	Δx	Δy	Δz	ΔR_1	ΔR_2	ΔR_3
O_1	1	0	0	8	2	-2
O_2	0	1	0	-7	5	3
O_3	0	0	1	4	-2	7

The group operation table is

Operation	Δx	Δy	Δz	ΔR_1	ΔR_2	ΔR_3
O_1	1	0	0	8	2	-2
O_2	1	1	0	1	7	1
O_3	0	1	1	-3	3	10

The relaxation procedure is given in the table 4.3.

Table 4.3 Relaxation Procedure

Initial Stage	x	y	z	R_1	R_2	R_3
	0	0	0	-32	-17	-19
$4O_1$	4	0	0	0	-9	-27
$3O_3$	0	3	3	-9	0	3
$1O_1$	1	0	0	-1	2	1
End of Stage 1	5	3	3	-1	2	1
Start of Stage 2	$10x$	$10y$	$10z$	$10R_1$	$10R_2$	$10R_3$
	50	30	30	-10	20	10
$-3O_2$	-3	-3	0	-13	-1	7
$2O_1$	2	0	0	3	3	3
End of Stage 2	49	27	30	3	3	3
Start of Stage 3	$100x$	$100y$	$100z$	$100R_1$	$100R_2$	$100R_3$
	490	270	300	30	30	30
$-4O_2$	-4	-4	0	-26	2	-26
$3O_3$	0	3	3	-35	11	4
$4O_1$	4	0	0	-3	19	-4
$-3O_2$	-3	-3	0	-6	-2	-7
$1O_3$	0	1	1	-9	1	3
$1O_1$	1	0	0	-1	3	1
End of Stage 3	488	267	304	-1	3	1

$100x = 488$, $100y = 267$ and $100z = 304$

Hence, the solution correct to two places of decimal is $x = 4.88$, $y = 2.67$ and $z = 3.04$. Therefore, the solution correct to one place of decimal is $x = 4.8$, $y = 2.7$ and $z = 3.0$.

4.3.3   Ill – Conditioned System of Equations

The solution of some system of linear equations are more sensitive to round – off error than others. Therefore, they create problems during computation of the solution. In such system, if we perform a small change in one of the values of the coefficient matrix or any right hand side vector causes a large change in the solution. Such systems are known as ill – conditioned. On the other hand, a system is well – conditioned if we perform small changes in the coefficients also cause small changes in the solution. In practical applications we often encountered such type of ill – conditioned systems.

Example 4.17 The system

$$7x + 5y = 6$$
$$7x + 5.02y = 6.02$$

has the solution $x = 0.14$ and $y = 1.00$. Now, consider small changes in the coefficients as

$$7.01x + 5y = 6$$
$$7x + 5.02y = 6.05$$

Then the solution of the new system is $x = -0.68$ and $y = 2.16$. Therefore, the given system is ill – conditioned.

Ill – conditioned system can be generally seen by calculating the value of the determinant of coefficient matrix A in the system Ax = B. The quantity K(A) defined by $K(A) = \|A\|.\|A^{-1}\|$ where A is non – singular and $\|A\|$ is the norm of matrix A, gives a measure of the condition of the matrix. K(A) is called the condition number of the matrix A.

When the condition number K(A) becomes large, the system is considered as being ill – conditioned. Matrices with condition numbers near 1 are said to be well – conditioned.

Example 4.18 Consider

$$A = \begin{bmatrix} 5 & 3 \\ 5 & 3.01 \end{bmatrix} \text{ then } A^{-1} = \begin{bmatrix} 60.20 & -60.00 \\ -100.00 & 100.00 \end{bmatrix}$$

Taking the Euclidean norm, we have $\|A\| = 8.2499$ and $\|A^{-1}\| = 164.9971$. Hence, $K(A) = \|A\|.\|A^{-1}\| = 1361.2096$ which is very large value. Therefore, A is ill- conditioned.

Example 4.19 Consider

$$A = \begin{bmatrix} 0.5 & 0.5 \\ 0.3 & -0.2 \end{bmatrix} \text{ then } A^{-1} = \begin{bmatrix} 0.80 & 2.00 \\ 1.20 & -2.00 \end{bmatrix}$$

Taking the Euclidean norm, we have $\|A\| = 0.7937$ and $\|A^{-1}\| = 3.1749$. Hence, $K(A) = \|A\|.\|A^{-1}\| = 2.5199$ which is very small. Therefore, A is well conditioned.

Remark: Euclidean norm of matrix A is defined as
$$E(A) = \|A\|_2 = (\Sigma_{i=1,j=1}^{n} |a_{ij}|^2)^{\frac{1}{2}}$$
For example, for 2 ×2 matrix, $E(A) = \|A\|_2 = \sqrt{a_{11}^2 + a_{12}^2 + a_{21}^2 + a_{22}^2}$

4.3.4   Method for Ill – Conditioned System of Equations

Consider the system of equations

$$a_1x + b_1y + c_1z = d_1$$
$$a_2x + b_2y + c_2z = d_2 \quad\quad .... (4.3.25)$$
$$a_3x + b_3y + c_3z = d_3$$

Let x', y', z' be an approximate solution. Substituting these values on the LHS of Eq. (4.3.25) we get the new values of d_1, d_2, d_3 say d_1', d_2', d_3'. Thus, the new system of equations is

$$a_1x' + b_1y' + c_1z' = d_1'$$
$$a_2x' + b_2y' + c_2z' = d_2' \quad\quad .... (4.3.26)$$
$$a_3x' + b_3y' + c_3z' = d_3'$$

Subtracting Eq. (4.3.26) from Eq. (4.3.25) we get,

$$a_1e_x + b_1e_y + c_1e_z = p_1$$
$$a_2e_x + b_2e_y + c_2e_z = p_2 \quad\quad .... (4.3.27)$$
$$a_3e_x + b_3e_y + c_3e_z = p_3$$

where, $e_x = x - x', e_y = y - y'$ and $e_z = z - z'$ and $p_i = d_i - d_i'$. Solve Eq. (4.3.27) for e_x, e_y, e_z. Since $e_x = x - x', e_y = y - y'$ and $e_z = z - z'$ we have $x = e_x + x', y = e_y + y'$ and $z = e_z + z'$ which is a better approximation for x, y and z respectively. Repeat the procedure to improve the solution to the desired accuracy.

Example 4.20   Improve the solution of

$$x + 4y + 7z = 5$$
$$2x + 5y + 8z = 7$$
$$3x + 6y + 9.1z = 9.1$$

by iterative method whose approximate solution is given by $x = 1.8, y = -1.2, z = 1$.

Solution: Given system of equations is

$$x + 4y + 7z = 5$$
$$2x + 5y + 8z = 7$$
$$3x + 6y + 9.1z = 9.1$$

Substitute value of $x = 1.8, y = -1.2, z = 1$ and the new approximation is

$$x' + 4y' + 7z' = 4$$
$$2x' + 5y' + 8z' = 5.6$$
$$3x' + 6y' + 9.1z' = 7.3$$

Then Eq. (4.3.26) is

$$e_x + 4e_y + 7e_z = 1$$
$$2e_x + 5e_y + 8e_z = 1.4$$
$$3e_x + 6e_y + 9.1e_z = 1.8$$

The solution is $e_x = 0.2, e_y = 0.2$ and $e_z = 0$. Hence, the new approximation is $x = 2, y = -1, z = 1$. With the new values of x, y, z and repeating the above steps $e_x = 0.00, e_y = 0.00$ and $e_z = 0.00$. Thus, $x = 2, y = -1, z = 1$ is the required solution.

4.4   EIGEN VALUES AND EIGEN VECTORES

The eigen value problem has wide range of applications in mathematics, physics, biology, sociology, economics and statistics. This problem plays an important role in the study of ordinary differential equations, matrices and analyzing growth models of population.

Definition 4.2   Let A be a square matrix of order $n \times n$. The number λ is said to be an *eigen value of A* if there exists a non-zero vector X of order n such that
$$A\,X = \lambda\,X, \quad X \neq 0 \qquad\qquad .... (4.4.1)$$
In this case, non-zero vector X is called an *eigen vector of A* corresponding to λ. Eq. (4.4.1) can be written as $A\,X = \lambda I\,X$ or $A\,X - \lambda I\,X = 0$ or
$$[A - \lambda I\,]X = 0 \qquad\qquad .... (4.4.2)$$
Where, I is the $n \times n$ identity matrix. In order for a non-zero vector X to satisfy this equation, $A - \lambda I$ must be singular, that is, $|A - \lambda I| = 0$. Therefore, if Eq. (4.4.2) can be re – written in a set of homogeneous linear equations form as

$$(a_{11} - \lambda)x_1 + a_{12}x_2 + \ldots\ldots + a_{1n}x_n = 0$$
$$a_{21}x_1 + (a_{22}-\lambda)\,x_2 + \ldots\ldots + a_{2n}x_n = 0$$
$$\cdots \quad \cdots \quad \cdots \quad \cdots \quad \cdots \quad \cdots \qquad .... (4.4.3)$$
$$a_{n1}x_1 + a_{n2}x_2 + \ldots\ldots + (a_{nn}-\lambda)x_n = 0$$

then $|A - \lambda I| = \begin{vmatrix} a_{11} - \lambda & a_{12} & a_{13} & \cdots & \cdots & a_{1n} \\ a_{21} & a_{22} - \lambda & a_{23} & \cdots & \cdots & a_{2n} \\ \cdots & \cdots & \cdots & \cdots & \cdots & \cdots \\ \cdots & \cdots & \cdots & \cdots & \cdots & \cdots \\ a_{n1} & a_{n2} & a_{n3} & \cdots & \cdots & a_{nn} - \lambda \end{vmatrix} = 0,$

which is called the characteristic equation of the matrix A. The polynomial, say $P(\lambda) = |A - \lambda I|$ is called the characteristic polynomial of A. The eigen values λ_i of A are simply the roots of the characteristic polynomial of A, which are distinct or repeated. If we substitute the values of λ_i in Eq. (4.4.1) we get corresponding eigen vectors. For each eigen value λ_i, there exists at least one corresponding eigen vector X_i such that $AX_i = \lambda_i X_i$, $i = 1,2,3, ..., n$.

The set of all eigenvalues, λ_i, of matrix A is called the *spectrum* of A and the largest of $|\lambda_i|$ is called the *spectral radius* of matrix A.

Remark: Eigen values and eigen vectors can be complex – valued as well as real-valued.

- For higher order matrices, eigen values and eigen vectors are found using other techniques.
- For each eigen value, we find eigen vector X by solving the characteristic equation $(A - \lambda I)X = 0$. The set of all vectors X satisfying $A\,X = \lambda\,X$ is called the *eigenspace of A* corresponding to λ.
- **Cayley – Hamilton theorem:** Every square matrix satisfies its own characteristic equation.
- The multiplicity of a eigenvalue to the eigen polynomial is equal to the number of linearly independent eigenvectors corresponding to this eigenvalue.
- The linearly independent eigenvectors are orthogonal to each other.

Properties of Eigen Values

Some important properties of eigen values are given below:

- The sum of the eigen values of a matrix A, is the sum of the elements of its principal diagonal. The sum of the entries of the principal diagonal is called the trace of A.

  i.e. $\lambda_1 + \lambda_2 + \lambda_3 + ... + \lambda_n = trace = a_{11} + a_{22} + ... + a_{nn}$

- If λ is an eigen value of a matrix A, then $\frac{1}{\lambda}$ is the eigen value of A^{-1}.

- For orthogonal matrix, if λ is an eigen value, then $\frac{1}{\lambda}$ is also its eigen value.

- If $\lambda_1, \lambda_2, \lambda_3, ... , \lambda_n$ are the eigen values of a matrix A, then A^n has the eigen values $\lambda_1^n, \lambda_2^n, \lambda_3^n, ... , \lambda_n^n$, where n is the positive integer.

Definition 4.3   An eigenvector V is said to be *normalized* if the coordinate of largest magnitude is equal to unity. (i.e. the largest co-ordinate in the vector V is the number 1)

Example 4.21   Find the eigen values and eigen vectors of the matrix

$$\begin{bmatrix} 3 & -1 & 1 \\ -1 & 5 & -1 \\ 1 & -1 & 3 \end{bmatrix}$$

Solution: The characteristic equation is

$$|A - \lambda I| = \begin{vmatrix} 3-\lambda & -1 & 1 \\ -1 & 5-\lambda & -1 \\ 1 & -1 & 3-\lambda \end{vmatrix} = -\lambda^3 + 11\lambda^2 - 36\lambda + 36 = 0$$

After solving this equation, the eigen values of A are $\lambda = 6, 2, 3$. If the corresponding eigenvectors are x_1, x_2 and x_3, we have

$$[A - \lambda I]X = \begin{bmatrix} 3-\lambda & -1 & 1 \\ -1 & 5-\lambda & -1 \\ 1 & -1 & 3-\lambda \end{bmatrix} \begin{bmatrix} x_1 \\ x_2 \\ x_3 \end{bmatrix} = \begin{bmatrix} 0 \\ 0 \\ 0 \end{bmatrix} \quad .... \text{(i)}$$

(i)   Puttting $\lambda = 6$ in (i) we have,

Therefore, $$\begin{bmatrix} -3 & -1 & 1 \\ -1 & -1 & -1 \\ 1 & -1 & -3 \end{bmatrix} \begin{bmatrix} x_1 \\ x_2 \\ x_3 \end{bmatrix} = \begin{bmatrix} 0 \\ 0 \\ 0 \end{bmatrix}$$

$$-3x_1 - x_2 + x_3 = 0 ,$$
$$-x_1 - x_2 - x_3 = 0$$
$$x_1 - x_2 - 3x_3 = 0$$

From the first two equations we get, $\dfrac{x_1}{3-1} = \dfrac{x_2}{-1-3} = \dfrac{x_3}{1+1}$ or $\dfrac{x_1}{2} = \dfrac{x_2}{-4} = \dfrac{x_3}{2}$

giving eigen vector $(1, -2, 1)^T$ or $\begin{bmatrix} 1 \\ -2 \\ 1 \end{bmatrix}$

(ii)   Puttting $\lambda = 2$ in (i) we have,

Therefore,
$$\begin{bmatrix} 1 & -1 & 1 \\ -1 & 3 & -1 \\ 1 & -1 & 1 \end{bmatrix} \begin{bmatrix} x_1 \\ x_2 \\ x_3 \end{bmatrix} = \begin{bmatrix} 0 \\ 0 \\ 0 \end{bmatrix}$$

$$x_1 - x_2 + x_3 = 0$$
$$-x_1 + 3x_2 - x_3 = 0$$
$$x_1 - x_2 + x_3 = 0$$

Since first and third equations are same, we have

$$x_1 - x_2 + x_3 = 0$$
$$-x_1 + 3x_2 - x_3 = 0$$

Hence, $\frac{x_1}{1-3} = \frac{x_2}{-1+1} = \frac{x_3}{3-1}$ or $\frac{x_1}{-2} = \frac{x_2}{0} = \frac{x_3}{2}$ giving eigen vector $(-1, 0, 1)^T$

(iii)   Puttting $\lambda = 3$ in (i) we have,

Therefore,
$$\begin{bmatrix} 0 & -1 & 1 \\ -1 & 2 & -1 \\ 1 & -1 & 0 \end{bmatrix} \begin{bmatrix} x_1 \\ x_2 \\ x_3 \end{bmatrix} = \begin{bmatrix} 0 \\ 0 \\ 0 \end{bmatrix}$$

$$-x_2 + x_3 = 0 \ ,$$
$$-x_1 + 2x_2 - x_3 = 0$$
$$x_1 - x_2 = 0$$

From first and third equations it is clear that $x_1 = x_2 = x_3$
Hence, corresponding eigen vector is $(1, 1, 1)^T$.

Example 4.22 Find the eigenvalues and eigenvectors of the matrix

$$\begin{bmatrix} -2 & 2 & -3 \\ 2 & 1 & -6 \\ -1 & -2 & 0 \end{bmatrix}$$

Solution: The characteristic equation is

$$|A - \lambda I| = \begin{vmatrix} -2 - \lambda & 2 & -3 \\ 2 & 1 - \lambda & -6 \\ -1 & -2 & -\lambda \end{vmatrix} = \lambda^3 - 3\lambda^2 - 17\lambda + 3 = 0$$

After solving this equation, the eigen values of A are $\lambda = 5, -3, -3$. If the corresponding eigenvectors are x, y and z, we have

$$[A - \lambda I]X = \begin{bmatrix} -2 - \lambda & 2 & -3 \\ 2 & 1 - \lambda & -6 \\ -1 & -2 & -\lambda \end{bmatrix} \begin{bmatrix} x \\ y \\ z \end{bmatrix} = \begin{bmatrix} 0 \\ 0 \\ 0 \end{bmatrix} \quad \text{......... (i)}$$

(i)   Puttting $\lambda = 5$ in (i) we have,

Therefore,
$$\begin{bmatrix} -7 & 2 & -3 \\ 2 & -4 & -6 \\ -1 & -2 & -5 \end{bmatrix} \begin{bmatrix} x \\ y \\ z \end{bmatrix} = \begin{bmatrix} 0 \\ 0 \\ 0 \end{bmatrix}$$

$$-7x + 2y - 3z = 0 \ ,$$
$$2x - 4y - 6z = 0$$
$$-x - 2y - 5z = 0$$

Hence, $\frac{x}{20-12} = \frac{y}{6+10} = \frac{z}{-4-4}$ or $\frac{x}{8} = \frac{y}{16} = \frac{z}{-8}$ giving corresponding eigen vector $(1, 2, -1)^T$.

(ii)   Puttting $\lambda = -3$ in (i) we have,

Therefore,
$$\begin{bmatrix} 1 & 2 & -3 \\ 2 & 4 & -6 \\ -1 & -2 & 3 \end{bmatrix}\begin{bmatrix} x \\ y \\ z \end{bmatrix} = \begin{bmatrix} 0 \\ 0 \\ 0 \end{bmatrix}$$

$$x + 2y - 3z = 0 ,$$
$$2x + 4y - 6z = 0$$
$$-x - 2y + 3z = 0$$

We get only one independent equation $x + 2y - 3z = 0$

Choosing $x = 0$ we have $2y = 3z$. Therefore, $\frac{x}{0} = \frac{y}{3} = \frac{z}{2}$ giving the eigen vector $(0, 3, 2)^T$. Choosing $z = 0$, we have $x = 2y$. Therefore, $\frac{x}{2} = \frac{y}{1} = \frac{z}{0}$ giving the eigen vector $(2, 1, 0)^T$. Any other eigenvector corresponding to $\lambda = -3$ will be a linear combination of $(0, 3, 2)^T$ and $(2, 1, 0)^T$.

4.5   POWER METHOD FOR APPROXIMATING EIGENVALUES

The eigenvalues of an $n \times n$ matrix A are obtained by solving its characteristic equation

$$\lambda^n + P_1\lambda^{n-1} + P_2\lambda^{n-2} + \dots\dots + P_n = 0$$

For large value of n, it is very difficult to solve this type of polynomial equations. Moreover, numerical techniques are very sensitive to rounding errors in finding approximating roots of high degree of polynomial equations.In this section, we look at an alternative method, known as power method, for approximating eigen values.This method is used to find the dominant eigenvalue of an $n \times n$ matrix.

Definition 4.4 Let $\lambda_1, \lambda_2, \lambda_3, \dots , \lambda_n$ be the eigenvalues of an $n \times n$ matrix A. If $|\lambda_1| > |\lambda_2| \geq \dots \geq |\lambda_n|$ then λ_1 is called the *dominant eigenvalue* of A. The eigenvectors corresponding to λ_1 are called *dominant eigen vectors* of A.

Like the Jacobi and Gauss – Seidel methods, the power method for approximating eigen values are iterative in nature. If X_0 is any vector then it can be written as a linear combination of n linearly independent eigenvectors $V_1, V_2, V_3, \dots , V_n$ corresponding to $\lambda_1, \lambda_2, \lambda_3, \dots , \lambda_n$, respectively.

Thus, we have $X_0 = c_1 V_1 + c_2 V_2 + \dots\dots + c_n V_n$ .... (4.5.1)

But we know $AV_i = \lambda_i V_i$ .... (4.5.2)

Now,   from Eq. (4.5.1) we have $AX_0 = c_1 A V_1 + c_2 A V_2 + \dots\dots + c_n AV_n$

.... (4.5.3)

Substituting Eq. (4.5.2) in Eq. (4.5.3) we have,

$$AX_0 = c_1 \lambda_1 V_1 + c_2\lambda_2 V_2 + \dots\dots + c_n\lambda_n V_n$$

$$A^2 X_0 = c_1 \lambda_1{}^2 V_1 + c_2 \lambda_2{}^2 V_2 + \dots \dots + c_n \lambda_n{}^2 V_n$$

$$\dots \qquad \dots \qquad \dots \qquad \dots$$

$$A^n X_0 = c_1 \lambda_1{}^n V_1 + c_2 \lambda_2{}^n V_2 + \dots \dots + c_n \lambda_n{}^n V_n$$

If we divide the last equation by $\lambda_1{}^n$, we have

$$\frac{1}{\lambda_1{}^n} A^n X_0 = c_1 V_1 + c_2 \left(\frac{\lambda_2}{\lambda_1}\right)^n V_2 + \dots \dots + c_n \left(\frac{\lambda_n}{\lambda_1}\right)^n V_n \qquad \dots \dots (4.5.4)$$

For large value of n, the terms $\left(\frac{\lambda_2}{\lambda_1}\right)^n, \dots \dots, \left(\frac{\lambda_n}{\lambda_1}\right)^n$ get converge to zero as

$|\lambda_2 / \lambda_1| < 1, \dots \dots, |\lambda_n / \lambda_1| < 1$. Therefore, for large value of n,

$$\frac{1}{\lambda_1{}^n} A^n X_0 = c_1 V_1 \qquad \dots \dots (4.5.5)$$

As long as $c_1 \neq 0$, Eq. (4.5.5) is the eigenvector corresponding to λ_1.
Since $n + 1 > n$, we have

$$\frac{1}{\lambda_1{}^{n+1}} A^{n+1} X_0 = c_1 V_1 \qquad \dots \dots (4.5.6)$$

Taking dot product of both the sides of Eq. (4.5.5) and Eq. (4.5.6) with any P which is not orthogonal to V_1, we have

$$\frac{1}{\lambda_1{}^n} (A^n X_0 . P) = c_1 V_1 . P$$

$$\frac{1}{\lambda_1{}^{n+1}} (A^{n+1} X_0 . P) = c_1 V_1 . P$$

Therefore, $\qquad \frac{1}{\lambda_1{}^{n+1}} (A^{n+1} X_0 . P) = \frac{1}{\lambda_1{}^n} (A^n X_0 . P) \neq 0$

So, $\qquad \frac{(A^{n+1} X_0 . P)}{(A^n X_0 . P)} = \frac{\lambda_1{}^{n+1}}{\lambda_1{}^n} = \lambda_1$

The rate of convergence is determined by the quotient $\frac{\lambda_2}{\lambda_1}$. If $\frac{\lambda_2}{\lambda_1}$ is small then the convergence will be faster.

Remarks: To find the numerically smallest eigen value of A, obtain the numerically largest eigen value of A^{-1} and take its reciprocal.
- The eigen values of A – PI are $\lambda_i - P$, where λ_i are the eigen values of A.
- To find the numerically smallest eigen value of A, obtain the dominant eigen value λ_1 of A and then find B = $A - \lambda_1 I$ and find the dominant eigen value of B. Then, the smallest eigen value of A is equal to the dominant eigen value of B + λ_1. This method to find the smallest eigenvalue valid, only if the eigenvalues of A are rational.

Example 4.23 Using power method, find the numerically largest eigen value

of $\qquad A = \begin{bmatrix} 10 & 2 & 1 \\ 2 & 10 & 1 \\ 2 & 1 & 10 \end{bmatrix}$ and the corresponding eigen vector.

Solution: Let $X_1 = \begin{bmatrix} 1 \\ 0 \\ 0 \end{bmatrix}$ be an arbitrary initial eigen vector.

$$AX_1 = \begin{bmatrix} 10 & 2 & 1 \\ 2 & 10 & 1 \\ 2 & 1 & 10 \end{bmatrix} \begin{bmatrix} 1 \\ 0 \\ 0 \end{bmatrix} = \begin{bmatrix} 10 \\ 2 \\ 2 \end{bmatrix} = 10 \begin{bmatrix} 1 \\ 0.2 \\ 0.2 \end{bmatrix} = 10X_2$$

$$AX_2 = \begin{bmatrix} 10 & 2 & 1 \\ 2 & 10 & 1 \\ 2 & 1 & 10 \end{bmatrix} \begin{bmatrix} 1 \\ 0.2 \\ 0.2 \end{bmatrix} = \begin{bmatrix} 10.6 \\ 4.2 \\ 4.2 \end{bmatrix} = 10.6 \begin{bmatrix} 1 \\ 0.3962 \\ 0.3962 \end{bmatrix} = 10.6X_3$$

$$AX_3 = \begin{bmatrix} 10 & 2 & 1 \\ 2 & 10 & 1 \\ 2 & 1 & 10 \end{bmatrix} \begin{bmatrix} 1 \\ 0.3962 \\ 0.3962 \end{bmatrix} = \begin{bmatrix} 11.1886 \\ 6.3582 \\ 6.3582 \end{bmatrix} = 11.1886 \begin{bmatrix} 1 \\ 0.5683 \\ 0.5683 \end{bmatrix}$$
$$= 11.1886X_4$$

$$AX_4 = \begin{bmatrix} 10 & 2 & 1 \\ 2 & 10 & 1 \\ 2 & 1 & 10 \end{bmatrix} \begin{bmatrix} 1 \\ 0.5683 \\ 0.5683 \end{bmatrix} = \begin{bmatrix} 11.7049 \\ 8.2513 \\ 8.2513 \end{bmatrix} = 11.7049 \begin{bmatrix} 1 \\ 0.7049 \\ 0.7049 \end{bmatrix}$$
$$= 11.7049X_5$$

$$AX_5 = \begin{bmatrix} 10 & 2 & 1 \\ 2 & 10 & 1 \\ 2 & 1 & 10 \end{bmatrix} \begin{bmatrix} 1 \\ 0.7049 \\ 0.7049 \end{bmatrix} = \begin{bmatrix} 12.1147 \\ 9.7539 \\ 9.7539 \end{bmatrix} = 12.1147 \begin{bmatrix} 1 \\ 0.8051 \\ 0.8051 \end{bmatrix}$$
$$= 12.1147X_6$$

$$AX_6 = \begin{bmatrix} 10 & 2 & 1 \\ 2 & 10 & 1 \\ 2 & 1 & 10 \end{bmatrix} \begin{bmatrix} 1 \\ 0.8051 \\ 0.8051 \end{bmatrix} = \begin{bmatrix} 12.4153 \\ 10.8561 \\ 10.8561 \end{bmatrix} = 12.4153 \begin{bmatrix} 1 \\ 0.8744 \\ 0.8744 \end{bmatrix}$$
$$= 12.4153X_7$$

$$AX_7 = \begin{bmatrix} 10 & 2 & 1 \\ 2 & 10 & 1 \\ 2 & 1 & 10 \end{bmatrix} \begin{bmatrix} 1 \\ 0.8744 \\ 0.8744 \end{bmatrix} = \begin{bmatrix} 12.6232 \\ 11.6184 \\ 11.6184 \end{bmatrix} = 12.6232 \begin{bmatrix} 1 \\ 0.9204 \\ 0.9204 \end{bmatrix}$$
$$= 12.6232X_8$$

$$AX_8 = \begin{bmatrix} 10 & 2 & 1 \\ 2 & 10 & 1 \\ 2 & 1 & 10 \end{bmatrix} \begin{bmatrix} 1 \\ 0.9204 \\ 0.9204 \end{bmatrix} = \begin{bmatrix} 12.7612 \\ 12.1244 \\ 12.1244 \end{bmatrix} = 12.7612 \begin{bmatrix} 1 \\ 0.9501 \\ 0.9501 \end{bmatrix}$$
$$= 12.7612X_9$$

$$AX_9 = \begin{bmatrix} 10 & 2 & 1 \\ 2 & 10 & 1 \\ 2 & 1 & 10 \end{bmatrix} \begin{bmatrix} 1 \\ 0.9501 \\ 0.9501 \end{bmatrix} = \begin{bmatrix} 12.8503 \\ 12.4511 \\ 12.4511 \end{bmatrix} = 12.8503 \begin{bmatrix} 1 \\ 0.9689 \\ 0.9689 \end{bmatrix}$$
$$= 12.8503X_{10}$$

$$AX_{10} = \begin{bmatrix} 10 & 2 & 1 \\ 2 & 10 & 1 \\ 2 & 1 & 10 \end{bmatrix} \begin{bmatrix} 1 \\ 0.9689 \\ 0.9689 \end{bmatrix} = \begin{bmatrix} 12.9067 \\ 12.6579 \\ 12.6579 \end{bmatrix} = 12.9067 \begin{bmatrix} 1 \\ 0.9807 \\ 0.9807 \end{bmatrix}$$
$$= 12.9067X_{11}$$

$$AX_{11} = \begin{bmatrix} 10 & 2 & 1 \\ 2 & 10 & 1 \\ 2 & 1 & 10 \end{bmatrix} \begin{bmatrix} 1 \\ 0.9807 \\ 0.9807 \end{bmatrix} = \begin{bmatrix} 12.9421 \\ 12.7877 \\ 12.7877 \end{bmatrix} = 12.9421 \begin{bmatrix} 1 \\ 0.9881 \\ 0.9881 \end{bmatrix}$$
$$= 12.9421 X_{12}$$

$$AX_{12} = \begin{bmatrix} 10 & 2 & 1 \\ 2 & 10 & 1 \\ 2 & 1 & 10 \end{bmatrix} \begin{bmatrix} 1 \\ 0.9881 \\ 0.9881 \end{bmatrix} = \begin{bmatrix} 12.9643 \\ 12.8691 \\ 12.8691 \end{bmatrix} = 12.9643 \begin{bmatrix} 1 \\ 0.9927 \\ 0.9927 \end{bmatrix}$$
$$= 12.9643 X_{13}$$

$$AX_{13} = \begin{bmatrix} 10 & 2 & 1 \\ 2 & 10 & 1 \\ 2 & 1 & 10 \end{bmatrix} \begin{bmatrix} 1 \\ 0.9927 \\ 0.9927 \end{bmatrix} = \begin{bmatrix} 12.9781 \\ 12.9197 \\ 12.9197 \end{bmatrix} = 12.9781 \begin{bmatrix} 1 \\ 0.9955 \\ 0.9955 \end{bmatrix}$$
$$= 12.9781 X_{14}$$

$$AX_{14} = \begin{bmatrix} 10 & 2 & 1 \\ 2 & 10 & 1 \\ 2 & 1 & 10 \end{bmatrix} \begin{bmatrix} 1 \\ 0.9955 \\ 0.9955 \end{bmatrix} = \begin{bmatrix} 12.9865 \\ 12.9505 \\ 12.9505 \end{bmatrix} = 12.9865 \begin{bmatrix} 1 \\ 0.9972 \\ 0.9972 \end{bmatrix}$$
$$= 12.9865 X_{15}$$

$$AX_{15} = \begin{bmatrix} 10 & 2 & 1 \\ 2 & 10 & 1 \\ 2 & 1 & 10 \end{bmatrix} \begin{bmatrix} 1 \\ 0.9972 \\ 0.9972 \end{bmatrix} = \begin{bmatrix} 12.9916 \\ 12.9692 \\ 12.9692 \end{bmatrix} = 12.9916 \begin{bmatrix} 1 \\ 0.9983 \\ 0.9983 \end{bmatrix}$$
$$= 12.9916 X_{16}$$

If we continue with the same procedure we get $\lambda_1 = 13$ and the corresponding eigen vector is $(1, 1, 1)^T$.

Example 4.24 Using power method, find the dominant eigen value of

$$A = \begin{bmatrix} 8 & -6 & 2 \\ -6 & 7 & -4 \\ 2 & -4 & 3 \end{bmatrix}$$

Solution: Let $X_1 = \begin{bmatrix} 1 \\ 0 \\ 0 \end{bmatrix}$ be an arbitrary initial eigen vector.

$$AX_1 = \begin{bmatrix} 8 & -6 & 2 \\ -6 & 7 & -4 \\ 2 & -4 & 3 \end{bmatrix} \begin{bmatrix} 1 \\ 0 \\ 0 \end{bmatrix} = \begin{bmatrix} 8 \\ -6 \\ 2 \end{bmatrix} = 8 \begin{bmatrix} 1 \\ -0.75 \\ 0.25 \end{bmatrix} = 8X_2$$

$$AX_2 = \begin{bmatrix} 8 & -6 & 2 \\ -6 & 7 & -4 \\ 2 & -4 & 3 \end{bmatrix} \begin{bmatrix} 1 \\ -0.75 \\ 0.25 \end{bmatrix} = \begin{bmatrix} 13 \\ -12.25 \\ 5.75 \end{bmatrix} = 13 \begin{bmatrix} 1 \\ -0.9423 \\ 0.4423 \end{bmatrix} = 13X_3$$

$$AX_3 = \begin{bmatrix} 8 & -6 & 2 \\ -6 & 7 & -4 \\ 2 & -4 & 3 \end{bmatrix} \begin{bmatrix} 1 \\ -0.9423 \\ 0.4423 \end{bmatrix} = \begin{bmatrix} 14.5384 \\ -14.3653 \\ 7.0961 \end{bmatrix} = 14.5384 \begin{bmatrix} 1 \\ -0.9881 \\ 0.4881 \end{bmatrix}$$
$$= 14.5384 X_4$$

$$AX_4 = \begin{bmatrix} 8 & -6 & 2 \\ -6 & 7 & -4 \\ 2 & -4 & 3 \end{bmatrix} \begin{bmatrix} 1 \\ -0.9881 \\ 0.4881 \end{bmatrix} = \begin{bmatrix} 14.9048 \\ -14.8691 \\ 7.4167 \end{bmatrix} = 14.9048 \begin{bmatrix} 1 \\ -0.9976 \\ 0.4976 \end{bmatrix}$$
$$= 14.9048 X_5$$

$$AX_5 = \begin{bmatrix} 8 & -6 & 2 \\ -6 & 7 & -4 \\ 2 & -4 & 3 \end{bmatrix} \begin{bmatrix} 1 \\ -0.9976 \\ 0.4976 \end{bmatrix} = \begin{bmatrix} 14.9808 \\ -14.9736 \\ 7.4832 \end{bmatrix} = 14.9808 \begin{bmatrix} 1 \\ -0.9995 \\ 0.4995 \end{bmatrix}$$
$$= 14.9808 X_6$$

$$AX_6 = \begin{bmatrix} 8 & -6 & 2 \\ -6 & 7 & -4 \\ 2 & -4 & 3 \end{bmatrix} \begin{bmatrix} 1 \\ -0.9995 \\ 0.4995 \end{bmatrix} = \begin{bmatrix} 14.996 \\ -14.9945 \\ 7.4965 \end{bmatrix} = 14.996 \begin{bmatrix} 1 \\ -0.9999 \\ 0.4999 \end{bmatrix}$$
$$= 14.996 X_7$$

$$AX_7 = \begin{bmatrix} 8 & -6 & 2 \\ -6 & 7 & -4 \\ 2 & -4 & 3 \end{bmatrix} \begin{bmatrix} 1 \\ -0.9995 \\ 0.4999 \end{bmatrix} = \begin{bmatrix} 14.9968 \\ -14.9961 \\ 7.4977 \end{bmatrix} = 14.9968 \begin{bmatrix} 1 \\ -1 \\ 0.5 \end{bmatrix}$$
$$= 14.9968 X_8$$

Therefore, the dominant eigen value $\lambda_1 = 15$ and the corresponding eigen vector is $(1, -1, 0.5)^T$.

Example 4.25 Using power method, find all the eigen values of

$$A = \begin{bmatrix} 1 & 6 & 1 \\ 1 & 2 & 0 \\ 0 & 0 & 2 \end{bmatrix}$$

Solution: Let $X_1 = \begin{bmatrix} 1 \\ 0 \\ 0 \end{bmatrix}$ be an arbitrary initial eigen vector.

$$AX_1 = \begin{bmatrix} 1 & 6 & 1 \\ 1 & 2 & 0 \\ 0 & 0 & 2 \end{bmatrix} \begin{bmatrix} 1 \\ 0 \\ 0 \end{bmatrix} = \begin{bmatrix} 1 \\ 1 \\ 0 \end{bmatrix} = 1 \begin{bmatrix} 1 \\ 1 \\ 0 \end{bmatrix} = 1X_2$$

$$AX_2 = \begin{bmatrix} 1 & 6 & 1 \\ 1 & 2 & 0 \\ 0 & 0 & 2 \end{bmatrix} \begin{bmatrix} 1 \\ 1 \\ 0 \end{bmatrix} = \begin{bmatrix} 7 \\ 3 \\ 0 \end{bmatrix} = 7 \begin{bmatrix} 1 \\ 0.4286 \\ 0 \end{bmatrix} = 7X_3$$

$$AX_3 = \begin{bmatrix} 1 & 6 & 1 \\ 1 & 2 & 0 \\ 0 & 0 & 2 \end{bmatrix} \begin{bmatrix} 1 \\ 0.4286 \\ 0 \end{bmatrix} = \begin{bmatrix} 3.5716 \\ 1.8572 \\ 0 \end{bmatrix} = 3.5716 \begin{bmatrix} 1 \\ 0.52 \\ 0 \end{bmatrix} = 3.5716 X_4$$

$$AX_4 = \begin{bmatrix} 1 & 6 & 1 \\ 1 & 2 & 0 \\ 0 & 0 & 2 \end{bmatrix} \begin{bmatrix} 1 \\ 0.52 \\ 0 \end{bmatrix} = \begin{bmatrix} 4.12 \\ 2.04 \\ 0 \end{bmatrix} = 4.12 \begin{bmatrix} 1 \\ 0.4951 \\ 0 \end{bmatrix} = 4.12 X_5$$

$$AX_5 = \begin{bmatrix} 1 & 6 & 1 \\ 1 & 2 & 0 \\ 0 & 0 & 2 \end{bmatrix} \begin{bmatrix} 1 \\ 0.4951 \\ 0 \end{bmatrix} = \begin{bmatrix} 3.9706 \\ 1.9902 \\ 0 \end{bmatrix} = 3.9706 \begin{bmatrix} 1 \\ 0.5012 \\ 0 \end{bmatrix} = 3.9706 X_6$$

$$AX_6 = \begin{bmatrix} 1 & 6 & 1 \\ 1 & 2 & 0 \\ 0 & 0 & 2 \end{bmatrix} \begin{bmatrix} 1 \\ 0.5012 \\ 0 \end{bmatrix} = \begin{bmatrix} 4.0072 \\ 2.0024 \\ 0 \end{bmatrix} = 4.0072 \begin{bmatrix} 1 \\ 0.4997 \\ 0 \end{bmatrix} = 4.0072 X_7$$

$$AX_7 = \begin{bmatrix} 1 & 6 & 1 \\ 1 & 2 & 0 \\ 0 & 0 & 2 \end{bmatrix} \begin{bmatrix} 1 \\ 0.4997 \\ 0 \end{bmatrix} = \begin{bmatrix} 3.9982 \\ 1.9994 \\ 0 \end{bmatrix} = 3.9982 \begin{bmatrix} 1 \\ 0.5000 \\ 0 \end{bmatrix} = 3.9982 X_8$$

$$AX_8 = \begin{bmatrix} 1 & 6 & 1 \\ 1 & 2 & 0 \\ 0 & 0 & 2 \end{bmatrix} \begin{bmatrix} 1 \\ 0.5000 \\ 0 \end{bmatrix} = \begin{bmatrix} 4 \\ 2 \\ 0 \end{bmatrix} = 4 \begin{bmatrix} 1 \\ 0.5 \\ 0 \end{bmatrix} = 4 X_9$$

Therefore, the dominant eigen value $\lambda_1 = 4$ and the corresponding eigen vector is $(1, 0.5, 0)^T$.

To find the least eigen value, let $B = A - 4I$ since $\lambda_1 = 4$

Hence, $B = \begin{bmatrix} 1 & 6 & 1 \\ 1 & 2 & 0 \\ 0 & 0 & 2 \end{bmatrix} - \begin{bmatrix} 4 & 0 & 0 \\ 0 & 4 & 0 \\ 0 & 0 & 4 \end{bmatrix} = \begin{bmatrix} -3 & 6 & 1 \\ 1 & -2 & 0 \\ 0 & 0 & -2 \end{bmatrix}$

Now, we will find the dominant eigenvalue of B.

Let $Y_1 = \begin{bmatrix} 1 \\ 0 \\ 0 \end{bmatrix}$ be an arbitrary initial eigen vector.

$$BY_1 = \begin{bmatrix} -3 & 6 & 1 \\ 1 & -2 & 0 \\ 0 & 0 & -2 \end{bmatrix} \begin{bmatrix} 1 \\ 0 \\ 0 \end{bmatrix} = \begin{bmatrix} -3 \\ 1 \\ 0 \end{bmatrix} = -3 \begin{bmatrix} 1 \\ -0.3333 \\ 0 \end{bmatrix} = -3 Y_2$$

$$BY_2 = \begin{bmatrix} -3 & 6 & 1 \\ 1 & -2 & 0 \\ 0 & 0 & -2 \end{bmatrix} \begin{bmatrix} 1 \\ -0.3333 \\ 0 \end{bmatrix} = \begin{bmatrix} -4.9998 \\ 1.6666 \\ 0 \end{bmatrix} = -4.9998 \begin{bmatrix} 1 \\ -0.3333 \\ 0 \end{bmatrix}$$
$$= -4.9998 Y_3$$

$$BY_3 = \begin{bmatrix} -3 & 6 & 1 \\ 1 & -2 & 0 \\ 0 & 0 & -2 \end{bmatrix} \begin{bmatrix} 1 \\ -0.3333 \\ 0 \end{bmatrix} = \begin{bmatrix} -4.9998 \\ 1.6666 \\ 0 \end{bmatrix} = -4.9998 \begin{bmatrix} 1 \\ -0.3333 \\ 0 \end{bmatrix}$$
$$= -4.9998 Y_4$$

Therefore, dominant eigenvalue of B = -5 (after rounding off)

∴ Smallest value of $A = -5 + 4 = -1$

Now, $\lambda_1 + \lambda_2 + \lambda_3$ = Trace = 5

∴ $4 - 1 + \lambda_3 = 5$

∴ $\lambda_3 = 2$

Therefore, eigenvalues are 4, -1, 2.

4.6   PROGRAMS IN C
4.6.1   Program to implement Gauss Elimination method

```
//Gauss Elimination Method
#include <stdio.h>
#include <math.h>
#include <conio.h>
void main()
{
        int num,i,j,k,m;
        float a[20][20],u,sum,x[20];
        clrscr();
        printf("\n\t\t\t :: GUASS-ELIMINATION METHOD :: ");
        printf("\n\t\t\t -----------------------------\n\n");
        printf("\n ENTER THE TOTAL NUMBER OF VARIABLES IN THE GIVEN
        SYSTEM =>");
        scanf("%d",&num);
        m=1;
        printf("\n");
        for(i=0;i<num;i++)
        {
            printf("\n ENTERING THE CO-EFFICIENTS OF EQUATION %d :",i+1);
            printf("\n ~~~~~~~~~~~~~~~~~~~~~~~~~~~~~~~~~~~~~~~~~~~~~~~\n");
                for(j=0;j<=num;j++)
                {
                  if(j!=num)
                  {
                        printf(" ENTER THE CO-EFFICIENT OF x%d =>",j+1);
                        scanf("%f",&a[i][j]);
                  }
                  else
                  {
                  printf(" ENTER THE CO-EFFICIENT OF y%d (VARIABLE OF
                  RIGHT HAND SIDE) =>",m);
                        scanf("%f",&a[i][j]);
                        m++;
                  }
                }

            printf("\n\n");
    }
    for(k=0;k<num-1;k++)
    {
        for(i=k+1;i<=num;i++)
```

```
                {
                        u=a[i][k]/a[k][k];
                        for(j=k;j<=num;j++)
                        {
                                a[i][j]=a[i][j]-u*a[k][j];
                        }
                }
        }
}
printf("\n\n THE MATRIX OF THE CO-EFFICIENTS OF THE SYSTEM OF ");
printf("EQUATIONS IS:\n");
printf(" ~~~~~~~~~~~~~~~~~~~~~~~~~~~~~~~~~~~~~~~~~~~~~~~~~~~~~");
printf("~~~~~~~~~~~~~~~\n");
for(i=0;i<num;i++)
{
        for(j=0;j<=num;j++)
        {
                printf(" %.2f \t",a[i][j]);
        }
        printf("\n");
}
x[num-1]=a[num-1][num]/a[num-1][num-1];
for(i=num-1;i>=0;i--)
{
        sum=0.0;
        for(j=i+1;j<num;j++)
        {
                sum=sum+a[i][j]*x[j];
        }
        x[i]=(a[i][num]-sum)/a[i][i];
}
printf("\n\n THE ROOTS OF THE SYSTEM OF EQUATIONS IS :\n");
printf(" ~~~~~~~~~~~~~~~~~~~~~~~~~~~~~~~~~~~~~~~~~~~~~~~~~\n");

for(i=num-1;i>=0;i--)
{
        printf(" x%d=%.2f \n",i+1,x[i]);
}
getch();  }
```

4.6.2   Program to implement Gauss Elimination method with pivoting
```
//Gauss Elimination Method With Pivoting
#include<stdio.h>
#include<conio.h>
#include<math.h>
```

```c
#include<stdlib.h>
void main()
{
        int Row,i,j,Pos,iCount;
        float Mat[20][20]={0};
        float Element,Max,Temp;
        clrscr();
        printf("\nGauss Elimination Method With Pivoting...\n");
        printf("Enter the total Number of Unknowns  : ");
        scanf("%d",&Row);
        for (i=0; i<Row; i++)
        {
                printf("\nEnter coefficient for Equation %d\n",i+1);
                for (j=0; j<Row+1; j++)
                {
                        printf("Co-efficient x[%d][%d]  : ",i+1,j+1);
                        scanf("%f",&Mat[i][j]);
                }
        }
        printf("\nEntered Equation are :\n");
        for (i=0; i<Row; i++)
        {
                for (j=0; j<Row; j++)
                        printf("%6.2f",Mat[i][j]);
                printf(" | %6.2f\n",Mat[i][j]);
        }
        getch();
        clrscr();
        for (iCount=0; iCount<Row; iCount++)
        {
//Pivoting.................................................................
                Max = Mat[iCount][iCount];
                Pos = iCount;
                for (i=iCount; i<Row; i++)
                {
                        if (Max<Mat[i][iCount])
                                Pos = i;

                }
                if (Pos!=iCount)
                {
                        for (i=0; i<=Row; i++)
                        {
                                Temp = Mat[iCount][i];
```

```
                                        Mat[iCount][i] = Mat[Pos][i];
                                        Mat[Pos][i] = Temp;
                            }
                }
//Pivoting Done.........................................................
printf("\n\nPivoted Matrix...................................................\n");
                for (i=0; i<Row; i++)
                {
                            for (j=0; j<Row; j++)
                                    printf("\t%6.2f",Mat[i][j]);
                            printf(" | %f\n",Mat[i][j]);
                }
                getch();
//Elimination.........................................................
                for (i=iCount+1; i<Row; i++)
                {
                        Element = -Mat[i][iCount]/Mat[iCount][iCount];
                        for (j=iCount; j<Row+1; j++)
                                Mat[i][j] += Element*Mat[iCount][j];
                }
//Elimination Done.........................................................
printf("\n\nIntermediate Matrix...................................................\n");
                for (i=0; i<Row; i++)
                {
                            for (j=0; j<Row; j++)
                                    printf("\t%6.2f",Mat[i][j]);
                            printf(" | %f\n",Mat[i][j]);
                }
                getch();
        }
        for (iCount=Row-1; iCount>=0; iCount--)
        {
                for (i=iCount-1; i>=0; i--)
                {
                        Element = -(Mat[i][iCount]/Mat[iCount][iCount]);
                        for (j=0; j<=Row; j++)
                                Mat[i][j] += Element*Mat[iCount][j];
                }
        printf("\n\nIntermediate Matrix...................................................\n");
                for (i=0; i<Row; i++)
                {
                            for (j=0; j<Row; j++)
                                    printf("\t%6.2f",Mat[i][j]);
```

```
                              printf(" | %f\n",Mat[i][j]);
                    }
                    getch();
          }
printf("\nResulting Matrix......................................................\n");
          for (i=0; i<Row; i++)
          {
                    for (j=0; j<Row; j++)
                              printf("\t%6.2f",Mat[i][j]);
                    printf(" | %f\n",Mat[i][j]);
          }
          clrscr();
          printf("\n\nRoots of are.........\n\n");
          for (i=0; i<Row; i++)
                    printf("%10.5f ",Mat[i][Row]/Mat[i][i]);
          printf("\n");
          return(0);  }
```

4.6.3   Program to implement Gauss Jordan method

```
//Gauss – Jordan Method
#include <stdio.h>
#include <math.h>
#include <conio.h>
void main()
{
          int num,i,j,k,m;
          float a[20][20],u,sum,x[20];
          clrscr();
          printf("\n\t\t\t :: GUASS-JORDAN METHOD :: ");
          printf("\n\t\t\t -----------------------------\n\n");
          printf("\n ENTER THE TOTAL NUMBER OF VARIABLES IN THE GIVEN
          SYSTEM =>");
          scanf("%d",&num);
          m=1;
          printf("\n");
          for(i=0;i<num;i++)
          {
              printf("\n ENTERING THE CO-EFFICIENTS OF EQUATION %d :",i+1);
              printf("\n ~~~~~~~~~~~~~~~~~~~~~~~~~~~~~~~~~~~~~~~~~~~~~~~~\n");
                    for(j=0;j<=num;j++)
                    {
                              if(j!=num)
                              {
                                      printf(" ENTER THE CO-EFFICIENT OF x%d =>",j+1);
```

```
                        scanf("%f",&a[i][j]);
            }
            else
            {
                    printf(" ENTER THE CO-EFFICIENT OF y%d
                    (VARIABLE OF RIGHT  HAND SIDE) =>",m);
                    scanf("%f",&a[i][j]);
                    m++;
            }
        }
        printf("\n\n");
    }
        for(k=0;k<num;k++)
        {
          for(i=0;i<num;i++)
          {
                    u=a[i][k]/a[k][k];
                    if(i!= k)
                    {
                       for(j=k+1;j<num+1;j++)
                       {
                                a[i][j]=a[i][j]-u*a[k][j];
                       }
                    }
          }
        }
    }
    printf("\n\n THE ROOTS OF THE SYSTEM OF EQUATIONS ARE :\n");
    printf(" ~~~~~~~~~~~~~~~~~~~~~~~~~~~~~~~~~~~~~~~~~~~~~~~~\n");
            for(i=0;i<num;i++)
            {
                x[i]= (a[i][num]/a[i][i]);
                printf(" x%d=%.2f \n",i+1,x[i]);
            }
            getch();  }
```

4.6.4   Program to implement Crout's Reduction method

```
//Crout's Reduction method
#include <stdio.h>
#include <math.h>
#include <conio.h>
void main()
{
        int num,i,j,k,m;
```

```
float a[20][20],x[20],b[20][20],u[20][20],c[20];
clrscr();
printf("\n\t\t\t :: CROUT'S REDUCTION METHOD :: ");
printf("\n\t\t\t ----------------------------\n\n");
printf("\n ENTER TOTAL NUMBER OF VARIABLES IN THE GIVEN SYSTEM
=>");
scanf("%d",&num);
m=1;
printf("\n");
for(i=0;i<num;i++)
{
printf("\n ENTERING THE CO-EFFICIENTS OF EQUATION %d :",i+1);
printf("\n ~~~~~~~~~~~~~~~~~~~~~~~~~~~~~~~~~~~~~~~~~~~~~~\n");
        for(j=0;j<=num;j++)
        {
                if(j!=num)
                {
                printf(" ENTER THE CO-EFFICIENT OF x%d =>",j+1);
                scanf("%f",&a[i][j]);
                }
                else
                {
                        printf(" ENTER THE CO-EFFICIENT OF y%d
                        (VARIABLE OF RIGHT HAND SIDE) =>",m);
                        scanf("%f",&a[i][j]);
                        m++;
                }
        }
            printf("\n\n");
}
for(i=0;i<num;i++)
        b[i][0]=a[i][0];
for(j=1;j<num+1;j++)
        u[0][j]=a[0][j]/b[0][0];
for(m=1;m<num;m++)
{
        for(i=m;i<num;i++)
        {
        for(k=0; k<m; k++)
                        a[i][m]=a[i][m]-b[i][k]*u[k][m];
        b[i][m] = a[i][m];
        }
        for(j=m+1; j<num+1; j++)
```

```
                    {
                            for(k=0;k<m; k++)
                            {
                                    a[m][j] = a[m][j] - b[m][k]*u[k][j];
                                    u[m][j] = a[m][j] / b[m][m];
                            }
                    }
                    for(k=0;k<num;k++)
                    {
                            i = (num-k-1);
                            x[i] = u[i][num];
                            for(j=i+1; j<num; j++)
                                    x[i] = x[i] - u[i][j]*x[j];
                    }
            }
            printf("The roots of the system of Equations are: \n");
            for(i=0;i<num;i++)
            {
                printf("x%d=%.2f \n",i+1,x[i]);
            }
            getch();  }
```

4.6.5   Program to implement Gauss – Jacobi method

```
//Gauss – Jacobi method
#include<stdio.h>
#include<conio.h>
#include<math.h>
#include<stdlib.h>
void main()
{
        int Row,i,j,Break=1,Iteration;
        float Mat[20][20]={0};
        float TempX[20],x[20];
        printf("\n\t\tGAUSS ⊣JACOBI METHOD\n\n");
        printf("Enter Total Number of Unknowns  : ");
        scanf("%d",&Row);
        for (i=0; i<Row; i++)
        {
                printf("\nEnter coefficient for Equation %d\n",i+1);
                for (j=0; j<Row+1; j++)
                {
                        printf("Co-efficient x[%d][%d]  : ",i+1,j+1);
                        scanf("%f",&Mat[i][j]);
```

```
        }
}
printf("\nEntered Equation are  :\n");
for (i=0; i<Row; i++)
{
      for (j=0; j<Row; j++)
            printf("%6.2f",Mat[i][j]);
      printf(" | %6.2f\n",Mat[i][j]);
 }
 getch();
 for (i=0; i<Row; i++)
 {
        x[i] = 0;
        TempX[0] = 0;
 }
 Iteration = 0;
 while (1)
  {
            Break = 1;
            printf("\n");
            for (i=0; i<Row; i++)
                    printf("%8.6f ",x[i]);
            for (i=0; i<Row; i++)
            {
                    TempX[i] = Mat[i][Row];
                    for (j=0; j<Row; j++)
                    {
                        if (i!=j)
                            TempX[i] -= Mat[i][j]*x[j];
                    }
                    TempX[i] /= Mat[i][i];
            }
            for (i=0; i<Row; i++)
            {
                    if (fabs(x[i]-TempX[i])>0.001)
                            Break = 0;
            }
            Iteration += 1;
            if (Break || Iteration>=50)
                    break;
            for (i=0; i<Row; i++)
                    x[i] = TempX[i];
        }
```

```
                if (Iteration >=50)
                {
                        printf("\nNo convergence....");
                        return(0);
                }
                printf("\n\nRoots of the equation are....\n");
                for (i=0; i<Row; i++)
                        printf("%7.4f ",x[i]);
                printf("\n");
                return(0);  }
```

4.6.6   Program to implement Gauss – Seidel method

```c
//Gauss – Seidel method
#include<stdio.h>
#include<conio.h>
#include<math.h>
void main()
{
        int Row,i,j,Break=1,Iteration;
        float Mat[20][20] = {0};
        float TempX[20],x[20];
        printf("\n\t\t GAUSS-SEIDEL METHOD...\n\n");
        printf("Enter the total Number of Unknowns  : ");
        scanf("%d",&Row);
        for (i=0; i<Row; i++)
        {
                printf("\nEnter co-efficient for Equation %d\n",i+1);
                for (j=0; j<Row+1; j++)
                {
                        printf("Co-efficient x[%d][%d]  : ",i+1,j+1);
                        scanf("%f",&Mat[i][j]);
                }
        }
        printf("\nEntered Equations are  :\n");
        for (i=0; i<Row; i++)
        {
                for (j=0; j<Row; j++)
                        printf("%6.2f",Mat[i][j]);
                printf(" | %6.2f\n",Mat[i][j]);
        }
        getch();
        for (i=0; i<Row; i++)
        {
```

```
                x[i] = 0;
                TempX[0] = 0;
        }
        Iteration = 0;
        while (1)
        {
                Break = 1;
                printf("\n");
                for (i=0; i<Row; i++)
                        printf("%8.6f ",x[i]);
                for (i=0; i<Row; i++)
                {
                        x[i] = Mat[i][Row];
                        for (j=0; j<Row; j++)
                        {
                                if (i!=j)
                                        x[i] -= Mat[i][j]*x[j];
                        }
                        x[i] /= Mat[i][i];
                }
                for (i=0; i<Row; i++)
                {
                        if (fabs(x[i]-TempX[i])>0.001)
                                Break = 0;
                }
                Iteration += 1;
                if (Break || Iteration>=50)
                        break;
                for (i=0; i<Row; i++)
                        TempX[i] = x[i];
        }
        if (Iteration >=50)
        {
                printf("\nNo convergence....");
                return(0);
        }
        printf("\n\nRoots of the equation are....\n");
        for (i=0; i<Row; i++)
                printf("%7.4f ",x[i]);
        printf("\n");
        getch();
        return(0);  }
```

4.6.7 Program to implement power method

```
//power method to find largest eigen value
#include<stdio.h>
#include<conio.h>
#include<math.h>
void main()
{
        int i,j,k,n;
        float a[20][20], x[20], y[20], z[20], p,q,r,s,t;
        clrscr();
        printf("\n\n Power Method - Numerically Largest Eigen Value...\n");
        printf("Enter the order of the matrix  :\n ");
        scanf("%d",&n);
        for (i=0; i<n; i++)
        {
                printf("\nEnter the coefficients of the matrix for row:
%d\n",i+1);
                for (j=0; j<n; j++)
                {
                        printf("Co-efficient a[%d][%d]  : ",i+1,j+1);
                        scanf("%f",&a[i][j]);
                }
                x[i] = 1;
        }
        k=0;
        Newline:
        for(i=0,i<n, i++)
        {      y[i] = 0;
                for(j=0; j<n;j++)
                {
                        y[i] = y[i] + x[j]* a[i][j];
                }

                z[i] = fabs(y[i]);
        }

        t = z[0];
        j=0;

        for(i=1; i<n; i++)
        {
                if(z[i] >= t)
                {
```

```
            t = z[i];
            j = i;
        }
}
if(t ==y[j])
        p = t;
else
        p =-t;
for(i=0; i<n; i++)
{
        x[i] = y[i] / p;
}
k = k + 1;
if(k>=50)
        printf("The numerically largest eigen value is: %f \n", p);
else
        goto Newline;
 getch();   }
```

EXERCISES

1.   Multiple Choice Questions

(1)   If all the elements of a matrix are zero then that matrix is known as a
_____.
(a)   Unit matrix   (b)   Null matrix   (c)   Singular matrix
(d)   Non – singular matrix   (e)   None of these

(2)   If the determinant of a square matrix A is zero then A is said to be
_____matrix.
(a)   Unit   (b)   Null   (c)   Singular
(d)   Non – singular   (e)   None of these

(3)   If all the elements except leading diagonal elements are zero then the
square matrix is said to be a _____ matrix
(a)   Diagonal   (b)   Unit   (c)   Triangular
(d)   Singular   (e)   None of these

(4)   A diagonal matrix of order n in which all the elements on leading diagonal
are equal to 1 (i.e. $a_{ii} = 1, i = 1, 2, ..., n$), is called a _____ .

(a)   Diagonal matrix   (b)   Scalar matrix   (c)   Unit matrix.
(d)   Triangular matrix   (e)   None of these

(5)   A square matrix is called an/a _____ if all the elements below
the   leading   diagonal   are   zero   (i.e. $a_{ij} = 0$ for all $i > j$)   and
_____ if all the elements above the leading diagonal are
zero (i.e. $a_{ij} = 0$ for all $i < j$).
(a)   Lower triangular matrix , Upper triangular matrix
(b)   Upper triangular matrix, Lower triangular matrix
(c)   Diagonal matrix, Symmetric matrix
(d)   Symmetric matrix, Diagonal matrix
(e)   None of these

(6)   A square matrix A is said to be _____ if $A^{-1} = A^T$ or $AA^T = A^TA = I$
(a)   Symmetric matrix   (b)   Hermitian matrix   (c)   Transpose matrix
(d)   Orthogonal matrix   (e)   None of these

(7)   In case of solving system of simultaneous linear equations which of these
is a direct method?.
(a)   Gauss Elimination method   (b)   Gauss – Jacobi method
(c)   Gauss – Seidel method   (d)   Graffe's root squaring method

(8)   In triangularization of Gauss – Elimination method......
(a)   Unit matrix is formed
(b)   Upper triangular matrix is formed
(c)   Lower triangular matrix is formed
(d)   Diagonal matrix is formed
(e)   None of these

(9)   The convergence criteria for Gauss – Seidel method is
   (a)   The diagonal elements of the co–efficient matrix must be dominant
   (b)   The co-efficient of the first row variables should be dominant than other rows
   (c)   The co-efficient of the last row variables should be dominant than other rows
   (d)   The co-efficient of the first column variables should be dominant than other columns.
   (e)   The co-efficient of the last column variables should be dominant than other columns

(10)   Which iterative method is better than other methods to solve simultaneous linear equations?
   (a)   Gauss – Elimination method
   (b)   Gauss – Jacobi method
   (c)   Gauss – Seidel method
   (d)   Crout's method
   (e)   Gauss – Jordan method

(11)   In a system of equations , if we perform a small change in one of the values of the coefficient matrix or any right hand side vector causes a large change in the solution. Such systems are known as _____.
   (a)   Ill – conditioned   (b)   Well – conditioned

(12)   If λ is an eigen value of a matrix A, then $\frac{1}{\lambda}$ is the eigen value of A^{-1}
   (a)   True   (b)   False

(13)   If λ and $\frac{1}{\lambda}$ both are eigen values of a matrix A then A is _____matrix
   (a)   Orthogonal   (b)   Unit   (c)   Diagonal
   (d)   Singular   (e)   None of these

Answers: (1) (b) (2) (c) (3) (a) (4) (c)   (5) (b) (6) (d) (7) (a) (8) (b)
          (9) (a) (10) (c) (11) (a) (12) (a) (13) (a)

2.   Problems

(1)   Express the matrix A as the sum of a symmetric and a skew – symmetric matrix where

$$A = \begin{bmatrix} 3 & -2 & 6 \\ 2 & 7 & -1 \\ 5 & 4 & 0 \end{bmatrix}$$

(2)   Find the inverse of the following matrices.

(i) $\begin{bmatrix} 1 & 3 & 3 \\ 1 & 4 & 3 \\ 1 & 3 & 4 \end{bmatrix}$ (ii) $\begin{bmatrix} 2 & 4 & 3 \\ 0 & 1 & 1 \\ 2 & 2 & -1 \end{bmatrix}$ (iii) $\begin{bmatrix} 2 & 5 & 3 \\ 3 & 1 & 2 \\ 1 & 2 & 1 \end{bmatrix}$

(3)   Solve the following systems of equations using matrix inversion method:

(i) $x + y + z = 1$ (ii) $x + y + z = 4$ (iii) $x + 4y + 9z = 16$
      $x + 2y + 3z = 1$ $2x - y + 3z = 1$ $2x + y + z = 10$
      $2x + 3y + z = 2$ $3x + 2y - z = 1$ $3x + 2y + 3z = 18$

(4)   Solve the following systems of equations by Gauss elimination method
      (Apply pivoting wherever it is required):

(i) $x + 2y - z = 3$, $3x - y + 2z = 1$, $2x - 2y + 3z = 2$

(ii) $5x - y + z = 10$, $2x + 4y = 12$, $x + y + 5z = -1$

(iii) $2x + 2y - z + u = 4$, $4x + 3y - z + 2u = 6$, $8x + 5y -$
       $3z + 4u = 12$, $3x + 3y - 2z + 2u = 6$

(iv) $2x + 2y + 4z = 18$, $x + 3y + 2z = 13$, $3x + y + 3z = 14$

(v) $x + y - z = 2$, $2x + 3y - 5z = 1$, $4x - 5y - 7z = 5$

(vi) $-10x + 6y + 3z = -100$, $6x - 5y + 5z = -100$,
       $3x + 6y - 10z = -100$

(5)   Solve the following systems of equations by Gauss Jordan method:

(i) $5x + 3y + z = 2$, $4x + 10y + 4z = -4$, $2x + 3y + 5z = 11$

(ii) $10x + y - z = 12$, $x + 10y - z = 12$, $x + y - 10z = 12$

(iii) $x + y + z = 7$, $3x + 3y + 4z = 24$, $2x + y + 3z = 16$

(iv) $x + 3y + 10z = 24$, $2x + 17y + 4z = 35$, $28x + 4y - z = 32$

(v) $2x + 4y + 8z = 41$, $4x + 6y + 10z = 56$, $6x + 8y + 10z = 64$

(vi) $x + y + z - w = 2$, $7x + y + 3z + w = 12$, $8x - y + z -$
       $3w = 5$, $10x + 5y + 3z + 2w = 20$

(6)   Solve the following systems of equations by factorization method:

(i) $2x - 3y + 10z = 3$, $-x + 4y + 2z = 20$, $5x + 2y + z = -12$

(ii) $2x - 6y + 8z = 24$, $3x + y + 2z = 16$, $5x + 4y - 3z = 2$

(iii) $4x + y + 2z = 12$, $2x - 3y + 8z = 20$, $-x + 11y + 4z = 33$

(7)   Solve the following systems of equations by Crout's reduction method:

(i) $x + 2y + 3z = 6$, $2x + 4y + z = 7$, $3x + 2y + 9z = 14$

(ii) $x + y + 2z = 4$, $3x + y - 3z = -4$, $2x - 3y - 5z = -5$

(iii) $x + 3y - z + 2w = 9$, $-2x + y + 2z - w = 2$,
       $3x - 4y + z + 3w = 3$, $-6x + 3y - 4z + 5w = 2$

(8)   Find the inverse of the following matrices using Crout's method:

(i) $\begin{bmatrix} 3 & -1 & 1 \\ -15 & 6 & -5 \\ 5 & -2 & 2 \end{bmatrix}$ (ii) $\begin{bmatrix} 1 & 1 & 1 \\ 1 & 2 & -3 \\ 2 & -1 & 3 \end{bmatrix}$ (iii) $\begin{bmatrix} 1 & -1 & 0 \\ -2 & 3 & -4 \\ -2 & 3 & -3 \end{bmatrix}$

(9)   Solve the following systems of equations by (i) Gauss – Jacobi (ii)
      Gauss – Seidel method:

(i) $5x + 3y + z = 2$, $4x + 10y + 4z = -4$, $2x + 3y + 8z = 20$

(ii) $10x + y + z = 12$, $2x + 10y + z = 13$, $2x + 7y + 10z = 19$

(iii) $8x + y + z = 8$, $2x + 4y + z = 4$, $x + 3y + 3z = 5$

(iv) $5x + 2y + z = 12$, $x + 4y + 2z = 15$, $x + 2y + 5z = 20$

(v) $10x - 2y - z - w = 3$, $-2x + 10y - z - w = 15$,
$-x - y + 10z - 2w = 27, -x - y - 2z + 10w = -9$
(vi) $4x + 2y + z = 14$, $x + 5y - z = 10$, $x + y + 8z = 20$

(10)   Solve the following systems of equations by relaxation method:
(i) $10x - 2y + z = 12$, $x + 9y - z = 10$, $2x - y + 11z = 20$
(ii) $3x + 9y - 2z = 11, 4x + 2y + 13z = 24$, $4x - 4y + 3z = 8$
(iii) $50x + 2y - 3z = 196, 3x + 65y + 2z = 81$,
$-x + y + 33z = 63$
(iv) $5x - 2y + z = 13$, $3x + 7y - 11z = 2$, $x + 20y - 2z = 8$

(11)   Show that the following systems of equations are ill – conditioned:
(i) $2x + y = 25$, $2.001x + y = 25.01$
(ii) $2x + y = 2$, $2x + 1.01y = 2.01$

(12)   Find whether the following matrices are ill – conditioned or well – conditioned?

(i) $\begin{bmatrix} 1 & 4 & 7 \\ 2 & 5 & 8 \\ 3 & 6 & 9.1 \end{bmatrix}$ (ii) $\begin{bmatrix} 3 & -1 & 3 \\ 1 & 0 & 4 \\ 2 & 2 & 1 \end{bmatrix}$

(13)   An approximate solution for the system of equations $x + 4y + 7z = 5$, $2x + 5y + 8z = 7$, $3x + 6y + 9.1z = 9.1$ is given by $x = 1.8, y = -1.2$ and $z = 1$. Improve this solution by the iterative method for ill – conditioned system of equations described in the section 4.3.4.

(14)   Find the eigen values and eigen vectors of the following matrices:

(i) $\begin{bmatrix} 2 & 0 & 1 \\ 0 & 2 & 0 \\ 1 & 0 & 2 \end{bmatrix}$ (ii) $\begin{bmatrix} 1 & -2 \\ -5 & 4 \end{bmatrix}$ (iii) $\begin{bmatrix} 6 & -2 & 2 \\ -2 & 3 & -1 \\ 2 & -1 & 3 \end{bmatrix}$

(15)   Find the numerically largest eigenvalues and the corresponding eigenvectors of the following matrices, using power method:

(i) $\begin{bmatrix} 1 & 3 & -1 \\ 3 & 2 & 4 \\ -1 & 4 & 10 \end{bmatrix}$ (ii) $\begin{bmatrix} 8 & 1 & 2 \\ 0 & 10 & -1 \\ 6 & 2 & 15 \end{bmatrix}$ Take unit vector as initial vector

(iii) $\begin{bmatrix} 1 & -3 & 2 \\ 4 & 4 & -1 \\ 6 & 3 & 5 \end{bmatrix}$ (iv) $\begin{bmatrix} 10 & 2 & 1 \\ 2 & 10 & 1 \\ 2 & 1 & 10 \end{bmatrix}$ (v) $\begin{bmatrix} 3 & 2 & 4 \\ -1 & 4 & 10 \\ 1 & 3 & -1 \end{bmatrix}$

(16)   Find the numerically largest and smallest eigenvalues of the following matrices, using the power method:

(i) $\begin{bmatrix} 1 & 6 & 1 \\ 1 & 2 & 0 \\ 0 & 0 & 3 \end{bmatrix}$ (ii) $\begin{bmatrix} 3 & 2 & 4 \\ 2 & 0 & 2 \\ 4 & 2 & 3 \end{bmatrix}$

Answers

(1) $\begin{bmatrix} 3 & 0 & 5.5 \\ 0 & 7 & 1.5 \\ 5.5 & 1.5 & 0 \end{bmatrix} + \begin{bmatrix} 0 & -2 & 5 \\ 2 & 0 & -2.5 \\ -5 & 2.5 & 0 \end{bmatrix}$

(2) (i) $\begin{bmatrix} 7 & -3 & -3 \\ -1 & 1 & 0 \\ -1 & 0 & 1 \end{bmatrix}$ (ii) $\frac{1}{4}\begin{bmatrix} 3 & -10 & -1 \\ -2 & 8 & 2 \\ 2 & -4 & -2 \end{bmatrix}$ (iii) $\frac{1}{4}\begin{bmatrix} -3 & 1 & 7 \\ -1 & -1 & -5 \\ 5 & 1 & -13 \end{bmatrix}$

(3) (i) $x = 1,\ y = 0,\ z = 0$ (ii) $x = -1,\ y = 3,\ z = 2$

   (iii) $x = 7,\ y = -9,\ z = 5$

(4) (i) $x = -1,\ y = 4,\ z = 4$ (ii) $x = 2.5556,\ y = 1.7222,\ z = -1.0556$

   (iii) $x = 1,\ y = 1,\ z = -1,\ u = -1$ (iv) $x = 1,\ y = 2,\ z = 3$

   (v) $x = 3,\ y = 0,\ z = 1$ (vi) $x = 175,\ y = 195,\ z = 160$

(5) (i) $x = 1,\ y = -2,\ z = 3$ (ii) $x = 1,\ y = 1,\ z = -1$

   (iii) $x = 3,\ y = 1,\ z = 3$ (iv) $x = 0.99,\ y = 1.50,\ z = 1.84$

   (v) $x = 1.5,\ y = 2.5,\ z = 3.5$ (vi) $x = 1,\ y = 1,\ z = 1,\ u = 1$

(6) (i) $x = -4,\ y = 3,\ z = 2$ (ii) $x = 1,\ y = 3,\ z = 5$

   (iii) $x = 1,\ y = 2,\ z = 3$

(7) (i) $x = 1,\ y = 1,\ z = 1$ (ii) $x = 1,\ y = -1,\ z = 2$

   (iii) $x = 1,\ y = 2,\ z = 2,\ w = 2$

(8) (i) $\begin{bmatrix} 2 & 0 & -1 \\ 5 & 1 & 0 \\ 0 & 1 & 3 \end{bmatrix}$ (ii) $\frac{1}{11}\begin{bmatrix} -3 & 4 & 5 \\ 9 & -1 & -4 \\ 5 & -3 & -1 \end{bmatrix}$ (iii) $\begin{bmatrix} 3 & -3 & 4 \\ 2 & -3 & 4 \\ 0 & -1 & 1 \end{bmatrix}$

(9) (i) $x = 1,\ y = -2,\ z = 3$ (ii) $x = 1,\ y = 1,\ z = 1$

   (iii) $x = 0.83,\ y = 0.32,\ z = 1.07$ (iv) $x = 1.08,\ y = 1.95,\ z = 3.16$; $x = 0.996, y = 1.95, z = 3.16$

   (v) $x = 1,\ y = 2,\ z = 3, w = 0$ (vi) $x = 2,\ y = 1.99,\ z = 1.99$

(10) (i) $x = 1.3,\ y = 1.2,\ z = 1.7$ (ii) $x = 1.35,\ y = 2.10,\ z = 2.84$

   (iii) $x = 4,\ y = 1,\ z = 2$ (iv) $x = 2.6,\ y = 0.3432,\ z = 0.741$

(12) (i) Ill – conditioned (ii) Well – conditioned

(14) (i) 1,2,3; (1,0,-1), (0, 1, 0), (1, 0 1) (ii) -1, 6; (1,1), (2, -5)

   (iii) 8,2, 2; (2, -1, 1), (1, 0 -2), (1,2,0)

(15) (i) 11.65, $(0.025, 0.422, 1)^T$ (ii) 16.447, $(0.243, -0.085, 1.0)^T$

   (iii) 7, $(4.5, 1, 15)^T$ (iv) 13; $(1, 1, 1)^T$

   (v) 7.4; $(0.8, 1, 0.4)^T$

(16) (i) 4, -1 (ii) 8, -1

Chapter 5   Finite Differences

Objectives

- To know the importance of finite differences
- To convert from one finite difference operator to another finite difference operator
- To understand the concept of factorial notation
- To understand how to propagate the error
- To understand the concept of summation of the given series

Learning Outcomes

After reading this lesson students should be able to

- Identify the difference between various finite difference operator and effectively convert from one operator to another operator
- Convert the given polynomial into factorial notation
- Find the error and correct the true value
- Effectively find the sum of the given series

5.1   INTRODUCTION

Finite differences play a significant role in the interpolation, Taylor's series and the solution of differential equations. Finite difference table can be utilized as a forward difference, backward difference or central difference in the interpolation depending upon the requirement.

Suppose a function $y = f(x)$ is not specified by a fixed formula then also we can find approximate values of $f(x)$ upto a desired degree of accuracy with the help of finite differences. Hence, the calculus of finite differences deal with the changes in the function due to the changes in the independent variable.

For the given set of values $(x_i, y_i), i = 1,2,3, ..., n$ of any function $y = f(x)$, independent variables x_i are known as arguments and the corresponding values of dependent variables y_i are known as entries.

5.2   FORWARD DIFFERENCES

Let $x_0, x_1, x_2, \ldots \ldots, x_n$ be n independent variables and let $y_0, y_1, y_2, \ldots \ldots, y_n$ be the corresponding values of dependent variables for the function $y = f(x)$. Let the equally spaced arguments $x_0, x_1, x_2, \ldots \ldots, x_n$ be defined as $x_0, x_0 + h, x_0 + 2h, \ldots \ldots \ldots, x_0 + nh$, where h is the length of the interval.

The operator Δ is defined as

$$\Delta f(x_i) = f(x_i + h) - f(x_i)$$

i.e.
$$\Delta f(x_i) = f(x_{i+1}) - f(x_i)$$

i.e.
$$\Delta y_i = y_{i+1} - y_i$$

Here, Δ is called the Newton's forward difference operator.

The subtraction of each value of y from the preceding value of y is denoted by Δ and the results are known as first order differences of y.

Thus, the first order differences are defined as

$$\Delta y_0 = y_1 - y_0$$
$$\Delta y_1 = y_2 - y_1$$
$$\ldots \quad \ldots \quad \ldots$$
$$\ldots \quad \ldots \quad \ldots$$
$$\Delta y_{n-1} = y_n - y_{n-1}$$

If we take the differences of first order differences then they are defined as

$$\Delta^2 y_0 = \Delta(\Delta y_0) = \Delta(y_1 - y_0) = \Delta y_1 - \Delta y_0$$
$$\Delta^2 y_1 = \Delta y_2 - \Delta y_1$$
$$\ldots \quad \ldots \quad \ldots$$
$$\ldots \quad \ldots \quad \ldots$$
$$\Delta^2 y_{n-1} = \Delta y_n - \Delta y_{n-1}$$

which are called Newton's second order forward differences. Similarly, Newton's third order forward   differences can be defined. In general,   the nth order difference is defined by

$$\Delta^n y_n = \Delta^{n-1} y_{n+1} - \Delta^{n-1} y_n$$

Newton's forward order differences of a function are summarized in a below tabular form.

Table 5.1 Forward Difference Table

x	y	Δy	$\Delta^2 y$	$\Delta^3 y$	$\Delta^4 y$
x_0	y_0	$\Delta y_0 = y_1 - y_0$	$\Delta^2 y_0 = \Delta y_1 - \Delta y_0$	$\Delta^3 y_0 = \Delta^2 y_1 - \Delta^2 y_0$	$\Delta^4 y_0 = \Delta^3 y_1 - \Delta^3 y_0$
x_1	y_1	$\Delta y_1 = y_2 - y_1$	$\Delta^2 y_1 = \Delta y_2 - \Delta y_1$	$\Delta^3 y_1 = \Delta^2 y_2 - \Delta^2 y_1$	
x_2	y_2	$\Delta y_2 = y_3 - y_2$	$\Delta^2 y_2 = \Delta y_3 - \Delta y_2$		
x_3	y_3	$\Delta y_3 = y_4 - y_3$			
x_4	y_4				

This table is called a diagonal difference table. Horizontal table can also be prepared but we will work on diagonal table only. In the Table 5.1, y_0 is called the leading term and $\Delta y_0, \Delta^2 y_0, \Delta^3 y_0, \Delta^4 y_0$ are called the leading differences.

Example 5.1   Given a set of values of a function $f(x)$ as follows:

x	0	1	2	3	4	5
$y = f(x)$	20	27	35	54	72	98

Construct Newton's forward difference table.

Solution: Newton's forward difference table:

x	y	Δy	$\Delta^2 y$	$\Delta^3 y$	$\Delta^4 y$	$\Delta^5 y$
0	20	7	1	10	-22	43
1	27	8	11	-12	21	
2	35	19	-1	9		
3	54	18	8			
4	72	26				
5	98					

5.2.1   Results on Forward Difference Operator

Result 1: If $f(x)$ is a constant function then $\Delta f(x) = 0$

Proof: It is given that $f(x)$ is a constant function. Let $f(x) = m$, where m is any constant.

Therefore, $\Delta f(x) = f(x + h) - f(x) = m - m = 0$

Result 2: Fon any two functions $f(x)$ and $g(x)$, $\Delta[f(x) + g(x)] = \Delta f(x) + \Delta g(x)$

Proof: $LHS = \Delta[f(x) + g(x)]$

$$= \Delta\left((f+g)(x)\right) = (f+g)(x+h) - (f+g)(x)$$

$$= f(x+h) + g(x+h) - f(x) - g(x)$$

$$= [f(x+h) - f(x)] + [g(x+h) - g(x)]$$

$$= \Delta f(x) + \Delta g(x) = RHS$$

Result 3: $\Delta[af(x) + b\,g(x)] = a\,\Delta f(x) + b\,\Delta g(x)$
for the constants a and b.

Proof: From Result 1 and Result 2 we can easily derive that

$$\Delta[af(x) + b\,g(x)] = a\,\Delta f(x) + b\,\Delta g(x)$$

Result 4: $\Delta\left(f(x)g(x)\right) = f(x+h)\,\Delta g(x) + g(x)\Delta f(x)$

Proof: $LHS = \Delta\left(f(x)g(x)\right)$

$$= \Delta\left((fg)(x)\right) = fg(x+h) - fg(x) = f(x+h)g(x+h) - f(x)g(x)$$

Adding and subtracting $f(x+h)g(x)$ we get,

$$\Delta\left(f(x)g(x)\right) = f(x+h)g(x+h) + f(x+h)g(x) - f(x+h)g(x)$$
$$- f(x)g(x)$$

$$= [f(x+h)g(x+h) - f(x+h)g(x)] + [f(x+h)g(x) - f(x)g(x)]$$

$$= f(x+h)\,[g(x+h) - g(x)] + g(x)[f(x+h) - f(x)]$$

$$= f(x+h)\,\Delta g(x) + g(x)\,\Delta f(x) = RHS$$

Remark: We can also prove that $\Delta\left(f(x)g(x)\right) = g(x+h)\,\Delta f(x) + f(x)\Delta g(x)$ by adding and subtracting $g(x+h)f(x)$.

Result 5:

$$\Delta\left(\frac{f(x)}{g(x)}\right) = \frac{g(x)\Delta f(x) - f(x)\Delta g(x)}{g(x)g(x+h)}$$

Proof:

$$LHS = \Delta\left(\frac{f(x)}{g(x)}\right) = \frac{f(x+h)}{g(x+h)} - \frac{f(x)}{g(x)}$$

$$= \frac{f(x+h)g(x) - f(x)g(x+h)}{g(x)g(x+h)}$$

Adding and subtracting $f(x)g(x)$ we get,

$$= \frac{f(x+h)g(x) - f(x)g(x) + f(x)g(x) - f(x)g(x+h)}{g(x)g(x+h)}$$

$$= \frac{g(x)[f(x+h)-f(x)]-f(x)[g(x+h)-g(x)]}{g(x)g(x+h)}$$

$$= \frac{g(x)\Delta f(x)-f(x)\,\Delta g(x)]}{g(x)g(x+h)} = RHS$$

Result 6: $\Delta[c.f(x)] = c\,\Delta f(x)$; c is any constant

Result 7: $\Delta^p\,\Delta^q\,f(x) = \Delta^{p+q}\,f(x)$, p,q are positive integres.

Example 5.2 Evaluate the following, the interval of differencing being h.

(i) $\Delta \log f(x)$ (ii) $\Delta^2 \sin 2x$ (iii) $\Delta[e^x \cos x]$ (iv) $\Delta[\tan^{-1}ax]$

(v) $\left(\dfrac{\Delta^2}{E}\right) e^x \dfrac{Ee^x}{\Delta^2 e^x}$

Solution:

(i)
$$\Delta \log f(x) = \log f(x+h) - \log f(x)$$
$$= \log\left[\frac{f(x+h)}{f(x)}\right] = \log\left[\frac{Ef(x)}{f(x)}\right]$$

We know that, $E = I + \Delta$

$$= \log\left[\frac{(I+\Delta)f(x)}{f(x)}\right] = \log\left[\frac{f(x)+\Delta f(x)}{f(x)}\right]$$

$$= \log\left[1 + \frac{\Delta f(x)}{f(x)}\right]$$

(ii) $\Delta \sin 2x = \sin 2(x+h) - \sin 2x$
$$= 2\cos(2x+h)\sin h$$
$$= 2\sin h \cos(2x+h)$$

$\therefore \quad \Delta^2 \sin 2x = \Delta(\Delta \sin 2x)$
$$= \Delta[2\sin h\cos(2x+h)]$$
$$= 2\sin h\,\Delta\cos(2x+h)$$
$$= 2\sin h\,[\cos(2(x+h)+h)-\cos(2x+h)]$$
$$= 2\sin h.-2\sin(2x+2h)\sin h$$
$$= -4\sin^2 h\,\sin(2x+2h)$$

(iii) $\Delta[e^x \cos x] = e^{x+h}\Delta\cos x + \cos x\,\Delta e^x$
$$= e^{x+h}[\cos(x+h)-\cos x]+\cos x[e^{x+h}-e^x]$$
$$= e^{x+h}\left[-2\sin\left(x+\frac{h}{2}\right)\sin\frac{h}{2}\right]+e^{x+h}\cos x\left[1-\frac{e^x}{e^{x+h}}\right]$$

$$= e^{x+h} \left[-2 \sin\left(x + \frac{h}{2}\right) \sin\frac{h}{2} + \cos x \, (1 - e^{-h}) \right]$$

(iv) $\Delta[tan^{-1}ax] = tan^{-1}(ax + ah) - tan^{-1}ax$

$$= tan^{-1}\left(\frac{ax+ah-ax}{1+(ax+ah)(ax)}\right) = tan^{-1}\left(\frac{ah}{1+a^2x^2+a^2hx}\right)$$

(v) $\left(\frac{\Delta^2}{E}\right) e^x \frac{Ee^x}{\Delta^2 e^x} = (\Delta^2 E^{-1}) e^x \frac{Ee^x}{\Delta^2 e^x}$

$$= \Delta^2 e^{x-h} \frac{Ee^x}{\Delta^2 e^x} = \Delta^2 e^x e^{-h} \frac{E \, e^x}{\Delta^2 \, e^x}$$

$$= e^{-h} E \, e^x$$

$$= e^{-h} e^{x+h}$$

$$= e^x$$

5.3   BACKWARD DIFFERENCES

Let the equally spaced arguments x_0, x_1, $x_2, \dots\dots$, x_n be defined as x_0, $x_0 + h$, $x_0 + 2h, \dots\dots\dots, x_0 + nh$, where h is the length of the interval and let y_0, y_1, $y_2, \dots\dots$, y_n be the corresponding functional values of the function $y = f(x)$.

The operator ∇ is defined as

$$\nabla f(x_i) = f(x_i) - f(x_i - h)$$

i.e. $\qquad\qquad \nabla f(x_i) = f(x_i) - f(x_{i-1})$

i.e. $\qquad\qquad \nabla y_i = y_i - y_{i-1}$

Here, ∇ is called the Newton's first order backward difference operator.
Thus, in particular the backward difference operator ∇ is defined as

$$\nabla y_1 = y_1 - y_0$$

$$\nabla y_2 = y_2 - y_1$$

$$\cdots \quad \cdots \quad \cdots$$

$$\cdots \quad \cdots \quad \cdots$$

$$\nabla y_n = y_n - y_{n-1}$$

If we take the higher order backward differences then they are defined as

$$\nabla^2 y_n = \nabla y_n - \nabla y_{n-1}, \nabla^3 y_n = \nabla^2 y_n - \nabla^2 y_{n-1}, \dots\dots, \nabla^n y_n = \Delta^{n-1}y_n - \Delta^{n-1}y_{n-1}$$

which are called Newton's second order, third order, ..., n^{th} order backward differences repectively.

Newton's backward order differences of a function are summarized in a below tabular form.

Table 5.2 Backward Difference Table

x	y	∇y	$\nabla^2 y$	$\nabla^3 y$	$\nabla^4 y$
x_0	y_0				
x_1	y_1	$\nabla y_1 = y_1 - y_0$			
x_2	y_2	$\nabla y_2 = y_2 - y_1$	$\nabla^2 y_2 = \nabla y_2 - \nabla y_1$		
x_3	y_3	$\nabla y_3 = y_3 - y_2$	$\nabla^2 y_3 = \nabla y_3 - \nabla y_2$	$\nabla^3 y_3 = \nabla^2 y_3 - \nabla^2 y_2$	
x_4	y_4	$\nabla y_4 = y_4 - y_3$	$\nabla^2 y_4 = \nabla y_4 - \nabla y_3$	$\nabla^3 y_4 = \nabla^2 y_4 - \nabla^2 y_3$	$\nabla^4 y_4 = \nabla^3 y_4 - \nabla^3 y_3$

In the Table 5.2, y_4 is called the leading term and $\nabla y_4, \nabla^2 y_4, \nabla^3 y_4, \nabla^4 y_4$ are called the leading differences.

Example 5.3   Construct the backward difference table for the function $f(x) = x^3 - 7x^2 + 9x - 11$ for $x = 1, 3, 5, 7, 9, 11$.
Solution: Backward difference table:

x	y	∇y	$\nabla^2 y$	$\nabla^3 y$	$\nabla^4 y$	$\nabla^5 y$
-1	-28					
1	-8	20				
3	-20	-12	-32			
5	-16	4	16	48		
7	52	68	64	48	0	
9	232	180	112	48	0	0

Example 5.4 Construct the backward difference table from the following data:
$\cos 10^0 = 0.9848$, $\cos 15^0 = 0.9659$, $\cos 20^0 = 0.9397$,
$cos\ 25^0 = 0.9063$. Find the values of $\nabla^2 y_{20}$ and $\nabla^3 y_{25}$.

Solution: Backward difference table:

x	y	∇y	$\nabla^2 y$	$\nabla^3 y$
10	0.9848			
15	0.9659	-0.0189		
20	0.9397	-0.0262	-0.0073	
25	0.9063	-0.0334	-0.0072	0.0001

From the table it is clear that $\nabla^2 y_{20} = -0.0073$ and $\nabla^3 y_{25} = 0.0001$.

5.4   CENTRAL DIFFERENCES

Let $x_0, x_1, x_2, \ldots \ldots, x_n$ be n independent variables of the function $y = f(x)$. Let $x_i = x_0 + nh$, where i is not restricted to integer values, h is the length of the interval. Then the central difference operator δ is defined as

$$\delta f(x) = f\left(x + \frac{h}{2}\right) - f\left(x - \frac{h}{2}\right)$$

where $y_i = f(x_i)$. Therefore, $\delta y_j = y_{j+\frac{h}{2}} - y_{j-\frac{h}{2}}$

Let $y_{\frac{1}{2}} = f\left(x_0 + \frac{h}{2}\right)$ then $\delta y_{\frac{1}{2}} = \delta f\left(x_0 + \frac{h}{2}\right)$

$$= f\left(x_0 + \frac{h}{2} + \frac{h}{2}\right) - f\left(x_0 + \frac{h}{2} - \frac{h}{2}\right)$$

$$= f(x_0 + h) - f(x_0) = f(x_1) - f(x_0) = y_1 - y_0$$

Therefore, $\delta y_{\frac{1}{2}} = y_1 - y_0, \delta y_{\frac{3}{2}} = y_2 - y_1, \delta y_{\frac{5}{2}} = y_3 - y_2, \ldots \ldots, \delta y_{\frac{n-1}{2}} = y_n - y_{n-1}$.

These are called first order central differences.

If we take the differences of first order differences then central differences are defined as $\delta^2 y_1 = y_{\frac{3}{2}} - y_{\frac{1}{2}}, \; \delta^2 y_2 = y_{\frac{5}{2}} - y_{\frac{3}{2}}, \; \delta^2 y_3 = y_{\frac{7}{2}} - y_{\frac{5}{2}}$ and so on.

Similarly, Newton's third order central differences can be defined as .

$\delta^3 y_{\frac{3}{2}} = \delta^2 y_2 - \delta^2 y_1, \; \delta^3 y_{\frac{5}{2}} = \delta^2 y_3 - \delta^2 y_2$ and so on.

In general, the nth order difference is defined by

$$\delta^n y_{\left(\frac{2i+1}{2}\right)} = \delta^{n-1} y_{i+1} - \delta^{n-1} y_i$$

Newton's central order differences of a function are summarized in a below tabular form.

Table 5.3 Central Difference Table

x	y	δy	$\delta^2 y$	$\delta^3 y$	$\delta^4 y$
x_0	y_0				
		$\delta y_{\frac{1}{2}} = y_1 - y_0$			
x_1	y_1		$\delta^2 y_1 = y_{\frac{3}{2}} - y_{\frac{1}{2}}$		
		$\delta y_{\frac{3}{2}} = y_2 - y_1$		$\delta^3 y_{\frac{3}{2}} = \delta^2 y_2 - \delta^2 y_1$	
x_2	y_2		$\delta^2 y_2 = y_{\frac{5}{2}} - y_{\frac{3}{2}}$		$\delta^4 y_2 = \delta^3 y_{\frac{5}{2}} - \delta^3 y_{\frac{3}{2}}$
		$\delta y_{\frac{5}{2}} = y_3 - y_2$		$\delta^3 y_{\frac{5}{2}} = \delta^2 y_3 - \delta^2 y_2$	
x_3	y_3		$\delta^2 y_3 = y_{\frac{7}{2}} - y_{\frac{5}{2}}$		
		$\delta y_{\frac{7}{2}} = y_4 - y_3$			
x_4	y_4				

5.5   OTHER OPERATORS

We have already seen the forward difference operator Δ , backward difference operator ∇ and central difference operator δ in the previous sections. Let's summarize these operators quickly.

$$\Delta f(x) = f(x + h) - f(x)$$
$$\nabla f(x) = f(x) - f(x - h)$$
$$\delta f(x) = f\left(x + \frac{h}{2}\right) - f(x - \frac{h}{2})$$

In this section we will study other operators and their relations with one another.

Shift Operator E (Enlargement Operator, Displacement Operator, Translation Operator)

Let $y_i = f(x_i)$ be a function. where, $x_i = x_0 + ih$, $i = 0,1,2,...,n$ be a set of values of the function $f(x)$ then the shift operator E is defined as

$$Ef(x) = f(x + h) \qquad \text{i.e. } Ey_x = y_{x+h}$$

Thus, when the operator E applies on f(x), the result is the next value of the function $f(x + h)$. Therefore, E is known as shift or translation operator.

$$E^2 f(x) = E^2 y_x = E(Ey_x) = E(y_{x+h}) = y_{x+2h} = f(x + 2h)$$
$$E^3 f(x) = E^3 y_x = E(E^2 y_x) = E(y_{x+2h}) = y_{x+3h} = f(x + 3h)$$
$$\cdots \quad \cdots \quad \cdots \quad \cdots \quad \cdots \quad \cdots \quad \cdots \quad \cdots$$
$$\cdots \quad \cdots \quad \cdots \quad \cdots \quad \cdots \quad \cdots \quad \cdots \quad \cdots$$
$$E^n f(x) = E^n y_x = y_{x+nh} = f(x + nh)$$

The inverse operator E^{-1} is defined as

$$E^{-1} f(x) = f(x - h)$$

In general,

$$E^{-n} f(x) = E^{-n} y_x = y_{x-nh} = f(x - nh)$$

Averaging Operator μ (Mean Operator)

The average or mean operator μ is defined as

$$\mu f(x) = \frac{1}{2}\left[f\left(x + \frac{h}{2}\right) + f\left(x - \frac{h}{2}\right)\right]$$

$$\mu y_x = \frac{1}{2}\left[y_{x+\frac{h}{2}} + y_{x-\frac{h}{2}}\right]$$

Differential Operator D

The differential operator D is defined as

$$Df(x) = \frac{d}{dx}f(x) = f'(x)$$

Therefore,

$$D^n f(x) = \frac{d^n}{dx^n}f(x)$$

5.5.1 Relation Between $\Delta, \nabla, E, \delta, \mu$ and D

(1) Relation Between Δ, ∇ and E

We know that $\Delta y_x = y_{x+1} - y_x = Ey_x - y_x = (E - I)y_x$

where, I is the identity operator. Hence, $\boxed{\Delta = E - I}$ .... (5.5.1)

Now, backward difference operator is defined as

$$\nabla y_x = y_x - y_{x-1} = y_x - E^{-1}y_x = y_x(I - E^{-1})$$

$$\boxed{\nabla = I - E^{-1}}$$ .... (5.5.2)

or $\quad \frac{I}{E} = I - \nabla \therefore \boxed{E = \frac{I}{1-\nabla}}$ .... (5.5.3)

Substitute the value of E in Eq. (5.4.1), we have

$$\Delta = \frac{I}{1-\nabla} - I = \frac{\nabla}{1-\nabla} \quad \therefore \boxed{\Delta = \frac{\nabla}{1-\nabla}}$$ .... (5.5.4)

Therefore, $\quad \frac{1}{1-\nabla} = \Delta + I$

$\therefore 1 - \nabla = \frac{I}{\Delta + I} \quad \therefore \nabla = I - \frac{I}{\Delta + I} = \frac{\Delta}{\Delta + I} \quad \therefore \boxed{\nabla = \frac{\Delta}{\Delta + I}}$ .... (5.5.5)

Now, $\quad E(\nabla y_x) = E(y_x - y_{x-h}) = y_{x+h} - y_x = \Delta y_x$

$$\therefore \quad \boxed{E\nabla = \Delta}$$ .... (5.5.6)

Similarly, $\nabla(Ey_x) = \nabla y_{x+h} = y_{x+h} - y_x = \Delta y_x \quad \therefore \nabla E = \Delta$

(2) Relation Between δ, E, Δ and ∇

We know that

$$\delta f(x) = f\left(x + \frac{h}{2}\right) - f\left(x - \frac{h}{2}\right)$$
$$\therefore \delta f(x) = E^{\frac{1}{2}} f(x) - E^{-\frac{1}{2}} f(x) = \left(E^{\frac{1}{2}} - E^{-\frac{1}{2}}\right)f(x)$$

Therefore, $\quad \boxed{\delta = E^{\frac{1}{2}} - E^{-\frac{1}{2}}}$ .... (5.5.7)

$$\delta = E^{\frac{1}{2}} - E^{-\frac{1}{2}} = E^{\frac{1}{2}} - \frac{I}{E^{\frac{1}{2}}} = \frac{E-I}{E^{\frac{1}{2}}} = \frac{\Delta}{(I+\Delta)^{\frac{1}{2}}} = \frac{\Delta}{\sqrt{I+\Delta}}$$

$$\therefore \quad \boxed{\delta = \frac{\Delta}{\sqrt{I+\Delta}}} \qquad \text{........ (5.5.8)}$$

Also, $\delta = E^{\frac{1}{2}} - E^{-\frac{1}{2}} = \frac{I}{\sqrt{I-\nabla}} - \sqrt{I} - \nabla = \frac{\nabla}{\sqrt{I-\nabla}} \quad \therefore \boxed{\delta = \frac{\nabla}{\sqrt{I-\nabla}}} \quad \text{... (5.5.9)}$

and

$$\delta = E^{\frac{1}{2}} - E^{-\frac{1}{2}} = E^{\frac{1}{2}}(1 - E) = E^{\frac{1}{2}}\nabla \quad \therefore \boxed{\delta = E^{\frac{1}{2}}\nabla} \qquad \text{........ (5.5.10)}$$

$$\delta = E^{\frac{1}{2}} - E^{-\frac{1}{2}} = E^{-\frac{1}{2}}(E - I) = E^{-\frac{1}{2}}\Delta \quad \therefore \boxed{\delta = E^{-\frac{1}{2}}\Delta} \qquad \text{........ (5.5.11)}$$

We have seen that,

$$\delta f(x) = \left(E^{\frac{1}{2}} - E^{-\frac{1}{2}}\right) f(x) = E^{\frac{1}{2}} f(x) - E^{-\frac{1}{2}} f(x)$$

$$= f\left(x + \frac{h}{2}\right) - f\left(x - \frac{h}{2}\right)$$

Now, $\delta^2 f(x) = \delta\left(\delta f(x)\right) = \delta f\left(x + \frac{h}{2}\right) - \delta f\left(x - \frac{h}{2}\right)$

$$= \left(E^{\frac{1}{2}} - E^{-\frac{1}{2}}\right) f\left(x + \frac{h}{2}\right) - \left(E^{\frac{1}{2}} - E^{-\frac{1}{2}}\right) f\left(x - \frac{h}{2}\right)$$

$$= E^{\frac{1}{2}}\left(f\left(x + \frac{h}{2}\right) - f\left(x - \frac{h}{2}\right)\right) - E^{-\frac{1}{2}}\left(f\left(x + \frac{h}{2}\right) - f\left(x - \frac{h}{2}\right)\right)$$

$$= f(x + h) - f(x) - f(x) + f(x - h)$$

$$\left(\because E^{\frac{1}{2}} f\left(x + \frac{h}{2}\right) = f\left(x + \frac{h}{2} + \frac{h}{2}\right) = f(x + h) = Ef(x)\right)$$

$$= f(x + h) + f(x - h) - 2f(x)$$

$$= Ef(x) + E^{-1} f(x) - 2f(x)$$

$$= (E + E^{-1} - 2)f(x)$$

$$\therefore \quad \boxed{\delta^2 = (E + E^{-1} - 2)} \qquad \text{........ (5.5.12)}$$

(3)   Relation Between $\mu, E \text{ and } \delta$

We know that

$$\mu f(x) = \frac{1}{2}\left[f\left(x + \frac{h}{2}\right) + f\left(x - \frac{h}{2}\right)\right]$$

$$= \frac{1}{2}\left[E^{\frac{1}{2}} f(x) + E^{-\frac{1}{2}} f(x)\right]$$

$$= \frac{1}{2}\left[E^{\frac{1}{2}} + E^{-\frac{1}{2}}\right] f(x)$$

Therefore,

$$\boxed{\mu = \frac{1}{2}\left[E^{\frac{1}{2}} + E^{-\frac{1}{2}}\right]} \qquad \text{........ (5.5.13)}$$

Squaring,

$$\mu^2 = \frac{1}{4}\left[E^{\frac{1}{2}} - E^{-\frac{1}{2}}\right]^2 = \frac{1}{4}(E + 2 + E^{-1}) = \frac{1}{4}(\delta^2 + 4) = I + \frac{1}{4}\delta^2$$

Therefore,

$$\boxed{\mu = \sqrt{I + \frac{1}{4}\delta^2}}$$

.... (5.5.14)

(4)   Relation Between D, E, Δ and ∇

We know that

$$Df(x) = \frac{d}{dx}f(x)$$

By Taylor's theorem, we have

$$f(x + h) = f(x) + \frac{h}{1!}f'(x) + \frac{h^2}{2!}f''(x) + \ldots\ldots$$

$$\therefore\ E f(x) = f(x) + \frac{h}{1!}Df(x) + \frac{h^2}{2!}D^2f(x) + \ldots\ldots (\because E f(x) = f(x + h))$$

$$= \left[1 + \frac{h}{1!}D + \frac{h^2}{2!}D^2 + \ldots\ldots\right]f(x)$$

$$= e^{hD}f(x)\ (\because \text{By Taylor's theorem } e^x = 1 + \frac{1}{1!}x + \frac{1}{2!}x^2 + \ldots\ldots)$$

Therefore,

$$\boxed{E = e^{hD}}$$

.... (5.5.15)

Now,

$$E = I + \Delta = e^{hD}$$

$$hD = \log e = \log(1 + \Delta) \qquad \text{(Apply } log \text{ on both the sides)}$$

By Taylor's theorem,

$$hD = \left(\Delta - \frac{\Delta^2}{2!} + \frac{\Delta^3}{3!} - \ldots\ldots\right)$$

$$\therefore\quad \boxed{D = \frac{1}{h}\left[\Delta - \frac{\Delta^2}{2!} + \frac{\Delta^3}{3!} - \ldots\ldots\right]}$$

.... (5.5.16)

Also, we have $\Delta = E - I = e^{hD} - I$

and $\nabla = I - E^{-1} = I - e^{-hD}$

Result: If n is an integer,

$$f(x + nh) = f(x) + \binom{n}{1}\Delta f(x) + \binom{n}{2}\Delta^2 f(x) + \ldots\ldots + \binom{n}{i}\Delta^i f(x)$$
$$+ \ldots\ldots$$

i.e.

$$f(x + nh) = \sum_{i=0}^{\infty}\binom{n}{i}\Delta^i f(x)$$

Proof: We prove this result my mathematical induction.

For $n = 1$,   LHS $= f(x + nh) = f(x + h) = Ef(x)$

RHS $= f(x) + \Delta f(x) = (I + \Delta)f(x) = Ef(x)$

LHS = RHS

Therefore, our result is true for $n = 1$. Suppose our result is true for $n - 1$
Hence,

$$f(x + (n-1)h) = E^{n-1}f(x) = \sum_{i=0}^{\infty} \binom{n-1}{i} \Delta^i f(x) \qquad \ldots\ldots (i)$$

To prove the result for n

i.e. $f(x + nh) = E^n f(x) = \sum_{i=0}^{\infty} \binom{n}{i} \Delta^i f(x)$

Now,

$$E^n f(x) = E\,(E^{n-1} f(x)) = (I + \Delta)E^{n-1} f(x)$$
$$= E^{n-1} f(x) + \Delta E^{n-1} f(x)$$
$$= \sum_{i=0}^{\infty} \binom{n-1}{i} \Delta^i f(x) + \sum_{i=0}^{\infty} \binom{n-1}{i} \Delta^{i+1} f(x) \qquad (\because \text{from (i)})$$
$$= \sum_{i=0}^{\infty} \binom{n-1}{i} \Delta^i f(x) + \sum_{i=1}^{\infty} \binom{n-1}{i-1} \Delta^i f(x)$$

We know that $\binom{n-1}{i} + \binom{n-1}{i-1} = \binom{n}{i}$

Therefore, $f(x + nh) = E^n f(x) = \sum_{i=0}^{\infty} \binom{n}{i} \Delta^i f(x)$

By mathematical induction we have proved that the result is true for all n.

As a special case, we get $f(x) = f_0 = \sum_{i=0}^{\infty} \binom{x}{i} \Delta^i f_0$

This formula refers general functional value f_x in terms of f_0 and its differences.

Example 5.5   Find the missing value in the following table:

x	1	2	3	4	5
y	34.4	39.7	45.3	---	63.1

Solution: Since, only four data points are given in the table, the polynomial is of degree three.
Therefore, $\Delta^4 y_0 = 0$. The forward difference table is

x	y	Δy	$\Delta^2 y$	$\Delta^3 y$	$\Delta^4 y$
1	34.4	5.3	0.3	$y_3 - 51.2$	$210.5 - 4y_3$
2	39.7	5.6	$y_3 - 50.9$	$159.3 - 3y_3$	
3	45.3	$y_3 - 45.3$	$108.4 - 2y_3$		
4	y_3	$63.1 - y_3$			
5	63.1				

Now, $\Delta^4 y_0 = 0$. Therefore, $210.5 - 4y_3 = 0$ hence, $y_3 = 52.625$

Alternate Solution: $\Delta^4 y_0 = 0$ $\therefore$ $(E - 1)^4 y_0 = 0$

$\therefore$ $(E^4 - 4E^3 + 6E^2 - 4E + 1)y_0 = 0$

$\therefore$ $y_4 - 4y_3 + 6y_2 - 4y_1 + y_0 = 0$.

Now, substitute all the values of y

$\therefore$ $63.1 - 4y_3 + 6(45.3) - 4(39.7) + 34.4 = 0$

$\therefore$ $210.5 - 4y_3 = 0 \Rightarrow y_3 = 52.625$

5.6   DIFFERENCES OF A POLYNOMIAL

Fundamental Theorem of Differential Calculus

The nth forward diffrence of a polynomial of degree n is constant and all higher order differences are zero when the values of the independent variable are at equal intervals.

i.e. If $f(x) = a_0 x^n + a_1 x^{n-1} + a_2 x^{n-2} + \ldots\ldots + a_n$ is a nth degree polynomial then

$\Delta^n f(x) = n! \, a_0 \, h^n$, where h is the interval of differencing.

Let $f(x) = a_0 x^n + a_1 x^{n-1} + a_2 x^{n-2} + \ldots\ldots + a_n$

$\Delta f(x) = f(x + h) - f(x)$

$\quad = a_0[(x + h)^n - x^n] + a_1[(x + h)^{n-1} - x^{n-1}] + \ldots\ldots +$ $a_{n-1}[(x + h) - x] + a_n h$

$\quad = a_0(hnx^{n-1} + \ldots) + a_1(\ldots + \ldots) + \ldots\ldots +$

$\quad = a_0 nhx^{n-1} + a_1{}' x^{n-2} + a_2{}' x^{n-3} + \ldots\ldots + a_{n-1}{}' x + a_n{}'$

Where, $a_1{}'$, $a_2{}'$, $\ldots\ldots$, $a_{n-1}{}'$, $a_n{}'$ are new coefficients.

Therefore, first difference of an nth degree polynomial is a polynomial of degree $(n - 1)$.

$\Delta^2 f(x) = \Delta f(x + h) - \Delta f(x)$

$\quad = a_0 nh [(x + h)^{n-1} - x^{n-1}] + a_1{}' [(x + h)^{n-2} - x^{n-2}] + \ldots\ldots +$ $a_{n-1}{}' h$

$\quad = a_0 n (n - 1)h^2 x^{n-2} + a_1{}'' x^{n-3} + \ldots\ldots + a_{n-1}{}''$

Hence, second differences is a polynomial of degree $(n - 2)$.

Similarly, if we continue the same process, the nth order differences is a polynomial of degree zero.

So, $\Delta^n f(x) = a_0 n (n - 1)(n - 2) \ldots\ldots\ldots 1 \, h^n = a_0 n! \, h^n$ which is a constant. Therefore, all higher order differences of a polynomial of degree n will be zero.

Example 5.6   Evaluate

$$\Delta^n[(1 - ax)(1 - bx^2)(1 - cx^3)(1 - dx^4)]$$

Solution: Given that,

$$= \Delta^n[(1 - ax)(1 - bx^2)(1 - cx^3)(1 - dx^4)]$$

$$= \Delta^{10}[abcd\, x^{10} + Ax^9 + Bx^8 + \ldots\ldots + 1]$$

The polynomial in the bracket is of degree 10. Therefore, as per the above theorem, $\Delta^n f(x) = \Delta^{10} f(x)$ is constant which is equal to $a_0\, n!\, h^n$. Here, $a_0 = abcd, n = 10$ and $h = 1$. Therefore,

$$\Delta^n[(1 - ax)(1 - bx^2)(1 - cx^3)(1 - dx^4)] = \Delta^{10}\, f(x) = abcd\,(10!)$$

Converse of the above theorem is also true.

Converse of the theorem: If the nth order differences of a function tabulated at equal intervals are constant, then function is a polynomial of degree n.

Example 5.7   Construct a forward difference table for $f(x) = x^3 + x - 1$, for $x = 1, 2, 3, 4, 5$.

Solution: The polynomial is of degree 3. Therefore, by the above theorem, the third order forward differences are constant and all higher order differences are zero.

x	y	Δy	$\Delta^2 y$	$\Delta^3 y$	$\Delta^4 y$
1	1	8	12	6	0
2	9	20	18	6	
3	29	38	24		
4	67	62			
5	129				

Example 5.8   Find the order of a polynomial for the data given below.

x	1	2	3	4	5
y	-1	3	19	53	111

Solution:

x	y	Δy	$\Delta^2 y$	$\Delta^3 y$	$\Delta^4 y$
1	-1	4	12	6	0
2	3	16	18	6	
3	19	34	24		
4	53	58			
5	111				

Here, third order differences are constant and fourth order forward difference is zero. So, by the converse of the fundamental theorem of differential calculus the polynomial is of degree three.

Example 5.9   Prove the following relations:

(i) $\Delta.\nabla = \Delta - \nabla = \delta^2$

(ii) $(I + \Delta)(I - \Delta) = 1$

(iii) $\Delta = \dfrac{\delta^2}{2} + \delta\sqrt{I + \dfrac{1}{4}\delta^2}$

(iv) $hD = \log(I + \Delta) = -\log(I - \nabla) = \sin h^{-1}(\mu\delta)$

(v) $\Delta + \nabla = \dfrac{\Delta}{\nabla} - \dfrac{\nabla}{\Delta}$

(vi) $\Delta^r y_n = \nabla^r y_{n+r}$

Solution:

(i)   We know that, $\Delta f(x) = f(x + h) - f(x)$ and
$$\nabla f(x) = f(x) - f(x - h)$$

Therefore, $(\Delta.\nabla)f(x) = \Delta(\nabla f(x)) = \Delta(f(x) - f(x - h))$
$$= \Delta f(x) - \Delta f(x - h)$$
$$= \Delta f(x) - [f(x) - f(x - h)] = \Delta f(x) - \nabla f(x)$$
$$= (\Delta - \nabla)f(x)$$

Thus, $\Delta.\nabla = \Delta - \nabla$

Now, $\Delta.\nabla = (E - I)(I - E^{-1}) = E + E^{-1} - 2 = \delta^2$ (from Eq. (5.5.12))

and $\Delta - \nabla = (E - I) - (I - E^{-1}) = E + E^{-1} - 2 = \delta^2$

Therefore, $\Delta.\nabla = \Delta - \nabla = \delta^2$

(ii) $(I + \Delta)(I - \Delta) = E.E^{-1} = I$

(iii)   RHS $= \dfrac{\delta^2}{2} + \delta\sqrt{I + \dfrac{1}{4}\delta^2} = \dfrac{1}{2}\delta\left[\delta + 2\sqrt{I + \dfrac{1}{4}\delta^2}\right]$

$$= \dfrac{1}{2}\delta\left[\delta + \sqrt{4 + \delta^2}\right]$$

$$= \dfrac{1}{2}\delta\left[\left(E^{\frac{1}{2}} - E^{-\frac{1}{2}}\right) + \sqrt{4 + \left(E^{\frac{1}{2}} - E^{-\frac{1}{2}}\right)^2}\right]$$

$$= \dfrac{1}{2}\delta\left[\left(E^{\frac{1}{2}} - E^{-\frac{1}{2}}\right) + \sqrt{\left(E^{\frac{1}{2}} + E^{-\frac{1}{2}}\right)^2}\right]$$

$$= \dfrac{1}{2}\left(E^{\frac{1}{2}} - E^{-\frac{1}{2}}\right)\left[E^{\frac{1}{2}} - E^{-\frac{1}{2}} + E^{\frac{1}{2}} + E^{-\frac{1}{2}}\right]$$

$$= \dfrac{1}{2} \times 2\left[E^{\frac{1}{2}} - E^{-\frac{1}{2}}\right]E^{\frac{1}{2}}$$

$$= E - I = \Delta = \text{LHS}$$

(iv)   We know that $E = e^{hD}$

,   We have already seen that $E = I + \Delta = e^{hD}$

$hD \, loge = logE = log(1 + \Delta)$ (Apply log on both the sides)

$$\therefore \quad hD = log(I + \Delta) \qquad ...... \text{ (i)}$$

Now, $E^{-1} = I - \nabla = e^{-hD}$

$$-hD \, loge = log(I - \nabla) = -logE$$

$$\therefore \quad hD = -log(I - \nabla) \qquad ...... \text{ (ii)}$$

Again, $\mu\delta = \left[\dfrac{E^{\frac{1}{2}} + E^{-\frac{1}{2}}}{2}\right] \left(E^{\frac{1}{2}} - E^{-\frac{1}{2}}\right)$

$$= \frac{E - E^{-1}}{2} = \frac{e^{hD} - e^{-hD}}{2} \qquad (\because E = e^{hD})$$

$$= \sinh(hD)$$

Therefore, $hD = \sin h^{-1}(\mu\delta) \qquad ..... \text{ (iii)}$

From (i), (ii) and (iii), $hD = log(I + \Delta) = -log(I - \nabla) = \sin h^{-1}(\mu\delta)$

(v)   RHS $= \dfrac{\Delta}{\nabla} - \dfrac{\nabla}{\Delta}$

$$= \left(\frac{\Delta}{\nabla} - \frac{\nabla}{\Delta}\right) y_x = \left(\frac{E - I}{I - E^{-1}} - \frac{I - E^{-1}}{E - I}\right) y_x$$

$$= \left(\frac{E - I}{\dfrac{E - I}{E}} - \frac{\dfrac{E - I}{E}}{E - I}\right) y_x = \left(E - \frac{I}{E}\right) y_x = (E - E^{-1}) y_x$$

$$= [(I + \Delta) - (I - \nabla)] y_x = (\Delta - \nabla) y_x = \text{LHS}$$

Therefore, $\Delta + \nabla = \dfrac{\Delta}{\nabla} - \dfrac{\nabla}{\Delta}$

(vi)   RHS $= \nabla^r \, y_{n+r}$

$$= (1 - E^{-1})^r y_{n+r} = \left(\frac{E - I}{E}\right)^r y_{n+r} = (E - I)^r \, E^{-r} y_{n+r}$$

$$= (E - I)^r \, y_n = \Delta^r y_n = \text{LHS} \qquad (\because E^{-r} y_{n+r} = y_n \text{ and } E - I = \Delta)$$

Therefore, $\Delta^r y_n = \nabla^r \, y_{n+r}$

5.7   FACTORIAL NOTATION

A factorial notation $[x]^n$ is defined as $[x]^n = x(x - 1)(x - 2) \ldots \ldots [x - (n - 1)]$ where n is a positive integer.

In particular, $[x] = x$

$$[x]^2 = x(x - 1)$$
$$[x]^3 = x(x - 1)(x - 2)$$

....

...   .

$$[x]^n = x(x - 1)(x - 2) \ldots \ldots (x - (n - 1))$$

If h is the interval of differencing then,

$$[x]^n = x(x-h)(x-2h) \dots \dots (x-(n-1)h)$$

Now, we will find the differences of $[x]^n$

$$\begin{aligned}
\Delta[x]^n &= [x+h]^n - [x]^n \\
&= (x+h)(x+h-h)(x+h-2h)(x+h-3h) \dots \dots (x+h- \\
&\quad (n-1)h) - x\,(x-h)(x-2h) \dots \dots (x-(n-1)h) \\
&= x\,(x-h)(x-2h) \dots \dots (x-(n-2)h)(x+h-x+(n-1)h) \\
&= n\,h\,[x]^{n-1} \qquad \dots \dots \text{(i)}
\end{aligned}$$

Similarly, $\quad \Delta^2[x]^n = \Delta(\Delta[x]^n) = \Delta(n\,h\,[x]^{n-1}) = nh\,\Delta([x]^{n-1})$

$$= nh[(n-1)h\,[x]^{n-2}] = n(n-1)h^2[x]^{n-2} \quad \text{(from (i))} \qquad \dots \dots \text{(ii)}$$

Continuing the same procedure we get,

$$\Delta^{n-1}[x]^n = n(n-1)(n-2) \dots \dots 2\,h^{n-1}[x]$$

Therefore, $\quad \Delta^n[x]^n = n(n-1)(n-2) \dots \dots 2\,h^{n-1}\Delta[x]$

$$\begin{aligned}
&= n(n-1)(n-2) \dots \dots 2.1\,h^{n-1}\,[(x+h)-x] \\
&= n!\,h^n \qquad \dots \dots \text{(iii)}
\end{aligned}$$

$$\Delta^{n+1}[x]^n = n!\,h^n - n!\,h^n = 0$$

If we take the interval of differentiating is 1 then,

$$\Delta^n[x]^n = n! \ \text{ and } \Delta^{n+1}[x]^n = 0$$

In general, $\quad \Delta^k[x]^n = n(n-1)(n-2) \dots \dots (n-k+1)\,h^k[x]^{n-k}$

$$(\text{ for any } k < n)$$

In particular, when h = 1,

$$\Delta[x]^n = n[x]^{n-1}$$

$$\Delta^2[x]^n = n(n-1)[x]^{n-2}$$

$$\dots \dots \dots \dots \dots \dots \dots \dots \dots \dots$$

$$\dots \dots \dots \dots \dots \dots \dots \dots \dots \dots$$

$$\Delta^n[x]^n = n!$$

So, when h = 1, the outcome of differencing $[x]^n$ is analogous to that of differentiating x^n. Hence, in this case the difference operator Δ is analogous to the differential operator D.

Remark:
- If a polynomial is given in factorial notation, then its different order of finite differences can be easily derived by the rule of differentiation.
- If the function is given in factorial notation, the polynomial function f(x) can be derived by termwise integration.

5.7.1 Reciprocal Factorial

If the interval of difference $h = 1$, the reciprocal factorial $[x]^{-n}$ is defined as

$$[x]^{-n} = \frac{1}{(x+1)(x+2)(x+3)\ldots\ldots\ldots+(x+n)}$$

$$\Delta[x]^{-n} = [x+h]^{-n} - [x]^{-n}$$

$$= \frac{1}{(x+2h)(x+3h)(x+4h)\ldots\ldots[x+(n+1)h]}$$

$$- \frac{1}{(x+h)(x+2h)\ldots\ldots(x+nh)}$$

$$= \frac{(x+h) - [x+(n+1)h]}{(x+h)(x+2h)(x+3h)\ldots\ldots(x+nh)[x+(n+1)h]}$$

$$= \frac{-nh}{(x+h)(x+2h)(x+3h)\ldots\ldots(x+nh)[x+(n+1)h]}$$

$$= -nh\,[x]^{-(n+1)}$$

$$\Delta^2[x]^{-n} = \Delta\left(\Delta\,[x]^{-n}\right) = \Delta\left[-nh\,[x]^{-(n+1)}\right]$$

$$= (-nh)[(-(n+1)h]\,[x]^{-(n+2)}$$

$$= (-1)^2\,n(n+1)h^2[x]^{-(n+2)}$$

....
....

In general,

$$\Delta^k[x]^{-n} = (-1)^k\,n(n+1)(n+2)\ldots\ldots\left(n+(k-1)\right)h^k\,[x]^{-(n+k)}$$

Result: If the interval of difference being unity, prove that

$$[x]^{-n} = \frac{1}{(x+n)^n}$$

Proof: By the definition of $[x]^n$, we have

$$[x]^n = x(x-1)(x-2)\ldots\ldots(x-(n-1))$$

$$= [x]^{n-1}(x-(n-1))$$

If $n = 0$, we have, $[x]^0 = [x]^{-1}(x+1)$ .... (5.7.1)

Now, we know that, $\Delta[x]^n = n\,h\,[x]^{n-1} = n\,[x]^{n-1}$ (for $h = 1$)

When $x = 1$, $\Delta[x]^1 = [x]^0$

Therefore, $[x]^0 = 1$, ($\because \Delta[x]^1 = (x+1) - x$ for $h = 1$)

Hence, from Eq. (5.7.1), we have

$$1 = [x]^{-1}(x+1)$$

$$\therefore \ [x]^{-1} = \frac{1}{(x+1)} \qquad\qquad\qquad \text{........ (5.7.2)}$$

Now, $\quad [x]^{n-1} = [x]^{n-2} \, (x - (n-2))$

When n = 0, $\ [x]^{-1} = [x]^{-2} \, (x+2)$

$$\therefore \ [x]^{-2} = \frac{1}{(x+2)} = \frac{1}{(x+1)(x+2)} \quad (\because Eq.\,(5.7.2)) \qquad \text{........ (5.7.3)}$$

Repeating the same procedure, we have,

$$[x]^{-n} = \frac{1}{(x+1)(x+2)(x+3)\,......\,...\,(x+n)}$$

$$\therefore \ [x]^{-n} = \frac{1}{(x+n)^n} \qquad\qquad\qquad \text{........ (5.7.4)}$$

5.7.2 Expressing a Polynomial in Factorial Notation

Let $f(x) = a_0 + a_1 x + \,.....\, + a_{n-1} x^{n-1} + a_n x^n$ be a polynomial of degree n. Let $f(x) = A + B\,[x] + C\,[x]^2 + \,.....\, + O[x]^{n-1} + P[x]^n$ .... (5.7.5) be a polynomial expressed in factorial notation where, A, B, C, ..., P are some unknown constants which need to be found out and $P \neq 0$.

Now, $\ \Delta f(x) = \Delta\,(A + B\,[x] + C\,[x]^2 + \,......\, + P[x]^n)$

$\qquad\qquad = B.1 + C.2\,[x]^1 + \,......\, + P.n[x]^{n-1}$

$\Delta^2 f(x) = \Delta(B.1 + C.2\,[x]^1 + \,......\, + P.n[x]^{n-1})$

$\qquad\qquad = C.2.1 + D.3.2[x]^1 + \,......\, + P.n.\,(n-1)[x]^{n-2}\,)$

Repeating the same procedure, we get

$$\Delta^n f(x) = P.n.\,(n-1).\,(n-2)\,......\,...\,2.1.\,[x]^0 = p.n!$$

Putting $x = 0$ in all the above values of finite differences of $f(x)$, we get

$$f(0) = A$$

$$\Delta f(0) = B.1! \quad \therefore \ B = \frac{\Delta f(0)}{1!}$$

$$\Delta^2 f(0) = C.2.1 = C.2! \quad \therefore \ C = \frac{\Delta^2 f(0)}{2!}$$

$$\Delta^3 f(0) = D.3.2.1 = D.3! \quad \therefore \ D = \frac{\Delta^3 f(0)}{3!}$$

$$\cdots\cdots\cdots\cdots\cdots\cdots\cdots\cdots\cdots\cdots\cdots\cdots$$

$$\cdots\cdots\cdots\cdots\cdots\cdots\cdots\cdots\cdots\cdots\cdots\cdots$$

$$\Delta^n f(0) = P.n.\,(n-1).\,(n-2)\,...\,2.1 = P.n! \quad \therefore \ P = \frac{\Delta^n f(0)}{n!}$$

Substituting the values of A, B, C, ..., P in Eq. (5.7.5) we get,

$$f(x) = f(0) + \frac{\Delta f(0)}{1!}\,[x] + \frac{\Delta^2 f(0)}{2!}\,[x]^2 + \,......\, + \frac{\Delta^n f(0)}{n!}\,[x]^n$$

5.7.3   Inverse Operator of Δ

If Δy_x is given and we want to find the value of y_x then it is called inverse finite difference operation or finite integration.

Hence, if $\Delta y_x = u_x$ then $y_x = \Delta^{-1} u_x$. The symbol Δ^{-1} is known as the inverse of the operator Δ. Δ^{-1} is analogous to D^{-1} in calculus. This operator is useful in finding the sum of n terms of a series.

Properties of Δ^{-1}

1. $\Delta^{-1}\left[p\,u_x + qv_x\right] = p\Delta^{-1}u_x + q\,\Delta^{-1}v_x$

2. $\Delta^{-1}[x]^r = \dfrac{[x]^{r+1}}{r+1}$, (here $h = 1$)

3. $\Delta^{-1}[x]^{-r} = -\dfrac{[x]^{-(r-1)}}{r-1}$

4. $\Delta^{-1}[px + q]^r = \dfrac{[px+q]^{(r+1)}}{a(r+1)}$

5. $\Delta^{-1}[px + q]^{-r} = -\dfrac{[px+q]^{-(r-1)}}{a(r-1)}$

Example 5.10   Express $f(x) = x^3 - 4x^2 + 9x - 11$ in factorial notation and hence show that $\Delta^3 f(x) = 6$ and $\Delta^4 f(x) = 0$

Solution: (Synthetic Division)

$$\text{Let } f(x) = A[x]^3 + B[x]^2 + C[x] + D$$

Using the method of synthetic division (see Appendix - II), we divide the polynomial by $x, x-1, x-2$ etc. successively to get the constants A, B, C and D.

		x^3	x^2	x	
1		1	-4	9	-11 = D
		0	1	-3	
2		1	-3	6 = C	
		0	2		
3		1	-1 = B		
		0			
		1 = A			

Thus, $f(x) = [x]^3 - [x]^2 + 6[x] - 11$

By the rule of simple differentiation, we have

$$\therefore \qquad \Delta f(x) = 3[x]^2 - 2[x] + 6$$
$$\therefore \qquad \Delta^2 f(x) = 3 \times 2[x] - 2$$
$$\therefore \qquad \Delta^3 f(x) = 6$$
$$\therefore \qquad \Delta^4 f(x) = 0$$

Alternate Method: (Direct Method)

Let $f(x) = x^3 - 4x^2 + 9x - 11 = A[x]^3 + B[x]^2 + C[x] + D$
$$= A\,x(x-1)(x-2) + Bx(x-1) + Cx + D \quad \text{........ (i)}$$

Putting $x = 0$ on both sides of (i), we get $-11 = D$

Putting $x = 1$, we get $\qquad -5 = C + D$

$\therefore \qquad\qquad\qquad C = 6$

Putting $x = 2$, we get $\qquad -1 = 2B + 2C + D$

$\therefore \qquad\qquad\qquad -1 = 2B + 1$

$\therefore \qquad\qquad\qquad -1 = B$

Now, equating the coefficients of x^3 on both sides of (i), we get $A = 1$

So, the required polynomial in factorial notation is
$$f(x) = [x]^3 - [x]^2 + 6[x] - 11$$
$$\therefore \qquad \Delta f(x) = 3[x]^2 - 2[x] + 6$$
$$\therefore \qquad \Delta^2 f(x) = 3 \times 2[x] - 2$$
$$\therefore \qquad \Delta^3 f(x) = 6$$
$$\therefore \qquad \Delta^4 f(x) = 0$$

Alternate Method:

Here, the polynomial is of degree three. Therefore, the maximum power of the polynomial in factorial notation can be three.

$$f(x) = f(0) + \frac{\Delta f(0)}{1!}[x] + \frac{\Delta^2 f(0)}{2!}[x]^2 + \frac{\Delta^3 f(0)}{3!}[x]^3$$

To find the values of $f(0), \Delta f(0), \Delta^2 f(0)$ and $\Delta^3 f(0)$ we need four values of $f(x)$ at $x = 0, 1, 2, 3$ For $x = 0, 1, 2, 3$ the corresponding values of f(x) = -11, -5, -1, 7.

Forward difference table is:

x	$f(x)$	$\Delta f(x)$	$\Delta^2 f(x)$	$\Delta^3 f(x)$
0	-11	6	-2	6
1	-5	4	4	
2	-1	8		
3	7			

Here, $f(0) = -11, \Delta f(0) = 6, \Delta^2 f(0) = -2, \Delta^3 f(0) = 6$

Therefore, the polynomial in factorial notation is

$$f(x) = -11 + \frac{6}{1!} [x] + \frac{-2}{2!} [x]^2 + \frac{6}{3!} [x]^3$$

$$\therefore\ f(x) = -11 + 6 [x] - [x]^2 + [x]^3$$

Example 5.11   Find the function whose first difference is

$$x^3 - 3x^2 + 5x - 9$$

Solution: Let $f(x)$ be the required function. It is given that

$$\Delta f(x) = x^3 - 3x^2 + 5x - 9$$

Let $x^3 - 3x^2 + 5x - 9 = x^3 + Bx^2 + Cx + D$

$$= x(x - 1)(x - 2) + Bx(x - 1) + Cx + D \ \ldots\text{(i)}$$

Putting $x = 0$ on both sides of (i), we get $D = -9$

Putting $x = 1$, we get $C + D = -6$ $\therefore C = 3$

Putting $x = 2$, we get $2B + 2C + D = -3$ $\therefore B = 0$

Therefore, $\Delta f(x) = x^3 + 3x - 9$

Integrating $\Delta f(x)$, we get

$$f(x) = \frac{[x]^4}{4} + 3\frac{[x]^2}{2} - 9[x] + c$$

where c is the constant of integration.

Example 5.12 Find the lowest degree polynomial which satisfies the following values:

x	0	1	2	3	4	5	6
$f(x)$	0	2	6	18	44	90	162

Solution: We know that

$$f(x) = f(0) + \frac{\Delta f(0)}{1!} [x] + \frac{\Delta^2 f(0)}{2!} [x]^2 + \ldots\ldots + \frac{\Delta^n f(0)}{n!} [x]^n \qquad \ldots\ldots\text{(i)}$$

Prepare a forward difference table to find $\Delta f(0), \Delta^2 f(0)$ etc.

x	$f(x)$	$\Delta f(x)$	$\Delta^2 f(x)$	$\Delta^3 f(x)$	$\Delta^4 f(x)$
0	0	2	2	6	0
1	2	4	8	6	0
2	6	12	14	6	0
3	18	26	20	6	
4	44	46	26		
5	90	72			
6	162				

Putting $f(0) = 0, \Delta f(0) = 2, \Delta^2 f(0) = 2, \Delta^3 f(0) = 6$ in (i), we get

$$f(x) = 0 + \frac{2}{1!}[x] + \frac{2}{2!}[x]^2 + \frac{6}{3!}[x]^3 = 2x + x(x-1) + x(x-1)(x-2)$$
$$= x^3 - 2x^2 + 3x$$

5.8   ERROR PROPAGATION

Let $y_i, i = 0,1,2,3, \dots \dots, 8$ be the entries of $f(x)$ at arguments $x_i, i = 0,1,2,3, \dots \dots, 8$ respectively.

Suppose an error ε is found in the entry y_5 of a difference table. The error is magnified and spreads as and when the higher order differences are formed. The difference table is used to study the concept of error propagation. The difference table is given below.

Table 5.4 Forward Difference Table to Find Error Propagation

x	y	Δy	$\Delta^2 y$	$\Delta^3 y$	$\Delta^4 y$
x_0	y_0	Δy_0	$\Delta^2 y_0$	$\Delta^3 y_0$	$\Delta^4 y_0$
x_1	y_1	Δy_1	$\Delta^2 y_1$	$\Delta^3 y_1$	$\Delta^4 y_1 + \varepsilon$
x_2	y_2	Δy_2	$\Delta^2 y_2$	$\Delta^3 y_2 + \varepsilon$	$\Delta^4 y_2 - 4\varepsilon$
x_3	y_3	Δy_3	$\Delta^2 y_3 + \varepsilon$	$\Delta^3 y_3 - 3\varepsilon$	$\Delta^4 y_3 + 6\varepsilon$
x_4	y_4	$\Delta y_4 + \varepsilon$	$\Delta^2 y_4 - 2\varepsilon$	$\Delta^3 y_4 + 3\varepsilon$	$\Delta^4 y_4 - 4\varepsilon$
x_5	$y_5 + \varepsilon$	$\Delta y_5 - \varepsilon$	$\Delta^2 y_5 + \varepsilon$	$\Delta^3 y_5 - \varepsilon$	$\Delta^4 y_5 + \varepsilon$
x_6	y_6	Δy_6	$\Delta^2 y_6$	$\Delta^3 y_6$	
x_7	y_7	Δy_7	$\Delta^2 y_7$		
x_8	y_8	Δy_8			
x_9	y_9				

We find following observations from the Table 5.4.
1.   Error spreads in a triangular pattern
2.   The error increases with the order of differences.
3.   The coefficients of $\varepsilon's$ in any column are the binomial coefficients of $(1 - \varepsilon)^n$ with alternating signs.
  e.g. in the first difference column, the errors are $\varepsilon, -\varepsilon$, in the second difference column, $\varepsilon, -2\varepsilon, \varepsilon$, in the third, $\varepsilon, -3\varepsilon, +3\varepsilon, -\varepsilon$, and in the fourth difference column, $\varepsilon, -4\varepsilon, +6\varepsilon, -4\varepsilon, \varepsilon$.

4. The algebraic sum of the errors in any difference column is zero.
5. The maximum error occurs opposite to the entry containing the error
6. If there are n number of points in the table then n^{th} differences are constant and $(n+1)^{th}$ differences vanish. The sum of all the values in $(n+1)^{th}$ differences column is zero or it is very near to zero.

> **Remark:** In case of two or more errrors, the successive differences will be irregular and exact location of errors may not be possible to find out.

Example 5.13   Find and correct an error in y in the following data.

x	0	1	2	3	4	5	6	7	8
y	11	14	17	21	28	36	49	67	91

Solution:

x	y	Δy	$\Delta^2 y$	$\Delta^3 y$	$\Delta^4 y$
0	11	3	0	1	1
1	14	3	1	2	-4
2	17	4	3	-2	6
3	21	7	1	4	-4
4	28	8	5	0	1
5	36	13	5	1	
6	49	18	6		
7	67	24			
8	91				

Here, the sum of all fourth differences is zero. Maximum value in the column is 6. Hence, $6\varepsilon = 6$ Therefore, $\varepsilon = 1$. Therefore, the incorrect functional value is 17. The values of fourth difference column are the coeffficients of $(1 - \varepsilon)^4$. Therefore, also the error $\varepsilon = 1$.

∴ The incorrect entry is $y_2 = 17$
Therefore, the required correct entry is $17 - 1 = 16$.

Example 5.14   In the following table, there is an error in the functional value y_3:

x	0	1	2	3	4	5	6
y	4	5	17	49	96	167	253

Find and correct value of y_3.

Solution: Let ε be the error in y_3. The forward difference table is:

x	y	Δy	$\Delta^2 y$	$\Delta^3 y$	$\Delta^4 y$	$\Delta^5 y$
0	4	1	11	$9+\varepsilon$	$-14-4\varepsilon$	$28+10\varepsilon$
1	5	12	$20+\varepsilon$	$-5-3\varepsilon$	$14+6\varepsilon$	$-32-10\varepsilon$
2	17	$32+\varepsilon$	$15-2\varepsilon$	$9+3\varepsilon$	$-18-4\varepsilon$	
3	$49+\varepsilon$	$47-\varepsilon$	$24+\varepsilon$	$-9-\varepsilon$		
4	96	71	15			
5	167	86				
6	253					

Six points are given in the table. Therefore, $\Delta^5 y$ should be constant and hence all the entries of the fifth difference should be equal.

Hence, $28+10\varepsilon = -32-10\varepsilon$ $\therefore -20\varepsilon = 60$ $\therefore \varepsilon = -3$

Therefore, the corrected entry for $y_3 = 49-3 = 46$

Example 5.15 Assuming $f(x)$ is a polynomial of degree three. One entry in the following table is incorrect. Use the difference table to identify and correct the error.

x	0	1	2	3	4	5	6	7
$f(x)$	0	1	3	11	22	45	81	133

Solution: The forward difference table is

x	$f(x)$	$\Delta f(x)$	$\Delta^2 f(x)$	$\Delta^3 f(x)$
0	0	1	1	5
1	1	2	6	-3
2	3	8	3	9
3	11	11	12	1
4	22	23	13	3
5	45	36	16	
6	81	52		
7	133			

Since $f(x)$ is a polynomial of degree 3, all the entries of third difference column i.e. $\Delta^3 f(x)$ must be constant. The sum of the entries of third difference column being 15, each entry under $\Delta^3 f(x)$ must be $\frac{15}{5} = 3$. Therefore, there are errors in the first four entries of the column $\Delta^3 f(x)$ (as fifth entry is already

3). Four entries can be written as $3 + (2)$, $3 - 3(2)$, $3 + 3(2)$, $3 - (2)$. Taking $\varepsilon = 2$ and comparing with the error propagation table, we find that the entry corresponding to $x = 3$ has an error.

$$\therefore f(x) + \varepsilon = 11$$

Therefore, the true value of $f(x)$ is $11 - \varepsilon = 11 - 2 = 9$.

Example 5.16   Using the method of seperation of symbols, prove that

1. $$u_0 + \frac{u_1 x}{1!} + \frac{u_2 x^2}{2!} + \frac{u_3 x^3}{3!} + \ ... \ ... + \infty$$

$$= e^x \left(u_0 + x\Delta u_0 + \frac{x^2}{2!}\Delta^2 u_0 + \frac{x^3}{3!}\Delta^3 u_0 + \ ... + \infty \right)$$

2. $$\Delta^n u_{x-n} = u_x - nu_{x-1} + \frac{n(n-1)}{2} u_{x-2} + \ ... \ ... + (-1)^n u_{x-n}$$

3. $$u_x = u_{x-1} + \Delta u_{x-2} + \ ... \ ... + \Delta^{n-1} u_{x-n} + u_{x-n}$$

Solution:

1.   LHS

$$= u_0 + \frac{u_1 x}{1!} + \frac{u_2 x^2}{2!} + \frac{u_3 x^3}{3!} + \ ... \ ...$$

$$= u_0 + \frac{x}{1!} Eu_0 + \frac{x^2}{2!} E^2 u_0 + \frac{x^3}{3!} E^3 u_0 + \ ... \ ...$$

$$= \left(1 + \frac{xE}{1!} + \frac{x^2 E^2}{2!} + \frac{x^3 E^3}{3!} + \ ... \ ... \right) u_0$$

$$= e^{xE} u_0 = e^{x(1+\Delta)} u_0 = e^x . e^{x\Delta} u_0$$

$$= e^x \left(1 + \frac{x\Delta}{1!} + \frac{x^2 \Delta^2}{2!} + \frac{x^3 \Delta^3}{3!} + \ ... \ ... \right) u_0$$

$$= e^x \left(u_0 + \frac{x}{1!}\Delta u_0 + \frac{x^2}{2!}\Delta^2 u_0 + \frac{x^3}{3!}\Delta^3 u_0 + \ ... \ ... \right)$$

$$= \text{RHS}$$

2.   RHS

$$= u_x - nu_{x-1} + \frac{n(n-1)}{2} u_{x-2} + \ ... \ ... + (-1)^n u_{x-n}$$

$$= u_x - nE^{-1} u_x + \frac{n(n-1)}{2} E^{-2} u_x + \ ... \ ...$$

$$+ (-1)^n E^{-n} u_x$$

$$= \left(1 - nE^{-1} + \frac{n(n-1)}{2} E^{-2} + \dots \dots \right.$$

$$\left. + (-1)^n E^{-n} \right) u_x$$

$$= (1 - E^{-1})^n u_x$$

$$= \left(1 - \frac{1}{E}\right)^n u_x = \left(\frac{E-1}{E}\right)^n u_x$$

$$= \Delta^n E^{-n} u_x \quad (\because \Delta = E - 1)$$

$$= \Delta^n u_{x-n} = \text{LHS}$$

3.   RHS

$$= u_{x-1} + \Delta u_{x-2} + \dots \dots + \Delta^{n-1} u_{x-n} + u_{x-n}$$

$$= E^{-1} u_x + \Delta E^{-2} u_x + \dots \dots + \Delta^{n-1} E^{-n} u_x + \Delta^n E^{-n} u_x$$

$$= E^{-1} \left(1 + \frac{\Delta}{E} + \frac{\Delta^2}{E^2} + \dots \dots + \frac{\Delta^{n-1}}{E^{n-1}}\right) u_x + \frac{\Delta^n}{E^n} u_x$$

$$= E^{-1} \left[\frac{\left(\frac{\Delta}{E}\right)^n - 1}{\frac{\Delta}{E} - 1}\right] u_x + \frac{\Delta^n}{E^n} u_x$$

(as formula for G. P. of finite series is $\left(\frac{a(r^n - 1)}{r-1}\right)$ here, $a = 1, r = \frac{\Delta}{E}$)

$$= E^{-1} \left[\frac{\Delta^n - E^n}{\Delta - E} \frac{1}{E^{n-1}}\right] u_x + \frac{\Delta^n}{E^n} u_x$$

$$= \left[-\left(\frac{\Delta^n - E^n}{E^n}\right)\right] u_x + \frac{\Delta^n}{E^n} u_x \quad (\because \Delta - E = -1)$$

$$= \left[-\left(\frac{\Delta^n}{E^n} - 1\right)\right] u_x + \frac{\Delta^n}{E^n} u_x = \left[1 - \frac{\Delta^n}{E^n} + \frac{\Delta^n}{E^n}\right] u_x$$

$$= u_x = \text{LHS}$$

Example 5.17 Find the sum of the series

$$1 + \frac{4}{1!}x + \frac{10}{2!} x^2 + \frac{20}{3!} x^3 + \frac{35}{4!} x^4 + \frac{56}{5!} x^5 + \dots \dots + \infty$$

Solution:

Compare the given series with the $u_0 + \frac{u_1 x}{1!} + \frac{u_2 x^2}{2!} + \frac{u_3 x^3}{3!} + \dots \dots + \infty$ (See Example 5.14(1)).

We have $u_0 = 1$, $u_1 = 4$, $u_2 = 10$, $u_3 = 20$, $u_4 = 35$, $u_5 = 56$

To apply the result given in Example 5.14 (1) we have to compute Δu_0, $\Delta^2 u_0$, $\Delta^3 u_0, \dots \dots$

u	$\Delta\,u$	$\Delta^2\,u$	$\Delta^3\,u$	$\Delta^4\,u$
$u_0 = 1$	3	3	1	0
$u_1 = 4$	6	4	1	0
$u_2 = 10$	10	5	1	
$u_3 = 20$	15	6		
$u_4 = 35$	21			
$u_5 = 56$				

$\therefore \quad u_0 = 1, \quad \Delta u_0 = 3, \quad \Delta^2 u_0 = 3, \quad \Delta^3 u_0 = 1, \quad \Delta^4 u_0 = \Delta^5 u_0 = 0$

$$\therefore \quad 1 + \frac{4}{1!}x + \frac{10}{2!}x^2 + \frac{20}{3!}x^3 + \frac{35}{4!}x^4 + \frac{56}{5!}x^5 + \dots\dots + \infty$$

$$= u_0 + \frac{u_1 x}{1!} + \frac{u_2 x^2}{2!} + \frac{u_3 x^3}{3!} + \frac{u_4 x^4}{4!} + \dots\dots + \infty$$

$$= e^x \left(u_0 + x\Delta u_0 + \frac{x^2}{2!}\Delta^2 u_0 + \frac{x^3}{3!}\Delta^3 u_0 + \dots\infty \right) \quad \text{(As Example 5.14(}i\text{))}$$

$$= e^x \left(1 + 3x + \frac{3x^2}{2} + \frac{x^3}{6} \right)$$

$$= \frac{1}{6}e^x (x^3 + 9x^2 + 18x + 6)$$

5.9   SUMMATION OF A SERIES

Suppose we want to find the sum of the series $u_1 + u_2 + u_3 + \dots\dots + u_n$.

For h = 1, let's define $u_x = \Delta y_x = y_{x+1} - y_x$

Therefore,

$$u_1 = y_2 - y_1$$
$$u_2 = y_3 - y_2$$
$$\dots\dots\dots\dots\dots$$
$$\dots\dots\dots\dots\dots$$
$$u_n = y_{n+1} - y_n$$

Adding both sides, we get $u_1 + u_2 + \dots\dots + u_n = y_{n+1} - y_1 = [y_x]_{x=1}^{x=n+1}$

Therefore,

$$\sum_{x=1}^{n} u_x = [y_x]_{x=1}^{x=n+1} = [\Delta^{-1} u_x]_{x=1}^{x=n+1} \quad (\because u_x = \Delta y_x \text{ Hence, } y_x = \Delta^{-1} u_x)$$

Example 5.18   Find the sum to n terms of the series $1.3.5 + 2.4.6 + 3.5.7 + \dots$

Solution: For h = 1, the xth term of the series $u_x = x\,(x+2)(x+4)$

$$= (x+4)[(x+3)-3](x+2)$$
$$= (x+4)(x+3)(x+2) - 3(x+4)(x+2)$$
$$= (x+4)(x+3)(x+2) - 3(x+4)\{(x+3)-1\}$$
$$= (x+4)^{(3)} - 3(x+4)^{(2)} + 3(x+4)^{(1)}$$

$$\sum_{x=1}^{n} u_x = [\Delta^{-1} u_x]_{x=1}^{x=n+1}$$

$$= \left[\Delta^{-1}\{(x+4)^{(3)} - 3(x+4)^{(2)} + 3(x+4)^{(1)}\}\right]_{x=1}^{x=n+1}$$

$$= \left[\frac{(x+4)^{(4)}}{4} - 3\frac{(x+4)^{(3)}}{3} + 3\frac{(x+4)^{(2)}}{2}\right]_{x=1}^{x=n+1}$$

$$= \frac{1}{4}\left[(n+5)^{(4)} - 5^{(4)}\right] - \left[(n+5)^{(3)} - 5^{(3)}\right] + \frac{3}{2}\left[(n+5)^{(2)} - 5^{(2)}\right]$$

$$= \frac{1}{4}[(n+5)(n+4)(n+3)(n+2) - 5.4.3.2]$$
$$- [(n+5)(n+4)(n+3) - 5.4.3] + \frac{3}{2}[(n+5)(n+4) - 5.4]$$

$$= \frac{1}{4}(n+5)(n+4)\{(n+3)(n+2) - 4(n+3) + 6\}$$

$$= \frac{1}{4}(n+5)(n+4)(n^2 + n)$$

$$= \frac{1}{4}n(n+1)(n+4)(n+5)$$

Example 5.19 Find the sum to n terms of the series

$$\frac{1}{2.3} + \frac{1}{3.4} + \frac{1}{4.5} + \dots\dots\dots$$

Solution: For h = 1, the xth term of the series is

$$u_x = \frac{1}{(x+1)(x+2)} = x^{(-2)}$$

Hence,

$$\sum_{x=1}^{n} u_x = [\Delta^{-1} u_x]_{x=1}^{x=n+1} = [\Delta^{-1}x^{(-2)}]_{x=1}^{x=n+1}$$

$$= \left[\frac{x^{(-1)}}{(-1)}\right]_{x=1}^{x=n+1} = -\left[\frac{1}{(x+1)}\right]_{x=1}^{x=n+1}$$

$$= -\left[\frac{1}{n+2} - \frac{1}{2}\right] = \frac{1}{2}\cdot\frac{n}{(n+2)}$$

Example 5.20   Prove that

$$\sum_{x=0}^{n} u_x = \binom{n+1}{1} u_0 + \binom{n+1}{2} \Delta u_0 + \binom{n+1}{3} \Delta^2 u_0 + \ldots\ldots + \Delta^n u_0$$

and hence, find $1^2 + 2^2 + 3^2 + \ldots + n^2$.

Solution:

$$RHS = \frac{1}{\Delta}\left[\binom{n+1}{1} \Delta u_0 + \binom{n+1}{2} \Delta^2 u_0 + \binom{n+1}{3} \Delta^3 u_0 + \ldots\ldots\right.$$
$$\left. + \Delta^{n+1} u_0\right]$$

$$= \frac{1}{\Delta}\left[\left\{1 + \binom{n+1}{1}\Delta + \binom{n+1}{2}\Delta^2 + \binom{n+1}{3}\Delta^3 + \ldots\ldots + \Delta^{n+1}\right\} - 1\right]u_0$$

$$= \frac{1}{\Delta}\left[(1+\Delta)^{(n+1)} - 1\right]u_0$$

$$= \left[\frac{E^{(n+1)} - 1}{E - 1}\right]u_0 \quad (as\ \Delta = E - 1)$$

$$= (1 + E + E^2 + \ldots\ldots + E^n)u_0$$

$$= u_0 + u_1 + u_2 + \ldots\ldots + u_n$$

$$= \sum_{x=0}^{n} u_x = LHS \qquad\qquad \ldots\ldots (i)$$

Now, let's take $u_x = 1^2 + 2^2 + 3^2 + \ldots\ldots + n^2$

Therefore, $\sum_{x=0}^{n} u_x = \sum_{x=0}^{n} x^2 = 1^2 + 2^2 + 3^2 + \ldots\ldots + n^2$

To apply result (i), we have to find $u_0, \Delta u_0, \Delta^2 u_0, \ldots\ldots$ The forward difference table is

x	u_x	$\Delta\ u_x$	$\Delta^2\ u_x$	$\Delta^3\ u_x$
0	0	1	2	0
1	1	3	2	0
2	4	5	2	0
3	9	7	2	
4	16	9		
5	25			

$$\sum_{x=0}^{n} u_x = \sum_{x=0}^{n} x^2 = \binom{n+1}{1} u_0 + \binom{n+1}{2} \Delta u_0 + \binom{n+1}{3} \Delta^2 u_0$$

$$= \binom{n+1}{1}(0) + \binom{n+1}{2}(1) + \binom{n+1}{3}(2)$$

$$= \frac{(n+1)n}{2} + \frac{(n+1)n(n-1)}{3.2.1}(2)$$

$$= \frac{n(n+1)}{6}[3 + 2n - 2]$$

$$= \frac{1}{6} n(n+1)(2n+1)$$

5.9.1 Montmort's Theorem

$$u_0 + u_1 x + u_2 x^2 + \dots \dots \infty = \frac{u_0}{1-x} + \frac{x\Delta u_0}{(1-x)^2} + \frac{x^2\Delta^2 u_0}{(1-x)^3} + \dots \dots \dots \infty$$

Proof: LHS $= u_0 + u_1 x + u_2 x^2 + \dots \dots$

$$= u_0 + xE\, u_0 + x^2 E^2\, u_0 + \dots \dots$$

$$= (1 + xE + x^2 E^2 + \dots \dots)\, u_0$$

$$= \frac{1}{1 - xE}\, u_0$$

(Formula for sum of infinite geometric progression is $\frac{a}{1-r}$ where, a = first term = 1, r = ratio = xE)

$$= \frac{1}{1 - x(1 - \Delta)}\, u_0 = \frac{1}{1 - x - x\Delta}\, u_0$$

$$= \frac{1}{(1-x)\left[\frac{1 - x - x\Delta}{1-x}\right]}\, u_0$$

$$= \frac{1}{(1-x)}\left[1 - \frac{x\Delta}{1-x}\right]^{-1} u_0$$

$$= \frac{1}{(1-x)}\left[1 + \frac{x\Delta}{1-x} + \frac{x^2\Delta^2}{(1-x)^2} + \dots \dots\right] u_0$$

$$= \frac{u_0}{1-x} + \frac{x\Delta u_0}{(1-x)^2} + \frac{x^2\Delta^2 u_0}{(1-x)^3} + \dots \dots \dots = RHS$$

Example 5.21 Use Montmort's theorem, to find the sum of the series

$$1.2 + 2.3\, x + 3.4\, x^2 + 4.5\, x^3 + \dots \dots \dots + \infty$$

Solution: Compare the given series $1.2 + 2.3\, x + 3.4\, x^2 + 4.5\, x^3 + \dots \dots \dots +$ ∞ with $u_0 + u_1 x + u_2 x^2 + \dots \dots \infty.$

We have, $u_0 = 1.2 = 2, u_1 = 2.3 = 6, u_2 = 3.4 = 12,$ $u_3 = 4.5 = 20$

To apply Montmort's theorem we have to compute Δu_0, $\Delta^2 u_0$, $\Delta^3 u_0$, ...

u	Δu	$\Delta^2 u$	$\Delta^3 u$
$u_0 = 2$	4	2	0
$u_1 = 6$	6	2	
$u_2 = 12$	8		
$u_3 = 20$			

∴ $u_0 = 2$, $\Delta u_0 = 4$, $\Delta^2 u_0 = 2$, $\Delta^3 u_0 = \Delta^4 u_0 = 0$

∴ $1.2 + 2.3\, x + 3.4\, x^2 + 4.5\, x^3 + \text{... ... ...} + \infty$

$$= u_0 + u_1 x + u_2 x^2 + \text{... ...} \infty = \frac{u_0}{1-x} + \frac{x \Delta u_0}{(1-x)^2} + \frac{x^2 \Delta^2 u_0}{(1-x)^3} + \text{... ... ...}$$

$$= \frac{2}{1-x} + \frac{4x}{(1-x)^2} + \frac{2x^2}{(1-x)^3}, x \neq 1 \quad = \frac{2}{(1-x)^3}$$

Example 5.22   Use Montmort's theorem, to find the sum of the series

$$1^3 + 2^3 x + 3^3 x^2 + 4^3 x^3 + \text{... ... ...} + \infty$$

Solution: Compare the given series $1^3 + 2^3 x + 3^3 x^2 + 4^3 x^3 + \text{... ...} + \infty$

with $u_0 + u_1 x + u_2 x^2 + \text{... ...} \infty$.

We have, $u_0 = 1^3 = 1, u_1 = 2^3 = 8, u_2 = 3^3 = 27,$ $u_3 = 4^3 = 64$

To apply Montmort's theorem we have to compute Δu_0, $\Delta^2 u_0$, $\Delta^3 u_0$, ...

u	Δu	$\Delta^2 u$	$\Delta^3 u$	$\Delta^4 u$
$u_0 = 1$	7	12	6	0
$u_1 = 8$	19	18	6	
$u_2 = 27$	37	24		
$u_3 = 64$	61			
$u_4 = 125$				

∴ $u_0 = 1$, $\Delta u_0 = 7$, $\Delta^2 u_0 = 12$, $\Delta^3 u_0 = 6$, $\Delta^4 u_0 = \Delta^5 u_0 = 0$

∴ $1^3 + 2^3 x + 3^3 x^2 + 4^3 x^3 + \text{... ... ...} + \infty$

$$= u_0 + u_1 x + u_2 x^2 + u_3 x^3 + \text{... ...} \infty$$

$$= \frac{u_0}{1-x} + \frac{x \Delta u_0}{(1-x)^2} + \frac{x^2 \Delta^2 u_0}{(1-x)^3} + \frac{x^3 \Delta^3 u_0}{(1-x)^4} + \text{... ... ...}$$

$$= \frac{1}{1-x} + \frac{7x}{(1-x)^2} + \frac{12x^2}{(1-x)^3} + \frac{6x^3}{(1-x)^4}, x \neq 1 \quad = \frac{x^2 + 4x + 1}{(1-x)^4}$$

EXERCISES

1. Multiple Choice Questions

(1) The first order Newton's forward difference operator is defined as

 (a) $\Delta y_1 = y_2 - y_1$

 (b) $\Delta y_1 = y_1 - y_2$

 (c) $\Delta y_1 = y_1 - y_0$

 (d) $\Delta y_1 = y_0 - y_1$

 (e) None of these

(2) If the nth order differences of a function tabulated at equal intervals are constant, then function is a polynomial of degree _____.

 (a) $n + 1$

 (b) n

 (c) $n - 1$

 (d) *can't decided*

 (e) None of these

(3) Select the correct option from the following:

 (a) $\Delta . \nabla = \nabla - \Delta$

 (b) $\Delta . \nabla = 1 - \nabla$

 (c) $\Delta . \nabla = \Delta - 1$

 (d) $\Delta . \nabla = \Delta - \nabla$

 (e) None of these

(4) A factorial notation $[x]^n$ is defined as

 (a) $[x]^n = x(x - 1)(x - 2) \dots \dots [x - (n - 1)]$

 (b) $[x]^n = x(x + 1)(x + 2) \dots \dots [x + (n - 1)]$

 (c) $[x]^n = x.x.x \dots \dots (n - 1)$ times

 (d) $[x]^n = 1.2.3 \dots \dots . n$ times

 (e) None of these

(5) If we assume h = 1 then the value of $\Delta^{-1}[x]^r = ?$

 (a) r. $[x]^{r-1}$

 (b) $\dfrac{[x]^{r+1}}{r+1}$

 (c) (r-1). $[x]^{r-1}$

 (d) $\dfrac{[x]^{r-1}}{r-1}$

 (e) None of these

Answers: (1) (a)   (2) (b)   (3) (d)   (4) (a)   (5) (b)

2. Problems

(1) Given the set of values

x:	0	1	2	3	4	5
f(x):	12	15	20	27	39	52

Construct forward difference table and hence find the values of $\Delta^2 f(3)$, $\Delta^3 f(2)$ and $\Delta^4 f(1)$.

(2) Show that $\Delta^3 y_i = y_{i+3} - 3y_{i+2} + 3y_{i+1} - y_i$

(3) Form the table of backward differences of the function $f(x) = x^3 - 3x^2 - 5x - 7$ for $x = -1, 0, 1, 2, 3, 4, 5$.

(4) Show that the operators δ, μ, E, Δ and ∇ commute with one another.

(5) Evaluate the following:

(a) $\Delta^2 \cos 2x$ (b) $\Delta^n (e^{ax+b})$ (c) $\Delta (x + \cos x)$

(d) $\Delta^2 \left(\frac{1}{x^2 + 5x + 6}\right)$ (e) $\Delta^n \left(\frac{1}{x}\right)$ (f) $\Delta \left(\frac{1}{f(x)}\right)$

(g) $\Delta^3 [(1 - x)(1 - 2x)(1 - 3x)]$
(*if the interval of differencing being unity*)

(h) $\Delta^{10}[(1 - x)(1 - 2x^2)(1 - 3x^3)(1 - 4x^4)]$
(*if the interval of differencing is 2*)

(i) $\left(\frac{\Delta^2}{E}\right) x^3$

(6) Prove the following results:

(a) $\mu = \frac{2 + \Delta}{2\sqrt{1+\Delta}}$ (b) $1 + \mu^2 \delta^2 = \left(1 + \frac{\delta^2}{2}\right)^2$

(c) $\Delta^3 y_2 = \nabla^3 y_5$ (d) $(E^{1/2} + E^{-1/2})(1 + \Delta)^{1/2} = 2 + \Delta$

(e) $\delta = 2 \sinh \left(\frac{hD}{2}\right)$ (f) $\delta = \Delta (1 + \Delta)^{-1/2} = \nabla(1 - \nabla)^{-1/2}$

(g) $\delta(E^{1/2} + E^{-1/2}) = \Delta E^{-1} + \Delta$

(h) $E^{1/2} = \mu + \frac{\delta}{2}$; $E^{-1/2} = \mu - \frac{\delta}{2}$

(i) $\mu\delta = \frac{1}{2}\Delta E^{-1} + \frac{\Delta}{2}$ (j) $\nabla = \delta E^{-1/2}$

(7) Assuming that the following values of y belong to a polynomial of degree 4, find the missing values in the table:

x:	0	1	2	3	4	5	6	7
f(x):	1	-1	1	-1	1	--	--	--

(8) Find the missing term in the following table (a) by using the difference table and (b) without using the difference table:

x:	0	1	2	3	4
y:	1	3	9	--	81

(9)   Find the missing values from the following table:

x:	100	200	300	400	500	600	700
y:	4	9	--	193	--	1329	2704

(10)   Express the following functions in terms of factorial polynomials and
hence find their differences taking $h = 1$.

(a) $x^4 - 3x^3 + 4x^2 - 7x + 6$
(b) $2x^3 - 3x^2 + 4x - 8$
(c) $x^4 - 12x^3 + 24x^2 - 30x + 9$. Also, show that $\Delta^5 f(x) = 0$.

(11)   Express $7x^4 + 12x^3 - 6x^2 + 5x - 3$ in terms of factorial polynomials,
taking $h = 2$ and hence find its forward differences.

(12)   Obtain the function whose first difference is $2x^3 + 3x^2 - 5x + 4$.

(13)   Calculate $\Delta^4 y$ if $y = (3x + 1)(3x + 4) \dots \dots (3x + 22)$

(14)   Find $\Delta^2 y$ and $\Delta^{-1} y$, when $y = \frac{1}{(3x+1)(3x+4)(3x+7)}$

(15)   Write the polynomial of lowest degree which satisfies the following set
of numbers:
$$0, 7, 26, 63, 124, 215, 342, 511$$

(16)   One entry in the following table is incorrect and y is a cubic polynomial
in x. Use the difference table to locate and correct the error:

x:	0	1	2	3	4	5	6	7
y:	25	21	18	18	27	45	76	123

(17)   Locate and correct the error in the following table of values:

x:	2.5	3.0	3.5	4.0	4.5	5.0	5.5
y:	4.32	4.83	5.27	5.47	6.26	6.79	7.23

(18)   Using the method of seperation of symbols, prove that

(a) $u_0 + \binom{n}{1} \Delta u_1 + \binom{n}{2}\Delta^2 u_2 + \dots \dots = u_n + \binom{n}{1}\Delta^2 u_{n-1} + \binom{n}{2}\Delta^4 u_{n-2} + \dots \dots$

(b) $u_0 + \binom{n}{1} u_1 x + \binom{n}{2} u_2 x^2 + \binom{n}{3} u_3 x^3 \dots \dots$
$= (1 + x)^n u_0 + \binom{n}{1} (1 + x)^{n-1} x\Delta u_0 + \binom{n}{2} (1 + x)^{n-2} x^2 \Delta^2 u_0 + \dots \dots$

(c) $u_x = u_{x-1} + \Delta u_{x-2} + \Delta^2 u_{x-3} + \Delta^3 u_{x-4} + \dots \dots$

(d) $\Delta^n e^x = e^{x+n} - \binom{n}{1} e^{x+n-1} + \binom{n}{2} e^{x+n-2} + \dots + (-1)^n e^x$

(19)   Find the nth term of the sequence $1, 4, 10, 20, 35, 56, \dots.$ Also find 7th
term.

(20) Show that
$$u_0 + \frac{u_1 x}{1!} + \frac{u_2 x^2}{2!} + \ldots \ldots + \infty = e^x (u_0 + x\Delta u_0 + \frac{x^2}{2!}\Delta^2 u_0 + \ldots \ldots +$$
∞) and hence find the sum of the series

(a) $1^3 + \frac{2^3}{1!} x + \frac{3^3}{2!} x^2 + \frac{4^3}{3!} x^3 + \ldots \ldots + \infty$

(b) $5 + \frac{8}{1!} x + \frac{13}{2!} x^2 + \frac{40}{3!} x^3 + \frac{109}{4!} x^4 + \frac{240}{5!} x^5 + \ldots \ldots + \infty$

(21) Use the method of finite differences to find the sum of the first n terms of the series:
(a) $1^3 + 2^3 + 3^3 + \ldots \ldots$
(b) $2.5 + 5.8 + 8.11 + 11.14 + \ldots \ldots$
(c) $1.4.7 + 2.5.8 + 3.6.9 + \ldots \ldots$
(d) $\frac{1}{2.3.4} + \frac{1}{3.4.5} + \frac{1}{4.5.6} + \ldots \ldots$

(22) Use Montmort's theorem to find the sum of the following series:
(a) $1.3 + 3.5x + 5.7x^2 + 7.9x^3 + \ldots \ldots + \infty$
(b) $1^2 + 2^2 x + 3^2 x^2 + 4^2 x^3 + \ldots \ldots + \infty$

Answers

(1)   1, -4, -7

(5)   (a) $-4 \sin^2 h \cos(2x + 2h)$ (b) $(e^{ah} - 1)^n e^{ax+b}$

(c) $1 - 2 \sin\left(x + \frac{1}{2}\right) \sin\frac{1}{2}$ (d) $-2/[(x + 2)(x + 3)(x + 4)]$

(e) $\dfrac{(-1)^n n!}{x \, (x+1)(x+2)...(x+n)}$ (f) $\dfrac{-\Delta f(x)}{f(x)f(x+1)}$

(g)   -36   (h) $24 \times 2^{10} \times 10!$

(i) $6x$

(7) $y_5 = 31, \; y_6 = 129, y_7 = 351$ (8) $y_4 = 31$

(9)   48; 564

(10) (a) $[x]^4 + 3[x]^3 + 2[x]^2 - 5[x]^1 + 6$

(b) $2[x]^3 + 3[x]^2 + 3[x]^1 - 8$

(c) $[x]^4 - 6[x]^3 + 13[x]^2 + [x] + 9$

(11) $y = 7[x]^4 + 96[x]^3 + 262[x]^2 + 97[x]^1 - 3; \; \Delta y = 56[x]^3 + 576[x]^2 + 1048[x]^1 + 194; \; \Delta^2 y = 336[x]^2 + 2304[x]^1 + 2096; \; \Delta^3 y = 1334[x]^1 + 4608; \; \Delta^4 y = 2688$

(12) $\frac{1}{2}[x]^4 + 3[x]^3 + 4[x] + c$

(13) $\Delta^4 y = 136080 \, (3x + 13)(3x + 16)(3x + 19)(3x + 22)$

(14) $\dfrac{108}{(3x+1)(3x+4).....(3x+13)}; \; -\dfrac{6}{6(3x+1)(3x+4)}$ (15) $x^3 + 2x^2 + 3x$

(16)   The entry corresponding to $x = 3$ is in error. True value is $y = 19$.

(17)   The entry corresponding to $x = 4.0$ is in error. True value is $y = 5.75$

(19) $\frac{1}{6} \, (n^3 + 6n^2 + 11n + 6), \; 7th \; term = 84$

(20) (a) $e^x \, (1 + 7x + 6x^2 + x^3)$ (b) $\frac{1}{3} e^x \, (10 \, x^3 + 3x^2 + 9x + 15 \,)$

(21) (a) $\frac{1}{4} n^2 \, (n + 1)^2$ (b) $3n^3 + 6n^2 + n$

(c) $\frac{1}{4} n(n + 1)(n + 6)(n + 7)$ (d) $\dfrac{n(n+5)}{12(n+2)(n+3)}$

(22) (a) $\dfrac{3+6x-x^2}{(1-x)^3}$ (b) $\dfrac{1+x}{(1-x)^3}$

Chapter 6   Interpolation

Objectives

- To know various applications of interpolation
- To enable students to obtain an intuitive and working understanding of different interpolation methods like Newton's forward, Newton's backward, Central interpolation, Lagrange's interpolation and Newton's divided for basic problems of numerical analyses and gain experience in the implementation of interpolation methods.
- To understand, analyze and predict the concept of error in these methods
- To understand the importance and the concept of piecewise interpolation
- To understand the concept of cubic spline approximation

Learning Outcomes

After reading this lesson students should be able to

- Apply different interpolation methods successfully
- Select correct interpolation method for a given problem
- Identify an error in different interpolation methods and rectify it
- Effectively solve the problems of piecewise interpolation
- Effectively solve the problems of cubic spline approximation

6.1   INTRODUCTION

Let $x_0, x_1, x_2, \ldots \ldots, x_n$ be n independent variables and let $y_0, y_1, y_2, \ldots \ldots, y_n$ be the corresponding values of dependent variables for the function $y = f(x)$. Then the process of estimating the value of unknown dependent variable y corresponding to any known value of x between the specified range $x_0 \leq x \leq x_n$ of independent variable x is known as *interpolation*.

The process of estimating the value of dependent variable y corresponding to the given value of independent variable x outside the range $x_0 \leq x \leq x_n$ is known as *extrapolation*.

Here, we assume $f(x)$ to be single valued, continuous and known explicitly, then the value of dependent variable y corresponding to any value of the independent variable x can be easily calculated. Conversely, if $f(x)$ is a function which is not known explicitly and if a set of values $(x_0, y_0), (x_1, y_1), (x_2, y_2), \ldots \ldots, (x_n, y_n)$ which satisfies a function are known then a function $\emptyset(x)$ is required to be found such that $f(x)$ and $\emptyset(x)$ agree at a given set of values. If $\emptyset(x)$ is a polynomial then it is called an interpolating polynomial and the process is called polynomial interpolation. If $\emptyset(x)$ is a trigonometric function then the process is called trigonometric interpolation and $\emptyset(x)$ is called a trigonometric polynomial. We are only interested in polynomial interpolation.

We write $f(x) \equiv \emptyset(x)$. Therefore, $f(x) = \emptyset(x) + R_{n+1}(x)$ where, $R_{n+1}(x)$ is the remainder or error occured during the process of approximating $f(x)$ by $\emptyset(x)$. As a justification for this approximation of the unknown function $\emptyset(x)$ by means of polynomial $f(x)$,the Weierstrass Approximation theorem is stated here without proof.

The Weierstrass Approximation theorem

Let $f(x)$ be a continuous function defined on closed interval $[a,b]$. Then $f(x)$ can be uniformly approximated by polynomial. i.e. Let $f(x)$ be a continuous function on a closed interval [a,b], then given $\varepsilon > 0$, there exists plynomial P(x) such that

$$|f(x) - P(x)| < \varepsilon, \text{for } \forall\, x \in [a,b]$$

6.1.1 Error in Interpolation

Let $f(x)$ be a function which is continuous and differentiable upto desired number of times and $p(x)$ be the interpolating polynomial of degree n such that

$$f(x_j) = p(x_j), \quad j = 0,1,2,3\dots,n \qquad \dots\dots (6.1.1)$$

Since $R_{n+1}(x)$ is the remainder in approximating $f(x)$ by $p(x)$

We have, $f(x) = p(x) + R_{n+1}$ or $R_{n+1} = f(x) - p(x)$ $\dots\dots (6.1.2)$

From Eq. (6.1.1) and Eq. (6.1.2), we have

$$R_{n+1}(x_j) = 0, \quad j = 0,1,2,3,\dots\dots,n \qquad \dots\dots (6.1.3)$$

i.e. $x - x_0, x - x_1, \dots\dots, x - x_n$ are all factors of $R_{n+1}(x)$.

Let $w(x) = (x - x_0)(x - x_1)\dots\dots(x - x_n)$

From the Eq. (6.1.3) we may write

$$R_{n+1}(x) = w(x)\,\emptyset(x) \qquad \dots\dots (6.1.4)$$

where, $w(x)$ is a polynomial of degree $(n+1)$ and $\emptyset(x)$ is any function.

Thus, from Eq. (6.1.2) and Eq. (6.1.4)

$$f(x) = p(x) + w(x)\,\emptyset(x) \qquad \dots\dots (6.1.5)$$

Now, the remainder at specific point $x = \alpha$ which is different from x_j , $j = 0,1,2,3,\dots\dots,n$ is given by

$$f(\alpha) = p(\alpha) + w(\alpha)\,\emptyset(\alpha) \quad (\because \text{Eq. (6.1.5)}) \qquad \dots\dots (6.1.6)$$

Define $F(x) = f(x) - p(x) - w(x)\,\emptyset(\alpha)$ $\dots\dots (6.1.7)$

Then, $F(x) = 0$ at α and x_j, $j = 0,1,2,3,\dots\dots,n$

$F(x)$ is continuously differentiable up to desired number of time as $f(x)$ is continuously differentiable up to any desired number of time.

Now, if we take $a = \min\{\alpha, x_0, x_1, \dots\dots, x_n\}$ and $b = \max\{\alpha, x_0, x_1, \dots\dots, x_n\}$ then $F(x)$ satisfies Rolle's theorem for all the sub intervals of $[a, b]$. By the repreated application of Rolle's theorem, we have

$$\therefore\quad F^{n+1}(\xi) = 0 \qquad \text{for every } \xi \in (a, b) \qquad \text{........ (6.1.8)}$$

Differentiating function $F(x)$, $(n + 1)$ times, we get

$$F^{n+1}(x) = f^{n+1}(x) - p^{n+1}(x) - w^{n+1}(x)\,\emptyset(\alpha) \qquad \text{........ (6.1.9)}$$

Since $p(x)$ is a polynomial of degree n and $w(x)$ is a polynomial of degree $(n + 1)$ with leading coefficient 1, we have

$$p^{n+1}(x) = 0 \quad \text{and} \quad w^{n+1}(x) = (n + 1)! \qquad \text{........ (6.1.10)}$$

From Eq. (6.1.9), we have

$$F^{n+1}(x) = f^{n+1}(x) - 0 - (n + 1)!\,\emptyset(\alpha)$$

From Eq. (6.1.8),

$$0 = F^{n+1}(\xi) = f^{n+1}(\xi) - (n + 1)!\,\emptyset(\alpha)$$

$$\therefore\quad \emptyset(\alpha) = \frac{f^{n+1}(\xi)}{(n + 1)!}$$

Therefore, from Eq. (6.1.4), we have

$$R_{n+1}(\alpha) = w(\alpha)\,\emptyset(\alpha) = w(\alpha)\frac{f^{n+1}(\xi)}{(n + 1)!}$$

In general,

$$R_{n+1}(x) = w(x)\frac{f^{n+1}(\xi)}{(n + 1)!}$$

$$= (x - x_0)(x - x_1)\dots\dots(x - x_n)\frac{f^{n+1}(\xi)}{(n + 1)!} \qquad \text{........ (6.1.11)}$$

where, ξ lies between the min and max of the numbers $x, x_0, x_1, \dots\dots, x_n$.

Remark:

1. If x_j, $j = 0,1,2,\dots\dots,n$ are equispaced and $h > 0$ be the interval of differencing then we have $x_1 = x_0 + h$, $x_2 = x_0 + 2h, \dots\dots, x_n = x_0 + nh$
    If we define $u = \frac{x - x_0}{h}$ then $x - x_1 = x - (x_0 + h) = (x - x_0) - h = uh - h = (u - 1)h$
    Similarly, $x - x_r = (u - r)h$. Then,

    $$R_{n+1}(x) = u(u - 1)(u - 2)\dots\dots(u - n).\,h^{n+1}\frac{f^{n+1}(\xi)}{(n + 1)!}$$

2. If $f^{n+1}(x)$ does not vary significantly over the range of interpolation $[x_0, x_n]$ and h is very small then we have

    $$h^{n+1}\,f^{n+1}(\xi) \approx \Delta^{n+1}f(x_0) = \Delta^{n+1}y_0$$

    Therefore,

    $$R_{n+1}(x) = \frac{u(u-1)(u-2)\dots\dots(u-n)}{(n+1)!}\Delta^{n+1}y_0 \qquad \text{........ (6.1.12)}$$

6.2   NEWTON'S FORWARD DIFFERENCE INTERPOLATION FORMULA

Consider an nth degree polynomial passing through $(n + 1)$ points $(x_0, y_0), (x_1, y_1), (x_2, y_2), , \ldots \ldots, (x_n, y_n)$ of interval size h such that y and $y_n(x)$ agree at the tabulated points. Let $x_i's$ are equidistant points.

Since $y_n(x)$ is an nth degree polynomial, it may be written as

$$y_n(x) = a_0 + a_1(x - x_0) + a_2(x - x_0)(x - x_1) + \ldots + a_n(x - x_0)$$
$$(x - x_1) \ldots \ldots (x - x_{n-1}) \qquad \ldots\ldots (6.2.1)$$

Applying the condition that y and $y_n(x)$ should agree at the tabulated points and putting, $x = x_0, x_1, x_2, x_3, \ldots \ldots, x_n$ we have

$$\left.\begin{array}{l} at \ \ x = x_0 \Rightarrow y_0 = a_0 \\ at \ \ \ x = x_1 \Rightarrow y_1 = a_0 + a_1(x_1 - x_0) \\ at \ \ x = x_2 \Rightarrow y_2 = a_0 + a_1(x_2 - x_0) + a_2(x_2 - x_0)(x_2 - x_1) \\ \qquad \cdots \qquad \cdots \qquad \cdots \\ \qquad \qquad \cdots \qquad \cdots \qquad \cdots \end{array}\right\} \ldots(6.2.2)$$

and so on.

Here, interval size is h and $x_i's$ are equidistant.

$$\therefore \ x_{i+1} - x_i = h \qquad i = 0,1,2,3, \ldots \ldots, n - 1$$
$$\therefore \ x_{i+m} - x_i = mh \qquad\qquad \ldots\ldots (6.2.3)$$

Now, from Eq.(6.2.2) and from Eq. (6.2.3) we have

$$a_0 = y_0$$

$$a_1 = \frac{y_1 - a_0}{x_1 - x_0} = \frac{y_1 - y_0}{x_1 - x_0} = \frac{y_1 - y_0}{h} = \frac{\Delta y_0}{h}$$

$$(\because \text{ from Eq.(6.2.3) } x_1 - x_0 = h)$$

$$a_2 = \frac{y_2 - a_0 - a_1(x_2 - x_0)}{(x_2 - x_0)(x_2 - x_1)} = \frac{y_2 - y_0 - \left(\frac{y_1 - y_0}{h}\right) 2h}{(2h).(h)}$$

$$= \frac{y_2 - y_0 - 2y_1 + 2y_0}{2h^2} = \frac{(y_2 - y_1) - (y_1 - y_0)}{2! \ h^2}$$

$$= \frac{\Delta y_1 - \Delta y_0}{2! \ h^2} = \frac{\Delta^2 y_0}{2! \ h^2}$$

Similarly,

$$a_3 = \frac{\Delta^3 y_0}{3! \ h^3}$$

$$\ldots\ldots\ldots\ldots\ldots \qquad \ldots\ldots\ldots\ldots\ldots$$
$$\ldots\ldots\ldots\ldots\ldots \qquad \ldots\ldots\ldots\ldots\ldots$$

$$\therefore \ a_n = \frac{\Delta^n y_0}{n! \ h^n}$$

Thus, $\quad a_0 = y_0, \; a_1 = \frac{\Delta y_0}{h}, \; a_2 = \frac{\Delta^2 y_0}{2! \, h^2}, \; \ldots \ldots \ldots \ldots, a_n = \frac{\Delta^n y_0}{n! \, h^n}$

Substitute all these values of constant in Eq. (6.2.1), we get

$$y_n(x) = y_0 + \frac{\Delta y_0}{h}(x - x_0) + \frac{\Delta^2 y_0}{2! \, h^2}(x - x_0)(x - x_1) + \ldots \ldots \ldots$$

$$+ \frac{\Delta^n y_0}{n! \, h^n}(x - x_0)(x - x_1) \ldots \ldots (x - x_{n-1}) \qquad \ldots \ldots (6.2.4)$$

Let

$$\frac{x - x_0}{h} = u$$

$\therefore \; x - x_0 = uh$

$\therefore \; x - x_1 = x - (x_0 + h) = (x - x_0) - h = uh - h = h\,(u - 1)$

$\therefore \; x - x_2 = x - (x_1 + h) = (x - x_1) - h = h\,(u - 1) - h = h\,(u - 2)$

$\qquad \ldots \qquad\qquad\qquad \ldots \qquad\qquad\qquad \ldots \qquad\qquad\qquad \ldots$

$\therefore \; x - x_{n-1} = h\left(u - (n - 1)\right)$

Putting these values of $\;x - x_0, x - x_1, \ldots \ldots, x - x_{n-1}\;$ in Eq. (6.2.4) we get

$$y_n(x) = y_0 + \frac{\Delta y_0}{1! h} uh + \frac{\Delta^2 y_0}{2! \, h^2} uh. h(u - 1) + \; \ldots + \frac{\Delta^n y_0}{n! \, h^n}(uh). h(u - 1). h(u - 2) \ldots h(u - (n - 1))$$

$$\therefore \; y_n(x) = y_0 + \frac{\Delta y_0}{1!} u + \frac{\Delta^2 y_0}{2!} u(u - 1) + \cdots + \frac{\Delta^n y_0}{n!} u(u - 1)(u - 2) \ldots \ldots (u - (n - 1)) \qquad \ldots \ldots (6.2.5)$$

In general,

$$\boxed{\begin{aligned} y_n(x) = y_k &+ \frac{\Delta y_k}{1!} u + \frac{\Delta^2 y_k}{2!} u(u - 1) + \; \ldots \ldots \\ &+ \frac{\Delta^{n-k} y_k}{(n-k)!} u(u - 1)(u - 2) \ldots \ldots (u - ((n - k) - 1)) \end{aligned}} \qquad \ldots \ldots (6.2.6)$$

This is known as Newton's forward difference interpolation formula. This formula is applicable if the value to be interpolated lies near the upper half of the table.

6.2.1   Estimation of Error in Newton's Forward Interpolation Formula

From Eq. (6.1.12), we have

$$R_{n+1}(x) = \frac{u(u - 1)(u - 2) \ldots \ldots (u - n)}{(n + 1)!} \Delta^{n+1} y_0 \qquad \ldots \ldots (6.2.7)$$

$$\therefore \; |R_{n+1}(x)| = \left| \frac{u(u - 1)(u - 2) \ldots \ldots (u - n)}{(n + 1)!} \right| |\Delta^{n+1} y_0|$$

If $0 < u < 1$, then

$$|(u - 2)(u - 3)(u - 4) \ldots \ldots (u - n)| \leq |(-2)(-3)(-4) \ldots \ldots (-n)|$$
$$\leq 2.3.4 \ldots \ldots n = 1.2.3.4 \ldots \ldots n = n!$$

and

$$|u(u-1)| = u(1-u) = u - u^2 = \frac{1}{4} - \frac{1}{4} + 2.\frac{1}{2}u - u^2$$

$$= \frac{1}{4} - \left(\frac{1}{2} - u\right)^2 \leq \frac{1}{4}$$

$$\therefore \ |R_{n+1}(x)| \leq \frac{n!}{4(n+1)!}|\Delta^{n+1}y_0|$$

Let

$$A_n(u) = \frac{u(u-1)(u-2)\dots\dots(u-n)}{(n+1)!} \qquad \dots\dots\dots(6.2.8)$$

then

$$|A_n(u)| \leq \frac{n!}{4(n+1)!} = \frac{1}{4(n+1)}$$

$$\therefore \ |R_{n+1}(x)| = \left(\frac{1}{4(n+1)}\right)|\Delta^{n+1}y_0| < 1$$

If n > 1 and 0 < u < 1 the error in Newton's forward difference formula is less than 1 in the last significant figure in ordinary calculation. The formula is suitable for interpolation at the top of the forward difference table.

From Eq. (6.2.8),

$$|A_n(u)| = \left|\frac{u(u-1)(u-2)\dots\dots(u-n)}{(n+1)!}\right|$$

For 0 < ε < 1, we have

$$|A_n(\varepsilon)| = \left|\frac{\varepsilon(\varepsilon-1)(\varepsilon-2)\dots\dots(\varepsilon-n)}{(n+1)!}\right| \qquad \dots\dots\dots(6.2.9)$$

and

$$|A_n(-\varepsilon)| = \left|\frac{-\varepsilon(-\varepsilon-1)(-\varepsilon-2)\dots\dots(-\varepsilon-n)}{(n+1)!}\right|$$

$$= \left|\frac{\varepsilon(\varepsilon+1)(\varepsilon+2)\dots\dots(\varepsilon+n)}{(n+1)!}\right| \qquad \dots\dots\dots(6.2.10)$$

For extrapolation, in the forward difference table, we must have u < 0. Eq. (6.2.9) and Eq. (6.2.10) indicates that, when u is negative the error in the extrapolation is greater than that of the error in the interpolation. Thus, the use of interpolation in computing a function value is preferable than the use of extrapolation in the forward difference.

Example 6.1 For the given values find the order of the polynomial which might be suitable to the given values:

x	2.0	2.1	2.2	2.3	2.4	2.5
$f(x)$	13.00	14.261	15.648	17.167	18.824	20.625

Solution: The forward difference table is:

x_i	$f(x_i)$	$\Delta f(x_i)$	$\Delta^2 f(x_i)$	$\Delta^3 f(x_i)$	$\Delta^4 f(x_i)$	$\Delta^5 f(x_i)$
2.0	13.00	1.261	0.126	0.006	0	0
2.1	14.261	1.3870	0.132	0.006	0	
2.2	15.648	1.51900	0.138	0.006		
2.3	17.167	1.65700	0.144			
2.4	18.824	1.80100				
2.5	20.625					

As we have discussed in the previous chapter that if n^{th} order differences are constant and $(n+1)^{th}$ order differences are zero then the polynomial best fitted to the given value will be of order n.

Therefore, in this example order of polynomial is 3.

Example 6.2   Construct a polynomial for the data given below.
Also find $y(x = 5)$.

x	4	6	8	10
y	1	3	8	16

Solution: The forward difference table is

x_i	y_i	Δy_i	$\Delta^2 y_i$	$\Delta^3 y_i$
4	1	2	3	0
6	3	5	3	
8	8	8		
10	16			

The forward difference formula is

$$y(x) = y_0 + \frac{\Delta y_0}{1!} u + \frac{\Delta^2 y_0}{2!} u(u-1) + \frac{\Delta^3 y_0}{3!} u(u-1)(u-2)$$

where,

$$u = \frac{x - x_0}{h} = \frac{x - 4}{2}$$

$$\therefore \ y(x) = 1 + 2\left(\frac{x-4}{2}\right) + \frac{3}{2}\left(\frac{x-4}{2}\right)\left(\frac{x-4}{2} - 1\right) + 0$$

$$= 1 + (x - 4) + \frac{3}{2} \left(\frac{x-4}{2}\right)\left(\frac{x-6}{2}\right)$$

$$= \frac{1}{8}(3x^2 - 22x + 48)$$

For $x = 5$, $y(5) = \frac{1}{8}(3(5)^2 - 22(5) + 48) = \frac{1}{8}(75 - 110 + 48) = 1.625$

Example 6.3   A population of a town is given below. Estimate population for the year 1969.

Year (x)	1965	1975	1985	1995	2005
Population (in 1000's) (y)	46	66	81	93	101

Solution:

Newton's forward difference table is

x_i	y_i	Δy_i	$\Delta^2 y_i$	$\Delta^3 y_i$	$\Delta^4 y_i$
1965	46	20	-5	2	-3
1975	66	15	-3	-1	
1985	81	12	-4		
1995	93	8			
2005	101				

Here, tabular points are equidistant and interval length h = 10. Since x = 1969 is near the upper half of the table or near the starting point of the table we use Newton's forward difference formula. Also, point x = 1969 lies between first and second point (i.e. between x = 1965 and x = 1975) therefore we consider forward differences at the first point.

The forward difference formula is

$$y(x) = y_0 + \frac{\Delta y_0}{1!}u + \frac{\Delta^2 y_0}{2!}u(u-1) + \frac{\Delta^3 y_0}{3!}u(u-1)(u-2)$$
$$+ \frac{\Delta^4 y_0}{4!}u(u-1)(u-2)(u-3)$$

where,

$$u = \frac{x - x_0}{h} = \frac{1969 - 1965}{10} = \frac{4}{10} = 0.4$$

$\therefore y(1965) = 46 + 20(0.4) + \frac{-5}{2}(0.4)(0.4 - 1) + \frac{2}{6}(0.4)(0.4 - 1)(0.4 - 2)$
$+ \frac{-3}{24}(0.4)(0.4 - 1)(0.4 - 2)(0.4 - 3)$

$$= 46 + 8 + 0.6 + 0.128 + 0.1248$$
$$= 54.8528 \text{ (up to four decimal places)}$$

Example 6.4   Using Newton's formula for interpolation, find the number of students getting marks not more than 55 from the following data.

Marks	40 – 50	50-60	60-70	70-80	80-90
No. of Students	41	52	61	45	41

Solution:

Marks	No. of Students	Δy_i	$\Delta^2 y_i$	$\Delta^3 y_i$	$\Delta^4 y_i$
Below 50	41	52	9	-25	37
Below 60	93	61	-16	12	
Below 70	154	45	-4		
Below 80	199	41			
Below 90	240				

Here, tabular points are equidistant and interval length h = 10. Since x = 55 is near the upper half of the table or near the starting point of the table, we use Newton's forward difference formula

The forward difference formula is

$$y(x) = y_0 + \frac{\Delta y_0}{1!} u + \frac{\Delta^2 y_0}{2!} u(u-1) + \frac{\Delta^3 y_0}{3!} u(u-1)(u-2)$$
$$+ \frac{\Delta^4 y_0}{4!} u(u-1)(-2)(u-3)$$

where,

$$u = \frac{x - x_0}{h} = \frac{55 - 50}{10} = \frac{5}{10} = 0.5$$

$\therefore y(55) = 41 + 52(0.5) + \frac{9}{2}(0.5)(0.5 - 1) + \frac{-25}{6}(0.5)(0.5 - 1)(0.5 - 2) + \frac{37}{24}(0.5)(0.5 - 1)(0.5 - 2)(0.5 - 3)$

   = $41 + 26 + (-1.125) + (-1.5625) + (-1.4453)$

   = $62.8672 \approx 63$ students

Example 6.5 Apply Newton's forward differene formula to calculate $\cos 32^0$. Given the folowing data.

x^0	25^0	30^0	35^0	40^0	45^0
$y = \cos x^0$	0.9063	0.8660	0.8192	0.7660	0.7071

Solution:

The forward difference table is

x	y	Δy	$\Delta^2 y$	$\Delta^3 y$	$\Delta^4 y$
25	0.9063	-0.0403	-0.0065	0.0001	0.0006
30	0.8660	-0.0468	-0.0064	0.0007	
35	0.8192	-0.0532	-0.0057		
40	0.7660	-0.0589			
45	0.7071				

Here, tabular points are equidistant and interval length h = 5. Since $x = 32$ is near the upper half of the table. we use Newton's forward difference formula. Also, point $x = 32$ lies between second and third point (i.e. between $x = 30$ and $x = 35$) therefore we consider forward differences at the second point.

The forward difference formula is

$$y(x) = y_0 + \frac{\Delta y_0}{1!} u + \frac{\Delta^2 y_0}{2!} u(u - 1) + \frac{\Delta^3 y_0}{3!} u(u - 1)(u - 2)$$
$$+ \frac{\Delta^4 y_0}{4!} u(u - 1)(u - 2)(u - 3)$$

where,

$$u = \frac{x - x_0}{h} = \frac{32 - 30}{5} = \frac{2}{5} = 0.4$$

$$\therefore y(32) = cos\ 32^0 = 0.8660 + (-0.0468)(0.4) + \frac{-0.0064}{2}(0.4)(0.4 - 1)$$

$$+ \frac{0.0007}{3!}(0.4)(0.4 - 1)(0.4 - 2)$$

$$= 0.8660 - 0.01872 + 0.000768 + 0.00004$$

$$= 0.8481$$

6.3 NEWTON'S BACKWARD DIFFERENCE INTERPOLATION FORMULA

Consider an nth degree polynomial passing through $(n + 1)$ points $(x_0, y_0), (x_1, y_1), (x_2, y_2), , \dots \dots, (x_n, y_n)$ of interval size h such that y and $y_n(x)$ agree at the tabulated points. Let $x_i's$ are equidistant points.

Since $y_n(x)$ is an nth degree polynomial, it may be written as

$$y_n(x) = a_0 + a_1(x - x_n) + a_2(x - x_n)(x - x_{n-1}) + \dots$$
$$+ a_n(x - x_n)(x - x_{n-1}) \dots (x - x_1) \qquad \dots\dots (6.3.1)$$

Applying the condition that y and $y_n(x)$ should agree at the tabulated points and putting , $x = x_n, x_{n-1}, x_{n-2}, \dots \dots, x_0$ we have

$$at\ x = x_n \Rightarrow y_n = a_0$$
$$at\quad x = x_{n-1} \Rightarrow y_{n-1} = a_0 + a_1(x_{n-1} - x_n)$$
$$at\quad x = x_{n-2} \Rightarrow y_{n-2} = a_0 + a_1(x_{n-2} - x_n) + a_2(x_{n-2} - x_n)(x_{n-2} - x_{n-1})$$
$$\cdots \quad \cdots \quad \cdots$$
$$\cdots \quad \cdots \quad \cdots$$

.... (6.3.2)

and so on.

Here, interval size is h and x_i's are equidistant.

$$\therefore\ x_n - x_{n-1} = h$$
$$\therefore\ x_{n-1} - x_n = -h$$
$$\therefore\ x_{n-i} - x_n = -ih \qquad \text{........ (6.3.3)}$$

Now, from Eq.(6.3.2) and from Eq. (6.3.3) we have

$$a_0 = y_n$$

$$a_1 = \frac{y_{n-1} - a_0}{x_{n-1} - x_n} = \frac{y_{n-1} - y_n}{x_{n-1} - x_n} = \frac{y_{n-1} - y_n}{-h} = \frac{y_n - y_{n-1}}{h}$$

$$= \frac{\nabla y_n}{h} \qquad (\because \text{ from Eq.(6.3.3) } x_{n-1} - x_n = -h\ )$$

$$a_2 = \frac{y_{n-2} - a_0 - a_1(x_{n-2} - x_n)}{(x_{n-2} - x_n)(x_{n-2} - x_{n-1})} = \frac{y_{n-2} - y_n - \left(\frac{y_n - y_{n-1}}{h}\right)(-2h)}{(-2h).(-h)}$$

$$= \frac{y_{n-2} - y_n - (y_n - y_{n-1})(-2)}{2h^2}$$

$$= \frac{y_{n-2} - y_n + 2y_n - 2y_{n-1}}{2h^2}$$

$$= \frac{y_{n-2} - 2y_{n-1} + y_n}{2h^2} = \frac{y_n - 2y_{n-1} + y_{n-2}}{2!\ h^2}$$

$$= \frac{(y_n - y_{n-1}) - (y_{n-1} - y_{n-2})}{2!\ h^2} = \frac{\nabla y_n - \nabla y_{n-1}}{2!\ h^2} = \frac{\nabla^2 y_n}{2!\ h^2}$$

Similarly, $a_3 = \frac{\nabla^3 y_n}{3!\ h^3}$

....

$$\therefore\ a_n = \frac{\nabla^n y_n}{n!\ h^n}$$

Thus, $a_0 = y_n,\ a_1 = \frac{\nabla y_n}{h},\ a_2 = \frac{\nabla^2 y_n}{2!\ h^2}, \ldots\ldots\ldots\ldots, a_n = \frac{\nabla^n y_n}{n!\ h^n}$

Substitute all these values of constant in Eq. (6.3.1), we get

$$y_n(x) = y_n + \frac{\nabla y_n}{h}(x - x_n) + \frac{\nabla^2 y_n}{2!\ h^2}(x - x_n)(x - x_{n-1}) + \ldots\ldots$$

$$+ \frac{\nabla^n y_n}{n!\ h^n}(x - x_n)(x - x_{n-1}) \ldots\ldots (x - x_1) \qquad \text{........ (6.3.4)}$$

Let
$$\frac{x - x_n}{h} = u$$

$\therefore\ x - x_n = uh$

$\therefore\ x - x_{n-1} = x - (x_n - h) = (x - x_n) + h = uh + h = h\,(u + 1)$

$\therefore\ x - x_{n-2} = x - (x_{n-1} - h) = (x - x_{n-1}) + h = h\,(u + 1) + h = h\,(u + 2)$

$\cdots \qquad\qquad \cdots \qquad\qquad \cdots \qquad\qquad \cdots$

$\therefore\ x - x_1 = h\,(u + n - 1)$

Putting these values of $x - x_n, x - x_{n-1}, \ldots \ldots, x - x_1$ in Eq. (6.3.4) we get

$y_n(x) = y_n + \frac{\nabla y_n}{1!h}\,uh + \frac{\nabla^2 y_n}{2!\,h^2}\,uh.\,h(u + 1) + \ldots + \frac{\nabla^n y_n}{n!\,h^n}\,(uh).\,h(u + 1).\,h(u + 2) \ldots h(u + n - 1)$

$\therefore\ y_n(x) = y_n + \frac{\nabla y_n}{1!}\,u + \frac{\nabla^2 y_n}{2!}\,u(u + 1) + \ldots + \frac{\nabla^n y_n}{n!}\,u(u + 1)(u + 2) \ldots \ldots (u + n - 1)$ .... (6.3.5)

In general,

$$
\boxed{\begin{aligned}
y_n(x) &= y_n + \frac{\nabla y_n}{1!}\,u + \frac{\nabla^2 y_n}{2!}\,u(u + 1) + \ldots \ldots \ldots \\
&\quad + \frac{\Delta^{k-1} y_n}{(k-1)!}\,u(u + 1)(u + 2) \ldots \ldots (u + ((k - 1) - 1))
\end{aligned}}
$$
.... (6.3.6)

This is known as Newton's backward difference interpolation formula. This formula is applicable if the value to be interpolated lies near the lower half of the table.

6.3.1 Estimation of Error in Newton's Backward Interpolation Formula

As discussed in section 6.2.1, for Newton's backward formula, the error is

$$R_{n+1}(x) = \frac{u(u + 1)(u + 2) \ldots \ldots (u + n)}{(n + 1)!}\,\nabla^{n+1} y_n$$

$$\therefore\ |R_{n+1}(x)| = \left|\frac{u(u + 1)(u + 2) \ldots \ldots (u + n)}{(n + 1)!}\right|\,|\nabla^{n+1} y_n|$$

If we take $\quad B_n(u) = \dfrac{u(u + 1)(u + 2) \ldots \ldots (u + n)}{(n + 1)!} \quad$ then

$$|B_n(u)| = \left|\frac{u(u + 1)(u + 2) \ldots \ldots (u + n)}{(n + 1)!}\right|$$

and $\quad |A_n(u)| = |B_n(u)|$ where, $A_n(u)$ is given as in Eq. (6.1.8)

Thus, the conclusion about the error in Newton's backward difference formula is same as Newton's forward formula. The proper interpolation is preferable in any situation than extrapolation.

Example 6.6   Given that $\sqrt{9} = 3, \sqrt{10} = 3.1623, \sqrt{11} = 3.3166, \sqrt{12} = 3.4641$ and $\sqrt{13} = 3.6055$, find $\sqrt{12.2}$ using Newton's backward difference formula.

Solution: The backward difference table is

x	y	∇y	$\nabla^2 y$	$\nabla^3 y$	$\nabla^4 y$
9	3				
10	3.1623	0.1623			
11	3.3166	0.1543	-0.008		
12	3.4641	0.1475	-0.0068	0.0012	
13	3.6055	0.1414	-0.0061	0.0007	-0.0005

Here, tabular points are equidistant and interval length h = 1. Since $x = 12.2$ is near the lower half of the table. we use Newton's backward difference formula. Also, point $x = 12.2$ lies between fourth and fifth point (i.e. between $x = 12$ and $x = 13$) therefore we consider backward differences at the fifth point. The backward difference formula is

$$y(x) = y_n + \frac{\nabla y_n}{1!} u + \frac{\nabla^2 y_n}{2!} u(u + 1) + \frac{\nabla^3 y_n}{3!} u(u + 1)(u + 2)$$
$$+ \frac{\nabla^4 y_n}{4!} u(u + 1)(u + 2)(u + 3)$$

where,

$$u = \frac{x - x_n}{h} = \frac{12.2 - 13}{1} = -0.8$$

$$\therefore y(12.2) = 3.6055 + (0.1414)(-0.8) + \frac{-0.0061}{2}(-0.8)(-0.8 + 1)$$
$$+ \frac{0.0007}{3!}(-0.8)(-0.8 + 1)(-0.8 + 2) + \frac{-0.0005}{4!}(-0.8)(-0.8 + 1)(-0.8 + 2)(-0.8 + 3)$$
$$= 3.6055 - 0.1131 + 0.000488 - 0.0000224 + 0.0000088$$
$$= 3.4929$$

Example 6.7   Using Newton's backward interpolation formula, find y(4.75).

x	2.5	3.0	3.5	4.0	4.5
y	9.27	12.45	15.70	19.52	23.75

Solution: The backward difference table is

x	y	∇y	$\nabla^2 y$	$\nabla^3 y$	$\nabla^4 y$
2.5	9.27				
3.0	12.45	3.18			
3.5	15.70	3.25	0.07		
4.0	19.52	3.82	0.57	0.5	
4.5	23.75	4.23	0.41	-0.16	-0.66

Here, tabular points are equidistant and interval length h = 0.5. Since $x = 4.75$ is near the lower half of the table. we use Newton's backward difference formula. In fact this point is not in the range of the tabulated values. *Hence, this is the case of extrapolation.* we consider backward differences at the fifth point. The backward difference formula is

$$y(x) = y_n + \frac{\nabla y_n}{1!} u + \frac{\nabla^2 y_n}{2!} u(u+1) + \frac{\nabla^3 y_n}{3!} u(u+1)(u+2)$$
$$+ \frac{\nabla^4 y_n}{4!} u(u+1)(u+2)(u+3)$$

where,

$$u = \frac{x - x_n}{h} = \frac{4.75 - 4.5}{0.5} = 0.5$$

$$\therefore y(4.75) = 23.75 + 4.23(0.5) + \frac{0.41}{2}(0.5)(0.5+1)$$

$$+ \frac{-0.16}{3!}(0.5)(0.5+1)(0.5+2) + \frac{-0.66}{4!}(0.5)(0.5+1)(0.5+2)(0.5+3)$$

$$= 23.75 + 2.115 + 0.15375 - 0.05 - 0.1805 = 25.7883$$

Remark: In the above example, the forward difference formula is

$$y(x) = y_0 + \frac{\Delta y_0}{1!} u + \frac{\Delta^2 y_0}{2!} u(u-1) + \frac{\Delta^3 y_0}{3!} u(u-1)(u-2)$$
$$+ \frac{\Delta^4 y_0}{4!} u(u-1)(u-2)(u-3)$$

where,

$$u = \frac{x - x_0}{h} = \frac{4.75 - 2.5}{0.5} = \frac{2.25}{0.5} = 4.5$$

$$\therefore y(4.75) = 9.27 + 3.18(4.5) + \frac{0.07}{2}(4.5)(4.5-1)$$

$$+ \frac{0.5}{3!}(4.5)(4.5-1)(4.5-2) + \frac{-0.66}{4!}(4.5)(4.5-1)(4.5-2)(4.5-3)$$

$$= 9.27 + 14.31 + 0.55125 + 3.28125 - 1.6242$$
$$= 25.7883$$

In the case of extrapolation, Newton's forward and backward intrpolation gives the same answer regardless of the position and the value of x.

6.4   CENTRAL DIFFERENCE INTERPOLATION FORMULAE

We have seen that Newton's forward and backward interpolation formulae are applicable if the value to be interpolated lies near the upper half or lower half of a set of tabular values respectively. If the value of a function to be interpolated lies at or near the center of the table, Newton's forward and backward formulae do not give accurate result. To get more accurate results at or near the center of the tabular values, a suitable formula needs to be developed. This formula is known as central difference formula.

The following five are generally used as central difference formulae.

1.   Gauss's forward interpolation formula
2.   Gauss's backward interpolation formula
3.   Stirling's formula
4.   Bessel's formula
5.   Laplace-Everett formula

6.4.1   Gauss's Forward Interpolation Formula

Newton's forward difference formula is

$$\therefore\ y_n(x) = y_0 + \frac{\Delta y_0}{1!}\, u + \frac{\Delta^2 y_0}{2!}\, u(u-1) + \ldots\ldots\ldots$$

$$+ \frac{\Delta^n y_0}{n!}\, u(u-1)(u-2)\ldots\ldots(u-(n-1)) \qquad\qquad \ldots\ldots (6.4.1)$$

where, $u = \dfrac{x - x_0}{h}$

$$\text{Now,}\ \left.\begin{array}{l} \Delta^2 y_0 = \Delta^2 E\, y_{-1} = \Delta^2(1+\Delta)y_{-1} = \Delta^2 y_{-1} + \Delta^3 y_{-1} \\ \Delta^3 y_0 = \Delta^3 E\, y_{-1} = \Delta^3(1+\Delta)y_{-1} = \Delta^3 y_{-1} + \Delta^4 y_{-1} \\ \text{Similarly,}\ \Delta^4 y_0 = \Delta^4 y_{-1} + \Delta^5 y_{-1} \end{array}\right\} \ldots\ldots(6.4.2)$$

and so on.

Substituting values of Eq. (6.4.2) in Eq. (6.4.1), we have

$$y = y_n(x) = y_0 + \Delta y_0\, u + \frac{u(u-1)}{2!}(\Delta^2 y_{-1} + \Delta^3 y_{-1})$$

$$+ \frac{u(u-1)(u-2)}{3!}(\Delta^3 y_{-1} + \Delta^4 y_{-1})$$

$$+ \frac{u(u-1)(u-2)(u-3)}{4!}(\Delta^4 y_{-1} + \Delta^5 y_{-1}) +$$

$$= y_0 + \Delta y_0\, u + \frac{u(u-1)}{2!}\Delta^2 y_{-1} + \left[\frac{u(u-1)}{2!} + \frac{u(u-1)(u-2)}{3!}\right]\Delta^3 y_{-1}$$

$$+\left[\frac{u(u-1)(u-2)}{3!}+\frac{u(u-1)(u-2)(u-3)}{4!}\right]\Delta^4 y_{-1}+\ldots\ldots\ldots$$

By simplifying this, we have

$$y = y_n(x) = y_0 + \Delta y_0\, u + \frac{u(u-1)}{2!}\Delta^2 y_{-1} + \frac{(u+1)u(u-1)}{3!}\Delta^3 y_{-1}$$

$$+\frac{(u+1)u(u-1)(u-2)}{4!}\Delta^4 y_{-1} + \frac{(u+1)u(u-1)(u-2)(u-3)}{5!}\Delta^5 y_{-1}$$

$$+\ldots\ldots$$

$$= y_0 + \Delta y_0\, u + \frac{u(u-1)}{2!}\Delta^2 y_{-1} + \frac{(u+1)u(u-1)}{3!}\Delta^3 y_{-1}$$

$$+\frac{(u+1)u(u-1)(u-2)}{4!}[\Delta^4 y_{-2} + \Delta^5 y_{-2}]$$

$$+\frac{(u+1)u(u-1)(u-2)(u-3)}{5!}[\Delta^5 y_{-2} + \Delta^6 y_{-2}] + \ldots\ldots\ldots\ldots$$

(by proceeding as in (6.4.2))

$$= y_0 + \Delta y_0\, u + \frac{u(u-1)}{2!}\Delta^2 y_{-1} + \frac{(u+1)u(u-1)}{3!}\Delta^3 y_{-1}$$

$$+\frac{(u+1)u(u-1)(u-2)}{4!}\Delta^4 y_{-2}$$

$$+\left[\frac{(u+1)u(u-1)(u-2)}{4!}+\frac{(u+1)u(u-1)(u-2)(u-3)}{5!}\right](\Delta^4 y_{-2}$$

$$+\Delta^5 y_{-2}) + \ldots\ldots\ldots$$

Proceeding and grouping the terms like this, we have

$$y = y_n(x) = y_0 + \Delta y_0\, u + \frac{\Delta^2 y_{-1}}{2!}u(u-1) + \frac{\Delta^3 y_{-1}}{3!}(u+1)u(u-1)$$

$$+\frac{\Delta^4 y_{-2}}{4!}(u+1)u(u-1)(u-2) + \ldots\ldots\ldots \qquad\ldots\ldots (6.4.3)$$

This is called Gauss's forward interpolation formula. The corresponding forward difference table is given below.

Table 6.1 Gauss Difference Table

y	Δy	$\Delta^2 y$	$\Delta^3 y$	$\Delta^4 y$	$\Delta^5 y$	
y_{-3}						
	Δy_{-3}					
y_{-2}		$\Delta^2 y_{-3}$				
	Δy_{-2}		$\Delta^3 y_{-3}$			
y_{-1}		$\Delta^2 y_{-2}$		$\Delta^4 y_{-3}$		
	Δy_{-1} ------▶		$\Delta^3 y_{-2}$ ------▶		$\Delta^5 y_{-3}$	**Backward line**
y_0 ------▶		$\Delta^2 y_{-1}$ -------▶		$\Delta^4 y_{-2}$ -------▶		**Central line**
	Δy_0 -------▶		$\Delta^3 y_{-1}$ -------▶		$\Delta^5 y_{-2}$ ---▶	**Forward line**
y_1		$\Delta^2 y_0$		$\Delta^4 y_{-1}$		
	Δy_1		$\Delta^3 y_0$			
y_2		$\Delta^2 y_1$				
	Δy_2					
y_3						

Remark:
- Gauss's forward intrpolation formula involves, all even order differences on the central line and odd order difference on the forward line alternatively as shown in the Table 6.1.
- For the more accuacry, choose the value (x_0, y_0) in such a way that $0 < u = \frac{x - x_0}{h} < 1$. Beacuase of this, one can use maximum number of available differences.

Example 6.8 Find $e^{-3.2}$ from the following data using Gauss forward interpolation formula.

x	2.0	2.5	3.0	3.5	4.0
$y = e^{-x}$	0.1353	0.0821	0.0498	0.0302	0.0183

Solution: The Gauss forward difference table is

x	y	Δy	$\Delta^2 y$	$\Delta^3 y$	$\Delta^4 y$
2.0	0.1353				
		-0.0532			
2.5	0.0821		0.0209		
		-0.0323		-0.0082	
3.0	0.0498		0.0127		0.0032
		-0.0196		-0.005	
3.5	0.0302		0.0077		
		-0.0119			
4.0	0.0183				

The Gauss's forward interpolation formula is

$$y = y_n(x) = y_0 + \Delta y_0 \, u + \frac{\Delta^2 y_{-1}}{2!} u(u-1) + \frac{\Delta^3 y_{-1}}{3!} (u+1)u(u-1)$$

$$+ \frac{\Delta^4 y_{-2}}{4!} (u+1)u(u-1)(u-2)$$

where, $u = \frac{x-x_0}{h} = \frac{3.2-3.0}{0.5} = 0.4$. Since, $0 < u < 1$, the condition is satisfied. Here, $y_0 = 0.0498$, $\Delta y_0 = -0.0196$, $\Delta^2 y_{-1} = 0.0127$, $\Delta^3 y_{-1} = -0.005$, $\Delta^4 y_{-2} = 0.0032$.

Putting these values in Gauss's forward interpolation formula, we get

$$y(3.2) = 0.0498 + \frac{-0.0196}{1!} (0.4) + \frac{0.0127}{2!} (0.4)(-0.6)$$

$$+ \frac{-0.005}{3!} (1.4)(0.4)(-0.6) + \frac{0.0032}{4!} (1.4)(0.4)(-0.6)(-1.6)$$

$$= 0.0498 - 0.00784 - 0.001524 + 0.00028 + 0.00007168$$

$$= 0.04078$$

6.4.2   Gauss's Backward Interpolation Formula

Newton's forward difference formula is

$$\therefore \; y_n(x) = y_0 + \frac{\Delta y_0}{1!} u + \frac{\Delta^2 y_0}{2!} u(u-1) + \dots$$

$$+ \frac{\Delta^n y_0}{n!} u(u-1)(u-2) \dots \dots (u-(n-1)) \qquad \dots\dots (6.4.4)$$

where,

$$u = \frac{x - x_0}{h}$$

Now, $\Delta y_0 = \Delta E y_{-1} = \Delta(1 + \Delta)y_{-1} = \Delta y_{-1} + \Delta^2 y_{-1}$

$$\left.\begin{array}{l} \Delta^2 y_0 = \Delta^2 y_{-1} + \Delta^3 y_{-1} \\ \Delta^3 y_0 = \Delta^3 y_{-1} + \Delta^4 y_{-1} \end{array}\right\} \qquad \dots\dots (6.4.5)$$

and so on.

Substituting values of Eq. (6.4.5) in Eq. (6.4.4), we have

$$y = y_n(x) = y_0 + u(\Delta y_{-1} + \Delta^2 y_{-1}) + \frac{u(u-1)}{2!} (\Delta^2 y_{-1} + \Delta^3 y_{-1})$$

$$+ \frac{u(u-1)(u-2)}{3!} (\Delta^3 y_{-1} + \Delta^4 y_{-1})$$

$$+ \frac{u(u-1)(u-2)(u-3)}{4!} (\Delta^4 y_{-1} + \Delta^5 y_{-1}) + \dots\dots$$

$$= y_0 + u \, \Delta y_{-1} + \left[u + \frac{u(u-1)}{2!} \right] \Delta^2 y_{-1} + \left[\frac{u(u-1)}{2!} + \frac{u(u-1)(u-2)}{3!} \right] \Delta^3 y_{-1}$$

$$+ \left[\frac{u(u-1)(u-2)}{3!} + \frac{u(u-1)(u-2)(u-3)}{4!} \right] \Delta^4 y_{-1} + \dots\dots\dots\dots$$

By simplifying this, we have

$$y = y_n(x) = y_0 + u\,\Delta y_{-1} + \frac{(u+1)u}{2!}\Delta^2 y_{-1} + \frac{(u+1)u(u-1)}{3!}\Delta^3 y_{-1}$$

$$+\frac{(u+1)u(u-1)(u-2)}{4!}\Delta^4 y_{-1} + \frac{(u+1)u(u-1)(u-2)(u-3)}{5!}\Delta^5 y_{-1}$$

$$+\ ......$$

$$= y_0 + u\,\Delta y_{-1} + \frac{(u+1)u}{2!}\Delta^2 y_{-1} + \frac{(u+1)u(u-1)}{3!}[\Delta^3 y_{-2} + \Delta^4 y_{-2}]$$

$$+\frac{(u+1)u(u-1)(u-2)}{4!}[\Delta^4 y_{-2} + \Delta^5 y_{-2}] + \ ....$$

$$\text{(by proceeding as in (6.4.5))}$$

$$= y_0 + u\,\Delta y_{-1} + \frac{(u+1)u}{2!}\Delta^2 y_{-1} + \frac{(u+1)u(u-1)}{3!}\Delta^3 y_{-2}$$

$$+\left[\frac{(u+1)u(u-1)}{3!} + \frac{(u+1)u(u-1)(u-2)}{4!}\right]\Delta^4 y_{-2} + \ ......$$

$$= y_0 + u\,\Delta y_{-1} + \frac{(u+1)u}{2!}\Delta^2 y_{-1} + \frac{(u+1)u(u-1)}{3!}\Delta^3 y_{-2}$$

$$+\frac{(u+2)(u+1)u(u-1)}{3!}\Delta^4 y_{-2} + \ ......$$

Proceeding and grouping the terms like this, we have

$$y = y_n(x) = y_0 + u\,\Delta y_{-1} + \frac{\Delta^2 y_{-1}}{2!}(u+1)u + \frac{\Delta^3 y_{-2}}{3!}(u+1)u(u-1)$$

$$+\frac{\Delta^4 y_{-2}}{4!}(u+2)(u+1)u(u-1) + \ ....\qquad ......(6.4.6)$$

This is called Gauss's backward interpolation formula.

> **Remark:**
> • Gauss's backward interpolation formula involves, all even order differences on the central line and odd order difference on the backward line alternatively as shown in the Table 6.1.
> • For the more accuarcy, choose the value (x_0, y_0) in such a way that $-1 < u = \frac{x-x_0}{h} < 0$. Beacuase of this, one can use maximum number of available differences.

Example 6.9   Given the data.

x	10	20	30	40	50
$y = log_{10}x$	1	1.3010	1.4771	1.6021	1.6990

Find the value of $log_{10} 27.5$ by Gauss backward interpolation formula.

Solution: The Gauss forward difference table is

x	y	Δy	$\Delta^2 y$	$\Delta^3 y$	$\Delta^4 y$
10	1				
		0.3010			
20	1.3010		-0.1249		
		0.1761		0.0738	
30	1.4771		-0.0511		-0.0508
		0.125		0.023	
40	1.6021		-0.0281		
		0.0969			
50	1.6990				

The Gauss's backward interpolation formula is

$$y = y_n(x) = y_0 + u\,\Delta y_{-1} + \frac{\Delta^2 y_{-1}}{2!}(u+1)u + \frac{\Delta^3 y_{-2}}{3!}(u+1)u(u-1)$$
$$+\frac{\Delta^4 y_{-2}}{4!}(u+2)(u+1)u(u-1) + \text{... ...}$$

where, $u = \frac{x-x_0}{h} = \frac{27.5-30.0}{10} = -0.25$. Since, $-1 < u < 0$, the condition is satisfied. Here, $y_0 = 1.4771$, $\Delta y_0 = 0.1761$, $\Delta^2 y_{-1} = -0.0511$, $\Delta^3 y_{-1} = 0.0738$, $\Delta^4 y_{-2} = -0.0508$

Putting these values in Gauss's backward interpolation formula, we get

$$y(27.5) = 1.4771 + \frac{0.1761}{1!}(-0.25) + \frac{-0.0511}{2!}(0.75)(-0.25)$$
$$+\frac{0.0738}{3!}(0.75)(-0.25)(-1.25) + \frac{-0.0508}{4!}(1.75)(0.75)(-0.25)(-1.25)$$
$$= 1.4771 - 0.0440 + 0.0048 + 0.0029 - 0.0009$$
$$= 1.4399 \text{ (upto four significant digits)}$$

6.4.3 Stirling's Interpolation Formula

Stirling's interpolation formula is derived by taking average of Gauss's forward and backward interpolation formulae. Gauss's forward interpolation formula is

$$y = y_n(x) = y_0 + \Delta y_0\, u + \frac{\Delta^2 y_{-1}}{2!}u(u-1) + \frac{\Delta^3 y_{-1}}{3!}(u+1)u(u-1)$$
$$+\frac{\Delta^4 y_{-2}}{4!}(u+1)u(u-1)(u-2) + \text{... ... ...}$$

Gauss's backward inerpolation formula is

$$y = y_n(x) = y_0 + \Delta y_{-1}u + \frac{\Delta^2 y_{-1}}{2!}(u+1)u + \frac{\Delta^3 y_{-2}}{3!}(u+1)u(u-1)$$
$$+\frac{\Delta^4 y_{-2}}{4!}(u+2)(u+1)u(u-1) + \text{... ... ...}$$

Taking average of these two equations such that differences of the same order are grouped

$$y = y_n(x) = y_0 + u\left(\frac{\Delta y_0 + \Delta y_{-1}}{2}\right) + \left[\frac{u(u-1)}{2!} + \frac{(u+1)u}{2!}\right]\frac{\Delta^2 y_{-1}}{2}$$

$$+ \frac{(u+1)u(u-1)}{3!}\left(\frac{\Delta^3 y_{-1} + \Delta^3 y_{-2}}{2}\right)$$

$$+ \left[\frac{(u+1)u(u-1)(u-2)}{4!} + \frac{(u+2)(u+1)u(u-1)}{4!}\right]\frac{\Delta^4 y_{-2}}{2} + \ldots\ldots\ldots\ldots$$

$$\therefore\ y = y_n(x) = y_0 + \left(\frac{\Delta y_0 + \Delta y_{-1}}{2}\right)u + \Delta^2 y_{-1}\frac{u^2}{2!}$$

$$+ \frac{u(u^2 - 1^2)}{3!}\left(\frac{\Delta^3 y_{-1} + \Delta^3 y_{-2}}{2}\right) + \frac{u^2(u^2 - 1^2)}{4!}\Delta^4 y_{-2} + \ldots \qquad \ldots\ldots\ldots (6.4.7)$$

Which is known as Striling's formula.

> **Remark:**
> - Stirling's formula involves, all even order differences on the central line and average of odd order differences of the same order lying on just below and just above the central line as given below:
>
> $$\begin{array}{cccc} & \Delta y_{-1} & \Delta^3 y_{-2} & \Delta^5 y_{-3} \\ \ldots\ldots\ y_0\ \ldots\ldots\ldots & \Delta^2 y_{-1} & \ldots\ldots\ldots\Delta^4 y_{-2}\ldots\ldots\ldots\ldots & \Delta^6 y_{-3} \\ & \Delta y_0 & \Delta^3 y_{-1} & \Delta^5 y_{-2} \end{array}$$
>
> - For the accuarcy, choose the value (x_0, y_0) in such a way that $\frac{-1}{2} <$ $u = \frac{x - x_0}{h} < \frac{1}{2}$. Better accuarcy is obtained if $\frac{-1}{4} < u < \frac{1}{4}$. Apart from this selection, choose u in such a way that we can use more number of differences.

Example 6.10   Use Stirling's formula to compute $sin\ 42^0$, given the following table of values of $sin\ x^0$.

x	20	30	40	50	60	70	80
$y = sinx^0$	0.3420	0.5020	0.6428	0.7660	0.8660	0.9397	0.9848

Solution: Given h = 10. Let $x_0 = 50$ such that $u = \frac{x - x_0}{h} = \frac{42 - 40}{10} = 0.2$

Since, $\frac{-1}{2} < u < \frac{1}{2}$, the condition is satisfied.

The central difference table is

x	y	Δy	$\Delta^2 y$	$\Delta^3 y$	$\Delta^4 y$	$\Delta^5 y$	$\Delta^6 y$
20	0.3420						
		0.16					
30	0.5020		-0.0192				
		0.1408		0.0016			
40	0.6428		-0.0176		-0.0072		
		0.1232		-0.0056		0.0097	
50	0.7660		-0.0232		0.0025		-0.0114
		0.1		-0.0031		-0.0017	
60	0.8660		-0.0263		0.0008		
		0.0737		-0.0023			
70	0.9397		-0.0286				
		0.0451					
80	0.9848						

The Stirling's formula is

$$y = y_n(x) = y_0 + \left(\frac{\Delta y_0 + \Delta y_{-1}}{2}\right) u + \Delta^2 y_{-1} \frac{u^2}{2!}$$

$$+ \frac{u(u^2 - 1^2)}{3!} \left(\frac{\Delta^3 y_{-1} + \Delta^3 y_{-2}}{2}\right) + \frac{u^2(u^2 - 1^2)}{4!} \Delta^4 y_{-2}$$

$$+ \frac{u(u^2 - 1^2)(u^2 - 2^2)}{5!} \left(\frac{\Delta^5 y_{-2} + \Delta^5 y_{-3}}{2}\right) + \frac{u^2(u^2 - 1^2)(u^2 - 2^2)}{6!} \Delta^6 y_{-3}$$

Substituting, $u = 0.2$, $y_0 = 0.6428$, $\Delta y_0 = 0.1232$, $\Delta y_{-1} = 0.1408$, $\Delta^2 y_{-1} = -0.0176$

$\Delta^3 y_{-1} = -0.0056$, $\Delta^3 y_{-2} = 0.0016$, $\Delta^4 y_{-2} = -0.0072$

$$\therefore \sin 42^0 = 0.6428 + \left(\frac{0.1232 + 0.1408}{2}\right)(0.2) + -0.0176\frac{(0.2)^2}{2!}$$

$$+ \frac{(0.2)((0.2)^2 - 1^2)}{3!} \left(\frac{-0.0056 + 0.0016}{2}\right) + \frac{(0.2)^2((0.2)^2 - 1^2)}{4!}(-0.0072)$$

$$= 0.6428 + 0.0264 - 0.000352 - 0.000064 + 0.00001152$$
$$= 0.6688 \text{ (upto three significant digits)}$$

6.4.4 Bessel's Interpolation Formula

Gauss forward interpolation formula is

$$y = y_n(x) = y_0 + \Delta y_0\, u + \frac{\Delta^2 y_{-1}}{2!} u(u - 1) + \frac{\Delta^3 y_{-1}}{3!}(u + 1)u(u - 1)$$

$$+ \frac{\Delta^4 y_{-2}}{4!}(u + 1)u(u - 1)(u - 2) + \ldots\ldots\ldots \qquad\qquad \ldots\ldots.. (6.4.8)$$

where, $\quad \Delta y_0 = y_1 - y_0 \implies y_0 = y_1 - \Delta y_0$

Similarly, $\quad y_{-1} = y_0 - \Delta y_{-1}$

$$\therefore \Delta^2 y_{-1} = \Delta^2 y_0 - \Delta^3 y_{-1}$$

$$y_{-2} = y_{-1} - \Delta y_{-2}$$

$$\therefore \Delta^4 y_{-2} = \Delta^4 y_{-1} - \Delta^5 y_{-2}$$

and so on.

Splitting the alternate terms of Gauss forward interpolation formula given in Eq. (6.4.8) into two equal parts, we have

$$y = y_n(x) = \left(\frac{y_0}{2} + \frac{y_0}{2}\right) + \Delta y_0 \, u + \left(\frac{1}{2}\Delta^2 y_{-1} + \frac{1}{2}\Delta^2 y_{-1}\right)\frac{u(u-1)}{2!}$$

$$+ \frac{\Delta^3 y_{-1}}{3!}(u+1)u + \left(\frac{1}{2}\Delta^4 y_{-2} + \frac{1}{2}\Delta^4 y_{-2}\right)\frac{(u+1)u(u-1)(u-2)}{4!}$$

$$+ \dots \dots \dots \qquad\qquad \dots\dots (6.4.9)$$

$$= \frac{y_0}{2} + \frac{1}{2}(y_1 - \Delta y_0) + \Delta y_0 \, u + \frac{1}{2}\Delta^2 y_{-1}\frac{u(u-1)}{2!}$$

$$+ \frac{1}{2}(\Delta^2 y_0 - \Delta^3 y_{-1})\frac{u(u-1)}{2!} + \frac{\Delta^3 y_{-1}}{3!}(u+1)u(u-1)$$

$$+ \frac{1}{2}\Delta^4 y_{-2}\frac{(u+1)u(u-1)(u-2)}{4!}$$

$$+ \frac{1}{2}(\Delta^4 y_{-1} - \Delta^5 y_{-2})\frac{(u+1)u(u-1)(u-2)}{4!} + \dots\dots\dots$$

$$= \left(\frac{y_0 + y_1}{2}\right) + \left(u - \frac{1}{2}\right)\Delta y_0 + \frac{u(u-1)}{2!}\left(\frac{\Delta^2 y_{-1} + \Delta^2 y_0}{2}\right)$$

$$+ \frac{u(u-1)}{2!}\left(\frac{u+1}{3} - \frac{1}{2}\right)\Delta^3 y_{-1} + \frac{(u+1)u(u-1)(u-2)}{4!}\left(\frac{\Delta^4 y_{-2} + \Delta^4 y_{-1}}{2}\right)$$

$$+ \dots\dots\dots$$

$$\therefore y = y_n(x) = \left(\frac{y_0 + y_1}{2}\right) + \left(u - \frac{1}{2}\right)\Delta y_0 + \frac{u(u-1)}{2!}\left(\frac{\Delta^2 y_{-1} + \Delta^2 y_0}{2}\right)$$

$$+ \frac{\left(u - \frac{1}{2}\right)u(u-1)}{3!}\Delta^3 y_{-1} + \frac{(u+1)u(u-1)(u-2)}{4!}\left(\frac{\Delta^4 y_{-2} + \Delta^4 y_{-1}}{2}\right)$$

$$+ \dots\dots\dots \qquad\qquad \dots\dots (6.4.10)$$

which is known as the Bessel's formula.

Remark:

- Bessel's formula involves, all odd order differences below the central line and average of even order differences of the same order lying on lines corresponding to y_0 and y_1 as given below:

Central y_0 line

$$\begin{pmatrix} y_0 \\ y_1 \end{pmatrix} \dots \dots \Delta y_0 \dots \dots \begin{pmatrix} \Delta^2 y_{-1} \\ \Delta^2 y_0 \end{pmatrix} \dots \dots \Delta^3 y_{-1} \dots \dots \begin{pmatrix} \Delta^4 y_{-2} \\ \Delta^4 y_{-1} \end{pmatrix} \dots \dots \dots \dots \dots$$

y_1 line

Bessel's formula is the modified version of Gauss forward interpolation formula.

- If we substitute $u = \frac{1}{2}$ in Eq. (6.4.10), the coefficients of all odd order differences are zero and the formula reduces to

$$y = \left(\frac{y_0 + y_1}{2}\right) - \frac{1}{8}\left(\frac{\Delta^2 y_{-1} + \Delta^2 y_0}{2}\right) + \frac{3}{128}\left(\frac{\Delta^4 y_{-2} + \Delta^4 y_{-1}}{2}\right)$$
$$- \frac{5}{1024}\left(\frac{\Delta^6 y_{-3} + \Delta^6 y_{-2}}{2}\right) + \dots$$

This formula is known as formula for interpolating to halves.

- Similar to Gauss forward interpolation formula, choose the value (x_0, y_0) in such a way that $0 < u = \frac{x - x_0}{h} < 1$. Better accuarcy is obtained if $\frac{1}{4} < u < \frac{3}{4}$.

Example 6.11 Use Bessel's formula to estimate $\sqrt[3]{66.16}$ for the given data

x	61	65	69	73	77
$y = \sqrt[3]{x}$	3.9365	4.0207	4.1016	4.1793	4.2543

Solution: Given h = 4. Let $x_0 = 65$ such that $u = \frac{x - x_0}{h} = \frac{66.16 - 65}{4} = 0.29$

Since, $0 < u < 1$, the condition is satisfied. In fact, $0.25 < u < 0.75$. Hence, this formula is the best suited. The central difference table is

x	y	Δy	$\Delta^2 y$	$\Delta^3 y$	$\Delta^4 y$
61	3.9365				
		0.0842			
65	4.0207		-0.0033		
		0.0809		0.0001	
69	4.1016		-0.0032		0.0004
		0.0777		0.0005	
73	4.1793		-0.0027		
		0.075			
77	4.2543				

The Bessel's formula is

$$y(x) = \left(\frac{y_0 + y_1}{2}\right) + \left(u - \frac{1}{2}\right)\Delta y_0 + \frac{u(u-1)}{2!}\left(\frac{\Delta^2 y_{-1} + \Delta^2 y_0}{2}\right)$$

$$+ \frac{\left(u - \frac{1}{2}\right)u(u-1)}{3!}\Delta^3 y_{-1} + \frac{(u+1)u(u-1)(u-2)}{4!}\left(\frac{\Delta^4 y_{-2} + \Delta^4 y_{-1}}{2}\right)$$

$$\therefore y(66.16) = \left(\frac{4.0207 + 4.1016}{2}\right) + \left(0.29 - \frac{1}{2}\right)(0.0809)$$

$$+ \frac{0.29(0.29 - 1)}{2!}\left(\frac{-0.0033 + 0.0032}{2}\right)$$

$$+ \frac{\left(0.29 - \frac{1}{2}\right)(0.29)(0.29 - 1)}{3!}(0.0001)$$

$$= 4.0612 + (-0.21)(0.0809) + (-0.1030)(0.00005)$$
$$+ (0.0072)(0.0001)$$

$$= 4.0612 - 0.01699 - 0.000005 + 0.0000007$$
$$= 4.0442 \quad \text{(up to three decimal places)}$$

6.4.5 Laplace – Everett Interpolation Formula

Gauss forward interpolation formula is

$$y = y_n(x) = y_0 + \Delta y_0\, u + \frac{\Delta^2 y_{-1}}{2!}u(u-1) + \frac{\Delta^3 y_{-1}}{3!}(u+1)u(u-1)$$

$$+ \frac{\Delta^4 y_{-2}}{4!}(u+1)u(u-1)(u-2) + \ldots\ldots\ldots \qquad \ldots\ldots\ldots (6.4.11)$$

Now, we have

$$\left.\begin{aligned}
\Delta y_0 &= y_1 - y_0 \\
\Delta^3 y_{-1} &= \Delta^2 y_0 - \Delta^2 y_{-1} \\
\Delta^5 y_{-2} &= \Delta^4 y_{-1} - \Delta^4 y_{-2}
\end{aligned}\right\} \qquad \ldots\ldots\ldots (6.4.12)$$

and so on.

Substitute values of Eq. (6.4.12) in Eq. (6.4.11), we get

$$y_n(x) = y_0 + u(y_1 - y_0) + \frac{u(u-1)}{2!}\Delta^2 + \frac{(u+1)u(u-1)}{3!}(\Delta^2 y_0 - \Delta^2 y_{-1})$$

$$+ \frac{(u+1)u(u-1)(u-2)}{4!}\Delta^4 y_{-2}$$

$$+ \frac{(u+2)(u+1)u(u-1)(u-2)}{5!}(\Delta^4 y_{-1} - \Delta^4 y_{-2}) + \ldots\ldots$$

$$= (1-u)y_0 + uy_1 + \left[\frac{u(u-1)}{2!} - \frac{(u+1)u(u-1)}{3!}\right]\Delta^2 y_{-1}$$

$$+ \frac{(u+1)u(u-1)}{3!}\Delta^2 y_0 +$$

$$+ \left[\frac{(u+1)u(u-1)(u-2)}{4!} - \frac{(u+2)(u+1)u(u-1)(u-2)}{5!}\right]\Delta^4 y_{-2}$$

$$+ \frac{(u+2)(u+1)u(u-1)(u-2)}{5!}\Delta^4 y_{-1} + \dots \dots \qquad \dots \dots (6.4.13)$$

$$= (1-u)y_0 + uy_1 + u(u-1)\left[\frac{1}{2!} - \frac{(u+1)}{3!}\right]\Delta^2 y_{-1}$$

$$+ \frac{(u+1)u(u-1)}{3!}\Delta^2 y_0 + (u+1)u(u-1)(u-2)\left[\frac{1}{4!} - \frac{(u+2)}{5!}\right]\Delta^4 y_{-2}$$

$$+ \frac{(u+2)(u+1)u(u-1)(u-2)}{5!}\Delta^4 y_{-1} + \dots \dots \dots$$

$$= (1-u)y_0 + uy_1 - \frac{u(u-1)(u-2)}{3!}\Delta^2 y_{-1} + \frac{(u+1)u(u-1)}{3!}\Delta^2 y_0$$

$$- \frac{(u+1)u(u-1)(u-2)(u-3)}{5!}\Delta^4 y_{-2}$$

$$+ \frac{(u+2)(u+1)u(u-1)(u-2)}{5!}\Delta^4 y_{-1} + \dots \dots \dots \qquad \dots \dots (6.4.14)$$

Let $u = 1 - v$ i.e. $1 - u = v$ then we have,

$$\frac{u(u-1)(u-2)}{3!} = \frac{(1-v)(-v)(-v-1)}{3!} = -\frac{(v+1)v(v-1)}{3!} \qquad \dots \dots (i)$$

$$\frac{(u+1)u(u-1)(u-2)(u-3)}{5!}$$

$$= \frac{(1-v+1)(1-v)(1-v-1)(1-v-2)(1-v-3)}{5!}$$

$$= \frac{(2-v)(1-v)(-v)(-v-1)(-v-2)}{5!}$$

$$= -\frac{(v+2)(v+1)v(v-1)(v-2)}{5!} \qquad \dots \dots (ii)$$

and so on.

Substitute (i) and (ii) in Eq. (6.4.14) we get,

$$y = y_n(x) = vy_0 + uy_1 + \frac{(v+1)v(v-1)}{3!}\Delta^2 y_{-1} + \frac{(u+1)u(u-1)}{3!}\Delta^2 y_0$$

$$+ \frac{(v+2)(v+1)v(v-1)(v-2)}{5!}\Delta^4 y_{-2}$$

$$+ \frac{(u+2)(u+1)u(u-1)(u-2)}{5!}\Delta^4 y_{-1} + \dots$$

$$= vy_0 + \frac{(v+1)v(v-1)}{3!}\Delta^2 y_{-1} + \frac{(v+2)(v+1)v(v-1)(v-2)}{5!}\Delta^4 y_{-2}$$

$$+ uy_1 + \frac{(u+1)u(u-1)}{3!}\Delta^2 y_0 + \frac{(u+2)(u+1)u(u-1)(u-2)}{5!}\Delta^4 y_{-1}$$

$$+ \dots \dots \dots$$

$$y = y_n(x) = \left[vy_0 + \frac{v(v^2-1^2)}{3!}\Delta^2 y_{-1} + \frac{v(v^2-1^2)(v^2-2^2)}{5!}\Delta^4 y_{-2} \right.$$

$$+ \dots \dots$$

$$\left. + \left[uy_1 + \frac{u(u^2-1^2)}{3!}\Delta^2 y_0 + \frac{u(u^2-1^2)(u^2-2^2)}{5!}\Delta^4 y_{-1} + \dots \right] \right] \dots \dots (6.4.15)$$

which is known as Laplace – Everett formula, where $u = \frac{x-x_0}{h}$ and $v = 1 - u$.

Remark:
- Laplace – Everett formula involves only even order differences lying on the central line (y_0) and below the central line (y_1).
- Laplace – Everett formula is a modified version of Gauss forward interpolation formula.
- Similar to Gauss forward interpolation formula, choose the value (x_0, y_0) in such a way that $0 < u = \frac{x-x_0}{h} < 1$ and therefore, $0 < v < 1$.

Relation Between Bessel's and Laplace – Everett Formulae

The Bessel's formula upto the third difference term is

$$y = y_n(x) = \left(\frac{y_0+y_1}{2}\right) + \left(u-\frac{1}{2}\right)\Delta y_0 + \frac{u(u-1)}{2!}\left(\frac{\Delta^2 y_{-1}+\Delta^2 y_0}{2}\right)$$

$$+ \frac{\left(u-\frac{1}{2}\right)u(u-1)}{3!}\Delta^3 y_{-1} \qquad \dots \dots (6.4.16)$$

Now, express odd – order differences in terms of lower even – order differences.

$$\therefore y_n(x) = \left(\frac{y_0+y_1}{2}\right) + \left(u-\frac{1}{2}\right)(y_1-y_0) + \frac{u(u-1)}{2!}\left(\frac{\Delta^2 y_{-1}+\Delta^2 y_0}{2}\right)$$

$$+ \frac{\left(u-\frac{1}{2}\right)u(u-1)}{3!}(\Delta^2 y_0 - \Delta^2 y_{-1})$$

$$= (1-u)y_0 + uy_1 + \frac{(u+1)u(u-1)}{3!}\Delta^2 y_0 - \frac{u(u-1)(u-2)}{3!}\Delta^2 y_{-1}$$

$$= \left[vy_0 + \frac{(v+1)v(v-1)}{3!}\Delta^2 y_{-1} \right] + \left[uy_1 + \frac{(u+1)u(u-1)}{3!}\Delta^2 y_0 \right] \dots (6.4.17)$$

where, $v = 1 - u$. One can easily verify that the Eq. (6.4.17) is Laplace – Everett formula up to second – order difference. Thus, we can see that Everett's formula truncated after second differences is similar to Bessel's formula truncated after third differences.

Example 6.12 The following table

x	0.51	0.52	0.53	0.54	0.55
$y = f(x)$	0.5292	0.5379	0.5465	0.5549	0.5633

gives the values of the probability integral $f(x) = \frac{1}{\sqrt{2\pi}} \int_0^x e^{-x^2} dx$. Find the value of $\frac{1}{\sqrt{2\pi}} \int_0^{0.533} e^{-x^2} dx$ using Laplace – Everett formula.

Solution: Given h = 0.01. Let $x_0 = 0.53$ such that $u = \frac{x - x_0}{h} = \frac{0.533 - 0.53}{0.01} = 0.3$. Since, $0 < u < 1$, the condition is satisfied. In fact, $0.25 < u < 0.75$. Hence, this formula is the best suited.

The Laplace – Everett formula is

$$y = y_n(x) = \left[vy_0 + \frac{v(v^2 - 1^2)}{3!} \Delta^2 y_{-1} + \frac{v(v^2 - 1^2)(v^2 - 2^2)}{5!} \Delta^4 y_{-2} \right.$$
$$\left. + \; ... \; ... \right]$$
$$+ \left[uy_1 + \frac{u(u^2 - 1^2)}{3!} \Delta^2 y_0 + \frac{u(u^2 - 1^2)(u^2 - 2^2)}{5!} \Delta^4 y_{-1} + \; ... \; ... \; ... \right]$$

where, $v = 1 - u = 1 - 0.3 = 0.7$

The central difference table is

x	y	Δy	$\Delta^2 y$	$\Delta^3 y$	$\Delta^4 y$
0.51	0.5292				
		0.0087			
0.52	0.5379		-0.0001		
		0.0086		-0.0001	
0.53	0.5465		-0.0002		0.0003
		0.0084		0.0002	
0.54	0.5549		0		
		0.0084			
0.55	0.5633				

From the table it is clear that,

$y_0 = 0.5465$, $\Delta^2 y_{-1} = -0.0002, \Delta^4 y_{-2} = 0.0003, y_1 = 0.5549, \Delta^2 y_0 = 0$

$\therefore y(0.533) = (0.7)(0.5465) + \frac{(0.7)[(0.7)^2 - 1^2]}{3!} (-0.0002)$

$+ \frac{(0.7)[(0.7)^2 - 1^2][(0.7)^2 - 2^2]}{5!} 0.0003 + \; ... \; ... + (0.3)(0.5549) + \; ... \; ...$

$= 0.3826 + (-0.0595)(-0.0002) + (0.01044)(0.0003) + (0.3)(0.5549)$

$= 0.3826 + 0.000012 + 0.000003132 + 0.16647$

$= 0.549085132 \approx 0.5491$ (up to four decimal places)

6.5   INTERPOLATION WITH UNEQUAL INTERVALS

In the previous sections, we have assumed that the values of $x_i's$ are equally spaced but what happened if $x_i's$ are not equally spaced? In that case Newton's forward and backward difference formulae are not applicable. It is therefore required to derive interpolation formulae which are applicable for unequally spaced values of arguments. In such cases, we use

- Lagrange's interpolation formula
- Newton's divided difference formula

6.5.1   Lagrange's Interpolation Formula

Let $y_0 = f(x_0), y_1 = f(x_1), y_2 = f(x_2), \dots \dots, y_n = f(x_n)$ be the values of the function $y = f(x)$ corresponding to the arguments $x_0, x_1, x_2, \dots \dots, x_n$ not necessarily equally spaced. Since there are (n+1) pairs of values (x_i, y_i) $i = 0,1,2,3 \dots, n$ the function $f(x)$ can be represented by a polynomial of degree n in x. Consider a polynomial of degree n in x,

$$y = f(x) = a_0(x - x_1)(x - x_2) \dots \dots (x - x_n)$$
$$+ a_1(x - x_0)(x - x_2) \dots \dots (x - x_n)$$
$$+ a_2(x - x_0)(x - x_1)(x - x_3) \dots \dots (x - x_n)$$
$$+ \dots \dots \dots \dots \dots \dots \dots \dots \dots \dots \dots \dots \dots$$
$$+ a_n(x - x_0)(x - x_1) \dots \dots (x - x_{n-1}) \qquad \dots\dots (6.5.1)$$

where, $a_0, a_1, a_2, \dots \dots, a_n$ are constants to be determined. Eq. (6.5.1) is true for all values of x. Let $x = x_0, y = y_0$ then Eq. (6.5.1) becomes,

$$y_0 = f(x_0) = a_0(x_0 - x_1)(x_0 - x_2) \dots \dots (x_0 - x_n)$$

$$\therefore a_0 = \frac{y_0}{(x_0 - x_1)(x_0 - x_2) \dots \dots (x_0 - x_n)}$$

When $x = x_1, y = y_1$ then Eq. (6.5.1) becomes,

$$y_1 = a_1(x_1 - x_0)(x_1 - x_2) \dots \dots (x_1 - x_n)$$

$$\therefore a_1 = \frac{y_1}{(x_1 - x_0)(x_1 - x_2) \dots \dots (x_1 - x_n)}$$

Similarly,

$$a_2 = \frac{y_2}{(x_2 - x_0)(x_2 - x_1)(x_2 - x_3) \dots \dots (x_2 - x_n)}$$

$$\dots\dots\dots\dots\dots\dots\dots\dots\dots\dots\dots\dots\dots\dots\dots\dots\dots\dots\dots\dots$$
$$\dots\dots\dots\dots\dots\dots\dots\dots\dots\dots\dots\dots\dots\dots\dots\dots\dots\dots$$

$$a_n = \frac{y_n}{(x_n - x_0)(x_n - x_1)(x_n - x_2) \dots \dots (x_n - x_{n-1})}$$

Substituting the values of $a_0, a_1, a_2, \dots \dots, a_n$ in Eq. (6.5.1) we get,

$$y = f(x) = \frac{(x - x_1)(x - x_2) \dots \dots \dots (x - x_n)}{(x_0 - x_1)(x_0 - x_2) \dots \dots \dots (x_0 - x_n)} y_0$$

$$+ \frac{(x - x_0)(x - x_2) \dots \dots \dots (x - x_n)}{(x_1 - x_0)(x_1 - x_2) \dots \dots \dots (x_1 - x_n)} y_1$$

$$+ \dots \dots \dots + \frac{(x - x_0)(x - x_1) \dots \dots \dots (x - x_{n-1})}{(x_n - x_0)(x_n - x_1)(x_n - x_2) \dots \dots \dots (x_n - x_{n-1})} y_n$$

$$\dots \dots (6.5.2)$$

This is called Lagrange's interpolation formula.

Remark: Lagrange's interpolation formula can be expressed as the sum of partial functions.

Dividing both sides of Eq. (6.5.2) by $(x - x_0)(x - x_1)(x - x_2) \dots \dots \dots (x - x_n)$, we get

$$\frac{f(x)}{(x - x_0)(x - x_1)(x - x_2) \dots \dots \dots (x - x_n)}$$

$$= \frac{y_0}{(x_0 - x_1)(x_0 - x_2) \dots \dots \dots (x_0 - x_n)} \cdot \frac{1}{(x - x_0)}$$

$$+ \frac{y_1}{(x_1 - x_0)(x_1 - x_2) \dots \dots \dots (x_1 - x_n)} \cdot \frac{1}{(x - x_1)} + \dots \dots$$

$$+ \frac{y_n}{(x_n - x_0)(x_n - x_1)(x_n - x_2) \dots \dots \dots (x_n - x_{n-1})} \cdot \frac{1}{(x - x_n)}$$

Advantages of Lagrange's Interpolation Formula

The major advantages of Lagrange's interpolation formula are given below.

1. It is easy to calculate the coefficients of the polynomial.
2. Lagrange's formula can be applied whether the values $x_i's$ given in the table are equidistant or not.
3. It shows the relationship between two variables. Hence, we can always find the value of the dependent variable.
4. We can find the value of the independent variable corresponding to given value of a function.

Disadvantages of Lagrange's Interpolation Formula

The disadvantages of Lagrange's interpolation formula are given below.

1. The calculation of the Lagrange's formula is very cumbersome.
2. It is difficult to find the exact order of the polynomial using Lagrange's formula.
3. Modification process is tedious in Lagrange's formula. i.e. If we want to add another interpolation value then the interpolation coefficients are required to be recalculated.

Example 6.13 Certain values of x and $log_{10}x$ are (200, 2.3010), (205, 2.3118), (206, 2.3139) and (209, 2.3201). Find $log_{10}202$ using Lagrange's interpolation formula.

Solution: Putting $x_0 = 200, x_1 = 205, x_2 = 206, x_3 = 209, y_0 = 2.3010$, $y_1 = 2.3118$, $y_2 = 2.3139$, $y_3 = 2.3201$ and $x = 202$ in the Lagrange's interpolation formula given in Eq. (6.5.2), we have

$$log_{10}202 = \frac{(202 - 205)(202 - 206)(202 - 209)}{(200 - 205)(200 - 206)(200 - 209)} \times 2.3010$$

$$+ \frac{(202 - 200)(202 - 206)(202 - 209)}{(205 - 200)(205 - 206)(205 - 209)} \times 2.3118$$

$$+ \frac{(202 - 200)(202 - 205)(202 - 209)}{(206 - 200)(206 - 205)(206 - 209)} \times 2.3139$$

$$+ \frac{(202 - 200)(202 - 205)(202 - 206)}{(209 - 200)(209 - 205)(209 - 206)} \times 2.3201$$

$$= \frac{(-3)(-4)(-7)}{(-5)(-6)(-9)} \times 2.3010 + \frac{(2)(-4)(-7)}{(5)(-1)(-4)} \times 2.3118 + \frac{(2)(-3)(-7)}{(6)(1)(-3)}$$

$$\times 2.3139 + \frac{(2)(-3)(-4)}{(9)(4)(3)} \times 2.3201$$

$$= 0.7159 + 6.4730 - 5.3991 + 0.5156$$

$$= 2.3054$$

Example 6.14 Using Lagrange's method find the interpolating polynomial for the given values

x	0	1	3	4
$y = f(x)$	-12	0	12	24

Solution: Putting $x_0 = 0, x_1 = 1, x_2 = 3, x_3 = 4$, $y_0 = -12$, $y_1 = 0$, $y_2 = 12$, $y_3 = 24$ in the Lagrange's interpolation formula given in Eq. (6.5.2), we have

$$f(x) = \frac{(x - 1)(x - 3)(x - 4)}{(0 - 1)(0 - 3)(0 - 4)} \times (-12) + \frac{(x - 0)(x - 3)(x - 4)}{(1 - 0)(1 - 3)(1 - 4)} \times 0$$

$$+ \frac{(x - 0)(x - 1)(x - 4)}{(3 - 0)(3 - 1)(3 - 4)} \times 12 + \frac{(x - 0)(x - 1)(x - 3)}{(4 - 0)(4 - 1)(4 - 3)} \times 24$$

$$= \frac{(x - 1)(x - 3)(x - 4)}{(-1)(-3)(-4)} \times (-12) + \frac{(x - 0)(x - 3)(x - 4)}{(1)(-2)(-3)} \times 0$$

$$+ \frac{(x - 0)(x - 1)(x - 4)}{(3)(2)(-1)} \times 12 + \frac{(x - 0)(x - 1)(x - 3)}{(4)(3)(1)} \times 24$$

$$= (x^2 - 4x + 3)(x - 4) + (x^2 - x)(x - 4)(-2) + 2(x^2 - x)(x - 3)$$

$$= (x^3 - 4x^2 + 3x - 4x^2 + 16x - 12) + (-2)(x^3 - x^2 - 4x^2 + 4x)$$
$$+ 2\,(x^3 - x^2 - 3x^2 + 3x)$$
$$= x^3 - 6x^2 + 17x - 12$$

Example 6.15   Use Lagrange's formula to express the function

$$\frac{x^2 + 9x - 1}{(x - 1)(x + 1)(x - 2)(x + 2)}$$

as a sum of partial function.

Solution: We have

$$\frac{x^2 + 9x - 1}{(x - 1)(x + 1)(x - 2)(x + 2)}$$

Here $f(x) = x^2 + 9x - 1$. Let $x_0 = 1, x_1 = -1, x_2 = 2$ and $x_3 = -2$

Hence, $f(x_0) = f(1) = 9$ $f(x_1) = f(-1) = -9$

$\qquad f(x_2) = f(2) = 21$ $f(x_3) = f(-2) = -15$

Therefore,

$$\frac{x^2 + 9x - 1}{(x - 1)(x + 1)(x - 2)(x + 2)} = \frac{y_0}{(x_0 - x_1)(x_0 - x_2)(x_0 - x_3)} \cdot \frac{1}{(x - x_0)}$$

$$+ \frac{y_1}{(x_1 - x_0)(x_1 - x_2)(x_1 - x_3)} \cdot \frac{1}{(x - x_1)}$$

$$+ \frac{y_2}{(x_2 - x_0)(x_2 - x_1)(x_2 - x_3)} \cdot \frac{1}{(x - x_2)}$$

$$+ \frac{y_3}{(x_3 - x_0)(x_3 - x_1)(x_3 - x_2)} \cdot \frac{1}{(x - x_3)}$$

$$= \frac{9}{(2)(-1)(3)} \cdot \frac{1}{(x - 1)} + \frac{-9}{(-2)(-3)(1)} \cdot \frac{1}{(x + 1)} + \frac{21}{(1)(3)(4)} \cdot \frac{1}{(x - 2)}$$

$$+ \frac{-15}{(-3)(-1)(-4)} \cdot \frac{1}{(x + 2)}$$

$$= -\frac{9}{6(x - 1)} - \frac{9}{6(x + 1)} + \frac{21}{12(x - 2)} + \frac{15}{12(x + 2)}$$

Example 6.16 Determine by Lagrange's method the percentage number of patients over 57 years, using the following data:

Age over (x) years	30	35	45	55
% number (y) of patients:	148	96	68	34

Solution: Putting $x_0 = 30, x_1 = 35, x_2 = 45, x_3 = 55,$

$y_0 = 148$, $y_1 = 96$, $y_2 = 68$, $y_3 = 34$ and $x = 57$ in the Lagrange's interpolation formula given in Eq. (6.5.2), we have

$$f(57) = \frac{(57-35)(57-45)(57-55)}{(30-35)(30-45)(30-55)} \times 148$$

$$+ \frac{(57-30)(57-45)(57-55)}{(35-30)(35-45)(35-55)} \times 96$$

$$+ \frac{(57-30)(57-35)(57-55)}{(45-30)(45-35)(45-55)} \times 68$$

$$+ \frac{(57-30)(57-35)(57-45)}{(55-30)(55-35)(55-45)} \times 34$$

$$= \frac{(22)(12)(2)}{(-5)(-15)(-25)} \times 148 + \frac{(27)(12)(2)}{(5)(-10)(-20)} \times 96$$

$$+ \frac{(27)(22)(2)}{(15)(10)(-10)} \times 68 + \frac{(27)(22)(12)}{(25)(20)(10)} \times 34$$

$$= -41.6768 + 62.208 - 53.856 + 48.4704$$

$$= 15.1456$$

> **Remark:**   This is the case of extrapolation where the given value of independent variable x lies outside the range $x_0 \le x \le x_n$.

6.5.2   Inverse Interpolation

Inverse interpolation is the process of finding the value of the argument corresponding to a given value of the function which is lying between two tabulated values.

Lagrange's Inverse Interpolation Formula

If we express x (dependent variable) as a function of y (independent variable) then the Lagrange's inverse interpolation formula can be written as

$$x = f(y) = \frac{(y-y_1)(y-y_2) \ldots \ldots (y-y_n)}{(y_0-y_1)(y_0-y_2) \ldots \ldots (y_0-y_n)} x_0$$

$$+ \frac{(y-y_0)(y-y_2) \ldots \ldots (y-y_n)}{(y_1-y_0)(y_1-y_2) \ldots \ldots (y_1-y_n)} x_1 + \ldots \ldots \ldots$$

$$+ \frac{(y-y_0)(y-y_1) \ldots \ldots (y-y_{n-1})}{(y_n-y_0)(y_n-y_1)(y_n-y_2) \ldots \ldots (y_n-y_{n-1})} x_n \qquad \ldots \ldots . (6.5.3)$$

Example 6.17   Find the value of x corresponding to y = 70 given

x	11	13	15	17
$y = f(x)$	22	51	102	176

Solution: Putting $x_0 = 11, x_1 = 13, x_2 = 15, x_3 = 17$, $y_0 = 22$, $y_1 = 51$, $y_2 = 102, y_3 = 176$ and $y = 70$ in the Lagrange's inverse interpolation formula given in Eq. (6.5.3), we have

$$x = \frac{(70 - 51)(70 - 102)(70 - 176)}{(22 - 51)(22 - 102)(22 - 176)} \quad (11)$$

$$+ \frac{(70 - 22)(70 - 102)(70 - 176)}{(51 - 22)(51 - 102)(51 - 176)} (13)$$

$$+ \frac{(70 - 22)(70 - 51)(70 - 176)}{(102 - 22)(102 - 51)(102 - 176)} (15)$$

$$+ \frac{(70 - 22)(70 - 51)(70 - 102)}{(176 - 22)(176 - 51)(176 - 102)} (17)$$

$$= \frac{(19)(-32)(-106)}{(-29)(-80)(-154)} (11) + \frac{(48)(-32)(-106)}{(29)(-51)(-125)} (13)$$

$$+ \frac{(48)(19)(-106)}{(80)(51)(-74)} (15) + \frac{(48)(19)(-32)}{(154)(125)(74)} (17)$$

$$= -1.9842 + 11.4489 + 4.8029 - 0.3483$$

$$= 13.9193$$

Inverse Interpolation Using Method of Successive Approximations (Inverse Interpolation Using Iterative Method, Inverse Interpolation Using Newton's Forward Difference Formula)

Newton's forward difference formula (from Eq. 6.2.6) is

$$y_u = y_0 + u\frac{\Delta y_0}{1!} + \frac{u(u-1)}{2!}\Delta^2 y_0 + \frac{u(u-1)(u-2)}{3!}\Delta^3 y_0 + \ldots$$

From this, we get

$$u = \frac{1}{\Delta y_0}\left[y_u - y_0 - \frac{u(u-1)}{2!}\Delta^2 y_0 - \frac{u(u-1)(u-2)}{3!}\Delta^3 y_0 \right.$$

$$\left. - \ldots \ldots\right] \qquad \ldots\ldots (6.5.4)$$

If we neglect the second and higher differences, we obtain the first approximation to u as

$$u_1 = \frac{1}{\Delta y_0}(y_u - y_0) \qquad \ldots\ldots (6.5.5)$$

To find the second approximation, including the term containing second differences in Eq. (6.5.4) and replacing u by u_1, we get

$$u_2 = \frac{1}{\Delta y_0}\left[y_u - y_0 - \frac{u_1(u_1 - 1)}{2!}\Delta^2 y_0\right] \qquad \text{...... (6.5.6)}$$

To find the third approximation, including the term containing third differences in Eq. (6.5.4) and replacing u by u_2, we get

$$u_3 = \frac{1}{\Delta y_0}\left[y_u - y_0 - \frac{u_2(u_2 - 1)}{2!}\Delta^2 y_0 - \frac{u_2(u_2 - 1)(u_2 - 2)}{3!}\Delta^3 y_0 \right] (6.5.7)$$

and so on. This process is repeated till two successive approximations of u agree with each other to the desired accuracy.

Remark: Here we have used Newton's forward difference interpolation formula instead of that reader can start with any other interpolation formula to find inverse interpolation.

Example 6.18   The following values of $y = f(x)$ are given.

x	2	3	4	5	6
$y = x^2$	4	9	16	25	36

Calculate the value of $\sqrt{6}$ using successive approximation, correct to four decimal places.

Solution: The forward difference table is

x	y	Δy	$\Delta^2 y$	$\Delta^3 y$	$\Delta^4 y$
2	4	5	2	0	0
3	9	7	2	0	
4	16	9	2		
5	25	11			
6	36				

Here, $y_u = 6$, $y_0 = 4$, $\Delta y_0 = 5$, $\Delta^2 y = 2$, $\Delta^3 y = 0$, $\Delta^4 y = 0$.
The successive approximations to u are:

$$u_1 = \frac{1}{\Delta y_0}(y_u - y_0) = \frac{1}{5}(6 - 4) = 0.4$$

$$u_2 = \frac{1}{\Delta y_0}\left[y_u - y_0 - \frac{u_1(u_1 - 1)}{2!}\Delta^2 y_0\right] = \frac{1}{5}\left[6 - 4 - \frac{0.4(0.4 - 1)}{2}(2)\right]$$
$$= 0.448$$

$$u_3 = \frac{1}{\Delta y_0}\left[y_u - y_0 - \frac{u_2(u_2 - 1)}{2!}\Delta^2 y_0 - \frac{u_2(u_2 - 1)(u_2 - 2)}{3!}\Delta^3 y_0 \right]$$

$$= \frac{1}{5}\left[6 - 4 - \frac{0.448(0.448 - 1)}{2}(2) - \frac{0.448(0.448 - 1)(0.448 - 2)}{6}(0)\right]$$

$$= 0.4494$$

$$u_4 = \frac{1}{\Delta y_0}\left[y_u - y_0 - \frac{u_3(u_3 - 1)}{2!}\Delta^2 y_0 - \frac{u_3(u_3 - 1)(u_3 - 2)}{3!}\Delta^3 y_0 \right.$$
$$\left. - \frac{u_4(u_4 - 1)(u_4 - 2)(u_4 - 3)}{4!}\Delta^4 y_0\right]$$

$$= \frac{1}{5}\left[6 - 4 - \frac{0.4494(0.4494 - 1)}{2}(2)\right] = 0.4495$$

Similarly, $u_5 = 0.4495$. Hence, $u = 0.4495$

Therefore, the square root of 6 is given by $x_0 + uh = 2 + 0.4495(1) = 2.4495$

6.5.3 Error in Lagrange's Interpolation Formula

The error in Lagrange's interpolation formula can be derived from the Eq. (6.1.11). Here the error is the difference between $y(x)$ and the Lagrange's polynomial $L_n(x)$ at a given point. Also we assume that function can be differentiated $(n + 1)$ times. Hence, we have

$$y(x) - L_n(x) = R_n(x) = \frac{\pi_{n+1}(x)}{(n + 1)!}y^{(n+1)}(\xi), \quad a < \xi < b$$

The quantity E_L where

$$E_L = \frac{max}{[a, b]}|R_n(x)|$$

is used as an estimate of error. Along with that if we assume that

$$|y^{(n+1)}(\xi)| \le M_{n+1}, \quad a < \xi < b$$

then

$$E_L \le \frac{M_{n+1}}{(n + 1)!}\frac{max}{[a, b]}|\pi_{n+1}(x)| \qquad \text{...... (6.5.8)}$$

Let's understand the concept of error by the following examples.

Example 6.19 The function $y = cosx$ is tabulated below

x	0	$\pi/4$	$\pi/2$	$3\pi/4$
$y = cosx$	1	0.70711	0	-0.70711

Find the value of $\cos\left(\frac{\pi}{6}\right)$ using Lagrange's interpolation formula. Estimate the error in the solution obtained. Verify it with the error formula.

Solution: Lagrange's formula is

$$\cos\left(\frac{\pi}{6}\right) = \frac{\left(\frac{\pi}{6} - \frac{\pi}{4}\right)\left(\frac{\pi}{6} - \frac{\pi}{2}\right)\left(\frac{\pi}{6} - \frac{3\pi}{4}\right)}{\left(0 - \frac{\pi}{4}\right)\left(0 - \frac{\pi}{2}\right)\left(0 - \frac{3\pi}{4}\right)} \times (1) \quad + \frac{\left(\frac{\pi}{6} - 0\right)\left(\frac{\pi}{6} - \frac{\pi}{2}\right)\left(\frac{\pi}{6} - \frac{3\pi}{4}\right)}{\left(\frac{\pi}{4} - 0\right)\left(\frac{\pi}{4} - \frac{\pi}{2}\right)\left(\frac{\pi}{4} - \frac{3\pi}{4}\right)}$$

$$\times (0.70711)$$

$$+ \frac{\left(\frac{\pi}{6} - 0\right)\left(\frac{\pi}{6} - \frac{\pi}{4}\right)\left(\frac{\pi}{6} - \frac{\pi}{2}\right)}{(3\pi/4 - 0)\left(3\pi/4 - \frac{\pi}{4}\right)\left(3\pi/4 - \frac{\pi}{2}\right)} \times (-0.70711)$$

$$= \frac{(-0.261799)(-1.047198)(-1.832596)}{(-0.785398)(-1.570796)(-2.3561945)} \quad (1)$$

$$+ \frac{(0.523599)(-1.047198)(-1.832596)}{(0.785398)(-0.785398)(-1.570796)} \quad (0.70711)$$

$$+ \frac{(0.523599)(-0.261799)(-1.047198)}{(2.3561945)(1.570796)(0.785398)}(-0.70711)$$

$$= 0.172839 + 0.7333005 - 0.0349190 = 0.8712205$$

Actual value of $\cos\left(\frac{\pi}{6}\right) = 0.8660254$

$\therefore$ *Error* $= |Actual\ value - Approximate\ value|$

$$= |0.8660254 - 0.8712205| = 0.0051951$$

Verification:

Since $y(x) = \cos(x)$, we have $y'(x) = -\sin(x)$, $y''(x) = -\cos(x)$, $y'''(x) = \sin(x)$, $y^{(4)}(x) = -\cos(x)$

Hence, $\left|y^{(4)}(\xi)\right| \leq 1$, When $x = \frac{\pi}{6}$,

$$|R_n(x)| \leq \left|\frac{\left(\frac{\pi}{6} - 0\right)\left(\frac{\pi}{6} - \frac{\pi}{4}\right)\left(\frac{\pi}{6} - \frac{\pi}{2}\right)\left(\frac{\pi}{6} - \frac{3\pi}{4}\right)}{24}\right| = \frac{1}{24} \cdot \frac{\pi}{12} \cdot \frac{\pi}{3} \cdot \frac{7\pi}{12}$$

$$= 0.020934$$

which agree with the actual error in the solution obtained.

6.5.4 Divided Differences

The modification process is tedious in Lagrange's formula. That means if we want to add another interpolation value then the interpolation coefficients are required to be recalculated. The process of recalculating the interpolation coefficients is not required in Newton's divided difference formula. Before deriving this formula, we need to understand the concept of divided differences.

Let $(x_0, y_0), (x_1, y_1), (x_2, y_2), \dots\dots$, be the given pair of values of the function $y = f(x)$, then the first order divided diffrence, denoted by $[x_0, x_1]$, for the arguments x_0, x_1 is defined by

$$\Delta_d y_0 = [x_0, x_1] = \frac{y_1 - y_0}{x_1 - x_0}$$

Similarly, $\Delta_d y_1 = [x_1, x_2] = \frac{y_2 - y_1}{x_2 - x_1}$ and $\Delta_d y_2 = [x_2, x_3] = \frac{y_3 - y_2}{x_3 - x_2}$ etc.

The second divided difference for the arguments x_0, x_1, x_2 is defined as

$$\Delta_d^2 y_0 = [x_0, x_1, x_2] = \frac{\Delta_d y_1 - \Delta_d y_0}{x_2 - x_0} = \frac{[x_1, x_2] - [x_0, x_1]}{x_2 - x_0}$$

The third divided difference for the arguments x_0, x_1, x_2, x_3 is defined as

$$\Delta_d^3 y_0 = [x_0, x_1, x_2, x_3] = \frac{\Delta_d^2 y_1 - \Delta_d^2 y_0}{x_3 - x_0} = \frac{[x_1, x_2, x_3] - [x_0, x_1, x_2]}{x_3 - x_0}$$

and so on. The divided difference is given in Table 6.1.

Table 6.1 Divided Difference

x	y	Divided difference		
		First	Second	Third
x_0	y_0			
		$\Delta_d y_0 = [x_0, x_1] = \frac{y_1 - y_0}{x_1 - x_0}$		
x_1	y_1		$\Delta_d^2 y_0 = [x_0, x_1, x_2] = \frac{\Delta_d y_1 - \Delta_d y_0}{x_2 - x_0}$	
		$\Delta_d y_1 = [x_1, x_2] = \frac{y_2 - y_1}{x_2 - x_1}$		$\Delta_d^3 y_0 = [x_0, x_1, x_2, x_3]$ $= \frac{\Delta_d^2 y_1 - \Delta_d^2 y_0}{x_3 - x_0}$
x_2	y_2		$\Delta_d^2 y_0 = [x_1, x_2, x_3] = \frac{\Delta_d y_2 - \Delta_d y_1}{x_3 - x_1}$	
		$\Delta_d y_2 = [x_2, x_3] = \frac{y_3 - y_2}{x_3 - x_2}$		
x_3				

Properties of Divided Differences

1. Divided difference of a constant is zero.
2. The divided differences are symmetrical in all their arguments. i.e. all their values are independednt of the order of the arguments.

Proof:

$$[x_0, x_1] = \frac{y_1 - y_0}{x_1 - x_0} = \frac{y_0 - y_1}{x_0 - x_1} = [x_1, x_0] \qquad \ldots \ldots (6.5.9)$$

Also note that

$$[x_0, x_1] = \frac{y_0}{x_0 - x_1} + \frac{y_1}{x_1 - x_0} \qquad \ldots \ldots (6.5.10)$$

$$[x_0, x_1, x_2] = \frac{[x_1, x_2] - [x_0, x_1]}{x_2 - x_0}$$

$$= \frac{1}{x_2 - x_0} \left\{ \left[\frac{y_1}{x_1 - x_2} + \frac{y_2}{x_2 - x_1} \right] - \left[\frac{y_0}{x_0 - x_1} + \frac{y_1}{x_1 - x_0} \right] \right\} \text{ by (6.5.10)}$$

$$= \frac{1}{x_2 - x_0} \left\{ -\frac{y_0}{x_0 - x_1} + y_1 \left[\frac{1}{x_1 - x_2} - \frac{1}{x_1 - x_0} \right] + \frac{y_2}{x_2 - x_1} \right\}$$

$$= \frac{1}{x_2 - x_0} \left\{ \frac{y_0}{x_1 - x_0} + \frac{y_1 (x_2 - x_0)}{(x_1 - x_2)(x_1 - x_0)} + \frac{y_2}{x_2 - x_1} \right\}$$

$$= \frac{y_0}{(x_0 - x_1)(0 - x_2)} + \frac{y_1}{(x_1 - x_0)(x_1 - x_2)}$$

$$+ \frac{y_2}{(x_2 - x_0)(x_2 - x_1)} \qquad \ldots \ldots (6.5.11)$$

From Eq. (6.5.11) it is clear that $[x_0, x_1, x_2]$ remains unchanged when any two of the arguments are interchanged and therefore, symmetric in threir arguments.

Continuing in a same way, we can prove that $[x_0, x_1, x_2, x_3, \ldots, x_n]$ is symmetrical in nature with respect to any two arguments. Hence, the divided differences are symmetrical in all their arguments.

3.   The divided difference operator Δ is linear.

i.e. $\Delta\left[f(x) \pm g(x)\right] = \Delta f(x) \pm \Delta g(x)$

Proof:

$$\Delta[f(x_0) \pm g(x_0)] = \frac{\{af(x_1) \pm bg(x_1)\} - \{af(x_0) \pm bg(x_0)\}}{x_1 - x_0}$$

$$= \frac{a\{f(x_1) - f(x_0)\}}{x_1 - x_0} \pm \frac{b\{g(x_1) - g(x_0)\}}{x_1 - x_0}$$

$$= a\, \Delta f(x_0) \pm b\, \Delta\, g(x_0)$$

In general, $\Delta\left[f(x) \pm g(x)\right] = \Delta f(x) \pm \Delta g(x)$

This property holds good for higher order differences also.

4.   The nth order divided difference of a polynomial of degree $'n'$ is constant and is equal to the coefficient of x^n.

Proof: Without loss of generality, let us assume that $f(x) = x^n$, $n \in N$.

$$[x_0, x_1] = \frac{f(x_1) - f(x_0)}{x_1 - x_0} = \frac{x_1^n - x_0^n}{x_1 - x_0}$$

$$= x_1^{n-1} + x_0 \, x_1^{n-2} + x_0^2 \, x_1^{n-3} + \ldots\ldots + x_0^{n-1}$$

$$= \text{a symmetric polynomial of degree } (n-1) \text{ in } x_0 \text{ and } x_1 \text{ with leading coefficient } 1.$$

Now,

$$[x_0, x_1, x_2] = \frac{[x_1, x_2] - [x_0, x_1]}{x_2 - x_0}$$

$$= \frac{(x_2^{n-1} + x_1 \, x_2^{n-2} + \ldots\ldots + x_1^{n-1}) + (x_0^{n-1} + x_1 \, x_0^{n-2} + \ldots\ldots + x_1^{n-1})}{x_2 - x_0}$$

$$= \frac{x_2^{n-1} - x_0^{n-1}}{x_2 - x_0} + \frac{x_1(x_2^{n-2} - x_0^{n-2})}{x_2 - x_0} + \ldots\ldots + \frac{x_1^{n-2}(x_2 - x_0)}{x_2 - x_0}$$

$$= (x_2^{n-2} + x_0 \, x_2^{n-3} + \ldots\ldots + x_0^{n-2}) + x_1(x_2^{n-3} + x_0 x_2^{n-4} + \ldots\ldots + x_0^{n-3})$$
$$+ x_1^{n-2}$$

$$= \text{a symmetric polynomial of degree } (n-2) \text{ in } x_0, x_1 \text{ and } x_2 \text{ with leading co-efficient } 1.$$

Continuing the same way, we can prove that $[x_0, x_1, x_2, \ldots, x_r]$ is a symmetric polynomial of degree

$(n-r)$ in $x_0, x_1, x_2, \ldots\ldots, x_r$ with leading coefficient 1.

Thus, the nth order divided difference of x^n will be a symmetric polynomial of degree $(n - n) = 0$ in $x_0, x_1, x_2, \ldots\ldots, x_n$ with leading coefficient 1.

Therefore, n^{th} order divided difference of a polynomial of degree $'n'$ i.e.

$$\Delta^n \left[a_0 \, x^n + a_1 x^{n-1} + \ldots\ldots + a_n \right] = a_0 \Delta^n x^n + a_1 \Delta^n x^{n-1} + \ldots\ldots + \Delta^n a_n$$

$$= a_0 . 1 + a_1 . 0 + \ldots\ldots + a_n . 0$$
$$= a_0 = constant$$

5.   Relation between divided difference and forward difference

If the arguments $x_0, x_1, x_2, \ldots\ldots, x_n$ are equally spaced with interval length h then

$$[x_0, x_1, x_2, \ldots, x_r] = \frac{\Delta^r f(x_0)}{r! \, h^r}; \qquad r = 1, 2, \ldots, n$$

Proof: Given that interval length is h. i.e. $x_r - x_{r-1} = h, \quad r = 1, 2, \ldots, n$

$$\Delta f(x_0) = [x_0, x_1] = \frac{f(x_1) - f(x_0)}{x_1 - x_0} = \frac{1}{h} \Delta f(x_0)$$

$$\Delta^2 f(x_0) = [x_0, x_1, x_2] = \frac{[x_1, x_2] - [x_0, x_1]}{x_2 - x_0} = \frac{\Delta f(x_1) - \Delta f(x_0)}{x_2 - x_0}$$

$$= \frac{\frac{1}{h} \Delta f(x_1) - \frac{1}{h} \Delta f(x_0)}{2h}$$

$$= \frac{\Delta^2 f(x_0)}{(1.h)(2.h)} = \frac{1}{2! \, h^2} \Delta^2 f(x_0)$$

Similarly, $\Delta^3 f(x_0) = [x_0, x_1, x_2, x_3] = \frac{1}{3! \, h^3} \Delta^3 f(x_0)$ and so on. In general,

$$[x_0, x_1, x_2, \dots \dots, x_r] = \frac{\Delta^r f(x_0)}{r! \, h^r}; \qquad r = 1, 2, \dots \dots, n$$

6.5.5   Newton's Divided Diffference Interpolation Formula

This formula is used particularly when the values of the function $y = f(x)$ are to be tabulated at unequal intervals. Consider a polynomial passing through $(n + 1)$ points of degree $'n'$ of the type

$$y_n(x) = a_0 + a_1(x - x_0) + a_2(x - x_0)(x - x_1) + \dots \dots + a_n(x - x_0)(x - x_1) \dots \dots (x - x_{n-1}) \qquad \dots \dots (6.5.12)$$

Applying the condition that y and $y_n(x)$ should agree at the tabulated points and putting, $x = x_0, x_1, x_2, x_3, \dots \dots, x_n$ we have

$$\left.\begin{array}{l} \qquad\qquad at\ x = x_0 \Rightarrow y_0 = a_0 \\ \qquad at\quad x = x_1 \Rightarrow y_1 = a_0 + a_1(x_1 - x_0) \\ at\quad x = x_2 \Rightarrow y_2 = a_0 + a_1(x_2 - x_0) + a_2(x_2 - x_0)(x_2 - x_1) \\ \qquad\qquad \cdots \qquad \cdots \qquad \cdots \\ \qquad\qquad\qquad \cdots \qquad \cdots \qquad \cdots \end{array}\right\} \dots \dots (6.5.13)$$

and so on.

Now, from Eq.(6.5.13) we have

$$a_0 = y_0$$

$$a_1 = \frac{y_1 - a_0}{x_1 - x_0} = \frac{y_1 - y_0}{x_1 - x_0} = \Delta_d \, y_0$$

$$a_2 = \frac{y_2 - a_0 - a_1(x_2 - x_0)}{(x_2 - x_0)(x_2 - x_1)} = \frac{y_2 - y_0 - \left(\frac{y_1 - y_0}{x_1 - x_0}\right)(x_2 - x_0)}{(x_2 - x_0)(x_2 - x_1)}$$

$$= \frac{y_2(x_1 - x_0) - y_0(x_1 - x_0) - (y_1 - y_0)(x_2 - x_0)}{(x_2 - x_0)(x_2 - x_1)(x_1 - x_0)}$$

$$= \frac{y_2 x_1 - y_2 x_0 - y_0 x_1 + y_0 x_0 - (y_1 x_2 - y_1 x_0 - y_0 x_2 + y_0 x_0)}{(x_2 - x_0)(x_2 - x_1)(x_1 - x_0)}$$

$$= \frac{x_1 y_2 - x_0 y_2 - x_1 y_0 + x_0 y_0 - x_2 y_1 + x_0 y_1 + x_2 y_0 - x_0 y_0}{(x_2 - x_0)(x_2 - x_1)(x_1 - x_0)}$$

$$\therefore a_2 = \frac{(x_1 y_2 - x_1 y_1 - x_0 y_2 + x_0 y_1) - (x_2 y_1 - x_2 y_0 - x_1 y_1 + x_1 y_0)}{(x_2 - x_0)(x_2 - x_1)(x_1 - x_0)}$$

$$(\because \text{Adding and subtracting } x_1 y_1)$$

$$= \frac{(x_1 - x_0)(y_2 - y_1) - (x_2 - x_1)(y_1 - y_0)}{(x_2 - x_0)(x_2 - x_1)(x_1 - x_0)}$$

$$= \frac{(x_1 - x_0)(y_2 - y_1)}{(x_2 - x_0)(x_2 - x_1)(x_1 - x_0)} - \frac{(x_2 - x_1)(y_1 - y_0)}{(x_2 - x_0)(x_2 - x_1)(x_1 - x_0)}$$

$$= \frac{(y_2 - y_1)}{(x_2 - x_0)(x_2 - x_1)} - \frac{(y_1 - y_0)}{(x_2 - x_0)(x_1 - x_0)}$$

$$= \frac{1}{(x_2 - x_0)}\left[\frac{(y_2 - y_1)}{(x_2 - x_1)} - \frac{(y_1 - y_0)}{(x_1 - x_0)}\right] = \frac{\Delta_d y_1 - \Delta_d y_0}{(x_2 - x_0)}$$

$$= \Delta_d^2 y_0$$

Similarly, $a_n = \Delta_d^{n-1} y_0$

Thus, $a_0 = y_0, a_1 = \Delta_d y_0, a_2 = \Delta_d^2 y_0, \ldots\ldots\ldots, a_n = \Delta_d^{n-1} y_0$

Substitute all these values of constant in Eq. (6.5.6), we get

$$y_n(x) = y_0 + \Delta_d y_0(x - x_0) + \Delta_d^2 y_0 (x - x_0)(x - x_1) + \ldots\ldots$$
$$\ldots. + \Delta_d^{n-1} y_0 (x - x_0)(x - x_1) \ldots\ldots (x - x_{n-1}) \qquad \ldots\ldots (6.5.14)$$

This is known as Newton's divided difference interpolation formula.

Example 6.20 Construct a table of divided difference for the following data:

x	2.5	3.0	4.5	4.75	6.0
y	8.85	11.45	20.66	22.85	38.60

Solution: The divided difference table is

x	y	$\Delta_d y$	$\Delta_d^2 y$	$\Delta_d^3 y$	$\Delta_d^4 y$
2.5	8.85	$\frac{11.45 - 8.85}{3.0 - 2.5} = 5.2$	$\frac{6.14 - 5.2}{4.5 - 2.5} = 0.47$	$\frac{1.50 - 0.47}{4.75 - 2.5} = 0.46$	$\frac{0.35 - 0.46}{6.0 - 2.5} = -0.031$
3.0	11.45	$\frac{20.66 - 11.45}{4.5 - 3.0} = 6.14$	$\frac{8.76 - 6.14}{4.75 - 3.0} = 1.50$	$\frac{2.56 - 1.50}{6.0 - 3.0} = 0.35$	
4.5	20.66	$\frac{22.85 - 20.66}{4.75 - 4.5} = 8.76$	$\frac{12.6 - 8.76}{6.0 - 4.5} = 2.56$		
4.75	22.85	$\frac{38.60 - 22.85}{6.0 - 4.75} = 12.6$			
6.0	38.60				

Example 6.21 Using Newton's divided difference formula, evaluate f(6) and f(14).

x	4	5	7	10	11	13
$f(x)$	48	100	294	900	1210	2028

Solution: We form the divided difference table since the intervals are unequal. The divided difference table is

x	$f(x)$	$\Delta_d f(x)$	$\Delta_d^2 f(x)$	$\Delta_d^3 f(x)$	$\Delta_d^4 f(x)$	$\Delta_d^5 f(x)$
4	48	52	15	1	0	0
5	100	97	21	1	0	
7	294	202	27	1		
10	900	310	33			
11	1210	409				
13	2028					

The divided difference formula is

$$f(x) = f(x_0) + [x_0, x_1](x - x_0) + [x_0, x_1, x_2] (x - x_0)(x - x_1)$$
$$+ [x_0, x_1, x_2, x_3] (x - x_0)(x - x_1)(x - x_2)$$

For $x = 6$,
$$f(6) = 48 + 52 (6 - 4) + 15(6 - 4)(6 - 5) + 1 (6 - 4)(6 - 5)(6 - 7)$$
$$= 48 + 104 + 30 - 2 = 180$$

For $x = 14$,
$$f(14) = 48 + 52 (14 - 4) + 15(14 - 4)(14 - 5)$$
$$+ 1 (14 - 4)(14 - 5)(14 - 7)$$
$$= 48 + 520 + 1350 + 630 = 2548$$

Example 6.22 Determine $f(x)$ as a polynomial in x for the following data:

x	- 4	-1	0	2	5
$f(x)$	1245	33	5	9	1335

Solution: The divided difference table is

x	$f(x)$	$\Delta_d f(x)$	$\Delta_d^2 f(x)$	$\Delta_d^3 f(x)$	$\Delta_d^4 f(x)$
-4	1245	-404	94	-14	3
-1	33	-28	10	13	
0	5	2	88		
2	9	442			
5	1335				

The divided difference formula is

$$f(x) = f(x_0) + [x_0, x_1](x - x_0) + [x_0, x_1, x_2](x - x_0)(x - x_1)$$
$$+ [x_0, x_1, x_2, x_3](x - x_0)(x - x_1)(x - x_2)$$
$$= 1245 + (-404)(x + 4) + (94)(x + 4) + (-14)(x + 4)(x + 1)(x - 0)$$
$$+ (3)(x + 4)(x + 1)x(x - 2) = 3x^4 - 5x^3 + 6x^2 - 14x + 5$$

6.6   HERMITE INTERPOLATING POLYNOMIAL

In the previous sections, we have discussed interpolating polynomials for $y = f(x)$, which make use of $(n + 1)$ function values. In this section, we derive an interpolating polynomial for $y = f(x)$ such that it assumes the same values as $f(x)$ and its derivatives will assume the same values as $f'(x)$ at $x = x_p, p = 0, 1, 2, \ldots, n$.

Given the set of data points (x_p, y_p, y_p'), $p = 0, 1, 2, \ldots, n$ it is required to find an interpolating polynomial of the least degree , say $H_{2n+1}(x)$, for $y = f(x)$ satisfying the conditions:

$$H_{2n+1}(x_p) = y_p \qquad\qquad \ldots\ldots (6.6.1)$$

$$H_{2n+1}'(x_p) = y_p' \qquad\qquad \ldots\ldots (6.6.2)$$

where $y_p = f(x_p)$ and $y_p' = f'(x_p)$ for $p = 0, 1, 2, \ldots, n$.

The polynomial $H_{2n+1}(x)$ is known as *Hermite's interpolating polynomial.* Since we have here $(2n + 2)$ conditions, the number of coefficients to be determined is $(2n + 2)$ and the degree of the polynomial $f(x)$ is $(2n + 1)$.

Let

$$H_{2n+1}(x) = \sum_{p=0}^{n} A_p(x)y_p + \sum_{p=0}^{n} B_p(x)y_p' \qquad\qquad \ldots\ldots (6.6.3)$$

where $A_p(x)$ and $B_p(x)$ are polynomials in x of degree $(2n + 1)$.
Using Eq. (6.6.1) in Eq. (6.6.3) we have,

$$\sum_{p=0}^{n} A_p(x)y_p + \sum_{p=0}^{n} B_p(x)y_p' = y_p$$

Therefore we obtain,

$$A_p(x_j) = \begin{cases} 0, & \text{if } p \neq j \\ 1, & \text{if } p = j \end{cases}; \quad B_p(x_j) = 0 \text{ for all } p \text{ and } j \qquad\qquad \ldots\ldots (6.6.4)$$

Fron Eq. (6.6.3), we have

$$H'_{2n+1}(x) = \sum_{p=0}^{n} A_p'(x)y_p + \sum_{p=0}^{n} B_p'(x)y_p' \qquad\qquad \ldots\ldots (6.6.5)$$

Using Eq. (6.6.2) in Eq. (6.6.5), we get

$$\sum_{p=0}^{n} A_p'(x)y_p + \sum_{p=0}^{n} B_p'(x)y_p' = y_p'$$

Therefore,

$$A_p'(x_j) = 0 \text{ for all } p \text{ and } j \qquad \text{and}$$

$$B_p'(x_j) = \begin{cases} 0, & \text{if } p \neq j \\ 1, & \text{if } p = j \end{cases} \qquad \dots \dots (6.6.6)$$

Since $A_p(x)$ and $B_p(x)$ are polynomials in x of degree $(2n+1)$, we write

$$A_p(x) = u_p(x)\big[L_p(x)\big]^2 \quad \text{and} \quad B_p(x) = v_p(x)\big[L_p(x)\big]^2 \qquad \dots \dots (6.6.7)$$

where,

$$L_p(x) = \frac{(x-x_0)(x-x_1)\dots\dots(x-x_{p-1})(x-x_{p+1})\dots\dots(x-x_n)}{(x_p-x_0)(x_p-x_1)\dots\dots(x_p-x_{p-1})(x_p-x_{p+1})\dots\dots(x_p-x_n)}$$

which is a polynomial of the nth degree used in the $(p+1)^{\text{th}}$ term of the Lagrange's formula. Since $\big[L_p(x)\big]^2$ is a polynomial of degree $2n$, $u_p(x)$ and $v_p(x)$ are linear polynomials.

Let $u_p(x) = a_p(x) + b_p \quad$ and $\quad v_p(x) = c_p(x) + d_p \qquad \dots \dots (6.6.8)$

We therefore write

$$A_p(x_j) = \big(a_p x_j + b_p\big)\big[L_p(x_j)\big]^2$$

$$A_p'(x_j) = a_p\big[L_p(x_j)\big]^2 + \big(a_p x_j + b_p\big)2\,L_p(x_j)L_p'(x_j)$$

Using Eq. (6.6.4) and Eq. (6.6.6) in these equations, we have

$$a_p x_p + b_p = 1 \qquad \because L_p(x_p) = 1 \qquad \dots \dots (6.6.9)$$

$$a_p + 2\big(a_p x_p + b_p\big)L_p'(x_p) = 0 \qquad \dots \dots (6.6.10)$$

From Eq. (6.6.9) and Eq. (6.6.10), we get

$$a_p = -2L_p'(x_p) \quad \text{and} \quad b_p = 1 + 2x_p L_p'(x_p) \qquad \dots \dots (6.6.11)$$

Also,

$$B_p(x_j) = \big(c_p x_j + d_p\big)\big[L_p(x_j)\big]^2$$

$$B_p'(x_j) = c_p\big[L_p(x_j)\big]^2 + \big(c_p x_j + d_p\big)2\,L_p(x_j)L_p'(x_j)$$

Using Eq. (6.6.4) and Eq. (6.6.6) in these equations, we have

$$c_p x_p + d_p = 0 \qquad \because L_p(x_p) = 1 \qquad \dots \dots (6.6.12)$$

$$c_p + 2\big(c_p x_p + d_p\big)L_p'(x_p) = 1 \qquad \dots \dots (6.6.13)$$

From Eq. (6.6.12) and Eq. (6.6.13), we get

$$c_p = 1 \quad and \quad d_p = -x_p \qquad \dots \dots (6.6.14)$$

Using Eq. (6.6.11) in Eq. (6.6.7), we have

$$A_p(x) = \{1 - 2xL_p'(x_p) + 2x_pL_p'(x_p)\}\left[L_p(x)\right]^2$$

$$= \{1 - 2(x-x_p)L_p'(x_p)\}\left[L_p(x)\right]^2 \qquad \text{........ (6.6.15)}$$

and using Eq. (6.6.14) in Eq. (6.6.7), we have

$$B_p(x) = (x-x_p)\left[L_p(x)\right]^2 \qquad \text{........ (6.6.16)}$$

Using Eq. (6.6.15) and Eq. (6.6.16) in Eq. (6.6.3), we get

$$H_{2n+1}(x) = \sum_{p=0}^{n}\{1 - 2(x-x_p)L_p'(x_p)\}\left[L_p(x)\right]^2 y_p$$

$$+ \sum_{p=0}^{n}(x-x_p)\left[L_p(x)\right]^2 y_p' \qquad \text{.........(6.6.17)}$$

which is the required Hermite's interpolation formula.

Remark: Hermite's interpolating polynomial is given by

$$y = \sum_{p=0}^{n} A_p(x)y_p + \sum_{p=0}^{n} B_p(x)y_p'$$

or

$$y = \sum_{p=0}^{n} u_p(x)\left[L_p(x)\right]^2 y_p + \sum_{p=0}^{n} v_p(x)\left[L_p(x)\right]^2 y_p'$$

or

$$y = \sum_{p=0}^{n}\left[y_p u_p(x) + y_p' v_p(x)\right]\left[L_p(x)\right]^2$$

Example 6.23 Express y as a polynomial in x from the following data, using Hermite's interpolating formula.

x:	0	1	2
y:	0	1	0
y':	0	2	4

Hence find the value of $y(1.5)$.

Solution: Let $L_0(x), L_1(x)$ and $L_2(x)$ be the second degree polynomials that are the multipliers of y_0, y_1 and y_2 in Lagrange's interpolation formula for the given data.

$$L_0(x) = \frac{(x - x_1)(x - x_2)}{(x_0 - x_1)(x_0 - x_2)} = \frac{(x - 1)(x - 2)}{(0 - 1)(0 - 2)} = \frac{1}{2}(x^2 - 3x + 2)$$

$$L_1(x) = \frac{(x - x_0)(x - x_2)}{(x_1 - x_0)(x_1 - x_2)} = \frac{(x - 0)(x - 2)}{(1 - 0)(1 - 2)} = 2x - x^2$$

$$L_2(x) = \frac{(x - x_0)(x - x_1)}{(x_2 - x_0)(x_2 - x_1)} = \frac{(x - 0)(x - 1)}{(2 - 0)(2 - 1)} = \frac{1}{2}(x^2 - x)$$

$$L'_0(x) = \frac{1}{2}(2x - 3), \qquad L'_1(x) = 2 - 2x, \qquad L'_2(x) = \frac{1}{2}(2x - 1)$$

$$L'_0(x_0) = -\frac{3}{2}, \quad L'_1(x_1) = 0, \quad L'_2(x_2) = \frac{3}{2}$$

$$A_0(x) = \{1 - 2(x - x_0)L'_0(x_0)\}[L_0(x)]^2$$

$$= \left\{1 - 2(x - 0)\left(-\frac{3}{2}\right)\right\} \cdot \frac{1}{4}(x^2 - 3x + 2)^2$$

$$= \frac{1}{4}(1 + 3x)(x^4 - 6x^3 + 13x^2 - 12x + 4)$$

$$= \frac{1}{4}(3x^5 - 17x^4 + 33x^3 - 23x^2 + 4)$$

$$A_1(x) = \{1 - 2(x - x_1)L'_1(x_1)\}[L_1(x)]^2 = \{1 - 2(x - 1)(0)\}$$

$$= x^4 - 4x^3 + 4x^2$$

$$A_2(x) = \{1 - 2(x - x_2)L'_2(x_2)\}[L_2(x)]^2$$

$$= \left\{1 - 2(x - 2)\left(\frac{3}{2}\right)\right\} \cdot \frac{1}{4}(x^2 - x)^2$$

$$= \frac{1}{4}(7 - 3x)(x^4 - 2x^3 + x^2) = \frac{1}{4}(-3x^5 + 13x^4 - 17x^3 + 7x^2)$$

$$B_0(x) = (x - x_0)[L_0(x)]^2 = x \cdot \frac{1}{4}(x^2 - 3x + 2)^2$$

$$= \frac{1}{4}(x^5 - 6x^4 + 13x^3 - 12x^2 + 4x)$$

$$B_1(x) = (x - x_1)[L_1(x)]^2 = (x - 1)(2x - x^2)^2 = x^5 - 5x^4 + 8x^3 - 4x^2$$

$$B_2(x) = (x - x_2)[L_2(x)]^2 = (x - 2) \cdot \frac{1}{4}(x^2 - x)^2$$

$$= \frac{1}{4}(x^5 - 4x^4 + 5x^3 - 2x^2)$$

Hermite's interpolating polynomial is given by

$$y = \sum_{p=0}^{2} A_p(x)y_p + \sum_{p=0}^{2} B_p(x)y'_p$$

Thus, $y = 0 \times \frac{1}{4}(3x^5 - 17x^4 + 33x^3 - 23x^2 + 4) + 1 \times (x^4 - 4x^3 + 4x^2) + 0 \times \frac{1}{4}(-3x^5 + 13x^4 - 17x^3 + 7x^2) + 0 \times \frac{1}{4}(x^5 - 6x^4 + 13x^3 - 12x^2 + 4x) + 2 \times (x^5 - 5x^4 + 8x^3 - 4x^2) + 4 \times \frac{1}{4}(x^5 - 4x^4 + 5x^3 - 2x^2)$

$= (2 + 1)x^5 + (1 - 10 - 4)x^4 + (-4 + 16 + 5)x^3 + (4 - 8 - 2)x^2$

$$\therefore \ y = 3x^5 - 13x^4 + 17x^3 - 6x^2$$
$$\therefore \ y(1.5) = 3(1.5)^5 - 13(1.5)^4 + 17(1.5)^3 - 6(1.5)^2$$
$$= 22.78125 - 65.8125 + 57.375 - 13.5$$
$$= 0.84375$$

6.7 PIECEWISE POLYNOMIAL INTERPOLATION

The interpolating polynomials of higher degree are not always easy to evaluate. It is time consuming and tedious task and there may be loss of significant digits involved in their calculations means higher round-off errors. To keep the degree of the interpolating polynomial small with significant accuracy it is desirable to consider piecewise polynomial interpolation. This involves finding a continuous function $y = f(x)$ approximated by a lower degree polynomial in each interval (x_{p-1}, x_p); $p = 1,2,3, \dots \dots, n$. In the following subsections we discuss two piecewise interpolation methods.

6.7.1 Piecewise Linear Interpolation

The function $f(x)$, discussed above, is called a piecewise linear interpolation if each of the polynomials on the subintervals are of degree less than or equal to 1. In this method, we approximate the function $y = f(x)$ at the (n+1) nodal points $x_0, x_1, \dots \dots, x_n$ by a linear polynomial in each interval (x_{p-1}, x_p).

Using the Lagrange's interpolation formula, the piecewise linear interpolation formula $P_p(x)$ is given by

$$P_p(x) = \left(\frac{x - x_p}{x_{p-1} - x_p}\right) y_{p-1} + \left(\frac{x - x_{p-1}}{x_p - x_{p-1}}\right) y_p, \ x \in (x_{p-1}, x_p),$$
$$p = 1,2,3, \dots \dots, n \qquad \dots\dots (6.7.1)$$

Then the overall interpolating polynomial is given by

$$P(x) = \sum_{p=1}^{n} P_p(x) \qquad \dots\dots (6.7.2)$$

Example 6.24 Find the piecewise linear polynomial for the following data:

x	0	1	2
y	1	2	21

Solution: For $0 \le x \le 1$ and $1 \le x \le 2$ using Eq. (6.6.18), we have
$$y = \left(\frac{x - x_1}{x_0 - x_1}\right) y_0 + \left(\frac{x - x_0}{x_1 - x_0}\right) y_1$$
$$y = \left(\frac{x - 1}{0 - 1}\right)(1) + \left(\frac{x - 0}{1 - 0}\right)(2) = x + 1$$

and

$$y = \left(\frac{x - x_2}{x_1 - x_2}\right) y_1 + \left(\frac{x - x_1}{x_2 - x_1}\right) y_2$$

$$y = \left(\frac{x - 2}{1 - 2}\right)(2) + \left(\frac{x - 1}{2 - 1}\right)(21) = 19x - 17$$

Therefore, the required interpolating polynomial is

$$P(x) = \begin{cases} x + 1 & if\ 0 \leq x \leq 1 \\ 19x - 17 & if\ 1 \leq x \leq 2 \end{cases}$$

6.7.2   Piecewise Cubic Interpolation

In this subsection, we consider piecewise cubic interpolation in which a cubic polynomial approximation is assumed over each subinterval (x_{p-1}, x_p). To obtain sufficient information to find these coefficients, we require continuity of the interpolating polynomials in neighbouring intervals as well as the continuity of a number of derivatives. Let the function $y = f(x)$ be approximated by a cubic polynomial $P_p(x)$ in each interval (x_{p-1}, x_p) satisfies the follwoing conditions:

$$P_p(x_{p-1}) = y_{p-1}, \qquad P_p(x_p) = y_p$$
$$P'_p(x_{p-1}) = y'_{p-1}, \qquad P'_p(x_p) = y'_p$$

Since these are Hermite type of conditions, $P_p(x)$ is called piecewise cubic Hermite interpolating polynomial. From Eqs. (6.6.3), (6.6.15) and (6.6.16) for the interval (x_{p-1}, x_p), $p = 1,2,3, \ldots., n$, we have

$$P_p(x) = A_{p-1}(x)y_{p-1} + A_p(x)y_p + B_{p-1}(x)y'_{p-1} + B_p(x)y'_p$$
$$p = 1,2,3,\ldots.,n \quad \ldots.... (6.7.3)$$

where $\qquad A_{p-1}(x) = \left\{1 - 2(x - x_{p-1})L'_{p-1}(x_{p-1})\right\}\left[L_{p-1}(x)\right]^2,$

$$L_{p-1}(x) = \frac{x - x_p}{x_{p-1} - x_p} \qquad and \qquad L'_{p-1}(x) = \frac{1}{x_{p-1} - x_p}$$

$$\therefore\ A_{p-1}(x) = \left(\frac{x - x_p}{x_{p-1} - x_p}\right)^2\left[1 + \frac{2(x_{p-1} - x)}{(x_{p-1} - x_p)}\right] \qquad \ldots.... (6.7.4)$$

Similarly,

$$A_p(x) = \left(\frac{x - x_{p-1}}{x_{p-1} - x_p}\right)^2\left[1 + \frac{2(x - x_p)}{(x_{p-1} - x_p)}\right] \qquad \ldots.... (6.7.5)$$

$$B_{p-1}(x) = \left(\frac{x - x_p}{x_{p-1} - x_p}\right)^2(x - x_{p-1}) \qquad \ldots.... (6.7.6)$$

$$B_p(x) = \left(\frac{x - x_{p-1}}{x_{p-1} - x_p}\right)^2(x - x_p) \qquad \ldots.... (6.7.7)$$

Then the overall piecewise cubic interpolating polynomial is given by

$$P(x) = \sum_{p=1}^{n} P_p(x) \qquad \qquad \text{........(6.7.8)}$$

Example 6.25 Find the interpolating polynomial for the following data using (i) piecewise linear intrepolation (ii) piecewise cubic Hermite interpolation.

x	0	1	2
y	1	5	29
y'	1	11	64

Solution:

(i) The piecewise linear interpolating polynomial is given by

$$y = \left(\frac{x - x_p}{x_{p-1} - x_p}\right) y_{p-1} + \left(\frac{x - x_{p-1}}{x_p - x_{p-1}}\right) y_p, \quad x_{i-1} \le x \le x_i$$

For $0 \le x \le 1$ and $1 \le x \le 2$ using Eq. (6.6.18), we have

$$y = \left(\frac{x - x_1}{x_0 - x_1}\right) y_0 + \left(\frac{x - x_0}{x_1 - x_0}\right) y_1$$

$$y = \left(\frac{x - 1}{0 - 1}\right) (1) + \left(\frac{x - 0}{1 - 0}\right) (5) = 4x + 1$$

and

$$y = \left(\frac{x - x_2}{x_1 - x_2}\right) y_1 + \left(\frac{x - x_1}{x_2 - x_1}\right) y_2$$

$$y = \left(\frac{x - 2}{1 - 2}\right) (5) + \left(\frac{x - 1}{2 - 1}\right) (29) = 24x - 19$$

Therefore, the required interpolating polynomial is

$$P(x) = \begin{cases} 4x + 1 & if \ 0 \le x \le 1 \\ 24x - 19 & if \ 1 \le x \le 2 \end{cases}$$

(ii) In $0 \le x \le 1$, $x_0 = 0$, $x_1 = 1$; $y_0 = 1$, $y_1 = 5$; $y_0' = 1$, $y_1' = 5$

$$L_0(x) = \frac{x - 1}{0 - 1} = 1 - x; \ L_1(x) = \frac{x - 0}{1 - 0} = x; \quad L'_0(x) = -1; \ L'_1(x) = 1$$

$$u_0(x) = \{1 - 2(x - x_0) L'_0(x_0)\} = 1 - 2x.(-1) = 1 + 2x$$

$$u_1(x) = \{1 - 2(x - x_1) L'_1(x_1)\} = 1 - 2(x - 1)(1) = 3 - 2x$$

$$v_0(x) = (x - x_0) = x; \ v_1(x) = (x - x_1) = x - 1$$

Hermite's interpolating polynomial is

$$y = \sum_{p=0}^{1} \{y_p \, u_p(x) + y_p' \, v_p(x)\} \{L_p(x)\}^2$$

$$= (1 + 2x + x)(1 - x)^2 + (15 - 10x + 11x - 11)x^2$$
$$= (1 + 3x)(1 - 2x + x^2) + (4 + x)x^2$$
$$= 4x^3 - x^2 + x + 1$$

In $1 \le x \le 2$, $x_0 = 1$, $x_1 = 2$; $y_0 = 5$, $y_1 = 29$; $y_0' = 11$, $y_1' = 65$

$$L_0(x) = \frac{x-2}{1-2} = 2 - x; \ L_1(x) = \frac{x-1}{2-1} = x - 1;$$

$$L'_0(x) = -1; \ L'_1(x) = 1$$

$$u_0(x) = \{1 - 2(x-x_0)L'_0(x_0)\} = 1 - 2(x - 1).(-1) = 2x - 1$$

$$u_1(x) = \{1 - 2(x-x_1)L'_1(x_1)\} = 1 - 2(x - 2)(1) = 5 - 2x$$

$$v_0(x) = (x-x_0) = x - 1; \ v_1(x) = (x-x_1) = x - 2$$

Hermite's interpolating polynomial is

$$y = \sum_{p=0}^{1} \{y_p \, u_p(x) + y_p' \, v_p(x)\}\{L_p(x)\}^2$$
$$= \{5(2x - 1) + 11(x - 1)\}(2 - x)^2 + \{29(5 - 2x) + 65(x - 2)\}(x - 1)^2$$
$$= (21x - 16)(4 - 4x + x^2) + (15 + 7x)(x^2 - 2x + 1)$$
$$= 28x^3 - 99x^2 + 125x - 49$$

Hence the required cubic Hermite interpolating polynomial is

$$y = \begin{cases} 4x^3 - x^2 + x + 1, & \text{for } 0 \le x \le 1 \\ 28x^3 - 99x^2 + 125x - 49, & \text{for } 1 \le x \le 2 \end{cases}$$

6.8 CUBIC SPLINE INTERPOLATION

In the previous sections we have discussed, for a given set of values of functions, how an nth degree interpolating polynomial can be constructed and used. When n is large compare to the order of the original function then the nth degree interpolating polynomial does not give accurate results at the end of the range. It is possible to create piecewise polynomials that remove such discontinuities at the junctions of the successive arcs. Such piecewise polynomials are called spline functions. These junction points are called nodal points or knots.

The name spline function is derived from a draftsman's device for drawing smooth curves in such a way that not only curve but also its slope and curvature are continuous functions.

Let a set of nodal points $(x_0, y_0), (x_1, y_1), (x_2, y_2), \ldots \ldots, (x_n, y_n)$ be given, where $a = x_0 < x_1 < x_2 < \ldots \ldots < x_n = b$ may not be equally spaced. We want to find a cubic spline function $S(x)$, such that it satisfies the following properties:

(i) $S(x_i) = y_i, i = 0, 1, 2, \ldots \ldots, n$

(ii) The function $S(x)$, its slope $S'(x)$ and its curvature $S''(x)$ are continuous in $[a, b]$.

(iii) On each of the intervals $(x_{i-1}, x_i), i = 1, 2, 3, \ldots, n$ $S(x)$ is a polynomial of degree ≤ 3.

Since $S(x)$ is a cubic polynomial, $S'(x)$ is quadratic and $S''(x)$ is a linear polynomial. By the Lagrange's interpolation formula in the interval (x_{i-1}, x_i),

$$S''(x) = \frac{x_i - x}{x_i - x_{i-1}} S''(x_{i-1}) + \frac{x - x_{i-1}}{x_i - x_{i-1}} S''(x_i) \qquad \ldots\ldots\ldots (6.8.1)$$

Integrating Eq. (6.8.1) twice with respect to x, we have

$$S(x) = \frac{(x_i - x)^3}{6h_i} M_{i-1} + \frac{(x - x_{i-1})^3}{6h_i} M_i + c_1 x + c_2 \qquad \ldots\ldots\ldots (6.8.2)$$

where $x_i - x_{i-1} = h_i$, $M_i = S''(x_i)$ and c_1 and c_2 are the constants of integration to be determined. These constants can be obtained by using $S(x_{i-1}) = y_{i-1}$ and $S(x_i) = y_i$ as $S(x)$ has to agree with $y = f(x)$. Hence, Eq. (6.8.2) becomes,

$$\frac{h_i^2}{6} M_{i-1} + c_1 x_{i-1} + c_2 = y_{i-1} \qquad \ldots\ldots\ldots (6.8.3)$$

$$\frac{h_i^2}{6} M_i + c_1 x_i + c_2 = y_i \qquad \ldots\ldots\ldots (6.8.4)$$

From Eq. (6.8.3) and Eq. (6.8.4), we get

$$c_1 = \frac{(y_i - y_{i-1})}{h_i} - \frac{(M_i - M_{i-1})}{6} h_i \qquad \ldots\ldots\ldots (6.8.5)$$

$$c_2 = \frac{(x_i y_{i-1} - x_{i-1} y_i)}{h_i} - \frac{1}{6}(x_i M_{i-1} - x_{i-1} M_i) h_i \qquad \ldots\ldots\ldots (6.8.6)$$

Using Eq. (6.8.5) and Eq. (6.8.6) in Eq. (6.8.2), we have

$$S(x) = \frac{(x_i - x)^3}{6h_i} M_{i-1} + \frac{(x - x_{i-1})^3}{6h_i} M_i + \frac{(y_i - y_{i-1})x}{h_i}$$

$$- \frac{(M_i - M_{i-1})}{6} h_i x + \frac{(x_i y_{i-1} - x_{i-1} y_i)}{h_i} - \frac{1}{6}(x_i M_{i-1} - x_{i-1} M_i) h_i \ldots (6.8.7)$$

$$= \left[\frac{(x_i - x)^3}{6h_i} - \frac{h_i}{6}(x_i - x) \right] M_{i-1} + \left[\frac{(x - x_{i-1})^3}{6h_i} - \frac{h_i}{6}(x - x_{i-1}) \right] M_i$$

$$+ \frac{1}{h_i}(x_i - x)y_{i-1} + \frac{1}{h_i}(x - x_{i-1})y_i$$

$$= \left[\frac{(x_i - x)\{(x_i - x)^2 - h_i^2\}}{6h_i} \right] M_{i-1}$$

$$+ \left[\frac{(x - x_{i-1})\{(x - x_{i-1})^2 - h_i{}^2\}}{6h_i} \right] M_i$$

$$+ \frac{1}{h_i}(x_i - x)y_{i-1} + \frac{1}{h_i}(x - x_{i-1})y_i \qquad \ldots\ldots\ldots (6.8.8)$$

where M_{i-1} and M_i are unknowns to be found by using the continuity of $S'(x)$ at the point x_i. Differentiating Eq. (6.8.7) with respect to x, we get

$$S'(x) = -\frac{(x_i - x)^2}{2h_i}M_{i-1} + \frac{(x - x_{i-1})^2}{2h_i}M_i - \frac{(M_i - M_{i-1})h_i}{6}$$

$$+ \frac{(y_i - y_{i-1})}{h_i}, \quad \text{for } x < x_i \qquad \ldots\ldots\ldots (6.8.9)$$

and

$$S'(x) = -\frac{(x_{i+1} - x)^2}{2h_{i+1}}M_i + \frac{(x - x_i)^2}{2h_{i+1}}M_{i+1} - \frac{(M_{i+1} - M_i)h_{i+1}}{6}$$

$$+ \frac{(y_{i+1} - y_i)}{h_{i+1}}, \quad \text{for } x > x_i \qquad \ldots\ldots\ldots (6.8.10)$$

From the continuity of function $S'(x)$ and $x = x_i$ and Eqs. (6.8.9) and (6.8.10), we have

$$\frac{h_i}{6} M_{i-1} + \frac{h_i}{3} M_i + \frac{1}{h_i}(y_i - y_{i-1})$$

$$= -\frac{h_{i+1}}{3} M_i - \frac{h_{i+1}}{6} M_{i+1} + \frac{1}{h_{i+1}}(y_{i+1} - y_i)$$

or

$$\frac{h_i}{6} M_{i-1} + \left(\frac{h_i + h_{i+1}}{3}\right) M_i + \frac{h_{i+1}}{6} M_{i+1} = \frac{1}{h_{i+1}}(y_{i+1} - y_i) - \frac{1}{h_i}(y_i - y_{i-1})$$

$$i = 1, 2, \ldots, (n - 1) \qquad \ldots\ldots\ldots (6.8.11)$$

Thus, total $(n - 1)$ equations in $(n - 1)$ unknowns with the conditions $M_0 = 0$ and $M_n = 0$ gives $(n + 1)$ equations in $(n + 1)$ unknowns $M_0, M_1, \ldots\ldots, M_n$ and hence can be easily found.

In the case when $x_i's$ are equally spaced i.e. $h_i = h$ for all i, $S(x)$ is given by

$$S(x) = \frac{1}{6h} [(x_i - x)^3 M_{i-1} + (x - x_{i-1})^3 M_i]$$

$$+ \frac{1}{h}(x_i - x)\left(y_{i-1} - \frac{h^2}{6}M_{i-1}\right) + \frac{1}{h}(x - x_{i-1})\left(y_i - \frac{h^2}{6}M_i\right) \qquad \ldots\ldots\ldots (6.8.12)$$

where $M_{i-1} + 4 M_i + M_{i+1} = \frac{6}{h^2}(y_{i-1} - 2y_i + y_{i+1})$, $i = 1, 2, 3, \ldots (n - 1)$, $M_0 = M_n = 0$

Example 6.26 Fit a cubic spline curve that passes through $(0, 1), (1, 4), (2, 0)$ and $(3, -2)$ with the natural boundary conditions $S''(0) = S''(3) = 0$

Solution: The values of $x_i{'}s$ are equally spaced with $h = 1$, we have $M_{i-1} +$ $4 M_i + M_{i+1} = 6 (y_{i-1} - 2y_i + y_{i+1})$ $i = 1, 2$ and $M_0 = S''(0) = M_n = S''(3) = 0$

For $i = 1$ and $i = 2$, we get

$$M_0 + 4 M_1 + M_2 = 6 (y_0 - 2y_1 + y_2) = 6(1 - 8 + 0) = -42$$
$$M_1 + 4 M_2 + M_3 = 6 (y_1 - 2y_2 + y_3) = 6(4 - 0 - 2) = 12$$

i.e. $4 M_1 + M_2 = -42$ and $M_1 + 4 M_2 = 12$ ($\because M_0 = M_3 = 0$)

Solving these two equations we get $M_1 = -12$, $M_2 = 6$

The cubic spline in $x_{i-1} \le x \le x_i$, is given by

$$S(x) = \frac{1}{6} [(x_i - x)^3 M_{i-1} + (x - x_{i-1})^3 M_i] + (x_i - x) \left(y_{i-1} - \frac{1}{6} M_{i-1} \right)$$

$$+ (x - x_{i-1}) \left(y_i - \frac{1}{6} M_i \right) \qquad \dots \dots \dots \dots \dots (1)$$

For $i = 1$, the cubic spline, for $0 \le x \le 1$, is given by

$$S_1(x) = \frac{1}{6} [(x - 0)^3 \times (-12)] + (1 - x) \left\{ 1 - \frac{1}{6} \times 0 \right\}$$

$$+ (x - 0) \left\{ 4 - \frac{1}{6} \times (-12) \right\}$$

$$= -2x^3 + (1 - x) + 6x$$

$$= -2x^3 + 5x + 1$$

For $i = 2$, the cubic spline, for $1 \le x \le 2$, is given by

$$S_2(x) = \frac{1}{6} [(2 - x)^3 \times (-12) + (x - 1)^3 \times (6)] + (2 - x) \left\{ 4 - \frac{1}{6} \times (-12) \right\}$$

$$+ (x - 1) \left\{ 0 - \frac{1}{6} \times (6) \right\}$$

$$= (-2)(8 - 12x + 6x^2 - x^3) + (x^3 - 3x^2 + 3x - 1) + (12 - 6x) + (1 - x)$$

$$= 3x^3 - 15x^2 + 20x - 4$$

For $i = 3$, the cubic spline, for $2 \le x \le 3$, is given by

$$S_3(x) = \frac{1}{6} [(3 - x)^3 \times (6) + (x - 2)^3 \times (0)] + (3 - x) \left\{ 0 - \frac{1}{6} \times (6) \right\}$$

$$+ (x - 2) \left\{ (-2) - \frac{1}{6} \times (0) \right\}$$

$$= (27 - 27x + 9x^2 - x^3) + (x - 3) + (4 - 2x)$$

$$= -x^3 + 9x^2 - 27x + 27 + x - 3 + 4 - 2x$$

$$= -x^3 + 9x^2 - 28x + 28$$

Hence, the required cubic spline approximation in each interval for the given function is given by

$$S(x) = \begin{cases} S_1(x) = -2x^3 + 5x + 1 & for\ 0 \le x \le 1 \\ S_2(x) = 3x^3 - 15x^2 + 20x - 4 & for\ 1 \le x \le 2 \\ S_3(x) = -x^3 + 9x^2 - 28x + 28 & for\ 2 \le x \le 3 \end{cases}$$

6.9   DOUBLE INTERPOLATION

So far we have discussed interpolation formulae to approximate a function of one variable. The problem of polynomial interpolation for functions of two or more variables is important but the formulae become complicated. For the sake of simplicity, interpolate the function with respect to the first variable keeping the other variables constant, then interpolate with respect to the second variable and so on. We illustrate the method for functions of two variables.

Example 6.27   Tabulate the values of the function $f(x, y) = x^2 - 2x + y^2$ for $x = 0, 1, 2, 3, 4$ and $y = 0, 1, 2, 3, 4$. Using this table, compute $f(2.5, 3.5)$ by double integration.

Solution: The values of function for the given values of x and y are given in the following table:

			y		
x	0	1	2	3	4
0	0	1	4	9	16
1	-1	0	3	8	15
2	0	1	4	9	16
3	3	4	7	12	19
4	8	9	12	17	24

Choose the tabular values corresponding to $x = 1, 2, 3$ and $y = 2, 3, 4$ near to $x = 2.5$ and $y = 3.5$. The best fit area for the required interpolation is shown in bold letters in the above tabular representation. Using Newton's forward difference formula,

At $x = 1$			
y	f	Δf	$\Delta^2 f$
2	3	5	2
3	8	7	
4	15		

At $x = 2$			
y	f	Δf	$\Delta^2 f$
2	4	5	2
3	9	7	
4	16		

At $x = 3$			
y	f	Δf	$\Delta^2 f$
2	7	5	2
3	12	7	
4	19		

$u = \frac{y - y_0}{h} = \frac{3.5 - 2}{1} = 1.5$. Hence,

$$f(1, 3.5) = f_0 + u\Delta f_0 + \frac{u(u-1)}{2!}\Delta^2 f_0 = 3 + (1.5)(5) + \frac{(1.5)(0.5)}{2}(2)$$
$$= 11.25$$

$$f(2, 3.5) = f_0 + u\Delta f_0 + \frac{u(u-1)}{2!}\Delta^2 f_0 = 4 + (1.5)(5) + \frac{(1.5)(0.5)}{2}(2)$$
$$= 12.25$$

$$f(3, 3.5) = f_0 + u\Delta f_0 + \frac{u(u-1)}{2!}\Delta^2 f_0 = 7 + (1.5)(5) + \frac{(1.5)(0.5)}{2}(2)$$
$$= 15.25$$

Therefore, the new table is as follows:

At y= 3.5			
x	f	Δf	$\Delta^2 f$
1	11.25	1	2
2	12.25	3	
3	15.25		

$u = \frac{x - x_0}{h} = \frac{2.5 - 1}{1} = 1.5$. Hence, by the Newton's forward difference formula,

$$f(2.5, 3.5) = f_0 + u\Delta f_0 + \frac{u(u-1)}{2!}\Delta^2 f_0$$
$$= 11.25 + (1.5)(1) + \frac{(1.5)(0.5)}{2}(2) = 13.5$$

6.10 PROGRAMS IN C

6.10.1 Program for Newton's forward interpolation method

```
//Program to implement Newton's forward interpolation method
#include<stdio.h>
#include<conio.h>
void main()
{
float  x [20],y1[10][10],xy=0,u=0,tempx=0,h,ans=0,main_ans=0;
float  factorial=1,uu=1;
        int n,i,j,temp,k;
         clrscr();
        printf("\nEnter the size :- ");
        scanf("%d",&n);
        for(i=0;i<n;i++)
        {
                        printf("\nEnter the value of x(%d) :- ",i+1);
                        scanf("%f",&x[i]);
                        printf("\nEnter the value of y(%d) :- ",i+1);
                        scanf("%f",&y1[i][0]);
        }
        printf("\nEnter the value of x");
        scanf("%f",&xy);
        for(i=0;i<n;i++)
        {
                if(xy>=x[i] && xy<=x[i+1])
                    {
                            tempx=x[i];
                            temp=i;
                    }
        }
        h=(x[1]-x[0]);
        printf("\nx1=%f :- ",tempx);
        printf("\nh=%f :- ",h);
        u=(xy-tempx)/h;
        printf("\nu=%f :- \n",u);
        for(i=0;i<n;i++)
        {
                for(j=0;j<n-i;j++)
                    {
                            y1[j][i+1]=(y1[j+1][i])-(y1[j][i]);

                    }
```

```
                }
        for(i=0;i<n;i++)
        {
                        for(j=0;j<n-i;j++)
                        {
                                        printf(" %.4f  |",y1[i][j]);
                        }
        printf("\n");
        }
        for(i=0;i<n-1;i++)
        {
                        ans=y1[temp][i];
                        if(i>=2)
                        {
                                for(j=1;j<=i;j++)
                                {
                                        factorial*=j;
                                }
        }
        for(j=0;j<i;j++)
        {
                        uu*=(u-j);
        }
        ans=((ans*uu)/factorial);
        main_ans+=ans;
        ans=0;
        factorial=uu=1;
        }
        printf("\n THE ANS IS:- %.4f",main_ans);
        getch();
}
```

6.10.2 Program for Newton's backward interpolation method

```
//Program to implement Newton's backward interpolation method
#include<stdio.h>
#include<conio.h>
void main()
{
float x[20],y1[10][10],xy=0,u=0,h,ans=0,main_ans=0,factorial=1,uu=1;
        int n,i,j,temp,k;
        clrscr();
        printf("\n\t\tNEWTON BACKWARD\n\n");
        printf("\nEnter total number of value :- ");
```

```
            scanf("%d",&n);
            for(i=0;i<n;i++)
            {
                        printf("\nEnter the value of x(%d) :- ",i+1);
                        scanf("%f",&x[i]);
                        printf("\nEnter the value of y(%d) :- ",i+1);
                        scanf("%f",&y1[i][0]);
            }
            printf("\nEnter the value of x");
            scanf("%f",&xy);
            for(i=0;i<n;i++)
            {
                        if(xy>=x[i] && xy<=x[i+1])
                        {
                                    temp=i+1;
                                    break;
                        }
            }
            h=(x[1]-x[0]);
            printf("\nh=%f :- ",h);
            u=(xy-x[temp])/h;
            printf("\nu=%f :- \n",u);
            for(i=0;i<n;i++)
            {
                        for(j=i;j<n;j++)
                        {
                                    y1[j+1][i+1]=(y1[j+1][i])-(y1[j][i]);
                        }
            }
            for(i=0;i<n;i++)
            {
                        printf("%d   %0.4f",i+1,x[i]);
                        for(j=0;j<=i;j++)
                        {
                                    printf(" %.4f  |",y1[i][j]);
                        }
                        printf("\n");
            }
            for(i=0;i<n-1;i++)
            {
                        ans=y1[temp][i];
                        if(i>=2)
                        {
```

```
                         for(j=1;j<=i;j++)
                         {
                                    factorial*=j;
                         }
                }
                for(j=0;j<i;j++)
                {
                            uu*=(u+j);
                }
                ans=((ans*uu)/factorial);
                main_ans+=ans;
                ans=0;
                factorial=uu=1;
        }
        printf("\n THE ANS IS:- %.4f",main_ans);
        getch();  }
```

6.10.3   Program for Lagrange's interpolation method

```
//Program to implement Lagrange's interpolation method
#include<stdio.h>
#include<conio.h>
float x[20];
float y[20];
int i,j,n,k;
float yx,temp=0.00;
float U=1.0,L=1.0,result=0.00;
void main()
{
        void insert();
        void display();
        void calc();
        clrscr();
        insert();
        display();
        calc();
        getch();
}
void insert()
{
        printf("enter how many no u want :: ");
        scanf("%d",&n);
        for(i=0;i<n;i++)
        {
```

```
                        printf("value for x(%d)=",i);
                        scanf("%f",&x[i]);
                        printf("value for y(%d)=",i);
                        scanf("%f",&y[i]);        }
            printf("Enter the value of y(x) : ");
            scanf("%f",&yx);
}
void display()
{
            printf("\n x | ");
            for(i=0;i<n;i++)
            {
                        printf(" %.2f ",x[i]);
            }
            printf("\n");
            printf("---------------------------------------------------\n");
                        printf(" y | ");
            for(i=0;i<n;i++)
            {
                        printf(" %.2f ",y[i]);
            }
}
void calc()
{
            printf("\n\ny(x) = ");
            for(i=0;i<n;i++)
            {
                        printf("y%d",i+1);
                        temp = x[i];
                        for(j=0;j<n;j++)
                        {
                                    if(i != j)
                                    {
                                                printf("(x - x%d)",j+1);
                                                U*=(yx-x[j]);
                                                L*=(temp-x[j]);
                                    }
                        }
                        result+=y[i]*(U/L);
                        printf("\n\t-------------------------- + \n\t");
                        for(k=0;k<n;k++)
                        {
                                    if(i != k)
```

```
                                        {
                                                printf("(x%d - x%d)",i+1,k+1);
                                        }
                        }
                        printf("\n\n\t");
                        U=1.00;
                        L=1.00;
                }
                printf("\nAnswer :: %f",result);
        }
```

6.10.4   Program for Lagrange's inverse interpolation method

```
//Program to implement Lagrange's inverse interpolation method
#include<stdio.h>
#include<conio.h>
float x[20];
float y[20];
int i,j,n,k;
float xy,temp=0.00;
float U=1.0,L=1.0,result=0.00;
void main()
{
        void insert();
        void display();
        void calc();
        clrscr();
        insert();
        display();
        calc();
        getch();
}
void insert()
{
        printf("enter how many no u want :: ");
        scanf("%d",&n);
        for(i=0;i<n;i++)
        {
                printf("value for x(%d)=",i);
                scanf("%f",&x[i]);
                printf("value for y(%d)=",i);
                scanf("%f",&y[i]);
        }
        printf("Enter the value of x(y) : ");
```

```
                scanf("%f",&xy);
}
void display()
{
        printf("\n x | ");
        for(i=0;i<n;i++)
        {
                printf(" %.2f ",x[i]);
        }
        printf("\n");
        printf("-----------------------------------------------\n");
                printf(" y | ");
        for(i=0;i<n;i++)
        {
                printf(" %.2f ",y[i]);
        }
}
void calc()
{
        printf("\n\nx(y) = ");
        for(i=0;i<n;i++)
        {
                printf("x%d",i+1);
                temp = y[i];
                for(j=0;j<n;j++)
                {
                                if(i != j)
                                {
                                        printf("(y - y%d)",j+1);
                                        U*=(xy-y[j]);
                                        L*=(temp-y[j]);
                                }
                }
                result+=x[i]*(U/L);
                printf("\n\t-------------------------- + \n\t");
                for(k=0;k<n;k++)
                {
                                if(i != k)
                                {
                                        printf("(y%d - y%d)",i+1,k+1);
                                }
                }
                printf("\n\n\t");
```

```
                U=1.00;
                L=1.00;
        }
        printf("\nAnswer :: %f",result);
}
```

6.10.5 Program for Newton's divided interpolation method

```
//Program to implement Newton's divided interpolation method
#include<stdio.h>
#include<conio.h>
void main()
{
        float x[20],y1[10][10],xy=0,ans=0,main_ans=0,xx=1;
        int n,i,j,temp=0,k,temp_loop=0;
        clrscr();
        printf("\nEnter the size :- ");
        scanf("%d",&n);
        for(i=0;i<n;i++)
        {
                printf("\nEnter the value of x(%d) :- ",i+1);
                scanf("%f",&x[i]);
                printf("\nEnter the value of y(%d) :- ",i+1);
                scanf("%f",&y1[i][0]);
        }
        printf("\nEnter the value of x");
        scanf("%f",&xy);
        for(i=0;i<n;i++)
          {
                for(j=0;j<n-i;j++)
                {
                        y1[j][i+1]=(y1[j+1][i]-y1[j][i])/(x[j+i+1]-x[j]);

                }
          }
        for(i=0;i<n;i++)
          {
                for(j=0;j<n-i;j++)
                {
                        printf(" %.4f  |",y1[i][j]);
                }
        printf("\n");
          }
        for(i=0;i<n;i++)
```

```
        {
                ans=y1[temp][i];
                for(j=0;j<i;j++)
                {
                        xx*=(xy-x[j]);
                }
                ans=ans*xx;
                main_ans+=ans;
                ans=temp_loop=0;
                xx=1;
        }
    printf("\n THE ANS IS:- %.4f",main_ans);
    getch();
}
```

EXERCISES

1. Multiple Choice Questions

(1)   In Interpolation......
    (a)   All the data points must be on the curve
    (b)   All data points need not be on the curve
    (c)   All data points can be scattered
    (d)   Data points above the curve must be same as data points below the curve
    (e)   None of these

(2)   Extrapolation means.........
    (a)   Given point must be outside the range of table points
    (b)   Given point must be inside the range of table points
    (c)   Given point may be inside or outside the table points
    (d)   All of these
    (e)   None of these

(3)   Open ended methods are also said to be......
    (a)   Interpolation
    (b)   Approximation
    (c)   Extrapolation
    (d)   All of these
    (e)   None of these

(4)   Which of these methods are used for intervals of equal length?
    (a)   Newton's forward, Newton's Backward & Newton's Divided
    (b)   Newton's forward & Newton's divided
    (c)   Newton's backward & Newton's divided
    (d)   Newton's forward, Newton's backward & Lagrange
    (e)   Lagrange, Newton's forward & Newton's divided

(5)   In any Newton's method, if suppose third order difference of y is constant then order of given polynomial is
    (a)   2
    (b)   3
    (c)   4
    (d)   5
    (e)   None of these

(6)   The value to be found for $x = 5.6$ and intervals are given like $1 - 2, 2 - 3, 3 - 6, 6 - 8, 8 - 10$ then
    (a)   Newton's forward difference formula will be used.
    (b)   Newton's backward difference formula will be used.
    (c)   Newton's divided difference formula will be used.
    (d)   Cubic spline method will be used.
    (e)   None of these

(7)   In which situation Lagrange's interpolation method can be used?
    (a)   Equal interval length
    (b)   Unequal interval length
    (c)   Both equal as well as unequal
    (d)   First equal, second unequal, third equal and so on....
    (e)   None of these

(8)   Disadvantage of Lagrange's interpolation formula is
    (a)   Time consuming task
    (b)   We can not find the order of polynomial
    (c)   Accuracy is not like Newton's method
    (d)   All of these

(9)   The value to be found for $x = 6.3$ and values of x are given like 1, 2, 3, 4, 5, 6 then in Newton's backward difference interpolation formula which line of x will be selected?
    (a)   Sixth
    (b)   Second
    (c)   Third
    (d)   Fourth
    (e)   Fifth

(10)   Inverse interpolation means......
    (a)   x is given and $y = f(x)$ to be found
    (b) $y = f(x)$ is given and x to be found
    (c)   to find inverse of the given number
    (d)   to find reverse of the given number
    (e)   None of these

(11)   What do you mean by spline?
    (a)   It is a wooden strip whose functionality is to interpolate the given data points
    (b)   It is a wooden strip whose functionality is to approximate the given data points
    (c)   It is a wooden strip whose functionality is to give smoothness to the curve.
    (d)   It is a polynomial which is used in differentiation.
    (e)   None of these

Answers: (1) (a) (2) (a)   (3) (c) (4) (d) (5) (b) (6) (c) (7) (c)
           (8) (d) (9) (a)   (10) (b) (11) (c)

2.   Problems

(1)   Find f(1.5), using appropriate Newton's formula from the following data.

x	0	1	2	3	4
f(x)	858.3	869.6	880.9	892.3	903.6

(2)   Find y at x = 0.95, using Newton's forward interpolation formula, from the given table:

x	1.0	1.1	1.2	1.3	1.4	1.5
y	0.841	0.891	0.932	0.964	0.985	1.015

(3)   Given $sin45^0 = 0.7071$, $sin50^0 = 0.7660$, $sin 55^0 = 0.8192$, $sin60^0 = 0.8660$, find $sin52^0$ using Newton's forward formula.

(4)   Construct Newton's forward interpolation polynomial for the following data:

x:	4	6	8	10
y:	1	3	8	16

Hence evaluate y for x = 5.

(5)   Evaluate $f(15)$, using Newton's formula, given the following data:

x:	10	20	30	40	50
y:	46	66	81	93	101

(6)   Find a cubic polynomial in x for the following data:

x:	0	1	2	3	4	5
y:	-3	3	11	27	57	107

(7)   The following data gives the values of the elliptic integral

$$f(x) = \int_0^x \frac{d\theta}{\sqrt{1 - \frac{1}{2} sin^2\theta}}$$

for certain equidistant values of x^0: Find the value of $f(23.5^0)$, using Newton's forward interpolation formula.

x:	21^0	22^0	23^0	24^0	25^0	26^0
y:	0.3706	0.3887	0.4068	0.4250	0.4433	0.4616

(8)   Find $log_{10}5.15$ and $log_{10}4.48$ from the following table:

x:	5.1	5.2	5.3	5.4	5.5
$lo_{10}x$:	0.7076	0.7160	0.7243	0.7324	0.7404

(9)   Compute $f(0.5)$ and $f(6.7)$ using appropriate Newton's formula from the following data:

x:	0	1	2	3	4	5	6	7
f(x):	0	7	26	63	124	215	342	511

(10) The following table gives the melting point of an alloy of lead and zinc; where T is the temperature in °C and P is the percentage of lead in the alloy. Find the melting point of the alloy containing 84% of lead using Newton's interpolation method.

P:	60	70	80	90
T :	226	250	276	304

(11) The sales in a particular department store for the last five years is given in the following table:

Year	1974	1976	1978	1980	1982
Sales (in lakhs)	40	43	48	52	57

Estimate the sales for the year 1979.

(12) The probability integral

$$P = \sqrt{\frac{2}{\pi}} \cdot \int_0^x exp\left(-\frac{1}{2} t^2\right) dt$$

has the following values

x:	1.00	1.05	1.10	1.15	1.20	1.25
P:	0.68268 9	0.70628 2	0.72866 8	0.74985 6	0.76986 1	0.78870 0

Calculate P for x = 1.235.

(13) Find the number of students whose weight is between 60 and 70 from the data given below:

Weight in kgs.	0 – 40	40 – 60	60 – 80	80 – 100	100 – 120
No. of students:	250	120	100	70	50

(14) From the data given below, find the value of y when x = 3.2 using Gauss forward interpolation formula.

x:	2.0	2.5	3.0	3.5	4.0
y :	246.2	409.3	537.2	636.3	715.9

(15) Use Gauss interpolation formula to find $y(41)$ with the help of the following data:

$y(30) = 3678.2$, $y(35) = 2995.1$, $y(40) = 2400.1$, $y(45) = 1876.2$ and $y(50) = 1416.4$.

(16) Apply Gauss's forward and backward formulas to obtain sin 45°, given in the following table:

x°:	20	30	40	50	60	70
$y = \sin x°$:	0.3420	0.5020	0.6428	0.7660	0.8660	0.9397

(17) Use Gauss's forward and backward interpolation formula to find the

population for the year 1936 from the following data:

Year(x):	1901	1911	1921	1931	1941	1951
Population(y):	12	15	20	27	39	52
(in thousands)						

(18)   Use Stirling's interpolation formula to find $f(35)$ from the table below.

x:	20	30	40	50
y :	512	439	346	243

(19)   Use Stirling's formula to evaluate $f(1.22)$, given

x:	1.0	1.1	1.2	1.3	1.4
f(x) :	0.841	0.891	0.932	0.963	0.985

(20)   Use Stirling's formula, show that $\tan 16^0 = 0.2867$, from the data given in the below table:

θ^0:	0	5	10	15	20	25	30
$y = \tan \theta^0$:	0	0.0875	0.1763	0.2679	0.3640	0.4663	0.5774

(21)   Use Bessel's formula to evaluate $f(0.305)$, where $f(x)$ is given below:

x:	0.1	0.2	0.3	0.4	0.5
f(x) :	2.74560	2.82922	2.97427	3.18993	3.49034

(22)   Compute $f(1.44)$ from the following table:

x:	0	0.5	1.0	1.5	2.0	2.5	3.0
f(x) :	0	0.191	0.341	0.433	0.477	0.494	0.499

applying (i) Stirling's formula (ii) Bessel's formula (iii) Laplace – Everett's formula.

(23)   The function $f(x)$ is given in the table below:

x:	20	24	28	32
f(x) :	2854	3162	3544	3992

Find $f(x)$ for $x = 25$ using Bessel's interpolation formula.

(24)   Apply Bessel's formula to find the value of F at $x = 1.95$, given that

x:	1.7	1.8	1.9	2.0	2.1	2.2	2.3
F :	2.979	3.144	3.283	3.391	3.463	3.997	4.491

Which other interpolation formula can be used in this example? Which is more appropriate? Give reasons.

(25)   Given the table

x:	310	320	330	340	350	360
logx:	2.49136	2.50515	2.51851	2.53148	2.54407	2.55630

Find the value of $\log 337.5$ by Everett's formula.

(26)   Use Everett's formula to obtain $f(1.15)$, given that $f(1) = 1.000, f(1.1) = 1.049, f(1.2) = 1.096, f(1.3) = 1.140$

(27)   Use Lagrange's interpolation formula to find the polynomial of least degree which attain the following tabular values.

x:	0	1	2	5
y:	2	3	12	147

(28)   Give the table of values

x:	150	152	154	156
$y = \sqrt{x}$:	12.247	12.329	12.410	12.490

Evaluate $\sqrt{155}$ using Lagrange's interpolation formula.

(29)   Find $y(9)$ by Lagrange's formula if

x:	8	10	12	14	16
y:	1000	1900	3250	5400	8950

(30)   Using Lagrange's interpolation formula, express the following function as sum of partial function:

$$\frac{x^2 + x - 3}{x^3 - 2x^2 - x + 2}$$

(31)   Use Lagrange's inverse interpolation formula to obtain the value of x when $y = 85$ from the following data:

x:	2	5	8	14
y:	94.8	87.9	81.3	68.7

(32)   Use Lagrange's inverse formula to find the root of the equation $f(x) = 0$ given that $f(30) = -30, f(34) = -13, f(38) = 3$ and $f(42) = 18$.

(33)   Find the table of values

x:	1.8	2.0	2.2	2.4	2.6
y:	2.9422	3.6269	4.4571	5.4662	6.6947

Find x when $y = 5.0$ using the method of successive approximation.

(34)   Find y at $x = 20$ by Newton's divided difference formula if

x:	12	18	22	24	32
$f(x)$:	146	836	1948	2796	9236

(35)   Find the interpolating polynomial fitting the points $(0,1), (1,1), (2,2), (4,5)$ by (i) Lagrange's formula and (ii) Newton's divided difference formula.

(36)   Use Newton's divided difference formula to find $f(1)$ and $f(9)$ from the following data:

x:	0	2	3	4	7	8
$f(x)$:	4	26	58	112	466	668

(37)   Find the value of y at $x = 5.603$ from the following data, using Newton's divided difference formula.

x:	5.600	5.602	5.605	5.607	5.608
y:	0.77557	0.77683	0.77871	0.77997	0.78059

(38)   Determine the Hermite polynomial of degree three approximating the function $y(x)$ for the following data:

x:	-1	0	1
y:	-10	-4	-2
y':	10	3	2

(39)   Express y as a polynomial in x from the following data, using Hermite's interpolating formula:

x:	0	1	2
y:	1	3	21
y':	0	6	36

(40)   Using Hermite's interpolation formula, estimate the value of $\ln 3.2$ from the following table.

x:	3	3.5	4.0
$y = \ln x$:	1.09861	1.25276	1.38629
$y' = \dfrac{1}{x}$:	0.33333	0.28571	0.25000

(41)   Obtain piecewise cubic Hermite polynomial for the following data:

x:	0	1	2
y:	1	3	35
y':	1	6	81

(42)   Find the interpolating polynomial for the following data using (i) piecewise linear interpolation (ii) piecewise cubic Hermite interpolation.

x:	1	2	3
y:	-1	4	21
y':	1	10	25

(43)   Fit a natural cubic spline to the data

x:	1	2	3	4
y:	1	2	5	11

and compute $y(1.5)$ and $y'(3)$. Is this spline smooth?

(44)   The following values of x and y are given:

x:	1	2	3	4
y:	1	5	11	8

Using cubic spline, show that (i) $y(1.5) = 2.575$ (ii) $y'(3) = 2.067$

(45)   Find the cubic spline approximation for the function $y = f(x)$ given in the following data. Assume that $y_0'' = y_3'' = 0$

x:	0	1	2	3
y:	-5	-4	3	22

(46)   Tabulate the values of the function $f(x, y) = x^2 + y^2 + y$ for $x = 0, 1, 2, 3, 4$ and $y = 0, 1, 2, 3, 4$. Using this table, compute $f(2.5, 1.5)$ by double integration.

Answers

(1)   875.2 (2) 0.806   (3)   0.788   (4)   1.625
(5)   56.8672 (6) $x^3 - 2x^2 + 7x - 3$ (7)   0.4159
(8)   0.7118, 0.6513   (9)   2.375, 455.533   (10)   286.96 °C
(11)   50.1172   (12)   0.783172   (13)   Approx. 54
(14)   579.8   (15)   2290.1   (16)   0.70689, 0.70689
(17)   32.625   (18)   395   (19)   0.934
(21)   2.98328   (22)   0.389, 0.388, 0.389 (23)   3250.875 approx.
(24)   3.347   (25) 2.52828 approx.   (26)   1.073
(27) $x^3 + x^2 - x + 2$ (28)   12.45   (29)   1405.860
(30) $\dfrac{1}{2(x-1)} + \dfrac{1}{(x-2)} - \dfrac{1}{2(x+1)}$ (31)   6.5928
(32)   37.23   (33)   2.3124   (34)   1305.36
(35) $y = -\dfrac{1}{12}(x^3 - 9x^2 + 8x + 1)$ (36)   10, 922
(37)   0.77746   (38) $y = x^3 - 2x^2 + 3x - 4$
(39) $y = x^4 + x^2 + 1$ (40) $\ln 3.2 = 1.16314$

(41) $y(x) = \begin{cases} 3x^3 - 2x^2 + x + 1, & 0 \le x \le 1 \\ 23x^3 - 66x^2 + 69x - 23, & 1 \le x \le 2 \end{cases}$

(42) $y(x) = \begin{cases} 5x - 6, & 1 \le x \le 2 \\ 17x - 30, & 2 \le x \le 3 \end{cases}$

$y(x) = \begin{cases} x^3 - 2x, & 1 \le x \le 2 \\ x^3 - 2x, & 2 \le x \le 3 \end{cases}$

(43) $S(x) = \begin{cases} \dfrac{1}{3}(x^3 - 3x^2 + 5x), & 1 \le x \le 2 \\ \dfrac{1}{3}(x^3 - 3x^2 + 5x), & 2 \le x \le 3 \\ \dfrac{1}{3}(-2x^3 - 24x^2 + 76x + 81), & 3 \le x \le 4 \end{cases}$

$y(1.5) = S_0(1.5) = \dfrac{11}{8},\ y'(3) = S_1'(3) = S_2'(3) = \dfrac{14}{8}$ and so it is a smooth spline

(45) $S(x) = \begin{cases} \dfrac{1}{5}(4x^3 + x - 25), & 0 \le x \le 1 \\ \dfrac{1}{5}(10x^3 - 18x^2 + 19x - 31), & 1 \le x \le 2 \\ \dfrac{1}{5}(-14x^3 + 126x^2 - 269x + 161), & 2 \le x \le 3 \end{cases}$

(46) $f(2.5, 1.5) = 10$

Chapter 7   Curve Fitting and Approximation

Objectives

- To know the concept of curve fitting
- To enable students to obtain an intuitive and working understanding of different curve fitting methods like method of group average, method of least square and method of moments for different form of curves
- To know the importance and the concept of the sum of the square of residuals for different types of curves
- To understand the importance and the concept of approximation of function
- To know the properties of Legendre's and Chebyshev polynomials
- To know the process of approximation by Taylor's series and Chebyshev polynomials
- To understand the concept of economizing the given power series

Learning Outcomes

After reading this lesson students should be able to

- Apply different curve fitting methods successfully
- Find the best fitting curve by applying appropriate curve fitting method
- Calculate the sum of the squares of the residuals for different types of curves
- Approximate the function using Taylor's series expansion
- Approximate the given polynomial using Chebyshev polynomial
- Economize the given power series by Lanczos economization method using Chebyshev polynomials

7.1   INTRODUCTION

In many branches of mathematics, engineering and science it is required to establish the relationship between two or more variables either to perform experiments or to derive certain formulas or to formulate a mathematical model. This can be accomplished by constructing a mathematical equation $y = f(x)$, called an *empirical equation*. The problem is to find such equation of the curve that best fit the given set of data. The process of finding such an equation of best fit is known as *curve fitting*. Curve fitting has several applications in the field of engineering, computer graphics and statistics. Regression analysis is one of the applications of curve fitting. Let the set of data points (x_i, y_i) $i = 1,2,3,......,n$ be given for the functional relationship $y = f(x)$. The variable y is called the dependent variable and x the independent variable. The relationship between two variables may be either linear or nonlinear. The best practice is to draw a scatter diagram to determine the functional relationship needed to fit the points. In this cahpter, we will discuss three standard methods: method of group averages, method of moments and method of least squares for evaluating constants occurring in best fitting equation for the given data. Amongst these methods, the method of least squares is the best to fit a unique curve to a given data.

7.2   METHOD OF GROUP AVERAGES

Let (x_i, y_i) $i = 1,2,3,......,n$ be n observations and assume the relationship between two variables x and y be linear i.e. a straight line passes through most of the plotted points and near the remaining points on a graph paper and the equation is

$$y = a + bx \qquad\qquad ......(7.2.1)$$

We want to find the values of the constants a and b.

From Figure 7.1, at the point $x = x_i$, the observed value of $y = y_i = P_i M_i$
From Eq.(7.2.1), the expected value of y corresponding to $x = x_i$ is $y = a + bx_i = Q_i M_i$. Now, we define the residual e_i corresponding to (x_i, y_i) as the difference between the observed value of y and the expected value of y. It is defined as

$$e_i = Q_i P_i = M_i P_i - M_i Q_i = y_i - (a + bx_i), \quad i = 1, 2, 3, ..., n$$

Some of the $e_i's$ are positive, some are negative and some are zero (for example, in Figure 7.1 e_1 is positive, e_3 is negative and e_n is zero).

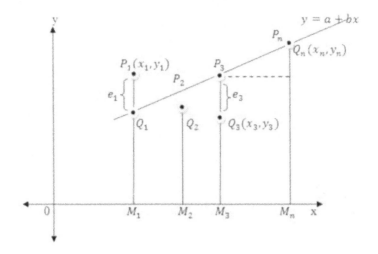

Figure 7.1

The method of group averages is based on the principle that the algebraic sum of the residuals of the plotted points is zero, i.e. $\sum_{i=1}^{n} e_i = 0$. Since we need to determine the values of two constants a and b, we require two equations containing a and b. For this purpose, we divide the data into two groups, first containing m set of values and the other containing $(n - m)$ set of values. Now, apply the principle of group averages to each of the two groups, i.e. apply the principle $\sum_{i=1}^{n} e_i = 0$ for each group, we have

$$\sum_{i=1}^{m} [y_i - (a + bx_i)] = 0$$

$$\sum_{i=m+1}^{n} [y_i - (a + bx_i)] = 0$$

$$\sum_{i=1}^{m} y_i = \sum_{i=1}^{m} (a + bx_i) \quad \text{and} \quad \sum_{i=m+1}^{n} y_i = \sum_{i=m+1}^{n} (a + bx_i)$$

$$\sum_{i=1}^{m} y_i = am + b\sum_{i=1}^{m} x_i \quad \text{and} \quad \sum_{i=m+1}^{n} y_i = a(n - m) + b\sum_{i=m+1}^{n} x_i$$

$$a + b\frac{\sum_{i=1}^{m} x_i}{m} = \frac{\sum_{i=1}^{m} y_i}{m} \quad \text{and} \quad a + b\frac{\sum_{i=m+1}^{n} x_i}{n - m} = \frac{\sum_{i=m+1}^{n} y_i}{n - m}$$

$$a + b\overline{x_1} = \overline{y_1} \quad \text{and} \quad a + b\overline{x_2} = \overline{y_2} \qquad \text{........ (7.2.2)}$$

where $\overline{x_1}$, $\overline{y_1}$ and $\overline{x_2}$, $\overline{y_2}$ are the averages of the first and second group respectively. Solving Eqs. in (7.2.2) for a and b, we get the best fitting straight line.

> **Remark:**
> - Since the groups can be divided in many ways, the values of constants may differ. Hence, the answers are not unique. So, the equation of best fit is not unique.
> - Choose two groups in such a way that both groups contain equal number of observations.
> - This method is suitable whenever the best fit requires two constants.

Example 7.1   Fit a straight line $y = a + bx$ to the following data by method of group averages.

x	10	20	30	40	50	60
y	22.8	27.3	34.5	40.9	45.4	50.6

Solution: Divide the given data into two groups each containing three pairs of values.

Group I		Group II	
x	y	x	y
10	22.8	40	40.9
20	27.3	50	45.4
30	34.5	60	50.6
60	84.6	150	136.9

It is given that $y = a + bx$. $\overline{x_1} = \frac{60}{3} = 20$, $\overline{y_1} = \frac{84.6}{3} = 28.2$ and $\overline{x_2} = \frac{150}{3} = 50$, $\overline{y_2} = \frac{136.9}{3} = 45.63$

Substituting these values in Eq. (7.2.2), we get

$$a + b\overline{x_1} = \overline{y_1} \Rightarrow a + 60b = 84.6 \quad \text{......... (1)}$$
$$a + b\overline{x_2} = \overline{y_2} \Rightarrow a + 150b = 136.9 \quad \text{......... (2)}$$

Solving Eqs. (1) and (2) for a and b by elimination method, we get $a = 49.733$ and $b = 0.581$

Hence, the required equation of straight line is $y = 49.733 + 0.581\,x$

Example 7.2   The relation between two quantities is given in the following table:

x:	2	3.5	4	8	14	20	24	30
y:	3.5	13.6	38.4	52.7	89.8	141.9	236.3	330.8

The probable law is $y = a + bx^2$. Find the values of a and b by the method of group averages.

Solution: The relation $y = a + bx^2$ is not linear. We have to convert it into linear relation.

$$y = a + bx^2$$

Putting $x^2 = X$, $y = a + bX$ .... (1)

which is linear. We divide the given data into two groups, each containing four pairs of values.

	Group I			Group II	
x	y	$X = x^2$	x	y	$X = x^2$
1	3.5	1	14	89.8	196
3	13.6	9	20	141.9	400
4	38.4	16	24	236.3	576
8	52.7	64	30	330.8	900
	108.2	90		798.8	2072

$$\overline{y_1} = \frac{108.2}{4} = 27.05, \overline{X_1} = \frac{90}{4} = 22.5 \quad \text{and} \quad \overline{y_2} = \frac{798.8}{4} = 199.7, \overline{X_2}$$
$$= \frac{2072}{4} = 518$$

Substituting these values in Eq. (7.2.2), we get

$$a + b\overline{X_1} = \overline{y_1} \Rightarrow a + 22.5b = 27.05 \qquad \text{........ (1)}$$
$$a + b\overline{X_2} = \overline{y_2} \Rightarrow a + 518b = 199.7 \qquad \text{........ (2)}$$

Solving Eqs. (1) and (2) for a and b by elimination method, we get $a = 19.21$ and $b = 0.35$ .Hence, the best linear fit is given by $y = 19.21 + 0.35X$ or $y = 19.21 + 0.35x^2$

Example 7.3   The observations in the following table fit a law of the form $y = ax^n$. Estimate the values of a and n and hence the formula by the method of group averages.

x:	10	20	30	40	50	60	70	80
y:	1.06	1.33	1.52	1.68	1.81	1.91	2.01	2.11

Solution: Given that $y = ax^n$

Taking logarithms on both sides, we get

$$\log_{10} y = \log_{10} a + n \log_{10} x$$

Therefore, $Y = A + nX$ .... (1)

where, $\log_{10} y = Y$, $\log_{10} a = A$ and $\log_{10} x = X$. Eq. (1) is linear in two variables X and Y.

Divide the data into two groups each containing four pairs of values, so that

Group – I

x	y	$X = \log_{10}x$	$Y = \log_{10}y$
10	1.06	1.0000	0.0253
20	1.33	1.3010	0.1239
30	1.52	1.4771	0.1818
40	1.68	1.6021	0.2253
		5.3802	0.5563

Group – II

x	y	$X = \log_{10}x$	$Y = \log_{10}y$
50	1.81	1.6989	0.2576
60	1.91	1.7781	0.2810
70	2.01	1.8451	0.3032
80	2.11	1.9031	0.3243
		7.2252	1.1661

$\overline{Y_1} = \dfrac{0.5563}{4} = 0.13907,\ \overline{X_1} = \dfrac{5.3802}{4} = 1.34505$ and $\overline{Y_2} = \dfrac{1.1661}{4}$

$= 0.2915,\ \overline{X_2} = \dfrac{7.2252}{4} = 1.8063$

From the Eq. (7.2.2) and Eq. (1), we get

$$A+n\overline{X_1} = \overline{Y_1} \Rightarrow A + 1.34505n = 0.13907 \quad \text{......... (2)}$$
$$A+n\overline{X_2} = \overline{Y_2} \Rightarrow A + 1.8063n = 0.2915 \quad \text{......... (3)}$$

Solving Eqs. (2) and (3) for A and n by elimination method, we get

$$A = -0.305 \quad i.e.\ \log_{10}a = -0.305$$

Therefore, $a = antilog\,(-0.305) = 0.4955$

and $n = 0.33$

Hence, the best linear fit is given by $y = 0.4955 + x^{0.33}$

7.2.1   Equation Involving Three Constants

Till now we have applied different methods to fit the observations to equations involving two constants such as $y = a + bx$, $y = a + bx^2, y = ax^n$ etc. In this sub section, we will see the equations of the form $y = a + bx + cx^2$, $y = ax^b + c, y = ab^x + c$ *and* $y = ae^{bx} + c$, each of which contains three constants. We have to eliminate one of the constants and thus, convert the given equations into linear form.   The following are the procedures to fit such equations to set of observations.

Fitting of the Curve of the Type $y = a + bx + cx^2$

Let (x_1, y_1) be a specific point on the curve satisfying the given equation. Then $y_1 = a + bx_1 + cx_1^2$

Therefore, $y - y_1 = b(x - x_1) + c(x^2 - x_1^2)$

$$\frac{y - y_1}{x - x_1} = b + c(x + x_1)$$

$\therefore\ Y = a + bX$ where, $\frac{y-y_1}{x-x_1} = Y$ and $(x + x_1) = X$

which is a linear form in X and Y. Here, b and c can be determined by the method of group averages and hence constant a.

Example 7.4 The following table gives the values of x and y.

x :	0	14	28	42	56
y :	38	58	70	84	75

Fit a second degree curve (or parabola) of the form $y = a + bx + cx^2$, by the method of group averages.

Solution: Given that $y = a + bx + cx^2$ .... (1)

Taking $(0, 38)$ as a specific point on the curve $y = a + bx + cx^2$

We get $38 = a + b(0) + c(0)^2$ $\therefore a = 38$

Hence, $y - 38 = b(x - 0) + c(x^2 - 0^2)$

$\therefore\ \dfrac{y - 38}{x} = b + cx$ $\therefore Y = b + cx$ where, $\dfrac{y - 38}{x} = Y$

We divide the data into two groups one containing 3 observations and the other containing 2 values

	Group I			Group II	
x	y	$Y = \dfrac{y - 38}{x}$	x	y	$Y = \dfrac{y - 38}{x}$
0	38	0	42	84	1.0952
14	58	1.4286	56	75	0.6607
28	70	1.1429			
42		2.5715	98		1.7559

$\overline{x_1} = \dfrac{42}{3} = 14, \overline{Y_1} = \dfrac{2.5715}{3} = 0.8572$ and $\overline{x_2} = \dfrac{98}{2} = 49,$

$$\bar{Y_2} = \frac{1.7559}{3} = 0.5853$$

$$0.8572 = b + c \ (14) \qquad \text{........ (2)}$$
$$0.5853 = b + c \ (98) \qquad \text{........ (3)}$$

Solving (2) and (3) we get

$$b = 0.903, \qquad c = -0.003$$

Substituting these values in (1), we get the required parabolic curve

$$y = 38 + 0.903x - 0.003x^2$$

Fitting of the Curve of the Type $y = ax^b + c$

The given equation can be re – written as $y - c = ax^b$ .... (7.2.3)

First we have to find the value of c. For that, let $(x_1, y_1), (x_2, y_2)$ and (x_3, y_3) be three specific points on the curve given in Eq. (7.2.3) such that x_1, x_2 and x_3 are in geometric progression i.e

$$x_1 . x_3 = x_2{}^2 \qquad \text{........ (1)}$$

Hence, Eq. (7.2.3) becomes $y_1 - c = ax_1{}^b$, $y_2 - c = ax_2{}^b$ and $y_3 - c = ax_3{}^b$

Therefore, $(y_1 - c).(y_3 - c) = a^2 \ (x_1.x_3)^b = a^2 \ (x_2{}^2)^b$ (from (1))

$$= (a \ x_2{}^b)^2 = (y_2 - c)^2$$

$$y_1 y_3 - c(y_1 + y_3) + c^2 = y_2{}^2 - 2cy_2 + c^2$$

$$\therefore \quad c = \frac{y_1 y_3 - y_2{}^2}{y_1 + y_3 - 2y_2}$$

Putting the value of c in Eq. (7.2.3) we have only two unknowns to determine. Taking logarithm on both the sides of Eq. (7.2.3), we get

$$\log_{10}(y - c) = \log_{10} a + b \ \log_{10} x \qquad \text{........ (7.2.4)}$$

$$\therefore Y = A + bX; \qquad where, \ Y$$
$$= \log_{10}(y - c), A = \log_{10} a, X = \log_{10} x$$

Example 7.5 Fit a curve of the form $y = ax^b + c$ to the following data:

x :	1	3	6	9	12	15
y :	25.2	76.5	166.8	258.3	555.9	1045

Solution: We have to take values of x_1, x_2, x_3 such that they are in geometric progression.

Let $x_1 = 1, x_2 = 3$ and $x_3 = 9$ since $x_1 . x_3 = x_2{}^2$

$$\therefore \quad c = \frac{y_1 y_3 - y_2{}^2}{y_1 + y_3 - 2y_2} = \frac{(25.2)(258.3) - (76.5)^2}{25.2 + 258.3 - 2(76.5)} = \frac{656.91}{130.5} = 5.0338$$

$$\therefore y = ax^b + 5.0338 \Rightarrow y - 5.0338 = ax^b$$
$$\therefore \log_{10}(y - 5.0338) = \log_{10} a + b \log_{10} x$$

Therefore, $Y = A + bX$ .... (1)

$where, Y = \log_{10}(y - 5.0338), A = \log_{10} a, X = \log_{10} x$

We divide the data into two groups each containing three data.

Group I			
x	y	$X = \log_{10} x$	$Y = \log_{10}(y - 5.0338)$
1	25.2	0	1.3046
3	76.5	0.4771	1.8541
6	166.8	0.7782	2.2089
		1.2553	5.3676

Group II			
x	y	$X = \log_{10} x$	$Y = \log_{10}(y - 5.0338)$
9	258.3	0.9542	2.4036
12	555.9	1.0792	2.7410
15	1045	1.1761	3.017
		3.2095	8.1616

$$\overline{X_1} = \frac{1.2553}{3} = 0.4184, \overline{Y_1} = \frac{5.3676}{3} = 1.7892 \text{ and } \overline{X_2} = \frac{3.2095}{3} = 1.0698,$$
$$\overline{Y_2} = \frac{8.1616}{3} = 2.7205$$

$$1.7892 = A + b\,(0.4184) \qquad .... (2)$$
$$2.7205 = A + b\,(1.0698) \qquad .... (3)$$

Solving (2) and (3) by elimination method, we get
$$A = 1.191, \ b = 1.43$$

Therefore, $a = (10)^A = (10)^{1.191} = 15.5239$

Hence, the required equation is $y = (15.5239)(x)^{1.43} + 5.0338$

Fitting of the Curve of the Type $y = ae^{bx} + c$

The given equation can be re – written as $y - c = ae^{bx}$ .... (7.2.5)

First we have to find the value of c. For that, let $(x_1, y_1), (x_2, y_2) \ and \ (x_3, y_3)$ be three specific points on the curve given in Eq. (7.2.5) such that $x_1, x_2 \ and \ x_3$ are in arithmetic progression i.e

$$x_1 + x_3 = 2\, x_2 \qquad\qquad \text{........ (1)}$$

Hence, Eq. (7.2.5) becomes $y_1 - c = ae^{bx_1},\quad y_2 - c = ae^{bx_2}$ and

$y_3 - c = ae^{bx_3}$ Therefore, $(y_1 - c).(y_3 - c) = a^2\, e^{b(x_1 + x_3)}$

$$= (a\, e^{bx_2})^2 = (y_2 - c)^2 \qquad \text{(from (1))}$$

$$y_1 y_3 - c(y_1 + y_3) + c^2 = y_2{}^2 - 2cy_2 + c^2 \;\therefore\; c = \frac{y_1 y_3 - y_2{}^2}{y_1 + y_3 - 2y_2}$$

Putting the value of c in Eq. (7.2.5) we have only two unknowns to determine. Taking logarithm on both the sides of Eq. (5.2.5), we get

$$\log_{10}(y - c) = \log_{10} a + bx\, \log_{10} e \qquad\qquad \text{........ (7.2.6)}$$

$\therefore Y = A + Bx;\qquad where,\; Y = \log_{10}(y - c),\; B = b\log_{10} e$

Example 7.6   Fit a curve of the form $y = ae^{bx} + c$ to the following data:

x :	10	12	15	20	24	30
y :	22.3	18.9	15.8	12.6	11.2	10.8

Solution: We have to take values of x_1, x_2, x_3 such that they are in arithmetic progression. Let $x_1 = 10, x_2 = 15$ and $x_3 = 20$
since $x_1 + x_3 = 2x_2$

$$\therefore\; c = \frac{y_1 y_3 - y_2{}^2}{y_1 + y_3 - 2y_2} = \frac{(22.3)(12.6) - (15.8)^2}{22.3 + 12.6 - 2(15.8)} = \frac{31.34}{3.3} = 9.497$$

$$\therefore y = ae^{bx} + 9.497 \;\Rightarrow\; y - 9.497 = ae^{bx}$$

$$\therefore\; \log_{10}(y - 9.497) = \log_{10} a + bx \log_{10} e$$

Therefore, $Y = A + Bx$ .... (1)

where, $Y = \log_{10}(y - 9.497),\; A = \log_{10} a,\; B = b\log_{10} e$
We divide the data into two groups each containing three data.

	Group I				Group II	
x	y	$Y = \log_{10}(y - 9.497)$	x	y	$Y = \log_{10}(y - 9.497)$
10	22.3	1.1073	20	12.6	0.4918
12	18.9	0.9733	24	11.2	0.2312
15	15.8	0.7995	30	10.8	0.1149
37		2.8801	74		0.8379

$$\overline{x_1} = \frac{37}{3} = 12.33\;, \overline{Y_1} = \frac{2.8801}{3} = 0.96 \text{ and } \overline{x_2} = \frac{74}{3} = 24.6667,\; \overline{Y_2}$$
$$= \frac{0.8379}{3} = 0.2793$$

$$0.96 = A + B\,(12.33) \qquad\qquad \text{........ (2)}$$
$$0.2793 = A + B\,(24.6667) \qquad\qquad \text{........ (3)}$$

Solving (2) and (3) by elimination method, we get
$$A = 1.64, \ B = -0.055$$
$$\therefore a = (10)^A = (10)^{1.64} = 43.6516, \ b = \frac{B}{\log 10 \ e} = \frac{-0.055}{0.4343} = -0.1266.$$
Hence, the required equation is $y = (43.6516)e^{(-0.1266)x} + 9.497$

Remark: If the curve is in the form $y = ab^x + c$ then $\log_{10}(y - c) = \log_{10} a + x \log_{10} b$. By assuming $Y = \log_{10}(y - c), A = \log_{10} a, \ B = \log_{10} b$ the given equation is converted into $Y = A + Bx$ which is linear in x and Y. Then we can proceed as discussed in this sub section.

7.3   PRINCIPLE OF LEAST SQUARES

One of the drawbacks of method of group averages is fitting of the curve is not unique and it depends on how we form the groups from the given data. The values of constants may vary depending on the number of observations choose to form the group. In this section, we discuss the method of least squares which gives unique values of constants and the most systematic approach to fit a unique curve based on given observations.

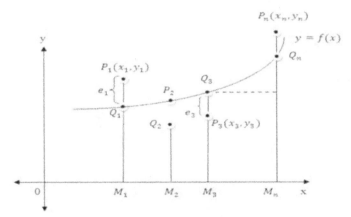

Figure 7.2

Let $$y = f(x)$$ .... (7.3.1)
be the curve be fitted to the set of observations (x_i, y_i) $i = 1,2,3, \dots \dots, n$.
At $x = x_1$, the observed (experimental) value of $y = y_1 = P_1 M_1$ and the corresponding expected or calculated value of y is $y = f(x_1) = Q_1 M_1$ ($\because$ from Eq. (7.3.1)). The difference e_1 of the observed and expected value (i.e. $e_1 = y_1 - f(x_1)$) of y is called an error or residual at $x = x_1$.

Therefore, we have $e_1 = y_1 - f(x_1) = P_1 M_1 - Q_1 M_1 = P_1 Q_1$
Similarly, $e_2 = y_2 - f(x_2) = P_2 M_2 - Q_2 M_2 = P_2 Q_2$
$$e_3 = y_3 - f(x_3) = P_3 M_3 - Q_3 M_3 = P_3 Q_3$$
$$\vdots$$

$$e_n = y_n - f(x_n) = P_n M_n - Q_n M_n = P_n Q_n$$

It is verified from the Figure 7.2 that some of the errors are positive and some of them are negative. Thus, to give equal weightage to each error, we square each of them and form the sum of the squares.

i.e.
$$E = e_1{}^2 + e_2{}^2 + e_3{}^2 + \dots\dots\dots + e_n{}^2$$

$$= \sum_{i=1}^{n} e_i{}^2 = \sum_{i=1}^{n} (y_i - f(x_i))^2$$

The curve of best fit is that for which the sum of the squares of deviations of the individual points from the curve i.e. errors is minimum. This is known as *the principle of the least squares.* From the Figure 7.2 it is clear that if E = 0 then all n points lie on the curve $y = f(x)$. If $E \neq 0$ then we should choose $f(x)$ such that the sum of the squares of errors (i.e. E) is minimum.

Remark: The principle of least squares does not help to determine the form of the curve $y = f(x)$ to fit a given data but it only determines the best possible values of the constants of the equation of the curve.

7.3.1 Fitting a Straight Line by Method of Least Squares

Suppose that the data points are (x_i, y_i) $i = 1,2,3,\dots\dots,n$ where x is the independent variable and y is the dependent variable. Let the fitting curve be the straight line $y = f(x) = a + bx$ to approximate the given set of data where, a and b represent the intercept and slope of the line respectively. To find the equation of the line of best fit we have to compute the constants a and b. As described in the section 5.3, the fitting curve $f(x)$ has the residual e from each data point. i.e. $e_1 = y_1 - f(x_1)$, $e_2 = y_2 - f(x_2), \dots\dots\dots, e_n = y_n - f(x_n)$. According to the principle of least squares, the best fitting curve has the property that

$$E = e_1{}^2 + e_2{}^2 + e_3{}^2 + \dots\dots\dots + e_n{}^2 = \sum_{i=1}^{n} e_i{}^2 = \sum_{i=1}^{n} (y_i - f(x_i))^2$$

$$= minimum$$

Thus, $E = \sum_{i=1}^{n}(y_i - f(x_i))^2 = \sum_{i=1}^{n}(y_i - (a + bx_i))^2$ is least. ..... (7.3.2)

The necessary conditions for Eq. (5.3.2) are

$$\frac{\partial E}{\partial a} = 0 \; and \; \frac{\partial E}{\partial b} = 0$$

Differentiating E partially with respect to a & b and equating them to zero, we get

$$\frac{\partial E}{\partial a} = 2\sum_{i=1}^{n}[y_i - (a + bx_i)].(-1) = 0$$

$$\frac{\partial E}{\partial b} = 2 \sum_{i=1}^{n} [y_i - (a + bx_i)].(-x_i) = 0$$

$$\therefore \sum_{i=1}^{n} [y_i - a - bx_i)] = 0 \quad and \quad \sum_{i=1}^{n} [x_i y_i - ax_i - bx_i^2] = 0$$

$$\therefore \sum_{i=1}^{n} y_i = na + b \sum_{i=1}^{n} x_i \quad (\because \sum_{i=1}^{n} a = na) \qquad \ldots\ldots(7.3.3)$$

$$\therefore \sum_{i=1}^{n} x_i y_i = a \sum_{i=1}^{n} x_i + b \sum_{i=1}^{n} x_i^2 \qquad \ldots\ldots(7.3.4)$$

Eqs. (7.3.3) and (7.3.4) are called normal equations. Solving Eqs. (7.3.3) and (7.3.4) simultaneously, we get the values of a and b and thus, the equation of the best fitting straight line.

Remark:
- Dropping the suffices i from Eqs. (7.3.3) and (7.3.4) the normal equations are

$$na + b \sum x = \sum y \qquad \ldots\ldots(1)$$
$$a \sum x + b \sum x^2 = \sum xy \qquad \ldots\ldots(2)$$

- Eq. (1) can be obtained by taking Σ on both sides of $y = a + bx$ and noting that $\Sigma a = na$ and (2) can be obtained by multiplying each of the term of $y = a + bx$ by x and then taking Σ on both sides.

Solving these equations by Cramer's rule

$$a = \frac{\begin{vmatrix} \sum y & \sum x \\ \sum xy & \sum x^2 \end{vmatrix}}{\begin{vmatrix} n & \sum x \\ \sum x & \sum x^2 \end{vmatrix}} \quad and \quad b = \frac{\begin{vmatrix} n & \sum y \\ \sum x & \sum xy \end{vmatrix}}{\begin{vmatrix} n & \sum x \\ \sum x & \sum x^2 \end{vmatrix}}$$

which gives,

$$a = \frac{n \sum xy - \sum x \sum y}{n \sum x^2 - (\sum x)^2} \quad and \quad b = \frac{\sum y \sum x^2 - \sum x \sum xy}{n \sum x^2 - (\sum x)^2}$$

Example 7.7 Fit a straight line to the following data by the method of least squares.

x	1	2	3	4	5
y	14	27	40	55	68

Solution: The equation of straight line is $y = a + bx$ $\qquad \ldots\ldots(1)$
The normal equations are

$$na + b \Sigma x = \Sigma y$$
$$a \Sigma x + b \Sigma x^2 = \Sigma xy$$

Here, $n = 5$, the other values $\Sigma x, \Sigma y, \Sigma x^2$ and Σxy are calculated from the following table.

x	y	xy	x^2
1	14	14	1
2	27	54	4
3	40	120	9
4	55	220	16
5	68	340	25
15	204	748	55

The normal equations become

$$5a + 15b = 204$$
$$15a + 55b = 748$$

Solving these equations by elimination method, we get

$$a = 0 \text{ and } b = 13.6$$

Substituting these values in (1) the best fit line is $y = 13.6x$

Alternate Method to Find a and b

We get $n = 5, \Sigma x = 15, \Sigma y = 204, \Sigma x^2 = 55$ and $\Sigma xy = 748$
Using Cramer's rule,

$$a = \frac{n \Sigma xy - \Sigma x \Sigma y}{n \Sigma x^2 - (\Sigma x)^2} = \frac{(5)(748) - (15)(204)}{(5)(55) - (15)^2} = 13.6$$

$$b = \frac{\Sigma y \Sigma x^2 - \Sigma x \Sigma xy}{n \Sigma x^2 - (\Sigma x)^2} = \frac{(204)(55) - (15)(748)}{(5)(55) - (15)^2} = 0$$

Substituting these values in (1) the best fit line is $y = 13.6x$

Example 7.8 Find the best fitting straight line to the data:

x	0	10	20	30	40
y	15	27	40	54	67

Solution: The equation of straight line is $y = a + bx$ .... (1)
The calculations can be made simpler by taking arbitrary origin for x and y.

Let $X = \frac{x - 30}{10}$, $Y = y - 54$

After these tranformations the new equation of the straight line be $Y = a + bX$ and the corresponding normal equations are

$$na + b \Sigma X = \Sigma Y \qquad .... (2)$$
$$a \Sigma X + b \Sigma X^2 = \Sigma XY \qquad .... (3)$$

Formulate the table

x	y	X	Y	XY	X^2
0	15	-3	-39	117	9
10	27	-2	-27	54	4
20	40	-1	-14	14	1
30	54	0	0	0	0
40	67	1	13	13	1
50	73	2	19	38	4
60	88	3	34	102	9
		0	-14	338	28

The equations (2) and (3) become

$$7a + (0)b = -14$$
$$(0)a + 28b = 338$$
$$a = -2 \quad \text{and} \quad b = 12.07$$

The new equation becomes $Y = a + bX = -2 + 12.07X$

$$\therefore y - 54 = -2 + 12.07\left(\frac{x-30}{10}\right)$$
$$\therefore y = 15.79 + 1.207x$$

Hence, the best fitting line is $y = 15.79 + 1.207x$.

Example 7.9 Fit a curve of the form $y = ax + bx^2$ to the following data by the method of least squares.

x	1	2	3	4	5
y	1.8	5.1	8.9	14.1	19.8

Solution: The given relation $\quad y = ax + bx^2 \quad$ .... (1)

is not linear. Therefore, the method of least squares cannot be applied directly. First we convert the given relation in the linear form.

The given relation is $y = ax + bx^2 \quad \therefore y = x(a + bx) \quad \therefore \frac{y}{x} = a + bx$

Therefore, we use transformation $Y = \frac{y}{x}$. Then the relation becomes

$$Y = a + bx \qquad \text{........ (2)}$$

The corresponding normal equations are

$$na + b\,\Sigma x = \Sigma Y \qquad \text{........ (3)}$$
$$a\,\Sigma x + b\Sigma\,x^2 = \Sigma\,xY \qquad \text{........ (4)}$$

Formulate the table

x	y	$Y = \dfrac{y}{x}$	xY	x^2
1	1.8	1.8	1.8	1
2	5.1	2.55	5.1	4
3	8.9	2.97	8.91	9
4	14.1	3.525	14.1	16
5	19.8	3.96	19.8	25
15		14.805	49.71	55

The equations (3) and (4) become
$$5a + 15b = 14.805$$
$$15a + 55b = 49.71$$
Solving these equations by elimination method, we get
$$a = 1.3725 \text{ and } b = 0.5295$$
Substituting these values in (2), we get
$$Y = 1.3725 + 0.5295x$$
Therefore,
$$\frac{y}{x} = 1.3725 + 0.5295x$$
Hence, the required equation of the curve is $y = 1.3725 + 0.5295x^2$

7.3.2   Fitting a Second Degree Curve (Parabola) $y = a + bx + cx^2$ by the Method of Least Squares

Suppose that the data points are (x_i, y_i) $i = 1,2,3, \dots \dots, n$ where x is the independent variable and y is the dependent variable. Let the fitting curve be the parabola $y = f(x) = a + bx + cx^2$ to approximate the given set of data. To find the equation of the parabola of best fit we have to compute the constants a, b and c. According to the principle of least squares, the best fitting curve has the property that

$$E = e_1{}^2 + e_2{}^2 + e_3{}^2 + \dots \dots + e_n{}^2 = \sum_{i=1}^{n} e_i{}^2 = \sum_{i=1}^{n} (y_i - f(x_i))^2$$
$$= minimum$$
Thus, $E = \sum_{i=1}^{n}(y_i - f(x_i))^2 = \sum_{i=1}^{n}(y_i - (a + bx_i + cx_i{}^2))^2$ is least.
$$\dots\dots (7.3.5)$$

The necessary conditions for Eq. (7.3.5) are
$$\frac{\partial E}{\partial a} = 0, \frac{\partial E}{\partial b} = 0 \text{ and } \frac{\partial E}{\partial c} = 0$$
Differentiating E partially with respect to a,b & c and equating them to zero, we get

$$\frac{\partial E}{\partial a} = 2 \sum_{i=1}^{n} [y_i - (a + bx_i + cx_i^2)].(-1) = 0$$

$$\frac{\partial E}{\partial b} = 2 \sum_{i=1}^{n} [y_i - (a + bx_i + cx_i^2)].(-x_i) = 0$$

$$\frac{\partial E}{\partial c} = 2 \sum_{i=1}^{n} [y_i - (a + bx_i + cx_i^2)].(-x_i^2) = 0$$

$$\therefore \sum_{i=1}^{n} [y_i - a - bx_i - cx_i^2)] = 0,$$

$$\sum_{i=1}^{n} [x_i y_i - ax_i - bx_i^2 - cx_i^3] = 0$$

and
$$\sum_{i=1}^{n} [x_i^2 y_i - ax_i^2 - bx_i^3 - cx_i^4] = 0$$

$$\therefore \sum_{i=1}^{n} y_i = na + b \sum_{i=1}^{n} x_i + c \sum_{i=1}^{n} x_i^2 \quad (\because \sum_{i=1}^{n} a = na) \qquad \ldots\ldots (7.3.6)$$

$$\sum_{i=1}^{n} x_i y_i = a \sum_{i=1}^{n} x_i + b \sum_{i=1}^{n} x_i^2 + c \sum_{i=1}^{n} x_i^3 \qquad \ldots\ldots (7.3.7)$$

$$\sum_{i=1}^{n} x_i^2 y_i = a \sum_{i=1}^{n} x_i^2 + b \sum_{i=1}^{n} x_i^3 + c \sum_{i=1}^{n} x_i^4 \qquad \ldots\ldots (7.3.8)$$

Eqs. (7.3.6), (7.3.7) and (7.3.8) are called normal equations. Solving Eqs. (7.3.6), (7.3.7) and (7.3.8) simultaneously, we get the values of a,b and c and thus, the euqation of the best fitting second degree curve for the given data.
Thus, the normal equations are

$$\Sigma y = na + b \ \Sigma x + c \ \Sigma x^2 \qquad \ldots\ldots (1)$$
$$\Sigma xy = a \ \Sigma x + b \ \Sigma x^2 + c \ \Sigma x^3 \qquad \ldots\ldots (2)$$
$$\Sigma x^2 y = a \ \Sigma x^2 + b \ \Sigma x^3 + c \ \Sigma x^4 \qquad \ldots\ldots (3)$$

Remark:
- Eq. (1) can be obtained by taking Σ on both sides of $y = a + bx + cx^2$ and noting that $\Sigma a = na$, (2) can be obtained by multiplying each of the term of $y = a + bx + cx^2$ by x and then taking Σ on both sides and Eq. (3) can be obtained by multiplying each of the term of $y = a + bx + cx^2$ by x^2 and then taking Σ on both sides.
- If the values of the independent variable are equally spaced then for our conveniency and ease in computations, it is sometimes required to change the origin and scale with the transformations of the form $X = \frac{x-A}{h}$ and $Y = \frac{y-B}{i}$.

- The values of A, B and h are chosen as follows:
1. If the number of observations of x is odd then
$$X = \frac{x-A}{h} = \frac{x-(middle\ value)}{interval\ length\ h}$$
2. If the number of observations of x is even then
$$X = \frac{x-A}{h} = \frac{x-(Average\ of\ two\ middle\ values)}{\frac{1}{2}(interval\ length\ h)}$$
3. Generally, the difference between two values of dependent variables is not same. Therefore,
$$Y = \frac{y-B}{i} = \frac{y-(average \quad or \quad near\ the\ average\ value)}{1}$$

Example 7.10 The following table shows the birth rate per 1000 population in a country during the years 1910 – 1950 in 5 year intervals. Find a least square parabola fitting the data. Calculate the trend value in the year 1935.

Year	1910	1915	1920	1925	1930	1935	1940	1945	1950
Birth rate per 1000 population	28.0	26.9	23.7	21.3	19.5	20.6	23.5	25.7	27.3

Solution: The second degree parabola is $\quad y = a + bx + cx^2 \qquad$ .... (1)

Since the values of *Year* are in A.P. with common difference is 5 and the number of observations is odd, we substitute $X = \frac{x-1930}{5}$ and $Y = y - 19.5$

Let the new equation of parabola be $\quad Y = a + bX + cX^2 \qquad$ .... (2)

The normal equations are

$$na + b\ \textstyle\sum X + c\ \sum X^2 \ = \ \sum Y \qquad \text{...\,.....(3)}$$
$$a\ \textstyle\sum X + b\ \sum X^2 + c\ \sum X^3 = \ \sum XY \qquad \text{...\,.....(4)}$$
$$a\ \textstyle\sum X^2 + b\ \sum X^3 + c\ \sum X^4 = \ \sum X^2 Y \qquad \text{...\,.....(5)}$$

Using the relevant values of below Table 7.1 in (3), (4), (5), we get

$$9a + 60c = 41 \qquad \text{........ (6)}$$
$$60b = -7.5 \qquad \text{........ (7)}$$
$$60a + 708c = 418.9 \qquad \text{........ (8)}$$

From (7), we get $b = 0.125$

Solving (6) and (8), we get $a = 1.405$ and $c = 0.473$

Using these values in (2), we get

$$Y = 1.405 + 0.125X + 0.473X^2$$

where, $X = \frac{x-1930}{5}$ and $Y = y - 19.5$

Table 7.1

Year	Birth rate per 1000 population	$X = \dfrac{x - 1930}{5}$	$Y = y - 19.5$	X^2	X^3	X^4	XY	X^2Y
1910	28.0	-4	8.5	16	-64	256	-34	136
1915	26.9	-3	7.4	9	-27	81	-22.2	66.6
1920	23.7	-2	4.2	4	-8	16	-8.4	16.8
1925	21.3	-1	1.8	1	-1	1	-1.8	1.8
1930	19.5	0	0	0	0	0	0	0
1935	20.6	1	1.1	1	1	1	1.1	1.1
1940	23.5	2	4	4	8	16	8	16
1945	25.7	3	6.2	9	27	81	18.6	55.8
1950	27.3	4	7.8	16	64	256	31.2	124.8
		0	41	60	0	708	-7.5	418.9

i.e. $\qquad y - 19.5 = 1.405 + 0.125X + 0.473X^2$

i.e. $\qquad y = 20.905 + 0.125X + 0.473X^2 \quad$ where, $X = \dfrac{x-1930}{5}$

which is the required parabolic relation between x and y.

The trend value in the year 1935 is $X = \dfrac{1935-1930}{5} = 1$

Therefore , $y = 21.503$

7.3.3 Fitting a Geometric Curve by the Method of Least Squares

Suppose that the data points are (x_i, y_i) $i = 1,2,3, \ldots\ldots, n$ where x is the independent variable and y is the dependent variable. The geometric curve is described by the equation $y = ax^b$.

Taking logarithms on both sides of the equation, we have

$$log_{10}y = log_{10}a + b\, log_{10}x$$
$$\therefore Y = A + bX$$

where, $Y = log_{10}y, A = log_{10}a$ and $X = log_{10}x$

which is linear in x and y. The same proof discussed in the case of fitting of straight line are applied. Hence, the normal equations are

$$nA + b\, \Sigma X = \Sigma Y$$
$$A\, \Sigma X + b\Sigma\, X^2 = \Sigma\, X$$

$$\therefore\ nA + B\, \Sigma log_{10}x = \Sigma log_{10}y$$
$$A\, \Sigma log_{10}x + B\Sigma\,(log_{10}x)^2 = \Sigma\, log_{10}x\ log_{10}y$$

By solving these equations we get

$$A = \frac{n \sum logx \ logy - \sum logx \sum logy}{n \sum (logx)^2 - (\sum logx)^2} \quad and$$

$$b = \frac{\sum logy \sum (logx)^2 - \sum logx \sum logxlogy}{n \sum (logx)^2 - (\sum logx)^2}$$

$$A = log_{10}a \Rightarrow a = 10^A$$

Thus, we can easily find a and b and hence, the best fitting geometric curve for the given data.

Example 7.11   Determine the values of a and b so that the equation $y = ax^b$ best fits the following data by the method of least squares :

x :	1	2	3	4	5
y :	7.1	27.8	62.1	110	161

Solution: The given relation $y = ax^b$ .... (1)
is not linear. Therefore, the method of least squares cannot be applied directly. First we convert the given relation in the linear form.

Taking logarithm on both the sides, we get

$$log_{10}y = log_{10}a + b. log_{10}x$$

$$\therefore \ Y = A + bX \quad .... (2)$$

where, $Y = log_{10}y$, $A = log_{10}a$ and $X = log_{10}x$

The corresponding normal equations are

$$nA + b\Sigma X = \Sigma Y \quad .... (3)$$

$$A\Sigma X + b\Sigma X^2 = \Sigma XY \quad .... (4)$$

Formulate the table

x	y	$X = log_{10}x$	$Y = log_{10}y$	X^2	XY
1	7.1	0	0.8513	0	0
2	27.8	0.3010	1.4440	0.0906	0.4347
3	62.1	0.4771	1.7931	0.2276	0.8555
4	110	0.6021	2.0414	0.3625	1.2291
5	161	0.6990	2.2068	0.4886	1.5426
15		2.0792	8.3366	1.1694	4.0618

Using the relevant values in (3) and (4) we get

$$5A + 2.0792b = 8.3366 \quad .... (5)$$

$$2.0792A + 1.1694b = 4.0618 \quad .... (6)$$

Solving (5) and (6), we get

$$A = log_{10}a = 0.855 \Rightarrow a = 10^{0.855} = 7.1614$$
$$b = 1.953$$

Using these values in (1), we get $y = ax^b = (7.1614)x^{(1.953)}$

7.3.4 Fitting an Exponential Curve by the Method of Least Squares

Suppose that the data points are (x_i, y_i) $i = 1,2,3,\dots\dots,n$ where x is the independent variable and y is the dependent variable. The exponential curve is described by the equations $y = ae^{bx}$ or $y = ab^x$.

(i) $y = ae^{bx}$

Taking logarithms on both sides of the equation, we have

$$log_{10}y = log_{10}a + bx\, log_{10}e$$
$$\therefore Y = A + Bx$$

where, $Y = log_{10}y, A = log_{10}a$ and $B = blog_{10}e$

which is linear in x and y. The same proof discussed in the case of fitting of straight line are applied. Hence, the normal equations are

$$nA + B\, \Sigma x = \Sigma Y$$
$$A\, \Sigma x + B\Sigma\, x^2 = \Sigma\, xY$$

$$\therefore\ nA + B\, \Sigma x = \Sigma log_{10}y$$
$$A\, \Sigma x + B\Sigma\, x^2 = \Sigma\, xlog_{10}y$$

By solving these equations we get

$$A = \frac{n\, \Sigma xlogy - \Sigma x \Sigma logy}{n\, \Sigma x^2 - (\Sigma x)^2} \quad and \quad B = \frac{\Sigma logy\, \Sigma x^2 - \Sigma x \Sigma xlogy}{n\, \Sigma x^2 - (\Sigma x)^2}$$

$$A = log_{10}a \Rightarrow a = 10^A \qquad\qquad B = blog_{10}e \Rightarrow b = \frac{B}{log_{10}e}$$

Thus, we can easily find a, b from the values of A, B and hence, the best fitting exponential curve for the given data.

(ii) $y = ab^x$

Taking logarithms on both sides of the equation, we have

$$log_{10}y = log_{10}a + x\, log_{10}b$$
$$\therefore Y = A + Bx$$

where, $Y = log_{10}y, A = log_{10}a$ and $B = log_{10}b$

which is linear in x and y. The normal equations are

$$nA + B\, \Sigma x = \Sigma Y$$
$$A\, \Sigma x + B\Sigma\, x^2 = \Sigma\, xY$$

$$\therefore\ nA + B\, \Sigma x = \Sigma log_{10}y$$
$$A\, \Sigma x + B\Sigma\, x^2 = \Sigma\, xlog_{10}y$$

By solving these equations we get

$$A = \frac{n \sum x \log y - \sum x \sum \log y}{n \sum x^2 - (\sum x)^2} \quad and \quad B = \frac{\sum \log y \sum x^2 - \sum x \sum x \log y}{n \sum x^2 - (\sum x)^2}$$

$$A = \log_{10} a \Rightarrow a = 10^A \qquad\qquad B = \log_{10} b \Rightarrow b = 10^B$$

Thus, we can easily find a, b from the values of A, B and hence, the best fitting exponential curve for the given data.

Example 7.12   Growth of bacteria (N) in a culture after t hrs. is given in the following table:

t :	0	1	2	3	4	5	6
N :	32	47	65	92	132	190	275

Fit a curve of the form $N = ab^t$ and estimate N when $t = 7$.

Solution: The given relation $N = ab^t$ .... (1)
is not linear. Therefore, the method of least squares cannot be applied directly. First we convert the given relation in the linear form.
Taking logarithm on both the sides, we get

$$\log_{10} N = \log_{10} a + t.\log_{10} b$$

$$\therefore\ Y = A + Bt \qquad\qquad ....\ (2)$$

where, $Y = \log_{10} N$, $A = \log_{10} a$ and $B = \log_{10} b$
The corresponding normal equations are

$$nA + B\Sigma t = \Sigma Y \qquad\qquad ....\ (3)$$

$$A\Sigma t + B\Sigma t^2 = \Sigma\ tY \qquad\qquad ....\ (4)$$

Formulate the table

t	N	$Y = \log_{10} N$	t^2	tY
0	32	1.5051	0	0
1	47	1.6721	1	1.6721
2	65	1.8129	4	3.6258
3	92	1.9638	9	5.8914
4	132	2.1206	16	8.4824
5	190	2.2788	25	11.394
6	275	2.4393	36	14.6358
21		13.7926	91	45.7015

Using the relevant values in (3) and (4) we get

$$7A + 21B = 13.7926 \qquad \text{........ (5)}$$
$$21A + 91B = 45.7015 \qquad \text{........ (6)}$$

Solving (5) and (6), we get
$$A = log_{10}a = 1.5071 \Rightarrow a = 10^{1.5071} = 32.144$$

and $\quad B = log_{10}b = 0.1544 \Rightarrow b = 10^{0.1544} = 1.4269$

Using these values in (1), we get
$$N = ab^t = (32.144)(1.4269)^t$$

When $t = 7$, $N = (32.144)(1.4269)^7 = 387.1281$

Alternate Method to Find a and b

We get $n = 7, \Sigma t = 21, Y = \Sigma logN = 13.7926, \Sigma t^2 = 91$ and $\Sigma tlogN = 45.7015$

Using Cramer's rule,

$$A = \frac{n \sum tlogN - \sum t \sum logN}{n \sum t^2 - (\sum t)^2} = \frac{(7)(45.7015) - (21)(13.7926)}{(7)(91) - (21)^2} = 0.1544$$

$$B = \frac{\sum logN \sum t^2 - \sum t \sum tlogN}{n \sum t^2 - (\sum t)^2} = \frac{(13.7926)(91) - (21)(45.7015)}{(7)(91) - (21)^2}$$
$$= 1.5071$$

$A = log_{10}a = 1.5071 \Rightarrow a = 10^{1.5071} = 32.144$ and

$B = log_{10}b = 0.1544 \Rightarrow b = 10^{0.1544} = 1.4269$

Substituting these values in (1) the best fit curve is
$$N = ab^t = (32.144)(1.4269)^t$$

Example 7.13 Fit a curve of the form $y = a.e^{bx}$ to the following data by the method of least squares :

x :	1	2	3	4	5	6
y :	1.53	2.75	4.69	7.64	16.02	31.53

Solution: The given relation $y = a.e^{bx}$ .... (1)
is not linear. Therefore, the method of least squares cannot be applied directly. First we convert the given relation in the linear form.
Taking logarithm on both the sides, we get

$$log_{10}y = log_{10}a + bx.log_{10}e$$
$$\therefore Y = A + Bx \qquad \text{........ (2)}$$

where, $Y = log_{10}y$, $A = log_{10}a$ and $B = blog_{10}e$
The corresponding normal equations are

$$nA + B\Sigma x = \Sigma Y \qquad \text{........ (3)}$$
$$A\Sigma x + B\Sigma x^2 = \Sigma xY \qquad \text{........ (4)}$$

Using the relevant values of the below Table 7.2 in (3) and (4) we get

$$6A + 21B = 4.8817 \qquad \text{........ (5)}$$
$$21A + 91B = 21.625 \qquad \text{........ (6)}$$

Solving (5) and (6), we get $A = log_{10}a = -0.094 \Rightarrow a = 10^{-0.094} = 0.8054$

and $B = b log_{10}e = 0.259 \Rightarrow b = \dfrac{0.259}{log_{10}e} = 0.5964$

Using these values in (1), we get $y = a.e^{bx} = (0.8054)e^{(0.5964)x}$

Table 7.2

x	y	$Y = log_{10}y$	x^2	xY
1	1.53	0.1847	1	0.1847
2	2.75	0.4393	4	0.8786
3	4.69	0.6712	9	2.0136
4	7.64	0.8831	16	3.5324
5	16.02	1.2047	25	6.0235
6	31.53	1.4987	36	8.9922
21		4.8817	91	21.625

7.4 CALCULATION OF THE SUM OF THE SQUARES OF THE RESIDUALS

Let $y = f(x)$ be the equation of the curve best fit for the given data. The sum of the squares of residuals

$$E = \sum_{i=1}^{n} \{y_i - f(x_i)\}^2 = 0$$

indicates the exact relationship between x and y. From the value of E, we can study the closeness of a curve to the ideal value zero and how closely the curve $y = f(x)$ fits the given data.

Let $\qquad\qquad y = a + bx \qquad\qquad$ .... (7.4.1)

be the equation of the straight line best fit for the given data. Now, we want to find the formula for the value of E when the straight line is the best fitting curve. The normal equations of Eq. (7.4.1) are given by,

$$\sum y = na + b \sum x \qquad \text{........ (1)}$$
and $$\sum xy = a \sum x + b \sum x^2 \qquad \text{........ (2)}$$

From (1) and (2) it is clear that,

$$\sum (y - a - bx) = 0 \qquad \text{........ (3)}$$
and $$\sum x(y - a - bx) = 0 \qquad \text{........ (4)}$$

Now,

$$E = \sum_{i=1}^{n} \{y_i - f(x_i)\}^2 = \sum \{y - (a + bx)\}^2$$

$$= \sum (y - a - bx)(y - a - bx)$$

$$= \sum y\,(y - a - bx) - a\sum(y - a - bx) - b\sum x\,(y - a - bx)$$

$$= \sum y\,(y - a - bx) - a\,.0 - b\,.0 \qquad (\because \text{ from (3) and (4))}$$

Therefore, $\qquad E = \sum y^2 - a\sum y - b\sum xy$

Thus, if we compute $\sum y^2, \sum y$ and $\sum xy$ then we can easily find the minimum value of E for a straight line.

Let $\qquad\qquad\qquad y = a + bx + cx^2 \qquad\qquad$ .... (7.4.2)

be the equation of the parabola best fit for the given data. Now, we want to find the formula for the value of E when the parabola is the best fitting curve.

The normal equations of Eq. (7.4.2) are given by,

$$\sum y = na + b\sum x + c\sum x^2 \qquad\qquad\qquad\text{........ (5)}$$
$$\sum xy = a\sum x + b\sum x^2 + c\sum x^3 \qquad\qquad\text{........ (6)}$$
$$\sum x^2 y = a\sum x^2 + b\sum x^3 + c\sum x^4 \qquad\qquad\text{........ (7)}$$

From (5), (6) and (7), it is clear that

$$\sum(y - a - bx - cx^2) = 0 \qquad\qquad\qquad\text{........ (8)}$$
$$\sum x(y - a - bx - cx^2) = 0 \qquad\qquad\qquad\text{........ (9)}$$
$$\sum x^2(y - a - bx - cx^2) = 0 \qquad\qquad\qquad\text{........ (10)}$$

Now, $\quad E = \sum\{y - (a + bx + cx^2)\}^2$

$$= \sum(y - a - bx - cx^2)(y - a - bx - cx^2)$$

$$= \sum y\,(y - a - bx - cx^2) - a\sum(y - a - bx - cx^2) - b\sum x(y - a - bx - cx^2) - c\sum x^2\,(y - a - bx - cx^2)$$

$$= \sum y\,(y - a - bx - cx^2) - a\,.0 - b\,.0 - c\,.0 \quad (\because \text{ from (8), (9) and (10))}$$

Therefore, $\quad E = \sum y^2 - a\sum y - b\sum xy - c\sum x^2\,y$

Thus, if we compute $\sum y^2, \sum y, \sum xy$ and $\sum x^2\,y$ then we can easily find the minimum value of E for a parabola.

Example 7.14 Find the straight line and the parabola of the best fit and calculate the sum of the squares of the residuals in both cases. Which curve is a better fit?

x :	0	1	2	3	4
y :	1	5	10	22	38

Solution: Let $\qquad\qquad y = a + bx \qquad\qquad$ .... (1)

be the equation of the straight line best fit for the given data.
The normal equations are

$$\sum y = na + b \sum x \qquad\qquad \text{........ (2)}$$

and

$$\sum xy = a \sum x + b \sum x^2 \qquad\qquad \text{........ (3)}$$

Formulate the table

x	y	x^2	x^3	x^4	xy	x^2y	y^2
0	1	0	0	0	0	0	1
1	5	1	1	1	5	5	25
2	10	4	8	16	20	40	100
3	22	9	27	81	66	198	484
4	38	16	64	256	152	608	1444
10	76	30	100	354	243	851	2054

Eq. (2) and (3) becomes

$$5a + 10b = 76$$
$$10a + 30b = 243$$

After solving these equations, we get $a = -3, b = 9.1$

Hence, the best fitting straight line is $y = -3 + 9.1x$

The sum of squares of residuals is $E_1 = \sum y^2 - a \sum y - b \sum xy$

$$= 2054 - 76(-3) - (243)(9.1) = 70.7$$

Let $\qquad\qquad y = a + bx + cx^2 \qquad\qquad \text{........ (4)}$

be the equation of the parabola best fit for the given data.

The normal equations are

$$\sum y = na + b \sum x + c \qquad\qquad \text{........ (5)}$$
$$\sum xy = a \sum x + b \sum x^2 + c \sum x^3 \qquad\qquad \text{........ (6)}$$
$$\sum x^2 y = a \sum x^2 + b \sum x^3 + c \sum x^4 \qquad\qquad \text{........ (7)}$$

Eqs. (5), (6) and (7) become

$$5a + 10b + 30c = 76$$
$$10a + 30b + 100c = 243$$
$$30a + 100b + 354c = 851$$

After solving these equations, we get $a = 1.429, b = 0.243, c = 2.214$

Hence, the best fitting parabola is $y = 1.429 + 0.243x + 2.214 x^2$

The sum of squares of residuals is

$$E_2 = \sum y^2 - a \sum y - b \sum xy - c \sum x^2 y$$
$$= 2054 - (1.429)(76) - (0.243)(243) - (2.214)(851) = 2.233$$

Since, $E_2 < E_1$, parabola is a better fit for the given data.

7.5   METHOD OF MOMENTS

Suppose n set of data points are (x_i, y_i) $i = 1,2,3, \ldots \ldots, n$ such that $x_i's$ are equally spaced. i.e. $x_2 - x_1 = x_3 - x_2 = \ldots \ldots = x_{n-1} - x_n = \Delta x$ (say) $= h = $ constant

Let $y = f(x)$ be the equation of the best fitting curve for the given data. We define the observed moments as follows:

The first moment, $\mu_1 = \sum y \, \Delta x = \Delta x \sum y$

The second moment, $\mu_2 = \sum xy \, \Delta x = \Delta x \sum xy$

The third moment, $\mu_3 = \sum x^2 y \, \Delta x = \Delta x \sum x^2 y$ and so on.

These are known as the moments of the observed values of y. For the given curve $y = f(x)$, we define the expected moments of the computed values of y as follows:

The first moment, $\gamma_1 = \int y \, dx = \int f(x) dx$

The second moment, $\gamma_2 = \int xy \, dx = \int x f(x) dx$

The third moment, $\gamma_3 = \int x^2 y \, dx = \int x^2 f(x) dx$ and so on.

The principle behind method of moments is the moments of the observed values of y are respectively equal to the moments of expected values of y.

i.e. $\mu_1 = \gamma_1, \quad \mu_2 = \gamma_2, \quad \mu_3 = \gamma_3$

In the Figure 7.3, let $P_i(x_i, y_i)$, $i = 1,2,3, \ldots \ldots, n$ be the n set of points of the best fit curve $y = f(x)$. $y_i = P_i M_i$ are the ordinates at M_i, $i = 1, 2, 3, \ldots \ldots n$. Let us consider the rectangles constructed with $P_1 M_1, P_2 M_2, \ldots \ldots, P_n M_n$ as lengths and $\Delta x = h$ as width. We take $y_1 = P_1 M_1$ as the mid point of the interval of width $\Delta x = h$ such that $AM_1 = \dfrac{\Delta x}{2} = \dfrac{h}{2}$ and hy_1 is the area of the rectangle.

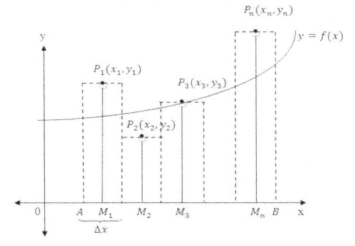

Figure 7.3 Method of Moments

Similarly, $y_n = P_n M_n$ is taken as the mid point of the interval of width $\Delta x = h$ such that $M_n B = \dfrac{\Delta x}{2} = \dfrac{h}{2}$ where, A and B are points on the x - axis.

Now, by definite integration, Sum of the areas of the $'n'$ rectangles

$$\gamma_1 = \int y \, dx = \int_{x_1 - \frac{h}{2}}^{x_n - \frac{h}{2}} y \, dx \quad or \quad \int_{x_1 - \frac{h}{2}}^{x_n - \frac{h}{2}} f(x) \, dx$$

Similarly,

$$\gamma_2 = \int xy \, dx = \int_{x_1 - \frac{h}{2}}^{x_n - \frac{h}{2}} x f(x) dx , \quad \gamma_3 = \int x^2 y \, dx = \int_{x_1 - \frac{h}{2}}^{x_n - \frac{h}{2}} x^2 f(x) \, dx$$

Since $\mu_1 = \gamma_1$, $\mu_2 = \gamma_2$, $\mu_3 = \gamma_3$ and so on, we have the following set of equations:

$$\Delta x \sum y = \int_{x_1 - \frac{h}{2}}^{x_n - \frac{h}{2}} f(x) dx , \quad \Delta x \sum xy = \int_{x_1 - \frac{h}{2}}^{x_n - \frac{h}{2}} x f(x) \, dx$$

$$\Delta x \sum x^2 y = \int_{x_1 - \frac{h}{2}}^{x_n - \frac{h}{2}} x^2 f(x) \, dx$$

These equations are useful to find the unknowns in the equation of $f(x)$. These equations are called *observation equations*.

Example 7.15   Fit a straight line to the following data by the method of moments:

x :	0	2	4	6	8
y :	0.4	1.5	2.7	4.2	5.5

Solution: The values of x are equally spaced with $\Delta x = h = 2$

Let $y = a + bx$ be the equation of the best fitting straight line for the given data. Since we have to find two constants a and b, it is sufficient to find the values of first two moments

x	y	xy
0	0.4	0
2	1.5	3
4	2.7	10.8
6	4.2	25.2
8	5.5	44
20	14.3	83

$$\mu_1 = \text{the first moment of the observed value of } y$$
$$= \Delta x \sum y = 2 \times 14.3 = 28.6$$

$$\mu_2 = \text{the second moment of the observed value of } y$$
$$= \Delta x \sum xy = 2 \times 83 = 166$$

Now, to find the expected values of y, the limits of integration are

$$x_1 - \frac{h}{2} \text{ to } x_n + \frac{h}{2} \quad i.e. \quad 0 - \frac{2}{2} \text{ to } 8 + \frac{2}{2} = -1 \text{ to } 9$$

Therefore, $\gamma_1 = \text{the first moment of the expected value of } y$

$$= \int_{x_1 - \frac{h}{2}}^{x_n - \frac{h}{2}} f(x)dx = \int_{-1}^{9} (a + bx) \, dx = \left[ax + b\frac{x^2}{2} \right]_{-1}^{9}$$

$$= (9a + 40.5b) - (-a + 0.5b) = 10a + 40b$$

$\gamma_2 = \text{the second moment of the expected value of } y$

$$= \int_{x_1 - \frac{h}{2}}^{x_n - \frac{h}{2}} xf(x)dx = \int_{-1}^{9} x(a + bx) \, dx = \int_{-1}^{9} (ax + bx^2) \, dx$$

$$= \left[a\frac{x^2}{2} + b\frac{x^3}{3} \right]_{-1}^{9} = (40.5a + 243b) - (0.5a - 0.33b)$$

$$= 40a + 243.33b.$$

The observation equations are

$$10a + 40b = 28.6$$
$$40a + 243.33b = 166$$

Solving these equations, we have $a = 0.383, \; b = 0.619$
Thus, the equation is $y = 0.383 + 0.619 x$

Example 7.16 By using the method of moments, fit a parabola of the form $y = a + bx + cx^2$ to the data given below:

x :	3	4	5	6	7
y :	31.9	34.6	33.8	27.0	31.6

Solution: The values of x are equally spaced with $\Delta x = h = 1$
Since we have to fit a parabola of the form $y = a + bx + cx^2$ we have to find three constants $a, b \text{ and } c$. Hence, it is sufficient to find the values of first three moments

x	y	xy	x^2y
3	31.9	95.7	287.1
4	34.6	138.4	553.6
5	33.8	169.0	845
6	27.0	162	972
7	31.6	221.2	1548.4
25	158.9	786.3	4206.1

$\mu_1 =$ the first moment of the observed value of y
$\quad = \Delta x \sum y = 1 \times 158.6 = 158.6$

$\mu_2 =$ the second moment of the observed value of
$\quad = \Delta x \sum xy = 1 \times 786.3 = 786.3$
$\mu_3 =$ the third moment of the observed value of y
$\quad = \Delta x \sum x^2 y = 1 \times 4206.1 = 4206.1$

Now, to find the expected values of y, the limits of integration are

$$x_1 - \frac{h}{2} \text{ to } x_n + \frac{h}{2} \quad i.e. \quad 3 - \frac{1}{2} \text{ to } 7 - \frac{1}{2} = 2.5 \text{ to } 7.5$$

Therefore, $\gamma_1 =$ the first moment of the expected value of y

$$= \int_{x_1 - \frac{h}{2}}^{x_n - \frac{h}{2}} f(x)dx = \int_{2.5}^{7.5} (a + bx + cx^2)\, dx = \left[ax + b\frac{x^2}{2} + c\frac{x^3}{3} \right]_{2.5}^{7.5}$$

$= 5a + 25b + 135.4167c$

$\gamma_2 =$ the second moment of the expected value of y

$$= \int_{x_1 - \frac{h}{2}}^{x_n - \frac{h}{2}} xf(x)dx = \int_{2.5}^{7.5} x(a + bx + cx^2)\, dx = \int_{2.5}^{7.5} (ax + bx^2 + cx^3)\, dx$$

$$= \left[a\frac{x^2}{2} + b\frac{x^3}{3} + c\frac{x^4}{4} \right]_{2.5}^{7.5} = 25a + 135.42b + 781.25c$$

$\gamma_3 =$ the third moment of the expected value of y

$$= \int_{x_1 - \frac{h}{2}}^{x_n - \frac{h}{2}} x^2 f(x)dx$$

$$= \int_{2.5}^{7.5} x^2(a + bx + cx^2)\, dx = \int_{2.5}^{7.5} (ax^2 + bx^3 + cx^4)\, dx$$

$$= \left[a\,\frac{x^3}{3} + b\,\frac{x^4}{4} + c\,\frac{x^5}{5} \right]_{2.5}^{7.5} = 135.42a + 781.25b + 4726.562c$$

The observation equations are

$$5a + 25b + 135.4167c = 158.6$$
$$25a + 135.42b + 781.25c = 786.3$$
$$135.42a + 781.25b + 4726.562c = 4206.1$$

Solving these equations, we have $a = 15.7217,\ b = 7.9427,\ c = -0.8734$.
Thus, the required equation is $y = 15.7217 + 7.9427\, x - 0.8734\, x^2$

Example 7.17 Using method of moments, fit a relation of the form $y = ab^x$ to the following data:

x:	2	3	4	5	6
y:	144	172.8	207.4	248.8	298.5

Solution: The required equation $y = ab^x$ is not linear. First we convert it into the linear form by taking logarithms on both the sides.

$$\log_{10} y = \log_{10} a + x\, \log_{10} b$$

i.e. $Y = A + xB$ where, $Y = \log_{10} y, A = \log_{10} a, B = \log_{10} b$ .... (1)

Eq. (1) is linear. The values of x are equally spaced with $\Delta x = h = 1$. Therefore, the method of moments can be used to fit the linear form (1).

Since we have to find two constants a and b, it is sufficient to find the values of first two moments

x	y	$Y = \log_{10} y$	xY
2	144	2.1584	4.3168
3	172.8	2.2375	6.7125
4	207.4	2.3168	9.2672
5	248.8	2.3959	11.9795
6	298.5	2.4749	14.8494
20		11.5835	47.1254

$\mu_1 =$ *the first moment of the observed value of y*
   $= \Delta x\ \Sigma Y = 1 \times 11.5835 = 11.5835$

$\mu_2 =$ *the second moment of the observed value of y*
   $= \Delta x\ \Sigma xY = 1 \times 47.1254 = 47.1254$

Now, to find the expected values of Y, the limits of integration are

$$x_1 - \frac{h}{2} \ \ to \ x_n + \frac{h}{2} \quad i.e. \ \ 2 - \frac{1}{2} \ \ to \ \ 6 + \frac{1}{2} = 1.5 \ to \ 6.5$$

Therefore, $\gamma_1 =$ the first moment of the expected value of y

$$= \int_{x_1-\frac{h}{2}}^{x_n-\frac{h}{2}} f(x)dx \ = \int_{1.5}^{6.5} (a+bx) \ dx \ = \left[ax + b\frac{x^2}{2} \right]_{1.5}^{6.5}$$

$$= (6.5a + 21.125b) - (1.5a + 1.125b) = 5a + 20b$$

$\gamma_2 =$ the second moment of the expected value of y

$$= \int_{x_1-\frac{h}{2}}^{x_n-\frac{h}{2}} xf(x)dx = \int_{1.5}^{6.5} x(a+bx) \ dx = \int_{1.5}^{6.5} (ax+bx^2) \ dx$$

$$= \left[a\frac{x^2}{2} + b\frac{x^3}{3} \right]_{1.5}^{6.5}$$

$$= (21.125a + 91.542b) - (1.125a + 1.125b) = 20a + 90.417b$$

The observation equations are $5a + 20b = 11.5835$

$$20a + 90.417b = 47.1254$$

Solving these equations, we have $A = \log_{10} a = 2.013 \Rightarrow a = 10^A = 103.04$, $B = \log_{10} b = 0.076 \Rightarrow b = 10^B = 1.1912$

Thus, the equation is $y = ab^x = (103.04)(1.1912)^x$

Example 7.18   Fit a curve of the form $y = ae^{bx}$ for the following data by the method of moments:

x:	1	2	3	4
y:	1.65	2.70	4.50	7.35

Solution: The required equation $y = ae^{bx}$ is not linear. First we convert it into the linear form by taking logarithms on both the sides.

$$\log_{10} y = \log_{10} a + bx \log_{10} e$$

i.e. $Y = A + xB$ where, $Y = \log_{10} y, A = \log_{10} a$, $B = b \log_{10} e$ ...... (1)

Eq. (1) is linear. The values of x are equally spaced with $\Delta x = h = 1$. Therefore, the method of moments can be used to fit the linear form (1).

Since we have to find two constants a and b, it is sufficient to find the values of first two moments

x	y	$Y = \log_{10} y$	xY
1	1.65	0.2175	0.2175
2	2.70	0.4314	0.8628
3	4.50	0.6532	1.9596
4	7.35	0.8663	3.4652
10		2.1684	6.5051

$\mu_1 = $ the first moment of the observed value of y
$= \Delta x \sum Y = 1 \times 2.1684 = 2.1684$
$\mu_2 = $ the second moment of the observed value of y
$= \Delta x \sum xY = 1 \times 6.5051 = 6.5051$

Now, to find the expected values of Y, the limits of integration are

$$x_1 - \frac{h}{2} \text{ to } x_n + \frac{h}{2} \quad i.e. \quad 1 - \frac{1}{2} \text{ to } 4 + \frac{1}{2} = 0.5 \text{ to } 4.5$$

Therefore, $\gamma_1 = $ the first moment of the expected value of y

$$= \int_{x_1-\frac{h}{2}}^{x_n-\frac{h}{2}} f(x)dx = \int_{0.5}^{4.5} (A + Bx)\, dx = \left[Ax + B\frac{x^2}{2} \right]_{0.5}^{4.5}$$

$$= (4.5A + 10.125B) - (0.5A + 0.125B) = 4A + 10B$$

$\gamma_2 = $ the second moment of the expected value of y

$$= \int_{x_1-\frac{h}{2}}^{x_n-\frac{h}{2}} xf(x)dx = \int_{0.5}^{4.5} x(A + Bx)\, dx = \int_{0.5}^{4.5} (Ax + Bx^2)\, dx$$

$$= \left[A\frac{x^2}{2} + B\frac{x^3}{3} \right]_{0.5}^{4.5} = (10.125A + 30.375B) - (0.125A + 0.0417B)$$

$$= 10A + 30.3333B$$

The observation equations are
$$4A + 10B = 2.1684$$
$$10A + 30.3333B = 6.5051$$

Solving these equations, we have $A = \log_{10} a = 0.034 \Rightarrow a = 10^A = 0.0814$,
$B = b\log_{10} e = 0.203 \Rightarrow b = \frac{B}{\log_{10} e} = \frac{0.203}{0.4343} = 0.4674$

Thus, the equation is $y = ae^{bx} = (0.0814)e^{(0.4674)x}$

7.6   APPROXIMATION OF FUNCTIONS

The approximation of a function is based on a particular class of functions like polynomials, exponential, trigonometric, rational etc. according to the requirement of an application or task. Since it is important to find a function which minimize an error in the software development process and it is more efficient and economical way to calculate the values of a function using an efficient approximation technique than to store a table of values and apply any interpolation techniques, the problem of approximating a function plays a significant role in numerical analysis.

Suppose $f_1, f_2, \ldots \ldots, f_n$ are the values of given function and $\emptyset_1, \emptyset_2, \ldots \ldots, \emptyset_n$ are the corresponding values of the approximating function. Then the error vector e is given by $e_i = f_i - \emptyset_i$. One way of choosing an approximating function is by least square method which states that the sum of the squares of deviations of the individual points from the curve i.e. errors is minimum. Other way of choosing an ideal approximating function is such that the maximum component of e is minimized.

In this section, we shall give a brief outline of Taylor's series approximation, Legendre polynomials and Chebyshev polynomials and their application in the economization of power series.

7.6.1   Taylor Series Representation

Taylor series expansion is not appropriate in computers as it is very difficult to determine a proper interval where the appoximation will be used.

If a function $f(x)$ has upto $(n + 1)$ derivatives in an interval $[a, b]$, then it may be expressed near $x = x_0$ in $[a, b]$ as

$$f(x) = f(x_0) + f'(x_0)(x - x_0) + f''(x_0)\frac{(x - x_0)^2}{2!} + f'''(x_0)\frac{(x - x_0)^3}{3!}$$

$$+ \ldots \ldots + f^n(x_0)\frac{(x - x_0)^n}{n!} + f^{n+1}(s)\frac{(x - x_0)^{n+1}}{(n + 1)!} \qquad \ldots \ldots (7.6.1)$$

where, $f'(x_0)$, $f''(x_0)$, $f'''(x_0)$ .... are the first, second, third order derivatives of $f(x)$ computed at $x = x_0$. The term

$$f^{n+1}(s)\frac{(x - x_0)^{n+1}}{(n + 1)!}$$

is called the remainder term. The term s is a number which is a function of x lies between x and x_0. The remainder term gives the truncation error if only the first n terms in the Taylor series are used to represent the function. Then the truncation error is

$$Truncation\ error = |f^{n+1}(s)| \frac{|(x - x_0)^{n+1}|}{(n + 1)!}$$

$$\leq M.\frac{|(x-x_0)^{n+1}|}{(n+1)!} \qquad where,\ M = \max |f^{n+1}(s)|\ for\ x\ in\ [a, b]. \qquad \ldots \ldots (7.6.2)$$

Example 7.19   Find the approximate value of $\cos\left(\frac{\pi}{2} + 0.2\right)$ using Taylor's series expansion.

Solution: Given that,

$$f(x) = \cos\left(\frac{\pi}{2} + x\right)$$
$$f'(x) = -\sin\left(\frac{\pi}{2} + x\right)$$
$$f''(x) = -\cos\left(\frac{\pi}{2} + x\right)$$
$$f'''(x) = \sin\left(\frac{\pi}{2} + x\right)$$

From Eq. (7.6.1), Taylor's series expansion is

$$f(x) = f(x_0) + f'(x_0)(x - x_0) + f''(x_0)\frac{(x - x_0)^2}{2!} + f'''(x_0)\frac{(x - x_0)^3}{3!}$$
$$+ \ldots \ldots$$

$$\therefore \cos\left(\frac{\pi}{2} + x\right) = \cos\left(\frac{\pi}{2} + x_0\right) + \left(-\sin\left(\frac{\pi}{2} + x_0\right)\right)(x - x_0)$$
$$+ \left(-\cos\left(\frac{\pi}{2} + x_0\right)\right)\frac{(x - x_0)^2}{2!} + \sin\left(\frac{\pi}{2} + x_0\right)\frac{(x - x_0)^3}{3!} + \ldots \ldots \ldots \ldots (1)$$

Putting $x_0 = 0$ in (1), we get

$$\cos\left(\frac{\pi}{2} + x\right) = \cos\frac{\pi}{2} - x\sin\frac{\pi}{2} - \frac{x^2}{2}\cos\frac{\pi}{2} + \frac{x^3}{6}\sin\frac{\pi}{2} + \ldots \ldots$$

$$= 0 - x - 0 + \frac{x^3}{6} + 0 - \frac{x^5}{120} + \ldots \ldots$$

$$\therefore \cos\left(\frac{\pi}{2} + 0.2\right) = -0.2 + \frac{0.2^3}{6} - \frac{0.2^5}{120} + \ldots \ldots$$

$$= -0.2 + 0.0013 - 0.0000026 + \ldots \ldots \ldots$$

$$\therefore \cos\left(\frac{\pi}{2} + 0.2\right) = -0.19866$$

7.6.2   Legendre Polynomials

The Legendre polynomial $P_n(x)$ defined on $[-1, 1]$ are given by

$$P_n(x) = \sum_{m=0}^{M}(-1)^m \frac{(2n - 2m)!\, x^{n-2m}}{2^n\, m!\, (n - m)!\, (n - 2m)!} \qquad \ldots \ldots (7.6.3)$$

where, $M = \frac{n}{2}$ or $\frac{(n-1)}{2}$ whichever is an integer.

The few Legendre polynomials are

$$P_0(x) = 1$$
$$P_1(x) = x$$
$$P_2(x) = \frac{1}{2}(3x^2 - 1)$$

$$P_3(x) = \frac{1}{2}(5x^3 - 3x)$$

$$P_4(x) = \frac{1}{8}(35x^4 - 30x^2 + 3)$$

$$P_5(x) = \frac{1}{8}(63x^5 - 70x^3 + 15x)$$

The Legendre polynomials satisfy the differential equation

$$(1 - x^2)y'' - 2xy' + n(n + 1)y = 0 \qquad \text{........ (7.6.4)}$$

The Legendre polynomials satisfy the recurrence relation

$$(2n + 1)x\, P_n(x) - nP_{n-1}(x) = (n + 1)P_{n+1}(x) \qquad \text{........ (7.6.5)}$$

Properties

1. $P_n(x)$ is an even polynomial if n is even and $P_n(x)$ is an odd polynomial if n is odd.

2. $P_n(x)$ are orthogonal polynomials (derived from Gram – Schmidt orthogonalization process) and satisfy

$$\int_{-1}^{1} P_m(x)P_n(x)\, dx = 0, \qquad m \neq n$$

$$= \frac{2}{2n + 1}, \qquad m = n$$

3. $P_n(-x) = (-1)^n P_n(x)$

7.6.3   Chebyshev Polynomials

The Chebyshev polynomial of degree n is defined by the relation

$$T_n(x) = \cos(n\cos^{-1}x) \quad where, -1 \leq x \leq 1 \qquad \text{........ (7.6.6)}$$

From which it is easily derived that $T_n(x) = T_{-n}(x)$ \qquad .... (7.6.7)

Let $\cos^{-1}x = \theta$ implies that $x = \cos\theta$. From Eq. (5.6.6), we get

$$T_n(x) = \cos n\theta \qquad \text{........ (7.6.8)}$$

Putting n = 0,1, we get $T_0(x) = \cos 0 = 1$, $T_1(x) = \cos\theta = x$

Now, Using the trigonometric formula

$$\cos(a \pm b) = \cos a.\cos b \mp \sin a.\sin b$$

For $n \geq 1$,

$$\cos(n - 1)\theta = \cos(n\theta - \theta) = \cos n\theta.\cos\theta + \sin n\theta.\sin\theta \qquad \text{........ (1)}$$

$$\cos(n + 1)\theta = \cos(n\theta + \theta) = \cos n\theta.\cos\theta - \sin n\theta.\sin\theta \qquad \text{........ (2)}$$

Using (1) and (2), we get

$$\cos(n - 1)\theta + \cos(n + 1)\theta = 2\cos n\theta.\cos\theta$$

Therefore,

$$T_{n-1}(x) + T_{n+1}(x) = 2x\, T_n(x)$$

This implies that,

$$T_{n+1}(x) = 2x\,T_n(x) - T_{n-1}(x) \qquad \text{........ (7.6.9)}$$

This is called the *triple recurrence relation* which can be used to compute successively all $T_n(x)$ since we know $T_0(x)$ and $T_1(x)$.

The first six Chebyshev polynomials are

$T_0(x) = 1$

$T_1(x) = x$

Substitute $n = 1, 2, 3, \ldots, 5$ in the Eq. (7.6.9), we get

$T_2(x) = 2x\,T_1(x) - T_0(x) = 2x(x) - 1 = 2x^2 - 1$

$T_3(x) = 2x\,T_2(x) - T_1(x) = 2x(2x^2 - 1) - x = 4x^3 - 3x$ .... (7.6.10)

$T_4(x) = 2x\,T_3(x) - T_2(x) = 2x(4x^3 - 3x) - (2x^2 - 1) = 8x^4 - 8x^2 + 1$

Similarly,

$T_5(x) = 16x^5 - 20x^3 + 5x$

$T_6(x) = 32x^6 - 48x^4 + 18x^2 - 1$

Using the Chebyshev polynomials given in Eq. (7.6.10), we can express powers of x in terms of

Chebyshev polynomials as

$$1 = T_0(x)$$

$$x = T_1(x)$$

$$x^2 = \frac{1}{2}\,[T_0(x) + T_2(x)]$$

$$x^3 = \frac{1}{4}\,[3T_1(x) + T_3(x)] \qquad \text{........ (7.6.11)}$$

$$x^4 = \frac{1}{8}\,[3T_0(x) + 4\,T_2(x) + T_4(x)]$$

$$x^5 = \frac{1}{16}\,[10T_1(x) + 5\,T_3(x) + T_5(x)]$$

$$x^6 = \frac{1}{32}\,[10T_0(x) + 15\,T_2(x) + 6\,T_4(x) + T_6(x)]$$

Also, we have

$T_n(x) = cosn\theta = real\ part\ (e^{in\theta})$

$\qquad = Rl\,(cos\theta + isin\theta)^n$

$\qquad = Rl\left[cos^n\theta + \binom{n}{1} cos^{n-1}\theta(i\,sin\theta) + \binom{n}{2} cos^{n-2}\theta\,(i\,sin\theta)^2 + \text{... ...}\right]$

$\qquad = \left[x^n + \binom{n}{2} x^{n-2}(x^2 - 1) + \binom{n}{4} x^{n-4}(x^2 - 1)^2 \text{... ...}\right]$

$\qquad = 2^{n-1}x^n + lower\ degree\ terms \qquad \text{........ (7.6.12)}$

Properties of Chebyshev Polynomials

1.   Recurrence relation

Chebyshev polynomial can be recursively defined using the following relation:

$$T_0(x) = 1, \ T_1(x) = x \text{ and } T_{n+1}(x) = 2x\,T_n(x) - T_{n-1}(x)$$

2.   Leading coefficient

The coefficient of x^n in $T_n(x)$ is always $2^{n-1} \ for \ n \ge 1$.

Proof: We can   prove this result by applying mathematical induction on definition of Chebyshev polynomial.

For n =1, $T_1(x) = x = 2^{1-1}x$

∴ The result is true for n = 1.

Let us assume that the result is true for n = k-1 and n = k

i.e $T_{k-1}(x) = 2^{(k-1)-1}\,x^{k-1} = 2^{(k-2)}\,x^{k-1}$ .... (3)

and $T_k(x) = 2^{(k-1)}\,x^k$ .... (4)

To prove the result for n = k+1.

By triple recurrence relation, $T_{k+1}(x) = 2x\,T_k(x) - T_{k-1}(x)$

From (3) and (4), we have $T_{k+1}(x) = 2x\left[2^{(k-1)}\,x^k - 2^{(k-2)}\,x^{k-1}\right]$

$$= 2^k\,x^{k+1} - 2^{(k-1)}x^k$$

$$= 2^k\,x^{k+1}\left[1 - \frac{1}{2x}\right]$$

The result is true for n = k+1.

Therefore, by mathematical induction, the result is true for $n \ge 1$.

3.   Symmetry

If n is even $T_n(x)$ is an even polynomial and if n is odd, $T_n(x)$ is an odd polynomial.

i.e. If n = 2m, $T_{2m}(-x) = T_{2m}(x)$ and for n = 2m+1,
    $T_{2m+1}(-x) = -T_{2m+1}(x)$

Proof: This property is derived by showing that $T_{2m}(x)$ involves only even powers of x and $T_{2m+1}(x)$ involves only odd powers of x. So, if we replace x by $-x$ in $T_{2m}(x)$ we get the same polynomials and in $T_{2m+1}(x)$ we get the negation of the given polynomials.

Therefore, $T_{2m}(-x) = T_{2m}(x)$ and $T_{2m+1}(-x) = -T_{2m+1}(x)$

4. Distinct zeros in [-1, 1]

$T_n(x)$ has n simple zeros $x_k = \cos(\frac{2k+1}{2n}\pi)$ for $k = 0,1,2,....,n-1$

These values are called the Chebyshev abscissas (nodes).

5. Extreme values

$T_n(x)$ assumes extreme values at $(n+1)$ points $x_k = \cos\frac{k\pi}{n}$, $k = 0,1,2,...,n$ and the extreme values at x_k is $(-1)^k$.

6. $|T_n(x)| \leq 1$ $for -1 \leq x \leq 1$

Proof: We know that by definition $T_n(x) = \cos n\theta$ and $|\cos n\theta| \leq 1$
Therefore, $|T_n(x)| \leq 1$

7. Orthogonality

$T_n(x)$ are orthogonal with respect to the weight function

$$W(x) = \frac{1}{\sqrt{1-x^2}}$$

$$\int_{-1}^{1} \frac{T_m(x)T_n(x)}{\sqrt{1-x^2}} dx = \begin{cases} 0, & m \neq n \\ \frac{\pi}{2}, & m = n \neq 0 \\ \pi, & m = n = 0 \end{cases}$$

Proof: Substitute $x = \cos\theta$, the integral becomes

$$\int_0^{\pi} T_m(\cos\theta) T_n(\cos\theta) d\theta = \int_0^{\pi} \cos m\theta.\cos n\theta \ d\theta$$

$$= \frac{1}{2}\int_0^{\pi} 2\cos m\theta \cos n\theta \ d\theta = \left[\frac{\sin(m+n)\theta}{2(m+n)} + \frac{\sin(m-n)\theta}{2(m-n)}\right]_0^{\pi}$$

$$= \begin{cases} 0, & m \neq n \\ \frac{\pi}{2}, & m = n \neq 0 \\ \pi, & m = n = 0 \end{cases}$$

8. The Chebyshev polynomial $T_n(x)$ satisfies the differential equation

$$(1-x^2)\frac{d^2y}{dx^2} - x\frac{dy}{dx} + n^2y = 0$$

Proof: We know that $y = T_n(x) = \cos n\theta$ where, $\theta = \cos^{-1}x$

$$\therefore x = \cos\theta \quad \therefore \frac{dx}{d\theta} = -\sin\theta$$

$$\therefore \frac{dy}{dx} = \frac{dy}{d\theta} \times \frac{d\theta}{dx} = \frac{-n\sin n\theta}{-\sin\theta} = \frac{n\sin n\theta}{\sin\theta}$$

$$\therefore \quad \frac{d^2y}{dx^2} = \frac{-n^2\cos n\theta \cdot \sin\theta + n\sin n\theta \cdot \cos\theta}{\sin^2\theta} = \frac{-n^2y + x\frac{dy}{dx}}{1-x^2}$$

$$\therefore \quad (1-x^2)\frac{d^2y}{dx^2} - x\frac{dy}{dx} + n^2y = 0$$

9.   Minimax property

If $P_n(x)$ is any polynomial of degree n with leading coefficient unity (monomial) and $T_n(x) = \frac{T_n(x)}{2^{n-1}}$ is the monic Chebyshev polynomial then

$$\max_{-1\le x\le 1} |T_n(x)| \le \max_{-1\le x\le 1} |P_n(x)|$$

This property is called the minimax property.

Proof: We have seen that $|T_n(x)| \le 1 \quad for -1 \le x \le 1$ .... (7.6.13)

Also, we have seen that $T_n(x)$ is a polynomial of degree n in x and that the coefficient of x^n in $T_n(x)$ is 2^{n-1}.

i.e $T_n(x) = 2^{n-1}x^n + \text{lower degree terms},\quad n \ge 1$ .... (7.6.14)

A Chebyshev polynomial whose highest degree term has a coefficient 1 is called a monic polynomial. Let $P_n(x)$ be a monic polynomial such that

$$|P_n(x)| = \frac{1}{2^{n-1}} T_n(x) = x^n + \text{lower degree terms} \quad \text{........ (7.6.15)}$$

Using Eqs. (7.6.12) and (7.6.13), we can write

$$|P_n(x)| = \frac{1}{2^{n-1}}, \quad -1 \le x \le 1 \text{ and } n \ge 1 \quad \text{... ..... (7.6.16)}$$

Eq. (7.6.15) indicates that the monic polynomial $P_n(x)$ has size $\frac{1}{2^{n-1}}$ on $-1 \le x \le 1$, and this becomes smaller as the degree n increases. In comparison,

$$\max_{-1\le x\le 1} |x^n| = 1$$

x^n is a monic polynomial whose size does not change with increasing n. Here, $P_n(x)$ is called minimax polynomial. Using this process best lower order approximation can be obtained, known as minimax approximation.

Example 7.20   Express the following as polynomials in x.

$$T_0(x) + 5T_1(x) + T_3(x)$$

Solution: Using Eq. (7.6.10)

$$T_0(x) = 1, T_1(x) = x \text{ and } T_3(x) = 4x^3 - 3x$$

Therefore,

$$T_0(x) + 5T_1(x) + T_3(x) = 1 + 5x + 4x^3 - 3x$$
$$= 1 + 2x + 4x^3$$

Example 7.21 Express the following polynomials as sum of Chebyshev polynomials. $1 + x^2 - 2x^3 + 3x^4$

Solution: Using Eq. (7.6.11)

$$1 = T_0(x), \quad x^2 = \frac{1}{2}[T_0(x) + T_2(x)], \quad x^3 = \frac{1}{4}[3T_1(x) + T_3(x)],$$

$$x^4 = \frac{1}{8}[3T_0(x) + 4T_2(x) + T_4(x)]$$

Therefore, $\quad 1 + x^2 - 2x^3 - 4x^4$

$$= T_0(x) + \frac{1}{2}[T_0(x) + T_2(x)] - \frac{2}{4}[3T_1(x) + T_3(x)]$$

$$- \frac{4}{8}[3T_0(x) + 4T_2(x) + T_4(x)]$$

$$= T_0(x) + \frac{1}{2}T_0(x) + \frac{1}{2}T_2(x) - \frac{3}{2}T_1(x) - \frac{1}{2}T_3(x) - \frac{3}{2}T_0(x) - 2T_2(x)$$

$$- \frac{1}{2}T_4(x)$$

$$= -\frac{3}{2}T_2(x) - \frac{3}{2}T_1(x) - \frac{1}{2}T_3(x) - \frac{1}{2}T_4(x)$$

$$= -\frac{1}{2}[3T_2(x) + 3T_1(x) + T_3(x) + T_4(x)$$

Chebyshev Polynomial Approximation

Let $f(x)$ be a continuous function defined on the interval $[-1, 1]$ and let $c_0 + c_1 x + c_2 x^2 + \ldots\ldots + c_n x^n$ be the required minimax or uniform polynomial approximation of $f(x)$. Let

$$\frac{a_0}{2} + \sum_{i=1}^{\infty} a_i T_i(x)$$

be the Chebyshev series expansion for $f(x)$. Then the truncated series or partial sum

$$P_n(x) = \frac{a_0}{2} + \sum_{i=1}^{n} a_i T_i(x) \qquad \ldots\ldots(7.6.17)$$

is very nearly solution to the problem

$$\max_{-1 \le x \le 1} \left| f(x) - \sum_{i=0}^{n} c_i x^i \right| = \min_{-1 \le x \le 1} \left| f(x) - \sum_{i=0}^{n} c_i x^i \right|$$

This means that the partial sum given in Eq. (7.6.17) is nearly the best uniform approximation to $f(x)$. The reason for this is as follows. Suppose we write

$$f(x) = \frac{a_0}{2} + a_1 T_1(x) + a_2 T_2(x) + \ldots\ldots + a_n T_n(x) + a_{n+1} T_{n+1}(x) + remainder \qquad \ldots\ldots(7.6.18)$$

Neglecting the remainder from Eq. (7.6.17), we get

$$f(x) - \left[\frac{a_0}{2} + \sum_{i=1}^{n} a_i\, T_i\,(x)\right] = a_{n+1}\, T_{n+1}(x) \qquad \ldots\ldots\ldots (7.6.19)$$

Since $a_{n+1}\, T_{n+1}(x)$ has $n+2$ equal maxima and minima, alternating in sign, then by Chebyshev equi-oscillation theorem, the polynomial in Eq. (7.6.17) of degree n is the best uniform approximation to $f(x)$.

Example 7.22 Find the best lower order approximation to the cubic polynomial $2x^3 + 3x^2$ using Chebyshev approximation.

Solution: From Eq. (7.6.11), we have

$$x^2 = \frac{1}{2}\,[T_0(x) + T_2(x)] \quad \text{and} \quad x^3 = \frac{1}{4}\,[3T_1(x) + T_3(x)]$$

$$\therefore\ 2x^3 + 3x^2 = 2\left(\frac{1}{4}\,[3T_1(x) + T_3(x)]\right) + 3\left(\frac{1}{2}\,[T_0(x) + T_2(x)]\right)$$

$$= \frac{3}{2}\,T_1(x) + \frac{1}{2}\,T_3(x) + \frac{3}{2}T_0(x) + \frac{3}{2}\,T_2(x)$$

Since $T_3(x)$ is a polynomial of degree 3, we approximate $f(x) = 2x^3 + 3x^2$ by $\frac{3}{2}T_0(x) + \frac{3}{2}\,T_1(x) + \frac{3}{2}\,T_2(x)$. Therefore, from Eq. (7.6.19), we have

$$f(x) - \left[\frac{a_0}{2} + \sum_{i=1}^{n} a_i\, T_i\,(x)\right] = a_{n+1}\, T_{n+1}(x)$$

$$\therefore\ (2x^3 + 3x^2) - \left(\frac{3}{2}T_0(x) + \frac{3}{2}\,T_1(x) + \frac{3}{2}\,T_2(x)\right) = \frac{1}{2}\,T_3(x)$$

The lower order approximation to the cubic $2x^3 + 3x^2$ using Chebyshev approximation is

$$\frac{3}{2}T_0(x) + \frac{3}{2}\,T_1(x) + \frac{3}{2}\,T_2(x) = \frac{3}{2}(1) + \frac{3}{2}(x) + \frac{3}{2}\,(2x^2 - 1)$$

$$= 3x^2 + \frac{3}{2}x \qquad\qquad (\because\ |T_3(x)| \le 1 \quad for - 1 \le x \le 1)$$

The error of this approximation on $[-1, 1]$ is

$$\max_{-1 \le x \le 1}\ \left|(2x^3 + 3x^2) - \left(\frac{3}{2}T_0(x) + \frac{3}{2}\,T_1(x) + \frac{3}{2}\,T_2(x)\right)\right|$$

$$= \max_{-1 \le x \le 1}\ \frac{1}{2}|\,T_3(x)| = \frac{1}{2}$$

Example 7.23 Find the best Chebyshev approximation of degree 3 or less to x^4 on $[-1,1]$.

Solution: From Eq. (7.6.11), we have

$$x^4 = \frac{1}{8}[3T_0(x) + 4T_2(x) + T_4(x)]$$

Since $T_4(x)$ is a polynomial of degree 4, we approximate $f(x) = x^4$ by $\frac{3}{8}T_0(x) + \frac{1}{2}T_2(x)$. Therefore, from Eq. (7.6.19), we have

$$f(x) - \left[\frac{a_0}{2} + \sum_{i=1}^{n} a_i T_i(x)\right] = a_{n+1} T_{n+1}(x)$$

$$\therefore \quad x^4 - \left(\frac{3}{8}T_0(x) + \frac{1}{2}T_2(x)\right) = \frac{1}{8}T_4(x)$$

The lower order approximation to the cubic x^4 using Chebyshev approximation is

$$\frac{3}{8}T_0(x) + \frac{1}{2}T_2(x) = \frac{3}{8}(1) + \frac{1}{2}(2x^2 - 1) = x^2 - \frac{1}{8}$$

The error of this approximation on $[-1, 1]$ is

$$\max_{-1 \le x \le 1} \left| x^4 - \left(\frac{3}{8}T_0(x) + \frac{1}{2}T_2(x)\right) \right| = \max_{-1 \le x \le 1} \frac{1}{8}|T_4(x)| = \frac{1}{8}$$

$$(\because |T_4(x)| \le 1 \quad for -1 \le x \le 1)$$

Lanczos Economization of Power Series

Consider the power series expansion of $f(x)$

$$f(x) = a_0 + a_1 x + a_2 x^2 + \ldots \ldots + a_n x^n \quad -1 \le x \le 1 \quad \text{........ (7.6.20)}$$

Using the relations given in Eq. (7.6.11), convert the given series into an expansion of Chebyshev polynomials. We get

$$f(x) = c_0 + c_1 T_1(x) + c_2 T_2(x) + \ldots \ldots + c_n T_n(x) \quad \text{........ (7.6.21)}$$

If large number of functions are given then expansion given in Eq. (7.6.21) converges more rapidly than the power series given by Eq. (7.6.20). If we truncate series given in Eq. (7.6.21) then the partial sum

$$P_n(x) = \sum_{i=0}^{n} c_i T_i(x) \quad \text{....... (7.6.22)}$$

is a good uniform approximation to $f(x)$ in the sense

$$\max_{-1 \le x \le 1} |f(x) - P_n(x)| \le |C_{n+1}| + |C_{n+2}| + \ldots \ldots \le \epsilon \quad \text{........ (7.6.23)}$$

For a given ϵ, it is possible to find the number of terms that should be retained in Eq. (7.6.22). This process is called *Lanczos economization of the power series*. Replacing each $T_i(x)$ in Eq. (7.6.22) by its polynomial form and rearranging the terms, we get the required economized polynomial approximation for $f(x)$.

Example 7.24 Economize the power series:

$$sinx \approx x - \frac{x^3}{6} + \frac{x^5}{120} - \frac{x^7}{5040} + \dots \dots$$

to three significant digit accuracy.

Solution: The truncated series is

$$sinx \approx x - \frac{x^3}{6} + \frac{x^5}{120} \qquad \dots \dots (1)$$

which is obtained by truncating the last term since $\frac{1}{5040} = 0.000198$ will produce a change in the fourth decimal place only. Now, we convert the powers of x in (1) into Chebyshev polynomials using the relations given in Eq. (7.6.11). We have

$$sinx \approx T_1(x) - \frac{1}{24}[3T_1(x) + T_3(x)]$$
$$+ \frac{1}{120 \times 16}[10T_1(x) + 5T_3(x) + T_5(x)]$$

After simplification, we get

$$sinx \approx \frac{169}{192} T_1(x) - \frac{5}{128} T_3(x) + \frac{1}{1920} T_5(x) \qquad \dots \dots (2)$$

Since $\frac{1}{1920} = 0.00052$ will produce a change in the fourth decimal place only, the truncated series is

$$sinx \approx \frac{169}{192} T_1(x) - \frac{5}{128} T_3(x)$$

Therefore, the economized series is given by

$$sinx \approx \frac{169}{192} x - \frac{5}{128}(4x^3 - 3x)$$
$$= \frac{383}{384} x - \frac{5}{32} x^3 = 0.9974x - 0.1526 x^3$$

Which gives $sinx$ to three significant digit accuracy.

Example 7.25 Economize the power series:

$$e^x \approx 1 + x + \frac{x^2}{2!} + \frac{x^3}{3!} + \frac{x^4}{4!} + \frac{x^5}{5!} + \dots \dots$$

using Lanczos economization with a tolerance of $\epsilon = 0.02$.

Solution: We have

$$f(x) = e^x = 1 + x + \frac{x^2}{2} + \frac{x^3}{6} + \frac{x^4}{24} + \frac{x^5}{120} + \dots \dots$$

Since $\frac{1}{120} = 0.008$, therefore

$$f(x) = e^x = 1 + x + \frac{x^2}{2} + \frac{x^3}{6} + \frac{x^4}{24} \qquad \dots \dots (1)$$

with a tolerance of $\epsilon = 0.02$.

Changing each power of x in (1) in terms of Chebyshev polynomials, we get

$$e^x = T_0(x) + T_1(x) + \frac{1}{4}[T_0(x) + T_2(x)] + \frac{1}{24}[3T_1(x) + T_3(x)] +$$
$$\frac{1}{192}[3T_0(x) + 4T_2(x) + T_4(x)]$$

$$= \frac{81}{64}T_0(x) + \frac{9}{8}T_1(x) + \frac{13}{48}T_2(x) + \frac{1}{24}T_3(x) + \frac{1}{192}T_4(x) \ \dots\dots (2)$$

We have $\frac{1}{192} = 0.005$

Since the magnitude of last term on RHS of (2) is less than 0.02.

Hence, the required economized polynomial approximation for e^x is given by

$$e^x = \frac{81}{64}T_0(x) + \frac{9}{8}T_1(x) + \frac{13}{48}T_2(x) + \frac{1}{24}T_3(x)$$

$$= \frac{x^3}{6} + \frac{13}{24}x^2 + x + \frac{191}{192}$$

7.7   PROGRAMS IN C

7.7.1   Program to fit a straight line using the method of group averages

```c
//A program to fit a straight line using the method of group averages
#include<conio.h>
#include<stdio.h>
void main()
{
        int i,N,m;
        float a,b,X[20],Y[20], x1,x2,x3,x4,sum1=0,sum2=0,sum3=0,sum4=0;
        clrscr();
        printf("\n\t::FITTING A STRAIGHT LINE USING THE METHOD OF
        GROUP AVERAGES ::");
        printf("\n\t----------------------------------------------------------");
        printf("\n\t HOW MANY NUMBER YOU WANT TO INSERT : ");
        scanf("%d",&N);
        if((N%2)==0)
        {
                m = N/2;
        }
        else
        {
                m = (N+1)/2;
        }
```

```
printf("\n\t ENTER THE VALUES OF X ::\n ");
for(i=0;i<N;i++)
{
        printf("\t\t");
        scanf("%f",&X[i]);

}
printf("\n\t ENTER THE VALUES OF Y::\n ");
for(i=0;i<N;i++)
{
        printf("\t\t");
        scanf("%f",&Y[i]);
}
for(i=0;i<m;i++)
{
        sum1 += X[i];
        sum3 += Y[i];
}
for(i=m;i<N;i++)
{
        sum2 += X[i];
        sum4 += Y[i];
}
clrscr();
printf("\n\t------------------");
printf("\n\t\t Group I ");
printf("\n\t------------------");
printf("\n\t X\tY");
printf("\n\t------------------\n");
for(i=0;i<m;i++)
{
        printf("\t%.2f\t%.2f",X[i],Y[i]);
        printf("\n");
}
printf("\n\t-----------------------\n");
printf("\t%.2f\t%.2f",sum1,sum3);
printf("\n\t---------------------");
printf("\n\t\t Group II ");
printf("\n\t---------------------");
printf("\n\t X\tY");
printf("\n\t---------------------\n");
for(i=m;i<N;i++)
{
```

```
                printf("\t%.2f\t%.2f",X[i],Y[i]);
                printf("\n");
        }
        printf("\n\t-----------------------\n");
        printf("\t%.2f\t%.2f",sum2, sum4);
        x1 = sum1/m;
        x3 = sum3/m;
        x2 = sum2/(N-m);
        x4 = sum4/(N-m);
        a = (x3-x4)/(x1-x2);
        b = x3 - x1*a;
        printf("\n\nThe values of a and b are: %f\t%f\n", a,b);
        if(b>0)
                printf("y = %fx + %f\n", a,b);
        else
                printf("y = %fx%f", a,b);
        getch();
}
```

7.7.2   Program to fit a straight line using least square method

```
//A program of straight line curve fitting
#include<conio.h>
#include<stdio.h>
#include<math.h>
#define n 20
float X[n]={0},Y[n]={0},X2[n]={0},Y2[n]={0},XY[n]={0};
void main()
{
        int i,ch,N;
        float a=0,b=0,c;
        float t_x=0,t_y=0,t_x2=0,t_y2=0,t_xy=0;
        clrscr();
        printf("\n\t\t:: FITTING A STRAIGHT LINE ::");
        printf("\n\t\t\t-----------------------------");
        printf("\n\t HOW MANY NUMBER YOU WANT TO INSERT : ");
        scanf("%d",&N);
        printf("\n\t ENTER VALUES OF X ::\n ");
        for(i=0;i<N;i++)
        {
                printf("\t\t");
                scanf("%f",&X[i]);
                t_x +=X[i];
        }
        printf("\n\t ENTER VALUES OF Y::\n ");
```

```
for(i=0;i<N;i++)
{
        printf("\t\t");
        scanf("%f",&Y[i]);
        t_y +=Y[i];
}
printf("\n\tEnter the value wich you want to find :: ");
scanf("%f",&c);
for(i=0;i<N;i++)
{
        X2[i]=X[i]*X[i];
        t_x2 +=X2[i];
        Y2[i]=Y[i]*Y[i];
        t_y2 +=Y2[i];
}
for(i=0;i<N;i++)
{
        XY[i]=X[i]*Y[i];
        t_xy +=XY[i];
}
clrscr();
printf("\n\t------------------------------------");
printf("\n\t X\t Y\t X2\t Y2\t XY");
printf("\n\t------------------------------------\n");
for(i=0;i<N;i++)
{

printf("\t%.2f\t%.2f\t%.2f\t%2.f\t%.2f",X[i],Y[i],X2[i],Y2[i],XY[i]);
        printf("\n");
}
printf("\n\t------------------------------------\n");
printf("\t%.2f\t%.2f\t%.2f\t%2.f\t%2.f",t_x, t_y,t_x2,t_y2,t_xy);
printf("\n\n\n\t\t 1. X ON Y");
printf("\n\t\t 2. Y ON X");
printf("\n\tCHOOSE ANY ONE :: ");
scanf("%d",&ch);
if(ch==2)
{
        a = ((t_y*t_x2)-(t_x*t_xy))/((N*t_x2)-(t_x*t_x));
        b = ((N*t_xy) - (t_x*t_y))/((N*t_x2) - (t_x*t_x));
        printf("\n\t\t\t:: ANSWER ::");
        printf("\n\t\t\t-----------");
        printf("\n\t\t\t a = %f",a);
```

```
                printf("\n\t\t\t b = %f",b);
                printf("\n\t\t\t x = %f",c);
                printf("\n\t\t\t y = a + bx");
                printf("\n\t\t\t y=%f+%fx",a,b);
                printf("\n\t\t\t y = %f",a+(b*c));
        }
        if(ch==1)
        {
                a = ((t_x*t_y2)-(t_y*t_xy))/((N*t_y2)-(t_y*t_y));
                b = ((N*t_xy) - (t_x*t_y))/((N*t_x2) - (t_x*t_x));
                printf("\n\t\t\t:: ANSWER ::");
                printf("\n\t\t\t-----------");
                printf("\n\t\t\t a = %f",a);
                printf("\n\t\t\t b = %f",b);
                printf("\n\t\t\t x = %f",c);
                printf("\n\t\t\t y = a + bx");
                printf("\n\t\t\t y=%f+%fx",a,b);
                printf("\n\t\t\t y = %f",a+(b*c));
        }
        getch();
}
```

7.7.3   Program to fit a geometric curve using least square method

```
//A program of curve fitting - power curve (Geometric curve)
#include<conio.h>
#include<stdio.h>
#include<math.h>
#define n 20
float X[n]={0},Y[n]={0},X2[n]={0},XY[n]={0},l_x[n]={0},l_y[n]={0};
void main()
{
        int i,N;
        float A=0,b=0,a;
        float t_x=0,t_y=0,t_x2=0,t_y2=0,t_xy=0, sum_x=0,sum_y=0;
        clrscr();
        printf("\n\t\t:: FITTING A POWER CURVE ::");
        printf("\n\t\t\t----------------------------");
        printf("\n\t HOW MANY NUMBER YOU WANT TO INSERT : ");
        scanf("%d",&N);
        printf("\n\t ENTER VALUES OF X ::\n ");
        for(i=0;i<N;i++)
        {
                printf("\t\t");
                scanf("%f",&X[i]);
```

```
            l_x[i]=log10(X[i]);

        }
        printf("\n\t ENTER VALUES OF Y::\n ");
        for(i=0;i<N;i++)
        {
                printf("\t\t");
                scanf("%f",&Y[i]);
                l_y[i]=log10(Y[i]);
        }
        for(i=0;i<N;i++)
        {
                sum_x += X[i];
                t_x += l_x[i];
                sum_y += Y[i];
                t_y += l_y[i];
                X2[i]=l_x[i]*l_x[i];
                t_x2 +=X2[i];
        }
        for(i=0;i<N;i++)
        {
                XY[i]=l_x[i]*l_y[i];
                t_xy +=XY[i];
        }
        clrscr();
        printf("\n\t---------------------------------------------");
        printf("\n\t X\t Y\t logx\t logy\t X2\t XY");
        printf("\n\t---------------------------------------------\n");
        for(i=0;i<N;i++)
        {
printf("\t%.2f\t%.2f\t%.2f\t%.2f\t%.2f\t%.2f",X[i],Y[i],l_x[i],l_y[i],X2[i],XY[i]);
                printf("\n");
        }
        printf("\n\t-----------------------------------------------------\n");
printf("\t%.2f\t%.2f\t%.2f\t%.2f\t%.2f\t%.2f",sum_x,sum_y,t_x,t_y,t_x2,t_xy);
        A = ((t_y*t_x2)-(t_x*t_xy))/((N*t_x2)-(t_x*t_x));
        b = ((N*t_xy) - (t_x*t_y))/((N*t_x2) - (t_x*t_x));
        printf("\n\n\n\t\t\t:: ANSWER ::");
        printf("\n\t\t\t------------");
        printf("\n\t\t\t A = %f",A);
        a = pow(10,A);
        printf("\n\tTherefore,\t a = %f",a);
        printf("\n\t\t\t b = %f",b);
```

```
        printf("\nThe required equation is y = %f(x)^%f", a,b);
        getch();
}
```

7.7.4   Program to fit an exponential curve using least square method

```
/A program of curve fitting - exponential curve
#include<conio.h>
#include<stdio.h>
#include<math.h>
#define n 20
float X[n]={0},Y[n]={0},X2[n]={0},XY[n]={0},l_x[n]={0},l_y[n]={0};
void main()
{
        int i,N;
        float A=0,B=0,b,a;
        float t_y=0,t_x2=0,t_y2=0,t_xy=0, sum_x=0,sum_y=0;
        clrscr();
        printf("\n\t\t:: FITTING AN EXPONENTIAL CURVE ::");
        printf("\n\t\t----------------------------");
        printf("\n\t HOW MANY NUMBER YOU WANT TO INSERT : ");
        scanf("%d",&N);
        printf("\n\t ENTER VALUES OF X ::\n ");
        for(i=0;i<N;i++)
        {
                printf("\t\t");
                scanf("%f",&X[i]);
        }
        printf("\n\t ENTER VALUES OF Y::\n ");
        for(i=0;i<N;i++)
        {
                printf("\t\t");
                scanf("%f",&Y[i]);
                l_y[i]=log10(Y[i]);
        }
        for(i=0;i<N;i++)
        {
                sum_x += X[i];
                sum_y += Y[i];
                t_y += l_y[i];
                X2[i]=X[i]*X[i];
                t_x2 +=X2[i];
        }
        for(i=0;i<N;i++)
        {
```

```
                    XY[i]=X[i]*l_y[i];
                    t_xy +=XY[i];
          }
          clrscr();
          printf("\n\t---------------------------------------------------");
          printf("\n\t X\t Y\t logy\t X2\t XY");
          printf("\n\t---------------------------------------------------\n");
          for(i=0;i<N;i++)
          {
          printf("\t%.2f\t%.2f\t%.2f\t%.2f\t%.2f",X[i],Y[i],l_y[i],X2[i],XY[i]);
                    printf("\n");
          }
          printf("\n\t----------------------------------------------------------\n");
          printf("\t%.2f\t%.2f\t%.2f\t%.2f\t%.2f",sum_x,sum_y,t_y,t_x2,t_xy);
                    A = ((t_y*t_x2)-(sum_x*t_xy))/((N*t_x2)-(sum_x*sum_x));
                    B = ((N*t_xy) - (sum_x*t_y))/((N*t_x2) - (sum_x*sum_x));
                    printf("\n\n\n\t\t\t:: ANSWER ::");
                    printf("\n\t\t\t------------");
                    printf("\n\t\t\t A = %f",A);
                    a = pow(10,A);
                    printf("\n\tTherefore,\t a = %f",a);
                    printf("\n\t\t\t B = %f",B);
                    b = pow(10,B);
                    printf("\n\tTherefore,\t b = %f",b);
                    printf("\nThe required equation is y = %f(%f)^x", a,b);
                    getch();
}
```

7.7.5 Program to fit a parabola using method of moments

```
//A program to fit a parabola using method of moments
#include<conio.h>
#include<stdio.h>
#include<math.h>
void main()
{
          int i,N,j,k;
          float a[20][20],c[20],b,X[20],Y[20], m1,m2,h;
          clrscr();
printf("\n\t::FITTING A PARABOLA USING METHOD OF MOMENTS ::");
          printf("\n\t-----------------------------------------------");
          printf("\n\t HOW MANY NUMBER YOU WANT TO INSERT : ");
          scanf("%d",&N);
          printf("Enter the initial value of x : \n");
```

```
scanf("%f", &X[0]);
printf("Enter the step size h for x : \n");
scanf("%f", &h);
for(i=1; i<N; i++)
{    X[i]= X[i-1]+ h;
}
printf("Enter the values of y : \n");
for(i=0; i<N; i++)
{    scanf("%f", &Y[i]);
}
m1 = X[0]- (h/2);
m2 = X[N-1]+ (h/2);
for(i=0;i<3;i++)
{    for(j=0;j<3;j++)
     {    a[i][j] = (pow(m2,(i+j+1))-pow(m1,(i+j+1)))/(i+j+1);
     }
}
for(i=0;i<3;i++)
{    a[i][3] = 0;
     for(j=0;j<N;j++)
     {    if(i==0)
                   a[i][3] = a[i][3]+ h*Y[j];
          else
                   a[i][3]= a[i][3]+ h*pow(X[j],i)*Y[j];
     }
}
for(k=0;k<3;k++)
{      for(i=0;i<3;i++)
       {    if(i!= k)
            {     for(j=k+1; j<4; j++)
                  {    a[i][j]= a[i][j] - ((a[i][k]*a[k][j])/a[k][k]);
                  }
            }
       }
}
for(i=0;i<3;i++)
{      c[i] = (a[i][3]/a[i][i]);
       printf("The value of c[%d] is : %f\n", i,c[i]);
}
printf("The required second degree parabola is : \n");
if(c[1] > 0 && c[2]>0)
       printf("y = %f+%fx+%fx^2\n",c[0],c[1],c[2]);
else if(c[1]<0 && c[2]<0)
```

```
                printf("y = %f%fx%fx^2\n",c[0],c[1],c[2]);
        else if(c[1]<0)
                printf("y = %f%fx%+fx^2\n",c[0],c[1],c[2]);
        else
                printf("y = %f+%fx%fx^2\n",c[0],c[1],c[2]);
        getch();
}
```

EXERCISES

1.   Multiple Choice Questions

(1)   What is the least square principal?
  - (a)   Summation of square of deviation of the given points from the actual points should be the least.
  - (b)   Square of summation of deviation of the given points from the actual points should be the least.
  - (c)   Square of summation of derivation of the given points from the actual points should be the least.
  - (d)   Summation of square of deviation of the given points from the actual points should maximum.
  - (e)   None of these

(2)   In Approximation......
  - (a)   All the data points must be on the curve
  - (b)   All data points need not be on the curve
  - (c)   All data points can be scattered
  - (d)   Data points above the curve must be same as data points below the curve
  - (e)   None of these

(3)   Which of the following method is used in curve fitting?
  - (a)   Newton's forward difference formula
  - (b)   Newton's backward difference formula
  - (c)   Newton's divided difference formula
  - (d)   Least Square method
  - (e)   None of these

(4)   The intersection point of regression line of x on y and regression line of y on x is
  - (a) $\left(\frac{\Sigma x}{n}, \frac{\Sigma y}{n}\right)$ (b) $\left(\frac{\Sigma y}{n}, \frac{\Sigma x}{n}\right)$ (c) $(\Sigma x , \Sigma y)$ (d) $\left(\frac{x}{n}, \frac{y}{n}\right)$
  - (e)   None of these

(5)   In regression line $x = a + by$, 'a' is known as
  - (a)   Slope   (b)   Intercept   (c)   Intersect
  - (d)   Addition – variable   (e)   None of these

(6)   The general equation of geometric curve is
       (a) $y = a + bx$ (b) $y = a.b^x$ (c) $y = a.x^b$
       (d) $y = a + bx + cx^2$ (e)   None of these

(7)   If the table values are given below:

x :	1	2	3	4
y :	1	4	9	16

then the intersection point of both regression lines (x on y and y on x) is
(a) (2.5, 7.5)   (b) (10, 30)   (c) (7.5, 2.5)   (d) (5, 15)
(e) None of these

Answers: (1) (a)   (2) (b)   (3) (d)   (4) (a)   (5) (b)   (6) (c)
(7) (a)

2.   Problems

Apply the method of group averages to the following problems (**1 to 13**):

(1)   The latent heat of vaporisation of steam r, is given in the following table
at different temperatures t:

t:	40	50	60	70	80	90	100	110
r:	1069.1	1063.6	1058.2	1052.7	1049.3	1041.8	1036.3	1030.8

For this range of temprature, a relation of the form $r = a + bt$ is known
to fit the data. Find the values of a and b.

(2)   Fit a straight line of the form $y = a + bx$ to the following data:

x:	0	5	10	15	20	25
y:	12	15	17	22	24	30

(3)   The relation between two quantities is given in the following table:

x:	1	2.5	4	6	8	10	12
y:	2.8	15.3	38.8	85.8	152.0	235.0	340.0

Obey the law $y = ax + bx^2$. Find the constants a and b.

(4)   Find the values of a and b in the relation $p = a + \left(\frac{b}{q}\right)$, that best fits the
following data:

x:	1	2.5	4	6	8	10	12
y:	2.8	15.3	38.8	85.8	152.0	235.0	340.0

(5)   Convert the equation $y = \frac{x}{a + bx}$ to a linear form and hence determine the
values of a and b which will best fit the following data:

x:	8	10	15	20	30	40
y:	13	14	15.4	16.3	17.2	17.8

(6)   Find a curve of the form $y = p\,x^q$, that fits the following data:

x:	0.013	0.027	0.042	0.073	0.108	0.151	0.233	0.341
y:	1.68	2.45	3.08	4.09	4.97	5.95	7.39	9.00

(7)   Fit a curve of the form $y = a\,b^x$ to the following data:

x:	2	3	4	5	6	7	8	9
y:	16	24	37	57	86	132	202	309

(8)   Fit a curve of the form $y = ax^2 + bx + c$ given

x:	10	20	30	40	50	60
y:	4.5	7.1	10.5	15.5	20.5	27.1

(9)   Fit a second degree parabola to the following data, assuming that the point (77.2, 216.3) lies on the parabola and reducing the equation into a linear form:

x:	77.2	70.0	64.3	50.7	38.2	30.1
y:	216.3	202.6	192.2	170.1	153.2	143.8

(10)   Fit a curve of the form $y = ab^x + c$ to the following data:

x:	0	1	2	3	4	5	6	7	8
y:	2.4	3.2	3.7	5.1	7.8	13.2	23.6	44.8	87.0

(11)   Fit a curve of the form $y = ax^b + c$ to the following data:

x:	0.5	1.0	1.5	2.0	2.5	3.0
y:	4.5	8.0	14.0	23.4	34.0	49.0

(12)   Fit a curve of the form $y = ax^b + c$ to the following data:

x:	0.5	1.0	2.0	4.0	8.0	12.0
y:	160	120	94	75	62	56

(13)   Fit a curve of the form $y = ae^{bx} + c$ for the following data.

x:	11	8	6	2	1
y:	10.99	11.34	11.65	12.46	12.71

By using method of least squares, fit a straight line to the following cases (**14 to 17**):

(14)

x:	1	2	3	4	5
y:	14	27	40	55	68

(15)

x:	0.5	1.0	1.5	2.0	2.5	3.0
y:	15	17	19	14	10	7

(16)

x:	2	4	6	8	10	12
y:	7.32	8.24	9.20	10.19	11.01	12.05

(17) The result of measurement of electric resistance R of a copper bar at various temperatures t °C are listed below:

t:	19	25	30	36	40	45	50
R:	76	77	79	80	82	83	85

Equation of stright line is $R = a + bt$ where, a and b are constants to be determined.

(18) Applying the method of least squares find an equation of the form $y = ax + bx^2$ that fits the following data:

x:	1	2	3	4	5	6
y:	2.6	5.4	8.7	12.1	16.0	20.2

(19) If $V(km/hr)$ and $R\ (kg/tonne)$ are related by a relation of the type $R = a + bV^2$, find by the method of least squares, a and b with the help of the following table:

V:	10	20	30	40	50
R:	8	10	15	21	30

(20) Using the method of least squares, fit a curve of the form $y = \dfrac{a}{b+x}$ to the following data

x:	30	40	50	60	70	80
y:	13.75	10.50	8.52	7.18	6.21	5.47

(21) Fit a second degree parabola of the form $y = a + bx + cx^2$ to the following data:

x:	0	10	20	30	40	50
y:	115	160	215	270	335	400

(22) Fit a parabola of the form $y = ax^2 + bx + c$ to the following data using the method of least squares.

x:	1.0	1.2	1.4	1.6	1.8	2.0
y:	0.98	1.40	1.86	2.55	2.28	3.20

(23) Fit a second degree parabola of the form $y = ax^2 + bx + c$ to the following data, taking x as the independent variable:

x:	1911	1912	1913	1914	1915
y:	10	12	8	10	14

(24) Find the gravitational constant g using the data below and the relation $d = \frac{1}{2} gt^2$, where d is distance in meters and t is the time in seconds.

t:	0.2	0.4	0.6	0.8	1.0
d:	0.1960	0.7850	1.7665	3.1405	4.9075

(**Hint:** Use the formula of exponential curve $y = ax^n$)

(25)   Fit a curve of the form $y = ax^b$, using the method of least squares, to the following data:

x:	2	4	7	10	20	40	60	80
y:	43	25	18	13	8	5	3	2

(26)   Fit a curve $y = ax^b$, using the method of least squares, to the following data:

x:	1	2	3	4	5	6
y:	2.98	4.26	5.21	6.10	6.80	7.50

(27)   The following data gives the number of students (%) passed in mathematics in a college in 8 years.

Years (x):	1988	1989	1990	1991	1992	1993	1994	1995
Student passed (%)(y):	30.5	23.2	13.9	15.3	11.3	17.1	9.6	12.9

By fitting a curve of the form $y = ab^x$ to this data estimate the percentage of the student will pass in Mathematics in the years 1996 and 1997.

(28)   Fit a curve $y = ae^{bx}$ to the following data

x:	1	2	3	4	5	6	7	8
y:	15.3	20.5	27.4	36.6	49.1	65.6	87.8	117.6

(29)   Determine the constants a and b by the method of least squares such that $y = a e^{bx}$ fits the following data.

x:	2	4	6	8	10
y:	4.077	11.084	30.128	81.897	222.62

(30)   Applying the method of least squares, fit a curve of the form $y = ab^x$ for the following data:

x:	2	3	4	5	6
y:	144	172.8	207.4	248.8	298.5

(31)   Fit a straight line and a second degree parabola to the following data. Find also the better fit.

x:	1	2	3	4	5	6
y:	18	23	29	36	40	46

(32)   Fit a straight line and the parabola of best fit to the following data and explain which is more reliable.

x:	1	2	3	4	5
y:	10	12	8	10	14

(33)   Fit a straight line of the form $y = ax + b$, to the following data by the method of moments.

x:	2	3	4	5
y:	27	40	55	68

(34)   By using the method of moments, fit a parabola to the following data:

x:	1	2	3	4
y:	1.7	1.81	2.3	3.2

(35)   Fit a curve of the form $y = a.e^{bx}$ to the following data:

x:	5	6	7	8	9	10
y:	133	55	23	7	2	2

(36)   Growth of bacteria (N) in a culture after t hrs. is given in the following table:

t :	0	1	2	3	4	5	6
N :	32	47	65	92	132	190	275

Fit a curve of the form $N = ab^t$ by the method of moments.

(37)   Obtain second degree polynomial approximation to $f(x) = (1 + x)^{1/2}$ over $[0,1]$ by means of Taylor series expansion about $x = 0$ and obtain approximate value of $\sqrt{1.05}$.

(38)   Obtain Taylor series expansion to approximate $sinx$. Using this evaluate $\sin(9.75)$.

(39)   Using Taylor series approximation find $(1.1)^{1/4}$ upto 3 decimal digits.

(40)   Expand $log_e(1 + x)$ by Taylor series about $x = 0$ up to third degree terms to obtain an approximate value of $log_e(1.2)$.

(41)   Let $f(x) = (1 - x)^{1/2}$. Using Taylor series expansion about the point $x = 0$, estimate $f(0.1)$ correct to 3 decimal places.

(42)   Find the best lower degree Chebyshev approximation to cubic polynomial $x^3 + 2x^2$.

(43)   Economize the power series:

$$sinx \approx x - \frac{x^3}{6} + \frac{x^5}{120} - \frac{x^7}{5040} + \text{... ...}$$

on the interval $[-1,1]$, allowing for a tolerance of 0.0005.

(44)   Economize the series given by

$$f(x) = 1 + \frac{1}{2}x + \frac{1}{4}x^2 + \frac{1}{16}x^3$$

Answers

(1) $a = 1090.26, b = -0.534$ (2) $y = 11.1 + 0.71x$

(3) $a = 1.24, b = 2.236$ (4) $a = 11.5253, b = 39.4658$

(5) $a = 0.2046, b = 0.0512$ (6) $y = (15.46) x^{0.51}$

(7) $y = 6.8155 (1.5272)^x$ (8) $a = 0.005, b = 0.105, c = 2.95$

(9) $y = 0.0094x^2 + 0.5319x + 119.2148$

(10) $y = 0.2992(2.07)^x + 2.26$

(11) $y = 2.8506\, x^{2.6170} + 3.4706$ (12) $y = 97.66\, x^{-0.448} + 23.4$

(13) $y = 3.1e^{1.01x} + 10$ (14) $y = 13.6x$

(15) $y = 20.2665 - 3.771x$ (16) $y = 6.37335 + 0.470714x$

(17) $R = 70.052 + 0.29t$ (18) $y = 2.41973x + 0.15589x^2$

(19) $a = 6.32, b = 0.0095$ (20) $y = \dfrac{454.5455}{3.2273 + x}$

(21) $y = 114.285 + 4.4786x + 0.025x^2$

(22) $y = -0.1875x^2 + 2.6239x - 1.4471$

(23) $y = 0.7143(x - 1913)^2 + 0.6(x - 1913) + 9.3714$

(24) $g = 9.8146\ m/sec^2$ (25) $y = 78x^{-0.8}$

(26) $y = 2.978(-0.5444)^b$ (27)   9.1%, 8.07%

(28) $y = 11.58e^{-0.2898x}$ (29) $a = 1.499, b = 0.5$

(30) $y = (100)(1.2)^x$ (31) $y = 5.6572\, x + 12.1998\ y = $ $-0.0536\ (x - 3.5)^2 + 5.6572\ (x - 3.5) + 32.1563$, parabola is a better fit

(32) $y = 0.6x + 9$, $y = 0.714\, x^2 + (-3.684)x + 13.998$, parabola is a better fit

(33) $y = 12.9375\, x + 2.2188$ (34) $y = 0.01\, x^2 + 0.45\, x + 1.09$

(35) $y = (10429.5667).\, e^{-0.8922\, x}$ (36) $N = (32.8473)(1.4168)^t$

(37) $1 + \dfrac{x}{2} - \dfrac{x^2}{8} + ...,\ 1.02468$

(38) $sinx = x - \dfrac{x^3}{3!} + \dfrac{x^5}{5!} - \dfrac{x^7}{7!} + ...,\ -0.3195$

(39)   1.0240625   (40)   0.191813846 (for x = 0.2)

(41)   0.9486875   (43) $sinx \approx \dfrac{383}{384}\, x - \dfrac{5}{32}\, x^3$

(44) $1 + \dfrac{35}{64}\, x + \dfrac{1}{4}\, x^2$

Chapter 8   Numerical Differentiation

Objectives

- To know the concept of numerical differentiation
- To enable students to obtain an intuitive and working understanding of different formulae of derivatives using Newton's forward and backward difference, Stirling's, Bessel's, Newton's divided and Lagrange's interpolation.
- To know the concept of maxima and minima of a tabulated function
- To understand the concept of partial derivatives based on finite differences
- To understand Richardson's extrapolation method

Learning Outcomes

After reading this lesson students should be able to

- Apply appropriate differentiation method successfully
- Calculate maxima and minima of a tabulated function
- Find partial derivatives based on finite differences
- Find derivatives using Richardson's extrapolation method

8.1   INTRODUCTION

If the function has a closed form like $f(x) = logx, f(x) = sinx$ etc. then several methods are available to find $\frac{dy}{dx}$ of a function in calculus. However, in many situations, it may happen that the function is not known exactly and it is defined in the tabular form only or the function is complicated then it is difficult to find the actual value of $f(x)$ but we first approximate the function by replacing $y = f(x)$ by the best interpolating polynomial $y = P(x)$. Thereafter, we differentiate this expression as many times as we desire.

The method of finding the derivative of a function using such numerical technique is called *numerical differentiation*. The choice of the interpolation formula to be used will depend on the value at which the derivative of $f(x)$ is computed. The value x may lie in the beginning or center or at the end of the series of arguments. If the values of x are equally spaced and derivative is required near the beginning or end of the table, Newton's forward or Newton's backward interpolation formula is used respectively. If the value of $\frac{dy}{dx}$ is required near the center of the table, one of the central difference interpolation formula (i.e. Stirling's or Bessel's) is used. If the values of x are not equally spaced, we use Newton's divided difference formula or Lagrange's interpolation formula for numerical differentiation.

Remark: It must be observed that the table of values does not completely define the function and the function may not be completely differentiable at all. We approximate the function $f(x_i)$ by the interpolating polynomial $P(x_i)$ but $f'(x_i)$ need not be approximately same as $P'(x_i)$ in all situations. The numerical differentiation is used only if the differences of tabulated values of $f(x)$ of some order are equal. Otherwise, in the case of finding higher order derivatives, the errors go on increasing. This is because the function $f(x_i)$ and its approximating polynomial $P(x_i)$ would agree at the set of data points but their slopes (i.e. $f'(x_i) - P'(x_i)$) at these points may differ significantly. So, numerical differentiation should be avoided if an alternative method is available.

8.2   FUNCTION TABULATED AT EQUAL INTERVALS

Consider the function $y = f(x)$ tabulated at n equally spaced values of x. Suppose the derivative is required lies near the beginning or end of the table of values and lies between the points x_0 and x_n or outside the range (x_0, x_n).

8.2.1   Derivatives Using Newton's Forward Difference Formula

Newton's forward interpolation formula is

$$y = y_0 + u\Delta y_0 + \frac{u(u-1)}{2!}\Delta^2 y_0 + \frac{u(u-1)(u-2)}{3!}\Delta^3 y_0 + \ldots\ldots (8.2.1)$$

where, $u = \frac{x - x_0}{h}$

Differentiating both sides of Eq. (8.2.1) with respect to x, we have

$$\frac{dy}{dx} = \frac{dy}{du} \cdot \frac{du}{dx}$$

Since

$$u = \frac{x - x_0}{h} \Rightarrow \frac{du}{dx} = \frac{1}{h}$$

$$\frac{dy}{dx} = \frac{1}{h}\frac{dy}{du}$$

$$= \frac{1}{h}\left\{\Delta y_0 + \frac{\Delta^2 y_0}{2!}[(u-1)+u]\right.$$

$$+ \frac{\Delta^3 y_0}{3!}[(u-1)(u-2) + u(u-2) + u(u-1)]$$

$$+ \frac{\Delta^4 y_0}{4!}[(u-1)(u-2)(u-3) + u(u-2)(u-3) + u(u-1)(u-3)$$

$$+ u(u-1)(u-2)] + \ldots\ldots\}$$

$$= \frac{1}{h}\left[\Delta y_0 + \frac{(2u-1)}{2}\Delta^2 y_0 + \frac{(3u^2 - 6u + 2)}{6}\Delta^3 y_0 \right.$$

$$+ \frac{(4u^3 - 18u^2 + 22u - 6)}{24}\Delta^4 y_0$$

$$\left. + \frac{(5u^4 - 40u^3 + 105u^2 - 100u + 24)}{120}\Delta^5 y_0 + \dots\right]$$

.... (8.2.2)

Differentiating Eq. (8.2.2) again with respect to x, we have

$$\frac{d^2 y}{dx^2} = \frac{d}{dx}\left(\frac{dy}{dx}\right) = \frac{d}{du}\left(\frac{dy}{dx}\right)\cdot\frac{du}{dx} = \frac{1}{h}\frac{d}{du}\left(\frac{dy}{dx}\right)$$

$$= \frac{1}{h^2}\left[\Delta^2 y_0 + (u-1)\Delta^3 y_0 + \frac{(6u^2 - 18u + 11)}{12}\Delta^4 y_0 \right.$$

$$\left. + \frac{(2u^3 - 12u^2 + 21u - 10)}{12}\Delta^5 y_0 + \dots\right]$$

... . (8.2.3)

Differentiating Eq. (8.2.3) again with respect to x, we have

$$\frac{d^3 y}{dx^3} = \frac{1}{h^3}\left[\Delta^3 y_0 + \frac{(12u - 18)}{12}\Delta^4 y_0 + \frac{(6u^2 - 24u + 21)}{12}\Delta^5 y_0 \right.$$

$$\left. + \dots \dots\right]$$

... . (8.2.4)

The formula obtained in Eq. (8.2.2), (8.2.3) and (8.2.4) is used to calculate first, second and third derivatives respectively at any point $x = x_k$ beginning of the table of values in terms of forward differences.

The formula will be further simplified if we want to compute the derivative at the tabulated point $x = x_0$ i.e. when $u = 0$. Substitute $u = 0$ in Eqs. (8.2.2) – (8.2.4), we get

$$\left(\frac{dy}{dx}\right)_{x=x_0} = D y_0 = \frac{1}{h}\left[\Delta y_0 - \frac{1}{2}\Delta^2 y_0 + \frac{1}{3}\Delta^3 y_0 - \frac{1}{4}\Delta^4 y_0 + \frac{1}{5}\Delta^5 y_0 \right.$$

$$\left. - \dots \dots\right]$$

... . (8.2.5)

$$\left(\frac{d^2 y}{dx^2}\right)_{x=x_0} = D^2 y_0$$

$$= \frac{1}{h^2}\left[\Delta^2 y_0 - \Delta^3 y_0 + \frac{11}{12}\Delta^4 y_0 - \frac{5}{6}\Delta^5 y_0 + \frac{137}{180}\Delta^6 y_0 \dots \dots\right]$$ .... (8.2.6)

$$\left(\frac{d^3 y}{dx^3}\right)_{x=x_0} = D^3 y_0$$

$$= \frac{1}{h^3}\left[\Delta^3 y_0 - \frac{3}{2}\Delta^4 y_0 + \frac{7}{4}\Delta^5 y_0 - \dots \dots\right]$$

.... (8.2.7)

In Chapter 5, we have derived the relations between the operators

$$1 + \Delta = E = e^{hD}$$

$$\therefore hD = \log(1 + \Delta) = \Delta - \frac{1}{2}\Delta^2 + \frac{1}{3}\Delta^3 - \frac{1}{4}\Delta^4 + \dots$$

$$\therefore D = \frac{1}{h}\left[\Delta - \frac{1}{2}\Delta^2 + \frac{1}{3}\Delta^3 - \frac{1}{4}\Delta^4 + \dots\right]$$

From this we get,

$$D^2 = \frac{1}{h^2}\left[\Delta^2 - \Delta^3 + \frac{11}{12}\Delta^4 - \frac{5}{6}\Delta^5 + \dots\right]$$

and

$$D^3 = \frac{1}{h^3}\left[\Delta^3 - \frac{3}{2}\Delta^4 + \dots\right]$$

Similarly, we can derive these formulas using operators at the tabulated point $x = x_0$ which are same as Eq. (8.2.5), (8.2.6) and (8.2.7) respectively.

Example 8.1 Compute $f'(0.2)$ and $f''(0)$ from the following tabular data.

x	0.0	0.2	0.4	0.6	0.8	1.0
$f(x)$	1.00	1.16	3.56	13.96	41.96	101.00

Solution: Since $x = 0$ *and* $x = 0.2$ are tabbular points and appear at and near beginning of the table, it is appropriate to use formulae based on Newton's forward difference to find the derivatives.

The forward difference table for the given data is

x	$f(x)$	$\Delta f(x)$	$\Delta^2 f(x)$	$\Delta^3 f(x)$	$\Delta^4 f(x)$	$\Delta^5 f(x)$
0.0	1.00	0.16	2.24	5.76	3.84	0.00
0.2	1.16	2.40	8.00	9.60	3.84	
0.4	3.56	10.40	17.60	13.44		
0.6	13.96	28.00	31.04			
0.8	41.96	59.04				
1.0	101.00					

Using forward difference formula given in Eq. (8.2.5), we have

$$\left(\frac{dy}{dx}\right)_{x=x_0} = Dy_0 = \frac{1}{h}\left[\Delta y_0 - \frac{1}{2}\Delta^2 y_0 + \frac{1}{3}\Delta^3 y_0 - \frac{1}{4}\Delta^4 y_0 + \frac{1}{5}\Delta^5 y_0 - \dots\dots\right]$$

Therefore,

$$f'(0.2) = \frac{1}{0.2}\left[2.40 - \frac{1}{2}(8.00) + \frac{1}{3}(9.60) - \frac{1}{4}(3.84)\right] = 3.2$$

Using forward difference formula given in Eq. (8.2.6), we have

$$\left(\frac{d^2y}{dx^2}\right)_{x=x_0} = D^2 y_0$$

$$= \frac{1}{h^2}\left[\Delta^2 y_0 - \Delta^3 y_0 + \frac{11}{12}\Delta^4 y_0 - \frac{5}{6}\Delta^5 y_0 + \frac{137}{180}\Delta^6 y_0 \ \dots \dots\right]$$

Hence,

$$f''(0) = \frac{1}{(0.2)^2}\left[(2.24) - (5.76) + \frac{11}{12}(3.84) - \frac{5}{6}(0.0)\right] = 0.00$$

Example 8.2 Find the value of $sec(1.11)$ from the following table:

x	1.10	1.12	1.14	1.16	1.18
$tan(x)$	1.9647	2.0659	2.1758	2.2957	2.4272

Solution: Since $\frac{d}{dx}(tanx) = sec^2 x \ and \ x = 1.11$ is not a tabbular point. Also, it appear near beginning of the table, it is appropriate to use formula based on Newton's forward difference to find the derivative.
The forward difference table for the given data is

x	$f(x)$	$\Delta f(x)$	$\Delta^2 f(x)$	$\Delta^3 f(x)$	$\Delta^4 f(x)$
1.10	1.9647	0.1012	0.0087	0.0013	0.0003
1.12	2.0659	0.1099	0.01	0.0016	
1.14	2.1758	0.1199	0.0116		
1.16	2.2957	0.1315			
1.18	2.4272				

Using forward difference formula given in Eq. (8.2.2), we have

$$\frac{d}{dx}(tanx) = sec^2 x$$

$$= \frac{1}{h}\left[\Delta y_0 + \frac{(2u-1)}{2}\Delta^2 y_0 + \frac{(3u^2-6u+2)}{6}\Delta^3 y_0 \right.$$
$$\left. + \frac{(4u^3-18u^2+22u-6)}{24}\Delta^4 y_0\right]$$

$$u = \frac{x-x_0}{h} = \frac{1.11-1.10}{0.02} = 0.5$$

$$\therefore sec^2(1.11)$$
$$= \left[0.1012 + \frac{2(0.5)-1}{2}(0.0087) + \frac{3(0.5)^2-6(0.5)+2}{6}(0.0013)\right.$$
$$\left. + \frac{4(0.5)^3-18(0.5)^2+22(0.5)-6}{24}(0.0003)\right]$$

$$= 50\left[0.1012 + 0 - 0.00005408 + 0.00001248\right] = 5.05792$$
$$\therefore sec(1.11) = 2.2489$$

8.2.2 Derivatives Using Newton's Backward Difference Formula

Newton's backward interpolation formula is

$$y = y_n + u\nabla y_n + \frac{u(u+1)}{2!}\nabla^2 y_n + \frac{u(u+1)(u+2)}{3!}\Delta^3 y_n + \ldots\ldots \quad (8.2.8)$$

where, $u = \frac{x - x_n}{h}$

Differentiating both sides of Eq. (8.2.8) with respect to x, we have

$$\frac{dy}{dx} = \frac{dy}{du} \cdot \frac{du}{dx}$$

Since

$$u = \frac{x - x_0}{h}, \qquad \frac{du}{dx} = \frac{1}{h}$$

$$\frac{dy}{dx} = \frac{1}{h}\frac{dy}{du}$$

$$= \frac{1}{h}\left\{ \nabla y_n + \frac{\nabla^2 y_n}{2!}\left[(u+1) + u\right]\right.$$

$$+ \frac{\nabla^3 y_n}{3!}\left[(u+1)(u+2) + u(u+2) + u(u+1)\right]$$

$$+ \frac{\nabla^4 y_n}{4!}\left[(u+1)(u+2)(u+3) + u(u+2)(u+3) + u(u+1)(u+3)\right.$$

$$\left.\left. + u(u+1)(u+2)\right] + \ldots\ldots\right\}$$

$$= \frac{1}{h}\left[\nabla y_n + \frac{(2u+1)}{2}\nabla^2 y_n + \frac{(3u^2 + 6u + 2)}{6}\nabla^3 y_n\right.$$

$$+ \frac{(4u^3 + 18u^2 + 22u + 6)}{24}\nabla^4 y_n$$

$$\left. + \frac{(5u^4 + 40u^3 + 105u^2 + 100u + 24)}{120}\Delta^5 y_0 + \ldots\ldots\right]$$

$$\ldots\ldots (8.2.9)$$

Differentiating Eq. (8.2.9) again with respect to x, we have

$$\frac{d^2 y}{dx^2} = \frac{d}{dx}\left(\frac{dy}{dx}\right) = \frac{d}{du}\left(\frac{dy}{dx}\right)\cdot\frac{du}{dx} = \frac{1}{h}\frac{d}{du}\left(\frac{dy}{dx}\right)$$

$$= \frac{1}{h^2}\left[\nabla^2 y_n + (u+1)\nabla^3 y_n + \frac{(6u^2 + 18u + 11)}{12}\nabla^4 y_n\right.$$

$$\left. + \frac{(2u^3 + 12u^2 + 21u + 10)}{12}\nabla^5 y_0\ldots\right] \qquad \ldots\ldots (8.2.10)$$

Differentiating Eq. (8.2.10) again with respect to x, we have

$$\frac{d^3y}{dx^3} = \frac{1}{h^3}\left[\nabla^3 y_n + \frac{(12u + 18)}{12}\nabla^4 y_n\right.$$

$$\left. + \frac{(6u^2 + 24u + 21)}{12}\Delta^5 y_0 \dots \dots\right] \qquad \dots\dots (8.2.11)$$

The formula obtained in Eq. (8.2.9), (8.2.10) and (8.2.11) is used to calculate first, second and third derivative respectively at any point $x = x_k$ near the end points of the table in terms of backward differences.

The formula will be further simplified if we want to compute the derivative at the tabulated point $x = x_n$ i.e. when $u = 0$. Substitute $u = 0$ in Eqs. (8.2.9) – (8.2.11), we get

$$\left(\frac{dy}{dx}\right)_{x=x_n} = Dy_0 = \frac{1}{h}\left[\nabla y_n + \frac{1}{2}\nabla^2 y_n + \frac{1}{3}\nabla^3 y_n + \frac{1}{4}\nabla^4 y_n + \frac{1}{5}\nabla^5 y_n\right.$$

$$\left. + \dots\dots\right] \qquad \dots\dots (8.2.12)$$

$$\left(\frac{d^2y}{dx^2}\right)_{x=x_n} = D^2 y_0$$

$$= \frac{1}{h^2}\left[\nabla^2 y_n + \nabla^3 y_n + \frac{11}{12}\nabla^4 y_n + \frac{5}{6}\nabla^5 y_n + \frac{137}{180}\nabla^6 y_n \dots\dots\right] \qquad \dots\dots (8.2.13)$$

$$\left(\frac{d^3y}{dx^3}\right)_{x=x_n} = D^3 y_0$$

$$= \frac{1}{h^3}\left[\nabla^3 y_n + \frac{3}{2}\nabla^4 y_n + \frac{7}{4}\nabla^5 y_n + \dots\dots\right] \qquad \dots\dots (8.2.14)$$

Now, we know that

$$E = e^{-hD} = \frac{1}{1 - \nabla}$$

$$\therefore -hD = \log(1 - \nabla) = -\left[\nabla + \frac{1}{2}\nabla^2 + \frac{1}{3}\nabla^3 + \frac{1}{4}\nabla^4 + \dots\right]$$

$$\therefore D = \frac{1}{h}\left[\nabla + \frac{1}{2}\nabla^2 + \frac{1}{3}\nabla^3 + \frac{1}{4}\nabla^4 + \dots\right]$$

From this we get,

$$D^2 = \frac{1}{h^2}\left[\nabla^2 + \nabla^3 + \frac{11}{12}\nabla^4 + \frac{5}{6}\nabla^5 + \dots\right]$$

and

$$D^3 = \frac{1}{h^3}\left[\nabla^3 + \frac{3}{2}\nabla^4 + \dots\right]$$

Similarly, we can derive these formulas using operators at the tabulated point $x = x_0$ which are same as Eq. (8.2.12), (8.2.13) and (8.2.14) respectively.

Example 8.3   The following data give the corresponding values of pressure and specific volume V of a superheated steam.

Volume V:	2	4	6	8	10
Pressure P:	105	42.7	25.3	16.7	13.0

Find the rate of change of pressure with respect to volume when $v = 10$. Also find $\frac{d^2y}{dx^2}$ when $v = 10$.

Solution: Since $V = 10$ appear near the end of the table, it is appropriate to use formulae based on Newton's backward difference to find the derivatives.

The backward difference table for the given data is

V	P	∇P	$\nabla^2 P$	$\nabla^3 P$	$\nabla^4 P$
2	105				
4	42.7	-62.3			
6	25.3	-17.4	44.9		
8	16.7	-8.6	8.8	-36.1	
10	13.0	-3.7	4.9	-3.9	32.2

Since $v = 10$ is a table value, using backward difference formula given in Eq. (8.2.12), we have

$$\left(\frac{dP}{dV}\right)_{v=v_n} = Dy_0 = \frac{1}{h}\left[\nabla P_n + \frac{1}{2}\nabla^2 P_n + \frac{1}{3}\nabla^3 P_n + \frac{1}{4}\nabla^4 P_n + \frac{1}{5}\nabla^5 P_n + \ldots\ldots\right]$$

$$\therefore \left(\frac{dP}{dV}\right)_{v=10} = P'(10) = \frac{1}{2}\left[-3.7 + \frac{1}{2}(4.9) + \frac{1}{3}(-3.9) + \frac{1}{4}(32.2)\right]$$

$$= 0.5[-3.7 + 2.45 - 1.3 + 8.05] = 2.75$$

$$\therefore P'(10) = 2.75$$

Now, from Eq. (8.2.13), we have

$$\left(\frac{d^2P}{dV^2}\right)_{v=v_n} = D^2y_0 = \frac{1}{h^2}\left[\nabla^2 P_n + \nabla^3 P_n + \frac{11}{12}\nabla^4 P_n\right]$$

$$\therefore \left(\frac{d^2P}{dV^2}\right)_{v=10} = P''(10) = \frac{1}{2^2}\left[4.9 - 3.9 + \frac{11}{12}(32.2)\right]$$

$$= 0.25\,[4.9 - 3.9 + 29.5166] = 7.6291$$

$$\therefore P''(10) = 7.6291$$

8.3 DERIVATIVES USING CENTRAL DIFFERENCE FORMULAE

In this section, we will study to find the derivatives using Stirling and Bessel's formulae for the point lies at the middle of the table of values and lies between the points x_0 and x_n.. We can similarly derive and use any other interpolation formula for calculating the derivatives.

8.3.1   Derivatives Using Stirling's Formula

Stirling's formula (From Eq. (6.4.7)) is

$$y = y_0 + \left(\frac{\Delta y_0 + \Delta y_{-1}}{2}\right)u + \Delta^2 y_{-1}\frac{u^2}{2!} + \frac{u(u^2 - 1^2)}{3!}\left(\frac{\Delta^3 y_{-1} + \Delta^3 y_{-2}}{2}\right)$$

$$+ \frac{u^2(u^2 - 1^2)}{4!}\Delta^4 y_{-2} + \dots \dots \dots \qquad \dots \dots \dots (8.3.1)$$

where, $u = \frac{x - x_0}{h}$

Differentiating both sides of Eq. (8.3.1) successively with respect to x and arguing as in Section 8.2.1, we have first, second and third derivatives as

$$\frac{dy}{dx}$$

$$= \frac{1}{h}\left[\begin{array}{l}\left(\frac{\Delta y_0 + \Delta y_{-1}}{2}\right) + u\Delta^2 y_{-1} + \left(\frac{3u^2 - 1}{6}\right)\left(\frac{\Delta^3 y_{-1} + \Delta^3 y_{-2}}{2}\right) \\ + \left(\frac{2u^3 - u}{12}\right)\Delta^4 y_{-2} + \frac{(5u^4 - 15u^2 + 4)}{120}\left(\frac{\Delta^5 y_{-2} + \Delta^5 y_{-3}}{2}\right) + \dots \dots\end{array}\right]$$

$$\dots \dots (8.3.2)$$

$$\frac{d^2y}{dx^2} = \frac{1}{h^2}\left[\Delta^2 y_{-1} + u.\left(\frac{\Delta^3 y_{-1} + \Delta^3 y_{-2}}{2}\right) + \left(\frac{6u^2 - 1}{12}\right)\Delta^4 y_{-2}\right.$$

$$\left. + \left(\frac{2u^3 - 3u}{12}\right)\left(\frac{\Delta^5 y_{-2} + \Delta^5 y_{-3}}{2}\right) + \cdots\right] \qquad \dots \dots (8.3.3)$$

$$\frac{d^3y}{dx^3} = \frac{1}{h^3}\left[\left(\frac{\Delta^3 y_{-1} + \Delta^3 y_{-2}}{2}\right) + u.\Delta^4 y_{-2}\right.$$

$$\left. + \left(\frac{2u^2 - 1}{4}\right)\left(\frac{\Delta^5 y_{-2} + \Delta^5 y_{-3}}{2}\right)\cdots\right] \qquad \dots \dots (8.3.4)$$

These formulae are used to find derivatives at general x for non tabular value. The formula will be further simplified if we want to compute the derivative at the tabulated point $x = x_0$ i.e. when $u = 0$. Substitute $u = 0$ in Eqs. (8.3.2) – (8.3.4), we get

$$\left(\frac{dy}{dx}\right)_{x=x_0} = \frac{1}{h}\left[\left(\frac{\Delta y_0 + \Delta y_{-1}}{2}\right) - \frac{1}{6}\left(\frac{\Delta^3 y_{-1} + \Delta^3 y_{-2}}{2}\right) + \frac{1}{30}\left(\frac{\Delta^5 y_{-2} + \Delta^5 y_{-3}}{2}\right)\right.$$
$$\left. - \dots\right] \qquad \dots\dots (8.3.5)$$

$$\left(\frac{d^2 y}{dx^2}\right)_{x=x_0} = \frac{1}{h^2}\left[\Delta^2 y_{-1} - \frac{1}{12}\Delta^4 y_{-2} + \frac{1}{90}\Delta^6 y_{-3} \dots\dots\right] \qquad \dots\dots (8.3.6)$$

$$\left(\frac{d^3 y}{dx^3}\right)_{x=x_0} = \frac{1}{h^3}\left[\left(\frac{\Delta^3 y_{-1} + \Delta^3 y_{-2}}{2}\right) + \dots\dots\right] \qquad \dots\dots (8.3.7)$$

8.3.2 Derivatives Using Bessel's Formula

Bessel's formula (From Eq. (6.4.10)) is

$$y = \left(\frac{y_0 + y_1}{2}\right) + \left(u - \frac{1}{2}\right)\Delta y_0 + \frac{u(u-1)}{2!}\left(\frac{\Delta^2 y_{-1} + \Delta^2 y_0}{2}\right)$$
$$+ \frac{\left(u - \frac{1}{2}\right)u(u-1)}{3!}\Delta^3 y_{-1} + \frac{(u+1)u(u-1)(u-2)}{4!}\left(\frac{\Delta^4 y_{-2} + \Delta^4 y_{-1}}{2}\right)$$
$$+ \dots\dots\dots \qquad \dots\dots (8.3.8)$$

where, $u = \frac{x - x_0}{h}$

Differentiating both sides of Eq. (8.3.8) successively with respect to x, we have the first, second and third derivatives as

$$\frac{dy}{dx} = \frac{1}{h}\left[\Delta y_0 + \frac{(2u-1)}{2!}\left(\frac{\Delta^2 y_{-1} + \Delta^2 y_0}{2}\right) + \frac{(3u^2 - 3u + 1/2)}{3!}\Delta^3 y_{-1}\right.$$
$$+ \frac{(4u^3 - 6u^2 - 2u + 2)}{4!}\left(\frac{\Delta^4 y_{-2} + \Delta^4 y_{-1}}{2}\right)$$
$$\left. + \frac{(5u^4 - 10u^3 + 5u - 1)}{5!}\Delta^5 y_{-2} + \dots\dots\right] \qquad \dots\dots (8.3.9)$$

$$\frac{d^2 y}{dx^2} = \frac{1}{h^2}\left[\left(\frac{\Delta^2 y_{-1} + \Delta^2 y_0}{2}\right) + \frac{(2u-1)}{2}\Delta^3 y_{-1}\right.$$
$$+ \frac{(6u^2 - 6u + 1)}{2}\left(\frac{\Delta^4 y_{-2} + \Delta^4 y_{-1}}{2}\right)$$
$$\left. + \frac{(4u^3 - 6u^2 + 1)}{24}\Delta^5 y_{-2}\right.$$
$$\left. + \dots\dots\right] \qquad \dots\dots (8.3.10)$$

$$\frac{d^3 y}{dx^3} = \frac{1}{h^3}\left[\Delta^3 y_{-1} + (6u-3)\left(\frac{\Delta^4 y_{-2} + \Delta^4 y_{-1}}{2}\right) + \dots\dots\right] \qquad \dots\dots (8.3.11)$$

These formulae are used to find derivatives at general x for non tabular value. The formula will be further simplified if we want to compute the derivative at the tabulated point $x = x_0$ i.e. when $u = 0$. Substitute $u = 0$ in Eqs. (8.3.9) – (8.3.11), we get

$$\left(\frac{dy}{dx}\right)_{x=x_0} = \frac{1}{h}\left[\Delta y_0 - \frac{1}{2}\left(\frac{\Delta^2 y_{-1} + \Delta^2 y_0}{2}\right) + \frac{1}{12}\Delta^3 y_{-1} + \frac{1}{12}\left(\frac{\Delta^4 y_{-2} + \Delta^4 y_{-1}}{2}\right)\right.$$
$$\left. - \frac{1}{120}\Delta^5 y_{-2} + \cdots\right] \qquad \ldots\ldots (8.3.12)$$

$$\left(\frac{d^2 y}{dx^2}\right)_{x=x_0} = \frac{1}{h^2}\left[\left(\frac{\Delta^2 y_{-1} + \Delta^2 y_0}{2}\right) - \frac{1}{2}\Delta^3 y_{-1} + \frac{1}{2}\left(\frac{\Delta^4 y_{-2} + \Delta^4 y_{-1}}{2}\right)\right.$$
$$\left. + \frac{1}{24}\Delta^5 y_{-2} + \cdots\right] \qquad \ldots\ldots (8.3.13)$$

$$\left(\frac{d^3 y}{dx^3}\right)_{x=x_0} = \frac{1}{h^3}\left[\Delta^3 y_{-1} - 3\left(\frac{\Delta^4 y_{-2} + \Delta^4 y_{-1}}{2}\right) + \cdots\right] \qquad \ldots\ldots (8.3.14)$$

Example 8.4 A slider in a machine moves along a fixed straight rod.Its distance x cm. along the rod is given below for various values of the time t seconds. Find the velocity of the slider and its acceleration when $t = 0.3$ second.

t:	0	0.1	0.2	0.3	0.4	0.5	0.6
x:	30.13	31.62	32.87	33.64	33.95	33.81	33.24

Solution: Since $t = 0.3$ appear near the middle of the table, we use Stirling's formulae. The central difference table for the given data is

t	x	Δx	$\Delta^2 x$	$\Delta^3 x$	$\Delta^4 x$	$\Delta^5 x$	$\Delta^6 x$
0	30.13						
		1.49					
0.1	31.62		−0.24				
		1.25		−0.24			
0.2	32.87		−0.48		0.26		
		0.77		0.02		−0.27	
0.3	33.64		−0.46		−0.01		0.29
		0.31		0.01		0.02	
0.4	33.95		−0.45		0.01		
		−0.14					
0.5	33.81		−0.43				
		−0.57					
0.6	33.24						

Since $t = 0.3$ is a table value, using Stirling's formula given in Eq. (8.3.5), we have

$$\left(\frac{dx}{dt}\right)_{t=t_0} = \frac{1}{h}\left[\left(\frac{\Delta y_0 + \Delta y_{-1}}{2}\right) - \frac{1}{6}\left(\frac{\Delta^3 y_{-1} + \Delta^3 y_{-2}}{2}\right) + \frac{1}{30}\left(\frac{\Delta^5 y_{-2} + \Delta^5 y_{-3}}{2}\right)\right.$$
$$\left. - \cdots\right]$$

$$\therefore \left(\frac{dx}{dt}\right)_{t=0.3} = \frac{1}{0.1}\left[\left(\frac{0.31+0.77}{2}\right) - \frac{1}{6}\left(\frac{0.01+0.02}{2}\right) + \frac{1}{30}\left(\frac{0.02-0.27}{2}\right)\right. \\ \left. - \cdots\right]$$

$$= 10[\, 0.54 - (0.1666)(0.015) + (0.0333)(-0.125)] = 5.3333$$

$$\therefore x'(0.3) = 5.3333$$

Now, from Eq. (8.3.6), we have

$$\left(\frac{d^2x}{dt^2}\right)_{t=t_0} = \frac{1}{h^2}\left[\Delta^2 y_{-1} - \frac{1}{12}\Delta^4 y_{-2} + \frac{1}{90}\Delta^6 y_{-3} - \cdots\cdots\right]$$

$$\therefore \left(\frac{d^2x}{dt^2}\right)_{t=0.3} = \frac{1}{(0.1)^2}\left[-0.46 - \frac{1}{12}(-0.01) + \frac{1}{90}(0.29) - \cdots\cdots\right]$$

$$= 100\,[-0.46 + 0.00083 + 0.0032] = -45.597 \qquad \therefore x''(0.3) = -45.597$$

Example 8.5 Using Bessel's formula, find the first and second derivative of $\sqrt{x}$ at $x = 17$ from the table below. Verify your result.

x:	11	13	15	17	19	21	23
$f(x)$:	3.3166	3.6055	3.8729	4.1231	4.3588	4.5825	4.7958

Solution: Since $x = 17$ appear near the middle of the table, we can use Bessel's formulae.

The central difference table for the given data is

x	$f(x)$	$\Delta f(x)$	$\Delta^2 f(x)$	$\Delta^3 f(x)$	$\Delta^4 f(x)$	$\Delta^5 f(x)$	$\Delta^6 f(x)$
11	3.3166						
		0.2889					
13	3.6055		−0.0215				
		0.2674		0.0043			
15	3.8729		−0.0172		−0.0016		
		0.2502		0.0027		0.0014	
17	4.1231		−0.0145		−0.0002		−0.002
		0.2357		0.0025		−0.0007	
19	4.3588		−0.012		−0.0009		
		0.2237		0.0016			
21	4.5825		−0.0104				
		0.2133					
23	4.7958						

Since $x = 17$ is a table value, using Bessel's formula given in Eq. (8.3.12), we have

$$\left(\frac{dy}{dx}\right)_{x=x_0} = \frac{1}{h}\left[\Delta y_0 - \frac{1}{2}\left(\frac{\Delta^2 y_{-1} + \Delta^2 y_0}{2}\right) + \frac{1}{12}\Delta^3 y_{-1} + \frac{1}{12}\left(\frac{\Delta^4 y_{-2} + \Delta^4 y_{-1}}{2}\right)\right.$$
$$\left. - \frac{1}{120}\Delta^5 y_{-2}\right]$$

$$\therefore \left(\frac{dy}{dx}\right)_{x=17} = \frac{1}{2}\left[0.2357 - \frac{1}{2}\left(\frac{(-0.0145) + (-0.012)}{2}\right) + \frac{1}{12}(0.0025)\right.$$
$$\left. + \frac{1}{12}\left(\frac{(-0.0002) + (-0.0009)}{2}\right) - \frac{1}{120}(-0.0007)\right]$$

$$= 0.5[\,0.2357 + 0.006625 + 0.000208 - 0.0000458 + 0.0000058]$$
$$= 0.1212$$

$$\therefore f'(17) = 0.1212$$

Now, from Eq. (8.3.13), we have

$$\left(\frac{d^2 y}{dx^2}\right)_{x=x_0} = \frac{1}{h^2}\left[\left(\frac{\Delta^2 y_{-1} + \Delta^2 y_0}{2}\right) - \frac{1}{2}\Delta^3 y_{-1} + \frac{1}{2}\left(\frac{\Delta^4 y_{-2} + \Delta^4 y_{-1}}{2}\right)\right.$$
$$\left. + \frac{1}{24}\Delta^5 y_{-2}\right]$$

$$\therefore \left(\frac{d^2 y}{dx^2}\right)_{x=17} = \frac{1}{(2)^2}\left[\left(\frac{(-0.0145) + (-0.012)}{2}\right) - \frac{1}{2}(0.0025)\right.$$
$$\left. + \frac{1}{2}\left(\frac{(-0.0002) + (-0.0009)}{2}\right) + \frac{1}{24}(-0.0007)\right]$$

$$= 0.25\,[-0.01325 - 0.00125 - 0.000275 - 0.000029] \quad = -0.003701$$
$$\therefore f''(17) = -0.003701$$

Verification:

$$\frac{d}{dx}\sqrt{x} = \frac{d}{dx}(x)^{1/2} = \frac{1}{2}(x)^{-1/2}$$

At the point $x = 17$, $\frac{d}{dx}\sqrt{x} = \frac{1}{2}(x)^{-1/2} = \frac{1}{2}(17)^{-1/2} = 0.1212$. Hence, the result is verified.

$$\frac{d^2}{dx^2}\sqrt{x} = \frac{d}{dx}\left(\frac{1}{2}(x)^{-\frac{1}{2}}\right) = \frac{1}{2}\cdot\left(-\frac{1}{2}\right)(x)^{-3/2}$$

Therefore, at the point $x = 17$,

$$\frac{d^2}{dx^2}\sqrt{x} = \frac{1}{2}\cdot\left(-\frac{1}{2}\right)(x)^{-3/2} = \frac{1}{2}\cdot\left(-\frac{1}{2}\right)(17)^{-3/2} = -0.003567$$

Hence, the result is verified. (There is a minor difference in the result due to truncation or rounding off error)

8.4   DERIVATIVES USING LAGRANGE'S INTERPOLATING POLYNOMIAL

For Equidistant Intervals

Let the different values of x, x_0, x_1, x_2 are equidistant with interval length h. Therefore,

$$x_i - x_{i-1} = h \quad \text{and} \quad x_i = x_0 + ih \quad i = 0,1,2,3 \quad \text{........ (8.4.1)}$$

The Lagrange's interpolating polynomial (from Eq. (6.5.2) is

$$y = f(x) = \frac{(x - x_1)(x - x_2)}{(x_0 - x_1)(x_0 - x_2)} y_0 + \frac{(x - x_0)(x - x_2)}{(x_1 - x_0)(x_1 - x_2)} y_1$$
$$+ \frac{(x - x_0)(x - x_1)}{(x_2 - x_0)(x_2 - x_1)} y_2 \quad \text{... ..... (8.4.2)}$$

In this case we have considered only three points x_0, x_1, and x_2 for computational convenience but it can be extended upto x_n. Differentiating both sides of Eq. (8.4.2) with respect to x, we get

$$f'(x) = \frac{(x - x_1) + (x - x_2)}{(x_0 - x_1)(x_0 - x_2)} y_0 + \frac{(x - x_0) + (x - x_2)}{(x_1 - x_0)(x_1 - x_2)} y_1$$
$$+ \frac{(x - x_0) + (x - x_1)}{(x_2 - x_0)(x_2 - x_1)} y_2$$

$$\therefore \ f'(x_0) = \frac{(x_0 - x_1) + (x_0 - x_2)}{(x_0 - x_1)(x_0 - x_2)} y_0 + \frac{(x_0 - x_0) + (x_0 - x_2)}{(x_1 - x_0)(x_1 - x_2)} y_1$$
$$+ \frac{(x_0 - x_0) + (x_0 - x_1)}{(x_2 - x_0)(x_2 - x_1)} y_2$$

But from Eq.(8.4.1), we have

$$x_1 - x_0 = h, \ x_2 - x_0 = 2h$$

$$\therefore \ f'(x_0) = \frac{(-h) + (-2h)}{(-h)(-2h)} y_0 + \frac{(-2h)}{(h)(-h)} y_1 + \frac{(-h)}{(2h)(h)} y_2$$

$$= \frac{-3h}{2h^2} y_0 + \frac{2h}{h^2} y_1 + \frac{-1}{2h} y_2$$

$$\therefore \ f'(x_0) = \frac{-3y_0 + 4y_1 - y_2}{2h} \quad \text{... ..... (8.4.3)}$$

which is first order formula.
Differentiating Eq. (8.4.2) twice with respect to x, we get

$$f''(x) = \frac{2}{(x_0 - x_1)(x_0 - x_2)} y_0 + \frac{2}{(x_1 - x_0)(x_1 - x_2)} y_1$$
$$+ \frac{2}{(x_2 - x_0)(x_2 - x_1)} y_2$$

$$\therefore f''(x_0) = \frac{2}{(x_0 - x_1)(x_0 - x_2)}y_0 + \frac{2}{(x_1 - x_0)(x_1 - x_2)}y_1$$
$$+ \frac{2}{(x_2 - x_0)(x_2 - x_1)}y_2$$

$$f''(x_0) = \frac{2}{(-h)(-2h)}y_0 + \frac{2}{(h)(-h)}y_1 + \frac{2}{(2h)(h)}y_2$$

$$\therefore f''(x_0) = \frac{y_0 + 2y_1 + y_2}{h^2} \qquad \qquad \dots\dots\dots (8.4.4)$$

which is second order derivative formula of Lagrange's interpolating polynomial based on three points x_0, x_1, x_2.

Now, the formula of Lagrange's interpolating polynomial based on four points x_0, x_1, x_2, x_3 is

$$y = f(x) =$$

$$\frac{(x - x_1)(x - x_2)(x - x_3)}{(x_0 - x_1)(x_0 - x_2)(x_0 - x_3)}y_0 + \frac{(x - x_0)(x - x_2)(x - x_3)}{(x_1 - x_0)(x_1 - x_2)(x_1 - x_3)}y_1$$

$$+ \frac{(x - x_0)(x - x_1)(x - x_3)}{(x_2 - x_0)(x_2 - x_1)(x_2 - x_3)}y_2 + \frac{(x - x_0)(x - x_1)(x - x_2)}{(x_3 - x_0)(x_3 - x_1)(x_3 - x_2)}y_3$$

$$\dots\dots (8.4.5)$$

Differentiating both sides of Eq. (8.4.5) with respect to x, we get

$$f'(x) = \frac{(x - x_1)(x - x_2) + (x - x_3)(x - x_1) + (x - x_3)(x - x_2)}{(x_0 - x_1)(x_0 - x_2)(x_0 - x_3)}y_0$$

$$+ \frac{(x - x_0)(x - x_2) + (x - x_3)(x - x_0) + (x - x_3)(x - x_2)}{(x_1 - x_0)(x_1 - x_2)(x_1 - x_3)}y_1$$

$$+ \frac{(x - x_0)(x - x_1) + (x - x_3)(x - x_0) + (x - x_3)(x - x_1)}{(x_2 - x_0)(x_2 - x_1)(x_2 - x_3)}y_2$$

$$+ \frac{(x - x_0)(x - x_1) + (x - x_2)(x - x_0) + (x - x_2)(x - x_1)}{(x_3 - x_0)(x_3 - x_1)(x_3 - x_2)}y_3$$

Substituting $x = x_0$ and taking $x_i - x_j = (i - j)h$, we get

$$f'(x_0) = \frac{(-h)(-2h) + (-3h)(-h) + (-3h)(-2h)}{(-h)(-2h)(-3h)}$$

$$+ \frac{0 + 0 + (-3h)(-2h)}{(h)(-h)(-2h)}y_1 + \frac{0 + 0 + (-3h)(-h)}{(2h)(h)(-h)}y_2$$

$$+ \frac{0 + 0 + (-2h)(-h)}{(3h)(2h)(h)}y_3$$

$$= \left(\frac{11h^2}{-6h^3}\right) y_0 + \left(\frac{6h^2}{2h^3}\right) y_1 + \left(\frac{3h^2}{-2h^3}\right) y_2 + \left(\frac{2h^2}{6h^3}\right) y_3$$

$$\therefore f'(x_0) = \frac{-11 y_0 + 18 y_1 - 9 y_2 + 2y_3}{6h} \qquad \dots\dots (8.4.6)$$

which is first order formula.

Differentiating Eq. (8.4.5) twice with respect to x, we get

$$f''(x) = \frac{2[(x - x_1) + (x - x_2) + (x - x_3)]}{(x_0 - x_1)(x_0 - x_2)(x_0 - x_3)} \, y_0$$

$$+ \frac{2[(x - x_0) + (x - x_2) + (x - x_3)]}{(x_1 - x_0)(x_1 - x_2)(x_1 - x_3)} \, y_1$$

$$+ \frac{2[(x - x_0) + (x - x_1) + (x - x_3)]}{(x_2 - x_0)(x_2 - x_1)(x_2 - x_3)} \, y_2$$

$$+ \frac{2[(x - x_0) + (x - x_1) + (x - x_2)]}{(x_3 - x_0)(x_3 - x_1)(x_3 - x_2)} \, y_3$$

Substituting $x = x_0$ and taking $x_i - x_j = (i - j)h$, we get

$$f''(x_0) = \frac{2[(-h) + (-2h) + (-3h)]}{(-h)(-2h)(-3h)} \, y_0 + \frac{2[0 + (-2h) + (-3h)]}{(h)(-h)(-2h)} \, y_1$$

$$+ \frac{2[0 + (-h)(-3h)]}{(2h)(h)(-h)} \, y_2 + \frac{2[0 + (-h) + (-2h)]}{(3h)(2h)(h)} \, y_3$$

$$= \left(\frac{-12h}{-6h^3}\right) y_0 + \left(\frac{-10h}{2h^3}\right) y_1 + \left(\frac{-8h}{-2h^3}\right) y_2 + \left(\frac{-6h}{6h^3}\right) y_3$$

$$= \frac{2 y_0 - 5 y_1 + 4y_2 - y_3}{h^2} \qquad \dots\dots (8.4.7)$$

which is second order derivative formula of Lagrange's interpolating polynomial based on four points x_0, x_1, x_2, x_3.

Example 8.6 Given the following values of $f(x) = e^x$, find the approximate value of $f'(1.0)$ and $f''(1.0)$, using Lagrange's interpolating polynomial.

x:	1.0	1.2	1.4	1.6
$f(x) = e^x$:	2.7183	3.3201	4.0552	4.9530

Solution: Here, interval length h = 0.2. Using first order differential formula given in Eq. (8.4.6)

$$f'(x_0) = \frac{-11 y_0 + 18 y_1 - 9 y_2 + 2y_3}{6h}$$

$$\therefore \; f'(1.0) = \frac{-11 (2.7183) + 18(3.3201) - 9(4.0552) + 2(4.9530)}{6(0.2)}$$

$$= \frac{(-29.9013) + 59.7618 - 36.4968 + 9.906}{1.2}$$

$$= \frac{3.2697}{1.2} = 2.72475$$

Using second order differential formula given in Eq. (8.4.7), we have

$$f''(x_0) = \frac{2\,y_0 - 5\,y_1 + 4y_2 - y_3}{h^2}$$

$$\therefore\ f''(1.0) = \frac{2(2.7183) - 5(3.3201) + 4(4.0552) - (4.9530)}{(0.2)^2}$$

$$= \frac{5.4366 - 16.6005 + 16.2208 - 4.9530}{0.04} = \frac{0.1039}{0.04} = 2.5975$$

8.5 FUNCTION TABULATED AT UNEQUAL INTERVALS

Consider the function $y = f(x)$ tabulated at n unequally spaced values of x. Then we may use Newton's divided difference formula or Lagrange's interpolation formula to find the value of $\frac{dy}{dx}$. Suppose the point at which the derivative is required lies between the points x_0 and x_n or outside the range (x_0, x_n).

8.5.1 Derivatives Using Newton's Divided Difference Formula

The Newton's divided difference formula (from Eq. (6.5.13) is

$$y = y_0 + \Delta_d\,y_0(x - x_0) + \Delta_d^2\,y_0\,(x - x_0)(x - x_1) + \Delta_d^3\,y_0\,(x - x_0)(x - x_1)(x - x_2) + \ldots\ldots + \Delta_d^{n-1}\,y_0\,(x - x_0)(x - x_1)\ldots\ldots(x - x_{n-1})$$

$$\ldots\ldots\ (8.5.1)$$

$$= y_0 + \Delta_d\,y_0(x - x_0) + \Delta_d^2\,y_0\,\{x^2 - (x_0 + x_1)x + x_0 x_1\}$$

$$+\Delta_d^3\,y_0\,\{x^3 - (x_0 + x_1 + x_2)\,x^2 + (x_0 x_1 + x_0 x_2 + x_1 x_2)x - x_0 x_1 x_2\}$$

$$+ \Delta_d^4\,y_0\,\{x^4 - (x_0 + x_1 + x_2 + x_3)\,x^3$$

$$+ (x_0 x_1 + x_0 x_2 + x_0 x_3 + x_1 x_2 + x_1 x_3 + x_2 x_3)x^2$$

$$- (x_0 x_1 x_2 + x_0 x_1 x_3 + x_0 x_2 x_3 + x_1 x_2 x_3)x + x_0 x_1 x_2 x_3\}$$

$$+ \ldots\ldots$$

Differentiating both sides of Eq. (8.5.1) with respect to x, we get

$$\frac{dy}{dx} = \Delta_d\,y_0 + \Delta_d^2\,y_0\{2x - (x_0 + x_1)\}$$

$$+\Delta_d^3\,y_0\,\{3x^2 - 2(x_0 + x_1 + x_2)x + (x_0 x_1 + x_0 x_2 + x_1 x_2)\} +$$

$$\Delta_d^4\,y_0\,\{4x^3 - 3(x_0 + x_1 + x_2 + x_3)x^2$$

$$+ 2(x_0 x_1 + x_0 x_2 + x_0 x_3 + x_1 x_2 + x_1 x_3 + x_2 x_3)x$$

$$- (x_0 x_1 x_2 + x_0 x_1 x_3 + x_0 x_2 x_3 + x_1 x_2 x_3)\} + \ldots\ldots \qquad \ldots\ldots\ (8.5.2)$$

$$\frac{d^2y}{dx^2} = 2\Delta_d^2\, y_0 + \{6x - 2(x_0 + x_1 + x_2)\}\,\Delta_d^3\, y_0 +$$

$$\{12x^2 - 6\,(x_0 + x_1 + x_2 + x_3)x$$
$$+ 2\,(x_0x_1 + x_0x_2 + x_0x_3 + x_1x_2 + x_1x_3 + x_2x_3\,)\}\,\Delta_d^4\, y_0$$

$$+ \text{......} \hspace{5cm} \text{......} (8.5.3)$$

$$\frac{d^3y}{dx^3} = 6\,\Delta_d^3\, y_0 + \{24x - 6\,(x_0 + x_1 + x_2 + x_3)\}\Delta_d^4\, y_0$$

$$+ \text{......} \hspace{5cm} \text{......} (8.5.4)$$

Example 8.7 Find the value of $f'(8)$ and $f''(9)$ from the following data, using an appropriate interpolation formula:

x:	4	5	7	10	11
$f(x)$:	48	100	294	900	1210

Solution: Since the values of x are not equally spaced, we can use any of the interpolation formulas meant for unequal intervals. Here, we will use Newton's divided difference formula.

The divided difference table for the given data is

x	$y = f(x)$	$\Delta_d y$	$\Delta_d^2 y$	$\Delta_d^3 y$	$\Delta_d^4 y$
4	48	$\dfrac{100-48}{5-4}=52$	$\dfrac{97-52}{7-4}=15$	$\dfrac{21-15}{10-4}=1$	$\dfrac{1-1}{11-4}=0$
5	100	$\dfrac{294-100}{7-5}=97$	$\dfrac{202-97}{10-5}=21$	$\dfrac{27-21}{11-5}=1$	
7	294	$\dfrac{900-294}{10-7}=202$	$\dfrac{310-202}{11-7}=27$		
10	900	$\dfrac{1210-900}{11-10}=310$			
11	1210				

The derivative of Newton's divided difference formula (from Eq. (8.5.2)) is

$$\frac{dy}{dx} = f'(x) = \Delta_d\, y_0 + \Delta_d^2\, y_0\{2x - (x_0 + x_1)\}$$

$$+\Delta_d^3\, y_0\,\{3x^2 - 2(x_0 + x_1 + x_2)x + (x_0x_1 + x_0x_2 + x_1x_2)\} +$$

$$\Delta_d^4 \, y_0 \, \{4x^3 - 3(x_0 + x_1 + x_2 + x_3)x^2$$
$$+ \, 2(x_0 x_1 + x_0 x_2 + x_0 x_3 + x_1 x_2 + x_1 x_3 + x_2 x_3)x$$
$$- (x_0 x_1 x_2 + x_0 x_1 x_3 + x_0 x_2 x_3 + x_1 x_2 x_3)\}$$
$$+ \, ... \, ...$$

$$\therefore f'(8) = 52 + 15\{2(8) - (4+5)\}$$
$$+ \, 1\{3(8)^2 - 2(4 + 5 + 7)(8)$$
$$+ \, [(4)(5) + (4)(7) + (5)(7)]\} + 0$$
$$= 52 + 105 + \{192 - 256 + 83\} = 52 + 105 + 19 \ = 176$$

$$\therefore f'(8) = 176$$

From Eq. (8.5.3), we have

$$\frac{d^2 y}{dx^2} = f''(x) = \ 2\Delta_d^2 \, y_0 + \{6x - 2(x_0 + x_1 + x_2)\} \Delta_d^3 \, y_0$$
$$\therefore \qquad f''(9) \ = \ 2(15) + \{6(9) - 2(4 + 5 + 7)\}(1)$$
$$= 30 + \{54 - 32\} = 30 + 22 \ = 52$$

$$\therefore f''(9) = 52$$

8.5.2 Derivatives Using Lagrange's Interpolating Polynomial

The Lagrange's interpolating polynomial (from Eq. (6.5.2) is

$$y = f(x) = \frac{(x - x_1)(x - x_2)}{(x_0 - x_1)(x_0 - x_2)} \, y_0 + \frac{(x - x_0)(x - x_2)}{(x_1 - x_0)(x_1 - x_2)} y_1$$
$$+ \, \frac{(x - x_0)(x - x_1)}{(x_2 - x_0)(x_2 - x_1)} \, y_2 \qquad\qquad ... \, ... \, (8.5.5)$$

Differentiating both sides of Eq. (8.5.5) with respect to x , we get

$$f'(x) = \frac{(x - x_1) + (x - x_2)}{(x_0 - x_1)(x_0 - x_2)} \, y_0 + \frac{(x - x_0) + (x - x_2)}{(x_1 - x_0)(x_1 - x_2)} y_1$$
$$+ \, \frac{(x - x_0) + (x - x_1)}{(x_2 - x_0)(x_2 - x_1)} \, y_2$$

$$\therefore f'(x_0) = \frac{(x_0 - x_1) + (x_0 - x_2)}{(x_0 - x_1)(x_0 - x_2)} \, y_0 + \frac{(x_0 - x_0) + (x_0 - x_2)}{(x_1 - x_0)(x_1 - x_2)} y_1$$
$$+ \, \frac{(x_0 - x_0) + (x_0 - x_1)}{(x_2 - x_0)(x_2 - x_1)} \, y_2$$

$$= \frac{(x_0 - x_1) + (x_0 - x_2)}{(x_0 - x_1)(x_0 - x_2)} \, y_0 + \frac{(x_0 - x_2)}{(x_1 - x_0)(x_1 - x_2)} y_1$$
$$+ \, \frac{(x_0 - x_1)}{(x_2 - x_0)(x_2 - x_1)} \, y_2 \qquad\qquad ... \, ... \, (8.5.6)$$

Similarly,

377 Numerical Analysis: A Programming Approach

$$f''(x) = \frac{2}{(x_0 - x_1)(x_0 - x_2)} y_0 + \frac{2}{(x_1 - x_0)(x_1 - x_2)} y_1$$
$$+ \frac{2}{(x_2 - x_0)(x_2 - x_1)} y_2$$

$$\therefore f''(x_0) = \frac{2}{(x_0 - x_1)(x_0 - x_2)} y_0 + \frac{2}{(x_1 - x_0)(x_1 - x_2)} y_1$$
$$+ \frac{2}{(x_2 - x_0)(x_2 - x_1)} y_2$$

$$\text{........ (8.5.7)}$$

Example 8.8 Find the value of cos 33° using the following data by Lagrange's interpolation formula.

x^0:	30	32	35	38
$y = \sin x^0$:	0.5	0.5299	0.5736	0.6157

Solution: Since the values of x are not equally spaced, we can use any of the interpolation formulas meant for unequal intervals.

The derivative of Lagrange's interpolating polynomial for unequally spaced values of x (from Eq. (8.5.6)) is

$$f'(x) = \frac{(x - x_1)(x - x_2) + (x - x_3)(x - x_1) + (x - x_3)(x - x_2)}{(x_0 - x_1)(x_0 - x_2)(x_0 - x_3)} y_0$$

$$+ \frac{(x - x_0)(x - x_2) + (x - x_3)(x - x_0) + (x - x_3)(x - x_2)}{(x_1 - x_0)(x_1 - x_2)(x_1 - x_3)} y_1$$

$$+ \frac{(x - x_0)(x - x_1) + (x - x_3)(x - x_0) + (x - x_3)(x - x_1)}{(x_2 - x_0)(x_2 - x_1)(x_2 - x_3)} y_2$$

$$+ \frac{(x - x_0)(x - x_1) + (x - x_2)(x - x_0) + (x - x_2)(x - x_1)}{(x_3 - x_0)(x_3 - x_1)(x_3 - x_2)} y_3$$

$$\therefore y$$
$$= \frac{(33 - 32)(33 - 35) + (33 - 38)(33 - 32) + (33 - 38)(33 - 35)}{(30 - 32)(30 - 35)(30 - 38)} (0.5)$$

$$+ \frac{(33 - 30)(33 - 35) + (33 - 38)(33 - 30) + (33 - 38)(33 - 35)}{(32 - 30)(32 - 35)(32 - 38)} (0.5299)$$

$$+ \frac{(33 - 30)(33 - 32) + (33 - 38)(33 - 30) + (33 - 38)(33 - 32)}{(35 - 30)(35 - 32)(35 - 38)} (0.5736)$$

$$+ \frac{(33 - 30)(33 - 32) + (33 - 35)(33 - 30) + (33 - 35)(33 - 32)}{(38 - 30)(38 - 32)(38 - 35)} (0.6157)$$

$$= \frac{(1)(-2) + (-5)(1) + (-5)(-2)}{(-2)(-5)(-8)} (0.5)$$

$$+ \frac{(3)(-2) + (-5)(3) + (-5)(-2)}{(2)(-3)(-6)} (0.5299)$$

$$+ \frac{(3)(1) + (-5)(3) + (-5)(1)}{(5)(3)(-3)} (0.5736)$$

$$+ \frac{(3)(1) + (-2)(3) + (-2)(1)}{(8)(6)(3)} (0.6157)$$

$$= \frac{3}{(-80)} (0.5) - \frac{11}{36} (0.5299) + \frac{17}{45} (0.5736) - \frac{5}{144} (0.6157)$$

$$= -0.01875 - 0.1619 + 0.2167 - 0.02138 = 0.01467$$

In degree, $\cos 33^0 = 0.01467 \times \frac{180}{\pi} = 0.8405$

8.6   MAXIMA AND MINIMA OF A TABULATED FUNCTION

The maximum and minimum values of a function can be obtained by equating the first derivative $\frac{dy}{dx}$ to zero and solving for x. The interpolation formula is used to find maximum or minimum value at the given point. Depending on the nature of the problem i.e. whether given tabular points are equally spaced or unequally spaced interpolation formula is used. Assuming that the given tabular points are equally spaced and the point at which the derivative is required lies near the beginning of the table. Then the derivative of Newton's forward difference formula for non – tabular value is

$$\frac{dy}{dx} = \frac{1}{h} \left[\Delta y_0 + \frac{(2u - 1)}{2} \Delta^2 y_0 + \frac{(3u^2 - 6u + 2)}{6} \Delta^3 y_0 \right.$$
$$\left. + \frac{(4u^3 - 18u^2 + 22u - 6)}{24} \Delta^4 y_0 + \dots \right]$$

But for maxima or minima $\frac{dy}{dx} = 0$

$$\Delta y_0 + \frac{(2u - 1)}{2} \Delta^2 y_0 + \frac{(3u^2 - 6u + 2)}{6} \Delta^3 y_0 + \dots = 0$$

Using the values of Δy_0, $\Delta^2 y_0$ etc. from the difference table we determine the equation in u. After solving this equation for u, we substitute the value of u and h in the equation $x = x_0 + uh$ for getting the value of x at which y is maximum.

Example 8.9   From the table below, for what value of x, y is minimum? Also find this value of y.

x:	3	4	5	6	7	8
y:	0.205	0.240	0.259	0.262	0.250	0.224

Solution: Since the values of x are equally spaced, we can use any of the interpolation formulas meant for equal intervals. Here, we use Newton's forward difference formula.

The forward difference table is

x	y	Δy	$\Delta^2 y$	$\Delta^3 y$	$\Delta^4 y$	$\Delta^5 y$
3	0.205	0.035	−0.016	0.000	0.001	−0.001
4	0.240	0.019	−0.016	0.001	0.000	
5	0.259	0.003	−0.015	0.001		
6	0.262	−0.012	−0.014			
7	0.250	−0.026				
8	0.224					

Taking $x_0 = 3, y_0 = 0.205, \ \Delta y_0 = 0.035, \Delta^2 y_0 = -0.016, \ \Delta^3 y_0 = 0$

Newton's forward difference formula is,

$$y = y_0 + \frac{\Delta y_0}{1!} u + \frac{\Delta^2 y_0}{2!} u(u-1) + \ldots + \frac{\Delta^n y_0}{n!} u(u-1)(u-2) \ldots \ldots (u-(n-1))$$

$$\therefore \ y = 0.205 + u(0.035) + \frac{u(u-1)}{2!}(-0.016) \qquad \ldots \ldots (1)$$

From Eq. (8.2.2), formula of derivative using Newton's forward interpolation formula is

$$\frac{dy}{dx} = \frac{1}{h} \left[\Delta y_0 + \frac{(2u-1)}{2} \Delta^2 y_0 + \frac{(3u^2 - 6u + 2)}{6} \Delta^3 y_0 \right]$$

$$\therefore \ \frac{dy}{dx} = \frac{1}{1} \left[0.035 + \frac{(2u-1)}{2}(-0.016) + \frac{(3u^2 - 6u + 2)}{6} (0) \right]$$

For y to be minimum, $\frac{dy}{dx} = 0$.

$$\therefore \ 0.035 - 0.008(2u - 1) = 0$$
$$\therefore \ u = 2.6875$$

Now, $x = x_0 + uh = 3 + (2.6875)(1) = 5.6875$

Hence, y is minimum at $x = 5.6875$

Substituting $u = 2.6875$ in (1), we get the minimum value of y

$$\therefore \ y = 0.205 + (2.6875)(0.035) + \frac{(2.6875)(2.6875 - 1)}{2!}(-0.016)$$
$$= 0.2628$$

Thus, minimum value of $y = 0.2628$ when $x = 5.6875$.

Remark: In these types of examples, we have to take upto the term containing $\Delta^3 y$ only, otherwise the equation $\frac{dy}{dx} = 0$ will be a higher degree equation which cannot be solved easily. If we get non linear higher degree equation then it can be solved by iterative method like False – position, Secant, Newton – Raphson etc. But in that case, the process of finding minimum or maximum value is cumbersome.

Example 8.10 Find the value of x, for which $f(x)$ is minimum in the range of x, given in the following data. Find also the minimum value of $f(x)$.

x:	2	3	4	5	6
y:	31.1875	12.0275	2.8655	3.7052	14.5440

Solution: From the table of values, it is seen that the minimum value of $f(x)$ occurs near $x = 4$, which lies in the middle of the table. Hence, we take $x_0 = 4$ and use Stirling's formula to obtain $\frac{dy}{dx}$.

The central difference table is

x	y	Δy	$\Delta^2 y$	$\Delta^3 y$	$\Delta^4 y$
2	31.1875				
		-19.16			
3	12.0275		9.998		
		-9.162		0.0037	
4	2.8655		10.0017		-0.0063
		0.8397		-0.0026	
5	3.7052		9.9991		
		10.8388			
6	14.5440				

By Stirling's formula, we have

$$\frac{dy}{dx} = \frac{1}{h}\left[\left(\frac{\Delta y_0 + \Delta y_{-1}}{2}\right) + u\Delta^2 y_{-1} + \left(\frac{3u^2 - 1}{6}\right)\left(\frac{\Delta^3 y_{-1} + \Delta^3 y_{-2}}{2}\right)\right]$$

where, $u = \frac{x - x_0}{h}$

$$\therefore \frac{dy}{dx} = \frac{1}{1}\left[\left(\frac{0.8397 - 9.162}{2}\right) + 10.0017u \right.$$
$$\left. + \left(\frac{3u^2 - 1}{6}\right)\left(\frac{-0.0026 + 0.0037}{2}\right)\right]$$

For y to be minimum, $\frac{dy}{dx} = 0$.

$$\therefore \ -4.16115 + 10.0017u + 0.00009167(3u^2 - 1) = 0$$

i.e. $-4.16115 + 10.0017u + 0.00027501\,u^2 - 0.00009167 = 0$

i.e. $0.00027501\,u^2 + 10.0017u - 4.16124167 = 0$

$$\therefore u = \frac{-10.0017 \pm \sqrt{10.0017^2 + 4(0.00027501)(4.16124167)}}{2 \times 0.00027501}$$

$$= \frac{-10.0017 \pm \sqrt{100.03858}}{0.00055002} = \frac{-10.0017 \pm 10.001929}{0.00055002}$$

$$= -36368.91 \quad or \quad 0.4163$$

Since $u = -36368.91$ is beyond the range, $u = 0.4163$

Now, $x = x_0 + uh = 4 + (0.4163)(1) = 4.4163$

Hence, $f(x)$ is minimum at $x = 4.4163$

Stirling's formula (From Eq. (6.4.7)) is

$$y = y_0 + \left(\frac{\Delta y_0 + \Delta y_{-1}}{2}\right)u + \Delta^2 y_{-1}\frac{u^2}{2!}$$
$$+ \frac{u(u^2 - 1^2)}{3!}\left(\frac{\Delta^3 y_{-1} + \Delta^3 y_{-2}}{2}\right) \qquad \dots\dots(1)$$

Substituting $u = 0.4163$ in (1), we get the minimum value of $f(x)$

$$\therefore f(x) = 2.8655 + \left(\frac{0.8397 - 9.162}{2}\right)(0.4163) + 10.0017\frac{(0.4163)^2}{2!}$$
$$+ \frac{0.4163(0.4163^2 - 1^2)}{3!}\left(\frac{-0.0026 + 0.0037}{2}\right)$$

$$= 2.8655 - 1.7323 + 0.86667 - 0.00003155 = 1.9998$$

Thus, $f(x)$ is minimum at $x = 4.4163$ and the minimum value of $f(x) = 1.9998$.

8.7   PARTIAL DERIVATIVES

In chapter 5, we have already proved that

$$D = \frac{1}{h}\left[\Delta - \frac{1}{2}\Delta^2 + \frac{1}{3}\Delta^3 - \frac{1}{4}\Delta^4 + \dots\right] \qquad \dots\dots(8.7.1)$$

$$D = \frac{1}{h}\left[\nabla + \frac{1}{2}\nabla^2 + \frac{1}{3}\nabla^3 + \frac{1}{4}\nabla^4 + \dots\right] \qquad \dots\dots(8.7.2)$$

Also, from Eq. (5.5.14) we have proved that $\mu = \sqrt{1 + \frac{1}{4}\delta^2}$ and we have the result $\delta = 2\sinh\left(\frac{hD}{2}\right)$. Combining these two results, we have

$$D = \frac{1}{h}\frac{\mu}{\sqrt{1 + \frac{1}{4}\delta^2}} \cdot \left(2\sin h^{-1}\frac{\delta}{2}\right)$$

$$= \frac{1}{h} \mu \left(1 + \frac{1}{4}\delta^2\right)^{-\frac{1}{2}} \cdot \left(\delta - \frac{1^2}{2^2 \cdot 3!}\delta^3 + \dots \dots \right)$$

$$= \frac{1}{h} \mu \left(1 - \frac{1}{8}\delta^2 + \frac{3}{8}\delta^4 - \dots \dots \right) \cdot \left(\delta - \frac{1^2}{2^2 \cdot 3!}\delta^3 + \dots \dots \right)$$

$$= \frac{1}{h} \mu \left(\delta - \frac{1^2}{3!}\delta^3 + \frac{1^2 \cdot 2^2}{5!}\delta^5 - \dots \dots \right) \qquad \dots \dots (8.7.3)$$

Using Eqs. (8.7.1) – (8.7.3), we get

$$f'(x_k) = Df_k = \frac{1}{h}\left(\Delta f_k - \frac{1}{2}\Delta^2 f_k + \frac{1}{3}\Delta^3 f_k - \frac{1}{4}\Delta^4 f_k + \frac{1}{5}\Delta^5 f_k\right.$$
$$\left. - \dots \right) \qquad \dots \dots (8.7.4)$$

$$f'(x_k) = Df_k = \frac{1}{h}\left(\nabla f_k + \frac{1}{2}\nabla^2 f_k + \frac{1}{3}\nabla^3 f_k + \frac{1}{4}\nabla^4 f_k + \frac{1}{5}\nabla^5 f_k\right.$$
$$\left. + \dots \right) \qquad \dots \dots (8.7.5)$$

$$f'(x_k) = Df_k = \frac{1}{h}\mu\left(\delta f_k - \frac{1^2}{3!}\delta^3 f_k + \frac{1^2 2^2}{5!}\delta^5 f_k - \frac{1^2 2^2 3^2}{7!}\delta^7 f_k\right.$$
$$\left. + \dots \right) \qquad \dots \dots (8.7.6)$$

where $f_k = f(x_k)$. Keeping only first term of Eqs. (8.7.4) – (8.7.6), we get

$$f'(x_k) = \frac{1}{h}\Delta f_k = \frac{f_{k+1} - f_k}{h} \qquad \dots \dots (8.7.7)$$

$$f'(x_k) = \frac{1}{h}\nabla f_k = \frac{f_k - f_{k-1}}{h} \qquad \dots \dots (8.7.8)$$

$$f'(x_k) = \frac{1}{h}\mu\delta f_k = \frac{f_{k+1} - f_{k-1}}{2h} \qquad \dots \dots (8.7.9)$$

Similarly,

$$f''(x_k) = \frac{1}{h}\Delta f'_k = \frac{1}{h^2}(\Delta f_{k+1} - \Delta f_k) = \frac{f_{k+2} - 2f_{k+1} + f_k}{h^2} \quad \dots (8.7.10)$$

$$f''(x_k) = \frac{1}{h}\nabla f'_k = \frac{1}{h^2}(\nabla f_k - \nabla f_{k-1}) = \frac{f_k - 2f_{k-1} + f_{k-2}}{h^2} \quad (8.7.11)$$

$$f''(x_k) = D^2 f_k = \frac{1}{h}D\left[2\sin h^{-1}\left(\frac{\delta}{2}\right)f_k\right]$$

$$= \frac{1}{h}D\left[\delta - \frac{1^2}{2^2 \cdot 3!}\delta^3 + \dots \dots \right]f_k$$

$$= \frac{1}{h^2}\left[\delta - \frac{1^2}{2^2 \cdot 3!}\delta^3 + \dots \dots \right]^2 f_k$$

Again, keeping only the first term, we get

$$f''(x_k) \approx \frac{1}{h^2}\, \delta^2 f_k = \frac{1}{h^2}\left(E^{\frac{1}{2}} - E^{-\frac{1}{2}}\right)^2 f_k \qquad \left(\because \delta = E^{\frac{1}{2}} - E^{-\frac{1}{2}}\right)$$

$$= \frac{1}{h^2}\,(E - 2 + E^{-1})\, f_k = \frac{f_{k+1} - 2f_k + f_{k-1}}{h^2} \qquad \ldots\ldots (8.7.12)$$

Let $f(x,y)$ be a function of two variables. Substitute $f(x_i, y_j) = f_{i,j}$. $x_i = x_0 + ih$ and $y_i = y_0 + jk$ where, h and k are step – sizes for x and y respectively. Then the approximate values for the partial derivatives of $f(x,y)$ are

$$\left(\frac{\partial f}{\partial x}\right)_{(x_i, y_j)} = \begin{cases} \dfrac{f_{i+1,j} - f_{i,j}}{h} \\[2mm] \dfrac{f_{i,j} - f_{i-1,j}}{h} \\[2mm] \dfrac{f_{i+1,j} - f_{i-1,j}}{2h} \end{cases}, \quad \left(\frac{\partial f}{\partial y}\right)_{(x_i, y_j)} = \begin{cases} \dfrac{f_{i,j+1} - f_{i,j}}{k} \\[2mm] \dfrac{f_{i,j} - f_{i,j-1}}{k} \\[2mm] \dfrac{f_{i,j+1} - f_{i,j-1}}{2k} \end{cases}$$

$$\left(\frac{\partial^2 f}{\partial x^2}\right)_{(x_i, y_j)} = \frac{f_{i+1,j} - 2f_{i,j} + f_{i-1,j}}{h^2}, \quad \left(\frac{\partial^2 f}{\partial y^2}\right)_{(x_i, y_j)} = \frac{f_{i,j+1} - 2f_{i,j} + f_{i,j-1}}{k^2}$$

$$\left(\frac{\partial^2 f}{\partial x\, \partial y}\right)_{(x_i, y_j)} = \frac{\partial}{\partial x}\left(\frac{\partial f}{\partial y}\right)_{(x_i, y_j)} = \frac{\partial}{\partial x}\left[\frac{f_{i,j+1} - f_{i,j-1}}{2k}\right]$$

$$= \frac{1}{2k}\left[\frac{f_{i+1,j+1} - f_{i-1,j+1}}{2h} - \frac{f_{i+1,j-1} - f_{i-1,j-1}}{2h}\right]$$

$$= \frac{f_{i+1,j+1} - f_{i-1,j+1} - f_{i+1,j-1} + f_{i-1,j-1}}{4hk}$$

8.8 RICHARDSON'S EXTRAPOLATION METHOD

In Richardson's extrapolation method, we combine two computed approximate values of $y'(x)$ using the same method or formula but with two different step sizes usually h and $h/2$ to obtain better approximation of the quantity. Also, using this method we can obtain higher order formula from a lower order formula and hence, improving the accuracy of estimates.

Consider Eqs. (8.7.7), (8.7.8) and (8.7.9) as a crude approximation for $f'(x_k)$. Let us consider

$$f'(x_0) = \frac{f_1 - f_{-1}}{2h} = \frac{1}{2h}\left[f(x_0 + h) - f(x_0 - h)\right]$$

$$= \frac{1}{2h}\left[\left\{f(x_0) + \frac{f'(x_0)}{1!}h + \frac{f''(x_0)}{2!}h^2 + \frac{f'''(x_0)}{3!}h^3 + \ldots\ldots\right\}\right.$$

$$\left. - \left\{f(x_0) - \frac{f'(x_0)}{1!}h + \frac{f''(x_0)}{2!}h^2 - \frac{f'''(x_0)}{3!}h^3 + \ldots\ldots\right\}\right]$$

$$= f'(x_0) + \frac{f'''(x_0)}{3!}h^3 + \frac{f^v(x_0)}{3!}h^4 + \ldots\ldots = g(h)$$

where, $\qquad g(h) = f'(x_0) + c_1 x^2 + c_2 x^4 + c_3 x^6 + \ldots\ldots \qquad\qquad \ldots\ldots (8.8.1)$

$g(h)$ is an approximation of $f'(x_0)$ with step size h.

A closer approximation of $f'(x_0)$ is obtained by changing the step size as $h/2$.
From Eq. (8.8.1), we have

$$g\left(\frac{h}{2}\right) = f'(x_0) + \frac{c_1 h^2}{4} + \frac{c_2 h^4}{16} + \frac{c_3 h^6}{64} + \ldots\ldots \qquad\qquad \ldots\ldots (8.8.2)$$

Eliminating c_1 from Eqs. (8.8.1) and (8.8.2), we have

$$4g\left(\frac{h}{2}\right) - g(h) = 3f'(x_0) - \frac{3}{4}c_2 h^4 - \frac{15}{16} c_3 h^6 - \ldots\ldots$$

or we can write this equation as

$$\frac{4g\left(\frac{h}{2}\right) - g(h)}{3} = f'(x_0) - \frac{1}{4}c_2 h^4 - \frac{5}{16} c_3 h^6 - \ldots\ldots$$

Putting $LHS = g^{(1)}(h)$, we get

$$g^{(1)}(h) = f'(x_0) - \frac{1}{4} c_2 h^4 - \frac{5}{16} c_3 h^6 - \ldots\ldots \qquad\qquad \ldots\ldots (8.8.3)$$

Then $g^{(1)}(h)$ is a closer approximation of $f'(x_0)$.
Now,

$$g^{(1)}\left(\frac{h}{2}\right) = f'(x_0) - \frac{1}{64} c_2 h^4 - \frac{5}{1024} c_3 h^6 - \ldots\ldots \qquad\qquad \ldots\ldots (8.8.4)$$

Eliminating c_2 from Eqs. (8.8.3) and (8.8.4), we have

$$16 g^{(1)}\left(\frac{h}{2}\right) - g^{(1)}(h) = 15 f'(x_0) + \frac{15}{64} c_3 h^6 + \ldots\ldots$$

or we can write this equation as

$$\frac{4^2 g^{(1)}\left(\frac{h}{2}\right) - g^{(1)}(h)}{4^2 - 1} = f'(x_0) + \frac{1}{64} c_3 h^6 + \ldots\ldots$$

Putting $LHS = g^{(2)}(h)$, we get

$$g^{(2)}(h) = f'(x_0) + \frac{1}{64} c_3 h^6 + \ldots\ldots \qquad\qquad \ldots\ldots (8.8.5)$$

$g^{(2)}(h)$ is a more closer approximation of $f'(x_0)$. The successive closer approximations of $f'(x_0)$ are obtained by

$$g^{(i)}(h) = \frac{4^i \, g^{(i-1)}\left(\frac{h}{2}\right) - g^{(i-1)}(h)}{4^i - 1}, \qquad i = 1, 2, \ldots\ldots \qquad\qquad \ldots\ldots (8.8.6)$$

where, $g^{(0)}(h) = g(h)$

The successive values of $g^{(i)}(h), i = 0,1,2,3, ...$ is given in the following Table 8.1.

Table 8.1

Step size i⟶	0	1	2	3
h	$g(h)$			
		$g^{(1)}(h)$		
$h/2$	$g(h/2)$		$g^{(2)}(h)$	
		$g^{(1)}(h/2)$		$g^{(3)}(h)$
$h/2^2$	$g(h/2^2)$		$g^{(2)}(h/2)$	
		$g^{(1)}(h/2^2)$		
$h/2^3$	$g(h/2^3)$			

Example 8.11 Find the values of $f'(0), f'(4)$ and $f'(8)$ from the following data using appropriate initial values based on finite differences and Richardson's extrapolation method.

x:	0	1	2	3	4	5	6	7	8
$y = f(x)$:	-5	-2	7	34	91	190	343	562	859

Solution: For computing $f'(0), f'(4)$ and $f'(8)$ we use approximate formulas of the forward, central and backward difference operators respectively.

For $x_0 = 0$, $g(h) = f'(0) = f'(x_0) = \frac{f_1 - f_0}{h}$

For $x_0 = 4$, $g(h) = f'(4) = f'(x_0) = \frac{f_1 - f_{-1}}{2h}$

For $x_0 = 8$, $g(h) = f'(8) = f'(x_0) = \frac{f_0 - f_{-1}}{h}$

The extrapolation table for $f'(0)$ is as follows:

Step size	$g(h)$	$g^{(1)}(h)$	$g^{(2)}(h)$	$g^{(3)}(h)$
8	$\frac{859-(-5)}{8}=108$			
		$\frac{2g(4)-g(8)}{2-1}=-60$		
4	$\frac{91-(-5)}{4}=24$		$\frac{4g^{(1)}(4)-g^{(1)}(8)}{4-1}=4$	
		$\frac{2g(2)-g(4)}{2-1}=-10$		4
2	$\frac{7-(-5)}{2}=6$		$\frac{4g^{(1)}(2)-g^{(1)}(4)}{4-1}=4$	
		$\frac{2g(1)-g(2)}{2-1}=0$		
1	$\frac{-2-(-5)}{1}=3$			

Therefore, $f'(0) = g^{(3)}(8) = 4$

Here, $g^{(2)}(8) = g^{(2)}(4) = g^{(3)}(8) = 4$. So, the value of $f'(0)$ is exactly 4.

The extrapolation table for $f'(4)$ is as follows:

Step size	$g(h)$	$g^{(1)}(h)$	$g^{(2)}(h)$
4	$\dfrac{859-(-5)}{8} = 108$		
		$\dfrac{4g(2)-g(4)}{4-1} = 76$	
2	$\dfrac{343-7}{4} = 84$		$\dfrac{16g^{(1)}(2)-g^{(1)}(4)}{16-1} = 76$
		$\dfrac{4g(1)-g(2)}{4-1} = 76$	
1	$\dfrac{190-34}{2} = 78$		

Therefore, $f'(4) = g^{(2)}(4) = 76$

The extrapolation table for $f'(8)$ is as follows:

Step size	$g(h)$	$g^{(1)}(h)$	$g^{(2)}(h)$	$g^{(3)}(h)$
8	$\dfrac{859-(-5)}{8} = 108$			
		$\dfrac{2g(4)-g(8)}{2-1} = 276$		
4	$\dfrac{859-91}{4} = 192$		$\dfrac{4g^{(1)}(4)-g^{(1)}(8)}{4-1} = 340$	
		$\dfrac{2g(2)-g(4)}{2-1} = 324$		340
2	$\dfrac{859-343}{2} = 258$		$\dfrac{4g^{(1)}(2)-g^{(1)}(4)}{4-1} = 340$	
		$\dfrac{2g(1)-g(2)}{2-1} = 336$		
1	$\dfrac{859-562}{1} = 297$			

Therefore, $f'(8) = g^{(3)}(8) = 340$

8.9 PROGRAMS IN C

8.9.1 Program to find derivative using Newton's forward interpolation formula

```c
//Differentiation using Newton's forward interpolation formula
//This program will give accurate value if entered value of x at which
differentiation is required lies in upper half of the table
#include<stdio.h>
#include<conio.h>
int fact(int);
void main()
{
        int n,k=-1,i,j,p,m,q;
        double product,res1;
        float x[10],y[10],d[10][10],sum,sum1,res,h,u,x1;
        clrscr();
printf("Differentiation using Newton's forward interpolation formula\n");
        printf("ENTER THE NUMBER OF POINTS : ");
        scanf("%d",&n);
        printf("\nENTER THE VALUES OF x and y :\n\nX   Y\n------------\n");
        for(i=1;i<=n;i++)
        {
                scanf("%f %f",&x[i],&y[i]);
        }
printf("\nENTER THE VALUE OF X AT WHICH DIFFERENTIATION IS REQUIRED : ");
        scanf("%f",&x1);
        for(i=0;i<n;i++)
        {
                if(x[i]>x1)
                {
                        k=i-1;
                        break;
                }
        }
        if(k==-1)
                k=n;
        h=x[2]-x[1];
        u=(x1-x[k])/h;
        for(i=1;i<=n-k;i++)
        {
                for(j=1;j<=n-i;j++)
                {
                        if(i==1)
                                d[i][j]=y[j+1]-y[j];
```

```
                        else
                                d[i][j]=d[i-1][j+1]-d[i-1][j];
                }
        }
        res1=d[1][k];
        for(j=2;j<=n-k;j++)
        {
                res=0;
                sum=0;
                for(p=0;p<=j-1;p++)
                {
                        product=1;
                        for(m=0;m<=j-1;m++)
                        {
                                if(m!=p)
                                        product*=(u-m);
                        }
                        sum+=product;
                }
                res+=sum;
                res1+=(res*d[j][k]/fact(j));
        }
        printf("\t\tTHE ANSWER IS : %f",res1/h);
        res1=d[2][k];
        for(j=3;j<=n-k;j++)
        {
                res=0;
                sum=0;
                for(p=0;p<=j-1;p++)
                {
                        sum1=0;
                        for(m=0;m<=j-1;m++)
                        {
                                if(m!=p)
                                {
                                        product=1;
                                        for(q=0;q<=j-1;q++)
                                        {
                                                if(q!=m && q!=p)
                                                        product*=(u-q);
                                        }
                                        sum1+=product;
                                }
                        }
```

```
                }
                        sum+=sum1;
                }
                res+=sum;
                res1+=(res*d[j][k])/fact(j);
        }
        printf("\n\t\tTHE ACCELERATION IS :%f",res1/(h*h));
        getch();
}
int fact(int y)
{
        int fv=1,j;
        for(j=1;j<=y;j++)
                fv=fv*j;
        return(fv);
}
```

8.9.2   Program to find derivative using Newton's backward interpolation formula

```
// Differentiation using Newton's backward interpolation formula.
//This program will give accurate value if entered value of x at which
differentiation is required lies in lower half of the table
#include<stdio.h>
#include<conio.h>
int fact(int);
void main()
{
        int n,k=-1,i,j,p,m,q;
        double product,res1;
        float x[10],y[10],d[10][10],sum,sum1,res,h,u,x1;
        clrscr();
printf("Differentiation using Newton's backward interpolation formula\n");
        printf("ENTER THE NUMBER OF POINTS : ");
        scanf("%d",&n);
        printf("\nENTER THE VALUES OF x and y :\n\nX    Y\n------------\n");
        for(i=1;i<=n;i++)
        {
                scanf("%f %f",&x[i],&y[i]);
        }
printf("\nENTER THE VALUE OF X AT WHICH DIFFERENTIATION IS REQUIRED : ");
        scanf("%f",&x1);
        for(i=1;i<=n;i++)
        {
                if(x1>=x[i] && x1<=x[i+1])
                {
```

```
                              k=i+1;
                              break;
                }
        }
        if(k==-1)
                k=n;
        h=x[2]-x[1];
        u=(x1-x[k])/h;
        for(i=1;i<=n-1;i++)
        {
                for(j=i+1;j<=n;j++)
                {
                        if(i==1)
                                d[i][j]=y[j]-y[j-1];
                        else
                                d[i][j]=d[i-1][j]-d[i-1][j-1];
                }
        }
        res1=d[1][k];
        for(j=2;j<=k-1;j++)
        {
                res=0;
                sum=0;
                for(p=0;p<=j-1;p++)
                {
                        product=1;
                        for(m=0;m<=j-1;m++)
                        {
                                if(m!=p)
                                        product*=(u+m);
                        }
                        sum+=product;
                }
                res+=sum;
                res1+=(res*d[j][k]/fact(j));
        }
        printf("\t\tTHE ANSWER IS : %f",res1/h);
        res1=d[2][k];
        for(j=3;j<=k-1;j++)
        {
                res=0;
                sum=0;
                for(p=0;p<=j-1;p++)
```

```
                {
                        sum1=0;
                        for(m=0;m<=j-1;m++)
                        {
                                if(m!=p)
                                {
                                        product=1;
                                        for(q=0;q<=j-1;q++)
                                        {
                                                if(q!=m && q!=p)
                                                product*=(u+q);
                                        }
                                        sum1+=product;
                                }
                        }
                sum+=sum1;
                }
                res+=sum;
                res1+=(res*d[j][k])/fact(j);
        }
        printf("\n\t\tTHE ACCELERATION IS  :%f",res1/(h*h));
        getch();
}
int fact(int y)
{
        int fv=1,j;
        for(j=1;j<=y;j++)
                fv=fv*j;
        return(fv);
}
```

8.9.3   Program to find derivative using Newton's divided difference formula

```
// Differentiation using Newton's divided difference formula.
#include<stdio.h>
#include<conio.h>
void main()
{
        int n,k=1,i,j,f,m,p,q;
        double product =1;
        float x[10],y[10],d[10][10],sum,sum1,mul,x1,res,res1,h;
        printf("ENTER THE NUMBER OF POINTS : ");
        scanf("%d", &n);
        printf("\nENTER THE VALUE OF X AND Y :\n");
```

```
        for(i=1;i<=n;i++)
                scanf("%f %f", &x[i], &y[i]);
printf("ENTER THE VALUE OF X AT WHICH INTERPOLATION IS REQUIRED : ");
        scanf("%f", &x1);
        for(i=1;i<=n-1;i++)
        {
                for(j=1;j<=n-i;j++)
                {
                        if(i==1)
                                d[i][j]=(y[j+1]-y[j])/(x[j+1]-x[j]);
                        else
                                d[i][j]=(d[i-1][j+1]-d[i-1][j])/(x[i+j]-x[j]);
                }
        }
        res1=d[1][k];
        for(j=2;j<=n-k;j++)
        {
                res=0;
                sum=0;
                for(m=0;m<=j-1;m++)
                {
                        product=1;
                        for(p=0;p<=j-1;p++)
                        {
                                if(p!=m)
                                        product*=(x1-x[k+p]);
                        }
                        sum+=product;
                }
                res+=sum;
                res1+=(res*d[j][k]);
        }
        printf("THE FIRST ORDER DERIVATIVE IS : %3.2f", res1);
        res1=d[2][k]*2;
        for(j=3;j<=n-k;j++)
        {
                res=0;
                sum=0;
                for(p=0;p<=j-1;p++)
                {
                        sum1=0;
                        for(m=0;m<=j-1;m++)
                        {
```

```
                        if(m!=p)
                        {
                                product=1;
                                for(q=0;q<=j-1;q++)
                                {
                                        if(q!=m && q!=p)
                                                product*=(x1-x[k+q]);
                                }
                                sum1+=product;
                        }
                }
                sum+=sum1;
        }
        res+=sum;
        res1+=(res*d[j][k]);
    }
    printf("\nTHE SECOND ORDER DERIVATIVE IS : %3.2f", res1);
    getch();
}
```

EXERCISES

1.   Multiple Choice Questions

(1)   If distance is given, to find velocity, which of the following is used?
(a)   Derivative (single)   (b)   Derivative (double)   (c)
Integration(single)
(d)   Least Square   (e)   None of these

(2)   If acceleration is given, to find distance, which of the following is used?
(a)   Derivative (single)   (b)   Derivative (double)
(c)   Integration(single)   (d)   Least Square   (e)   None of these

(3)   If acceleration is given, to find velocity, which of the following is used?
(a)   Derivative (single)   (b)   Derivative (double)
(c)   Integration(single)   (d)   Least Square   (e)   None of these

(4)   If the interval length of the given set of tabulated points is unequal then in
differentiation which of the following methods will be used?
(a)   Newton's forward difference
(b)   Newton's backward difference
(c)   Newton's divided difference
(d)   None of these

(5)   The maximum and minimum values of a function can be obtained by equating the _____ derivative to zero and solving for x.

   (a) Second   (b) First   (c) First and Second   (d) None of these

(6)   In the comparison of differentiation and integration, differentiation is
   (a)   Reliable   (b) Not so reliable   (c)   Accurate
   (d)   All of these   (e)   None of these

Answers: (1) (a)   (2) (e)   (3) (c)   (4) (c)   (5) (b)   (6) (b)

2.   Problems

(1)   From the following table of values of x and y, obtain $\frac{dy}{dx}$ and $\frac{d^2y}{dx^2}$ for $x = 1.2$

x	1.0	1.2	1.4	1.6	1.8	2.0	2.2
y	2.7183	3.3201	4.0552	4.9530	6.0496	7.3891	9.0250

(2)   Find $f'(x)$ at $x = 1.5$ using the following table:

x:	1.5	2.0	2.5	3.0	3.5	4.0
$f(x)$:	3.375	7.000	13.625	24.000	38.875	59.000

(3)   Find the value of $\cos(1.74)$ from the following table:

x:	1.7	1.74	1.78	1.82	1.86
$sinx$:	0.9916	0.9857	0.9781	0.9691	0.9584

(4)   Find the values of $\frac{dy}{dx}$ and $\frac{d^2y}{dx^2}$ at $x = 1.1$, from the following data, using Newton's forward difference formula:

x:	1.0	1.2	1.4	1.6	1.8	2.0
y:	0	0.128	0.544	1.296	2.432	4

(5)   The following data gives corresponding values of pressure and specific volume of a super heated steam.

v:	2	4	6	8	10
p:	105	42.7	25.3	16.7	13

   Find the rate of change of pressure with respect to volume when $v = 2$

(6)   Compute the values of $y'(0.02)$ and $y''(0.02)$ for the function $y = f(x)$ given by the following table values:

x:	0.0	0.05	0.10	0.15	0.20	0.25
y:	0.00	0.10017	0.20134	0.30452	0.41075	0.52110

(7)   Find the second derivatives of the function $f(x)$ tabulated below at the points $x = 2.0$ and $x = 3.5$, using Newton's backward interpolation formula

x:	1.5	2.0	2.5	3.0	3.5	4.0
$f(x)$:	3.375	7.000	13.625	24.000	38.875	59.000

(8)   Find the first two derivatives of $\sqrt[3]{x}$ at $x = 56$ given the table below

x:	50	51	52	53	54	55	56
$y = \sqrt[3]{x}$:	3.6840	3.7084	3.7325	3.7563	3.7798	3.8030	3.8259

(9)   The specific heats of silica glass at various temperature are as follows:

x (°C)	100	200	300	400	500
s (in calories	0.2372	0.2416	0.2460	0.2504	0.2545
per °C per gram					

Find the rate of change of specific heat with respect to temperature at 120 °C and at 450 °C using Newton's backward interpolation formula.

(10)   From the following values of x and y, find $\frac{dy}{dx}$ when $x = 6$

x	4.5	5.0	5.5	6.0	6.5	7.0	7.5
y	9.69	12.90	16.71	21.18	26.37	32.34	39.15

(11)   A rod is rotating in a plane. The following table gives the angle θ (radians) through which the rod has turned for various values of the time t second:

t:	0	0.2	0.4	0.6	0.8	1.0	1.2
θ:	0	0.12	0.49	1.12	2.02	3.20	4.67

Calculate the angular velocity and the angular acceleration of the rod, when $t = 0.6$ second.

(12)   Compute $f'(8)$, $f''(8)$, $f'(0.82)$ and $f''(0.82)$ using Stirling's formula, from the table given below:

x:	0.4	0.6	0.8	1.0	1.2
$y = f(x)$:	1.08107	1.18546	1.33743	1.54308	1.81066

(13)   Use the Stirling's interpolation formula to obtain the result:

$$\frac{d}{dx}[f(x)] = \frac{2}{3}[f(x+1) - f(x-1)] - \frac{1}{12}[f(x+2) - f(x-2)]$$

(14)   Find the values of $f'(0.48)$, $f'(0.5)$ and $f'(0.53)$ from the following data using the Stirling formula.

x:	0.35	0.40	0.45	0.50	0.55	0.60	0.65
$y = f(x)$:	1.521	1.506	1.488	1.467	1.444	1.418	1.389

(15) y is a function of x satisfying the differential equation $xy'' + ay' + (x - b)y = 0$, where a and b are known to be integers. Find the constants a and b from the table below:

x:	0.8	1.0	1.2	1.4	1.6	1.8	2.0	2.2
y:	1.73036	1.95532	2.19756	2.45693	2.73309	3.02549	3.33334	3.65563

(Hint: Find $y'(1.4)$, $y''(1.4)$, $y'(1.6)$, $y''(1.6)$ using Stirling's formula then solve two equations to obtain a and b)

(16)   Obtain the value of $f'(0.04)$, using Bessel's formula, from the table given below:

x:	0.01	0.02	0.03	0.04	0.05	0.06
$f(x)$:	0.1023	0.1047	0.1071	0.1096	0.1122	0.1148

(17)   Using Bessel's formula, find $f'(7.5)$ from the following table:

x:	7.47	7.48	7.49	7.50	7.51	7.52	7.53
$f(x)$:	0.193	0.195	0.198	0.201	0.203	0.206	0.208

(18)   Find the values of $\frac{dy}{dx}$ at $x = 800, x = 900$ and at $x = 1100$ from the following data, using Bessel's formula:

x:	0	300	600	900	1200	1500	1800
$f(x)$:	135	149	157	183	201	205	193

(19)   Find $f'(0.25)$ and $f'(0.22)$ from the following data using Newton's divided difference formula.

x:	0.15	0.21	0.23	0.27	0.32	0.35
$y = f(x)$:	0.1761	0.3222	0.3617	0.4314	0.5051	0.5441

(20)   Find $f'(10)$ from the following data using Newton's divided difference formula.

x:	3	5	11	27	34
$f(x)$:	-13	23	899	17315	35606

(21)   Compute $f'(0.8)$ and $f''(0.8)$, using the following table:

x:	0.4	0.6	0.7	0.9	1.2
$y = f(x)$:	1.08107	1.18546	1.25517	1.43309	1.81066

(22)   Find the values of $f'(4)$ and $f''(4)$ from the following data, using Newton's divided difference formula:

x:	1	2	4	8	10
$f(x)$:	0	1	5	21	27

(23)   Find the value of $\cos 33^0$ and $\sec 37^0$ using the following data, by Lagrange's interpolation formula.

x:	30	32	35	38
$y = tan\ x^0$:	0.5774	0.6249	0.7002	0.7813

(24)   Given the following values of $f(x) = logx$, find the approximate value of $f'(2.0)$ and $f''(2.0)$, using the Lagrange's interpolation formula. Compare your result with exact value.

x:	2.0	2.2	2.6
$y = f(x)$:	0.69315	0.78846	0.95551

(25)   Find the values of $f'(x)$ at $x = 2$ and $x = 5$ from the following data, using Lagarange's interpolation formula.

x:	0	1	3	6
$f(x)$:	18	10	-18	40

(26)   From the following table, find x, correct to four decimal places, where y is minimum. Also, find this value of y.

x:	3	4	5	6	7	8
y:	0.205	0.240	0.259	0.262	0.250	0.224

(27)   From the following table, find the value of x for which y is maximum and find this value of y.

x:	1.2	1.3	1.4	1.5	1.6
y:	0.9320	0.9636	0.9855	0.9975	0.9996

(28) Find the value of x for which $f(x)$ is maximum in the range of x given, using the following table. Find also the maximum value of $f(x)$.

x:	60	75	90	105	120
$f(x)$:	28.2	38.2	43.2	40.9	37.7

(**Hint:** The maximum value appears to be in the neighbourhood of $x = 90$, use Stirling's formula)

(29) From the following table find the value of x for which $f(x)$ is maximum. Also find the maximum value of $f(x)$ from the table of values given below.

x:	-1	1	2	3
$f(x)$:	7	5	19	51

(**Hint:** Intervals are not equally spaced, so use Newton's divided difference formula)

(30) By use of appropriate initial values based on finite differences and repeated Richardson extrapolation, find $f'(1)$ from the following table:

x:	0.6	0.8	0.9	1.0	1.1	1.2	1.4
$f(x)$:	0.707178	0.859892	0.925863	0.984007	1.033743	1.074575	1.127986

$h = 0.4, 0.2, 0.1$

(31) Find the values of $f'(0)$ and $f''(0)$ from the following table, using appropriate initial values based on finite differences and Richardson's extrapolation method:

x:	0	1	2	3	4	5	6	7	8
$f(x)$:	-1	0	5	20	51	104	185	300	455

(32) Find the values of $f'(3)$ and $f''(3)$ from the following data of values of $f(x)$, using appropriate initial values based on finite differences and Richardson's extrapolation method:

x:	-1	1	2	3	4	6	7
$f(x)$:	1	1	16	81	256	625	2401

Answers

(1)   3.3205; 3.318   (2)   4.75   (3)   −0.1825
(4)   0.630; 6.60   (5)   -52.4   (6)   4.00028; 0.800
(7)   12; 21   (9)   0.00004429; 0.00004125   (10)   9.66
(11)   3.82 radian/sec, 6.75 radian./ sec^2 (12)   0.8881; 1.3375;
0.9150; 1.3357   (14)   −0.4249; −0.44; −0.4634
(15) $a = 8.0273$, $b = 6.0143$ (16)   0.25625   (17)
0.2183   (18)   0.08846; 0.08044; 0.05182   (19)
$f'(0.25) = 1.7363$, $f'(0.22) = $ 1.9734   (20)   232.869   (21)
0.88811; 1.33744   (22)   2.8333; 0.8611
(23) $\cos 33^0 = 0.8389$, $\sec 37^0 = 1.2524$
(24) $f'(2.0) = 0.49619$, exact value = 0.5; $f''(2.0) = −0.19642$,
exact value = −0.25
(25)   −15.4444; 28.8889   (26) $x = 5.6875$, $y = 0.2628$
(27)   1.58; 1.00   (28)   92.11; 43.27
(29) $f(x) = x^3 + 3x^2 − 2x + 3$, $x = 0.291$, $f(x) = 2.6967$
(30)   0.54030   (31)   1, -2
(32)   108; 108

Chapter 9   Numerical Integration

Objectives

- To know the importance and the concept of numerical integration
- To enable students to understand Newton-Cote's formula
- To derive different integration formulae from the Newton-Cote's formula
- To find the error in integration formulae
- To interpret different integration formulae
- To know the concept of numerical integration using cubic spline
- To understand the importance of Romberg's method
- To find the value of integral or sum of a series using Euler – Maclaurin summation formula
- To understand various integration methods based on undetermined co-efficients
- To know the procedure of finding double integrals using numerical integration methods

Learning Outcomes

After reading this lesson students should be able to

- Apply appropriate integration formulae successfully
- Calculate error in given numerical integration example
- Interprete different integration formulae and obtained result using that formula
- Evaluate the value of integral using cubic spline
- Improve results obtained by different integration formulae using Romberg's method
- Obtain value of integral or sum of a series using Euler – Maclaurin summation formula
- Apply different numerical integration methods based on undetermined coefficients like Gauss-Legendre, and Gauss – Chebyshev
- Evaluate double integrals using numerical integration methods

9.1 INTRODUCTION

Consider the definite integral

$$I = \int_{x=a}^{b} f(x) \ dx \qquad \dots\dots(9.1.1)$$

where $f(x)$ is explicitly defined and integrable function and $[a, b]$ a finite interval. Then $f(x)$ can be evaluated exactly. However, in some cases function is not known explicitly but it is defined by a set of tabulated values. In such situations, numerical integration provides approximate solution. The problem of numerical integration is solved by representing $f(x)$ by an interpolating polynomial $P_n(x)$ and then integrating it between given limits.
Therefore,

$$I = \int_{x=a}^{b} f(x) \ dx \quad \approx \quad \int_{x=a}^{b} P_n(x) \ dx \qquad \dots\dots(9.1.2)$$

The polynomial $P_n(x)$ can be easily integrated analytically. Thus, the process of evaluating a definite integral by approximating an integrand from an interpolating polynomial is called a *numerical integration*. This is graphically shown in Figure 9.1. When this process is applied to a function of a single variable, it is sometimes called *numerical quadrature* or simply *quadrature*. When it is applied to a function of two independent variables, the process is called *numerical cubature* or simply *cubature*.
Eq. (9.1.2) can also be expressed as follows:

$$\int_{x=a}^{b} P_n(x) \ dx = \sum_{i=0}^{n} w_i P_n(x_i) \qquad \dots\dots(9.1.3)$$

where, $a = x_0 < x_1 < \dots < x_n = b$. Since $P_n(x)$ coincides with $f(x)$ at all the points $x_i, i = 0,1,2 \dots\dots, n$, it can also be expressed as

$$I = \int_{x=a}^{b} f(x) \ dx = \sum_{i=0}^{n} w_i(x_i) \qquad \dots\dots(9.1.4)$$

Here, x_i are called sampling points and w_i are called weighting coefficients or weights. There are various integration methods of selecting sampling points. Sampling points can be equally spaced or unequally spaced. Based on equally or unequally spaced sampling points there are two types of numerical techniques using which we can evaluate a definite integral.
1.   Newton – Cote's quadrature
2.   Gaussian quadrature

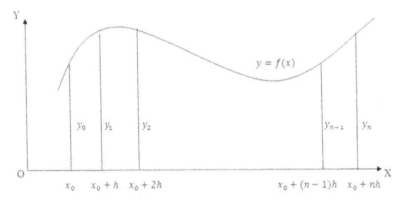

Figure 9.1 Numerical Integration

9.2   NEWTON – COTE'S QUADRATURE FORMULA

Let $y_0, y_1, y_2, \ldots\ldots, y_n$ be the set of values of the function $y = f(x)$ corresponding to $x = x_0, x_1, x_2, \ldots\ldots, x_n$. Let us divide the interval $[a, b]$ into n sub-intervals of width h.   Therefore, $x_0 = a, x_1 = x_0 + h, x_2 = x_0 + 2h, \ldots, x_n = x_0 + nh = b$.

Now,

$$I = \int_{x_0}^{x_n} f(x)\ dx = \int_{0}^{n} y(x_0 + uh)\ hdu$$

where, $u = (x - x_0)/h \Rightarrow du = dx\ /h \Rightarrow dx = hdu$

when $x = x_0 \Rightarrow u = (x_0 - x_0)/h\ = 0$
when $x = x_n \Rightarrow u = (x_n - x_0)/h\ = nh/h\ = n$

Replacing y by Newton's forward interpolating polynomial, we get

$$I = h \int_{0}^{n} \left[y_0 + \frac{u}{1!}\ \Delta y_0 + \frac{u(u-1)}{2!}\ \Delta^2 y_0 + \frac{u(u-1)(u-2)}{3!}\ \Delta^3 y_0 \right.$$
$$\left. + \ldots\ldots \right]\ du$$

$$= h \int_{0}^{n} \left[y_0 + u\ \Delta y_0 + \frac{u^2 - u}{2}\ \Delta^2 y_0 + \frac{u^3 - 3u^2 + 2u}{6}\ \Delta^3 y_0 + \ldots\ldots \right]\ du$$

Integrating term by term, we get

$$I = h \left[y_0 u + \frac{u^2}{2} \Delta y_0 + \frac{1}{2} \left(\frac{u^3}{3} - \frac{u^2}{2} \right) \Delta^2 y_0 + \frac{1}{6} \left(\frac{u^4}{4} - u^3 + u^2 \right) \Delta^3 y_0 \right.$$

$$\left. + \ldots \ldots \right]_0^n$$

$$= h \left[n y_0 + \frac{n^2}{2} \Delta y_0 + \frac{1}{2} \left(\frac{n^3}{3} - \frac{n^2}{2} \right) \Delta^2 y_0 + \frac{1}{6} \left(\frac{n^4}{4} - n^3 + n^2 \right) \Delta^3 y_0 \right.$$

$$+ \frac{1}{24} \left(\frac{n^5}{5} - \frac{3n^4}{2} + \frac{11n^3}{3} - 3n^2 \right) \Delta^4 y_0$$

$$+ \frac{1}{120} \left(\frac{n^6}{6} - 2n^5 + \frac{35n^4}{4} - \frac{50n^3}{3} + 12\,n^2 \right) \Delta^5 y_0$$

$$+ \frac{1}{720} \left(\frac{n^7}{7} - \frac{15n^6}{6} + 17n^5 - \frac{225n^4}{4} + \frac{274n^3}{3} \right.$$

$$\left. \left. - 60n^2 \right) \Delta^6 y_0 + \ldots \ldots \right] \qquad \qquad \ldots \ldots (9.2.1)$$

Eq. (9.2.1) is known as Newton – Cote's quadrature or general quadrature formula. By putting different values of n we get a number of special quadrature formula.

9.3   TRAPEZOIDAL RULE

Putting $n = 1$ in Eq. (9.2.1) then there are only two values $y_0 = f(x_0) = f(a)$ and $y_1 = f(x_1) = f(b)$. In this case we assume that the interpolating polynomial is linear. Hence, the second and higher order differences are not possible.

$$\int_{x_0}^{x_0+h} f(x)dx = h \left[y_0 + \frac{1}{2} \Delta y_0 \right]$$

$$= h \left[y_0 + \frac{1}{2} (y_1 - y_0) \right]$$

$$= \frac{h}{2} (y_0 + y_1) \qquad \qquad \ldots \ldots (9.3.1)$$

9.3.1   Composite Trapezoidal Rule

Let $y_0, y_1, y_2, \ldots \ldots, y_n$ be the set of values of the function $y = f(x)$ corresponding to $x = x_0, x_1, x_2, \ldots \ldots, x_n$. Let us divide the interval $[a, b]$ into n equal sub-intervals of width h. Therefore, $x_0 = a, x_1 = x_0 + h, x_2 = x_0 + 2h, x_3 = x_0 + 3h, \ldots, x_{n-1} = x_0 + (n-1)h, x_n = x_0 + nh = b$ and the Trapezoidal rule is applied in each of the intervals.

$$I = \int_{x_0=a}^{x_n=b} f(x)\, dx = \int_{x_0}^{x_0+nh} f(x)\, dx$$

$$= \int_{x_0}^{x_0+h} f(x)\,dx + \int_{x_0+h}^{x_0+2h} f(x)\,dx + \int_{x_0+2h}^{x_0+3h} f(x)\,dx + \cdots + \int_{x_0+(n-1)h}^{x_0+nh} f(x)\,dx$$

$$= \frac{h}{2}(y_0 + y_1) + \frac{h}{2}(y_1 + y_2) + \frac{h}{2}(y_2 + y_3) + \ldots\ldots$$

$$+ \frac{h}{2}(y_{n-1} + y_n) \qquad\qquad\qquad \text{(from Eq. (9.3.1))}$$

$$= \frac{h}{2}[(y_0 + y_1) + (y_1 + y_2) + (y_2 + y_3) + \ldots\ldots + (y_{n-1} + y_n)]$$

$$= \frac{h}{2}[(y_0 + y_n) + 2(y_1 + y_2 + y_3 + \ldots\ldots + y_{n-1})]$$

$$\therefore I = \int_{x_0=a}^{x_n=b} f(x)\,dx = \frac{h}{2}\begin{bmatrix} Sum\ of\ first\ and\ last\ ordinates \\ +2\ (Sum\ of\ remaining\ ordinates) \end{bmatrix} \,..(9.3.2)$$

Eq. (9.3.2) is known as *Composite Trapezoidal Rule*.

9.3.2   Error in Trapezoidal Rule

Let $y = f(x)$ be a continuous function having continuous derivatives in the interval $[a\ ,\ b]$. By expanding this function using Taylor's series in the neighbourhood of $x = x_0$, we get

$$\int_{x_0}^{x_0+h} y\,dx = \int_{x_0}^{x_0+h} \left[y_0 + \frac{(x-x_0)}{1!}y_0' + \frac{(x-x_0)^2}{2!}y_0'' + \ldots\ldots \right] dx$$

$$= \left[y_0.x + \frac{(x-x_0)^2}{2!}y_0' + \frac{(x-x_0)^3}{3!}y_0'' + \ldots\ldots \right]_{x_0}^{x_0+h}$$

$$= hy_0 + \frac{h^2}{2!}y_0' + \frac{h^3}{3!}y_0'' + \ldots\ldots = A, say \qquad\qquad \ldots\ldots.(9.3.3)$$

Now, from Eq. (9.3.1),

$$\int_{x_0}^{x_0+h} y\,dx = \frac{h}{2}(y_0 + y_1) = \frac{h}{2}[y_0 + y(x_0 + h)]$$

$$= \frac{h}{2}\left[y_0 + y_0 + \frac{h}{1!}y_0' + \frac{h^2}{2!}y_0'' + \ldots\ldots \right]$$

$$= hy_0 + \frac{h^2}{2}y_0' + \frac{h^3}{2 \times 2!}y_0'' + \ldots\ldots$$

$$= B, say \qquad\qquad \dots\dots(9.3.4)$$

From Eqs. (9.3.3) and (9.3.4), the error in the Trapezoidal rule in the interval $[x_0, x_0 + h = x_1]$ is

$$A - B = h^3 \left(\frac{1}{3!} - \frac{1}{2 \times 2!}\right) y_0''$$

$$= -\frac{1}{12} h^3 \, y_0'' \qquad \text{(omitting higher powers of h)}$$

Similarly errors in the intervals $[x_1, x_2], [x_2, x_3], \dots\dots, [x_{n-1}, x_n]$ are
$-\frac{1}{12} h^3 \, y_1''$, $-\frac{1}{12} h^3 \, y_2''$, $\dots\dots$, $-\frac{1}{12} h^3 \, y_{n-1}''$

Thus, the total error is

$$E_T = -\frac{1}{12} h^3 \, (y_0'' + y_1'' + y_2'' + \dots\dots + y_{n-1}'')$$

$$= -\frac{1}{12} h^3 \, [f''(\xi_1) + f''(\xi_2) + f''(\xi_3) + \dots\dots + f''(\xi_n)]$$

where, $x_0 < \xi_1 < x_1, \ x_1 < \xi_2 < x_2, \dots\dots\dots, \ x_{n-1} < \xi_n < x_n$
then

$$E_T \simeq -\frac{1}{12} h^3 . n \, f''(\xi)$$

where, $f''(\xi)$, $x_0 < \xi < x_n$ is the maximum of
$f''(\xi_1), f''(\xi_2), \dots\dots, f''(\xi_n)$,

Now, for composite Trapezoidal rule, $h = \frac{x_n - x_0}{n}$

$$\therefore E_T \simeq -\frac{1}{12} \left(\frac{x_n - x_0}{n}\right)^3 . n \, f''(\xi)$$

$$= -\frac{1}{12} (x_n - x_0) . h^2 f''(\xi), \ x_0 < x_n \qquad\qquad \dots\dots(9.3.5)$$

Hence, the error in Trapezoidal rule is $O(h^2)$.

9.3.3   Geometrical Interpretation of Trapezoidal Rule

The Trapezoidal formula geometrically interprets that the definite integral of the curve $y = f(x)$ between the limits x_0 and x_1 is approximated by the straight line joining $C(x_0, y_0)$ and $D(x_1, y_1)$.

Thus, the area bounded by the curve $y = f(x)$, $x = x_0$, $x = x_1$ and the x - axis is approximated by the area of the trapezoidal region bounded by the straight line CD, the x – axis, and the ordinates at $x = x_0$ and $x = x_1$. This is represented by the shaded area of the trapezium CABD in the Figure 9.2.

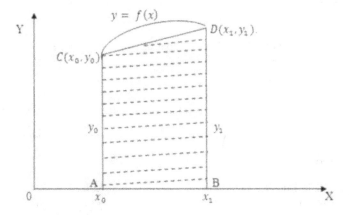

Figure 9.2   Trapezoidal Rule

The composite Trapezoidal formula geometrically interprets that the definite integral of the curve $y = f(x)$ between the limits x_0 and x_n is approximated by n straight lines joining

$\{P_0(x_0, y_0), P_1(x_1, y_1)\}, \{P_1(x_1, y_1), P_2(x_2, y_2)\}, \{P_2(x_2, y_2), P_3(x_3, y_3)\}, \dots \dots,$

$\{P_{n-1}(x_{n-1}, y_{n-1}), P(x_n, y_n)\}.$

Thus, the area bounded by the curve $y = f(x)$, $x = x_0$, $x = x_n$ and the x - axis is approximated by the sum of the areas of the trapeziums

$P_0 Q_0 Q_1 P_1 + P_1 Q_1 Q_2 P_2 + P_2 Q_2 Q_3 P_3 + \dots \dots \dots + P_{n-1} Q_{n-1} Q_n P_n$.   This   is represented by the shaded area given in Figure 9.3.

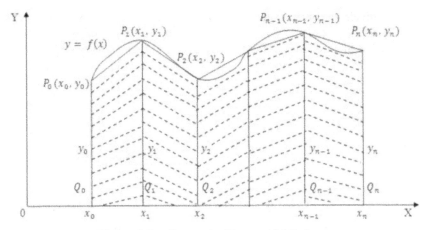

Figure 9.3   Composite Trapezoidal Rule

Remarks:

- This rule is applicable to any number of sub – intervals, even or odd.
- It gives exact result for a polynomial of degree one.
- It is based on two sampling points.
- The accuracy of the computed result can be improved or error may be reduced by increasing the number of sub-intervals or by decreasing the length of the interval h.

9.4   SIMPSON'S ONE – THIRD RULE

Putting $n = 2$ in Eq. (9.2.1) then there are only three values $y_0 = f(x_0) = f(a)$, $y_1 = f(x_0 + h) = f(x_1)$ and $y_2 = f(x_0 + 2h) = f(x_2) = f(b)$. In this case we assume that the interpolating polynomial is parabola i.e. second degree polynomial. Hence, the higher order differences than second order are not possible.

$$\int_{x_0}^{x_0+2h} f(x)dx = h\left[2y_0 + 2\Delta y_0 + \frac{1}{2}\left(\frac{8}{3} - 2\right)\Delta^2 y_0\right]$$

$$= h\left[2y_0 + 2\,(y_1 - y_0) + \frac{1}{3}\,(y_2 - 2y_1 + y_0)\right]$$

$$= \frac{h}{3}\,(y_0 + 4y_1 + y_2) \qquad\qquad\dots\dots\dots (9.4.1)$$

9.4.1   Composite Simpson's One – Third Rule

Let us divide the interval $[a \;,\; b]$ into $2n$ equal sub-intervals by points $a = x_0, \; x_1 = \; x_0 + h, x_2 = \; x_0 + 2h, \dots\dots, x_{2n} = \; x_0 + 2nh = b$ of width $h = (b - a)/2n$. The Simpson's one – third rule is applied in each of the n sub – intervals.

$$I = \int_{x_0=a}^{x_{2n}=b} f(x)\; dx = \int_{x_0}^{x_0+2nh} f(x)\; dx$$

$$= \int_{x_0}^{x_0+2h} f(x)\; dx + \int_{x_0+2h}^{x_0+4h} f(x)\; dx$$

$$+ \int_{x_0+4h}^{x_0+6h} f(x)\; dx + \dots\dots\dots + \int_{x_0+(2n-2)h}^{x_0+2nh} f(x)\; dx$$

$$= \frac{h}{3}\,(y_0 + 4y_1 + y_2) + \frac{h}{3}\,(y_2 + 4y_3 + y_4) + \frac{h}{3}\,(y_4 + 4y_5 + y_6) + \dots\dots$$

$$+ \frac{h}{3} (y_{2n-2} + 4y_{2n-1} + y_{2n})$$

$$= \frac{h}{3} [(y_0 + 4y_1 + y_2) + (y_2 + 4y_3 + y_4) + (y_4 + 4y_5 + y_6) + \dots + (y_{2n-2}$$
$$+ 4y_{2n-1} + y_{2n})]$$

$$= \frac{h}{3} [(y_0 + y_{2n}) + 4 (y_1 + y_3 + y_5 + \dots \dots + y_{2n-1}) + 2(y_2 + y_4 + \dots$$
$$+ y_{2n-2})]$$

$$\therefore I = \int_{x_0=a}^{x_{2n}=b} f(x) \, dx = \frac{h}{3} \begin{bmatrix} Sum\ of\ first\ and\ last\ ordinates \\ +4\ (Sum\ of\ all\ odd\ ordinates) \\ + 2(Sum\ of\ all\ even\ ordinates) \end{bmatrix} \quad \dots (9.4.2)$$

Eq. (9.4.2) is known as *Composite Simpson's One – Third Rule*.

Remarks:
- To apply this formula, the number of sub - intervals n must be even. i.e. the number of ordinates must be odd.
- This rule is based on three sampling points.
- This rule gives exact result for a polynomial of degree less than or equal to three.

9.4.2 Error in Simpson's One – Third Rule

Let $y = f(x)$ be a continuous function having continuous derivatives in the interval $[a , b]$. By expanding this function using Taylor's series in the neighbourhood of $x = x_0$, we get

$$\int_{x_0}^{x_0+2h} y \, dx = \int_{x_0}^{x_0+2h} \left[y_0 + \frac{(x - x_0)}{1!} y_0' + \frac{(x - x_0)^2}{2!} y_0'' + \dots \dots \right] dx$$

$$= \left[y_0 . x + \frac{(x - x_0)^2}{2!} y_0' + \frac{(x - x_0)^3}{3!} y_0'' + \dots \dots \right]_{x_0}^{x_0+2h}$$

$$= 2hy_0 + \frac{4h^2}{2!} y_0' + \frac{8h^3}{3!} y_0'' + \dots \dots$$

$$= 2hy_0 + 2h^2 y_0' + \frac{4}{3}h^3 y_0'' + \frac{2}{3} h^4 y_0''' + \frac{4}{15}h^5 y_0^{iv} + \dots \dots \qquad \dots \dots (9.4.3)$$

$$= A, say$$

Now, from Eq. (9.4.1),

$$\int_{x_0}^{x_0+2h} y \, dx = \frac{h}{3} (y_0 + 4y_1 + y_2) = \frac{h}{3} [y_0 + 4y (x_0 + h) + y (x_0 + 2h)]$$

$$= \frac{h}{3}\left[y_0 + 4\left\{ y_0 + \frac{h}{1!}y_0' + \frac{h^2}{2!}y_0'' + \ldots\ldots \right\} \right.$$

$$\left. + \left\{ y_0 + \frac{2h}{1!}y_0' + \frac{4h^2}{2!}y_0'' + \ldots \right\} \right]$$

$$= 2\,hy_0 + 2h^2 y_0' + \frac{4}{3}h^3 y_0'' + \frac{2}{3}h^4 y_0''' + \frac{5}{18}h^5 y_0^{iv} + \ldots\ldots$$

$$= B, say \qquad\qquad \ldots\ldots(9.4.4)$$

From Eqs. (9.4.3) and (9.4.4), the error in the Simpson's one – third rule in the interval $[x_0, x_0 + 2h = x_2]$ is

$$A - B = h^5 \left(\frac{4}{15} - \frac{5}{18} \right) y_0^{iv}$$

$$= -\frac{1}{90} h^5 y_0^{iv} \qquad \text{(omitting higher powers of h)}$$

Similarly errors in the intervals $[x_2, x_4], [x_4, x_6], \ldots\ldots, [x_{2n-2}, x_{2n}]$ are $-\frac{1}{90} h^5 y_2^{iv}, -\frac{1}{90} h^5 y_4^{iv}, \ldots\ldots, -\frac{1}{90} h^5 y_{2n-2}^{iv}$

Thus, the total error is

$$E_T = -\frac{1}{90} h^5 (y_0^{iv} + y_2^{iv} + y_4^{iv} + \ldots\ldots + y_{2n-2}^{iv})$$

$$= -\frac{1}{90} h^5 [f^{iv}(\xi_1) + f^{iv}(\xi_2) + f^{iv}(\xi_3) + \ldots\ldots + f^{iv}(\xi_n)]$$

where, $x_0 < \xi_1 < x_2, \; x_2 < \xi_2 < x_4, \ldots\ldots\ldots, \; x_{2n-2} < \xi_n < x_{2n}$
then

$$E_T \simeq -\frac{1}{90} h^5 . n\, f^{iv}(\xi)$$

where, $f''(\xi), \; x_0 < \xi < x_n$ is the maximum of $f''(\xi_1), \; f''(\xi_2), \ldots\ldots, f''(\xi_n)$
Now, for composite Simpson's one – third rule, $h = \frac{x_{2n} - x_0}{2n}$

$$\therefore E_T \simeq -\frac{1}{90} \left(\frac{x_{2n} - x_0}{2n} \right)^5 . n\, f^{iv}(\xi)$$

$$= -\frac{1}{180} (x_{2n} - x_0).h^4 f^{iv}(\xi), \; x_0 < \xi < x_{2n} \qquad \ldots\ldots(9.4.5)$$

Hence, the error in Simpson's one – third rule is $O(h^4)$.

9.4.3   Geometrical Interpretation of Simpson's One – Third Rule

The Simpson's one – third formula geometrically interprets that the definite integral of the curve $y = f(x)$ between the limits x_0 and x_2 is approximated by the parabola joining $P_0(x_0, y_0), P_1(x_1, y_1)$ and $P_2(x_2, y_2)$.
Thus, the area bounded by the curve $y = f(x)$, $x = x_0$, $x = x_2$ and the x - axis

is approximated by the area bounded by the parabola taken, the x – axis, and the ordinates at $x = x_0$ and $x = x_2$. This is represented by the shaded area in the Figure 9.4.

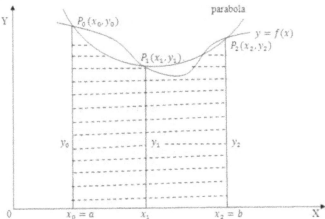

Figure 9.4   Simpson's One - Third Rule

9.5   SIMPSON'S THREE – EIGHTHS RULE

Putting $n = 3$ in Eq. (9.2.1) then there are only four values $y_0 = f(x_0) = f(a)$, $y_1 = f(x_0 + h) = f(x_1)$, $y_2 = f(x_0 + 2h) = f(x_2)$ and $y_3 = f(x_0 + 3h) = f(x_3) = f(b)$. In this case we assume that the interpolating polynomial is third order polynomial. Hence, the higher order differences than third order are not possible.

$$\int_{x_0}^{x_0+3h} f(x)dx = h\left[3y_0 + \frac{9}{2}\Delta y_0 + \frac{1}{2}\left(9 - \frac{9}{2}\right)\Delta^2 y_0 + \frac{1}{6}\left(\frac{81}{4} - 27 + 9\right)\Delta^3 y_0\right]$$

$$= h\left[3y_0 + \frac{9}{2}(y_1 - y_0) + \frac{9}{4}(y_2 - 2y_1 + y_0) + \frac{3}{8}(y_3 - 3y_2 + 3y_1 - y_0)\right]$$

$$= \frac{3h}{8}(y_0 + 3y_1 + 3y_2 + y_3) \qquad\qquad \dots\dots (9.5.1)$$

9.5.1   Composite Simpson's Three – Eighths Rule

Let us divide the interval $[a , b]$ into $3n$ equal sub-intervals by points $a = x_0$, $x_1 = x_0 + h, x_2 = x_0 + 2h, x_3 = x_0 + 3h \dots\dots, x_{3n} = x_0 + 3nh = b$ of width $h = (b - a)/3n$. The Simpson's three – eighth rule is applied in each of the n sub – intervals.

$$I = \int_{x_0=a}^{x_{3n}=b} f(x)\, dx = \int_{x_0}^{x_0+3nh} f(x)\, dx$$

$$= \int_{x_0}^{x_0+3h} f(x)\, dx + \int_{x_0+3h}^{x_0+6h} f(x)\, dx$$

$$+ \int_{x_0+6h}^{x_0+9h} f(x)\, dx + \dots\dots + \int_{x_0+(3n-3)h}^{x_0+3nh} f(x)\, dx$$

$$= \frac{3h}{8}(y_0 + 3y_1 + 3y_2 + y_3) + \frac{3h}{8}(y_3 + 3y_4 + 3y_5 + y_6)$$

$$+ \frac{3h}{8}(y_6 + 3y_7 + 3y_8 + y_9) + \dots + \frac{3h}{8}(y_{3n-3} + 3y_{3n-2} + 3y_{3n-1} + y_{3n})$$

$$= \frac{3h}{8}\left[\begin{array}{l}(y_0 + 3y_1 + 3y_2 + y_3) + (y_3 + 3y_4 + 3y_5 + y_6)\\ + (y_6 + 3y_7 + 3y_8 + y_9) + \dots\dots + (y_{3n-3} + 3y_{3n-2} + 3y_{3n-1} + y_{3n})\end{array}\right]$$

$$= \frac{3h}{8}\left[(y_0 + y_{3n}) + 3(y_1 + y_2 + y_4 + y_5 + \dots\dots) + 2(y_3 + y_6 + \dots\right.$$

$$\left. + y_{3n-3})\right] \qquad\qquad \dots\dots (9.5.2)$$

Eq. (9.5.2) is known as *Composite Simpson's Three – Eighths Rule*. The error in Simpson's three – eighths rule is

$$E_T = -\frac{3}{80} \cdot h^5 f^{iv}(\xi), \; x_0 < \xi < x_{3n} = -\frac{3}{240} \cdot (x_{3n} - x_0) \cdot h^4 f^{iv}(\xi), \; x_0 < \xi < x_{3n}$$

Remarks:
- To apply this formula, the number of sub - intervals n should be taken as multiple of 3.
- This rule is based on four sampling points.

- The Simpson's 3/8 rule is slightly more accurate than Simpson's 1/3 rule as the truncation error of Simpson's 3/8 rule is $E_T = -\frac{3}{80} \cdot h^5 f^{iv}(\xi) = -\frac{(b-a)^5}{6480} f^{iv}(\xi)$ as $h = \frac{b-a}{3}$ while the truncation error of Simpson's 1/3 rule is $E_T = -\frac{1}{90} \cdot h^5 f^{iv}(\xi) = -\frac{(b-a)^5}{2880} f^{iv}(\xi)$ as $h = \frac{b-a}{2}$.

9.6   BOOLE'S RULE

Putting $n = 4$ in Eq. (9.2.1) and assume that the interpolating polynomial is fourth order polynomial. Hence, the higher order differences than fourth order are not possible.

$$\int_{x_0}^{x_0+4h} f(x)dx = h\left[4y_0 + 8\Delta y_0 + \frac{1}{2}\left(\frac{64}{3} - \frac{16}{2}\right)\Delta^2 + \frac{1}{6}(64 - 64 + 16)\Delta^3 y_0 \right.$$

$$\left. + \frac{1}{24}\left(\frac{1024}{5} - 384 + \frac{704}{3} - 48\right)\Delta^4 y_0\right]$$

$$= 4h\left[y_0 + 2(y_1 - y_0) + \frac{5}{3}(y_2 - 2y_1 + y_0) + \frac{2}{3}(y_3 - 3y_2 + 3y_1 - y_0)\right.$$
$$\left. + \frac{7}{90}(y_4 - 4y_3 + 6y_2 - 4y_1 + y_0)\right]$$

$$= \frac{2h}{45}(7y_0 + 32y_1 + 12y_2 + 32y_3 + 7y_4) \qquad\qquad ....(9.6.1)$$

9.6.1   Composite Boole's Rule

Let us divide the interval $[a\ ,\ b]$ into $4n$ equal sub-intervals with interval length $h = (b - a)/4n$. The Boole's rule is applied in each of the n sub – intervals.

$$I = \int_{x_0=a}^{x_{4n}=b} f(x)\,dx = \int_{x_0}^{x_0+4nh} f(x)\ dx$$

$$= \int_{x_0}^{x_0+4h} f(x)\ dx + \int_{x_0+4h}^{x_0+8h} f(x)\ dx + ...+ \int_{x_0+(4n-4)h}^{x_0+4nh} f(x)\ dx$$

$$= \frac{2h}{45}[(7y_0 + 32y_1 + 12y_2 + 32y_3 + 7y_4)$$
$$+ (7y_4 + 32y_5 + 12y_6 + 32y_7 + 7y_8) + ...+ (7y_{4n-4}$$
$$+ 32y_{4n-3} + 12y_{4n-2} + 32y_{4n-1} + 7y_{4n})]$$
$$= \frac{2h}{45}[7(y_0 + y_{4n}) + 32(y_1 + y_5 + y_9 + ...) + 12(y_2 + y_6 + y_{10} + \cdots)$$
$$+ 32(y_3 + y_7 + y_{11} + \cdots) + 14(y_4 + y_8 + y_{12} + ...+ y_{4n-4})] \qquad ....(9.6.2)$$

This is known as *Composite Boole's rule.* The error in Boole's rule is

$$E_T = -\frac{8}{945}.h^7 f^{vi}(\xi),\ x_0 < \xi < x_{4n}$$

$$= -\frac{8}{3780}.(x_{4n} - x_0).h^6 f^{vi}(\xi),\ x_0 < \xi < x_{4n}$$

where, $h = \frac{b-a}{4}$

Remarks:
- To apply this formula, the number of sub - intervals n should be taken as multiple of 4.
- This rule is based on five sampling points.

9.7   WEDDLE'S RULE

Putting $n = 6$ in Eq. (9.2.1) and assume that the interpolating polynomial is sixth order polynomial. Hence, the higher order differences than sixth order are not possible.

$$\int_{x_0}^{x_0+6h} f(x)dx$$

$$= h \left[6y_0 + 18\Delta y_0 + \frac{1}{2}(72-18)\Delta^2 y_0 + \frac{1}{6}(324 - 216 + 36)\Delta^3 y_0 \right.$$
$$\left. + \frac{1}{24}\left(\frac{7776}{5} - 1944 + 792 - 108\right)\Delta^4 y_0 + \dots\dots \right]$$

$$= h \left[6y_0 + 18\Delta y_0 + 27\Delta^2 y_0 + 24\,\Delta^3 y_0 + \frac{123}{10}\Delta^4 y_0 + \frac{33}{10}\Delta^5 y_0 \right.$$
$$\left. + \frac{41}{140}\Delta^6 y_0 \right]$$

Now, if we take $\frac{42}{140} = \frac{3}{10}$ as a co-efficient of $\Delta^6 y_0$ instead of $\frac{41}{140}$ then error made will be negligible.

$$= h \left[6y_0 + 18(y_1 - y_0) + 27(y_2 - 2y_1 + y_0) + 24(y_3 - 3y_2 + 3y_1 - y_0) \right.$$
$$\left. + \frac{123}{10}(y_4 - 4y_3 + 6y_2 - 4y_1 + y_0) + \dots\dots \right]$$

$$= \frac{3h}{10}(y_0 + 5y_1 + y_2 + 6y_3 + y_4 + 5y_5 + y_6) \qquad \dots\dots (9.7.1)$$

9.7.1   Composite Weddle's Rule

Let us divide the interval $[a , b]$ into $6n$ equal sub-intervals with interval $h = (b-a)/6n$. The Weddle's rule is applied in each of the n sub – intervals.

$$I = \int_{x_0=a}^{x_{6n}=b} f(x)\, dx = \int_{x_0}^{x_0+6nh} f(x)\, dx$$

$$= \int_{x_0}^{x_0+6h} f(x)\, dx + \int_{x_0+6h}^{x_0+12h} f(x)\, dx + \dots\dots + \int_{x_0+(6n-6)h}^{x_0+6nh} f(x)\, dx$$

$$= \frac{3h}{10} [(y_0 + 5y_1 + y_2 + 6y_3 + y_4 + 5y_5 + y_6)$$
$$+ (y_6 + 5y_7 + y_8 + 6y_9 + y_{10} + 5y_{11} + y_{12}) + \dots\dots$$
$$+ (y_{6n-6} + 5y_{6n-5} + y_{6n-4} + 6y_{6n-3} + y_{6n-2} + 5y_{6n-1}$$
$$+ y_{6n})]$$

$$= \frac{3h}{10} [(y_0 + y_{6n}) + 5(y_1 + y_7 + y_{13} + \dots\dots) + (y_2 + y_8 + y_{14} + \cdots)$$
$$+ 6(y_3 + y_9 + y_{12} + \cdots) + (y_4 + y_{10} + y_{16} + \cdots)$$
$$+ 5(y_5 + y_{11} + y_{17} + \cdots) + 2(y_6 + y_{12} + y_{18} + y_{6n-6})] \qquad \dots\dots (9.7.2)$$

Eq. (9.7.2) is known as *Composite Weddle's Rule*. The error in Weddle's Rule is

$$E_T = -\frac{1}{140}.h^7 f^{vi}(\xi), \quad x_0 < \xi < x_{6n}$$

$$= -\frac{1}{540} \cdot (x_{6n} - x_0) \cdot h^6 f^{vi}(\xi), \quad x_0 < \xi < x_{6n}$$

where, $h = \frac{b-a}{6}$

> **Remarks:**
> - To apply this formula the number of sub - intervals n should be taken as multiple of 6.
> - This rule is based on seven sampling points.

Example 9.1   Evaluate

$$I = \int_0^6 \frac{1}{5x + 4} \, dx,$$

correct to three decimal palces, using (i) Trapezoidal rule   (ii) Simpson's 1/3 rule   (iii) Simpson's 3/8 rule   and (iv) Weddle's rule.

Solution: It is given that $y = 1/(5x + 4)$, $a = 0$, $b = 6$. We take six intervals so that Weddle's rule is applicable. Then, $h = 1$ and corresponding values of y are given as follows:

x	0	1	2	3	4	5	6
y	0.25	0.111	0.071	0.053	0.042	0.034	0.029

(i)   Trapezoidal rule is

$$\int_0^6 \frac{1}{5x + 4} \, dx = \frac{h}{2} \left[(y_0 + y_6) + 2(y_1 + y_2 + y_3 + y_4 + y_5) \right]$$

$$= \frac{1}{2} \left[(0.25 + 0.029) + 2(0.111 + 0.071 + 0.053 + 0.042 + 0.034) \right]$$

$$= 0.5[\, (0.279) + 2(0.311)] \quad = \quad 0.4505$$

(ii)   Since the number of intervals is six (even), we can apply Simpson's 1/3 rule. Simpson's 1/3 rule is

$$\int_0^6 \frac{1}{5x + 4} \, dx = \frac{h}{3} \left[(y_0 + y_6) + 4(y_1 + y_3 + y_5) + 2(y_2 + y_4) \right]$$

$$= \frac{1}{3} \left[(0.25 + 0.029) + 4(0.111 + 0.053 + 0.034) + 2(0.071 + 0.042) \right]$$

$$= 0.333[(0.279) + 4(0.198) + 2(0.113)] \quad = \quad 0.432$$

(iii)   Since the number of intervals is six (multiple of 3), we can apply Simpson's 3/8 rule. Simpson's 3/8 rule is

$$\int_0^6 \frac{1}{5x + 4} \, d = \frac{3h}{8} \left[(y_0 + y_6) + 3(y_1 + y_2 + y_4 + y_5) + 2y_3 \right]$$

$$= \frac{3}{8}[(0.25 + 0.029) + 3(0.111 + 0.071 + 0.042 + 0.034) + 2(0.053)]$$

$$= 0.375[(0.279) + 3(0.258) + 2(0.053)] = 0.435$$

(iv)   Since the number of intervals is six (multiple of 6), we can apply Weddle's rule. Weddle's rule is

$$\int_0^6 \frac{1}{5x + 4} \, dx = \frac{3h}{10} [y_0 + 5y_1 + y_2 + 6y_3 + y_4 + 5y_5 + y_6]$$

$$= \frac{3}{10}[0.25 + 5(0.111) + (0.071) + 6(0.053) + (0.042) + 5(0.034) + (0.029)]$$

$$= 0.3(1.435) = 0.4305$$

Example 9.2 A solid of revolution is formed by rotating about the x − axis, the area between the x − axis, the lines $x = 0$ and $x = 1$ and a curve through the points with the following co-ordinates:

x	0.00	0.25	0.50	0.75	1.00
y	1.0000	0.9896	0.9589	0.9089	0.8415

Estimate the volume of the solid formed using Simpson's 1/3 rule upto three decimal places.

Solution: Here, interval length $h = 0.25$. If V is the volume of the solid formed, then we know that

$$V = \int_0^1 \pi . y^2 \, dx$$

By Simpson's 1/3 rule,

$$\int_0^1 \pi . y^2 \, dx = \pi . \frac{h}{3} [(y_0^2 + y_4^2) + 4(y_1^2 + y_3^2) + 2(y_2^2)]$$

$$= \frac{0.25 \times \pi}{3}[\{(1 + (0.8415)^2\} + 4\{(0.9896)^2 + (0.9089)^2\} + 2(0.9589)^2]$$

$$= \frac{0.25 \times 3.1416}{3}[1.7081 + 7.2216 + 1.839] = 0.2618 (10.7687) = 2.8192$$

Example 9.3 The relationship between volume V of a tank at different level h as recorded as follows:

$h(m.)$:	10	11	12	13	14
$V(m^3.)$:	950	1070	1200	1350	1530

If t denotes the time in minutes, the rate of fall of the level which is in mt/min. when it is emptied is given by $dh/dt = -48\sqrt{h}/V$. Estimate the time taken for the water level to fall from 14 to 10 ft. using Simpson's 1/3rd formula.

Solution: It is given that,

$$\frac{dh}{dt} = -48\frac{\sqrt{h}}{V} \qquad \therefore \quad \frac{V}{\sqrt{h}}dh = -48\,dt$$

$$\therefore \int_{14}^{10} \frac{V}{\sqrt{h}}dh = \int -48\,dt \qquad \therefore \quad -\int_{10}^{14} \frac{V}{\sqrt{h}}dh = -48\int dt \qquad \text{.........(1)}$$

So, we need to find the value of $\frac{V}{\sqrt{h}}$.

$h(m.)$:	10	11	12	13	14
$V/\sqrt{h}\,(m^3.)$:	300.416	322.617	346.410	374.423	408.909

By Simpson's 1/3rd rule,

$$\int_{10}^{14} \frac{V}{\sqrt{h}}dh = \frac{h}{3}\left[(y_0 + y_4) + 4(y_1 + y_3) + 2y_2\right]$$

$$= \frac{1}{3}\left[(300.416 + 408.909) + 4(322.617 + 374.423) + 2(346.410)\right]$$

$$= \frac{1}{3}\left[(709.325) + 4(697.04) + 2(346.410)\right]$$

$$= \frac{1}{3}(4190.305) = 1396.7683$$

and $\qquad -48\int dt = -48t$

From (1), we have

$$\therefore \quad -\int_{10}^{14} \frac{V}{\sqrt{h}}dh = -48\int dt$$

$$\therefore \quad -1396.7683 = -48t \qquad \therefore \quad t = \frac{-1396.7683}{-48} = 29.0993$$

Example 9.4 The velocity v of a particle at a distance S from a point on its path is given by the table below.

S metre	0	10	20	30	40	50	60
V m/sec	47	58	64	65	61	52	38

Estimate the time taken to travel 60 metres by using Simpson's 1/3 rule. Compare your answer with Simpson's 3/8 rule.

Solution: We know that velocity $v = \frac{ds}{dt}$

$$\therefore dt = \frac{1}{v}ds \;\Rightarrow\; \int dt = \int \frac{1}{v}ds \;\Rightarrow\; t = \int_0^{60} \frac{1}{v}ds$$

S metre	0	10	20	30	40	50	60
$y = \dfrac{1}{v}$ m/sec	0.02127	0.01724	0.015625	0.01538	0.01639	0.01923	0.026316

By Simpson's 1/3 rule,

$$\int_0^{60} y\,ds = \frac{h}{3}\left[(y_0 + y_6) + 4(y_1 + y_3 + y_5) + 2(y_2 + y_4)\right]$$

$$= \frac{10}{3}\left[(0.02127 + 0.026316) + 4(0.01724 + 0.01538 + 0.01923)\right.$$
$$\left. + 2(0.015625 + 0.01639)\right]$$

$$\therefore\ t\ = 1.06338\ sec$$

By Simpson's 3/8 rule,

$$\int_0^{60} y\,ds = \frac{3h}{8}\left[(y_0 + y_6) + 3(y_1 + y_2 + y_4 + y_5) + 2y_3\right]$$

$$= \frac{3(10)}{8}\left[(0.02127 + 0.026316)\right.$$

$$+ 3(0.01724 + 0.015625 + 0.01639 + 0.01923) + 2(0.01538)]$$

$$\therefore\ t\ = 1.06425\ sec$$

Example 9.5   A rocket is launched from the ground. Its acceleration is registered during the first 80 seconds and is given in the table below. Using Simpson's 1/3rd rule, find the velocity of the rocket at t = 80 seconds.

t (Sec):	0	10	20	30	40	50	60	70	80
$f\ (cm/sec^2)$:	30	31.63	33.34	35.47	37.75	40.33	43.25	46.69	50.67

Solution: If we take velocity as v, we know that,

$$Acceleration\ f = \frac{dv}{dt} \Rightarrow f\,dt = dv$$

$$\therefore \int dv = \int f\,dt \Rightarrow Velocity\ v = \int_0^{80} f\,dt$$

By Simpson's 1/3 rule,

$$\int_0^{80} f\,dt = \frac{h}{3}\left[(y_0 + y_8) + 4(y_1 + y_3 + y_5 + y_7) + 2(y_2 + y_4 + y_6)\right]$$

$$= \frac{10}{3}\left[\begin{array}{l}(30 + 50.67) + 4(31.63 + 35.47 + 40.33 + 46.69) \\ + 2(33.34 + 37.75 + 43.25)\end{array}\right]$$

$$= 3.3333\,[\,(80.67) + 4(154.12) + 2(114.34)\,]$$

$$= 3.3333\,(925.83)\ = 3086.07\ cm/sec$$

Thus, the required velocity is given by $v = 3.0861\ km/sec$

Example 9.6 From the following data, estimate the value of $\int_1^5 logx\, dx$ using Simpson's 1/3 rule. Also, obtain the value of h, so that the value of the integral will be accurate up to five decimal places.

x	1.0	1.5	2.0	2.5	3.0	3.5	4.0	4.5	5.0
$y = logx$	0.0000	0.4055	0.6931	0.9163	1.0986	1.2528	1.3863	1.5041	1.6094

Solution: Given that, $a = 1.0, b = 5.0, h = 0.5$

By Simpson's 1/3 rule,

$$\int_1^5 logx\, dx = \frac{h}{3}[(y_0 + y_8) + 4(y_1 + y_3 + y_5 + y_7) + 2(y_2 + y_4 + y_6)]$$

$$= \frac{0.5}{3}[(0 + 1.6094) + 4(0.4055 + 0.9163 + 1.2528 + 1.5041)$$
$$+ 2(0.6931 + 1.0986 + 1.3863)]$$

$$= 0.1667[(1.6094) + 4(4.0787) + 2(3.178)]$$
$$= 0.1666(24.2802) = 4.0475$$

The error in Simpson's 1/3 rule is given by

$$E_T = \frac{1}{180}(x_{2n} - x_0).h^4 f^{iv}(\xi) \quad \text{(ignoring the sign)}$$

Now,

$$y = logx, y' = \frac{1}{x}, y'' = -\frac{1}{x^2}, y''' = \frac{2}{x^3}, y^{(iv)} = -\frac{6}{x^4}$$

$$\therefore \max_{1 \le x \le 5} f^{iv}(\xi) = 6, \quad \min_{1 \le x \le 5} f^{iv}(\xi) = 0.0096$$

$\therefore$ The error bounds are given by

$$\frac{(0.0096)(4)h^4}{180} < E_T < \frac{(6)(4)h^4}{180}$$

Given that the result is accurate upto five decimal places, then

$$\frac{(6)(4)h^4}{180} = \frac{24h^4}{180} < 10^{-5} \qquad \therefore h^4 < 0.000075 \ or \ h < 0.09$$

The actual value of integral is

$$\int_1^5 logx\, dx = [x\, logx - x]_1^5 = [(5log5 - 5) - (1log1 - 1)]$$

$$= 5log5 - 4 = 4.0472$$

Example 9.7 Calculate an approximate value of $\int_0^{\pi/2} sinx\, dx$ by
(i) Trapezoidal rule
(ii) Simpson's 1/3 rule
(iii) Boole's rule, using 8 sub-intervals. Calculate the percentage error from its true value in each cases.

Solution: Given that, $a = 0, b = \pi/2$, $n = 8 \Rightarrow h = \dfrac{b-a}{n} = \dfrac{\pi/2 - 0}{8} = \dfrac{\pi}{16}$

x	$sinx$	x	$sinx$
0	0.00000	$\dfrac{5\pi}{16}$	0.83147
$\dfrac{\pi}{16}$	0.19509	$\dfrac{6\pi}{16}$	0.92388
$\dfrac{2\pi}{16}$	0.38268	$\dfrac{7\pi}{16}$	0.98079
$\dfrac{3\pi}{16}$	0.55557	$\dfrac{8\pi}{16}$	1.00000
$\dfrac{4\pi}{16}$	0.70711		

(i)   By Trapezoidal rule,

$$\int_0^{\frac{\pi}{2}} sinx\, dx = \frac{h}{2} [(y_0 + y_8) + 2(y_1 + y_2 + y_3 + y_4 + y_5 + y_6 + y_7)]$$

$$= \frac{\pi/16}{2} [(0 + 1) + 2(0.19509 + 0.38268 + 0.55557 + 0.70711$$

$+0.83147 + 0.92388 + 0.98079]$

$= 0.09817[1 + 2(4.57659)] = 0.09817(10.15318) = 0.99674$

(ii)   By Simpson's 1/3 rule,

$$\int_0^{\pi/2} sinx\, dx = \frac{h}{3} [(y_0 + y_8) + 4(y_1 + y_3 + y_5 + y_7) + 2(y_2 + y_4 + y_6)]$$

$$= \frac{\pi/16}{3} [(0 + 1) + 4(0.19509 + 0.55557 + 0.83147 + 0.98079)$$

$$+ 2(0.38268 + 0.70711 + 0.92388)]$$

$$= 0.06545[1 + 4(2.56292) + 2(2.01367)]$$

$$= 0.06545 (15.27902) = 1.00001$$

(iii)   By Boole's rule,

$$\int_0^{\pi/2} sinx\, dx = \frac{2h}{45} [7y_0 + 32y_1 + 12y_2 + 32y_3 + 14y_4 + 32y_5 + 12y_6$$

$$+ 32y_7 + 7y_8]$$

$$= \frac{2(\pi/16)}{45} [7(0) + 32(0.19509) + 12(0.38268) + 32(0.55557)$$

$+14(0.70711) + 32(0.83147) + 12(0.92388) + 32(0.98079) + 7(1)]$

$= 0.00873\,[0 + 6.24288 + 4.59216 + 17.77824 + 9.89954 + 26.60704$
$\qquad + 11.08656 + 31.38528 + 7]$
$= 0.00873\,(114.5917) = 1.00039$

But the actual value of the integral is $\int_0^{\pi/2} sinx\,dx = [-cosx]_0^{\pi/2} = 1$

Therefore, in case of Trapezoidal rule, the percentage error

$= \left|\dfrac{Actual\ value - Approximate\ value}{Actual\ value}\right| \times 100 = \left|\dfrac{1 - 0.99674}{1}\right| \times 100$

$= 0.00326 \times 100 = 0.326 \qquad i.e.\,32.6\%$

In case of Simpson's 1/3 rule, the percentage error

$= \left|\dfrac{Actual\ value - Approximate\ value}{Actual\ value}\right| \times 100 = \left|\dfrac{1 - 1.00001}{1}\right| \times 100$

$= 0.00001 \times 100 = 0.001 \qquad i.e.\,0.1\%$

In case of Boole's rule, the percentage error

$= \left|\dfrac{Actual\ value - Approximate\ value}{Actual\ value}\right| \times 100 = \left|\dfrac{1 - 1.00039}{1}\right| \times 100$

$= 0.00039 \times 100 = 0.039 \qquad i.e.\,3.9\%$

9.8 NUMERICAL INTEGRATION USING CUBIC SPLINES

If $s(x)$ is the cubic spline in the interval (x_{i-1}, x_i), then

$$I = \int_{x_0}^{x_n} y\,dx = \sum_{i=1}^{n} \int_{x_{i-1}}^{x_i} s(x)dx$$

$$= \sum_{i=1}^{n} \int_{x_{i-1}}^{x_i} \frac{1}{6h}\Big[\{(x_i - x)^3 M_{i-1} + (x - x_{i-1})^3 M_i\}$$

$$+ \frac{1}{h}(x_i - x)\left(y_{i-1} - \frac{h^2}{6} M_{i-1}\right)$$

$$+ \frac{1}{h}(x - x_{i-1})\left(y_i - \frac{h^2}{6} M_i\right)\Big]\,dx \quad (from\ Eq.\,(6.8.12)$$

After carrying out the integration and simplification of this expression, we get

$$I = \sum_{i=1}^{n}\left[\frac{h}{2}(y_{i-1} + y_i) - \frac{h^3}{24}(M_{i-1} + M_i)\right] \qquad \ldots\ldots (9.8.1)$$

where, M_i are calculated from the recurrence relation.

$$M_{i-1} + 4M_i + M_{i+1} = \frac{6}{h^2}(y_{i-1} - 2y_i + y_{i+1}), \qquad \ldots\ldots (9.8.2)$$

for $i = 1, 2, \ldots\ldots, n - 1$

Example 9.8 Evaluate $I = \int_0^1 \sin \pi x \, dx$ using the cubic spline method.

Solution: Divide the interval $[0, 1]$ into two equal parts. Then $h = 0.5$ and the values of $y = \sin \pi x$ are as follows:

x	0.0	0.5	1.0
y	0.0	1.0	0.0

From Eq. (6.8.12), We know that

$$M_0 = M_n = 0$$

Therefore, $M_0 = M_2 = 0$ and from Eq. (9.8.2), we get $M_1 = -12$. Hence, Eq. (9.8.1) gives,

$$I = \sum_{i=1}^{2} \left[\frac{h}{2} (y_{i-1} + y_i) - \frac{h^3}{24} (M_{i-1} + M_i) \right]$$

$$\therefore I = \frac{1}{4} (y_0 + y_1) - \frac{1}{192} (M_0 + M_1) + \frac{1}{4} (y_1 + y_2) - \frac{1}{192} (M_1 + M_2)$$

$$= \frac{1}{4} + \frac{1}{16} + \frac{1}{4} + \frac{1}{16} = \frac{5}{8} = 0.6250$$

9.9   ROMBERG'S METHOD

In section 8.8, we have discussed Richardson's extrapolation method. If we apply Richardson's extrapolation method on numerical integration methods in a systematic way then it is known as Romberg's method of integration.

We know that the error in the Trapezoidal rule is $O(h^2)$. To evaluate the integral $I = \int_{x_0}^{x_n} y \, dx$, consider the composite Trapezoidal rule $I_T(h)$ for I with the width of the interval h. It is given by

$$I = I_T(h) + c_1 h^2 + c_2 h^4 + c_3 h^6 + \dots \dots \qquad \dots \dots (9.9.1)$$

Now, change the width of the interval as $h/2$ in Eq. (9.9.1), we have

$$I = I_T \left(\frac{h}{2} \right) + c_1 \frac{h^2}{4} + c_2 \frac{h^4}{16} + c_3 \frac{h^6}{64} + \dots \dots \qquad \dots \dots (9.9.2)$$

Eliminating c_1 from Eqs. (9.9.1) and (9.9.2), we have

$$I = \frac{4 I_T \left(\frac{h}{2} \right) - I_T(h)}{4 - 1} - \frac{1}{4} c_2 h^4 - \frac{5}{16} c_3 h^6 - \dots \dots$$

$$= I_T^{(1)}(h) - \frac{1}{4} c_2 h^4 - \frac{5}{16} c_3 h^6 - \dots \dots \qquad \dots \dots (9.9.3)$$

where, $\qquad I_T^{(1)}(h) = \dfrac{4 I_T \left(\frac{h}{2} \right) - I_T(h)}{4 - 1}$

is a closer approximation to I than $I_T(h)$. Again, changing the width h to $h/2$ in Eq. (9.9.3), we get

$$I = I_T^{(1)}\left(\frac{h}{2}\right) - \frac{1}{64}c_2h^4 - \frac{5}{1024}c_3h^6 - \dots\dots \qquad\dots\dots(9.9.4)$$

Eliminating c_2 from Eqs. (9.9.3) and (9.9.4), we have

$$I = I_T^{(2)}(h) + \frac{1}{64}c_3h^6 + \dots\dots \qquad\dots\dots(9.9.5)$$

where, $\qquad I_T^{(2)}(h) = \dfrac{4^2 \cdot I_T^{(1)}\left(\frac{h}{2}\right) - I_T^{(1)}(h)}{4^2 - 1}$

$I_T^{(2)}(h)$ is a still closer approximation to I.

In general, the successive closer approximations of I are given by

$$I_T^{(r)}(h) = \frac{4^r \cdot I_T^{(r-1)}\left(\frac{h}{2}\right) - I_T^{(r-1)}(h)}{4^r - 1}; \quad r = 1,2,\dots \qquad\dots\dots(9.9.6)$$

where $I_T^{(0)}(h) = I_T(h)$

Similarly, we know that the error in the Simpson's 1/3 rule is $O(h^4)$. To evaluate the integral $I = \int_{x_0}^{x_n} y\, dx$, if we consider the composite Simpson's 1/3 rule $I_s(h)$ for I with the width of the interval h. It is given by

$$I = I_s(h) + d_1h^4 + d_2h^6 + d_3h^8 + \dots\dots \qquad\dots\dots(9.9.7)$$

Arguing, as above, the extrapolation formula for Simpson's 1/3 rule is given by the recurrence relation

$$I_s^{(r)}(h) = \frac{4^{r+1} \cdot I_s^{(r-1)}\left(\frac{h}{2}\right) - I_s^{(r-1)}(h)}{4^{r+1} - 1}; \quad r = 1,2,\dots \qquad\dots\dots(9.9.8)$$

Example 9.9 Find the approximate value of

$$I = \int_0^1 \frac{1}{1+x^2}\, dx$$

using composite Trapezoidal rule with h = 0.5, 0.25, 0.125 and then Romberg's method. Hence, obtain an approximate value of π.

Solution: Let $h = 0.5$, $y = \frac{1}{1+x^2}$. We tabulate the value of y

$x:$	0	0.5	1
$y = \dfrac{1}{1+x^2}:$	1.0	0.80	0.50

By Trapezoidal rule,

$$I_T = \frac{h}{2}[(y_0 + y_2) + 2y_1]$$

$$= \frac{0.5}{2}[(1.0 + 0.50) + 2(0.80)] = 0.775$$

Let $h = 0.25$, we have

x :	0	0.25	0.5	0.75	1
$y = \dfrac{1}{1+x^2}$:	1.0	0.9412	0.8	0.64	0.50

Then, $I_T = \dfrac{h}{2}[(y_0 + y_4) + 2(y_1 + y_2 + y_3)]$

$= \dfrac{0.25}{2}[(1.0 + 0.50) + 2(0.9412 + 0.8 + 0.64)] = 0.7828$

Let $h = 0.125$, the tabular values are

x :	0	0.125	0.25	0.375	0.5	0.625	0.75	0.875	1
$y = \dfrac{1}{1+x^2}$:	1.0	0.9846	0.9412	0.8767	0.8	0.7191	0.64	0.5664	0.50

Then, $I_T = \dfrac{h}{2}[(y_0 + y_8) + 2(y_1 + y_2 + y_3 + \ldots + y_7)]$

$= \dfrac{0.125}{2}[(1.0 + 0.50)$
$+ 2(0.9846 + 0.9412 + 0.8767 + 0.8 + 0.7191 + 0.64$
$+ 0.5664)]$

$= 0.784750$

Now, let us apply Romberg's method

I_T / h	$I_T(h)$	$I_T{}^{(1)}(h)$	$I_T{}^{(2)}(h)$
$\dfrac{1}{2}$	0.7750		
		$\dfrac{4 I_T\left(\frac{1}{4}\right) - I_T\left(\frac{1}{2}\right)}{4-1} = 0.7854$	
$\dfrac{1}{4}$	0.7828		$\dfrac{4^2 I_T{}^{(1)}\left(\frac{1}{4}\right) - I_T{}^{(1)}\left(\frac{1}{2}\right)}{4^2-1} = 0.7854$
		$\dfrac{4 I_T\left(\frac{1}{8}\right) - I_T\left(\frac{1}{4}\right)}{4-1} = 0.7854$	
$\dfrac{1}{8}$	0.78475		

Hence, $I = 0.7854$. By actual integration

$$\int_0^1 \dfrac{1}{1+x^2}\,dx = \tan^{-1}(1) = 0.784475$$

$$I = \tan^{-1}(1) = \dfrac{\pi}{4}$$

$$\therefore \dfrac{\pi}{4} = 0.784475 \Rightarrow \pi = 4 \times 0.784475 = 3.1416$$

Example 9.10 Apply Romberg's integration method to evaluate

$$I = \int_{1.0}^{1.8} \frac{x}{coshx} \, dx$$

by applying composite Simpson's 1/3 rule with h = 0.8, 0.4, 0.2, 0.1.

Solution: Let $h = 0.8$, $y = \frac{x}{coshx}$. We tabulate the value of y

x :	1.0	1.8
$y = \frac{x}{coshx}$:	0.64805	0.57925

By Simpson's 1/3 rule,

$$I_s = \frac{h}{3}[(y_0 + y_2)] = \frac{0.8}{3}[(0.64805 + 0.57925)] = 0.32728$$

Let $h = 0.4$, we have

x :	1.0	1.4	1.8
$y = \frac{x}{coshx}$:	0.64805	0.65089	0.57925

Then, $I_s = \frac{h}{3}[(y_0 + y_2) + 4y_1] = \frac{0.4}{3}[(0.64805 + 0.57925) + 4(0.65089)] = 0.51078$

Let $h = 0.2$, the tabular values are

x :	1.0	1.2	1.4	1.6	1.8
$y = \frac{x}{coshx}$:	0.64805	0.66274	0.65089	0.62077	0.57925

Then, $I_s = \frac{h}{3}[(y_0 + y_4) + 4(y_1 + y_3) + 2y_2)] = \frac{0.2}{3}[(0.64805 + 0.57925) + 4(0.66274 + 0.62077) + 2(0.65089)] = 0.51087$

Let $h = 0.1$, the tabular values are

x :	1.0	1.1	1.2	1.3	1.4	1.5	1.6	1.7	1.8
y :	0.64805	0.65927	0.66274	0.65959	0.65089	0.63764	0.62077	0.60106	0.57925

Then, $I_s = \frac{h}{3}[(y_0 + y_9) + 4(y_1 + y_3 + y_5 + y_7) + 2(y_2 + y_4 + y_8)]$
$= \frac{0.1}{3}[(0.64805 + 0.57925)$
$+ 4(0.65927 + 0.65959 + 0.63764 + 0.60106)$
$+ 2(0.66274 + 0.65089 + 0.62077)] = 0.510878$

Now, let us apply Romberg's method

I_T	$I_T(h)$	$I_T^{(1)}(h)$	$I_T^{(2)}(h)$	$I_T^{(3)}(h)$
h				
0.8	0.32728			
		$\dfrac{4\,I_T(0.4) - I_T(0.8)}{4-1}$ $= 0.57195$		
0.4	0.51078		$\dfrac{4^2\,I_T^{(1)}(0.4) - I_T^{(1)}(0.8)}{4^2-1}$ $= 0.50683$	$\dfrac{4^3\,I_T^{(2)}(0.4) - I_T^{(1)}(0.8)}{4^3-1}$ $= 0.51094$
		$\dfrac{4\,I_T(0.2) - I_T(0.4)}{4-1}$ $= 0.5109$		
0.2	0.51087		$\dfrac{4^2\,I_T^{(1)}(0.2) - I_T^{(1)}(0.4)}{4^2-1}$ $= 0.510879$	
		$\dfrac{4\,I_T(0.1) - I_T(0.2)}{4-1}$ $= 0.51088$		
0.1	0.510878			

Hence, $I = 0.5109$

9.10   EULER – MACLAURIN SUMMATION FORMULA

Let $f(x)$ be a real, non – negative, continuous and continuously differentiable function up to all orders defined in the interval $[a, b]$. Let $[a, b]$ be divided into n equal sub-intervals by the points $a = x_0, x_1, x_2, \dots\dots, x_n = b$ such that $x_i = x_0 + ih$, $i = 0, 1, 2, \dots\dots, n$ and $h = \frac{b-a}{n}$ be the length of each sub – interval, then the Euler – Maclaurin summation formula is

$$\sum_{i=0}^{n} f(x_i) = \frac{1}{h}\int_{x_0}^{x_n} f(x)dx - \frac{1}{2}[f(x_n) + f(x_0)] - \frac{h}{12}[f'(x_n) - f'(x_0)]$$

$$-\frac{h^3}{720}[f'''(x_n) - f'''(x_0)] + \frac{h^5}{30240}[f^v(x_n) - f^v(x_0)] - \dots\dots$$

Proof: Let us define a function $F(x)$ such that $F(x + h) - F(x) = f(x)$

$$\therefore \ \Delta F(x) = f(x) \quad \Rightarrow \quad F(x) = \Delta^{-1}f(x) \qquad \dots\dots (9.10.1)$$

Now, $\Delta F(x_i) = f(x_i)$ (from Eq. (9.10.1))

$$\therefore \ F(x_1) - F(x_0) = \Delta F(x_0) = f(x_0)$$

Similarly, $F(x_2) - F(x_1) = \Delta F(x_1) = f(x_1)$

$$\dots \dots \dots \dots \dots \dots \dots \dots \dots \dots \dots \dots \dots \dots \dots$$

$$F(x_n) - F(x_{n-1}) = \Delta F(x_{n-1}) = f(x_{n-1})$$

Adding these results, we get

$$F(x_n) - F(x_0) = \sum_{i=0}^{n-1} f(x_i) \qquad \dots\dots (9.10.2)$$

We know that $\Delta = E - 1$ and $E = e^{hD}$
From Eq. (9.10.1), we have

$$F(x) = \Delta^{-1} f(x) = (E - 1)^{-1} f(x) = (e^{hD} - 1)^{-1} f(x)$$

$$= \left[\left(1 + hD + \frac{h^2 D^2}{2!} + \frac{h^3 D^3}{3!} + \dots\dots\right) - 1\right]^{-1} f(x)$$

$$\left(\because e^x = 1 + x + \frac{x^2}{2!} + \frac{x^3}{3!} + \dots\dots\right)$$

$$= \left[\left(hD + \frac{h^2 D^2}{2!} + \frac{h^3 D^3}{3!} + \dots\dots\right)\right]^{-1} f(x)$$

$$= (hD)^{-1} \left[1 + \frac{hD}{2!} + \frac{h^2 D^2}{3!} + \frac{h^3 D^3}{4!} + \dots\dots\right]^{-1} f(x)$$

$$= (hD)^{-1} \left[1 - \left(\frac{hD}{2} + \frac{h^2 D^2}{6} + \frac{h^3 D^3}{24} + \frac{h^4 D^4}{120} + \dots\dots\right)\right.$$

$$+ \left(\frac{hD}{2} + \frac{h^2 D^2}{6} + \frac{h^3 D^3}{24} + \frac{h^4 D^4}{120} + \dots\dots\right)^2$$

$$\left. - \left(\frac{hD}{2} + \frac{h^2 D^2}{6} + \frac{h^3 D^3}{24} + \frac{h^4 D^4}{120} + \dots\dots\right)^3 + \dots\dots\right] f(x)$$

$$= \frac{1}{h} D^{-1} \left[1 - \frac{hD}{2} + \frac{h^2 D^2}{12} - \frac{h^4 D^4}{720} + \dots\dots\right] f(x)$$

$$= \left[\frac{1}{h} D^{-1} - \frac{1}{2} + \frac{hD}{12} - \frac{h^3 D^3}{720} + \frac{h^5 D^5}{30240} - \dots\dots\right] f(x)$$

$$= \frac{1}{h} \int f(x)\, dx - \frac{1}{2} f(x) + \frac{h}{12} f'(x) - \frac{h^3}{720} f'''(x) + \frac{h^5}{30240} f^v(x)$$

$$- \dots\dots \qquad \dots\dots (9.10.3)$$

Putting $x = x_n$ and $x = x_0$ in Eq. (9.10.3) and then subtracting, we obtain

$$F(x_n) - F(x_0) = \frac{1}{h} \int_{x_0}^{x_n} f(x)\, dx - \frac{1}{2} [f(x_n) - f(x_0)]$$

$$+ \frac{h}{12}[f'(x_n) - f'(x_0)] - \frac{h^3}{720}[f'''^{(x_n)} - f'''^{(x_0)}]$$

$$+ \frac{h^5}{30240}[f^v(x_n) - f^v(x_0)] - \dots \dots \qquad \dots \dots (9.10.4)$$

Now,

$$\sum_{i=0}^{n} f(x_i) = \sum_{i=0}^{n-1} f(x_i) + f(x_n) \qquad \dots \dots (9.10.5)$$

From Eq. (9.10.1), (9.10.4) and (9.10.5), we have

$$\sum_{i=0}^{n} f(x_i) = \frac{1}{h} \int_{x_0}^{x_n} f(x)dx + \frac{1}{2}[f(x_n) + f(x_0)] + \frac{h}{12}[f'(x_n) - f'(x_0)]$$

$$- \frac{h^3}{720}[f'''^{(x_n)} - f'''^{(x_0)}] + \frac{h^5}{30240}[f^v(x_n) - f^v(x_0)] - \dots \dots \dots (9.10.6)$$

i.e. $\frac{1}{h}\int_{x_0}^{x_n} f(x)dx = \sum_{i=0}^{n} f(x_i) - \frac{1}{2}[f(x_n) + f(x_0)]$

$- \frac{h}{12}[f'(x_n) - f'(x_0)] + \frac{h^3}{720}[f'''(x_n) - f'''(x_0)] - \frac{h^5}{30240}[f^v(x_n) - f^v(x_0)] + \dots \dots$

$$= \left\{ \frac{1}{2}f(x_0) + f(x_1) + f(x_2) + \dots \dots + f(x_{n-1}) + \frac{1}{2}f(x_n) \right\}$$

$$- \frac{h}{12}[f'(x_n) - f'(x_0)] + \frac{h^3}{720}[f'''(x_n) - f'''(x_0)]$$

$$- \frac{h^5}{30240}[f^v(x_n) - f^v(x_0)] + \dots \dots$$

$$\int_{x_0}^{x_0+nh} y\, dx = \frac{h}{2}[y_0 + 2y_1 + 2y_2 + \dots + 2y_{n-1} + y_n] - \frac{h^2}{12}(y_n' - y_0')$$

$$+ \frac{h^4}{720}(y_n''' - y_0''') - \frac{h^5}{30240}(y_n^v - y_0^v) + \dots \dots \qquad \dots \dots (9.10.7)$$

which is known as Euler – Maclaurin formula. We observe that the first term on the right hand side of Eq. (9.10.7) represents the approximate value of the integral obtained from the Trapezoidal rule while the other terms represent the successive corrections to this value.

Example 9.11   Apply Euler – Maclaurin summation formula to find
$$1^2 + 2^2 + 3^2 + \dots \dots + n^2$$

Solution: Here, $f(x) = x^2$, $x_0 = 1$, $x_n = n$, $h = 1$
$$\therefore f'(x) = 2x, f''(x) = 2$$

From Eq. (9.10.6), we have

$$\sum_{i=0}^{n} f(x_i) = \frac{1}{h}\int_{x_0}^{x_n} f(x)dx + \frac{1}{2}[f(x_n) + f(x_0)] + \frac{h}{12}[f'(x_n) - f'(x_0)]$$

$$- \frac{h^3}{720} [f'''(x_n) - f'''(x_0)] + \frac{h^5}{30240} [f^v(x_n) - f^v(x_0)] - \dots\dots$$

$$\therefore \ 1^2 + 2^2 + \dots + x^2$$

$$= \int_1^n x^2 \, dx + \frac{1}{2}(n^2 + 1) + \frac{1}{12}(2n - 2) - \frac{1}{720}(2 - 2)$$

$$= \left[\frac{x^3}{3}\right]_1^n + \frac{1}{2}(n^2 + 1) + \frac{(n-1)}{6} \qquad = \frac{(n^3 - 1)}{3} + \frac{1}{2}(n^2 + 1) + \frac{(n-1)}{6}$$

$$= \frac{1}{6}(2n^3 + 3n^2 + n) = \frac{n(n+1)(2n+1)}{6}$$

Example 9.12 Apply Euler – Maclaurin summation formula to evaluate

$$\frac{1}{30^2} + \frac{1}{32^2} + \frac{1}{34^2} + \dots\dots + \frac{1}{50^2}$$

Solution: Here, $f(x) = \frac{1}{x^2}$, $x_0 = 30$, $x_n = 50$, $h = 2$,

Now, $x_n = a + (n - 1)d \ \Rightarrow 50 = 30 + (n - 1)2 \ \Rightarrow n = 11$

$$\therefore \ f'(x) = -\frac{2}{x^3}, f''(x) = \frac{6}{x^4}, f'''(x) = \frac{-24}{x^5}$$

From Eq. (9.10.6), we have

$$\sum_{i=0}^{11} f(x_i) = \frac{1}{2} \int_{30}^{50} \frac{1}{x^2} \, dx + \frac{1}{2}[f(50) + f(30)] + \frac{2}{12}[f'(50) - f'(30)]$$

$$- \frac{2^3}{720}[f'''(50) - f'''(30)] - \dots\dots$$

$$= -\frac{1}{2}\left[\frac{1}{50} - \frac{1}{30}\right] + \frac{1}{2}\left[\frac{1}{50^2} + \frac{1}{30^2}\right] + \frac{2}{12}\left[-\frac{2}{50^3} + \frac{2}{30^3}\right] - \frac{2^3}{720}\left[\frac{-24}{50^5} + \frac{-24}{30^5}\right]$$

$$= -0.5(0.02 - 0.0333) + 0.5(0.0004 + 0.0011) + 0.1667(-0.000016 +$$
$$0.000074) - 0.01111(-0.0000000768 - 0.0000009876)$$

$$= 0.00665 + 0.00075 + 0.0000096686 + 0.00000001183$$

$$= 0.00740968 \qquad upto \ 4 \ decimal \ places$$

9.11 METHODS BASED ON UNDETERMINED CO-EFFICIENTS

We know that the integral is approximated by a finite linear combination of values of $f(x)$ in the form

$$I = \int_a^b w(x)f(x) \, dx \ \approx \ \sum_{i=0}^{n} \lambda_i f_i \qquad\qquad \dots\dots(9.11.1)$$

where, x_i, $i = 0, 1, \dots, n$ are called the abscissas or nodes distributed within the limits of integration $[a, b]$ and λ_i, $i = 0, 1, \dots, n$ are called the weights of the integration formula.

In the preceding sections, we have seen integration formulae like Trapezoidal rule, Simpson's rule, Weddle's rule in which the range of integration was divided in predefined equally spaced intervals.

These integration formulae are nothing but a weighted sum of function values at given points within the domain of integration.

For example, Trapezoidal and Simpson's rules are

$$I = \int_{x_0=a}^{x_n=b} f(x)\, dx = h\left[\frac{1}{2}f_0 + f_1 + f_2 + f_3 + \dots \dots + \frac{1}{2}f_n\right] \quad \text{and}$$

$$I = \int_{x_0=a}^{x_n=b} f(x)\, dx = h\left[\frac{1}{3}f_0 + \frac{4}{3}f_1 + \frac{2}{3}f_2 + \frac{4}{3}f_3 + \dots \dots + \frac{1}{3}f_n\right] \quad \text{respectively}$$

and can be expressed as

$$I = h\sum_{i=0}^{n} \lambda_i f_i$$

In the integration method in Eq. (9.11.1), the values $x_i's$ and the weights $\lambda_i's$ can also be obtained by making the formula exact for polynomials of degree upto m. There are two possibilities for m:

$$if \begin{cases} m = n \ (i.e.\ all\ the\ values\ are\ known) & \text{the corrsponding methods are called Newton} - \text{Cotes methods} \\ m = 2n\ (i.e.\ values\ are\ to\ be\ determined) & \text{the corresponding methods are called Gaussian integration methods} \end{cases}$$

Gaussian integration methods or Gaussian quadrature formula utilizes the same number of values of $f(x)$ like other numerical integration formulae when $x_i's$ are not equally spaced but are at the points of subdivision of the interval which are symmetrically placed with respect to the mid – point of the interval of integration.

Suppose we want to evaluate $\int_a^b f(x)dx$. The requirement of the Gaussian formula is that limits of finite integral over $[a, b]$ should be in the form of $\int_{-1}^{1} f(x)dx$.

For this purpose, let $\qquad x = \alpha z + \beta \qquad \qquad$ .... (9.11.2)

where α and β are unknowns and chosen in such a way that they satisfy the following conditions:

when $x = a, z = -1 \quad$ and $\quad x = b,\ z = 1$

Putting these conditions in Eq. (9.11.2), we get

$$\qquad\qquad a = \beta - \alpha \qquad .... (1)$$

and $\qquad\qquad\quad b = \alpha + \beta \qquad .... (2)$

From (1) and (2), we get

$$\alpha = \frac{b-a}{2} \quad and \quad \beta = \frac{b+a}{2}$$

Putting these values in Eq. (9.11.2), we get

$$x = \frac{1}{2}\left[(b-a)z + (b+a)\right] \;\Rightarrow\; dx = \frac{1}{2}(b-a)dz \qquad .... (9.11.3)$$

$$\therefore \int_a^b f(x)dx = \int_{-1}^1 f\left[\frac{1}{2}(b-a)z + \frac{1}{2}(b+a)\right]\frac{1}{2}(b-a)\,dz$$

$$= \frac{1}{2}(b-a)\int_{-1}^1 g(z)dz = \frac{(b-a)}{2}\sum_{i=1}^n \lambda_i\, g(z_i) \quad \dots\dots (9.11.4)$$

where, λ_i and z_i are weights and nodes (i.e. sampling points) for the integral domain (-1, 1).

$$\int_{-1}^1 g(z)dz = \lambda_1\, g(z_1) + \lambda_2\, g(z_2) + \dots\dots + \lambda_n\, g(z_n) \qquad \dots\dots (9.11.5)$$

$\int_{-1}^1 g(z)\,dz$ can be evaluated using gaussian quadrature formule which are explained in the next sub – sections.

9.11.1   Gauss – Legendre Integration Method

This method uses Gaussian quadrature formula, in which $z_1, z_2, z_3, \dots\dots, z_n$ are assumed as the roots of the Legendre's polynomial $P_n(x)$ of degree n.

Let $\qquad g(z) = a_0 + a_1 z + a_2 z^2 + \dots\dots + a_{2n-1}\, z^{2n-1} \qquad \dots\dots (9.11.6)$

be a power series expanded in the interval (-1 , 1). By the properties of definite integrals, we have

$$\int_{-1}^1 g(z)dz = 2\int_0^1 (a_0 + a_2 z^2 + a_4 z^4 + \dots\dots + a_{2n-2}\, z^{2n-2})\,dz$$

$$= 2a_0 + \frac{2}{3}a_2 + \frac{2}{5}a_4 + \dots\dots + \frac{2}{2n-1}a_{2n-2} \qquad \dots\dots (9.11.7)$$

Substituting $\qquad z = z_i$ and $g(z_i) = a_0 + a_1 z_i + a_2 z_i^2 + a_3 z_i^3 + \dots\dots + a_{2n-1}\, z_i^{2n-1}$ $i = 1,2,3,\dots\dots, n$ in Eq. (9.11.4), we get

$$\int_{-1}^1 g(z)dz = \lambda_1\,(a_0 + a_1 z_1 + a_2 z_1^2 + \dots + a_{2n-1}\, z_1^{2n-1})$$

$$+ \lambda_2\,(a_0 + a_1 z_2 + a_2 z_2^2 + \dots + a_{2n-1}\, z_2^{2n-1})$$

$$+ \dots\dots + \lambda_n\,(a_0 + a_1 z_n + a_2 z_n^2 + \dots + a_{2n-1}\, z_n^{2n-1})$$

$$= a_0(\lambda_1 + \lambda_2 + \dots\dots + \lambda_n) + a_1(\lambda_1 z_1 + \lambda_2 z_2 + \dots\dots + \lambda_n z_n)$$

$$+ a_2(\lambda_1 z_1^2 + \lambda_2 z_2^2 + \dots\dots + \lambda_n z_n^2) + \dots + a_{2n-1}(\lambda_1 z_1^{2n-1}$$

$$+\lambda_2 z_2^{2n-1} + \dots + \lambda_n z_n^{2n-1}) \qquad\qquad \dots\dots (9.11.8)$$

Since R.H.S. of Eq. (9.11.7) and (9.11.8) are equal, equating co-efficients of z_i, we get

$$\left.\begin{array}{l} \lambda_1 + \lambda_2 + \lambda_3 + \ldots\ldots + \lambda_n = 2 \\ \lambda_1 z_1 + \lambda_2 z_2 + \ldots\ldots + \lambda_n z_n = 0 \\ \lambda_1 z_1{}^2 + \lambda_2 z_2{}^2 + \ldots\ldots + \lambda_n z_n{}^2 = \frac{2}{3} \\ \ldots\ldots\ldots\ldots\ldots\ldots\ldots\ldots\ldots\ldots\ldots\ldots\ldots\ldots\ldots \\ \lambda_1 z_1{}^{2n-1} + \lambda_2 z_2{}^{2n-1} + \ldots + \lambda_n z_n{}^{2n-1} = 0 \end{array}\right\} \quad \ldots\ldots (9.11.9)$$

By solving these $2n$ equations given in Eq.(9.11.9), we can obtain values of $2n$ unknowns z_i and λ_i, $i = 1,2,3,\ldots\ldots,n$. Practically it is very difficult to solve Eqs. (9.11.8), it needs lot of computations.

When $z_1, z_2, \ldots\ldots, z_n$ are the roots of the Legendre equation $P_n(z) = 0$, the values of $\lambda_i's$, $i = 1,2,3,\ldots\ldots,n$ can be easily obtained. The Legendre polynomial is

$$P_n(z) = \frac{1}{2^n . n!} \frac{d^n}{dz^n} (z^2 - 1)^n$$

Since, $z_1, z_2, \ldots\ldots, z_n$ are the roots of the Legendre equation, we have

$$\frac{d^n}{dz^n} (z^2 - 1)^n = 0 \qquad \ldots\ldots (9.11.10)$$

Two Points Gauss – Legendre Integration Method

Putting n = 2 in Eq. (9.11.10), we get

$$\frac{d^2}{dz^2} (z^2 - 1)^2 = 0 \quad \Rightarrow \quad \frac{d^2}{dz^2} (z^4 - 2z^2 + 1) = 0$$

$$\therefore 12z^2 - 4 = 0 \Rightarrow z = \pm \sqrt{1/3}$$

Let $z_1 = \sqrt{\frac{1}{3}}$ and $z_2 = -\sqrt{\frac{1}{3}}$. Then from Eq. (9.11.8), we have

$$\lambda_1 + \lambda_2 = 2$$

$$\lambda_1 z_1 + \lambda_2 z_2 = 0 \Rightarrow \lambda_1 \left(\sqrt{1/3}\right) + \lambda_2 \left(\sqrt{1/3}\right) = 0$$

$$\text{Thus, } \lambda_1 = \lambda_2 = 1$$

Three Points Gauss – Legendre Integration Method

Putting n = 3 in Eq. (9.11.10), we get

$$\frac{d^3}{dz^3} (z^2 - 1)^3 = 0 \quad \Rightarrow \quad \frac{d^3}{dz^3} (z^6 - 3z^4 + 3z^2 - 1) = 0$$

$$\therefore 120z^3 - 72z = 0 \Rightarrow 24z (5z^2 - 3) = 0 \Rightarrow z = 0, \pm \sqrt{3/5}$$

Let $z_1 = \sqrt{\frac{3}{5}}$, $z_2 = 0$ and $z_3 = -\sqrt{\frac{3}{5}}$. Then from Eq. (9.11.8), we have

$$\lambda_1 + \lambda_2 + \lambda_3 = 2$$

$$\lambda_1 z_1 + \lambda_2 z_2 + \lambda_3 z_3 = 0 \Rightarrow \lambda_1\left(-\sqrt{3/5}\right) + \lambda_3\left(\sqrt{\frac{3}{5}}\right) = 0 \Rightarrow -\lambda_1 + \lambda_3 = 0$$

$$\lambda_1 z_1^2 + \lambda_2 z_2^2 + \lambda_3 z_3^2 = \frac{2}{3} \Rightarrow \frac{3}{5}\lambda_1 + \frac{3}{5}\lambda_3 = \frac{2}{3} \Rightarrow \lambda_1 + \lambda_3 = \frac{10}{9}$$

Solving these equations, we get $\lambda_1 = \frac{5}{9}, \lambda_2 = \frac{8}{9}, \lambda_3 = \frac{5}{9}$

The nodes (i.e. sampling points) and their corresponding weights for the Gauss – Legendre integration method for n = 2 to 6 are given in Table 9.1.

Table 9.1 Nodes and Weights for Gauss – Legendre Integration Method

n	z_i	λ_i
2	$z_1 = -0.57735;$ $z_2 = 0.57735$	$\lambda_1 = 1.00000; \lambda_2 = 1.00000$
3	$z_1 = -0.77460;$ $z_2 = 0;$	$\lambda_1 = \lambda_3 = 0.55556;$
	$z_3 = 0.77460$	$\lambda_2 = 0.88889$
4	$z_1 = -0.86114;$ $z_2 = -0.33998;$	$\lambda_1 = \lambda_4 = 0.34785;$
	$z_3 = 0.33998,$ $z_4 = 0.86114$	$\lambda_2 = \lambda_3 = 0.65215;$
5	$z_1 = -0.90618;$ $z_2 = -0.53847;$ $z_3 = 0;$	$\lambda_1 = \lambda_5 = 0.23693;$
	$z_4 = 0.53847;$ $z_5 = 0.90618$	$\lambda_2 = \lambda_4 = 0.47863;$ $\lambda_3 = 0.56889$
6	$z_1 = -0.93247;$ $z_2 = -0.66121;$	$\lambda_1 = \lambda_6 = 0.17132;$
	$z_3 = -0.23862;$ $z_4 = 0.23862;$	$\lambda_2 = \lambda_5 = 0.36076;$
	$z_4 = 0.66121;$ $z_5 = 0.93247;$	$\lambda_3 = \lambda_4 = 0.46791;$

The values of $z_i{'}s$ and $\lambda_i{'}s$, given in the Table 9.1, are used in the Gaussian integration formula (Eq. (9.11.4)) and the value of $\int_{-1}^{1} g(z)dz$ is obtained.

Example 9.13   Determine unknown weights A and B and abscissa in the following integration formula so that it gives best possible accuracy.

$$\int_{-1}^{1} f(x)\, dx \simeq A\, f(-1) + B\, f(x_1)$$

Solution: Compare above integration formula with $\int_{-1}^{1} f(x)\, dx \simeq \lambda_1 f(x_0) + \lambda_2 f(x_1)$. Three unknowns A, B and x_1 are given which need to be determined. As we have three unknowns, three equations $f(x) = 1, x, x^2$ are required and also given that, $x_0 = -1$. Instead of λ_1, λ_2 we have A and B. From Eq. 9.11.9, we have

$$\lambda_1 + \lambda_2 = 2 \Rightarrow A + B = 2 \qquad \text{........ (1)}$$
$$\lambda_1 z_1 + \lambda_2 z_2 = 0 \Rightarrow A x_0 + B x_1 = 0 \qquad \text{........ (2)}$$

$$\lambda_1 z_1^2 + \lambda_2 z_2^2 = 0 \implies A x_0^2 + B x_1^2 = \frac{2}{3} \quad \text{........ (3)}$$

Since $x_0 = -1$, from (2), $\quad -A + B x_1 = 0 \implies A = B x_1 \quad \text{........ (4)}$

From (3), $\quad A + B x_1^2 = \frac{2}{3} \quad \text{........ (5)}$

From (4) and (5), $\quad A + (B x_1) x_1 = \frac{2}{3} \implies A + A x_1 = \frac{2}{3}$

$$-A + B x_1 = 0$$

Hence, $\quad x_1 (A + B) = \frac{2}{3} \implies x_1(2) = \frac{2}{3} \implies x_1 = \frac{1}{3}$

Therefore, $\quad A + A \left(\frac{1}{3}\right) = \frac{2}{3} \implies A = \frac{1}{2} \quad \therefore \quad B = \frac{3}{2} \ (from \ (1))$

$$\therefore \quad \int_{-1}^{1} f(x)\, dx \simeq \frac{1}{2} f(-1) + \frac{3}{2} f\left(\frac{1}{3}\right)$$

Example 9.14   Determine a, b, c such that

$$\int_{0}^{h} f(x)\, dx \simeq h \left\{ a f(0) + b f\left(\frac{h}{3}\right) + c f(h) \right\}$$

is exact for polynomial as high degree as possible.

Solution: Three unknowns a, b and c are given which need to be determined. As we have three unknowns, three equations $f(x) = 1, x, x^2$ are required and also given that, $x_0 = 0, x_1 = \frac{h}{3}, x_2 = h$.

Let $f(x) = 1$

$$\therefore \quad \int_{0}^{h} 1\, dx \simeq h \left\{ a(1) + b\,(1) + c \right\}$$

$[x]_0^h = h(a + b + c) \implies h(a + b + c) = h \implies a + b + c = 1 \quad \text{........(1)}$

Let $f(x) = x$

$$\therefore \quad \int_{0}^{h} x\, dx \simeq h \left\{ a(0) + b \left(\frac{h}{3}\right) + c(h) \right\}$$

$\left[\frac{x^2}{2}\right]_0^h = h\left(\frac{bh}{3} + ch\right) \implies \frac{h^2}{2} = h^2 \left(\frac{b}{3} + c\right) \implies \frac{2b}{3} + 2c = 1 \quad \text{........ (2)}$

Let $f(x) = x^2$

$$\therefore \quad \int_{0}^{h} x^2\, dx \simeq h \left\{ a(0) + b \left(\frac{h^2}{9}\right) + c(h^2) \right\}$$

$\left[\frac{x^3}{3}\right]_0^h = h\left(\frac{bh^2}{9} + ch^2\right) \implies \frac{h^3}{3} = h^3 \left(\frac{b}{9} + c\right) \implies \frac{b}{3} + 3c = 1 \quad \text{........ (3)}$

After solving Eqs. (1) – (3), we get $\quad a = 0, \ b = \frac{3}{4}, \ c = \frac{1}{4}$

$$\therefore \quad \int_{0}^{h} f(x)\, dx \simeq h \left\{ 0.f(0) + \frac{3}{4}.f\left(\frac{h}{3}\right) + \frac{1}{4}.f(h) \right\}$$

9.11.2 Gauss – Chebyshev Integration Method

The methods of the form

$$I = \int_{-1}^{1} \frac{1}{\sqrt{(1-x^2)}} f(x)\, dx = \sum_{i=0}^{n} \lambda_i f_i, \quad where, \quad w(x) = \frac{1}{\sqrt{(1-x^2)}}$$

are called Gauss- Chebyshev integration methods. These methods are exact for polynomials of degree upto 2n. This method uses Gaussian quadrature formula, in which $z_1, z_2, z_3, ..., z_n$ are assumed as the roots of the Chebyshev polynomials

$$T_n(z) = \cos(n \cos^{-1} z) = 0 \quad where, \quad -1 \le z \le 1 \qquad (from\ Eq.\ 7.6.6))$$

Therefore, by property of Chebyshev polynomial, we get

$$z_i = \cos\left(\frac{(2k+1)\pi}{2n}\right), \quad k = 0,1,2,...,n-1$$

All the weights are equal and are given by $\lambda_i = \pi/n$. To apply this integration method, we use the transformation

$$x = -1 + \frac{2(z-\alpha)}{(\beta - \alpha)}$$

where α and β are unknowns and chosen in such a way that they satisfy the following conditions:
when $x = a, z = -1$ *and* $x = b, z = 1$ and multiply the integrand by

$$\frac{(1-x^2)^{-1/2}}{(1-x^2)^{-1/2}}$$

This implies that

$$\therefore \int_{a}^{b} f(x)dx = \frac{(b-a)}{2} \int_{-1}^{1} g\left(\frac{(z+1)(b-a)}{2} + a\right) \frac{(1-z^2)^{1/2}}{(1-z^2)^{1/2}} dz$$

$$........ (9.11.11)$$

We then use the Gauss – Chebyshev integration to calculate the RHS of Eq. (9.11.11) producing the approximation

$$\therefore \int_{a}^{b} f(x)dx = \frac{\pi(b-a)}{2n} \sum_{i=1}^{n} g\left(\frac{(z_i+1)(b-a)}{2} + a\right)(1-z_i^2)^{1/2}$$

$$........ (9.11.12)$$

where the z_i are the Gauss – Chebyshev integration nodes over [-1, 1]. We will not go into the detail of these integration methods. The nodes (i.e. sampling points) and their corresponding weights for the Gauss – Chebyshev integration method for n = 2 to 5 are given in Table 9.2.

Table 9.2 Nodes and Weights for Gauss – Chebyshev Integration Method

n	z_i	λ_i
2	$z_1 = -0.707107;\quad z_2 = 0.707107$	$\lambda_1 = 1.5708;\ \lambda_2 = 1.5708$
3	$z_1 = -0.866025;\quad z_2 = 0;$ $z_3 = 0.866025$	$\lambda_1 = \lambda_2 = \lambda_3 = 1.0472;$
4	$z_1 = -0.382683;\quad z_2 = -0.92388;$ $z_3 = 0.382683,\quad z_4 = 0.92388$	$\lambda_1 = \lambda_4 = 0.785398;$ $\lambda_2 = \lambda_3 = 0.785398;$
5	$z_1 = -0.587785; z_2 = -0.951057;\ z_3 = 0;$ $z_4 = 0.587785;\quad z_5 = 0.951057$	$\lambda_1 = \lambda_2 = 0.628319;$ $\lambda_3 = \lambda_4 = \lambda_5 = 0.628319;$

The values of $z_i{}'s$ and $\lambda_i{}'s$, given in the Table 9.2, are used in the Gaussian integration formula (Eq. (9.11.4)) and the value of $\int_{-1}^{1} g(z)dz$ is obtained.

Example 9.15 Evaluate

$$\int_{2}^{4} (5x^4 + 3x^2 + 1)\, dx, \quad \text{using}$$

(i)   Gauss's two – point quadrature formula
(ii)   Gauss – Legendre three – point formula

Solution: Here, $a = 2$ and $b = 4$. Hence, from Eq. (9.11.3), we have

$$x = \frac{(b-a)}{2} z + \frac{(b+a)}{2} = \frac{(4-2)}{2} z + \frac{(4+2)}{2} = z + 3;$$

$$\therefore\ g(z) = 5(z+3)^4 + 3(z+3)^2 + 1$$

(i)   Two – point formula

Given $n = 2$, $a = 2$ and $b = 4$. From Eq.(9.11.4), we have

$$\int_{a}^{b} f(x)dx = \frac{1}{2}(b-a)\int_{-1}^{1} g(z)dz = \frac{(b-a)}{2}\sum_{i=1}^{2}\lambda_i\, g(z_i)$$

$$= \frac{(b-a)}{2}\ [\lambda_1 g(z_1) + \lambda_2 g(z_2)]$$

For Two – point formula, from Table 9.1, we have

$$z_1 = -0.57735;\quad z_2 = 0.57735,\ \lambda_1 = 1.00000;\ \lambda_2 = 1.00000$$

$$\int_{2}^{4} (5x^4 + 3x^2 + 1)\, dx = \frac{1}{2}(b-a)\int_{-1}^{1} g(z)dz$$

$$= \frac{(b-a)}{2}\ [\lambda_1 g(z_1) + \lambda_2 g(z_2)]$$

$$= \frac{(4-2)}{2}\ [1.0000\ \{5(z_1+3)^4 + 3(z_1+3)^2 + 1\}$$

$$+\ 1.0000\{5(z_2+3)^4 + 3(z_2+3)^2 + 1\}]$$

$$= 1.[1.0000\{5(-0.57735+3)^4 + 3(-0.57735+3)^2 + 1\}$$
$$+ 1.0000\{5(0.57735+3)^4 + 3(0.57735+3)^2 + 1\}]$$
$$= [(172.2395 + 17.6077 + 1) + (818.8715 + 38.3923 + 1)] = 1049.111$$

(ii)   Three – point formula

Given $n = 3$, $a = 2$ and $b = 4$. Therefore, from Eq.(9.11.4), we have

$$\int_a^b f(x)dx = \frac{1}{2}(b-a)\int_{-1}^1 g(z)dz = \frac{(b-a)}{2}\sum_{i=1}^3 \lambda_i\, g(z_i)$$

$$= \frac{(b-a)}{2}[\lambda_1 g(z_1) + \lambda_2 g(z_2) + \lambda_3 g(z_3)]$$

Now, $x = z+3$ $\therefore$ $g(z) = 5(z+3)^4 + 3(z+3)^2 + 1$

For Three – point formula, from Table 9.1, we have

$z_1 = -0.77460$; $z_2 = 0$; $z_3 = 0.77460$; $\lambda_1 = \lambda_3 = 0.55556$; $\lambda_2 = 0.88889$

$$\int_2^4 (5x^4 + 3x^2 + 1)\, dx = \frac{1}{2}(b-a)\int_{-1}^1 g(z)dz$$

$$= \frac{(b-a)}{2}[\lambda_1 g(z_1) + \lambda_2 g(z_2) + \lambda_3 g(z_3)]$$

$$= \frac{(4-2)}{2}[0.55556\{5(z_1+3)^4 + 3(z_1+3)^2 + 1\}$$
$$+ 0.88889\{5(z_2+3)^4 + 3(z_2+3)^2 + 1\}$$
$$+ 0.55556\{5(z_3+3)^4 + 3(z_3+3)^2 + 1\}]$$

$$= 1.[0.55556\{5(-0.77460+3)^4 + 3(-0.77460+3)^2 + 1\}$$
$$+ 0.88889\{5(0+3)^4 + 3(0+3)^2 + 1\}$$
$$+ 0.55556\{5(0.77460+3)^4 + 3(0.77460+3)^2 + 1\}]$$

$$= [0.55556(122.6316 + 14.8572 + 1) + 0.88889(405 + 27 + 1)$$
$$+ 0.55556(1014.9713 + 42.7428 + 1)]$$
$$= (76.9388 + 384.8894 + 588.1792)$$

$$= 1050.0074$$

Example 9.16 Evaluate $\int_0^1 \frac{dx}{1+x^2}$, using (i) 2 – point and (ii) 3 – point Gauss – Legendre's quadrature formula. Compare the result with exact value.

Solution: Here, $a = 0$ and $b = 1$. Hence, from Eq. (9.11.3), we have

$$x = \frac{(b-a)}{2}z + \frac{(b+a)}{2} = \frac{(1-0)}{2}z + \frac{(1+0)}{2} = \frac{1}{2}z + \frac{1}{2};$$

$$\therefore g(z) = \frac{1}{1 + \left(\frac{1}{2}z + \frac{1}{2}\right)^2} = \frac{4}{4 + (z+1)^2} = \frac{4}{z^2 + 2z + 5}$$

(i)   Two – point formula

Given $n = 2$, $a = 0$ and $b = 1$. From Eq.(9.11.4), we have

$$\int_a^b f(x)dx = \frac{1}{2}(b-a)\int_{-1}^1 g(z)dz = \frac{(b-a)}{2}\sum_{i=1}^2 \lambda_i\, g(z_i)$$

$$= \frac{(b-a)}{2}[\lambda_1 g(z_1) + \lambda_2 g(z_2)]$$

For Two – point formula, from Table 9.1, we have

$z_1 = -0.57735$; $z_2 = 0.57735$, $\lambda_1 = 1.00000$; $\lambda_2 = 1.00000$

$$\int_0^1 \frac{dx}{1+x^2} = \frac{1}{2}(b-a)\int_{-1}^1 g(z)dz = \frac{(b-a)}{2}[\lambda_1 g(z_1) + \lambda_2 g(z_2)]$$

$$= \frac{(1-0)}{2}\left[1.0000\left\{\frac{4}{z_1{}^2 + 2z_1 + 5}\right\} + 1.0000\left\{\frac{4}{z_2{}^2 + 2z_2 + 5}\right\}\right]$$

$$= \frac{4}{2}\times\left[1.0000\left\{\frac{1}{(-0.57735)^2 + 2(-0.57735) + 5}\right\}\right.$$

$$\left. + 1.0000\left\{\frac{1}{(0.57735)^2 + 2(0.57735) + 5}\right\}\right]$$

$$= 2 \times [0.239313 + 0.154130] = 0.786886$$

(ii)   Three – point formula

Given $n = 3$, $a = 0$ and $b = 1$. Therefore, from Eq.(9.11.4), we have

$$\int_a^b f(x)dx = \frac{1}{2}(b-a)\int_{-1}^1 g(z)dz = \frac{(b-a)}{2}\sum_{i=1}^3 \lambda_i\, g(z_i)$$

$$= \frac{(b-a)}{2}[\lambda_1 g(z_1) + \lambda_2 g(z_2) + \lambda_3 g(z_3)]$$

Now, $x = \frac{1}{2}z + \frac{1}{2}$ $\therefore g(z) = \frac{4}{z^2 + 2z + 5}$

For Three – point formula, from Table 9.1, we have

$z_1 = -0.77460$; $z_2 = 0$; $z_3 = 0.77460$; $\lambda_1 = \lambda_3 = 0.55556$; $\lambda_2 = 0.88889$

$$\int_0^1 \frac{dx}{1+x^2} = \frac{1}{2}(b-a)\int_{-1}^1 g(z)dz$$

$$= \frac{(b-a)}{2}[\lambda_1 g(z_1) + \lambda_2 g(z_2) + \lambda_3 g(z_3)]$$

$$= \frac{(1-0)}{2}\left[0.55556\left\{\frac{4}{z_1^2 + 2z_1 + 5}\right\} + 0.88889\left\{\frac{4}{z_2^2 + 2z_2 + 5}\right\}\right.$$
$$\left. + 0.55556\left\{\frac{4}{z_3^2 + 2z_3 + 5}\right\}\right]$$

$$= \frac{4}{2} \times \left[0.55556\left\{\frac{1}{(-0.77460)^2 + 2(-0.77460) + 5}\right\}\right.$$
$$+ 0.88889\left\{\frac{1}{(0)^2 + 2(0) + 5}\right\}$$
$$\left. + 0.55556\left\{\frac{1}{(0.77460)^2 + 2(0.77460) + 5}\right\}\right]$$

$$= 2 \times [0.55556\,(0.24686) + 0.88889(0.2) + 0.55556(0.139876)]$$
$$= 2 \times (0.392633) = 0.785266$$

The exact value of $\int_0^1 \frac{dx}{1+x^2} = [\tan^{-1} x]_0^1 = \tan^{-1} 1 = \pi/4 = 0.785398$

Example 9.17 Evaluate the integral

$$\int_{-1}^{1} (1 - x^2)^{3/2} \cos x \, dx, \quad \text{using}$$

(i)   Gauss – Legendre three – point formula
(ii)   Gauss – Chebyshev three – point formula

Solution: In this example, limits of integration is -1 to 1. So, no need to apply transformation.

(i)   Gauss – Legendre three point formula is given by

$$\int_{-1}^{1} f(x)dx = \sum_{i=1}^{3} \lambda_i \, g(z_i) = [\lambda_1 g(z_1) + \lambda_2 g(z_2) + \lambda_3 g(z_3)]$$

Given that, $g(z) = (1 - z^2)^{3/2} \cos z$
For Three – point formula, from Table 9.1, we have
$z_1 = -0.77460;\ z_2 = 0;\ z_3 = 0.77460;\ \lambda_1 = \lambda_3 = 0.55556;\ \lambda_2 = 0.88889$

$$\int_{-1}^{1} (1 - x^2)^{3/2} \cos x \, dx = [\lambda_1 g(z_1) + \lambda_2 g(z_2) + \lambda_3 g(z_3)]$$

$$= \left[0.55556 \times (1 - z_1^2)^{\frac{3}{2}} \cos z_1 + 0.88889 \times (1 - z_2^2)^{\frac{3}{2}} \cos z_2 + 0.55556\right.$$
$$\left. \times (1 - z_3^2)^{\frac{3}{2}} \cos z_3\right]$$

$$= \left[0.55556 \times (1 - (-0.77460)^2)^{\frac{3}{2}} \cos(-0.77460) + 0.88889 \right.$$

$$\times (1 - (0)^2)^{\frac{3}{2}} \cos(0) + 0.55556$$

$$\left. \times (1 - (0.77460)^2)^{\frac{3}{2}} \cos(0.77460) \right]$$

$$= [0.55556 \times (0.180803) + 0.88889 \times (1) + 0.55556 \times 0.180803]$$

$$= 1.08978$$

(ii)   Gauss – Chebyshev three point formula is given by

$$\int_{-1}^{1} \frac{f(x)}{\sqrt{(1-x^2)}} \, dx = \frac{\pi}{3} \sum_{i=1}^{3} \lambda_i \, g(z_i) = \frac{\pi}{3} [\lambda_1 g(z_1) + \lambda_2 g(z_2) + \lambda_3 g(z_3)]$$

Given that, $g(z) = (1 - z^2)^2 \cos z$

For Three – point formula, from Table 9.2, we have

$z_1 = -0.866025; \quad z_2 = 0; \quad z_3 = 0.866025; \qquad \lambda_1 = \lambda_2 = \lambda_3 = 1.0472$

$$\int_{-1}^{1} (1-x^2)^{3/2} \cos x \, dx = \frac{\pi}{3} [\lambda_1 g(z_1) + \lambda_2 g(z_2) + \lambda_3 g(z_3)]$$

$$= [1.0472 \times (1 - z_1{}^2)^2 \cos z_1 + 1.0472 \times (1 - z_2{}^2)^2 \cos z_2 + 1.0472$$

$$\times (1 - z_3{}^2)^2 \cos z_3]$$

$$= [1.0472 \times (1 - (-0.866025)^2)^2 \cos(-0.866025) + 1.0472$$

$$\times (1 - (0)^2)^2 \cos(0) + 1.0472$$

$$\times (1 - (0.866025)^2)^2 \cos(0.866025)]$$

$$= [1.0472 \times (0.040491) + 1.0472 \times (1) + 1.0472 \times 0.040491]$$

$$= 1.132004$$

9.12   DOUBLE INTEGRALS

The double integral

$$\int_{c}^{d} \int_{a}^{b} f(x,y) dx \, dy$$

is evaluated by two successive integration in x and y directions considering one variable at a time. Repeated application of Trapezoidal and Simpson's rules is used to evaluate double integrals.

9.12.1   Trapezoidal Rule

Consider the integral

$$I = \int_{y_0 = c}^{y_m = d} \int_{x_0 = a}^{x_n = b} f(x,y) dx \, dy$$

Dividing the interval (a, b) into n equal sub – intervals each of length h and the interval (c, d) into m equal sub-intervals each of length k, we have

$$x_i = x_0 + ih, \qquad x_0 = a, \qquad x_n = b$$
$$y_j = y_0 + jk, \qquad y_0 = c, \qquad y_m = d$$

and the region of integration is the area bounded by the lines $x = a, x = b, y = c$ and $y = d$ in the $xy-$ plane. We know that the accuracy of the computed result can be improved or truncation error can be reduced by increasing the number of sub-intervals or by decreasing the length of the interval h. Consider this in mind, we divide the area of integration into smaller rectangles each of dimensions h & k and evaluate the required double integral over each of the sub-rectangles and add them to get the value of the given double integral.

We first evaluate the integral

$$I_1 = \int_{y_0}^{y_1} \int_{x_0}^{x_1} f(x,y)\, dx\, dy$$

The rectangular area represented by I_1 is bounded by $x = x_0, x = x_1, y = y_0$ and $y = y_1$ as shown below by ABCD in the Figure 9.5.

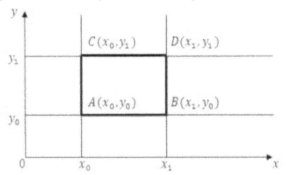

Figure 9.5

Let us apply Trapezoidal rule for the interval (x_0, x_1) to evaluate

$$I_1 = \int_{y_0}^{y_1} \int_{x_0}^{x_1} f(x,y)\, dx\, dy = \int_{y_0}^{y_1} \frac{h}{2}\,[f(x_0,y) + f(x_1,y)]\, dy$$

(Applying simple Trapezoidal rule for the inner integral)

$$= \frac{h}{2} \int_{y_0}^{y_1} f(x_0,y)\, dy + \frac{h}{2} \int_{y_0}^{y_1} f(x_1,y)\, dy \qquad \dots\dots (9.12.1)$$

Now, apply the Trapezoidal rule for the interval (y_0, y_1), we have

$$I_1 = \frac{h}{2} \left[\frac{k}{2}\,\{f(x_0,y_0) + f(x_0,y_1)\} + \frac{k}{2}\,\{f(x_1,y_0) + f(x_1,y_1)\} \right]$$

(Applying simple Trapezoidal rule for both integrals)

$$= \frac{hk}{4}\,[f(x_0,y_0) + f(x_0,y_1) + f(x_1,y_0) + f(x_1,y_1)] \qquad \dots\dots (9.12.2)$$

$$= \frac{hk}{4} \times \text{ sum of the values of the integrand f(x, y) at the corners of ABCD}$$

Now, consider

$$I_2 = \int_{y_0}^{y_2} \int_{x_0}^{x_2} f(x,y)\, dx\, dy = \int_{y_0}^{y_2} \left[\int_{x_0}^{x_1} f(x,y)\, dx + \int_{x_1}^{x_2} f(x,y)\, dx \right] dy$$

$$= \int_{y_0}^{y_2} \int_{x_0}^{x_1} f(x,y)\, dx\, dy + \int_{y_0}^{y_2} \int_{x_1}^{x_2} f(x,y)\, dx\, dy$$

$$= \left(\int_{y_0}^{y_1} + \int_{y_1}^{y_2} \right) \int_{x_0}^{x_1} + \left(\int_{y_0}^{y_1} + \int_{y_1}^{y_2} \right) \int_{x_1}^{x_2}$$

$$= \left(\int_{y_0}^{y_1} \int_{x_0}^{x_1} + \int_{y_1}^{y_2} \int_{x_0}^{x_1} + \int_{y_0}^{y_1} \int_{x_1}^{x_2} + \int_{y_1}^{y_2} \int_{x_1}^{x_2} \right) \qquad \ldots\ldots (9.12.3)$$

But, from Eq. (9.12.2), we have

$$\int_{y_0}^{y_1} \int_{x_0}^{x_1} f(x,y)\, dx\, dy = \frac{hk}{4} \left[f(x_0,y_0) + f(x_0,y_1) + f(x_1,y_0) + f(x_1,y_1) \right]$$

$$\int_{y_1}^{y_2} \int_{x_0}^{x_1} f(x,y)\, dx\, dy = \frac{hk}{4} \left[f(x_0,y_1) + f(x_0,y_2) + f(x_1,y_1) + f(x_1,y_2) \right]$$

$$\int_{y_0}^{y_1} \int_{x_1}^{x_2} f(x,y)\, dx\, dy = \frac{hk}{4} \left[f(x_1,y_0) + f(x_1,y_1) + f(x_2,y_0) + f(x_2,y_1) \right]$$

$$\int_{y_1}^{y_2} \int_{x_1}^{x_2} f(x,y)\, dx\, dy = \frac{hk}{4} \left[f(x_1,y_1) + f(x_1,y_2) + f(x_2,y_1) + f(x_2,y_2) \right]$$

From Eq. (9.12.3), we have

$$I_2 = \frac{hk}{4} \left[\{ f(x_0,y_0) + f(x_0,y_2) + f(x_2,y_0) + f(x_2,y_2) \} \right.$$

$$\left. + 2\{ f(x_1,y_2) + f(x_1,y_0) + f(x_0,y_1) + f(x_2,y_1) \} + 4\{ f(x_1,y_1) \} \right]$$

Now, the region of integration is shown in Figure 9.6.

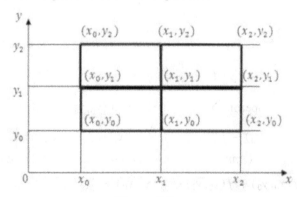

Figure 9.6

Therefore,

$$I_2 = \frac{hk}{4} \times$$

[{sum of the values of the integrand $f(x,y)$ at the corner points } +
4 × {value of $f(x,y)$ at the center point (x_1, y_1)} +
2 × {sum of the values of $f(x,y)$ at the remaining points}]

If we continue the same procedure, we get

$$I_n = \int_{y_0}^{y_n} \int_{x_0}^{x_n} f(x,y)\, dx\, dy$$

$$= \frac{hk}{4} \times$$

[{sum of the values of the integrand $f(x,y)$ at the four corner points } +
4 × {value of $f(x,y)$ at the center point I} + 2 ×
{sum of the values of $f(x,y)$ at the remaining points}]   ... . (9.12.4)
Eq. (9.12.4) is known as the Trapezoidal rule for double integration.

9.12.2   Simpson's Rule

Let us apply simple Simpson's rule to find $\iint f(x,y)dx\, dy$ over the area consisting of 4 adjacent sub – rectangles as shown in the Figure 9.7 as Simpson's rule is applicable only for even number of intervals. First we consider the integral

$$I_1 = \int_{y_0}^{y_2} \int_{x_0}^{x_2} f(x,y)\, dx\, dy$$

The region I_1 is shown in the Figure 9.7.

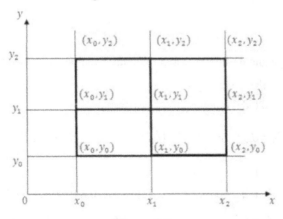

Figure 9.7

Using the simple Simpson's 1/3 rule for the interval I_1, we get

$$I_1 = \int_{y_0}^{y_2} \left[\int_{x_0}^{x_2} f(x,y) \, dx \right] dy$$

$$= \int_{y_0}^{y_2} \frac{h}{3} \left[f(x_0, y) + 4f(x_1, y) + f(x_2, y) \right]$$

$$= \frac{h}{3} \int_{y_0}^{y_2} f(x_0, y) + \frac{4h}{3} \int_{y_0}^{y_2} f(x_1, y) + \frac{h}{3} \int_{y_0}^{y_2} f(x_2, y) \qquad \text{........(9.12.5)}$$

Now, apply the simple Simpson's 1/3 rule to the Eq. (9.12.5) for the interval (y_0, y_2), we have

$$I_1 = \frac{hk}{9} \{ [f(x_0, y_0) + 4f(x_0, y_1) + f(x_0, y_2)] + 4 [f(x_1, y_0) + 4f(x_1, y_1) + f(x_1, y_2)] + [f(x_2, y_0) + 4f(x_2, y_1) + f(x_2, y_2)] \}$$

Using Simpson's rule for all the three integrals,

$$= \frac{hk}{9} [\{f(x_0, y_0) + f(x_2, y_0) + f(x_0, y_2) + f(x_2, y_2)\} + 4\{f(x_1, y_0) + f(x_0, y_1) + f(x_2, y_1) + f(x_1, y_2) +\} + 16f(x_1, y_1)]$$

If we continue the same procedure, we get

$$I_n = \int_{y_0}^{y_n} \int_{x_0}^{x_n} f(x,y) \, dx \, dy = \frac{hk}{9} \times$$

[{*sum of the values of the integrand* $f(x,y)$ *at the corner points* }
+ 16 × {*value of* $f(x,y)$ *at the center point I*}
+ 4 × {*sum of the values of* $f(x,y)$ *at the remaining points*}] ......(9.12.6)

The formula given in Eq. (9.12.6) is known as Simpson's rule for double integral.

Example 9.18 Evaluate

$$\int_0^{\pi/2} \int_0^{\pi/2} \sqrt{\sin(x + y)} \, dx dy$$

using (i) Trapezoidal rule (ii) Simpson's rule by taking $h = k = \pi/4$.

Solution: From the below Figure ,

(i)   By Trapezoidal rule,

$$I = \frac{hk}{4} [(f_A + f_C + f_G + f_I) + 4f_E + 2(f_B + f_D + f_F + f_H)]$$

$$= \frac{\pi^2}{64} [(0 + 1 + 1 + 0) + 4(1)$$

$$\qquad\qquad + 2 \, (0.840896 + 0.840896 + 0.840896 + 0.840896)]$$

$$= \frac{\pi^2}{64} [2 + 4 + 6.727168] = 0.154213 \, [12.727168] = 1.962695$$

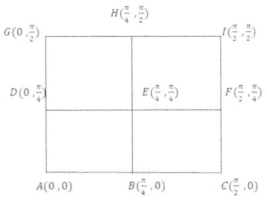

Now, $f(x, y) = \sqrt{sin(x + y)}$. The values of the integrand are given by

x \ y	0	$\dfrac{\pi}{4}$	$\dfrac{\pi}{2}$
0	$f_A = \sqrt{sin(0 + 0)}$ $= 0.0$	$f_D = \sqrt{sin\left(0 + \dfrac{\pi}{4}\right)}$ $= 0.840896$	$f_G = \sqrt{sin\left(0 + \dfrac{\pi}{2}\right)} = 1$
$\pi/4$	$f_B = \sqrt{sin\left(\dfrac{\pi}{4} + 0\right)}$ $= 0.840896$	$f_E = \sqrt{sin\left(\dfrac{\pi}{4} + \dfrac{\pi}{4}\right)} = 1$	$f_H = \sqrt{sin\left(\dfrac{\pi}{4} + \dfrac{\pi}{2}\right)}$ $= 0.840896$
$\pi/2$	$f_C = \sqrt{sin(\pi/2 + 0)}$ $= 1$	$f_F = \sqrt{sin\left(\dfrac{\pi}{2} + \dfrac{\pi}{4}\right)}$ $= 0.840896$	$f_I = \sqrt{sin\left(\dfrac{\pi}{2} + \dfrac{\pi}{2}\right)} = 0.0$

(ii)   By Simpson's rule,

$$I = \frac{hk}{9} \left[(f_A + f_C + f_G + f_I) + 16 f_E + 4(f_B + f_D + f_F + f_H) \right]$$

$$= \frac{\pi^2}{144} \left[(0 + 1 + 1 + 0) + 16(1) + 4\,(0.840896 + 0.840896 + 0.840896 + 0.840896) \right]$$

$$= \frac{\pi^2}{144} \left[2 + 16 + 13.454336 \right] = 0.068539 \,[31.454336] = 2.155849$$

Remark: The exact value of the double integral ≈ 2.19485

Example 9.19 Evaluate

$$\int_1^2 \int_1^2 \frac{dx\, dy}{x + y + 4},$$

using Trapezoidal rule by taking $h = 0.5$, $k = 0.25$.

Solution: As shown in the below figure,

$$I = \int_{ACOM} \frac{dxdy}{x+y+4} = \iint_{ACIG} + \iint_{GIOM} \frac{dxdy}{x+y+4}$$

y	1	1.25	1.5	1.75	2
x					
1	$f_A = 0.166667$	$f_D = 0.16$	$f_G = 0.153846$	$f_J = 0.148148$	$f_M = 0.142857$
1.5	$f_B = 0.153846$	$f_E = 0.148148$	$f_H = 0.142857$	$f_K = 0.137931$	$f_N = 0.133333$
2	$f_C = 0.142857$	$f_F = 0.137931$	$f_I = 0.133333$	$f_L = 0.129032$	$f_O = 0.125$

By Trapezoidal rule,

$I = \frac{hk}{4}[(f_A + f_C + f_G + f_I) + 4f_E + 2(f_B + f_D + f_F + f_H)] + \frac{hk}{4}[(f_G + f_I + f_M + f_O) + 4f_K + 2(f_H + f_J + f_L + f_N)]$

$= \frac{1}{32}\{[(0.166667 + 0.142857 + 0.153846 + 0.133333) + 4(0.148148)$

$\qquad + 2(0.153846 + 0.16 + 0.137931 + 0.142857)]$
$\qquad + [(0.153846 + 0.133333 + 0.142857 + 0.125)$
$\qquad + 4(0.137931)$
$\qquad + 2(0.142857 + 0.148148 + 0.129032 + 0.133333)]\}$

$= \frac{1}{32}\{[0.596703 + 0.592592 + 2(0.594634)]$

$\qquad + [0.555036 + 0.551724 + 2(0.55337)]\}$

$= \frac{1}{32}\{2.378563 + 2.2135] = \frac{1}{32}(4.592063) = 0.143502$

Remark: The exact value of the double integral ≈ 0.143347

9.13   PROGRAMS IN C

9.13.1   Program to implement Trapezoidal rule

```c
// Trapezoidal rule (two point formula)
#include<stdio.h>
#include<conio.h>
void main()
{
        int n,j,k;
        float x[20],fx[20],h,ans,temp;
        clrscr();
        printf("\t\t-------------------------------------------");
        printf("\n\t\t\t   TRAPEZOIDAL RULE \n");
        printf("\t\t-------------------------------------------\n");
        printf("\t\tHOW MANY VALUES YOU WANT TO INSERT ?... ");
        scanf("%d",&n);
        printf("\n");
        for(k=0;k<=n-1;k++)
        {
                printf(" ENTER THE VALUE OF x[%d] : ",k+1);
                scanf("%f",&x[k]);
                printf(" ENTER THE VALUE OF f(x[%d]) : ",k+1);
                scanf("%f",&fx[k]);
        }
        h= x[1] - x[0];
        temp=0.0;
        temp=(fx[0]+fx[n-1]);
        for(j=1;j<n-1;j++)
        {
                temp = temp + (2 * fx[j]);
        }
        ans = (h/2) * temp;
        printf("\n\t\tANSWER ::: %f",ans);
        getch();  }
```

9.13.2   Program to implement Simpson's one – third rule

```c
// Simpson's one – third rule (three point formula)
#include<stdio.h>
#include<conio.h>
void main()
{
        int n,j,k;
        float x[20],fx[20],h,ans,temp;
        clrscr();
```

```
        printf("\t\t\t\t SIMPSON'S 1/3rd RULE \n");
        printf("\t\t----------------------------------------------\n");
        printf("\n\t\tHOW MANY VALUES YOU WANT TO INSERT ?... ");
        scanf("%d",&n);
        printf("\n");
        for(k=0;k<=n-1;k++)
        {
                printf(" ENTER THE VALUE OF x[%d] : ",k+1);
                scanf("%f",&x[k]);
                printf(" ENTER THE VALUE OF f(x[%d]) : ",k+1);
                scanf("%f",&fx[k]);
        }
        h= x[1] - x[0];
        temp=0.0;
        temp=(fx[0]+fx[n-1]);
        for(j=1;j<n-1;j++)
        {
                if(j%2 == 0)
                {
                        temp = temp + (2 * fx[j]);
                }
                else
                {
                        temp = temp + (4 * fx[j]);
                }
        }
        ans = (h/3) * temp;
        printf("\n\t\tANSWER ::: %f",ans);
        getch();   }
```

9.13.3   Program to implement Simpson's 3/8th rule

```
// Simpson's 3/8th rule (Four point formula)
#include<stdio.h>
#include<conio.h>
void main()
{
        int n,j,k;
        float x[20],fx[20],h,ans,temp;
        clrscr();
        printf("\t\t\t\t SIMPSON'S 3/8th RULE \n");
        printf("\t\t----------------------------------------------\n");
        printf("\t\tHOW MANY VALUE YOU WANT TO INSERT ?... ");
        scanf("%d",&n);
```

```
printf("\n");
for(k=0;k<=n-1;k++)
{
        printf(" ENTER THE VALUE OF x[%d] : ",k+1);
        scanf("%f",&x[k]);
        printf(" ENTER THE VALUE OF f(x[%d]) : ",k+1);
        scanf("%f",&fx[k]);
}
h= x[1] - x[0];
temp=0.0;
temp=(fx[0]+fx[i-1]);
for(j=1;j<n-1;j++)
{
        if(j%3 == 0)
        {
                temp = temp + (2 * fx[j]);
        }
        else
        {
                temp = temp + (3 * fx[j]);
        }
}
ans = (3*h/8) * temp;
printf("\n\t\tANSWER ::: %f",ans);
getch(); }
```

9.13.4   Program to implement Weddle's rule

```
// Weddle's rule (Six point formula)
#include<stdio.h>
#include<conio.h>
void main()
{
        int n,j,k;
        float x[20],fx[20],h,ans,temp;
        clrscr();
        printf("\t\t\t WEDDLE'S RULE \n");
        printf("\t\t-----------------------------");
        printf("\n\t\tHOW MANY VALUES YOU WANT TO INSERT ?... \n");
        scanf("%d",&n);
        printf("\n");
        for(k=0;k<=n-1;k++)
        {
                printf(" ENTER THE VALUE OF x[%d] : ",k+1);
```

```
            scanf("%f",&x[k]);
            printf(" ENTER THE VALUE OF f(x[%d]) : ",k+1);
            scanf("%f",&fx[k]);
        }
        h= x[1] - x[0];
        for(j=0;j<n-5;j+=6)
        {
ans = ans + (3*h/10)*(fx[j]+5*fx[j+1]+fx[j+2]+6*fx[j+3]+fx[j+4]+5*fx[j+5]+fx[j+6]);
        }
        printf("\n\t\tANSWER ::: %f",ans);
        getch();  }
```

EXERCISES

1.   Multiple Choice Questions

(1)   The process of finding the value of definite integral from the set of
      numerical values of the functions which are given is known as
      (a)   Numerical Integration (b)   Interpolation   (c)   Approximation
      (d)   Curve fitting   (e)   Extrapolation

(2)   Which of the following is the method of integration
      (a)   Trapezoidal   (b)   Simpson's 1/3   (c)   Simpson's 3/8
      (d)   All of these   (e)   None of these

(3)   Which of the following is not a method of integration
      (a)   Trapezoidal   (b)   Weddle   (c)   Boole
      (d)   Newton's 1/3   (e)   Simpson's 1/3

(4)   The rule which approximates the area under the curve by connecting
      successive points on the curve by forming trapezoids is known as
      (a)   Trapezoidal rule   (b)   Simpson's 1/3   (c)   Simpson's 3/8
      (d)   Boole's Rule   (e)   None of these

(5)   Simpson's 1/3 rule approximates the area under the curve by connecting
      _____points.
      (a)   1   (b) 2   (c) 3   (d) 4   (e)   None of these

(6)   Which of the following integration rule gives better result?
      (a)   Trapezoidal rule   (b)   Simpson's 1/3   (c)   None of these

(7)   The formula of Simpson's 1/3 rule is
      (a) $I = \frac{h}{2} [y_1 + 2y_2 + 2y_3 + \ldots\ldots + y_n]$

      (b) $I = \frac{h}{3} [y_1 + 4y_2 + 2y_3 + 4y_4 + \ldots\ldots + y_n]$

      (c) $I = \frac{h}{3} [y_1 + 2y_2 + 4y_3 + 2y_4 + \ldots\ldots + y_n]$

(d) $I = \frac{3h}{8} [y_1 + 3y_2 + 3y_3 + 2y_4 + 3y_5 + 3y_6 + 2y_7 + ... + y_n]$

(e) $I = \frac{1}{h} [y_1 + 2y_2 + 2y_3 + 2y_4 + ... + y_n]$

(8)   The formula of Trapezoidal rule is

(a) $I = \frac{h}{2} [y_1 + 2y_2 + 2y_3 + ... + y_n]$

(b) $I = \frac{h}{3} [y_1 + 4y_2 + 2y_3 + 4y_4 + ... + y_n]$

(c) $I = \frac{h}{3} [y_1 + 2y_2 + 4y_3 + 2y_4 + ... + y_n]$

(d) $I = \frac{3h}{8} [y_1 + 3y_2 + 3y_3 + 2y_4 + 3y_5 + 3y_6 + 2y_7 + ... + y_n]$

(e) $I = \frac{1}{h} [y_1 + 2y_2 + 2y_3 + 2y_4 + ... + y_n]$

(9)   Error in computation is less in Simpson's 1/3 rule compare to Trapezoidal rule.

(a)   True   (b)   False

(10)   In Newton- Cote's formula, which value of n we should put to derive Simpson's $1/3^{rd}$ rule?

(a)   1   (b)   2   (c)   3   (d)   4   (e)   5

(11)   The table of values for a function $f(x)$ are given as: $1.8 - 6.050, 2.0 - 7.389, 2.4 - 11.023, 2.6 - 12.464, 3.0 - 20.086, 3.8 - 44.701$ then which of the following integration rule can be applied?

(a)   Trapezoidal   (b)   Simpson's $1/3^{rd}$ (c)   Simpson's 3/8

(d)   Weddle's   (e)   None of these

(12)   If number of intervals is 6 and of equal length then which of these rules gives better result?

(a)   Trapezoidal   (b)   Simpson's   (c)   Trapezoidal &
        Simpson's   (d)   None of these

Answers: (1) (a) (2) (d) (3) (d) (4) (a) (5) (c) (6) (b) (7) (b) (8) (a)
(9) (a) (10) (b) (11) (a) (12) (b)

2.   Problems

(1)   Find the value of $\int_0^\pi sinx\ dx$, by taking 10 sub-intervals, using

(i)   Trapezoidal rule   (ii) Simpson's 1/3rd rule

(2)   Evaluate $\int_0^1 dx/(1 + x^2)$ using Trapezoidal rule by dividing the range into 10 sub – intervals. Hence, obtain an approximate value of π. Also, find the error committed in the computation.

(3)   Compute the following integral by trapezoidal rule, taking eight sub – intervals, correct to four decimal places.

$$\int_1^5 log_{10} x\ dx$$

(4)   Calculate the value of $\int_0^1 \frac{x\ dx}{1+x}$ correct upto four decimal places, taking six intervals by
        (i)   Trapezoidal rule   (ii)   Simpson's one – third rule

(5)   Evaluate $\int_0^{\pi/2} \sqrt{1 - 0.162\ sin^2\theta}\ d\theta$, by Simpson's one – third rule and Weddle's rule, correct upto four decimal places, taking 12 points. Hence, calculate an error in both the cases.

(6)   Determine N, the number of sub – intervals, from the error formula

$$-\frac{(b-a)^5}{180\ N^4} \cdot f^{iv}(\xi)$$

so that the composite Simpson's one –third rule gives the value of the integral $\int_0^1 \frac{dx}{1+x}$ correct to three places of decimal. Compare the result with the exact value.

(7)   Evaluate $\int_0^1 dx/(1 + x^2)$ using
        (i)   Trapezoidal rule by taking $h = 1/4$
        (ii)   Simpson's 1/3 rule by taking $h = 1/4$
        (iii)   Simpson's 3/8 rule by taking $h = 1/6$
        (iv)   Weddle's rule by taking $h = 1/6$

(8)   The velocity v (km / min) of a moped which starts from rest is given at fixed intervals of time t as follows:

t:	2	4	6	8	10	12	14	16	18	20
v:	10	18	25	29	32	20	11	5	2	0

Estimate the distance covered in 20 minutes by Simpson's 1/3 rule.

(9)   Find an approximate value of $log_e 5$ by calculating to 4 decimal places, by Simpson's 1/3 rule, $\int_0^5 \frac{dx}{4x+5}$, dividing the range into 10 equal parts.

(10)   S is the specific heat of a body at temperature $0^0 C$. Find the total heat required to raise the temperature of the body of weight 1 gram from $0^0\ C$ to $12^0\ C$, using the following data of values and Simpson's 3/8 rule.

θ:	0	2	4	6	8	10	12
S:	1.00664	1.00543	1.00435	1.00331	1.00233	1.00149	1.00078

(11)   A river is 45 m wide. The depth d in meters at a distance x meters from one bank is given in the following data:

x:	0	5	10	15	20	25	30	35	40	45
y:	0	3	6	8	7	7	6	4	3	0

Find the cross – section of the river by Simpson's three – eight's rule.
(**Hint:** Use A = $\int y\ dx$)

(12)   A reservoir is in the form of a surface of revolution and D is the diameter in meters at a depth of p meters beneath the surface of the water. Find the amounts of water in m^3, that the reservoir holds when full, from the following data using Simpson's one – third rule.

p:	0	5	10	15	20	25	30
D:	36	35	33	29	22	16	9

(**Hint:** Volume $= \pi \int_0^{30} \left(\frac{D}{2}\right)^2 dp$)

(13)   A curve is given by the table:

x:	0	1	2	3	4	5	6
y:	0	2	2.5	2.3	2	1.7	1.5

The x –coordinate of the C.G. of the area bounded by the curve, the end ordinates and the x – axis is given by $A\bar{x} = \int_0^6 xy\,dx$, where A is the area. Find $\bar{x}$ by using Simpson's 1/3 rule.

(14)   A curve passes through the points (1, 0.2), (2, 0.7), (3, 1.0), (4, 1.3), (5, 1.5), (6, 1.7), (7, 1.9), (8, 2.1), (9, 2.3) and (10, 2.4). Find the volume of the solid generated by revolving the area between the curve, the x – axis and the ordinates $x = 1$ and $x = 10$ about the x – axis, using Simpson's three – eight's rule.

(15)   The velocity of an electric train which starts from rest is given in the following data:

t(min):	0	1	2	3	4	5	6	7	8	9	10	11	12
$v\left(\dfrac{km}{hour}\right)$:	0	10	25	40	55	60	62	57	42	30	20	13	0

Find the total distance covered in 12 minutes using Weddle's rule.

(16)   Compute the value of $\int_{0.2}^{1.4}(sinx - log_e x + e^x)\,dx$,, using trapezoidal, Simpson's one third and Weddle's rule with h = 0.2.

(17)   From the following table of values of x and y, find $\frac{dy}{dx}$ at $x = 2$ using the cubic spline method.

x:	2	3	4
y:	11	49	123

(18)   Evaluate $I = \int_0^1 \cos(x^2)\,dx$, using trapezoidal rule with $h = \frac{1}{2}, \frac{1}{4}, \frac{1}{8}$ and then apply Romberg's method to improve the result.

(19)   Evaluate $I = \int_0^{1/2} \frac{x}{sinx}\,dx$, using Simpson's one – third rule with $h = \frac{1}{4}, \frac{1}{8}, \frac{1}{16}$ and then obtain a better estimate by using Romberg's method.

(20) Evaluate $I = \int_0^1 \frac{1}{1+x}\, dx$, using trapezoidal rule with $h = \frac{1}{2}, \frac{1}{4}, \frac{1}{8}$ and then use Romberg's Method for getting more accurate result. Hence, evaluate $\log_e 2$.

(21) Apply Euler – Maclaurin summation formula to find
$$1^3 + 2^3 + 3^3 + \ldots\ldots + n^3$$

(22) Use Euler – Maclaurin formula to evaluate $I = \int_0^1 \sin \pi x \, dx$ (Take $h = 0.5, 0.25$) Compare your result with exact value.

(23) Find the sums, by Euler – Maclaurin formula up to three significant figures.

(i) $\frac{1}{51^2} + \frac{1}{53^2} + \frac{1}{55^2} + \ldots\ldots + \frac{1}{99^2}$

(ii) $\frac{1}{201^2} + \frac{1}{203^2} + \frac{1}{205^2} + \ldots\ldots + \frac{1}{299^2}$

(iii) $\frac{1}{21^3} + \frac{1}{23^3} + \frac{1}{25^3} + \ldots\ldots + \frac{1}{35^3}$

(24) Determine a , b and c such that the formula
$$\int_0^2 f(x)dx = 2 \left\{ af(0) + bf\left(\frac{2}{3}\right) + cf(2) \right\}$$
is exact for polynomials of as high order as possible.

(25) Determine algebraically the unknown abscissas x_1, x_2 and the common weight w for the quadrature formula $\int_{-1}^1 f(x)dx \approx w\, [f(x_1) + f(0) + f(x_2)]$ subject to requirement that the degree of precision be as high as possible.

(26) Construct the rule of the form
$$I(f) = \int_{-1}^1 f(x)\, dx \approx A_0\, f\left(\frac{-1}{2}\right) + A_1\, f(0) + A_2 f\left(\frac{1}{2}\right)$$
which is exact for all polynomial of degree less than or equal to 2.

(27) Construct the rule of the form
$$I(f) = \int_{-1}^1 f(x)\, dx \approx w_1\, f\left((-0.6)^{1/2}\right) + w_2\, f(0) + w_3 f\left((0.6)^{1/2}\right)$$
which is exact for all polynomial of degree less than or equal to 2.

(28) Evaluate $\int_2^3 \frac{\cos 2x}{1 + \sin x}\, dx$ using Gauss- Legendre's two and three point formula

(29) Evaluate the integral
$$\int_{-1}^1 (1 - x^2)^{1/2} \cos x \, dx, \quad \text{using}$$

(i) Gauss – Legendre two and three point formula
(ii) Gauss – Chebyshev two and three point formula

(30)   By using Gauss – Legendre's two – point formula, evaluate the following:

(i) $\int_{-1}^{1} \frac{\cos 2x}{1 + \sin x} dx$ (iv) $\int_{0}^{\pi/2} \log(1 + x) \, dx$

(ii) $\int_{0}^{2} (1 + x) \, dx$ (v) $\int_{0}^{\pi/2} \frac{d\theta}{\sqrt{1 + \sin^2}}$

(iii) $\int_{0}^{1} x \cdot e^{-x} dx$ (vi) $\int_{5}^{12} \frac{1}{x} \, dx$

(31)   By using Gauss – Legendre's three – point formula, evaluate the following:

(i) $\int_{0}^{1} \cos x \cdot e^{-x^2} dx$ (iv) $\int_{0}^{\pi/2} \sin x \, dx$

(ii) $\int_{2}^{4} (2x^4 + 2) \, dx$ (v) $\int_{5}^{12} \frac{1}{x} \, dx$

(iii) $\int_{0}^{1} \frac{1}{1 + x} \, dx$ (vi) $\int_{-1}^{1} (3x^2 + 5x^4) \, dx$

(32)   Evaluate $\int_{1}^{3} \int_{1}^{2} (x^2 + y^2) \, dx \, dy$ by Simpson's one – third rule taking h = k = 0.5.

(33)   Evaluate $\int_{0}^{1} \int_{0}^{1} x \, e^y \, dx \, dy$ by trapezoidal rule taking h = k = 0.5.

(34)   Evaluate $\int_{0}^{\pi/2} \int_{0}^{\pi/2} \sin(x + y) \, dx \, dy$ using (i) trapezoidal rule (ii) Simpson's one – third rule taking $h = k = \pi/4$.

(35)   Evaluate $\int_{1}^{5} \int_{1}^{5} \frac{1}{\sqrt{x^2 + y^2}} \, dx \, dy$ by trapezoidal rule with 4 sub – intervals.

Answers

(1) 1.9843 ; 2.00091   (2)   0.78498, $\pi = 3.13992$, Error = 0.00167   (3)
1.7505   (4)   0.3051, 0.3068   (5)   1.5051, 1.5050
(6)   N = 4   (7)   0.7854, 0.7854, 0.78535, 0.7854
(8)   309.33   (9)   1.61   (10)   12.04113 Approx.
(11) 221.25 m²   (12)   18078.56 m³   (13)   3.032
(14) 77.0358 m³
(15) 6.93 km   (16)   4.0715, 4.05214, 4.05145   (17)   29.0
(18) 0.9045   (19)   0.50707   (20)   0.6931

(21) $\left(\frac{n(n+1)}{2}\right)^2$ (22)   0.6258, 0.6359, Exact value = 0.63662
(23)   (i) 0.00499   (ii)   0.000833   (iii)   0.000427
(24) $a = 0, b = 3/4, c = 1/4$ (25) $w = 1/3, x_1 = 1, x_2 = -1$
(26) $A_0 = A_2 = 4/3$, $A_1 = -2/3$ (27) $w_1 = w_3 = 5/9$, $w_2 = -5/9$
(28) 0.203508, 0.202714   (29)   (i) 1.39113, 1.38684   (ii) 1.38642, 1.38243
(30)   (i) 0.20351   (ii) 4.0   (iii) 0.2647401   (iv) 0.858   (v) 1.311028
(vi) 0.87286
(31)   (i) 1.498624 (ii) 400.8028 (iii) 0.693122 (iv) 1.00008 (v) 0.87535
(vi) 4.0   (32)   14.667   (33)   0.876   (34)   1.7976, 2.0091
(35)   3.9975

Chapter 10   Difference Equations

Objectives

- To understand the importance of difference equation
- To know the relation between difference equation and differential equation
- To find the complementary function and particular integral
- To obtain the general or complete solution in case of homogeneous or non – homogeneous equation

Learning Outcomes

After reading this lesson students should be able to

- Differentiate between difference equation and differential equation
- Apply different rules to find complementary function
- Apply different rules to find particular integral
- Find complete solution in the case of homogeneous and non – homogeneous equation

10.1   INTRODUCTION

Difference equations are useful in the study of electrical networks, in many statistical problems including probability theory and to solve differential equations. The difference equation is in fact the discrete counterpart of the differential equations. Differential equations describe continuous systems and with these equations, rates of change are defined in terms of other values in the system while difference equations are a discrete parallel to this where we use old values from the system to calculate new values.

10.2   DEFINITIONS

Definition 10.1   *A difference equation* is a relation between the independent variable x, dependent variable y and the successive differences of the dependent variable. For example,

$$\Delta y_{n+2} - 3y_n = n^3 \qquad \text{........ (1)}$$

$$\Delta^2 y_n - 3\Delta y_n + 6y_n = 0 \qquad \text{........ (2)}$$

$$\Delta^3 y_n - 5\Delta^2 y_n + \Delta y_n - y_n = n \qquad \text{........ (3)}$$

are difference equations.

Now, we know that $\Delta = E - 1$, $\Delta^n = (E - 1)^n$

$$\Delta y_n = (E - 1)\, y_n = E y_n - y_n = y_{n+1} - y_n$$
$$\Delta^2 y_n = (E - 1)^2\, y_n = y_{n+2} - 2y_{n+1} + y_n$$
$$\Delta^3 y_n = (E - 1)^3\, y_n = y_{n+3} - 3y_{n+2} + 3y_{n+1} - y_n$$

Hence, $Eq.\,(1), (2)\,and\,(3)$ can also be written as

$$(y_{n+3} - y_{n+2}) - 3y_n = n^3 \Rightarrow y_{n+3} - y_{n+2} - 3y_n = n^3$$
$$(y_{n+2} - 2y_{n+1} + y_n) - 3(y_{n+1} - y_n) + 6y_n = 0 \Rightarrow y_{n+2} - 5y_{n+1} + 10y_n$$
$$= 0$$

$$(y_{n+3} - 3y_{n+2} + 3y_{n+1} - y_n) - 5(y_{n+2} - 2y_{n+1} + y_n) + (y_{n+1} - y_n) -$$
$$y_n = 0 \Rightarrow y_{n+3} - 8y_{n+2} + 14y_{n+1} - 8y_n = n$$

The equations (1), (2) and (3) can also be expressed in terms of the operator E as

$$(E^3 - E^2 - 3)y_n = n^3$$
$$(E^2 - 5E - 10)y_n = 0$$
$$(E^3 - 8E^2 - 14E - 8)y_n = n$$

Difference equations are also called recurrence relations.

Remark: We have assumed that the interval of differencing h = 1.

Definition 10.2   The *order of a difference equation* is the difference between the highest and lowest subscript of $y's$ occurring in the difference equation divided by the unit of increment.
For exmple, the order of $y_{n+2} - 5y_{n+1} + 10y_n = 0$ is $[(n + 2) - n]/1 = 2$
the order of $y_{n+2} - 3y_{n+1} + 11y_{n-1} = n^3$ is $[(n + 2) - (n - 1)]/1 = 3$
the order of $y_{n+4} - 3y_{n+3} = 0$ is $[(n + 4) - (n + 3)]/1 = 1$

Remark: The order of a difference equation is free from $\Delta's$ and the highest power of Δ does not give order of the difference equation.

The *degree of a difference equation* free from $\Delta's$ is the highest power of $y's$ occurring in the difference equation.
For example, $y_{n+2}^4 - 3y_{n+1}y_n + 11y_{n-1}^2 = n^3$ is of order 3 but degree 4.

Definition 10.3   *Solution of a difference equation* is an expression for y_n which satisfies the given difference equation.

Definition 10.4   The *general solution of a difference equation* is that in which the number of arbitrary constants is equal to the order of the difference equation.

Definition 10.5   A *particular solution* (or particular integral) *of a difference equation* is that solution which is obtained from the general solution by giving particular values to the constants.

10.3 LINEAR DIFFERENCE EQUATIONS

A difference equation in which y_n, y_{n+1}, y_{n+2} ... ... occur in the first degree and are not multiplied together is known as a linear difference equation. The general form of a linear difference equation with constant co-efficients is

$$a_0\, y_{x+n} + a_1\, y_{x+n-1} + a_2\, y_{x+n-2} + \ ...\ ... + a_{n-1}\, y_{x+1} + a_n\, y_x = \varphi(x)$$
$$\text{...... (10.3.1)}$$

$$or\ (a_0\, E^n + a_1 E^{n-1} + a_2 E^{n-2} + \ ...\ ... + a_{n-1}E + a_n)y_x = \varphi(x)$$
$$\text{........ (10.3.2)}$$

where, $a_0, a_1, a_2, ..., a_{n-1}, a_n$ and $f(x)$ are known functions of x. If $a_0, a_1, a_2, ..., a_{n-1}, a_n$ are constants and if we denote the polynomial

$a_0\, E^n + a_1 E^{n-1} + a_2 E^{n-2} + \ ...\ ... + a_{n-1}E + a_n$ by $f(E)$, then Eq. (10.3.1) and (10.3.2) can be written as

$$f(E)y_x = \varphi(x) \qquad \text{........ (10.3.3)}$$

If $\varphi(x) = 0$ in the Eq. (10.3.3) i.e. $f(E)y_x = 0$ then it is called the homogeneous equation corresponding to Eq. (10.3.3).

Otherwise $(\varphi(x) \neq 0$, i.e. $f(E)y_x = \varphi(x))$ is called the non – homogeneous linear equation.

10.3.1 Properties of Linear Difference Equations

As discussed in the previous section, the homogeneous difference equation of order n of the form

$$a_0\, y_{x+n} + a_1\, y_{x+n-1} + a_2\, y_{x+n-2} + \ ...\ ... + a_{n-1}\, y_{x+1} + a_n\, y_x = 0$$
$$\text{........ (10.3.4)}$$

is called a homogeneous difference equation with constant co-efficients.

(1) If $y_x = \xi(x)$ is a solution of Eq. (10.3.4), then $y_x = c.\xi(x)$ is also a solution of Eq. (10.3.4).

(2) If $\xi_1(x), \xi_2(x), \xi_3(x), ..., \xi_n(x)$ are n independent solutions of Eq. (10.3.4), then

$$y_x = c_1\xi_1(x) + c_2\xi_2(x) + \ ...\ ... + c_n\xi_n(x) \qquad \text{........ (10.3.5)}$$

is also a solution of Eq. (10.3.4). In fact, it is a general solution of Eq. (10.3.4), denote it by u_x where, $c_1, c_2, c_3, ..., c_n$ are arbitrary constants.

(3) If $y_x = v_x$ is a particular solution of Eq. (10.3.3) then the total solution of Eq. (10.3.3) is

$$y_x = u_x + v_x \qquad \text{........ (10.3.6)}$$

In Eq. (10.3.6), u_x is called the complementary function (C.F.) and v_x is called the particular integral (P.I.) of the solution of Eq. (10.3.3). Thus the complete solution of the Eq. (10.3.4) is

$$y_x = C.F. + P.I.$$

10.3.2 Rules for Finding Complementary Function

To find the complementary function of $f(E)y_x = \varphi(x)$ is the general solution of $f(E)y_x = 0$. To find the general solution of $f(E)y_x = 0$ we require as many arbitrary constants as the order of this equation. We replace E by m then the auxiliary equation $f(m) = 0$ is

$a_0 m^n + a_1 m^{n-1} + a_2 m^{n-2} + \ldots \ldots + a_{n-1} m^1 + a_n = 0$, which is the nth degree algebraic equation in m.

Consider the first order linear equation $(E - m_1)y_x = 0$

$$i.e. \;\; y_{x+1} - m_1 y_x = 0$$

Dividing this equation by $m_1{}^{(x+1)}$, we get

$$\frac{y_{x+1}}{m_1{}^{(x+1)}} - \frac{y_x}{m_1{}^x} = 0 \quad\quad i.e. \quad \Delta\left(\frac{y_x}{m_1{}^x}\right) = 0$$

$$\therefore \;\; \frac{y_x}{m_1{}^x} = c_1 \text{ , a constant}$$

or $$y_x = c_1 m_1{}^x$$

Thus, the solution of $(E - m_r)y_x = 0$ is $y_x = c_r m_r{}^x$, $r = 1,2,3, \ldots \ldots, n$.

(1)   If $m_1, m_2, m_3, \ldots \ldots, m_n$ are all real and distinct roots of auxiliary equation (A.E.) , then C.F. of Eq. (10.3.3) is $c_1 m_1^x + c_2 m_2^x + c_3 m_3^x + \ldots \ldots + c_n m_n^x$

(2)   If two roots of A.E. , say m_1 and m_2 are equal
In this case, $c_1 m_1{}^x + c_2 m_1^x + c_3 m_3^x + \ldots \ldots + c_n m_n^x$ can not be the solution of Eq. (10.3.3), as the firsr two terms become $c_1 m_1{}^x + c_2 m_1^x = (c_1 + c_2)m_1^x = c. m_1^x$ So, there will be only (n – 1) arbitrary constants. Now. let us consider the part of the C.F. corresponding to the equal roots m_1 and m_2 . i.e. let us solve the second order equation $(E - m_1)^2 y_x = 0$ i.e. $y_{x+2} - 2 m_1 y_{x+1} + m_1{}^2 y_x = 0$

Let $y_x = z_x m_1{}^x$ be a solution of this equation. Then,

$$z_{x+2} m_1{}^{x+2} - 2m_1 z_{x+1} m_1{}^{x+1} + m_1{}^2 z_x m_1{}^x = 0$$

$i.e.$ $\quad\quad (z_{x+2} - 2z_{x+1} + z_x) m_1{}^{x+2} = 0$

$\therefore (z_{x+2} - 2z_{x+1} + z_x) = 0$ $\quad as \;\; m_1{}^{x+2} \neq 0$

$i.e.$ $\quad (E - 1)^2 z_x = 0$ or $\quad \Delta^2 z_x = 0$

$\therefore \quad z_x = c_1 x + c_2$

$\therefore$ The solution of $(E - m_1)^2 y_x = 0$ is $y_x = (c_1 x + c_2) m_1{}^x$

The general solution of Eq. $f(E)y_x = 0$ is $y_x = (c_1 x + c_2) m_1{}^x + c_3 m_3^x + \ldots \ldots + c_n m_n^x$

i.e. C.F. of Eq. (10.3.3) is $(c_1 x + c_2) m_1{}^x + c_3 m_3^x + \ldots \ldots + c_n m_n^x$

Remark: If three roots say m_1, m_2 and m_3 are equal then the part of the C.F. corresponding to equal roots is $(c_1 x^2 + c_2 x + c_3) m_1{}^x + c_4 m_4^x + \ldots \ldots +$ $c_n m_n^x$. Similaly, if r roots of A.E. say $m_1, m_2, \ldots \ldots, m_r$ are equal then the part of the C.F. corresponding to these r equal roots is
$(c_1 x^{r-1} + c_2 x^{r-2} + \ldots \ldots + c_r) m_1{}^x + \ldots + c_n m_n^x$

(3)   If two of the roots of the A.E. are imaginary, which will be conjugate of each other

i.e. let $m_1 = \alpha + i\beta$, $m_2 = \alpha - i\beta$ then the C.F. of Eq. (10.3.3) is

$$y_x = A\,(\alpha + i\beta)^x + B(\alpha - i\beta)^x$$

put $\alpha = r \cos\theta$, $\beta = r\sin\theta$, we get

$$y_x = A[r\,(\cos\theta + i\sin\theta)]^{\,x} + B\,[r\,(\cos\theta - i\sin\theta)]^{\,x}$$
$$= A\,r^x\,(\cos\theta x + i\sin\theta x) + B\,r^x\,(\cos\theta x - i\sin\theta x)$$
$$= r^x\,\{(A + B)\,\cos\theta x + i\,(A - B)\,\sin\theta x\,\}$$
$$= r^x\,(c_1 \cos\theta x + c_2 \sin\theta x),$$

where, $r = modulus\ of\ (\alpha + i\beta) = \sqrt{\alpha^2 + \beta^2}$, $\theta = amplitude\ of\ (\alpha + i\beta) = \tan^{-1}\left(\frac{\beta}{\alpha}\right)$

(4)   Repeated complex roots. i.e. if four roots are of the type $\alpha \pm i\beta$ each twice

i.e. $m_1 = m_3 = \alpha + i\beta$ and $m_2 = m_4 = \alpha - i\beta$ then the part of the C.F. is $r^x\,\{\,(c_1 x + c_2)\,\cos\theta x + (c_3 x + c_4)\,\sin\theta x\}$,

where, $r = \sqrt{\alpha^2 + \beta^2}$, $\theta = \tan^{-1}\left(\frac{\beta}{\alpha}\right)$

Example 10.1   Solve the following difference equation:

$$y_{x+3} - 2y_{x+2} - 5y_{x+1} + 6y_x = 0$$

Solution: The given equation can be written in operator form as $(E^3 - 2E^2 - 5E + 6)y_x = 0$.
Therefore, the auxiliary equation is $E^3 - 2E^2 - 5E + 6 = 0$
if we substitute $E = 1$ then equality is satisfied. So, let $E = -1$ be a root.

1	1	-2	-5	6
	0	1	-1	-6
	1	-1	-6	0

The equation becomes $(E - 1)(E^2 - E - 6) = 0$

$$\therefore (E - 1)\ (E - 3)(E + 2) = 0$$
$$\therefore (E - 1) = 0, (E - 3) = 0, (E + 2) = 0$$

Hence, the roots of the given equation are 1, 3, -2
Since the equation is homogeneous equation, the complete solution is

$$y_x = C_1\,(1)^x + C_2(3)^x + C_3(-2)^x\ = C_1 + C_2(3)^x + C_3(-2)^x$$

Example 10.2   Solve the difference equation: $u_{n+3} + u_{n+2} - 8u_{n+1} - 12 u_n = 0$

Solution: The given equation can be written in operator form as $(E^3 + E^2 - 8E - 12)u_n = 0$
Therefore, the auxiliary equation is $E^3 + E^2 - 8E - 12 = 0$
By trial and error if we substitute $E = 3$ then equality is satisfied. So, let $E = 3$ be a root.

3	1	1	-8	-12
	0	3	12	12
	1	4	4	0

The equation becomes $(E - 3)(E^2 + 4E + 4) = 0$
$$\therefore (E - 3)(E + 2)^2 = 0$$
$$\therefore (E - 3) = 0, (E + 2)^2 = 0$$
Hence, the roots of the given equation are 3, -2, -2
Since the equation is homogeneous equation and roots are repeated, the complete solution is $u_n = C_1 (3)^n + (C_2 + C_3 n)(-2)^n$

Example 10.3 Solve the equation $u^2_{n+1} - 3u_n u_{n+1} + 2u^2_n = 0$

Solution: Divide the given difference equation by u_n^2, we get
$$\left(\frac{u_{n+1}}{u_n}\right)^2 - 3\left(\frac{u_{n+1}}{u_n}\right) + 2 = 0$$
Let $\frac{u_{n+1}}{u_n} = y_n$, the equation becomes
$$y^2_n - 3y_n + 2 = 0$$
i.e. $(y_n - 2)(y_n - 1) = 0$
The roots are $y_n = 2, \ y_n = 1$
i.e. $\dfrac{u_{n+1}}{u_n} = 2, \quad \dfrac{u_{n+1}}{u_n} = 1 \quad \Rightarrow \ u_{n+1} = 2u_n , \quad u_{n+1} = u_n$
i.e. $u_{n+1} - 2u_n = 0 \quad and \quad u_{n+1} - u_n = 0$
i.e. $(E - 2)u_n = 0 , (E - 1)u_n = 0$
$\therefore$ The complete solution is $u_n = C_1 (2)^n \quad or \quad u_n = C_1 (1)^n = C_1$

Example 10.4   Solve the equation: $\Delta^3 y_x + 3\Delta^2 y_x - 13\Delta y_x - 15 y_x = 0$

Solution: The given equation is
$$(E - 1)^3 y_x + 3(E - 1)^2 y_x - 13(E - 1)y_x - 15y_x = 0$$
$\therefore [(E^3 - 3E^2 + 3E - 1) + 3(E^2 - 2E + 1) - (13E - 13) - 15]y_x = 0$
i.e. $(E^3 - 16E)y_x = 0$
$\therefore$ The auxiliary equation is $E^3 - 16E = 0$
Therefore, $E (E^2 - 16) = 0$

i. e. $E = 0$, $E^2 - 16 = 0$

i. e. $E = 0$, $(E - 4)(E + 4) = 0$

$E = 0$, $E = 4$, $E = -4$

The complete solution of the given equation is $y_x = C_1 (0)^x + C_2 (4)^x + C_3 (-4)^x$ *i. e.* $y_x = C_2 (4)^x + C_3 (-4)^x$

Example 10.5   Solve $y_{x+3} + 8y_x = 0$

Solution: The given equation can be written in operator form as
$$(E^3 + 8)y_x = 0$$
The auxiliary equation is $(E^3 + 8) = 0$
The roots of the equation are
$$E = -1, \qquad E = \frac{1 \pm i\sqrt{3}}{2}$$

Thus, roots are imaginary and conjugate of each other.

Let $m_1 = \alpha + i\beta = \frac{1}{2} + \frac{i\sqrt{3}}{2}$, $m_2 = \alpha - i\beta = \frac{1}{2} - \frac{i\sqrt{3}}{2}$

Therefore, the complete solution is $y_x = r^x (c_1 \cos\theta x + c_2 \sin\theta x)$

where, $r = \sqrt{\alpha^2 + \beta^2} = \sqrt{\left(\frac{1}{2}\right)^2 + \left(\frac{\sqrt{3}}{2}\right)^2} = 1$, $\theta = \tan^{-1}\left(\frac{\beta}{\alpha}\right) =$

$\tan^{-1}\left(\frac{\sqrt{3}/2}{1/2}\right) = \frac{\pi}{3}$

$$y_x = C_1 (-1)^x + 1^x (C_2 \cos\frac{\pi}{3}x + C_3 \sin\frac{\pi}{3}x)$$

Example 10.6   The integers 0, 1, 1, 2, 3, 5, 8, 13, 21, ... are said to form a Fibonacci sequence. Form the Fibonacci difference equation and solve it.

Solution: In this Fibonacci sequence, each number, after second, is the sum of its two previous numbers. If y_n is the nth number then
$$y_n = y_{n-1} + y_{n-2} \quad for\ n > 2$$
i. e. $y_{n+2} - y_{n+1} - y_n = 0 \quad for\ n > 0$

The given difference equation can be written in operator form as
$$(E^2 - E - 1)y_n = 0$$
The auxiliary equation is $E^2 - E - 1 = 0$ *i. e.* $E = \frac{1}{2}(1 \pm \sqrt{5})$

Thus, the solution is
$$y_n = C_1 \left(\frac{1 + \sqrt{5}}{2}\right)^n + C_2 \left(\frac{1 - \sqrt{5}}{2}\right)^n, \quad for\ n > 0$$

When $n = 1$, $y_1 = 0$ (first term of the sequence)
$$C_1 \left(\frac{1 + \sqrt{5}}{2}\right)^n + C_2 \left(\frac{1 - \sqrt{5}}{2}\right)^n = 0 \qquad\qquad ...\ ......(1)$$

When $n = 2$, $y_2 = 1$ (second term of the sequence)

$$C_1 \left(\frac{1+\sqrt{5}}{2}\right)^n + C_2 \left(\frac{1-\sqrt{5}}{2}\right)^n = 1 \qquad \ldots\ldots\ldots (2)$$

Solving (1) and (2), we get

$$C_1 = \frac{5-\sqrt{5}}{10} \quad and \quad C_2 = \frac{5+\sqrt{5}}{10}$$

Therefore, the complete solution is

$$y_n = \frac{5-\sqrt{5}}{10}\left(\frac{1+\sqrt{5}}{2}\right)^n + \frac{5+\sqrt{5}}{10}\left(\frac{1-\sqrt{5}}{2}\right)^n$$

10.3.3   Rules for Finding Particular Integral

The particular integral (P.I.) of the solution of the equation $f(E)y_x = \varphi(x)$ is the function v_x, where $y_x = v_x$, is a particular solution of the equation $f(E)y_x = \varphi(x)$. The P.I. depends on $\varphi(x)$ and it is defined as

$$P.I.= \frac{1}{f(E)}\varphi(x)$$

where, $\frac{1}{f(E)}$ is the inverse operator of $f(E)$.

$$i.e. \quad f(E)\left\{\frac{1}{f(E)}\varphi(x)\right\} = \varphi(x)$$

Case I : When $\varphi(x) = a^x$, where a is a constant

$$P.I.= \frac{1}{f(E)}a^x = \frac{1}{f(a)}a^x, \quad if \ f(a) \neq 0$$

If $f(a) = 0$, then for the equation

(1) $(E-a)y_x = a^x$ then $P.I = \frac{1}{E-a}.a^x = x\,a^{x-1} = \frac{x^{(1)}}{1!}a^{x-1}$

(2) $(E-a)^2 y_x = a^x$ then $P.I = \frac{1}{(E-a)^2}.a^x = \frac{x(x-1)}{2!}a^{x-2} = \frac{x^{(2)}}{2!}a^{x-2}$

(3) $(E-a)^3 y_x = a^x$ then $P.I = \frac{1}{(E-a)^3}.a^x = \frac{x(x-1)(x-2)}{3!}a^{x-3} = \frac{x^{(3)}}{3!}a^{x-3}$

In general, for the equation $(E-a)^r y_x = a^x$ then

$$P.I = \frac{1}{(E-a)^r}.a^x = \frac{x^{(r)}}{r!}a^{x-r}$$

Example 10.7 Solve $2y_{x+2} - 7y_{x+1} - 9y_x = 5^x$

Solution: The given difference equation can be written in operator form as

$$(2E^2 - 7E - 9)y_x = 5^x$$

∴ The auxilliary equation is $2E^2 - 7E - 9 = 0$

or $(2E-9)(E+1) = 0$

The roots are $\qquad\qquad E = -1, \; E = 9/2$

Since the given difference equation is non – homogeneous, the complete solution is

$$y_x = C.F. + P.I.$$

Now, $\qquad\qquad C.F. = C_1 \cdot (-1)^x + C_2 \cdot \left(\frac{9}{2}\right)^x$

and $\qquad\qquad P.I. = \dfrac{1}{2E^2 - 7E - 9} \cdot 5^x$

$$= \dfrac{1}{2(5)^2 - 7(5) - 9} \cdot 5^x \qquad (Replace\ E\ by\ a = 5) = \frac{1}{6} \cdot 5^x$$

Thus, the complete solution is

$$y_x = C_1 \cdot (-1)^x + C_2 \cdot \left(\frac{9}{2}\right)^x + \frac{1}{6} \cdot 5^x$$

Example 10.8   Solve $y_{x+2} - 8y_{x+1} + 15y_x = 3^x$

Solution: The given difference equation can be written in operator form as

$$(E^2 - 8E + 15)y_x = 3^x$$

$\therefore$ The auxilliary equation is $E^2 - 8E + 15 = 0$

or $\qquad\qquad (E - 3)(E - 5) = 0$

The roots are $\qquad\qquad E = 3, \; E = 5$

Since the given difference equation is non – homogeneous, the complete solution is $\qquad y_x = C.F. + P.I.$

Now, $\qquad\qquad C.F. = C_1 \cdot 3^x + C_2 \cdot 5^x$

and $\qquad\qquad P.I. = \dfrac{1}{E^2 - 8E + 15} \cdot 3^x$

$$= \dfrac{1}{3^2 - 8(3) + 15} \cdot 3^x \qquad (Replace\ E\ by\ a = 3)$$

Here denominator is zero.

$$\therefore \; P.I. = \dfrac{1}{(E-3)(E-5)} \cdot 3^x = \dfrac{1}{(E-3)} \dfrac{1}{(3-5)} \cdot 3^x = -\frac{1}{2}\dfrac{1}{(E-3)} \cdot 3^x$$

$$= -\frac{1}{2}\dfrac{x^{(1)}}{1!} \, 3^{x-1} \text{ (Using the formula of (1) of Case I)}$$

$\therefore$ The complete solution is $\qquad y_x = C_1 \cdot 3^x + C_2 \cdot 5^x - \dfrac{x}{2} 3^{x-1}$

Example 10.9   Solve $u_{n+3} - 5u_{n+2} + 3u_{n+1} + 9u_n = 2^n + 3^n$

Solution: The given difference equation can be written in operator form as

$$(E^3 - 5E^2 + 3E - 9)y_n = 2^n + 3^n$$

$\therefore$ The auxilliary equation is $E^3 - 5E^2 + 3E - 9 = 0$

Putting $E = 3$, we get $f(E) = 0$. Therefore, $(E - 3)$ is one of the factor.

3	1	-5	3	9
	0	3	-6	-9
	1	-2	-3	0

The equation becomes $(E - 3)(E^2 - 2E - 3) = 0$

$$\therefore (E - 3)\ (E - 3)(E + 1) = 0$$

$$\therefore (E - 3)^2 = 0, (E + 1) = 0$$

Hence, the roots of the given equation are $3, 3, -1$

Since the given difference equation is non – homogeneous, the complete solution is

$$u_n = C.F. + P.I.$$

Now, $\qquad C.F.= (C_1 + C_2 n).3^n + C_3.(-1)^n$

and $\qquad P.I. = \dfrac{1}{(E - 3)^2(E + 1)}.(2^n + 3^n)$

$$= \dfrac{1}{(E - 3)^2(E + 1)}\ 2^n + \dfrac{1}{(E - 3)^2(E + 1)}\ 3^n$$

$$= \dfrac{1}{(2 - 3)^2(2 + 1)}\ 2^n + \dfrac{1}{(3 - 3)^2(3 + 1)}\ 3^n$$

$$= \dfrac{1}{3}\ 2^n + \dfrac{1}{4}\dfrac{1}{(E - 3)^2}.3^n$$

$\qquad\qquad$ (*as by replacing E by* 3, *denominator becomes zero*)

$$= \dfrac{1}{3}\ 2^n + \dfrac{1}{4}\dfrac{n^{(2)}}{2!}.3^{n-2} = \dfrac{1}{3}\ 2^n + \dfrac{n(n - 1)}{8}.3^{n-2}$$

$\therefore$ The complete solution is $u_n = (C_1 + C_2 n).3^n + C_3.(-1)^n + \dfrac{1}{3}\ 2^n$

$$+ \dfrac{n(n - 1)}{8}.3^{n-2}$$

Case II: If $\varphi(x)$ is a polynomial in x of degree n then

$$P.I. = \dfrac{1}{f(E)}\ \varphi(x) = [f(1 + \Delta)]^{-1}\varphi(x)$$

$$= (a_0 + a_1 \Delta + a_2\Delta^2 + \ldots\ldots + a_r \Delta^r)\ \varphi(x)$$

OR

If $\varphi(x)$ is a polynomial in x of degree n, then we take

$$a_1 x^n + a_2 x^{n-1} + \ldots\ldots + a_{n+1}$$

as the particular solution of the difference equation. Putting this solution in the given difference equation, the values of $a_1, a_2, \ldots\ldots, a_{n+1}$ are determined.

Example 10.10 Solve the following difference equations

(1) $y_{n+2} - y_{n+1} - y_n = n^2 + 2n - 1$

(2) $u_{n+2} - 2u_{n+1} + u_n = 3n + 2$

Solution:

(1)   The given difference equation can be written in operator form as

$$(E^2 - E - 1)y_n = n^2 + 2n - 1$$

∴ The auxilliary equation is $E^2 - E - 1 = 0$ i.e. $E = \frac{1}{2}(1 \pm \sqrt{5})$

Since the given difference equation is non – homogeneous, the complete solution is

$$y_n = C.F. + P.I.$$

Now, $C.F. = C_1 \left(\frac{1+\sqrt{5}}{2}\right)^n + C_2 \left(\frac{1-\sqrt{5}}{2}\right)^n, \quad for \ n > 0$

and $P.I. = \dfrac{1}{E^2 - E - 1} \cdot n^2 + 2n - 1$

$$= \dfrac{1}{(1+\Delta)^2 - (1+\Delta) - 1} \cdot n^2 + 2n - 1$$

$$= \dfrac{n^2 + 2n - 1}{\Delta^2 + \Delta - 1}$$

$$= \dfrac{n^2 + 2n - 1}{-1\{1 - (\Delta^2 + \Delta)\}} = -\{1 - (\Delta^2 + \Delta)\}^{-1}(n^2 + 2n - 1)$$

$$= -\{1 + (\Delta^2 + \Delta) + (\Delta^2 + \Delta)^2 + \dots\}(n^2 + 2n - 1)$$

Expressing $n^2 + 2n - 1$ in terms of factorial polynomial. We have

$n^2 + 2n - 1 = [n]^2 + 3[n]^1 - 1$

$= -(1 + \Delta + 2\Delta^2 + \dots\dots)([n]^2 + 3[n]^1 - 1)$

$= -\{([n]^2 + 3[n]^1 - 1) + \Delta([n]^2 + 3[n]^1 - 1) + 2\Delta^2([n]^2 + 3[n]^1 - 1)\}$

$= -\{([n]^2 + 3[n]^1 - 1) + (2[n] + 3) + 2(2)\}$

$= -\{(n^2 + 2n - 1) + (2n + 3) + 4\} = -(n^2 + 4n + 6)$

∴ The complete solution is y_n

$$= C_1 \left(\frac{1 + \sqrt{5}}{2}\right)^n + C_2 \left(\frac{1 - \sqrt{5}}{2}\right)^n - (n^2 + 4n + 6)$$

Another Method:

$$C.F. = C_1 \left(\frac{1 + \sqrt{5}}{2}\right)^n + C_2 \left(\frac{1 - \sqrt{5}}{2}\right)^n, \quad for \ n > 0$$

Suppose the P.I. is $a_1 n^2 + a_2 n + a_3$. Putting in given difference equation, we have

$[a_1(n+2)^2 + a_2(n+2) + a_3] - [a_1(n+1)^2 + a_2(n+1) + a_3] - [a_1 n^2 + a_2 n + a_3]$

$= n^2 + 2n - 1$

or $\qquad n^2\,(-a_1) + n(2a_1 - a_2) + (3a_1 + a_2 - a_3) = n^2 + 2n - 1$

Therefore, $\qquad\qquad\qquad -a_1 = 1$

$$2a_1 - a_2 = 2$$

$$3a_1 + a_2 - a_3 = -1$$

Hence, $\quad a_1 = -1,\ a_2 = -4,\ a_3 = -6$

Thus, $\quad P.I. = -(n^2 + 4n + 6)$

$\therefore$ The complete solution is $\ y_n$

$$= C_1\left(\frac{1+\sqrt5}{2}\right)^n + C_2\left(\frac{1-\sqrt5}{2}\right)^n - (n^2 + 4n + 6)$$

(2) The given difference equation can be written in operator form as

$$(E^2 - 2E + 1)\,u_n = 3n + 2$$

$\therefore$ The auxilliary equation is $E^2 - 2E + 1 = 0\quad i.e.\quad (E-1)^2 = 0$

$\therefore E = 1, 1$

Since the given difference equation is non – homogeneous, the complete solution is

$$u_n = C.F. + P.I.$$

$$C.F. = (C_1 + C_2n)\,.\,1^n = (C_1 + C_2n)$$

and $\qquad\qquad P.I. = \dfrac{1}{E^2 - 2E + 1}\,.\,(3n + 2)$

$$= \frac{1}{(E-1)^2}\,.\,(3n+2)$$

$$= \frac{3n+2}{\Delta^2}\qquad (as\ E = 1 + \Delta)$$

Expressing $3n + 2$ in terms of factorial polynomial. We have $3[n]^1 + 2\,[n]^0$

$$= \frac{3[n]^1 + 2\,[n]^0}{\Delta^2} = 3\,\Delta^{-2}[n]^1 + 2\,\Delta^{-2}[n]^0$$

$$= 3\,\frac{[n]^3}{6} + 2\,\frac{[n]^2}{2} = \frac{[n]^3}{2} + [n]^2 = \frac{n(n-1)(n-2)}{2} + n(n-1)$$

$$= \frac{n(n-1)}{2}\,[(n-2) + 2] = \frac{1}{2}n^2(n-1)$$

$\therefore$ The complete solution is $\ u_n = (C_1 + C_2n) + \dfrac{1}{2}n^2(n-1)$

Case III: If $\varphi(x)$ is a constant then the $P.I.$ of the difference equation will be a constant C provided that 1 is not a characteristic root of the difference equation.

Example 10.11 Solve $y_n - 4y_{n-1} + 5\,y_{n-2} = 3$

Solution: The given difference equation can be written in operator form as

$$(E^2 - 4E + 5)\, y_n = 3$$

∴ The auxilliary equation is $E^2 - 4E + 5 = 0$ i.e. $E = \dfrac{4 \pm \sqrt{16-20}}{2} = 2 \pm i$

∴ $E = 2 + i$ and $E = 2 - i$

Since the given difference equation is non – homogeneous, the complete solution is

$$u_n = C.F. + P.I.$$

Now, $C.F. = C_1(2 + i)^n + C_2(2 - i)^n , n \geq 0$

Here, 1 is not the root. Therefore, the $P.I.$ shall be a constant P. Putting it into the given difference equation, we get

$$P - 4P + 5P = 3 \Rightarrow P = \frac{3}{2}$$

$$P.I. = \frac{3}{2}$$

∴ The complete solution is $y_n = C_1(2 + i)^n + C_2(2 - i)^n + \dfrac{3}{2}$

Case IV: If $\varphi(x) = a^x F(x)$ where $F(x)$ is some polynomial in x of degree n.

$$P.I. = \frac{1}{f(E)}\, a^x F(x) = a^x \frac{1}{f(aE)} F(x)$$

Example 10.12 Solve the equations

(1) $y_{n+2} - 5y_{n+1} - 6y_n = n(n - 1)2^n$

(2) $y_{x+2} + 7y_{x+1} - 8y_x = 2^x x^2$

Solution:

(1) The given equation can be written in operator form as
   $$(E^2 - 5E - 6)\, y_n = n(n - 1)2^n$$

∴ The auxilliary equation is $E^2 - 5E - 6 = 0$ i.e. $(E - 6)(E + 1) = 0$

∴ The roots are $E = 6, \; E = -1$

Since the given difference equation is non – homogeneous, the complete solution is

$$u_n = C.F. + P.I.$$

Now, $C.F. = C_1(6)^n + C_2(-1)^n$

and $P.I. = \dfrac{1}{E^2 - 5E - 6} \cdot 2^n \, [n]^2$

$$= 2^n \cdot \frac{1}{4E^2 - 10E - 6} \cdot [n]^2$$

$$= 2^{n-1} \cdot \frac{1}{2(1 + \Delta)^2 - 5(1 + \Delta) - 3} \cdot [n]^2$$

$$= 2^{n-1} \frac{1}{-6 - \Delta + 2\Delta^2} [n]^2$$

$$= -\frac{2^{n-1}}{6} \left\{ \frac{1}{1 + \left(\frac{\Delta - 2\Delta^2}{6}\right)} \right\} [n]^2 = -\frac{2^{n-1}}{6} \left\{ 1 + \left(\frac{\Delta - 2\Delta^2}{6}\right) \right\}^{-1} [n]^2$$

$$= -\frac{2^{n-1}}{6} \left\{ 1 - \left(\frac{\Delta - 2\Delta^2}{6}\right) + \left(\frac{\Delta - 2\Delta^2}{6}\right)^2 \right\} [n]^2$$

$$= -\frac{2^{n-1}}{6} \left\{ 1 - \frac{\Delta}{6} + \frac{3\Delta^2}{6} \right\} [n]^2$$

$$= -\frac{2^{n-1}}{6} \left\{ n(n-1) - \frac{2n}{6} + \frac{6}{6} \right\} = -\frac{2^{n-1}}{36} (6n(n-1) - 2n + 6)$$

$$= -\frac{2^{n-1}}{36} (6n^2 - 8n + 6)$$

$\therefore$ The complete solution is y_n

$$= C_1(6)^n + C_2(-1)^n - \frac{2^{n-1}}{18} (3n^2 - 4n + 3)$$

(2)   The given difference equation reduces to $(E^2 - 7E - 8) y_x = 2^x x^2$

$\therefore$ The auxilliary equation is $E^2 - 7E - 8 = 0$ i.e. $(E - 8)(E + 1) = 0$

$\therefore$ The roots are $E = 8$, $E = -1$

Since the given difference equation is non – homogeneous, the complete solution is

$$y_x = C.F. + P.I.$$

Now, $C.F. = C_1(8)^x + C_2(-1)^x$

and $P.I. = \dfrac{1}{E^2 - 7E - 8} \cdot 2^x x^2$

$$= 2^x \cdot \frac{1}{(2E)^2 - 7(2E) - 8} \cdot x^2 = 2^x \cdot \frac{1}{4E^2 - 14E - 8} \cdot x^2$$

$$= 2^{x-1} \cdot \frac{1}{2E^2 - 7E - 4} \cdot x^2 = 2^{x-1} \cdot \frac{1}{2(1 + \Delta)^2 - 7(1 + \Delta) - 4} \cdot x^2$$

$$= 2^{x-1} \frac{1}{-9 - 3\Delta + 2\Delta^2} x^2$$

$$= -\frac{2^{x-1}}{9} \left\{ \frac{1}{1 + \left(\frac{3\Delta - 2\Delta^2}{9}\right)} \right\} x^2 = -\frac{2^{x-1}}{9} \left\{ 1 + \left(\frac{3\Delta - 2\Delta^2}{9}\right) \right\}^{-1} x^2$$

$$= -\frac{2^{x-1}}{9} \left\{ 1 - \left(\frac{3\Delta - 2\Delta^2}{9}\right) + \left(\frac{3\Delta - 2\Delta^2}{9}\right)^2 \right\} x^2$$

$$= -\frac{2^{x-1}}{9}\left\{1 - \frac{\Delta}{3} + \frac{\Delta^2}{3} + \ldots\right\}([x]^2 + [x]^1)$$

(As factorial polynomial corresponding to x^2 is $[x]^2 + [x]^1$)

$$= -\frac{2^{x-1}}{9}\left\{[x]^2 + [x]^1 - \frac{1}{3}(2x + 1) + \frac{1}{3}(2)\right\}$$

$$= -\frac{2^{x-1}}{9}\left(x(x - 1) + x - \frac{2x}{3} - \frac{1}{3} + \frac{2}{3}\right)$$

$$= -\frac{2^{n-1}}{9}\left(x^2 - \frac{2x}{3} + \frac{1}{3}\right) = -\frac{2^{n-1}}{27}(3x^2 - 2x + 1)$$

∴ The complete solution is $y_n = C_1(8)^x + C_2(-1)^x - \frac{2^{n-1}}{27}(3x^2 - 2x + 1)$

Case V: (1) If $\varphi(x) = sinkx$

$$P.I. = \frac{1}{f(E)} sinkx = \left(\frac{e^{ikx} - e^{-ikx}}{2i}\right) = \frac{1}{2i}\left(\frac{1}{f(E)}a^n - \frac{1}{f(E)}b^n\right)$$

where, $a = e^{ik}$ and $b = e^{-ik}$. Then proceed as in Case I.

(2)   If $\varphi(x) = coskx$

$$P.I. = \frac{1}{f(E)} coskx = \left(\frac{e^{ikx} + e^{-ikx}}{2}\right) = \frac{1}{2}\left(\frac{1}{f(E)}a^n + \frac{1}{f(E)}b^n\right)$$

where, $a = e^{ik}$ and $b = e^{-ik}$. Then proceed as in Case I.

Example 10.13 Solve $y_{n+2} - 2cos\alpha\, y_{n+1} + y_n = cos\,\alpha n$

Solution: The given equation can be written in operator form as

$$(E^2 - 2cos\alpha\, E + 1)y_n = cos\,\alpha n$$

The auxiliary equation is $(E^2 - 2cos\alpha\, E + 1) = 0$

$$\therefore\ E = \frac{2cos\alpha \pm \sqrt{4cos^2\alpha - 4}}{2} = cos\alpha \pm i\,sin\alpha$$

Since the given difference equation is non – homogeneous, the complete solution is

$$y_n = C.F. + P.I.$$

Now, $C.F. = 1^n\left[C_1\ cos\,\alpha n + C_2\ sin\,\alpha n\right]$

i.e. $C.F. = C_1\ cos\,\alpha n + C_2\ sin\,\alpha n$

and $P.I. = \frac{1}{E^2 - 2cos\alpha\, E + 1}.cos\,\alpha n$

$$= \frac{1}{E^2 - E(e^{i\alpha} + e^{-i\alpha}) + 1}.\left(\frac{e^{i\alpha n} + e^{-i\alpha n}}{2}\right)$$

$$= \frac{1}{2} \left[\frac{1}{(E - e^{i\alpha})(E - e^{-i\alpha})} e^{i\alpha n} + \frac{1}{(E - e^{i\alpha})(E - e^{-i\alpha})} e^{-i\alpha n} \right]$$

$$\text{Put } E = e^{i\alpha} \qquad\qquad \text{Put } E = e^{-i\alpha}$$

$$= \frac{1}{2} \left[\frac{1}{(E - e^{i\alpha})(e^{i\alpha} - e^{-i\alpha})} e^{i\alpha n} + \frac{1}{(E - e^{-i\alpha})(e^{-i\alpha} - e^{-i\alpha})} e^{-i\alpha n} \right]$$

$$= \frac{1}{4i \sin\alpha} \left[\frac{1}{(E - e^{i\alpha})} e^{i\alpha n} + \frac{1}{(E - e^{-i\alpha})} e^{-i\alpha n} \right]$$

$$= \frac{1}{4i \sin\alpha} \left[n.\, e^{i\alpha(n-1)} - n.\, e^{-i\alpha(n-1)} \right]$$

$$= \frac{n}{2\sin\alpha} \left[\frac{e^{i\alpha(n-1)} - e^{-i\alpha(n-1)}}{2i} \right] = \frac{n \sin(n-1)\alpha}{2\sin\alpha}$$

$\therefore$ The complete solution is $y_n = C_1 \cos \alpha n + C_2 \sin \alpha n + \dfrac{n \sin(n-1)\alpha}{2\sin\alpha}$

Example 10.14 Solve $\Delta^2 y_x + \Delta y_x = sinx$

Solution: The given equation is $\Delta^2 y_x + \Delta y_x = sinx$

$$(E - 1)^2 y_x + (E - 1)y_x = sinx$$

$$\{(E - 1)^2 + (E - 1)\}y_x = sinx$$

i.e. $\qquad\qquad \{(E - 1)E\}y_x = sinx$

i.e. $\qquad\qquad (E - 1)y_{x+1} = sinx$

Let $y_{x+1} = u_x$. Therefore, $(E - 1)u_x = sinx$

The auxiliary equation is $(E - 1) = 0$. Hence, the root is $E = 1$.

Since the given difference equation is non – homogeneous, the complete solution is

$$y_n = C.F. + P.I.$$

Now, $\quad C.F. = C_1.(1)^x = C_1$

and $\qquad\qquad P.I. = \dfrac{1}{(E - 1)} . sinx = \dfrac{1}{(E - 1)} \left(\dfrac{e^{ix} - e^{-ix}}{2i} \right)$

$$= \frac{1}{2i} \left[\frac{1}{e^i - 1} . e^{ix} - \frac{1}{e^{-i} - 1} . e^{-ix} \right] = \frac{1}{2i} \left[\frac{(e^{-i} - 1)e^{ix} - (e^i - 1).e^{-ix}}{(e^i - 1)(e^{-i} - 1)} \right]$$

$$= \frac{1}{2i} \left[\frac{\{e^{i(x-1)} - e^{-i(x-1)}\} - (e^{ix} - e^{-ix})}{1 - (e^i + e^{-i}) + 1} \right]$$

$$= \frac{1}{2i} \left[\frac{2i \sin(x - 1) - 2i\, sinx}{2 - 2\cos 1} \right] = \frac{\sin(x - 1) - sinx}{2(1 - \cos 1)}$$

$\therefore$ The complete solution is $u_x = y_{x+1} = C_1 + \dfrac{\sin(x - 1) - sinx}{2(1 - \cos 1)}$

i.e $\quad y_x = C_1 + \dfrac{\sin(x - 2) - \sin(x - 1)}{2(1 - \cos 1)}$

EXERCISES

Problems

(1)   Solve $y_{n+2} - 6y_{n+1} + 9y_n = 0$ given $y_0 = 1$, $y_1 = 0$

(2)   Solve the equation $y_{n+3} - 5y_{n+2} + 8y_{n+1} - 4y_n = 0$ given $y_0 = 3$, $y_1 = 2$ and $y_4 = 22$

(3)   Solve the equation: $(\Delta^2 - 3\Delta + 2)y_n = 0$

(4)   Solve the equation: $y_{x+3} - 9y_{x+2} + 43y_{x+1} - 75y_x = 0$

(5)   Solve the following difference equations:

   (i) $y_{x+2} - 7y_{x+1} + 12y_x = 0$ (ii) $u_{n+2} - 3u_{n+1} + 2u_n = 5^n + 2^n$

   (iii) $y_{n+2} - 5y_{n+1} + 6y_n = 6^n + 5$

(6)   Solve the following difference equations:

   (i) $(\Delta^4 + 2\Delta^3 - 3\Delta^2 - 4\Delta + 4)\,u_x = 0$

   (ii) $(\Delta^3 - 3\Delta^2 + 3\Delta - 1)\,y_x = 3\,(2^{x+1} + 3^{x-1})$

(7)   Solve $y_{n+2} - 4y_{n+1} + 3y_n = n.\,4^n$

(8)   Solve $y_{n+2} + y_{n+1} - 56y_n = 2^n.\,(n^2 - 3)$

(9)   Solve $u_{n+2} - 4u_{n+1} + 5u_n = 2$

(10)   Solve $(E^2 - 5E + 6)y_n = 4^n.\,(n^2 - n + 5)$

(11)   Solve the following difference equations:

   (i) $y_{x+1} - e^{2x}y_x = 0$ (Hint: $y_{x+1} = e^{2x}y_x$ Taking logarithms on both sides)

   (ii) $y_{n+1}^2 - 3\,y_n\,y_{n+1} + 2y_n^2 = 0$ (Hint: Divide the equation by y_n^2)

(12)   Solve $y_{n+2} - 16y_n = \cos\dfrac{n}{2}$

Answers

(1) $y_n = (1 - n)3^n$ (2) $y_n = 6 + (n - 3).\,2^n$ (3) $y_n = C_1.\,2^n + C_2.\,3^n$

(4) $y_x = C_1.\,3^x + 5^x\,(C_2\,\cos\theta x + C_3\,\sin\theta x)$ where, $\theta = \tan^{-1}\left(\dfrac{4}{3}\right)$

(5)   (i) $y_x = C_1.\,4^n + C_2.\,3^n$ (ii) $u_n = C_1 + C_2.\,2^n + \dfrac{5^n}{12} - n.\,2^{n-1}$

   (iii) $y_n = C_1.\,3^n + C_2.\,2^n + \dfrac{6^n}{12} + \dfrac{5}{2}$

(6)   (i) $u_x = (C_1 + C_2 n).\,(-1)^n + (C_3 + C_4 n).\,2^n$

   (ii) $y_x = (C_1 + C_2 x + C_3 x^2)2^x + (x^3 - 3x^2 + 2x).\,2^{x-3} + 3^x$

(7) $y_n = C_1 + C_2.\,3^n + \dfrac{4^n\,(3n-16)}{9}$

(8) $y_n = C_1.\,7^n + C_2.\,(-8)^n - \dfrac{2^{n-1}}{25}\,n^2 + \dfrac{2n}{5} - \dfrac{64}{25}$

(9) $u_n = C_1(2 + i)^n + C_2.\,(2 - i)^n + 1$

(10) $y_n = C_1.\,2^n + C_2.\,3^n + \dfrac{4^n\,(n^2 - 13n + 61)}{2}$

(11)   (i) $y_x = C\,e^{x(x-1)}$ (ii) $y_n = C_1$ or $y_n = C_2.\,2^n$

(12) $y_n = C_1.\,4^n + C_2.\,(-4)^n + \dfrac{\cos\left(\frac{n}{2}-1\right) - 16\cos\frac{n}{2}}{257 - 32\,\cos 1}$

Chapter 11   Numerical Solution of Ordinary Differential Equations

Objectives

- To know the difference between initial value and boundary value problem
- To know the difference between single step and multi – step methods
- To derive and apply different single step formulae
- To derive and apply different multi step formulae
- To know the concept of boundary value problem

Learning Outcomes

After reading this lesson students should be able to

- Know the concept of each single step method
- Apply appropriate single step formula successfully
- Know the concept of each multi – step method
- Apply appropriate multi step formula successfully
- Evaluate boundary value problem

11.1   INTRODUCTION

In science, engineering, economics, physics and in most areas, a large number of problems can be formulated into differential equations. For example, Newton's second law of motion, orbital motion of planets, population growth and simple model of economic growth etc. are governed by ordinary differential equations. It is, therefore, an essential mathematical tool for modelling many processes.

An ordinary differential equation, called an ODE, is an equation involving a function or functions of one independent variable and its ordinary derivative or derivatives. An ODE of order n is an equation of the form

$$F\left(x, y, y', y'', \ldots \ldots, y^{(n)}\right) = 0 \qquad \ldots\ldots\ldots (11.1.1)$$

Where, y is a function of independent variable x, $y' = dy/dx$ the first derivative with respect to x,

$y^{(n)} = d^n y/dx^n$ is the nth derivative with respect to x. For example, $dy/dx = x + y$, $d^2 y/dx^2 + y = 0$ etc.

The solution of an ordinary differential equation means finding an explicit expression for y in terms of a finite number of elementary functions of x. Such a solution of a differential equation is known as the closed or finite form of solution. Using integral calculus, it is possible to find closed form solutions for some of the simple differential equations. For example, the general solution of the simplest equation $Y'(t) = k(t)$ is $Y(t) = \int k(s)ds + c$ with c an arbitrary constant. But since there exists a large number of ordinary differential equations whose solutions cannot be obtained in closed form by the known analytical methods, the design of suitable numerical algorithms for accurately approximating solutions is essential.

The numerical methods for solving ordinary differential equations are methods of integrating a system of first order differential equations, since higher order ordinary differential equations can be reduced to a set of first order ODE's. For example, consider a second order differential equation of the form

$$y'' = f(x, y, y')$$

Let $k = y'$, then the above equation reduces to a system of two first order differential equations, such as $y' = k$, $k' = f(x, y, k)$. Therefore, we restrict ourselves to consider an ordinary differential equation of first order and first degree as

$$\frac{dy}{dx} = f(x, y) \qquad\qquad \dots\dots\dots (11.1.2)$$

In this chapter, we shall deal with different methods of solving the ordinary differential equations, first for solving initial value problems and then the boundary value problems. These numerical methods generate solutions in one of the following two forms:

(1)   An approximate power series for y in x from which the values of y corresponding to specified values of x can be obtained by direct substitution

(2)   Approximate values of y, corresponding to only specified values of x

The methods of Picard and Taylor series belong to the first category while the methods of Runge – Kutta, Euler, Milne and Adam – Bashforth belong to the second category.

11.2   BASIC TERMINOLOGIES OF DIFFERENTIAL EQUATIONS

1.   Order of Equations

The order of a differential equation is the highest derivative that appears in the equation.

For example, $\frac{dy}{dx} = f(x, y)$ and $y'' = f(x, y, y')$ are examples of first and second order differential equations.

2.   Degree of Equations

The degree of a differential equation is the power of the highest order derivative.

For example, $(y'')^2 - 11y' - 3 = 0$ is the second degree, second – order equation.

$xy'' + y^3 y' - 4y - 9 = 0$ is a first – degree, second order equation.

3. Initial Value Problem and Boundary Value Problem

We have already discussed that (Eq. 11.1.1) an ODE of order n is an equation of the form

$$F(x, y, y', y'', \dots \dots, y^{(n)}) = 0$$

Its general solution contains n arbitrary constants and is of the form

$$\varphi(x, y, c_1, c_2, c_3, \dots \dots, c_n) = 0$$

In order to find these n arbitrary constants, n conditions are required. These n conditions can be provided by the values of dependent variable or its derivatives for n specific values of the independent variable. If all the n conditions are specified only for the initial value of the independent variable, then the problem is called an *initial value problem (IVP)*.

For example, Solving the differential equation

$$\frac{d^2 y}{dx^2} = f\left(x, y, \frac{dy}{dx}\right)$$

subject to $y(0) = a$, $y'(0) = b$

It is also possible to specify the conditions for two or more values of independent variable x. Such problems are called the *boundary – value problem (BVP)*.

For example, solving the differential equation $y'' + 9y' - 6y = 3$, subject to the conditions $y(x_0) = a_1$, $y(x_k) = a_2$ and $y(x_n) = a_3$

In the following sections, we shall discuss various numerical methods for finding the solution of an initial value problem.

11.3 SINGLE – STEP METHODS

There are two main approaches that could be used to estimate the values of $y(x)$. They are known as single – step and multistep methods.

The information about the curve at one point is utilized and the solution is not iterated then they are referred to as single – step methods. In these methods, only one previous point is needed i.e. to estimate the value y_i , we need conditions at the previous point y_{i-1} only. The methods of Picard, Taylor, Euler and Runge – Kutta belong to this category.

11.3.1 Picard's Method

This method is also known as Picard successive approximation method. E. Picard, a French mathematician, developed this method in the early 20th century.

Consider the first order equation

$$y' = f(x, y) \qquad \qquad \dots\dots (11.3.1)$$

with $y(x_0) = y_0$. Integrating Eq. (11.3.1) with respect to x between limits x_0 and x, we get

$$\int_{y_0}^{y} dy = \int_{x_0}^{x} f(x, y) \, dx \quad \Rightarrow \quad y - y_0 = \int_{x_0}^{x} f(x, y) \, dx$$

$$\therefore \quad y = y_0 + \int_{x_0}^{x} f(x, y) \, dx \qquad \qquad \dots \dots (11.3.2)$$

Eq. (11.3.2) is known as integral equation as it contains the unknown y under the integral sign. This equation can be solved by an iterative process in successive steps.

Let us assume that y_0 is an initial approximation of y. The better approximation $y^{(1)}$ to the solution is obtained by putting $y = y_0$ in $f(x, y)$ and integrating Eq. (11.3.2), we get

$$y^{(1)} = y_0 + \int_{x_0}^{x} f(x, y_0) \, dx \qquad \qquad \dots \dots (11.3.3)$$

Now, in Eq. (11.3.3), the integrand is a function of x only and hence, it can be integrated between limits x_0 and x. For a second approximation $y^{(2)}$, $y^{(1)}$ becomes the initial approximation of y. Putting $y = y^{(1)}$ in $f(x, y)$ and integrating Eq. (11.3.2), we get

$$y^{(2)} = y_0 + \int_{x_0}^{x} f(x, y^{(1)}) \, dx \qquad \qquad \dots \dots (11.3.4)$$

Continuing this process, the nth approximation is given be the equation

$$y^{(n)} = y_0 + \int_{x_0}^{x} f(x, y^{(n-1)}) \, dx \qquad \qquad \dots \dots (11.3.5)$$

Eq. (11.3.5) is known as Picard's interation formula.
Thus, this method gives a sequence of approximations $y_1, y_2, y_3, \dots \dots$, each giving a better result than the preceding one.

Example 11.1 Solve $dy/dx = x^2 + y^2$ given $y(0) = 0$. Obtain the values of $y(0.1)$ and $y(0.2)$ using Picard's method.

Solution: Given that $f(x, y) = x^2 + y^2$, $x_0 = 0$, $y_0 = 0$
Picard's iterative formula for the solution is

$$y^{(n)} = y_0 + \int_{x_0}^{x} f(x, y^{(n-1)}) \, dx$$

$$\therefore \quad y = y_0 + \int_{x_0}^{x} f(x, y) \, dx \Rightarrow y = 0 + \int_{0}^{x} (x^2 + y^2) \, dx \qquad \dots \dots (1)$$

First Approximation
Putting $y = y_0$ in (1), we get

$$y^{(1)} = 0 + \int_{0}^{x} (x^2 + y_0^2) \, dx = \int_{0}^{x} x^2 \, dx = \frac{x^3}{3}$$

Second Approximation
Putting $y = y^{(1)}$ in (1), we get

$$y^{(2)} = 0 + \int_{0}^{x} (x^2 + (y^{(1)})^2) \, dx = \int_{0}^{x} \left(x^2 + \frac{x^6}{9}\right) dx = \frac{x^3}{3} + \frac{x^7}{63}$$

Third Approximation
Putting $y = y^{(2)}$ in (1), we get

$$y^{(3)} = 0 + \int_0^x \left(x^2 + \left(y^{(2)}\right)^2\right) dx$$

$$= \int_0^x \left(x^2 + \frac{x^6}{9} + 2\frac{x^3}{3}\cdot\frac{x^7}{63} + \frac{x^{14}}{3969}\right) dx$$

$$= \int_0^x \left(x^2 + \frac{x^6}{9} + 2\frac{x^{10}}{189} + \frac{x^{14}}{3969}\right) dx = \frac{x^3}{3} + \frac{x^7}{63} + \frac{2x^{11}}{2079} + \frac{x^{15}}{59535}$$

This process can be continued further although it may be a difficult task. If we stop at $y^{(3)}$, then

$$y(x) = \frac{x^3}{3} + \frac{x^7}{63} + \frac{2x^{11}}{2079} + \frac{x^{15}}{59535}$$

$\therefore \ y(0.1) = 0.0003333, \quad y(0.2) = 0.00266686$

Example 11.2 Find the solution, correct to four decimal positions, of the first order ordinary differential equation

$$\frac{dy}{dx} = 2x - y \text{ for } x = 1.1 \quad \text{when } y(1) = 3.$$

Solution: Given that $f(x,y) = 2x - y$, $x_0 = 1$, $y_0 = 3$

Instead of finding $y(x)$ as a power series in x, which is valid for all values of x, as in the previous problem, we will find better and better approximations for $y(1.1)$ successively as follows:

Picard's iterative formula for the solution is

$$y^{(n)} = y_0 + \int_{x_0}^x f\left(x, y^{(n-1)}\right) dx$$

$\therefore \ y = y_0 + \int_{x_0}^x f(x,y) \, dx \ \Rightarrow \ y = 3 + \int_1^{1.1} (2x - y) \, dx \quad .... (1)$

First Approximation

Putting $y = 3$ in (1), we get

$$y^{(1)} = 3 + \int_1^{1.1} (2x - 3) \, dx = 3 + \left[2\frac{x^2}{2} - 3x\right]_1^{1.1} = 2.91$$

Second Approximation

Putting $y = 2.91$ in (1), we get

$$y^{(2)} = 3 + \int_1^{1.1} (2x - 2.91) \, dx = 3 + \left[2\frac{x^2}{2} - 2.91x\right]_1^{1.1} = 2.919$$

Third Approximation

Putting $y = 2.919$ in (1), we get

$$y^{(3)} = 3 + \int_1^{1.1} (2x - 2.919) \, dx = 3 + \left[2\frac{x^2}{2} - 2.919x\right]_1^{1.1} = 2.9181$$

Fourth Approximation

Putting $y = 2.9181$ in (1), we get

$$y^{(4)} = 3 + \int_1^{1.1} (2x - 2.9181) \, dx = 3 + \left[2\frac{x^2}{2} - 2.9181x \right]_1^{1.1} = 2.91819$$

Looking at third and fourth approximations, we conclude that there is no change in the first four decimal places, therefore the value of $y(1.1)$ correct to four decimal digits is 2.9182 (rounded).

Picard's Method For Simultaneous First Order Differential Equations

In the case of a first order single differential equation, Picard's iteration formulae for the solutions of the simultaneous equations

$$\frac{dy}{dx} = f(x, y, z), \qquad \frac{dz}{dx} = g(x, y, z); \quad y(x_0) = y_0 \text{ and } z(x_0) = z_0$$

can be derived as

$$y^{(n)} = y_0 + \int_{x_0}^{x} f\left(x, y^{(n-1)}, z^{(n-1)}\right) dx \qquad \dots\dots (11.3.6)$$

and

$$z^{(n)} = z_0 + \int_{x_0}^{x} g\left(x, y^{(n-1)}, z^{(n-1)}\right) dx \qquad \dots\dots (11.3.7)$$

Let us understand this method for simultaneous equations by following example.

Example 11.3   Apply Picard's method with 2 iterations to find $y(0.1)$ and $z(0.1)$, given the simultaneous equations $\frac{dy}{dx} = x + z$, $\frac{dz}{dx} = x - y^2$ and $y(0) = 2; z(0) = 1$.

Solution: We know that Picard's iteration formulae for the solutions of the simultaneous equations

$$\frac{dy}{dx} = f(x, y, z), \qquad \frac{dz}{dx} = g(x, y, z); \quad y(x_0) = y_0 \text{ and } z(x_0) = z_0$$

can be derived as

$$y^{(n)} = y_0 + \int_{x_0}^{x} f\left(x, y^{(n-1)}, z^{(n-1)}\right) dx \qquad \dots\dots (1)$$

and

$$z^{(n)} = z_0 + \int_{x_0}^{x} g\left(x, y^{(n-1)}, z^{(n-1)}\right) dx \qquad \dots\dots (2)$$

Given that $f(x, y, z) = x + z$, $g(x, y, z) = x - y^2$,

Taking $x_0 = 0$, $y_0 = y^{(0)} = 2$; $z_0 = z^{(0)} = 1$ in (1) and (2), we get

$$y^{(1)} = 2 + \int_0^x (x + 1) \, dx = 2 + x + \frac{x^2}{2} \qquad (from \ (1))$$

$$z^{(1)} = 1 + \int_0^x (x - 4) \, dx = 1 - 4x + \frac{x^2}{2} \qquad (from \ (2))$$

$$y^{(2)} = 2 + \int_0^x \left(x + 1 - 4x + \frac{x^2}{2} \right) dx$$

$$= 2 + x - \frac{3x^2}{2} + \frac{x^3}{6} \qquad \dots \dots (3)$$

$$z^{(2)} = 1 + \int_0^x \left[x - \left(2 + x + \frac{x^2}{2} \right)^2 \right] dx$$

$$= 1 - 4x - \frac{3x^2}{2} - x^3 - \frac{x^4}{4} - \frac{x^5}{20} \qquad \dots \dots (4)$$

Substituting $x = 0.1$ in (3), we get

$$y(0.1) = 2 + 0.1 - \frac{3}{2}(0.01) + \frac{1}{6}(0.001) = 2.0852$$

Substituting $x = 0.1$ in (4), we get

$$z(0.1) = 1 - 4(0.1) - \frac{3}{2}(0.01) - 0.001 - \frac{1}{4}(0.0001) - \frac{1}{20}(0.00001)$$

$$= 0.5840$$

Remark: Picard's method is of considerable theoretical value, but can be applied to a limited class of equations in which successive integrations can be calculated easily. In other words, the method fails if $f(x, y)$ occurring in the differential equation $dy/dx = f(x, y)$, $y(x_0) = y_0$ is not easily integrable.

11.3.2 Taylor Series Method

To find the numerical solution of the equation

$$\frac{dy}{dx} = f(x, y), \qquad y(x_0) = y_0 \qquad \dots \dots (11.3.8)$$

We expand the function $y(x)$ about a point $x = x_0$ using Taylor's series as follows:

$$y(x) = y(x_0) + (x - x_0) y'(x_0) + (x - x_0)^2 \frac{y''(x_0)}{2!} + \dots \dots$$

$$+ (x - x_0)^n \frac{y^n(x_0)}{n!}$$

$$i.e. \ y(x) = y_0 + (x - x_0) y_0' + (x - x_0)^2 \frac{y_0''}{2!} + \dots \dots$$

$$+ (x - x_0)^n \frac{y_0^n}{n!} \qquad \dots \dots (11.3.9)$$

where $y_0', y_0'', \dots \dots$ are the first, second order derivatives and so on. Since the solution is not known, the derivatives in the above expansion are not known explicitly. Here, it is assumed that $f(x, y)$ is differentiable and hence, the derivatives can be obtained directly from the given differential equation itself. To get approximately the value of $y(x_0 + h)$, we replace $x = x_0 + h = x_1$ in Eq. (11.3.9). Then, we have

$y(x_0 + h) = y(x_1) = y_1$

$$= y_0 + h\,y_0' + h^2\,\frac{y_0''}{2!} + \dots\dots + h^n\,\frac{y_0^n}{n!}\ \dots\dots \quad (11.3.10)$$

If $y' = f(x,y)$ is given then we must repeatedly differentiate $f(x,y)$ implicitly with respect to x and evaluate them at x_0.

Now, $y' = f(x,y)$ and y is a function of x, then

$$y'' = \frac{d}{dx}\left(\frac{dy}{dx}\right) = \frac{d}{dx}[f(x,y)]$$

$$= \frac{\partial}{\partial x} f(x,y) + \frac{\partial}{\partial y} f(x,y)\cdot\frac{dy}{dx}$$

$$= \frac{\partial}{\partial x} f(x,y) + \frac{\partial}{\partial y} f(x,y)\cdot f(x,y)$$

If we take $f_x(x,y) = \frac{\partial}{\partial x} f(x,y),\ f_y(x,y) = \frac{\partial}{\partial y} f(x,y),\ f_{xx}(x,y) =$
$\frac{\partial^2}{\partial x^2} f(x,y),\ f_{yy}(x,y) = \frac{\partial^2}{\partial y^2} f(x,y)$ and $f_{xy}(x,y) = \frac{\partial}{\partial x\,\partial y} f(x,y)$ then

$$\therefore\quad y'' = f_x(x,y) + f_y(x,y) \times f(x,y) \qquad \dots\dots (11.3.11)$$

Similarly,

$y''' = f_{xx}(x,y) + 2f(x,y)f_{xy}(x,y) + f^2(x,y)f_{yy}(x,y) + f_x(x,y)f_y(x,y) +$
$f(x,y)f_y^2(x,y)$ \qquad \dots\dots (11.3.12)

Thus, $y(x_1 + h) = y(x_2)$

$= y(x_1) + hf(x_1,y_1) + \dfrac{h^2}{2!}\left[f_x(x_1,y_1) + f_y(x_1,y_1) \times f(x_1,y_1)\right]$

$+ \dfrac{h^3}{3!}\big[f_{xx}(x_1,y_1) + 2f(x_1,y_1)f_{xy}(x_1,y_1) + f^2(x_1,y_1)f_{yy}(x_1,y_1)$
$\qquad + f_x(x_1,y_1)f_y(x_1,y_1) + f(x_1,y_1)f_y^2(x_1,y_1)\big] + \dots\dots$

i.e. $y_2 = y_1 + hf(x_1,y_1) + \dfrac{h^2}{2!}\left[f_x(x_1,y_1) + f_y(x_1,y_1) \times f(x_1,y_1)\right]$

$+ \dfrac{h^3}{3!}\big[f_{xx}(x_1,y_1) + 2f(x_1,y_1)f_{xy}(x_1,y_1) + f^2(x_1,y_1)f_{yy}(x_1,y_1)$
$\qquad + f_x(x_1,y_1)f_y(x_1,y_1) + f(x_1,y_1)f_y^2(x_1,y_1)\big]$
$\qquad + \dots\dots \qquad\qquad \dots\dots (11.3.13)$

Similarly, taking (x_2,y_2) as the starting point, we get

$$y_3 = y_2 + hf(x_2,y_2) + \frac{h^2}{2!}\left[f_x(x_2,y_2) + f_y(x_2,y_2) \times f(x_2,y_2)\right] + \dots\dots\dots$$

Proceeding in this way, we can compute $y_4,\ y_5, \dots\dots$ In this method, we require only one previous value to compute next value. For example, to find the value of y_n by this method, we require the information at only one preceding point $y = y_{n-1}$ at $x = x_{n-1}$. So, this method is a single step method.

In general,

$$y_{i+1} = y_i + hf(x_i, y_i) + \frac{h^2}{2!} \left[f_x(x_i, y_i) + f_y(x_i, y_i) \times f(x_i, y_i) \right]$$
$$+ \,......\qquad\qquad ..\,.....\,(11.3.14)$$

This method is known as the Taylor series formula and can be applied recursively to obtain $y(x)$ for successsive values of x. Since the series given in Eq. (11.3.14) is an infinite series, we truncate the formula after a few terms resulting in a truncation error in the computed value. If we truncate the series after the term with h^{n-1}, the truncation error is given by

$$E_T = \frac{h^n}{n!} y^{(n)}(\xi), \; where \; x \le \xi \le x + h$$

or approximately ph^n, where p is a constant. In this case, the truncaton error per step is of order $h^n \left(\, i.e.\, O(h^n) \right)$. If the number of terms is more or the step length h is small then the truncation error will be reduced and hence, we will get better approximation.

Remark: Taylor series method works well as long as the successive derivatives can be calculated easily. If $f(x, y)$ is somewhat complicated and the calculation of higher order derivatives becomes tedious then this method cannot be used efficiently. Therefore, it is not much useful practically. But it is useful for finding starting values for the application of multi step methods like Milne – Simpson's, Adams – Bashforth etc.

Example 11.4 Use Taylor series method to compute $y(0.1)$ and $y(0.3)$, correct to five decimal places, if $y(x)$ satisfies $\frac{dy}{dx} = xy - 2x$ with $y(0) = 3$.

Solution: Given that, $y' = xy - 2x$,

$x_0 = 0, \; y_0 = 3.$ We take step length $h = 0.1$

$y' = xy - 2x$	$\Rightarrow y_0' = x_0 y_0 - 2x_0$	$\Rightarrow y_0' = 0$
$y'' = xy' + y - 2$	$\Rightarrow y_0'' = x_0 y_0' + y_0 - 2$	$\Rightarrow y_0'' = 1$
$y''' = xy'' + 2y'$	$\Rightarrow y_0''' = x_0 y_0'' + 2y_0'$	$\Rightarrow y_0''' = 0$
$y^{iv} = xy''' + 3y''$	$\Rightarrow y_0^{iv} = x_0 y_0''' + 3y_0''$	$\Rightarrow y_0^{iv} = 3$
$y^v = xy^{iv} + 4y'''$	$\Rightarrow y_0^v = x_0 y_0^{iv} + 4y_0'''$	$\Rightarrow y_0^v = 0$

By Taylor series expansion

$$y_1 = y(0.1) = y_0 + h y_0' + h^2 \frac{y_0''}{2!} + h^3 \frac{y_0'''}{3!} + h^4 \frac{y_0^{iv}}{4!} + h^5 \frac{y_0^v}{5!} + \,...\,...+$$

$$= 3 + (0.1)(0) + (0.1)^2 \left(\frac{1}{2}\right) + (0.1)^3 \left(\frac{0}{6}\right) + (0.1)^4 \left(\frac{3}{24}\right) + \,...\,...$$

$\therefore \; y(0.1) = 3 + 0.005 + 0.0000125 = 3.0050125$

$\qquad\qquad \therefore \; y(0.1) = 3.00501 \; (up \; to \; five \; decimal \; places)$

To find $y(0.3)$. We compute the value in two ways.

(A)   Here, we first find $y(0.3)$ by taking step length $h = 0.3$

$$y(0.3) = y_0 + h\,y_0' + h^2\,\frac{y_0''}{2!} + h^3\,\frac{y_0'''}{3!} + h^4\,\frac{y_0^{iv}}{4!}\ \ldots\ldots +$$

$$= 3 + (0.3)(0) + (0.3)^2\left(\frac{1}{2}\right) + (0.3)^3\left(\frac{0}{6}\right) + (0.3)^4\left(\frac{3}{24}\right) + \ldots\ldots$$

$$\therefore\ y(0.3) = 3 + 0.045 + 0.0010125 = 3.0460125 \approx 3.04601$$

(B) We compute $y(0.3)$ by taking $h = 0.1$. So, first we compute $y(0.2)$ and then $y(0.3)$.

Now, $(x_1, y_1) = (0.1, 3.00501)$

$y_1' = x_1 y_1 - 2x_1 = (0.1)(3.00501) - 2(0.1) = 0.100501$

$y_1'' = x_1 y_1' + y_1 - 2 = (0.1)(0.100501) + 3.00501 - 2 = 1.0150601$

$y_1''' = x_1 y_1'' + 2y_1' = (0.1)(1.0150601) + 2(0.100501) = 0.302508$

$y_1^{iv} = x_1 y_1''' + 3y_1'' = (0.1)(0.302508) + 3(1.0150601) = 3.0754311$

$y_1^{v} = x_1 y_1^{iv} + 4y_1''' = (0.1)(3.0754311) + 4(0.302508) = 1.5175751$

$$y_2 = y(0.2) = y_1 + h\,y_1' + h^2\,\frac{y_1''}{2!} + h^3\,\frac{y_1'''}{3!} + h^4\,\frac{y_1^{iv}}{4!} + h^5\,\frac{y_1^{v}}{5!} + \ldots\ldots +$$

$$= 3.00501 + (0.1)(0.100501) + (0.1)^2\left(\frac{1.0150601}{2}\right)$$

$$+ (0.1)^3\left(\frac{0.302508}{6}\right) + (0.1)^4\left(\frac{3.0754311}{24}\right) + (0.1)^5\left(\frac{1.5175751}{120}\right) + \cdots$$

$$\therefore\ y(0.2) = 3.00501 + 0.0100501 + 0.0050753 + 0.000050418$$
$$+ 0.0000128 + 0.000000126$$

$\therefore\ y(0.2) = 3.0201987$

Now, $(x_2, y_2) = (0.2, 3.0201987)$

$y_2' = x_2 y_2 - 2x_2 = (0.2)(3.0201987) - 2(0.2) = 0.2040397$

$y_2'' = x_2 y_2' + y_2 - 2 = (0.2)(0.2040397) + 3.0201987 - 2 = 1.0611066$

$y_2''' = x_2 y_2'' + 2y_2' = (0.2)(1.0611066) + 2(0.2040397) = 0.6203007$

$y_2^{iv} = x_2 y_2''' + 3y_2'' = (0.2)(0.6203007) + 3(1.0611066) = 3.3073799$

$y_2^{v} = x_2 y_2^{iv} + 4y_2''' = (0.2)(3.3073799) + 4(0.6203007) = 3.1426787$

$$y_3 = y(0.3) = y_2 + h\,y_2' + h^2\,\frac{y_2''}{2!} + h^3\,\frac{y_2'''}{3!} + h^4\,\frac{y_2^{iv}}{4!} + h^5\,\frac{y_2^{v}}{5!} + \ldots\ldots +$$

$$= 3.0201987 + (0.1)(0.2040397) + (0.1)^2\left(\frac{1.0611066}{2}\right) + (0.1)^3\left(\frac{0.6203007}{6}\right)$$

$$+ (0.1)^4\left(\frac{3.3073799}{24}\right) + (0.1)^5\left(\frac{3.1426787}{120}\right) + \ldots\ldots$$

$$\therefore\ y(0.3) = 3.0201987 + 0.02040397 + 0.005305533 + 0.000103$$
$$+ 0.000013781 + 0.00000026189$$

$\therefore\ y(0.3) = 3.0460256 \approx 3.04602$ (*correct to five decimal places*)

The exact solution of the given equation is $y = 2 + e^{x^2/2}$

	Exact Value	Error (Exact value – approximate value)
$y(0.1)$	3.0050125	$= 3.0050125 - 3.00501 = 2.5 \times 10^{-6}$
$y(0.3)$	3.0460279	$= 3.0460279 - 3.04601 = 1.79 \times 10^{-5}$ (by A)
		$= 3.0460279 - 3.04602 = 7.9 \times 10^{-6}$ (by B)

Thus, if we compute $y(x)$ through the sequence of the values of x, it gives us more accurate results

Taylor Series Method for Simultaneous First Order Differential Equations

In the case of a first order single differential equations, Taylor series method for the solutions of the simultaneous equations

$$\frac{dy}{dx} = f(x, y, z), \qquad \frac{dz}{dx} = g(x, y, z); \quad y(x_0) = y_0 \text{ and } z(x_0) = z_0$$

can be solved by using following two Taylor series

$$y(x_0 + h) = y_0 + h\, y_0' + h^2 \frac{y_0''}{2!} + h^3 \frac{y_0'''}{3!} + h^4 \frac{y_0^{iv}}{4!} + \dots \dots \qquad \text{and}$$

$$z(x_0 + h) = z_0 + h\, z_0' + h^2 \frac{z_0''}{2!} + h^3 \frac{z_0'''}{3!} + h^4 \frac{z_0^{iv}}{4!} + \dots \dots$$

Example 11.5 Solve the following simultaneous differential equations, using Taylor series method for $x = 0.1$ and $x = 0.2$ given $\frac{dy}{dx} = 2x + z$,

$\frac{dz}{dx} = x^2 + y^2$; $y(0) = 1$ and $z(0) = 1$.

Solution: Given that, $y' = 2x + z$, $z' = x^2 + y^2$;

$y' = 2x + z$	$z' = x^2 + y^2$
$y'' = 2 + z'$	$z'' = 2x + 2yy'$
$y''' = z''$	$z''' = 2 + 2yy'' + 2y'^2$
$y^{iv} = z'''$	$z^{iv} = 2yy''' + 2y''y' + 4y'y''$

Using $x_0 = 0$, $y_0 = 1$; $x_0 = 0$, $z_0 = 1$

$y_0' = 2x_0 + z_0 \Rightarrow y_0' = 1$ $z_0' = x_0^2 + y_0^2 \Rightarrow z_0' = 1$

$y_0'' = 2 + z_0' \Rightarrow y_0'' = 3$ $z_0'' = 2x_0 + 2y_0y_0' \Rightarrow z_0'' = 2$

$y_0''' = z_0'' \Rightarrow y_0''' = 2$ $z_0''' = 2 + 2y_0y_0'' + 2y_0'^2 \Rightarrow z_0''' = 10$

$y_0^{iv} = z_0''' \Rightarrow y_0^{iv} = 10$ $z_0^{iv} = 2y_0y_0''' + 2y_0''y_0' + 4y_0'y_0''$

$\Rightarrow z_0^{iv} = 22$

By Taylor series expansion $y_1 = y(x_0 + h) = y(0 + 0.1)$

$$= y_0 + h\, y_0' + h^2 \frac{y_0''}{2!} + h^3 \frac{y_0'''}{3!} + h^4 \frac{y_0^{iv}}{4!} + \dots \dots +$$

$$\therefore \ y(0.1) = 1 + (0.1)(1) + (0.1)^2 \left(\frac{3}{2}\right) + (0.1)^3 \left(\frac{2}{6}\right) + (0.1)^4 \left(\frac{10}{24}\right) + \dots \dots$$

$$= 1 + 0.1 + 0.015 + 0.000333 + 0.00004167 = 1.115375$$

$$z_1 = z(x_0 + h) = z(0 + 0.1)$$

$$= z_0 + h\,z_0' + h^2\,\frac{z_0''}{2!} + h^3\,\frac{z_0'''}{3!} + h^4\,\frac{z_0^{iv}}{4!} + \ldots\ldots +$$

$$\therefore z(0.1) = 1 + (0.1)(1) + (0.1)^2\left(\frac{2}{2}\right) + (0.1)^3\left(\frac{10}{6}\right) + (0.1)^4\left(\frac{22}{24}\right) + \ldots\ldots$$

$$= 1 + 0.1 + 0.01 + 0.001667 + 0.00009167 = 0.11175867$$

$$y(0.2) = 1 + (0.2)(1) + (0.2)^2\left(\frac{3}{2}\right) + (0.2)^3\left(\frac{2}{6}\right) + (0.2)^4\left(\frac{10}{24}\right) + \ldots\ldots$$

$$= 1 + 0.2 + 0.06 + 0.002667 + 0.0006667 = 1.2633337$$

$$\therefore z(0.2) = 1 + (0.2)(1) + (0.2)^2\left(\frac{2}{2}\right) + (0.2)^3\left(\frac{10}{6}\right) + (0.2)^4\left(\frac{22}{24}\right) + \ldots\ldots$$

$$= 1 + 0.2 + 0.04 + 0.0133333 + 0.0014667 = 1.2548$$

Taylor Series Method for Second Order Differential Equation

Any second or higher order ordinary differential equations can be reduced to a set of lower order ODE's. Consider a second order differential equation of the form

$$y'' = f(x, y, y')$$ .... (11.3.15)

with $\qquad\qquad y(x_0) = y_0$ .... (11.3.16)

Therefore, $\qquad y'(x_0) = y_0'$ .... (11.3.17)

Let $y' = k$, hence $y'' = k'$ then Eq.(11.3.15) reduces to a system of two first order differential equations, such as

$$y' = k, \quad k' = f(x, y, k)$$ .... (11.3.18)

Therefore, we have $k' = f(x, y, k)$ with initial conditions $y(x_0) = y_0$, $k(x_0) = k_0 = y_0'$ and Taylor series method is

$$k_1 = k_0 + h\,k_0' + h^2\,\frac{k_0''}{2!} + h^3\,\frac{k_0'''}{3!} + h^4\,\frac{k_0^{iv}}{4!} + \ldots\ldots \qquad \ldots\ldots (11.3.19)$$

where, $k_1 = k(x_1)$

Now,

$$y_1 = y_0 + h\,y_0' + h^2\,\frac{y_0''}{2!} + h^3\,\frac{y_0'''}{3!} + h^4\,\frac{y_0^{iv}}{4!} + \ldots\ldots$$

$$\therefore y_1 = y_0 + h\,k_0 + h^2\,\frac{k_0'}{2!} + h^3\,\frac{k_0''}{3!} + h^4\,\frac{k_0'''}{4!} + \ldots \qquad \ldots\ldots (11.3.20)$$

as $k(x_0) = k_0 = y_0'$

Eq. (11.3.18) gives k' and differentiating it with respect to x we get $k', k'', \ldots\ldots$ hence $k_0', k_0'', k_0''' \ldots\ldots$. Using Eqs. (11.3.19) and (11.3.20) we can obtain the values of $k_1, k_1', k_1'' \ldots\ldots$ at (x_1, y_1). Similarly, we get k_2 using

$$k_2 = k_1 + h\,k_1' + h^2\,\frac{k_1''}{2!} + h^3\,\frac{k_1'''}{3!} + h^4\,\frac{k_1^{iv}}{4!} + \ldots\ldots \qquad \ldots\ldots (11.3.21)$$

and we get y_2 using

$$y_2 = y_1 + h\, y_1' + h^2\, \frac{y_1''}{2!} + h^3\, \frac{y_1'''}{3!} + h^4\, \frac{y_1^{iv}}{4!} + \dots\dots \qquad\dots\dots\dots (11.3.22)$$

Example 11.6 Solve the equation $y'' - 2y' + y = x + 1, y(0) = 1,\ y'(0) = 0$ for $y(0.1)$ and $y(0.2)$, using Taylor series method of the fourth order. Compare the numerical solutions with the exact solutions.

Solution: Given that, $y'' = 2y' - y + x + 1,\ x_0 = 0,\ y_0 = 1$ and $y_0' = 0$

$y'' = 2y' - y + x + 1 \quad \Rightarrow \quad y_0'' = 2y_0' - y_0 + x_0 + 1 \qquad \Rightarrow \qquad y_0'' = 0$

$y''' = 2y'' - y' + 1 \quad \Rightarrow \quad y_0''' = 2y_0'' - y_0' + 1 \qquad \Rightarrow \qquad y_0''' = 1$

$y^{iv} = 2y''' - y'' \quad \Rightarrow \quad y_0^{iv} = 2y_0''' - y_0'' \qquad\qquad \Rightarrow \qquad y_0^{iv} = 2$

By Taylor series expansion,

$y_1 = y(x_0 + h) = y(0 + 0.1)$

$$= y_0 + h\, y_0' + h^2\, \frac{y_0''}{2!} + h^3\, \frac{y_0'''}{3!} + h^4\, \frac{y_0^{iv}}{4!} + \dots\dots +$$

$$\therefore\ y(0.1) = 1 + (0.1)(0) + (0.1)^2 \left(\frac{0}{2}\right) + (0.1)^3 \left(\frac{1}{6}\right) + (0.1)^4 \left(\frac{2}{24}\right)$$

$$= 1.0002$$

$$y(0.2) = 1 + (0.2)(0) + (0.2)^2 \left(\frac{0}{2}\right) + (0.2)^3 \left(\frac{1}{6}\right) + (0.2)^4 \left(\frac{2}{24}\right) = 1.0015$$

The given equation is $(D^2 - 2D + 1)y = x + 1$

A.E. is $m^2 - 2m + 1 = 0 \quad \therefore\ m = 1,1$

$\therefore\ C.F. = (Ax + B)e^x$

$$P.I. = \frac{1}{(D-1)^2}\,(x + 1) = (1 - D)^{-2}\,(x + 1)$$

$$= (1 + 2D + 3\,D^2 + \dots\dots)(x + 1) = x + 3$$

$\therefore$ Solution of the given equation is : $\quad y = (Ax + B)e^x + x + 3 \qquad \dots\dots (1)$

When $x = 0, y = 1 \ \therefore\ b + 3 = 1 \Rightarrow B = -2$

Differentiating (1) with respect to x, we have

$y' = (Ax - 2)e^x + Ae^x + 1$

When $x = 0, y' = 0 \ \therefore\ A - 1 = 0 \Rightarrow A = 1$.

Therefore, solution for the given equation is $y(x) = (x - 2)e^x + x + 3$

Hence, $y(0.1) = 1.0002,\ y(0.2) = 1.0015$.

11.3.3 Euler's Method

Euler's method is the oldest and the simplest, single step method. This method is not widely used because of its low accuracy. However, it serves as a starting point for predictor – corrector methods This method gives the solution as a set of tabulated values of variables x and y.

Consider a first order differential equation $\frac{dy}{dx} = f(x, y)$ with initial conditions

$$y(x_0) = y_0. \qquad\qquad \dots\dots (11.3.23)$$

Consider the first two terms of the Taylor series expansion, we have

$$y(x) = y(x_0) + (x - x_0)\, y'(x_0) \qquad \text{........ (11.3.24)}$$

From Eq. (11.3.23) and Eq. (11.3.24), we have

$$y(x) = y(x_0) + (x - x_0)\, f(x_0, y_0)$$

The value of $y(x)$ at $x = x_1$ is given by

$$y(x_1) = y(x_0) + (x_1 - x_0)\, f(x_0, y_0)$$

Let $x_1 - x_0 = h$, we get

$$y_1 = y_0 + h\, f(x_0, y_0)$$

Similarly, the value of $y(x)$ at $x = x_2$ is given by

$$y_2 = y_1 + h\, f(x_1, y_1)$$

In general, using recursive relation we have

$$y_{i+1} = y_i + h\, f(x_i, y_i) \qquad \text{........ (11.3.25)}$$

The formula given in Eq. (11.3.25) is known as Simple Euler's formula. The method in which we use simple Euler's formula for solving an equation is called Simple Euler's method. It can be used recursively to find values of $y_1, y_2, y_3, \ldots\ldots$ starting from the initial condition $y(x_0) = y_0$. A new value of y can be evaluated using the previous value of y as the initial condition.

Geometrical Interpretation

Let us assume that we have to find the approximate value of y, say y_n when $x = x_n$. We divide the interval $[x_0, x_n]$ into n sub-intervals by the points $x = x_0, x_1, x_2, \ldots, x_n$ each of width h i.e. $x_{i+1} - x_i = h$ $i = 1, 2, 3, \ldots n - 1$.

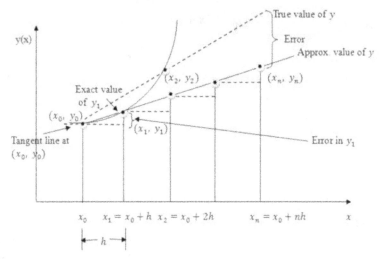

Figure 11.1 Illustration of Euler's method

Let (x_0, y_0) be the initial point lies on the solution curve. To find the value of y of the curve at $x = x_1$. Now, draw a tangent line from the point (x_0, y_0) with the slope $f(x_0, y_0)$. The point where this line intersects the vertical line erected at $x_1 = x_0 + h$ gives the next value of y, say y_1. The slope of the curve at this point is given by $f(x_0 + h, y_1)$. Again draw a tangent line from $(x_0 + h, y_1)$ with the slope $f(x_0 + h, y_1)$. The point where this line intersects the vertical line erected at $x_2 = x_1 + h$ gives the next value of y, say y_2 and so on. The truncation error involved in each step is $O(h^2)$.

Remark: In Euler's method the actual curve is approximated by a sequence of short straight lines. The disadvantage of this method is, unless the number of intervals is more (i.e. the value of h is small), the error is bound to be quite significant. The straight line deviates much from the actual curve. Therefore, the accuracy cannot be obtained. Since the method is very slow, the modification is required which is given in the next section.

Example 11.7 Given $\frac{dy}{dx} = \frac{y-x}{y+x}$ with initial condition $y = 1$ at $x = 0$; find y for $x = 0.1$ by Euler's method, correct up to four decimal places, taking step size h = 0.02.

Solution: The formula for Euler's method is $y_{i+1} = y_i + h f(x_i, y_i)$

Given that $\frac{dy}{dx} = \frac{y-x}{y+x}$, $x_0 = 0, y_0 = 1, h = 0.02$

Therefore, the Euler's method becomes $y_{i+1} = y_i + 0.02 \times f(x_i, y_i)$
For i = 0,

$$y_1 = y_0 + 0.02 \times f(x_0, y_0) = y_0 + 0.02 \times \left(\frac{y_0 - x_0}{y_0 + x_0}\right)$$

$$\therefore \quad y_1 = 1 + 0.02 \times \left(\frac{1 - 0}{1 + 0}\right) = 1.02$$

Therefore, the second point is obtained as $(x_1, y_1) = (x_0 + h, y_1) = (0.02, 1.02)$
For i = 1,

$$y_2 = y_1 + 0.02 \times f(x_1, y_1) = y_1 + 0.02 \times \left(\frac{y_1 - x_1}{y_1 + x_1}\right)$$

$$\therefore \quad y_2 = 1.02 + 0.02 \times \left(\frac{1.02 - 0.02}{1.02 + 0.02}\right) = 1.0392$$

Therefore, the third point is obtained as $(x_2, y_2) = (x_1 + h, y_2) = (0.04, 1.0392)$
For i = 2,

$$y_3 = y_2 + 0.02 \times f(x_2, y_2) = y_2 + 0.02 \times \left(\frac{y_2 - x_2}{y_2 + x_2}\right)$$

$$\therefore \quad y_3 = 1.0392 + 0.02 \times \left(\frac{1.0392 - 0.04}{1.0392 + 0.04}\right) = 1.0577$$

Therefore, the fourth point is obtained as $(x_3, y_3) = (x_2 + h, y_3) = (0.06, 1.0577)$
For i = 3,

$$y_4 = y_3 + 0.02 \times f(x_3, y_3) = y_3 + 0.02 \times \left(\frac{y_3 - x_3}{y_3 + x_3}\right)$$

$$\therefore \quad y_4 = 1.0577 + 0.02 \times \left(\frac{1.0577 - 0.06}{1.0577 + 0.06}\right) = 1.0756$$

Therefore, the fifth point is obtained as
$(x_4, y_4) = (x_3 + h, y_4) = (0.08, 1.0756)$

For $i = 4$,

$$y_5 = y_4 + 0.02 \times f(x_4, y_4) = y_4 + 0.02 \times \left(\frac{y_4 - x_4}{y_4 + x_4}\right)$$

$$\therefore \quad y_5 = 1.0756 + 0.02 \times \left(\frac{1.0756 - 0.08}{1.0756 + 0.08}\right) = 1.0928$$

Therefore, the sixth and final point is obtained as $(x_5, y_5) = (x_4 + h, y_5) = (0.1, 1.0928)$

Thus, the required approximate value of y at $x = 0.1$ is 1.0928.

Improved Euler Method (Heun's Method)

In the previous section, we have seen Euler's method which is the oldest and the simplest single step method. However, its major disadvantage is large trucation errors. In Euler's method, we have taken only first two terms of the Taylor series. In this method first three terms of the Taylor series are taken or we can say that the curve $y = f(x)$ in the interval is approximated by a line whose slope is the average of the slopes at the end points of the interval.

i.e.
$$y_{i+1} = y_i + \left(\frac{m_1 + m_2}{2}\right) h \qquad \dots \dots (11.3.26)$$

This approach is known as Heun's method and gives a better approximation than Euler's method.

Consider a first order differential equation $\frac{dy}{dx} = y'(x) = f(x, y)$

Let the slope is the average of the slopes at $y'(x_i)$ $(i.e.\ f(x_i, y_i))$ and $y'(x_{i+1})$ $(i.e.\ f(x_{i+1}, y_{i+1}))$

Therefore,

$$m = \frac{f(x_i, y_i) + f(x_{i+1}, y_{i+1})}{2}$$

Hence, Eq. (11.3.26) becomes

$$y_{i+1} = y_i + \frac{h}{2} \left[f(x_i, y_i) + f(x_{i+1}, y_{i+1}) \right] \qquad \dots \dots (11.3.27)$$

This cannot be evaluated until the value of y_{i+1} inside the function $f(x_{i+1}, y_{i+1})$ is already available to us. This value can be predicted using the Euler's formula as

$$y_{i+1} = y_i + \{h \times f(x_i, y_i)\} \qquad \dots \dots (11.3.28)$$

Then, Heun's formula becomes

$$y_{i+1} = y_i + \frac{h}{2} \left[f(x_i, y_i) + f(x_{i+2}, y^p{}_{i+1}) \right] \qquad \dots \dots (11.3.29)$$

This is the improved version of Euler's method. Since we can correct the value of y_{i+1} using the predicted value $y^p{}_{i+1}$ obtained by Euler's method, it is classified

as a one step *predictor – corrector method.*
Eq. (11.3.28) gives the predictor value and Eq. (11.3.29) gives the corrector value.
From the Eq. (11.3.28) and (11.3.29), we obtain

$$y_{i+1} = y_i + \frac{h}{2}\left[f(x_i, y_i) + f(x_{i+1}, y_i + h \times f(x_i, y_i))\right] \qquad \ldots\ldots\ldots (11.3.30)$$

This method is of order h^2.

Modified Euler's Method (Euler – Cauchy Method)

In Euler's method we have used the slope at the starting point of the solution curve to determine the next point of the solution curve. This technique will work only under the assumption that the function is linear. We have also seen the improvement in Euler's method by taking the slope whose value is the average of the slopes at the end points of the interval.
In modified Euler's method, the solution curve is approximated by the line passing through (x_i, y_i) with slope at the estimated midpoints of (x_i, y_i) and (x_{i+1}, y_{i+1}) to approximate y_{i+1}. Thus, the equation of the line is

$$y_{i+1} - y_i = (x_{i+1} - x_i) f\left(\frac{x_i + x_{i+1}}{2}, \frac{y_i + y_{i+1}}{2}\right)$$

i.e. $\qquad y_{i+1} = y_i + f\left(\frac{x_i + x_{i+1}}{2}, \frac{y_i + y_{i+1}}{2}\right)h \qquad \ldots\ldots\ldots (11.3.31)$

The value of y_{i+1} can be predicted using the Euler's formula as

$$y_{i+1} = y_i + \{h \times f(x_i, y_i)\} \qquad \ldots\ldots\ldots (11.3.32)$$

From Eq. (11.3.31) and Eq. (11.3.32), we get

$$y_{i+1} = y_i + hf\left(x_i + \frac{h}{2}, y_i + \frac{hf(x_i, y_i)}{2}\right) \qquad \ldots\ldots\ldots (11.3.33)$$

Eq. (11.3.33) is known as the modified Euler's method.
This method is also of order h^2. The local truncation error is $O(h^3)$ and global truncation error is $O(h^2)$.

Example 11.8 Given the equation

$$\frac{dy}{dx} = \frac{2y}{x} + x^3, \qquad \text{with } y(1) = 0.5$$

Estimate $y(1.4)$ using Improved Euler's method using $h = 0.2$. Compare the value with the exact solution.

Solution: Given $y' = f(x, y) = \frac{2y}{x} + x^3$; $\ x_0 = 1, \ y_0 = 0.5, \ h = 0.2$
From Eq. (11.3.30), the improved Euler's formula is

$$y_{i+1} = y_i + \frac{h}{2}\left[f(x_i, y_i) + f(x_{i+1}, y_i + h \times f(x_i, y_i))\right]$$

Iteration 1:

For i = 0,

$$y_1 = y(x_0 + h) = y_0 + \frac{h}{2}\left[f(x_0, y_0) + f(x_1, y_0 + h \times f(x_0, y_0))\right] \dots (1)$$

Putting $x_0 = 1$, $y_0 = 0.5$, $h = 0.2$ in (1), we get

$$y(1.2) = 0.5 + \frac{0.2}{2}\left[f(1, 0.5) + f(1.2, 0.5 + 0.2 \times f(1, 0.5))\right] \quad \dots\dots (2)$$

Now, $f(x_0, y_0) = \dfrac{2y_0}{x_0} + x_0{}^3 = \dfrac{2(0.5)}{1} + (1)^3 = 2$

Hence, $f(1, 0.5) = 2$

Substitute this value in (2), we get

$$y(1.2) = 0.5 + 0.1\left[2 + f(1.2, 0.9)\right] = 1.0228$$

Iteration 2:

For i = 1,

$$y_2 = y(x_1 + h) = y_1 + \frac{h}{2}\left[f(x_1, y_1) + f(x_2, y_1 + h \times f(x_1, y_1))\right] \dots (3)$$

Putting $x_1 = 1.2$, $y_1 = 1.0228$, $h = 0.2$ in (3), we get

$$y(1.4) = 1.0228 + \frac{0.2}{2}\left[f(1.2, 1.0228)\right.$$
$$\left. + f(1.4, 1.0228 + 0.2 \times f(1.2, 1.0228))\right] \qquad \dots\dots (4)$$

Now, $f(x_1, y_1) = \dfrac{2y_1}{x_1} + x_1{}^3 = \dfrac{2(1.0228)}{1.2} + (1.2)^3 = 3.43267$

Hence, $f(1.2, 1.0228) = 3.43267$

Substitute this value in (4), we get

$$y(1.4) = 1.0228 + 0.1\left[3.43267 + f(1.4, 1.709334)\right] = 1.8847$$

Exact Solution: Given equation is

$$\frac{dy}{dx} - \frac{2y}{x} = x^3$$

Which is a linear equation of the first order.

Integrating Factor: $e^{\int p\,dx} = e^{-2\int \frac{dx}{x}} = e^{-2logx} = \dfrac{1}{x^2}$

Solution

$$\frac{y}{x^2} = \int x^3 \cdot \frac{1}{x^2}\,dx + C \;\Rightarrow\; \frac{y}{x^2} = \frac{x^2}{2} + C$$

Using initial conditions *when* $x = 1,\; y = 0.5 \;\Rightarrow\; C = 0$

Therefore, the exact solution of the given equation is $y = \dfrac{1}{2}x^4$ $\dots\dots$ (5)

From (5), we get $y(1.2) = 1.0368$ *and* $y(1.4) = 1.9208$

Example 11.9 Using Euler's modified method, obtain a solution of the equation

$$\frac{dy}{dx} = x + |\sqrt{y}|,$$

with initial conditions $y(0) = 1$, for the range $0 \leq x \leq 0.6$ in steps of 0.2.

Solution: Given $y' = f(x, y) = x + |\sqrt{y}|$; $x_0 = 0$, $y_0 = 1$, $h = 0.2$
From Eq. (11.3.33), the modified Euler's formula is

$$y_{i+1} = y_i + hf\left(x_i + \frac{h}{2}, y_i + \frac{hf(x_i, y_i)}{2}\right)$$

Iteration 1:
For i = 0,

$$y_1 = y(x_0 + h) = y_0 + hf\left(x_0 + \frac{h}{2}, y_0 + \frac{h}{2}f(x_0, y_0)\right) \quad\dots\dots\,(1)$$

Putting $x_0 = 0$, $y_0 = 1$, $h = 0.2$ in (1), we get

$$y(0.2) = 1 + 0.2 f\left(0 + \frac{0.2}{2}, 1 + \frac{0.2}{2}f(0,1)\right) \quad\dots\dots\,(2)$$

Now, $f(x_0, y_0) = x_0 + |\sqrt{y_0}| = 0 + |\sqrt{1}|$
Hence, $f(0, 1) = 1$
Substitute this value in (2), we get

$y(0.2) = 1 + 0.2 \times f\left(0.1, 1 + \frac{0.2}{2} \times 1\right) = 1 + 0.2 f(0.1, 1.1) = 1 + 0.2 \times$
$1.1488 = 1.2298$

Iteration 2:
For i = 1,

$$y_2 = y(x_1 + h) = y_1 + hf\left(x_1 + \frac{h}{2}, y_1 + \frac{h}{2}f(x_1, y_1)\right) \quad\dots\dots\,(3)$$

Putting $x_1 = 0.2$, $y_1 = 1.2298$, $h = 0.2$ in (3), we get

$$y(0.4) = 1.2298 + 0.2 f\left(0.2 + \frac{0.2}{2}, 1.2298 + \frac{0.2}{2}f(0.2, 1.2298)\right) \quad\dots(4)$$

Now, $f(x_1, y_1) = x_1 + |\sqrt{y_1}| = 0.2 + |\sqrt{1.2298}|$
Hence, $f(0.2, 1.2298) = 1.3090$
Substitute this value in (4), we get

$y(0.4) = 1.2298 + 0.2 \times f(0.3, 1.2298 + 0.1 \times 1.3090)$
$= 1.2298 + 0.2 \times f(0.3, 1.3607) = 1.2298 + 0.2 \times 1.4665 = 1.5231$

Iteration 3:
For i = 2,

$$y_3 = y(x_2 + h) = y_2 + hf\left(x_2 + \frac{h}{2}, y_2 + \frac{h}{2}f(x_2, y_2)\right) \quad\dots\dots\,(5)$$

Putting $x_2 = 0.4$, $y_2 = 1.5231$, $h = 0.2$ in (5), we get

$$y(0.6) = 1.5231 + 0.2 f\left(0.4 + \frac{0.2}{2}, 1.5231 + \frac{0.2}{2} f(0.4, 1.5231)\right) \quad ..(6)$$

Now, $\quad f(x_2, y_2) = x_2 + |\sqrt{y_2}| = 0.4 + |\sqrt{1.5231}|$

Hence, $f(0.4, 1.5231) = 1.6341$

Substitute this value in (6), we get

$$y(0.6) = 1.5231 + 0.2 \times f(0.5, 1.5231 + 0.1 \times 1.6341)$$
$$= 1.5231 + 0.2 \times f(0.5, 1.68651) = 1.5231 + 0.2 \times 1.7987 = 1.8828$$

Hence, $y(0.6) = 1.8828 \; approx.$

11.3.4 Runge – Kutta Methods

These family of one – step methods were developed by two German mathematicians, Runge and Kutta. These methods are well – known as Runge – Kutta methods. As already discussed, the Taylor series method is not easy to apply as it involves labour work in finding the higher order derivatives. Euler's method is practically less efficient as it requires h to be small for getting reasonable accuracy. In Runge – Kutta methods the derivatives of higher order are not required, only the functional values at some selected points are required. These methods are designed to give greater accuracy. Due to these reasons, Runge – Kutta (R – K methods) are widely used methods for finding initial values. These methods are distinguished by their orders in the sense that they agree with Taylor's series solution upto the term in h^r where r differs from method to method and is called the order of that method.

(1) First Order Runge – Kutta Method:

From Eq. (11.3.25), Euler's formula is $y_{i+1} = y_i + h f(x_i, y_i)$

In particular, Euler's formula is

$$y_1 = y_0 + h f(x_0, y_0) = y_0 + h y_0' \qquad [\because y' = f(x, y)]$$

Expanding by Taylor's series, we get

$$y_1 = y(x_0 + h) = y_0 + h y_0' + \frac{h^2}{2} y_0'' + \ldots \ldots$$

It means that the Euler's method agrees with the Taylor's series solution upto the term in h. Therefore, Euler's method is the Runge – Kutta method of the first order.

(2) Second Order Runge – Kutta Method:

From Eq. (11.3.27), we have $y_{i+1} = y_i + \frac{h}{2} [f(x_i, y_i) + f(x_{i+1}, y_{i+1})]$

In particular,

$$y_1 = y_0 + \frac{h}{2} [f(x_0, y_0) + f(x_0 + h, y_1)] \qquad \ldots \ldots (11.3.34)$$

Putting $y_1 = y_0 + h f(x_0, y_0)$ in the right hand side of Eq. (11.3.34), we get

$$y_1 = y_0 + \frac{h}{2} [f_0 + f(x_0 + h, y_0 + h f_0)] \qquad \ldots\ldots (11.3.35)$$

where, $f_0 = f(x_0, y_0)$

Expanding LHS of Eq. (11.3.35) by Taylor's series, we get

$$y_1 = y(x_0 + h) = y_0 + h y_0' + \frac{h^2}{2!} y_0'' + \frac{h^3}{3!} y_0''' + \ldots\ldots \qquad \ldots\ldots (11.3.36)$$

Expanding $f(x_0 + h, y_0 + h f_0)$ by Taylor's series for a function of two variables, Eq. (11.3.35) gives

$$y_1 = y_0 + \frac{h}{2} \left[f_0 + \left\{ f(x_0, y_0) + h \left(\frac{\partial f}{\partial x}\right)_0 + h f_0 \left(\frac{\partial f}{\partial y}\right)_0 + O(h^2) \right\} \right]$$

where, $O(h^2) = $ *terms involving second and higher powers of h*

$$= y_0 + \frac{1}{2} \left[h f_0 + h f_0 + h^2 \left\{ \left(\frac{\partial f}{\partial x}\right)_0 + \left(\frac{\partial f}{\partial y}\right)_0 \right\} + O(h^3) \right]$$

$$= y_0 + h f_0 + \frac{h^2}{2} f_0' + O(h^3) \qquad \left(\because \frac{df(x,y)}{dx} = \frac{\partial f}{\partial x} + f \frac{\partial f}{\partial y} \right)$$

$$= y_0 + h y_0' + \frac{h^2}{2!} y_0'' + O(h^3) \qquad \ldots\ldots (11.3.37)$$

Comparing Eq. (11.3.36) and Eq. (11.3.37), it means that the modified Euler's method agrees with the Taylor's series solution upto the term in h^2.

Therefore, the modified Euler's method is the Runge – Kutta method of the second order. Hence, the second order Runge – Kutta formula is

$$y_1 = y(x_0 + h) = y_0 + \frac{1}{2} (k_1 + k_2)$$

where, $\quad k_1 = h f(x_0, y_0)$

and $\quad k_2 = h f(x_0 + h, y_0 + k_1)$

We state the Runge – Kutta formulas of the third and fourth order without proof.

(3)   Third Order Runge – Kutta Method:

The third order Runge – Kutta formula is

$$y_1 = y(x_0 + h) = y_0 + \frac{1}{6} (k_1 + 4 k_2 + k_3)$$

where, $\quad k_1 = h f(x_0, y_0)$

$$k_2 = h f \left(x_0 + \frac{h}{2}, y_0 + \frac{k_1}{2} \right)$$

and $\quad k_3 = h f(x_0 + h, y_0 + 2k_2 - k_1)$

(4)   Fourth Order Runge – Kutta Method:

The fourth order Runge – Kutta formula is

,
where,

$$y_1 = y(x_0 + h) = y_0 + k$$

$$k = \frac{1}{6}(k_1 + 2k_2 + 2k_3 + k_4)$$

$$k_1 = h\,f(x_0, y_0)$$

$$k_2 = h\,f\left(x_0 + \frac{h}{2}, y_0 + \frac{k_1}{2}\right)$$

$$k_3 = h\,f\left(x_0 + \frac{h}{2}, y_0 + \frac{k_2}{2}\right)$$

and

$$k_4 = h\,f(x_0 + h, y_0 + k_3)$$

Remark: The Runge – Kutta fourth order formula is widely used and simply referred as Runge – Kutta formula.

Example 11.10   Given that $dy/dx = x + y^2$, $y(0) = 1, h = 0.1$. Apply Runge – Kutta fourth order method to find approximate value of y for $x = 0.2$.

Solution: Given $f(x, y) = x + y^2$ and $h = 0.1$

Step 1: $x_0 = 0,$ $y_0 = 1$

$k_1 = h\,f(x_0, y_0) = 0.1 \times f(0,1) = 0.1 \times (0 + 1^2) = 0.1$

$k_2 = h\,f\left(x_0 + \dfrac{h}{2}, y_0 + \dfrac{k_1}{2}\right) = 0.1 \times f\left(0 + \dfrac{0.1}{2}, 1 + \dfrac{0.1}{2}\right)$

$\qquad\qquad = 0.1 \times f(0.05, 1.05)$

$\qquad\qquad = 0.1 \times (0.05 + 1.05^2) = 0.11525$

$k_3 = h\,f\left(x_0 + \dfrac{h}{2}, y_0 + \dfrac{k_2}{2}\right) = 0.1 \times f\left(0 + \dfrac{0.1}{2}, 1 + \dfrac{0.11525}{2}\right)$

$\qquad\qquad = 0.1 \times f(0.05, 1.057625)$

$\qquad\qquad = 0.1 \times (0.05 + 1.057625^2) = 0.11686$

$k_4 = h\,f(x_0 + h, y_0 + k_3) = 0.1 \times f(0 + 0.1, 1 + 0.11686)$

$\qquad\qquad = 0.1 \times f(0.1, 1.11686)$

$\qquad\qquad = 0.1 \times (0.1 + 1.11686^2) = 0.13474$

$\therefore\ k = \dfrac{1}{6}(k_1 + 2k_2 + 2k_3 + k_4)$

$\qquad = \dfrac{1}{6}(0.1 + 2(0.11525) + 2(0.11686) + 0.13474) = 0.11649$

$\therefore\ y_1 = y(x_0 + h) = y(0.1) = y_0 + k = 1 + 0.11649 = 1.11649$

Step 2: $x_1 = 0.1,$ $y_1 = 1.11649$

$k_1 = h f(x_1, y_1) = 0.1 \times f(0.1, 1.11649)$
$$= 0.1 \times (0.1 + 1.11649^2) \ = 0.13465$$

$k_2 = h f\left(x_1 + \dfrac{h}{2}, y_1 + \dfrac{k_1}{2}\right) = 0.1 \times f\left(0.1 + \dfrac{0.1}{2}, 1.11649 + \dfrac{0.13465}{2}\right)$
$$= 0.1 \times f(0.15, 1.1838) = 0.1 \times (0.15 + 1.1838^2) = 0.15514$$

$k_3 = h f\left(x_1 + \dfrac{h}{2}, y_1 + \dfrac{k_2}{2}\right) = 0.1 \times f\left(0.1 + \dfrac{0.1}{2}, 1.11649 + \dfrac{0.15514}{2}\right)$
$$= 0.1 \times f(0.15, 1.19406) = 0.1 \times (0.15 + 1.19406^2) = 0.15757$$

$k_4 = h f(x_1 + h, \ y_1 + k_3) = 0.1 \times f(0.1 + 0.1, 1.11649 + 0.15757)$
$$= 0.1 \times f(0.2, 1.27406) = 0.1 \times (0.2 + 1.27406^2) = 0.18232$$

$$\therefore \ k = \frac{1}{6} (k_1 + 2k_2 + 2k_3 + k_4)$$

$$= \frac{1}{6} (0.13465 + 2(0.15514) + 2(0.15757) + 0.18232) = 0.157065$$

$$\therefore \ y_2 = y(x_1 + h) = y(0.2) = y_1 + k = 1.11649 + 0.157065 = 1.273555$$

Example 11.11 Show that the Runge – Kutta formula of the fourth order for the solution of the equation $dy/dx = f(x)$, $y(x_0) = y_0$ (RHS is a function of x only) reduces to Simpson's rule of integration.

Solution: Let us find $y(x_0 + 2h)$ from the equation

$$\frac{dy}{dx} = f(x), \ y(x_0) = y_0$$

$k_1 = 2hf(x_0); \ k_2 = 2hf(x_0 + h); \ k_3 = 2hf(x_0 + h); \ k_4 = 2hf(x_0 + 2h)$

Now, Apply Runge – Kutta formula of the fourth order,

$$y(x_0 + 2h) = y(x_0) + \frac{1}{6} (k_1 + 2k_2 + 2k_3 + k_4)$$

$y(x_0 + 2h) - y(x_0)$
$$= \frac{1}{6} [2hf(x_0) + 2 \times 2hf(x_0 + h) + 2 \times 2hf(x_0 + h)$$
$$+ \ 2hf(x_0 + 2h)]$$

$$= \frac{h}{3} [f(x_0) + 2 f(x_0 + h) + 2 f(x_0 + h) + f(x_0 + 2h)]$$

$$= \frac{h}{3} [f(x_0) + 4 f(x_0 + h) + f(x_0 + 2h)] \qquad \text{....... (1)}$$

But LHS of Eq. (1) is,

$$\int_{x_0}^{x_0 + 2h} \left(\frac{dy}{dx}\right) dx \ = \int_{x_0}^{x_0 + 2h} f(x) dx$$

Thus, Eq. (1) reduces to

$$\int_{x_0}^{x_0+2h} f(x)dx = \frac{h}{3} [f(x_0) + 4f(x_0 + h) + f(x_0 + 2h)]$$

which is Simpson's rule of numerical integration.

Example 11.12   Find $y(0.1)$ and $y(0.2)$ given $y' = \sqrt{y^2 - 2xy}, y(0) = 1$
taking $h = 0.1$ by
(i) second order (ii) third order (iii) fourth order Runge – Kutta method.

Solution: Given $f(x, y) = \sqrt{y^2 - 2xy}; \quad h = 0.1$

(1)   Second order

Step 1: $x_0 = 0, \quad y_0 = 1$

$k_1 = h f(x_0, y_0) = 0.1 \times f(0, 1) = 0.1 \times \sqrt{1^2 - 2(0)(1)} = 0.1$

$\quad k_2 = h f(x_0 + h, y_0 + k_1) = 0.1 \times f(0 + 0.1, 1 + 0.1) = 0.1 \times f(0.1, 1.1)$

$\qquad\qquad\qquad = 0.1 \times \sqrt{1.1^2 - 2(0.1)(1.1)} = 0.09950$

$y_1 = y(x_0 + h) = y(0.1) = y_0 + \dfrac{1}{2}(k_1 + k_2) = 1 + \dfrac{1}{2}(0.1 + 0.09950)$

$\qquad = 1.09975$

Step 2: $x_1 = 0.1, \quad y_1 = 1.09975$

$\qquad k_1 = h f(x_1, y_1) = 0.1 \times f(0.1, 1.09975)$

$\qquad\qquad = 0.1 \times \sqrt{1.09975^2 - 2(0.1)(1.09975)} = 0.099474$

$k_2 = h f(x_1 + h, y_1 + k_1) = 0.1 \times f(0.1 + 0.1, 1.09975 + 0.099474)$

$= 0.1 \times f(0.2, 1.199224) = 0.1 \times \sqrt{1.199224^2 - 2(0.2)(1.199224)}$

$= 0.097900$

$y_2 = y(x_1 + h) = y(0.2) = y_1 + \dfrac{1}{2}$

$= 1.09975 + \dfrac{1}{2}(0.099474 + 0.097900) = 1.198437$

(2)   Third order

Step 1: $x_0 = 0, \quad y_0 = 1$

$k_1 = h f(x_0, y_0) = 0.1 \times f(0, 1) = 0.1 \times \sqrt{1^2 - 2(0)(1)} = 0.1$

$k_2 = h f\left(x_0 + \dfrac{h}{2}, y_0 + \dfrac{k_1}{2}\right) = 0.1 \times f\left(0 + \dfrac{0.1}{2}, 1 + \dfrac{0.1}{2}\right)$

$\qquad = 0.1 \times f(0.05, 1.05) = 0.1 \times \sqrt{1.05^2 - 2(0.05)(1.05)} = 0.099875$

$k_3 = h f(x_0 + h, y_0 + 2k_2 - k_1)$

$\qquad = 0.1 \times f(0 + 0.1, 1 + 2(0.099875) - 0.1)$

$\qquad = 0.1 \times f(0.1, 1.09975) = 0.1 \times \sqrt{1.09975^2 - 2(0.1)(1.09975)}$

$\qquad = 0.099474$

$$y_1 = y(x_0 + h) = y(0.1) = y_0 + \frac{1}{6}(k_1 + 4k_2 + k_3)$$

$$= 1 + \frac{1}{6}(0.1 + 4(0.099875) + 0.099474) = 1.099829$$

Step 2: $\quad x_1 = 0.1, \qquad y_1 = 1.099829$

$$k_1 = h f(x_1, y_1) = 0.1 \times f(0.1, 1.099829)$$

$$= 0.1 \times \sqrt{1.099829^2 - 2(0.1)(1.099829)} = 0.099482$$

$$k_2 = h f\left(x_1 + \frac{h}{2}, y_1 + \frac{k_1}{2}\right) = 0.1 \times f\left(0.1 + \frac{0.1}{2}, 1.099829 + \frac{0.099482}{2}\right)$$

$$= 0.1 \times f(0.15, 1.14957) = 0.1 \times \sqrt{1.14957^2 - 2(0.15)(1.14957)}$$

$$= 0.098825$$

$$k_3 = h f(x_1 + h, y_1 + 2k_2 - k_1)$$

$$= 0.1 \times f(0.1 + 0.1, 1.099829 + 2(0.098825) - 0.099482)$$

$$= 0.1 \times f(0.2, 1.197997)$$

$$= 0.1 \times \sqrt{1.197997^2 - 2(0.2)(1.197997)} = 0.097775$$

$$y_2 = y(x_1 + h) = y(0.2) = y_1 + \frac{1}{6}(k_1 + 4k_2 + k_3)$$

$$= 1.099829 + \frac{1}{6}(0.099482 + 4(0.098825) + 0.097775) = 1.19859$$

(3)   Fourth order

Step 1: $\quad x_0 = 0, \qquad y_0 = 1$

$$k_1 = h f(x_0, y_0) = 0.1 \times f(0, 1) = 0.1 \times \sqrt{1^2 - 2(0)(1)} = 0.1$$

$$k_2 = h f\left(x_0 + \frac{h}{2}, y_0 + \frac{k_1}{2}\right) = 0.1 \times f\left(0 + \frac{0.1}{2}, 1 + \frac{0.1}{2}\right)$$

$$= 0.1 \times f(0.05, 1.05)$$

$$= 0.1 \times \sqrt{1.05^2 - 2(0.05)(1.05)} = 0.099875$$

$$k_3 = h f\left(x_0 + \frac{h}{2}, y_0 + \frac{k_2}{2}\right) = 0.1 \times f\left(0 + \frac{0.1}{2}, 1 + \frac{0.099875}{2}\right)$$

$$= 0.1 \times f(0.05, 1.049938)$$

$$= 0.1 \times \sqrt{1.049938^2 - 2(0.05)(1.049938)} = 0.099869$$

$$k_4 = h f(x_0 + h, y_0 + k_3) = 0.1 \times f(0 + 0.1, 1 + 0.099869)$$

$$= 0.1 \times f(0.1, 1.099869)$$

$$= 0.1 \times \sqrt{1.099869^2 - 2(0.1)(1.099869)} = 0.099486$$

$$\therefore \ k = \frac{1}{6}(k_1 + 2k_2 + 2k_3 + k_4)$$

$$= \frac{1}{6}(0.1 + 2(0.099875) + 2(0.099869) + 0.099486) = 0.099829$$

$$\therefore \ y_1 = y(x_0 + h) = y(0.1) = y_0 + k = 1 + 0.099829 = 1.099829$$

Step 2: $x_1 = 0.1,$ $y_1 = 1.099829$

$k_1 = h\,f(x_1, y_1) = 0.1 \times f(0.1, 1.099829)$

$\quad = 0.1 \times \sqrt{1.099829^2 - 2(0.1)(1.099829)} \;=\; 0.099482$

$k_2 = h\,f\left(x_1 + \dfrac{h}{2}, y_1 + \dfrac{k_1}{2}\right) = 0.1 \times f\left(0.1 + \dfrac{0.1}{2}, 1.099829 + \dfrac{0.099482}{2}\right)$

$\quad = 0.1 \times f(0.15, 1.14957)$

$\quad = 0.1 \times \sqrt{1.14957^2 - 2(0.15)(1.14957)} \;=\; 0.098825$

$k_3 = h\,f\left(x_1 + \dfrac{h}{2}, y_1 + \dfrac{k_2}{2}\right) = 0.1 \times f\left(0.1 + \dfrac{0.1}{2}, 1.099829 + \dfrac{0.098825}{2}\right)$

$\quad = 0.1 \times f(0.15, 1.149242)$

$\quad = 0.1 \times \sqrt{1.149242^2 - 2(0.15)(1.149242)} \;=\; 0.098792$

$k_4 = h\,f(x_1 + h,\ y_1 + k_3) \;=\; 0.1 \times f(0.1 + 0.1, 1.099829 + 0.098792)$

$\quad = 0.1 \times f(0.2, 1.198621) \;=\; 0.1 \times \sqrt{1.198621^2 - 2(0.2)(1.198621)}$

$\quad = 0.097839$

$\therefore\ k = \dfrac{1}{6}\,(k_1 + 2k_2 + 2k_3 + k_4)$

$\quad = \dfrac{1}{6}(0.099482 + 2(0.098825) + 2(0.098792) + 0.097839) = 0.098759$

$\therefore\ y_2 = y(x_1 + h) = y(0.2) = y_1 + k = 1.099829 + 0.098759 =$
1.198588

Runge – Kutta Method for Simulataneous First Order Differential Equations

Consider the equations $dy/dx = f_1\,(x, y, z),\quad dz/dx = f_2\,(x, y, z)$ with the initial conditions $y(x_0) = y_0,\ z(x_0) = z_0$

The formulas are given as

$\quad y(x_0 + h) = y_0 + k \qquad\qquad\qquad\qquad z(x_0 + h) = z_0 + l$

where,

$k = \dfrac{1}{6}\,(k_1 + 2k_2 + 2k_3 + k_4) \qquad\qquad l = \dfrac{1}{6}\,(l_1 + 2l_2 + 2l_3 + l_4)$

$k_1 = h\,f_1(x_0, y_0, z_0) \qquad\qquad\qquad\qquad l_1 = h\,f_2(x_0, y_0, z_0)$

$k_2 = h\,f_1\left(x_0 + \dfrac{h}{2}, y_0 + \dfrac{k_1}{2}, z_0 + \dfrac{l_1}{2}\right)\ l_2 = h\,f_2\left(x_0 + \dfrac{h}{2}, y_0 + \dfrac{k_1}{2}, z_0 + \dfrac{l_1}{2}\right)$

$k_3 = h\,f_1\left(x_0 + \dfrac{h}{2}, y_0 + \dfrac{k_2}{2}, z_0 + \dfrac{l_2}{2}\right)\ l_3 = h\,f_2\left(x_0 + \dfrac{h}{2}, y_0 + \dfrac{k_2}{2}, z_0 + \dfrac{l_2}{2}\right)$

and

$k_4 = h\,f_1(x_0 + h,\ y_0 + k_3, z_0 + l_3)\qquad l_4 = h\,f_2(x_0 + h,\ y_0 + k_3, z_0 + l_3)$

Example 11.13 Solve the system of simultaneous differential equations

$$\frac{dy}{dx} = 5x + z; \quad \frac{dz}{dx} = y^2 - z; \quad y(0) = 0; \; z(0) = 1$$

for $y(0.1)$ and $z(0.1)$, using Runge – Kutta method of fourth order.

Solution: Given $f_1(x,y,z) = 5x + z$ $\qquad f_2(x,y,z) = y^2 - z$

$$x_0 = 0, \; y_0 = 0, \; z_0 = 1, \qquad h = 0.1$$

$k_1 = h\,f_1(x_0, y_0, z_0) = 0.1 \times f_1(0,0,1) = 0.1 \times \big(5(0) + (1)\big) = 0.1$

$l_1 = h\,f_2(x_0, y_0, z_0) = 0.1 \times f_2(0,0,1) = 0.1 \times (0^2 - 1) = -0.1$

$k_2 = h\,f_1\left(x_0 + \dfrac{h}{2}, y_0 + \dfrac{k_1}{2}, z_0 + \dfrac{l_1}{2}\right)$

$\quad = 0.1 \times f_1\left(0 + \dfrac{0.1}{2}, 0 + \dfrac{0.1}{2}, 1 + \dfrac{-0.1}{2}\right)$

$\quad = 0.1 \times f_1(0.05, 0.05, 0.95) = 0.1 \times (5(0.05) + 0.95) = 0.12$

$l_2 = h\,f_2\left(x_0 + \dfrac{h}{2}, y_0 + \dfrac{k_1}{2}, z_0 + \dfrac{l_1}{2}\right)$

$\quad = 0.1 \times f_2\left(0 + \dfrac{0.1}{2}, 0 + \dfrac{0.1}{2}, 1 + \dfrac{-0.1}{2}\right)$

$\quad = 0.1 \times f_2(0.05, 0.05, 0.95) = 0.1 \times (0.05^2 - 0.95) = -0.09475$

$k_3 = h\,f_1\left(x_0 + \dfrac{h}{2}, y_0 + \dfrac{k_2}{2}, z_0 + \dfrac{l_2}{2}\right)$

$\quad = 0.1 \times f_1\left(0 + \dfrac{0.1}{2}, 0 + \dfrac{0.12}{2}, 1 + \dfrac{-0.09475}{2}\right)$

$\quad = 0.1 \times f_1(0.05, 0.06, 0.952625) = 0.1 \times (5(0.05) + 0.952625)$

$\quad = 0.120263$

$l_3 = h\,f_2\left(x_0 + \dfrac{h}{2}, y_0 + \dfrac{k_2}{2}, z_0 + \dfrac{l_2}{2}\right)$

$\quad = 0.1 \times f_2\left(0 + \dfrac{0.1}{2}, 0 + \dfrac{0.12}{2}, 1 + \dfrac{-0.09475}{2}\right)$

$\quad = 0.1 \times f_2(0.05, 0.06, 0.952625) = 0.1 \times (0.06^2 - 0.952625)$

$\quad = -0.0949025$

$k_4 = h\,f_1(x_0 + h, \; y_0 + k_3, z_0 + l_3)$

$\quad = 0.1 \times f_1(0 + 0.1, 0 + 0.120263, 1 - 0.0949025)$

$\quad = 0.1 \times f_1(0.1, 0.120263, 0.9050975)$

$\quad = 0.1 \times (5(0.1) + 0.9050975) = 0.140510$

$l_4 = h\,f_2(x_0 + h, \; y_0 + k_3, z_0 + l_3) = 0.1 \times f_2(0 + 0.1, 0 + 0.120263, 1 - 0.0949025)$

$\quad = 0.1 \times f_2(0.1, 0.120263, 0.9050975)$

$\quad = 0.1 \times (0.120263^2 - 0.9050975) = -0.089063$

$$k = \frac{1}{6}(k_1 + 2k_2 + 2k_3 + k_4)$$

$$= \frac{1}{6}(0.1 + 2(0.12) + 2(0.120263) + 0.140510) = 0.120173$$

$$l = \frac{1}{6}(l_1 + 2l_2 + 2l_3 + l_4)$$

$$= \frac{1}{6}(-0.1 + 2(-0.09475) + 2(-0.0949025) - 0.089063) = -0.094728$$

Now, $y(x_0 + h) = y(0.1) = y_0 + k = 0 + 0.120173 = 0.120173$
           $z(x_0 + h) = z(0.1) = z_0 + l = 1 - 0.094728 = 0.905272$

Runge – Kutta Method for the Solution of a Second – Order Differential Equation

Consider the second order differential equation

$$\frac{d^2y}{dx^2} = y'' = f(x, y, y')$$

with initial conditions $y(x_0) = y_0$ and $y'(x_0) = y_0'$. Then the formulas are

$$y(x_0 + h) = y_0 + h\left[y_0' + \frac{1}{6}(k_1 + k_2 + k_3)\right]$$

$$y'(x_0 + h) = y_0' + \frac{1}{6}(k_1 + 2k_2 + 2k_3 + k_4)$$

where,

$$k_1 = h f(x_0, y_0, y_0')$$

$$k_2 = h f\left(x_0 + \frac{h}{2}, y_0 + \frac{h}{2}y_0' + \frac{h}{8}k_1, y_0' + \frac{k_1}{2}\right)$$

$$k_3 = h f\left(x_0 + \frac{h}{2}, y_0 + \frac{h}{2}y_0' + \frac{h}{8}k_1, y_0' + \frac{k_2}{2}\right)$$

and $$k_4 = h f\left(x_0 + h, y_0 + hy_0' + \frac{hk_3}{2}, y_0' + k_3\right)$$

Example 11.14 Solve the equation $y'' + 2xy' - 4y = 0$, $y(0) = 0.2, y'(0) = 0.5$ for $y(0.1)$ by Runge – Kutta method of the fourth order.

Solution: Given that $f(x, y, y') = y'' = 4y - 2xy'$; $x_0 = 0$, $y_0 = 0.2$, $y_0' = 0.5, h = 0.1$

$$k_1 = h f(x_0, y_0, y_0') = 0.1 \times f(0, 0.2, 0.5) = 0.1 \times [4(0.2) - 2(0)(0.5)]$$
$$= 0.08$$

$$k_2 = h f\left(x_0 + \frac{h}{2}, y_0 + \frac{h}{2}y_0' + \frac{h}{8}k_1, y_0' + \frac{k_1}{2}\right)$$

$$= 0.1 \times f\left(0 + \frac{0.1}{2}, 0.2 + \frac{0.1}{2}(0.5) + \frac{0.1}{8}(0.08), 0.5 + \frac{0.08}{2}\right)$$

$$= 0.1 \times f(0.05, 0.226, 0.54) = 0.1 \times [4(0.226) - 2(0.05)(0.54)]$$
$$= 0.085$$

$$k_3 = hf\left(x_0 + \frac{h}{2}, y_0 + \frac{h}{2}y_0' + \frac{h}{8}k_1, y_0' + \frac{k_2}{2}\right)$$

$$= 0.1 \times f\left(0 + \frac{0.1}{2}, 0.2 + \frac{0.1}{2}(0.5) + \frac{0.1}{8}(0.08), 0.5 + \frac{0.085}{2}\right)$$

$$= 0.1 \times f(0.05, 0.226, 0.5425) = 0.1 \times [4(0.226) - 2(0.05)(0.5425)]$$

$$= 0.084975$$

$$k_4 = hf\left(x_0 + h, y_0 + hy_0' + \frac{hk_3}{2}, y_0' + k_3\right)$$

$$= 0.1 \times f\left(0 + 0.1, 0.2 + (0.1)(0.5) + \frac{(0.1)(0.084975)}{2}, 0.5 + 0.084975\right)$$

$$= 0.1 \times f(0.1, 0.254249, 0.584975)$$

$$= 0.1 \times [4(0.254249) - 2(0.1)(0.584975)] = 0.0900001$$

$$\text{Now,} \quad y(x_0 + h) = y_0 + h\left[y_0' + \frac{1}{6}(k_1 + k_2 + k_3)\right]$$

$$\therefore \ y(x_0 + h) = y(0.1) = 0.2 + 0.1\left[0.5 + \frac{1}{6}(0.08 + 0.085 + 0.084975)\right]$$

$$= 0.254166$$

Remark: Value of k_4 is not required if we are not interested to find the value of $y'(0.1)$. $y'(0.1)$ is required if we want to find the next step (i.e. $y(0.2)$). Hence, in our case value of k_4 is not required.

11.4   MULTI – STEP METHODS

As we have discussed, single – step methods use the conditions at the last computed point y_i only to compute the next point y_{i+1}. They do not require the information available at previous steps $y_{i-1}, y_{i-2}, y_{i-3}, \dots$ ...etc. In *predictor – corrector* methods, also known as multi – step methods, we require to know the solution y at more than one previous points $x_{i-1}, x_{i-2}, x_{i-3}, etc.$ to compute the value of y at next point x_{i+1}. In these methods, the efficiency of estimation is improved by using more than one previous points. A predictor formula is used to predict the value of y at x_{i+1} and then a corrector formula is used to improve the value of y_{i+1}. If necessary, this value is again substituted in the right hand side of the corrector formula to get a still better approximation of y. This process is repeated until we get the desired convergence. One of the major disadvantage with multi – step methods is that they are not self – starting as prior values are required to evaluate the value of y at x_{i+1}. Only initial value condition is not enough in these methods. These starting values can be obtained using any of the single step methods discussed earlier. Because of this procedure, these methods become slightly complex. Inspite of these disadvantages, these methods have the advantage of giving an estimate of error from successive approximations to y_i. In the following section we consider two multi-step methods: Milne – Simpson method and Adams – Bashforth- Moulton method. Runge – Kutta fourth order method is generally used to start the predictor method. In these predictor – corrector methods, four prior values are required for finding the value of y at x_{i+1}.

Remark: Modified Euler's method is also considered as predictor – corrector method but for maintaning the flow we have kept it with simple Euler's and improved Euler's method.

11.4.1 Milne - Simpson's Predictor – Corrector Method

The Milne – Simpson's method is one of the powerful multi – step method. It uses a Milne formula as a predictor and Simpson's formula as a corrector. In this method, the information of four immediately preceding equispaced values of y, namely, $y_{i-3}, y_{i-2}, y_{i-1}$ and y_i is required, to find the value of y_{i+1}. Let us derive Milne's predictor formula. Consider a differential equation

$$\frac{dy}{dx} = f(x, y) \qquad \ldots\ldots\ldots(11.4.1)$$

with the initial condition $y(x_0) = y_0$.

Integrating both sides of Eq. (11.4.1) with respect to x between the limits x_0 and x_4, we get

$$\int_{x_0}^{x_4} \frac{dy}{dx}\, dx = \int_{x_0}^{x_4} f(x, y)\, dy \qquad \ldots\ldots\ldots(11.4.2)$$

$$y_4 - y_0 = \int_{x_0}^{x_4} f(x, y)\, dy \qquad \ldots\ldots\ldots(11.4.3)$$

By Newton's forward integration formula,

$$f(x, y) = f_0 + u\Delta f_0 + \frac{u(u-1)}{2}\Delta^2 f_0 + \frac{u(u-1)(u-2)}{6}\Delta^3 f_0$$
$$+ \ldots\ldots\ldots \qquad \ldots\ldots\ldots(11.4.4)$$

$$y' = y_0' + u\Delta y_0' + \frac{u(u-1)}{2}\Delta^2 y_0' + \frac{u(u-1)(u-2)}{6}\Delta^3 y_0' + \ldots\ldots\ldots$$

where, $u = \frac{x - x_0}{h}$, $x = x_0 + uh$, $y = dy/dx = f(x, y) = y'$, $y_0 = y_0'$, $\Delta y_0 = \Delta y_0'$, $\Delta^2 y_0 = \Delta^2 y_0'$ etc.

Putting Eq. (11.4.4) in Eq. (11.4.3), we get

$$y_4 = y_0 + \int_{x_0}^{x_4} [f_0 + u\Delta f_0 + \frac{u(u-1)}{2}\Delta^2 f_0 + \frac{u(u-1)(u-2)}{6}\Delta^3 f_0$$
$$+ \ldots\ldots]dx \qquad \ldots\ldots\ldots(11.4.5)$$

Since $dx = hdu$ and limits for u are 0 to 4 Eq. (11.4.5) becomes,

$$y_4 = y_0 + h\int_0^4 \left[f_0 + u\Delta f_0 + \frac{u(u-1)}{2}\Delta^2 f_0 + \frac{u(u-1)(u-2)}{6}\Delta^3 f_0 \right.$$
$$\left. + \ldots \right] du \qquad \ldots\ldots\ldots(11.4.6)$$

Now,

$$\int_0^4 du = 4; \quad \int_0^4 u\, du = \left[\frac{u^2}{2}\right]_0^4 = 8; \quad \int_0^4 \frac{u(u-1)}{2!}\, du = \frac{1}{2}\left[\frac{u^3}{3} - \frac{u^2}{2}\right]_0^4 = 20;$$

similarly, $\int_0^4 \dfrac{u(u-1)(u-2)(u-3)}{6}\, du = \dfrac{8}{3}$;

$$\int_0^4 \frac{u(u-1)(u-2)(u-3)(u-4)}{24}\, du = \frac{14}{45}$$

Using these values in Eq. (11.4.6), we have

$$y_4 = y_0 + h\left[4f_0 + 8\Delta f_0 + 20\Delta^2 f_0 + \frac{8}{3}\Delta^3 f_0 + \frac{14}{45}\Delta^4 f_0 + \dots\dots\right]. (11.4.7)$$

Putting the differences, such as $\Delta f_0 = f_1 - f_0$, $\Delta^2 f_0 = f_2 - 2f_1 + f_0$ etc.
Eq. (11.4.7) can be further simplified to

$$y_4 = y_0 + h\left[4f_0 + 8(f_1 - f_0) + 20(f_2 - 2f_1 + f_0) + \frac{8}{3}(f_3 - 3f_2 + 3f_1 - f_0)\right.$$
$$\left. + \frac{14}{45}\Delta^4 f_0 + \dots\dots\right]$$

$$y_4 = y_0 + h\left[\frac{8}{3}f_1 - \frac{4}{3}f_2 + \frac{8}{3}f_3\right] + \frac{14}{45}h\Delta^4 f_0$$
$$+ \dots\dots \qquad\qquad \dots\dots. (11.4.8)$$

It can also be written as

$$y_4 = y_0 + \frac{4h}{3}[2y_1' - y_2' + 2y_3'] + \frac{14}{45}h\Delta^4 y_0'$$
$$+ \dots\dots \qquad\qquad \dots\dots. (11.4.9)$$

Neglecting fourth and higher order differences, we get from Eq. (11.4.9)

$$y_4 = y_0 + \frac{4h}{3}[2y_1' - y_2' + 2y_3'] \qquad\qquad \dots\dots. (11.4.10)$$

The error in Eq. (11.4.10) is $\frac{14}{45}h\Delta^4 y_0' + \dots\dots$

i.e. $\frac{14}{45}h(E-1)^4 y_0' + \dots\dots = \frac{14}{45}h(e^{hD}-1)^4 y_0' + \dots\dots = \frac{14}{45}h(hD)^4 y_0',$
since h is small

i.e. $\frac{14}{45}h^5 y_0^{(5)} + \dots\dots = \frac{14}{45}h^5 y^{(5)}(\xi)$, where, $x_0 \le \xi \le x_4$

Eq. (11.4.10) is known as Milne's predictor formula.
In general Milne's predictor formula can be wriiten as

$$y_{n+1} = y_{n-3} + \frac{4h}{3}[2y_{n-2}' - y_{n-1}' + 2y_n'] + \frac{14}{45}h^5 y^{(5)}(\xi)\dots\dots (11.4.11)$$

where, $x_{n-3} \le \xi \le x_{n+1}$
Similarly, integrating Eq. (11.4.2) over the interval x_0 to x_2 or $u = 0$ to 2 and
repeating the above steps, we have

$$y_2 = y_0 + \frac{h}{3}[y_0' + 4y_1' + y_2'] \qquad\qquad \dots\dots. (11.4.12)$$

The error in Eq. (11.4.12) is

$$-\frac{1}{90} h\Delta^4 y_0' + \dots \dots = -\frac{1}{90} h(E-1)^4 y_0' + \dots \dots$$

$$= -\frac{1}{90} h(e^{hD}-1)^4 y_0' + \dots \dots$$

$$= -\frac{1}{90} h \, (hD)^4 \, y_0' \quad \text{since h is small}$$

$$= -\frac{1}{90} h^5 \, y_0^{(5)} + \dots \dots = -\frac{h^5}{90} y^{(5)}(\xi), \qquad \text{where,} \qquad x_0 \leq \xi \leq x_2$$

Eq. (11.4.12) is known as Milne's corrector *(extrapolation)* formula.

In general Milne's corrector formula can be wriiten as

$$y_{n+1} = y_{n-1} + \frac{h}{3} \, [y_{n-1}' + 4y_n' + y_{n+1}'] \quad -\frac{h^5}{90} \, y^{(5)}(\xi) \dots \dots (11.4.13)$$

where, $x_{n-1} \leq \xi \leq x_{n+1}$

Remark: At least four values are needed prior to the required value for evaluating Milne – Simpson's predictor corrector formula. If these initial values are not given it can be obtained either by using Taylor's series method, Euler's method or Runge – Kutta method.

Example 11.15 Evaluate $y(0.4)$ if $y(x)$ is the solution of

$$\frac{dy}{dx} = \frac{y^2 + x^2 y^2}{2}$$

assuming $y(0) = 1, y(0.1) = 1.06, y(0.2) = 1.12, y(0.3) = 1.21$ using Milne's predictor – corrector method.

Solution: Given that, $y' = \frac{y^2 + x^2 y^2}{2}$

$$x_0 = 0, \qquad y_0 = 1$$
$$x_1 = 0.1, \quad y_1 = 1.06$$
$$x_2 = 0.2, \quad y_2 = 1.12$$
$$x_3 = 0.3, \quad y_3 = 1.21 \qquad \text{and} \qquad h = 0.1$$

Now,

$$y_1' = \frac{y_1{}^2 + x_1{}^2 y_1{}^2}{2} = \frac{(1.06)^2 + (0.1)^2 (1.06)^2}{2} = 0.567418$$

$$y_2' = \frac{y_2{}^2 + x_2{}^2 y_2{}^2}{2} = \frac{(1.12)^2 + (0.2)^2 (1.12)^2}{2} = 0.652288$$

$$y_3' = \frac{y_3{}^2 + x_3{}^2 y_3{}^2}{2} = \frac{(1.21)^2 + (0.3)^2 (1.21)^2}{2} = 0.797934$$

From Eq. (11.4.11), Milne's predictor formula is

$$y_{n+1} = y_{n-3} + \frac{4h}{3} \, [2 y_{n-2}' - y_{n-1}' + 2 y_n'] \qquad \dots \dots (1)$$

Taking n = 3 in (1), we have

$$y_4^{(0)} = y_0 + \frac{4h}{3} [2 y_1' - y_2' + 2 y_3']$$

$$y_4^{(0)} = 1 + \frac{4(0.1)}{3} [2 (0.567418) - (0.652288) + 2 (0.797934)] = 1.2771$$

$$(y_4')^{(0)} = \frac{y_4^2 + x_4^2 (y_4^{(0)})^2}{2} = \frac{(1.2771)^2 + (0.4)^2 (1.2771)^2}{2} = 0.945971$$

From Eq. (11.4.13), Milne's corrector formula is

$$y_{n+1} = y_{n-1} + \frac{h}{3} [y_{n-1}' + 4y_n' + y_{n+1}'] \qquad \ldots\ldots(2)$$

Taking n = 3 in (2), we have

$$y_4^{(1)} = y_2 + \frac{h}{3} [y_2' + 4y_3' + (y_4')^{(0)}]$$

$$y_4^{(1)} = 1.12 + \frac{0.1}{3} [(0.652288) + 4(0.797934) + (0.945971)] = 1.279667$$

$$(y_4')^{(1)} = \frac{y_4^2 + x_4^2 y_4^2}{2} = \frac{(1.279667)^2 + (0.4)^2 (1.279667)^2}{2} = 0.94977$$

Now,

$$y_4^{(2)} = 1.12 + \frac{0.1}{3} [(0.652288) + 4(0.797934) + (0.94977)] = 1.279793$$

$$(y_4')^{(2)} = \frac{y_4^2 + x_4^2 y_4^2}{2} = \frac{(1.279793)^2 + (0.4)^2 (1.279793)^2}{2} = 0.949965$$

$$y_4^{(3)} = 1.12 + \frac{0.1}{3} [(0.652288) + 4(0.797934) + (0.949965)] = 1.27980$$

$$(y_4')^{(3)} = \frac{y_4^2 + x_4^2 y_4^2}{2} = \frac{(1.279780)^2 + (0.4)^2 (1.27980)^2}{2} = 0.94998$$

$$y_4^{(4)} = 1.12 + \frac{0.1}{3} [(0.652288) + 4(0.797934) + (0.94998)] = 1.27980$$

Since $y_4^{(3)} = y_4^{(4)}$, convergence upto four decimal places has occurred.
∴ The corrected value of $y(0.4) = 1.27980$

Example 11.16 Compute the Taylor series solution of $dy/dx = x^2 + y^2, y(0) = 1$, up to x^5 terms and hence compute values of $y(0.1), y(0.2)$ and $y(0.3)$. Use Milne's predictor – corrector method to compute $y(0.4)$.

Solution: Given that, $y' = x^2 + y^2$, with $x_0 = 0 \Rightarrow y_0 = 1, y_0' = 1$
$y_0'' = 2x_0 + 2y_0 y_0' \quad \therefore y_0'' = 2$
$y_0''' = 2 + 2y_0 y_0'' + 2(y_0')^2 \quad \therefore y_0''' = 8$
$y_0^{(iv)} = 2y_0 y_0''' + 2y_0' y_0'' + 4y_0' y_0'' = 2y_0 y_0''' + 6y_0' y_0'' \quad \therefore y_0^{(iv)} = 28$
$y_0^{(v)} = 2y_0 y_0^{(iv)} + 2y_0' y_0''' + 6y_0' y_0''' + 6(y_0'')^2 \quad \therefore y_0^{(v)} = 144$

The Taylor series solution is given by

$$y(0.1) = y_0 + h\, y_0' + h^2 \frac{y_0''}{2!} + h^3 \frac{y_0'''}{3!} + h^4 \frac{y_0^{iv}}{4!} + h^5 \frac{y_0^{v}}{5!} + \dots \dots +$$

$$= 1 + (0.1)(1) + (0.1)^2 \frac{2}{2!} + (0.1)^3 \frac{8}{6} + (0.1)^4 \frac{28}{24} + (0.1)^5 \frac{144}{120} = 1.1115$$

similarly,

$$y(0.2) = 1 + (0.2)(1) + (0.2)^2 \frac{2}{2!} + (0.2)^3 \frac{8}{6} + (0.2)^4 \frac{28}{24} + (0.2)^5 \frac{144}{120}$$

$$= 1.2529$$

$$y(0.3) = 1 + (0.3)(1) + (0.3)^2 \frac{2}{2!} + (0.3)^3 \frac{8}{6} + (0.3)^4 \frac{28}{24} + (0.3)^5 \frac{144}{120}$$

$$= 1.4384$$

$$\begin{array}{ll} x_0 = 0, & y_0 = 1 \\ x_1 = 0.1, & y_1 = 1.1115 \\ x_2 = 0.2, & y_2 = 1.2529 \\ x_3 = 0.3, & y_3 = 1.4384 \qquad \text{and} \qquad h = 0.1 \end{array}$$

Now,

$$\begin{aligned} y_1' &= x_1{}^2 + y_1{}^2 = (0.1)^2 + (1.1115)^2 = 1.24543 \\ y_2' &= x_2{}^2 + y_2{}^2 = (0.2)^2 + (1.2529)^2 = 1.60976 \\ y_3' &= x_3{}^2 + y_3{}^2 = (0.3)^2 + (1.4384)^2 = 2.15899 \end{aligned}$$

From Eq. (11.4.11), Milne's predictor formula is

$$y_{n+1} = y_{n-3} + \frac{4h}{3} \left[2\, y_{n-2}' - y_{n-1}' + 2\, y_n' \right] \qquad \dots \dots (1)$$

Taking n = 3 in (1), we have

$$y_4^{(0)} = y_0 + \frac{4h}{3} \left[2\, y_1' - y_2' + 2\, y_3' \right]$$

$$y_4^{(0)} = 1 + \frac{4(0.1)}{3} \left[2\,(1.24543) - (1.60976) + 2\,(2.15899) \right] = 1.69321$$

$$(y_4')^{(0)} = x_4{}^2 + (y_4^{(0)})^2 = (0.4)^2 + (1.69321)^2 = 3.02696$$

From Eq. (11.4.13), Milne's corrector formula is

$$y_{n+1} = y_{n-1} + \frac{h}{3} \left[y_{n-1}' + 4y_n' + y_{n+1}' \right] \qquad \dots \dots (2)$$

Taking n = 3 in (2), we have

$$y_4^{(1)} = y_2 + \frac{h}{3} \left[y_2' + 4y_3' + (y_4')^{(0)} \right]$$

$$y_4^{(1)} = 1.2529 + \frac{0.1}{3} \left[(1.60976) + 4(2.15899) + (3.02696) \right] = 1.69532$$

$$(y_4')^{(1)} = x_4{}^2 + y_4{}^2 = (0.4)^2 + (1.69532)^2 = 3.034110$$

Now,

$$y_4^{(2)} = 1.2529 + \frac{0.1}{3} \left[(1.60976) + 4(2.15899) + (3.034110) \right] = 1.69556$$

$$(y_4')^{(2)} = x_4{}^2 + y_4{}^2 = (0.4)^2 + (1.69556)^2 = 3.034924$$

$$y_4^{(3)} = 1.2529 + \frac{0.1}{3}\ [(1.60976) + 4(2.15899) + (3.034924)] = 1.69558$$

$$(y_4')^{(3)} = x_4^2 + y_4^2 = (0.4)^2 + (1.69558)^2 = 3.034992$$

$$y_4^{(4)} = 1.2529 + \frac{0.1}{3}\ [(1.60976) + 4(2.15899) + (3.034992)] = 1.69559$$

Since $y_4^{(3)} = y_4^{(4)}$, convergence upto four decimal places has occurred.

∴ The corrected value of $y(0.4) = 1.6955$

11.4.2 Adam – Bashforth's Predictor – Corrector Method

It is another predictor – corrector method, where the information of four immediately preceding equispaced values of y, namely, $y_{i-3}, y_{i-2}, y_{i-1}$ and y_i is required, to find the value of y_{i+1}. Consider a differential equation

$$\frac{dy}{dx} = f(x, y) \qquad\qquad \dots\dots(11.4.14)$$

with the initial condition $y(x_0) = y_0$.

Integrating both sides of Eq. (11.4.14) with respect to x between the limits x_n and x_{n+1}, we get

$$\int_{x_n}^{x_{n+1}} \frac{dy}{dx}\ dx = \int_{x_n}^{x_{n+1}} f(x, y)\ dy \qquad\qquad \dots\dots(11.4.15)$$

$$y_{n+1} - y_n = \int_{x_n}^{x_{n+1}} f(x, y)\ dy \qquad\qquad \dots\dots(11.4.16)$$

By Newton's backward integration formula,

$$f(x, y) = f_n + u\nabla f_n + \frac{u(u+1)}{2}\nabla^2 f_n + \frac{u(u+1)(u+2)}{6}\nabla^3 f_n$$
$$+ \dots\dots\dots \qquad\qquad \dots\dots(11.4.17)$$

$$y' = y_n' + u\nabla y_n' + \frac{u(u+1)}{2}\nabla^2 y_n' + \frac{u(u+1)(u+2)}{6}\nabla^3 y_n' + \dots\dots\dots$$

where, $u = \frac{x - x_n}{h}$, $x = x_n + uh$, $dy/dx = f(x, y) = y'$, $y_n = y_n'$, $\nabla y_n = \nabla y_n'$, $\nabla^2 y_n = \nabla^2 y_n'$ etc.

Putting Eq. (11.4.17) in Eq. (11.4.16), we get

$$y_{n+1} = y_n + \int_{x_n}^{x_{n+1}} [f_n + u\nabla f_n + \frac{u(u+1)}{2}\nabla^2 f_n + \frac{u(u+1)(u+2)}{6}\nabla^3 f_n$$
$$+ \dots]dx \qquad\qquad \dots\dots(11.4.18)$$

Since $dx = hdu$ and limits for u are 0 to 1 Eq. (11.4.18) becomes,

$$y_{n+1} = y_n + h\int_0^1 \left[f_n + u\nabla f_n + \frac{u(u+1)}{2}\nabla^2 f_n + \frac{u(u+1)(u+2)}{6}\nabla^3 f_n \right.$$
$$\left. + \dots \right] du \qquad\qquad \dots\dots(11.4.19)$$

Now,

$$\int_0^1 du = 1; \int_0^1 u\, du = \left[\frac{u^2}{2}\right]_0^1 = \frac{1}{2}; \int_0^1 \frac{u(u+1)}{2!}\, du = \frac{1}{2}\left[\frac{u^3}{3} + \frac{u^2}{2}\right]_0^1 = \frac{5}{12};$$

similarly, $\displaystyle\int_0^1 \frac{u(u+1)(u+2)(u+3)}{6}\, du = \frac{3}{8}$;

$$\int_0^1 \frac{u(u+1)(u+2)(u+3)(u+4)}{24}\, du = \frac{251}{720}$$

Using these values in Eq. (11.4.19), we have

$$y_{n+1} = y_n + h\left[f_n + \frac{1}{2}\nabla f_n + \frac{5}{12}\nabla^2 f_n + \frac{3}{8}\nabla^3 f_n + \frac{251}{720}\nabla^4 f_n \right.$$
$$\left. + \dots\dots\right] \qquad\qquad \dots\dots(11.4.20)$$

Putting the differences, such as $\nabla f_n = f_n - f_{n-1}$, $\nabla^2 f_n = f_n - 2f_{n-1} + f_{n-2}$, $\nabla^3 f_n = f_n - 3f_{n-1} + 3f_{n-2} - f_{n-3}$ etc.

Eq. (11.4.20) can be further simplified to

$$y_{n+1} = y_n + \frac{h}{24}\left[f_n + \frac{1}{2}(f_n - f_{n-1}) + \frac{5}{12}(f_n - 2f_{n-1} + f_{n-2})\right.$$
$$\left. + \frac{3}{8}(f_n - 3f_{n-1} + 3f_{n-2} - f_{n-3}) + \frac{251}{720}\nabla^4 f_n + \dots\dots\right]$$

$$y_{n+1} = y_n + \frac{h}{24}[55f_n - 59f_{n-1} + 37 f_{n-2} - 9f_{n-3}] + \frac{251}{720} h\nabla^4 f_n$$
$$+ \dots\dots \qquad\qquad \dots\dots(11.4.21)$$

It can also be written as

$$y_{n+1} = y_n + \frac{h}{24}[55y'_n - 59y'_{n-1} + 37y'_{n-2} - 9y'_{n-3}] + \frac{251}{720} h\,\nabla^4 y'_n$$
$$+ \dots\dots \qquad\qquad \dots\dots(11.4.22)$$

Neglecting fourth and higher order differences, we get from Eq. (11.4.22)

$$y_{n+1} = y_n + \frac{h}{24}[55y'_n - 59y'_{n-1} + 37y'_{n-2} - 9y'_{n-3}] \qquad \dots\dots(11.4.23)$$

The error in Eq. (11.4.23) is $\frac{251}{720} h\nabla^4 y'_n + \dots\dots$

i.e. $\quad \frac{251}{720} h(1 - E^{-1})^4 y'_n + \dots\dots = \frac{251}{720} h(1 - e^{-hD})^4 y'_n + \dots\dots =$
$\frac{251}{720} h\,(hD)^4\, y'_n$,

i.e. $\quad \frac{251}{720} h^5 y_n^{(5)} + \dots\dots$, since h is small $= \frac{251}{720} h^5 y^{(5)}(\xi)$, where, $x_{n-3} \le \xi \le x_{n+1}$

Eq. (11.4.23) is known as Adam - Bashforth's predictor formula.

In general Adam's predictor formula can be wriiten as

$$y_{n+1} = y_n + \frac{h}{24} [55 y_n' - 59y_{n-1}' + 37y_{n-2}' - 9y_{n-3}']$$

$$+ \frac{251}{720} h^5 y^{(5)}(\xi) \qquad\qquad \text{.........(11.4.24)}$$

where, $x_{n-3} \le \xi \le x_{n+1}$

Adam's corrector formula can be derived by using Newton's backward interpolation formula about f_{n+1} instead of f_n. Thus, from Eq. (11.4.16), we have

$$y_{n+1} = y_n + h \int_{-1}^{0} \left[f_{n+1} + u\nabla f_{n+1} + \frac{u(u+1)}{2} \nabla^2 f_{n+1} \right.$$

$$+ \frac{u(u+1)(u+2)}{6} \nabla^3 f_{n+1}$$

$$\left. + \frac{u(u+1)(u+2)(u+3)}{24} \nabla^4 f_{n+1} + \ldots \right] du \quad \text{.....(11.4.25)}$$

Carrying out the integration and repeating the above steps, we get the corrector formula as

$$y_{n+1} = y_n + \frac{h}{24} [9 y_{n+1}' + 19y_n' - 5y_{n-1}' + y_{n-2}']$$

$$- \frac{19}{720} h^5 y^{(5)}(\xi) \qquad\qquad \text{.........(11.4.26)}$$

where, $x_{n-2} \le \xi \le x_{n+1}$

The truncation error in Adam-Bashforth's predictor formula is approximately thirteen times more than that in the corrector formula with opposite sign.

Example 11.17   Find the values of $y(0.1), y(0.2)$ and $y(0.3)$ using Runge – Kutta method of the fourth order, given that

$$\frac{dy}{dx} = y(x + y), \qquad y(0) = 1.$$

Also find the value of $y(0.4)$ by Adam-Bashforth's method.

Solution: Given $y' = f(x, y) = y(x + y)$; $h = 0.1$

Step 1: $x_0 = 0$, $y_0 = 1$

$k_1 = h f(x_0, y_0) = 0.1 \times f(0,1) = 0.1 \times (1)(0 + 1) = 0.1$

$k_2 = h f\left(x_0 + \frac{h}{2}, y_0 + \frac{k_1}{2}\right) = 0.1 \times f\left(0 + \frac{0.1}{2}, 1 + \frac{0.1}{2}\right)$

$\quad = 0.1 \times f(0.05, 1.05) = 0.1 \times (1.05)(0.05 + 1.05) = 0.1155$

$k_3 = h f\left(x_0 + \frac{h}{2}, y_0 + \frac{k_2}{2}\right) = 0.1 \times f\left(0 + \frac{0.1}{2}, 1 + \frac{0.1155}{2}\right)$

$= 0.1 \times f(0.05, 1.05775) = 0.1 \times (1.05775)(0.05 + 1.05775) = 0.1172$

$k_4 = h f(x_0 + h, y_0 + k_3) = 0.1 \times f(0 + 0.1, 1 + 0.1172)$

$= 0.1 \times f(0.1, 1.1172) = 0.1 \times (1.1172)(0.1 + 1.1172) = 0.1360$

$$\therefore k = \frac{1}{6}(k_1 + 2k_2 + 2k_3 + k_4)$$

$$= \frac{1}{6}(0.1 + 2(0.1155) + 2(0.1172) + 0.1360) = 0.1169$$

$$\therefore y_1 = y(x_0 + h) = y(0.1) = y_0 + k = 1 + 0.1169 = 1.1169$$

Step 2: $x_1 = 0.1$, $y_1 = 1.1169$

$$k_1 = h f(x_1, y_1) = 0.1 \times f(0.1, 1.1169) = 0.1 \times (1.1169)(0.1 + 1.1169)$$
$$= 0.1359$$

$$k_2 = h f\left(x_1 + \frac{h}{2}, y_1 + \frac{k_1}{2}\right) = 0.1 \times f\left(0.1 + \frac{0.1}{2}, 1.1169 + \frac{0.1359}{2}\right)$$

$$= 0.1 \times f(0.15, 1.18485) = 0.1 \times (1.18485)(0.15 + 1.18485) = 0.15815$$

$$k_3 = h f\left(x_1 + \frac{h}{2}, y_1 + \frac{k_2}{2}\right) = 0.1 \times f\left(0.1 + \frac{0.1}{2}, 1.1169 + \frac{0.15815}{2}\right)$$

$$= 0.1 \times f(0.15, 1.19598) = 0.1 \times (1.19598)(0.15 + 1.19598) = 0.16098$$

$$k_4 = h f(x_1 + h, y_1 + k_3) = 0.1 \times f(0.1 + 0.1, 1.1169 + 0.16098)$$

$$= 0.1 \times f(0.2, 1.27788) = 0.1 \times (1.27788)(0.2 + 1.27788) = 0.18885$$

$$\therefore k = \frac{1}{6}(k_1 + 2k_2 + 2k_3 + k_4)$$

$$= \frac{1}{6}(0.1359 + 2(0.15815) + 2(0.16098) + 0.18885) = 0.1605$$

$$\therefore y_2 = y(x_1 + h) = y(0.2) = y_1 + k = 1.1169 + 0.1605 = 1.2774$$

Step 3: $x_2 = 0.2$, $y_2 = 1.2774$

$$k_1 = h f(x_2, y_2) = 0.1 \times f(0.2, 1.2774)$$
$$= 0.1 \times (1.2774)(0.2 + 1.2774) = 0.1887$$

$$k_2 = h f\left(x_2 + \frac{h}{2}, y_2 + \frac{k_1}{2}\right) = 0.1 \times f\left(0.2 + \frac{0.1}{2}, 1.2774 + \frac{0.1887}{2}\right)$$

$$= 0.1 \times f(0.25, 1.37175) = 0.1 \times (1.37175)(0.25 + 1.37175) = 0.22246$$

$$k_3 = h f\left(x_2 + \frac{h}{2}, y_2 + \frac{k_2}{2}\right) = 0.1 \times f\left(0.2 + \frac{0.1}{2}, 1.2774 + \frac{0.22246}{2}\right)$$
$$= 0.1 \times f(0.25, 1.38863) = 0.1 \times (1.38863)(0.25 + 1.38863) = 0.22754$$

$$k_4 = h f(x_2 + h, y_2 + k_3) = 0.1 \times f(0.2 + 0.1, 1.2774 + 0.22754)$$

$$= 0.1 \times f(0.3, 1.50494) = 0.1 \times (1.50494)(0.3 + 1.50494) = 0.27163$$

$$\therefore k = \frac{1}{6}(k_1 + 2k_2 + 2k_3 + k_4)$$

$$= \frac{1}{6}(0.1887 + 2(0.22246) + 2(0.22754) + 0.27163) = 0.22672$$

$$\therefore y_3 = y(x_2 + h) = y(0.3) = y_2 + k = 1.2774 + 0.22672 = 1.5041$$

Hence, we have

$$x_0 = 0, \qquad y_0 = 1$$
$$x_1 = 0.1, \qquad y_1 = 1.1169$$
$$x_2 = 0.2, \qquad y_2 = 1.2774$$
$$x_3 = 0.3, \qquad y_3 = 1.5041 \qquad \text{and} \qquad h = 0.1$$

Now,

$$y_0' = y_0(x_0 + y_0) = 1(0 + 1) = 1$$
$$y_1' = y_1(x_1 + y_1) = (1.1169)(0.1 + 1.1169) = 1.3592$$
$$y_2' = y_2(x_2 + y_2) = (1.2774)(0.2 + 1.2774) = 1.8872$$
$$y_3' = y_3(x_3 + y_3) = (1.5041)(0.3 + 1.5041) = 2.7135$$

From Eq. (11.4.23), Adam-Bashforth's predictor formula is

$$y_{n+1} = y_n + \frac{h}{24}\left[55y_n' - 59y_{n-1}' + 37y_{n-2}' - 9y_{n-3}'\right] \qquad \dots\dots(1)$$

Taking n = 3 in (1), we have

$$y_4^{(0)} = y_3 + \frac{h}{24}\left[55y_3' - 59y_2' + 37y_1' - 9y_0'\right]$$

$$y_4^{(0)} = 1.5041 + \frac{(0.1)}{24}\left[55(2.7135) - 59(1.8872) + 37(1.3592) - 9(1)\right]$$

$$= 1.8341$$

$$(y_4')^{(0)} = y_4^{(0)}\left(x_4 + y_4^{(0)}\right) = (1.8341)(0.4 + 1.8341) = 4.0976$$

From Eq. (11.4.26), Adam's corrector formula is

$$y_{n+1}^{(i)} = y_n + \frac{h}{24}\left[y_{n-2}' - 5y_{n-1}' + 19y_n' + 9\,y_{n+1}'^{(i-1)}\right] \qquad \dots\dots(2)$$

Taking n = 3 and i = 1 in (2), we have

$$y_4^{(1)} = y_3 + \frac{h}{24}\left[y_1' - 5y_2' + 19y_3' + 9\,y_4'^{(0)}\right]$$

$$y_4^{(1)} = 1.5041 + \frac{0.1}{24}\left[(1.3592) - 5(1.8872) + 19(2.7135) + 9(4.0976)\right]$$

$$= 1.8389$$

$$(y_4')^{(1)} = y_4^{(1)}\left(x_4 + y_4^{(1)}\right) = (1.8389)(0.4 + 1.8389) = 4.1171$$

Now,

$$y_4^{(2)} = 1.5041 + \frac{0.1}{24}\left[(1.3592) - 5(1.8872) + 19(2.7135) + 9(4.1171)\right]$$

$$= 1.8397$$

$$(y_4')^{(2)} = y_4^{(2)}\left(x_4 + y_4^{(2)}\right) = (1.83966)(0.4 + 1.83966) = 4.1202$$

$$y_4^{(3)} = 1.5041 + \frac{0.1}{24}\left[(1.3592) - 5(1.8872) + 19(2.7135) + 9(4.1202)\right]$$

$$= 1.83977$$

Since $y_4^{(2)} = y_4^{(3)}$, convergence upto four decimal places has occurred.

$\therefore$ The corrected value of $y(0.4) = 1.8397$

11.4.3 Difference Between Runge – Kutta Method and Predictor – Corrector Method

Runge – Kutta Method	Predictor – Corrector Method
• It is self starting method as it does not require more than the initial value of y.	• It is not self starting method as it requires more than one previous points to compute the value of y at next point.
• Functions evaluation is time consuming as it requires several functions to calculate the final value of y.	• Functions evaluation is not so time consuming
• Once we calculate the value of y it can not be improved.	• The efficiency of estimation is improved by using more than one previous points. A predictor formula is used to predict the value of y at x_{i+1} and then a corrector formula is used to improve the value of y_{i+1}.
• We can easily change step size in this method.	• Easy change in the step size is not possible in these methods.
• Estimate of truncation error is not easily obtainable.	• Estimate of truncation error is easily obtainable.

11.5 BOUNDARY VALUE PROBLEMS

As we have discussed earlier in this chapter, the general solution of an ordinary differential equation (ODE) of order n contains n arbitrary constants and is of the form

$$\varphi(x, y, c_1, c_2, c_3, \ldots\ldots, c_n) = 0$$

In order to find these n arbitrary constants, n conditions are required. These n conditions can be provided by the values of dependent variable or its derivatives for n specific values of the independent variable. If all the n conditions are specified for two or more values of independent variable x then such problems are called the *boundary – value problem (BVP)*. These problems for ODE occur in various branches of science and engineering.

Let us consider the simplest boundary value problem associated with a second order differential equation as

(a) $\qquad\qquad y'' + \alpha(x)y' + \beta(x)y = \gamma(x) \qquad\qquad$ .... (11.5.1)

with the boundary conditions $y(x_0) = a$ and $y(x_n) = b \qquad$ .... (11.5.2)

(b) $\qquad\qquad y^{iv} + \alpha(x)y = \beta(x) \qquad\qquad\qquad$ .... (11.5.3)

with the boundary conditions $y(x_0) = y'(x_0) = a$ and $y(x_n) = y'(x_n) = b$

$\qquad\qquad\qquad\qquad\qquad\qquad\qquad\qquad\qquad$ .... (11.5.4)

Though there exist many numerical methods such as the finite difference method, the shooting method, the cubic spline method, the collection method for solving such boundary value problems, the finite difference method is the most commonly used and a popular method. The finite difference method is explained in the next sub section.

11.5.1 Finite – Difference Method

In this method of solving boundary value problem, the derivatives appearing in the differential equation and the boundary conditions are replaced by appropriate finite – difference approximations and then solving the resulting linear system of algebraic equations by any standard procedure.

The finite – difference approximations to the various derivation are derived as under:

If $y(x)$ and its derivatives are single valued continuous functions of x then by Taylor series expansion, we have

$$y(x + h) = y(x) + hy'(x) + \frac{h^2}{2!} y''(x) + \frac{h^3}{3!} y'''(x) + \text{...........}(11.5.5)$$

and

$$y(x - h) = y(x) - hy'(x) + \frac{h^2}{2!} y''(x) - \frac{h^3}{3!} y'''(x) + \text{...........}(11.5.6)$$

From Eq. (11.5.5), we get

$$y'(x) = \frac{1}{h} [y(x + h) - y(x)] - \frac{h}{2} y''(x) - \text{......}$$

Therefore, we have $\quad y'(x) = \frac{1}{h} [y(x + h) - y(x)] + O(h)$

which is the forward difference approximation of $y'(x)$ with an error of order h. From Eq.(11.5.6), we get

$$y'(x) = \frac{1}{h} [y(x) - y(x - h)] + O(h) \text{ ......}$$

which is the backward difference approximation of $y'(x)$ with an error of order h. A central difference approximation for $y'(x)$ can be obtained by subtracting Eq. (11.5.5) from Eq. (11.5.6). We have

$$y'(x) = \frac{1}{2h} [y(x + h) - y(x - h)] + O(h^2) \qquad \text{.......}(11.5.7)$$

which is a central difference approximation formula with an error of the order h^2. This central difference formula to $y'(x)$ gives a better approximation than forward or backward difference approximations and hence, it is usually used in finite difference method of solving boundary value problem.

Adding Eq. (11.5.5) and Eq.(11.5.6), we get

$$y''(x) = \frac{1}{h^2} [y(x + h) - 2y(x) + y(x - h)] + O(h^2) \qquad \text{.......}(11.5.8)$$

which is the central difference approximation of $y''(x)$. In a similar manner, it is possible to derive finite – difference approximations to higher derivatives.

To solve the boundary value problem defined by Eqs. (11.5.1) and (11.5.2) , let the interval $[x_0 , x_n]$ be divided into n equal parts each of width h , so that $h = (x_n - x_0)/n$ and $x_i = x_0 + ih;\ i = 0,1,2, ...,n$.

Let the corresponding values of y at these points be $y_i = y(x_i);\ i = 0,1,2, ...,n$. From equations (11.5.1) and (11.5.2), values of $y'(x)$ and $y''(x)$ at the point $x = x_i$ can be written as

$$y_i' = \frac{1}{2h} [y_{i+1} - y_{i-1}] + O(h^2) \qquad\qquad ...\ ...\ ... (11.5.9)$$

$$y_i'' = \frac{1}{h^2} [y_{i+1} - 2y_i + y_{i-1}] + O(h^2) \qquad ...\ ...\ ... (11.5.10)$$

Since Eq. (11.5.1) holds good at the point $x = x_i$, we get
$$y_i'' + \alpha_i y_i' + \beta_i y_i = \gamma_i \qquad\qquad .... (11.5.11)$$
where, $y_i' = y'(x_i),\ \gamma_i = \gamma(x_i)$

Substituting the expressions for y_i' and y_i'' in Eq.(11.5.11)

$$\left(\frac{y_{i+1} - 2y_i + y_{i-1}}{h^2}\right) + \alpha_i \left(\frac{y_{i+1} - y_{i-1}}{2h}\right) + \beta_i y_i = \gamma_i$$

$$y_{i+1} - 2y_i + y_{i-1} + \frac{h}{2} \alpha_i (y_{i+1} - y_{i-1}) + h^2 \beta_i y_i = h^2 \gamma_i$$

After simplification, we get

$$\left(1 - \frac{h}{2} \alpha_i\right) y_{i-1} + (-2 + h^2 \beta_i) y_i + \left(1 + \frac{h}{2} \alpha_i\right) y_{i+1} = h^2 \gamma_i \quad .... (11.5.12)$$

$$i = 1, 2, ...,n - 1\ .\ \text{with}\ \ y_0 = a\ \text{and}\ y_n = b$$

Substituting $i = 1, 2, ...,n - 1$ in Eq. (11.5.12), we get

$$\left(1 - \frac{h}{2} \alpha_1\right) y_0 + (-2 + h^2 \beta_1) y_1 + \left(1 + \frac{h}{2} \alpha_1\right) y_2 = h^2 \gamma_1$$

$$\left(1 - \frac{h}{2} \alpha_2\right) y_1 + (-2 + h^2 \beta_2) y_2 + \left(1 + \frac{h}{2} \alpha_2\right) y_3 = h^2 \gamma_2$$

$$(11.5.13)$$

$$...\ ...\ ...\ ...\ ...\ ...\ ...\ ...\ ...\ ...\ ...\ ...\ ...\ ....$$
$$...\ ...\ ...\ ...\ ...\ ...\ ...\ ...\ ...\ ...\ ...\ ...\ ....$$

$$\left(1 - \frac{h}{2} \alpha_{n-1}\right) y_{n-2} + (-2 + h^2 \beta_{n-1}) y_{n-1} + \left(1 + \frac{h}{2} \alpha_{n-1}\right) y_n = h^2 \gamma_{n-1}$$

Eq. (11.5.13) is a linear system of $(n - 1)$ algebraic equations in the $(n - 1)$ unknowns $y_1, y_2, ...,y_{n-1}$.

Remark: The central difference approximations to the third and fourth derivatives are as under:

$$y_i''' = \frac{1}{2h^3}[y_{i+2} - 2y_{i+1} + 2y_{i-1} - y_{i-2}]$$

$$y_i^{iv} = \frac{1}{h^4}[y_{i+2} - 4y_{i+1} + 6y_i - 4y_{i-1} + y_{i-2}]$$

- The accuracy of finite difference method depends upon the width of the sub-interval h and on the order of approximation. As length of interval is reduced, the accuracy improves but the number of equations to be solved also increases.

Example 11.18 Solve the equation $y''(x) - xy(x) = 0$ for $y(x_i)$, $x_i = 0, \frac{1}{3}, \frac{2}{3}$, given that $y(0) + y'(0) = 1$ and $y(1) = 1$

Solution: The differential equation is approximated as

$$\frac{1}{h^2}[y_{i+1} - 2y_i + y_{i-1}] = x_i y_i$$

$$\therefore \ 9y_{i+1} - 18y_i + 9y_{i-1} = x_i y_i \qquad \left(since \ h = \frac{1}{3}\right) \qquad .... (1)$$

Substituting $i = 0, 1, 2$ in (1), we have

$$y_1 - 2y_0 + y_{-1} = 0 \qquad .... (2)$$

$$9y_2 - 18y_1 + 9y_0 = \frac{1}{3}y_1 \ \Rightarrow \ y_2 - 2y_1 + y_0 = \frac{1}{27}y_1$$

$$\Rightarrow \ y_2 - \left(2 + \frac{1}{27}\right)y_1 + y_0 = 0 \ \Rightarrow \ y_2 - \frac{55}{27}y_1 + y_0 = 0 \qquad ...... (3)$$

$$9y_3 - 18y_2 + 9y_1 = x_2 y_2 \ \Rightarrow \ 9y_3 - 18y_2 + 9y_1 = \frac{2}{3}y_2$$

$$\Rightarrow \ y_3 - 2y_2 + y_1 = \frac{2}{27}y_2 \ \Rightarrow \ y_3 - \left(2 + \frac{2}{27}\right)y_2 + y_1 = 0$$

$$\Rightarrow \ y_3 - \frac{56}{27}y_2 + y_1 = 0 \qquad ...... (4)$$

The first boundary condition is

$$y_0 + y_0' = 1 \ \Rightarrow \ y_0 + \frac{y_1 - y_{-1}}{2h} = 1 \quad \left(\because y_i' = \frac{y_{i+1} - y_{i-1}}{2h}\right)$$

$$\therefore \ 2y_0 + 3(y_1 - y_{-1}) = 2 \ \Rightarrow \ y_{-1} = \frac{2y_0 + 3y_1 - 2}{3} \qquad ...... (5)$$

The second boundary condition is

$$y_3 = 1 \qquad .... (6)$$

Putting Eq. (5) and (6) in Eq. (2), (3) and (4), we get

$$-2y_0 + 3y_1 = 1 \qquad .... (7)$$

$$y_0 - \frac{55}{27}y_1 + y_2 = 0 \qquad .... (8)$$

$$y_1 - \frac{56}{27} y_2 + 1 = 0 \qquad \qquad \text{........ (9)}$$

Solving equations (7), (8) and (9), we get

$$y_0 = -\frac{82}{83} = -0.9880, \quad y_1 = y\left(\frac{1}{3}\right) = -\frac{27}{83} = -0.3253,$$

$$y_2 = y\left(\frac{2}{3}\right) = \frac{27}{83} = 0.3253$$

Example 11.19   The deflection of a beam is governed by the equation

$$\frac{d^4 y}{dx^4} + 81y = \emptyset(x)$$

where $\emptyset(x)$ is given by the table

x:	1/3	2/3	1
$\emptyset(x)$:	81	162	243

and boundary condition $y(0) = y'(0) = y''(1) = y'''(1) = 0$. Estimate the deflection at the pivotal points of the beam using three sub – intervals.

Solution: Since $h = 1/3$ pivotal points are $x_0 = 0, x_1 = \frac{1}{3}, x_2 = \frac{2}{3}, x_3 = 1$
The corresponding y values are y_0, y_1, y_2 and y_3.
The given differential equation is approximated to

$$\frac{1}{h^4} [y_{i+2} - 4y_{i+1} + 6y_i - 4y_{i-1} + y_{i-2}] + 81y_i = \emptyset(x_i) \qquad \text{... ..... (1)}$$

Substituting $i = 1, 2, 3$ in (1), we have

at $i = 1$, $81(y_3 - 4y_2 + 7y_1 - 4y_0 + y_{-1}) = 81 \Rightarrow y_3 - 4y_2 + 7y_1 - 4y_0 + y_{-1} = 1$
$\qquad \qquad$ ....(2)

at $i = 2$, $81(y_4 - 4y_3 + 7y_2 - 4y_1 + y_0) = 162 \Rightarrow y_4 - 4y_3 + 7y_2 - 4y_1 + y_0 = 2$
$\qquad \qquad$ ......(3)

at $i = 3$, $81(y_5 - 4y_4 + 7y_3 - 4y_2 + y_1) = 243 \Rightarrow y_5 - 4y_4 + 7y_3 - 4y_2 + y_1 = 3$
$\qquad \qquad$ ....(4)

Also, we have $\qquad \qquad y_0 = 0 \qquad \qquad$ .... (5)

Since $\quad y_i' = (y_{i+1} - y_{i-1})/2h$

$\therefore$ for $i = 0$, $0 = y_0' = \dfrac{y_1 - y_{-1}}{2h} \Rightarrow = y_{-1} \qquad \text{... ..... (6)}$

Also, $y_i'' = [y_{i+1} - 2y_i + y_{i-1}] / h^2$

$\therefore$ for $i = 3$, $0 = y_3'' = \dfrac{1}{h^2} [y_4 - 2y_3 + y_2] \Rightarrow y_4 = 2y_3 - y_2 \text{ ... . (7)}$

Also, $y_i''' = [y_{i+2} - 2y_{i+1} + 2y_{i-1} - y_{i-2}] / 2h^3$

$\therefore$ for $i = 3$, $0 = y_3'''$
$= [y_5 - 2y_4 + 2y_2 - y_1] / 2h^3 \Rightarrow y_5 = 2y_4 - 2y_2 + y_1 \qquad \text{... ..... (8)}$

Using Eq. (5) and (6) in Eq.(2), we get

$$y_3 - 4y_2 + 8y_1 = 1 \qquad \text{........ (9)}$$

Using Eq. (5) and (7) in Eq. (3), we get

$$-2y_3 + 6y_2 - 4y_1 = 2 \Rightarrow -y_3 + 3y_2 - 2y_1 = 1 \qquad \text{........ (10)}$$

Using Eq. (7) and (8) in Eq. (4), we get

$$3y_3 - 4y_2 + 2y_1 = 3 \qquad \text{......... (11)}$$

Solving Eqs. (9), (10) and (11), we get $y_1 = 8/13, y_2 = 22/13, y_3 = 37/13$

Thus, $y\left(\frac{1}{3}\right) = 0.6154$, $y\left(\frac{2}{3}\right) = 1.6923$, $y(1) = 2.8462$

11.6 PROGRAMS IN C

11.6.1 Program to implement Euler's method

```
//Program to implement Euler's method to find the root of given equation
#include<stdio.h>
#include<conio.h>
#include<math.h>
#define Function(x,y) (2-pow(y,2))/(5*x)
void main()
{
        int n,i;
        float x,ys,yi,ym,ye,ReqX,h,m1,x1;
        clrscr();
        printf("\n\t\t Euler's method....");
        printf("\n Enter the initial value of x   : ");
        scanf("%f",&x);
        printf("\n Enter the initial value of y   : ");
        scanf("%f",&ys);
        printf("\n Enter the required value for x  : ");
        scanf("%f",&ReqX);
        printf("\n Enter the step size h   : ");
        scanf("%f",&h);
        n = (int)((ReqX - x) / h + .5);
        printf("-----------------------------------------------------------------\n");
        printf("\t\t\t Euler's Method                      \n");
        printf("Iteration\tx\ty Simple\ty Improved\ty Modified  \n");
        printf("-----------------------------------------------------------------\n");
        printf("\n\n");
```

```
        yi=ym=ys;
        for (i=1; i<=n; i++)
        {
                m1 = h * Function(x,ys);
                x1 = x + h;
                ys = ys + m1;
            yi = yi + (h/2)*(Function(x,yi)+Function(x1,yi+h*Function(x,yi)));
                ym = ym +h*Function(x+h/2, ym +(h/2)*Function(x,ym));
                 printf("%d \t  %f\t%f\t%f\t%f\t \n",i,x1,ys,yi,ym);
                x = x1;
        }
printf("\n\n Answer : ySimple-%f\t yImproved-%f\t yModified-%f\t\n ",ys, yi,
ym);
        getch();
        return(0);
}
```

11.6.2   Program to implement Runge – Kutta second order method
//Program to implement Runge – Kutta second order method to find the root of
given equation

```
#include<stdio.h>
#include <math.h>
#include<conio.h>
#define F(x,y)  ((y)+(x)*(x))
void main()
{
        float y0,x0,y1,n,h,k1,k2,k;
        float xa[20], ya[20];
        int i,t;
        printf("\n\t\t\t RUNGE KUTTA SECOND ORDER METHOD");
        printf("\t\t-----------------------------------\n");
        printf("\n Enter the value of x0: ");
        scanf("%f",&x0);
        printf("\n Enter the value of y0: ");
        scanf("%f",&y0);
        printf("\n Enter the value of h: ");
        scanf("%f",&h);
        printf("\n Enter the value of last point: ");
        scanf("%f",&n);
        printf("\n\n\t--------------------------------------------------");
        printf("\n\tNO.\tX\tY\tk1\tk2\tk\ty1");
        printf("\n\t--------------------------------------------------");
        for(x0,i=0; x0<n; x0=x0+h,i++)
```

```
        {
                k1 = h * F(x0,y0);
                k2 = h * F(x0+h,y0+k1);
                k = (k1 + k2)/2.0;
                y1 = y0 + k;
    printf("\n\t%d\t%.4f\t%.4f\t%.4f\t%.4f\t%.4f\t%.4f",i,x0,y0,k1,k2,k,y1);
                printf("\n");
                ya[i]=y1;
                xa[i]=x0;
                y0=y1;
        }
        //Only for answer printing purpose
        printf("\n\n\t\t\t :: ANSWER ::");
        printf("\n\t\t\t------------\n\t");
        printf("i  |");
        for(t=1;t<=i;t++)
        {
           printf("  %d   ",t);
        }
        printf("\n\t------------------------------------------------------");
        printf("\n\n\tx:: |");
        for(t=0;t<i;t++)
        {
           printf(" %.4f ",xa[t]);
        }
        printf("\n\n\ty:: |");
        for(t=0;t<i;t++)
        {
           printf(" %.4f ",ya[t]);
        } getch();  }
```

11.6.3   Program to implement Runge – Kutta fourth order method

```
//Program to implement Runge – Kutta fourth order method to find the root of
given equation
#include<stdio.h>
#include <math.h>
#include<conio.h>
#define F(x,y)  1/((x)+(y))
void main()
{
        float y0,x0,y1,n,h,k1,k2,k3,k4,k;
        float xa[20],ya[20];
        int i,t;
        printf("\n\t\t\t RUNGE KUTTA FOURTH ORDER METHOD");
```

```c
        printf("\n\t\t---------------------------------------------\n");
        printf("\nEnter the value of x0: ");
        scanf("%f",&x0);
        printf("\nEnter the value of y0: ");
        scanf("%f",&y0);
        printf("\nEnter the value of h: ");
        scanf("%f",&h);
        printf("\nEnter the value of last point: ");
        scanf("%f",&n);
        printf("\n\t-----------------------------------------------------------------");
        printf("\n\tNO.\tX\tY\tk1\tk2\tk3\tk4\tk\tY1");
        printf("\n\t-----------------------------------------------------------------");
        for(x0,i=0; x0<n; x0=x0+h,i++)
        {
                k1 = h * F(x0,y0);
                k2 = h * F(x0+h/2,y0+k1/2);
                k3 = h * F(x0+h/2.0,y0+k2/2);
                k4 = h * F(x0+h,y0+k3);
                k = (k1 + 2*k2 + 2*k3 + k4)/6;
                y1 = y0 + k;
printf("\n\t%d\t%.4f\t%.4f\t%.4f\t%.4f\t%.4f\t%.4f\t%.4f\t%.4f",i,x0,y0,k1,k2,k3
,k4,k,y1);
                printf("\n");
                ya[i]=y1;
                xa[i]=x0;
                y0=y1;
        }
        //This code is only for answer printing purpose
        printf("\n\n\t\t\t :: ANSWER ::\n");
        printf("\t\t\t ------------\n\t");
        printf("i  |");
        for(t=1;t<=i;t++)
        {
          printf("\t %d ",t);
        }
        printf("\n\t--------------------------------------------");
        printf("\n\n\tx:: |");
        for(t=0;t<i;t++)
        {
            printf("%.4f ",xa[t]);
        }
        printf("\n\n\ty:: |");
        for(t=0;t<i;t++)
```

```
        {
                printf(" %.4f ",ya[t]);
        }
getch();   }
```

11.6.4   Program to implement Milne – Simpson's predictor corrector method

```
// Milne – Simpson's predictor corrector method
#include<stdio.h>
#include <math.h>
#include<conio.h>
#define F(x,y)  1+(y*y)
void main()
{
        float y0,x0,y1,y2,y3, y_pre, y_cor,f0,f1,f2,f3,x1,x2,x3,x4,y[10],n,h,f,c;
        int i;
printf("\n\t\t\t MILNE SIMPSON'S PREDICTOR CORRECTOR METHOD.....");
        printf("\n\t\t----------------------------------------------------------");
        clrscr();
        printf("\nEnter the First four values of x: \n");
        scanf("%f %f %f %f",&x0,&x1,&x2,&x3);
        printf("\nEnter the corresponding four values of y: \n");
        scanf("%f %f %f %f",&y0,&y1,&y2,&y3);
        h = x1 - x0;
        printf("\tX \t\t\t Final Corrected Values of Y \t \n");
        printf("\n---------------------------------------------------------------\n");
        for(i=1; i<10;i++)
        {
                f1 = F(x1,y1);
                f2 = F(x2, y2);
                f3 = F(x3, y3);
                y_pre = y0+(4*h/3)*(2*f1-f2+2*f3);
                x4 = x3 + h;
                c = y2 + (h/3)*(f2+4*f3);
                A:
                y_cor = c + (h/3)*F(x4, y_pre);
                if(fabs(y_pre - y_cor)< 0.00001)
                        printf("\t%f\t%f\n", x4 , y_cor);
                else
                {
                        y_pre = y_cor;
                        goto A;
                }
```

```
                    x1=x2;
                    x2=x3;
                    x3=x4;
                    y0=y1;
                    y1=y2;
                    y2=y3;
                    y3= y_cor;
        }
        getch(); }
```

11.6.5   Program to implement Adam – Bashforth's predictor corrector method

```
// Adam – Bashforth's predictor corrector method
#include<stdio.h>
#include <math.h>
#include<conio.h>
#define F(x,y)  (1/2)*(x+y)
void main()
{
        float y0,x0,y1,y2,y3, y_pre, y_cor,f0,f1,f2,f3,x1,x2,x3,x4,y[10],n,h,c;
        int i;
printf("\n\t\t\t ADAM - BASHFORTH'S PREDICTOR CORRECTOR METHOD.....");
        printf("\n\t\t-------------------------------------------------------------");
        clrscr();
        printf("\nEnter the First four values of x: \n");
        scanf("%f %f %f %f",&x0,&x1,&x2,&x3);
        printf("\nEnter the corresponding four values of y: \n");
        scanf("%f %f %f %f",&y0,&y1,&y2,&y3);
        h = x1 - x0;
        printf("\tX \t\t\t Final Corrected Values of Y\t \n");
        printf("\n-----------------------------------------------------------------\n");
        for(i=1; i<10;i++)
        {
                f0 = F(x0,y0);
                f1 = F(x1,y1);
                f2 = F(x2, y2);
                f3 = F(x3, y3);
                y_pre = y3+(h/24)*(-9*f0+37*f1-59*f2+55*f3);
                x4 = x3 + h;
                c = y3 + (h/24)*(f1-5*f2+19*f3);
                A:
                y_cor = c + (9*h/24)*F(x4, y_pre);
                if(fabs(y_pre - y_cor)< 0.00001)
```

```
                        printf("\t%f\t%f\n", x4 , y_cor);
            else
            {
                        y_pre = y_cor;
                        goto A;  }
            x0=x1;
            x1=x2;
            x2=x3;
            x3=x4;
            y0=y1;
            y1=y2;
            y2=y3;
            y3= y_cor;
      }
      getch(); }
```

EXERCISES

1.   Multiple Choice Questions

(1)   If differential equation is $3\left(\dfrac{dy}{dx}\right)^2 + 6\,(d^2y / dx^2)^3 - 11 = 0$ then order of
equation is
(a)   1   (b) 2   (c) 3   (d) 4   (e) 5

(2)   If differential equation is $3\left(\dfrac{dy}{dx}\right)^2 + 6\,(d^2y / dx^2)^3 - 11 = 0$ then degree of
equation is
(a)   1   (b) 2   (c) 3   (d) 4   (e) 5

(3)   Which of this method is a multi step method?
(a)   Euler's method
(b)   Modified Euler's method
(c)   Taylor's method
(d)   Runge – Kutta 2nd order method
(e)   Runge – Kutta 4th order method

(4)   Which of the following is the disadvantage of Picard's method?
(a)   It fails, if the given differential equation is not easily integrated
(b)   It fails, if the given equation is not easily differentiated
(c)   It is not very accurate as compare to other single-step methods
(d)   Truncation error is very high compare to other methods
(e)   None of these

(5)   Which of the following method can't be used efficiently if the calculation of higher order derivatives becomes tedious?
    (a)   Picard's method
    (b)   Taylor series method
    (c)   Euler's method
    (d)   R-K method
    (e)   None of these

(6)   Which of the following method is very slow and less accurate compare to other methods
    (a)   Picard's method
    (b)   Runge Kutta method
    (c)   Simple Euler's method
    (d)   Modified Euler's method
    (e)   None of these

(7)   Which of the following method is not self – starting method?
    (a)   Euler's method
    (b)   Runge – Kutta method
    (c)   Picard's method
    (d)   Milne – Simpson method
    (e)   None of these

(8)   At least how many past solution points are needed in the Adams – Bashforth method for the solution of the next point?
    (a)   1   (b)   2   (c)   3   (d)   4   (e)   5

(9)   Which formula is a particular case of R- K formula of second order?
    (a)   Euler's method
    (b)   Taylor's method
    (c)   Modified Euler's method
    (d)   Picard's method
    (e)   None of these

(10)   Once we calculate the value of y it cannot be improved in _____method.
    (a)   Runge – Kutta
    (b)   Milne – Simpson
    (c)   Adams – Bashforth- Moulton
    (d)   Modified Euler's
    (e)   None of these

Answers: (1) (b) (2) (c) (3) (b) (4) (a) (5) (b) (6) (c) (7) (d) (8) (d)
           (9) (c) (10) (a)

2.   Problems

(1)   Find $y(0.1)$, using Picard's method, given that $dy/dx = (y-x)/(y+x)$ and $y(0) = 1$.

(2)   Apply Picard's method to obtain, correct to four decimal places, solution of the differential equation $dy/dx = x^2 + y^2$ for $x = 0.4$, given that $y = 0$ when $x = 0$.

(3)   Find $y(0.05)$ and $y(0.1)$, using Picard's method with 3 iterations, given that $dy/dx = 1 + 2xy$, $y(0) = 0$

(4)   Find $y(0.1)$ and $y(0.2)$, using Picard's method with 2 iterations, given that $dy/dx = x + x^4y$, $y(0) = 3$.

(5)   Use Picard's method with 3 iterations to find $y(0.3)$ and $z(0.3)$, given that $dy/dx = xz + 1$, $dz/dx = -xy$; $y(0) = 0$; $z(0) = 1$.

(6)   Use Taylor series method to find $y(4.1)$ and $y(4.2)$, given that $dy/dx = 1/(x^2 + y)$, $y(4) = 4$.

(7)   Use Taylor series method to obtain $y(0.1)$, correct to four decimal places, given that $dy/dx = x - y^2$, $y(0) = 1$.

(8)   Use Taylor series method to compute $y(0.1)$ and $y(0.2)$, correct to four decimal places, given that $dy/dx = \sqrt{x+y}$, $y(0) = 1$.

(9)   Use Taylor series method to find $y(0.1)$ and $z(0.1)$, given that $dy/dx = z - x, dz/dx = y + x$, $y(0) = 1$ and $z(0) = 1$.

(10)   Use Taylor series method of the fourth order to solve the simultaneous differential equations $dy/dx = 2x + yz$; $dz/dx = 2xz + y$, find $y(0.1)$ and $z(0.1)$, given that $y(0) = 1$ and $z(0) = -1$.

(11)   Use Taylor series method to find $y(0.2)$ and $y(0.4)$, given that $y'' = xy, y(0) = 1, y'(0) = 1$.

(12)   Use Taylor series method to find $y(0.1)$ and $y(0.2)$, given that $y'' - x^2y' - 2xy = 1$, $y(0) = 1, y'(0) = 0$.

(13)   Solve the following differential equation by Euler's method for $x = 0.1, 0.2, 0.3$; taking $h = 0.1$; $dy/dx = x^2 - y$, $y(0) = 1$. Compare the result with exact solution.

(14)   Solve the initial value problem $yy' = x$, $y(0) = 1.5$ using Euler's method, taking $h = 0.1$ and hence find $y(0.2)$.

(15)   Find $y(1.9)$, $y(1.8)$ and $y(1.7)$ by using simple, improved and modified Euler's method respectively, if $dy/dx = x + \sqrt{y}$, $y(2) = 4$. Take $h = -0.1$.

(16)   Using Euler's method solve the differential equation $dy/dx = x + y$, $y(0) = 1$ for $x = 0$ $(0.2)1.0$ and compare the result with the exact solution.

(17)   Find the value of $y(1.9)$, using improved Euler's method, given that $dy/dx = (x-y)/(x+y)$, $y(2) = 1$.

(18) Use improved Euler's method to find $y(0.1)$ given
$dy/dx = (y - x)/(y + x), y(0) = 1$

(19) Find $y(-0.2)$ and $y(-0.4)$, by using modified Euler's method, given that
$dy/dx = x^2 + y^2$, $y(0) = 1$ and $h = -0.2$.

(20) Given that $dy/dx = x + y^2$, $y(0) = 1$. Find an approximate value of y
at $x = 0.5$ by modified Euler's method.

(21) Given that $dy/dx = 2 + \sqrt{xy}$, $y(1) = 1$. Find an approximate value of
y at $x = 2$ in steps of 0.2, using modified Euler's method.

(22) Find the value of $y(0.1), y(0.2)$ using Runge – Kutta (i) second order (ii)
third order (iii) fourth order; given that $y' = x - 2y, y(0) = 1, h = 0.1$.

(23) Find the value of $y(1.1)$, using Runge – Kutta (i) third order (ii) fourth
order; given that $y' = y^2 + xy, y(1) = 1$, taking $h = 0.1$.

(24) Using Runge – Kutta method of fourth order, find $y(0.2)$, given that
$y' = 3x + \frac{y}{2}$, $y(0) = 1$, taking $h = 0.1$

(25) Using R-K method of fourth order, find $y(1.2), y(1.4)$, given that
$$dy/dx = \frac{2xy + e^x}{x^2 + xe^x}, \quad \text{with } x_0 = 1, \ y_0 = 0, h = 0.2.$$

(26) The angular displacement θ of a simple pendulum is given by the equation
$$\frac{d^2\theta}{dt^2} + \frac{g}{l} \sin\theta = 0$$
where $l = 98$ cm and $g = 980$ cm/sec^2. If $\theta = 0$ and
$d\theta/dt = 4.472$ at $t = 0$, use Runge – Kutta fourth order method to find
θ and $d\theta/dt$ when $t = 0.2$ sec.

(27) Using Runge – Kutta method of fourth order find $y(0.1)$ and $z(0.1)$,
given that $dy/dx = z + x$; $dz/dx = y - x$; $y(0) = 1; z(0) = 1$.

(28) Using Runge – Kutta method of fourth order find $y(0.1)$ and $z(0.1)$,
given that $dy/dx = \sin x - z + 1$; $dz/dx = \cos x - y$; $y(0)1$;
$z(0) = 2$.

(29) Using Runge – Kutta method of fourth order find $y(0.1)$ and $y(0.2)$,
taking $h = 0.1$, given that $y'' - x (y')^2 + y^2 = 0; y(0) = 1; y'(0) = 0$.

(30) Solve $y' = x^2 + y^2 - 2$ using Milne's method at $x = 0.3$ given
$y(0) = 1$. Find the values of y at $x = 0.1$ and 0.2 using Taylor series.

(31) Given $y' = (1 + x^2)/2$ and $y(0) = 1, y(0.1) = 1.06$, $y(0.2) = 1.12$,
$y(0.3) = 1.21$. Evaluate $y(0.4)$ by Milne's predictor – corrector
method.

(32) Given that
$dy/dx = y - x^2$; $y(0) = 1, y(0.2) = 1.2186, y(0.4) = 1.4682$ and
$y(0.6) = 1.7379$. Find $y(-0.2)$ and $y(-0.4)$ by Milne's predictor –
corrector method.

(33) Find the value of $y(0.3)$, using Adam – Bashforth's predictor –
corrector method, given that
$dy/dx = (x + y)e^{-x}$, $y(-0.1) = 0.9053, y(0) = 1, y(0.1)$

$= 1.1046$ and $y(0.2) = 1.2173$.

(34)   Find $y(0.2), y(0.4)$ and y(0.6) using Runge – Kutta method of fourth order given that $dy/dx = 1/(x + y)$, $y(0) = 2$. Hence, compute $y(0.8)$ using Adam – Bashforth's method.

(35)   Given that
$$dy/dx = (y^2 + xy^2)/2 \; ; y(2) = 1, y(2.1) = 1.1799, y(2.2) = 1.4493$$
$$and \; y(2.3) = 1.8957. \text{ Find } y(1.9) \text{ by Adam – Bashforth's}$$
predictor – corrector method.

(36)   Given that $dy/dx = 3 e^x + 2y; y(0) = 0$, find $y(-0.1)$ and $y(0.1)$ by Taylor's series method, $y(0.2)$ by Runge – Kutta method, $y(0.3)$ by Milne's method and $y(0.4)$ by Adam – Bashforth's method.

(37)   Solve the equation $y''(x) - \frac{14}{x} y'(x) + x^3 y(x) = 2x^3$, for $y\left(\frac{1}{3}\right)$ and $y\left(\frac{2}{3}\right)$, given that $y(0) = 2$ and $y(1) = 0$.

(38)   Solve the equation $y''(x) + (1 - x)y'(x) + xy(x) = x$, given that $y(0) = 0, y(1) = 0, \; h = \frac{1}{4}$.

(39)   Solve the boundary value problem
$$d^4y/dx^4 + 125 x^2 y = 125x \text{ where, } y(0) = 0,$$
$$y'(0) = 0, y(1) = 2, y''(1) = 0 \text{ and } h = 0.2.$$

Answers

(1) $y = 0.9828$ (2) $y = 0.0214$ (3) $y(0.05) = 0.0501$,
$y(0.1) = 0.1007$ (4) $y(0.1) = 3.0050$, $y(0.2) = 3.0202$
(5) $y(0.3) = 0.3450$, $z(0.3) = 0.9909$
(6) $y(4.1) = 4.005$, $y(4.2) = 4.0098$ (7) $y(0.1) = 0.9138$
(8) $y(0.1) = 1.1049$, $y(0.2) = 1.2193$ (9) $y(0.1) = 1.1003$, $z(0.1) =$
1.1100 (10) $y(0.1) = 0.9185, z(0.1) = -0.9137$ (11) $y(0.2) =$
1.00133, $y(0.4) = 1.10947$ (12) $y(0.1) = 1.0053$, $y(0.2) = 1.0227$
(13) $y(0.1) = 0.9, exact\ solution = 0.9052$, $y(0.2) = 0.8110$,
$exact\ solution = 0.8213$, $y(0.3) = 0.7339$, $exact\ solution = 0.7492$
(14) $y(0.2) = 1.5067$ (15) $y(1.9) = 3.6, y(1.8) = 3.2304, y(1.7) =$
$2.880716)$

x	0	0.2	0.4	0.6	0.8	1.0
Using Euler y:	1	1.2	1.48	1.856	2.3472	2.94664
Exact y:	1	1.2428	1.5836	2.0442	2.6511	3.4366

(17) $y(1.9) = 0.9671$ (18) $y(0.1) = 1.09166$
(19) $y(-0.2) = 0.8360, y(-0.4) = 0.7018$ (20) $y(0.5) = 2.2352$
(21) $y(2) = 5.051$
(22) $y(0.1) = 0.825 , y(0.2) = 0.6905\ using\ R - K\ second\ order$
        $y(0.1) = 0.8225 , y(0.2) = 0.68625\ using\ R - K\ third\ order$
        $y(0.1) = 0.82342 , y(0.2) = 0.68791\ using\ R - K\ fourth\ order$
(23) $y(1.1) = 1.2413\ using\ RK\ third\ order$, $y(1.1) = 1.2415\ using\ R -$
        $K\ fourth\ order$
(24) $y(0.2) = 1.1672$ (25) $y(1.2) = 0.1402, y(1.4) = 0.2705$
(26) $\theta(0.2) = 0.8367$, $(d\theta/dt)_{0.2} = 3.6545$
(27) $y(0.1) = 1.1102$, $z(0.1) = 1.1003$
(28) $y(0.1) = 0.9048$, $z(0.1) = 2.0046$
(29) $y(0.1) = 0.9950$, $y(0.2) = 0.9801$
(30) $y(0.3) = 0.61483$ (31) $y(0.4) = 1.27967$
(32) $y(-0.2) = 0.8213$, $y(-0.4) = 0.6899$ (33) $y(0.3) = 1.3361$
(34) $y(0.8) = 2.3164$ (35) $y(1.9) = 0.8715$
(36) $y(-0.1) = -0.2583, y(0.1) = 0.3487$, $y(0.2) = 0.8113$, $y(0.4) =$
1.4168 (37) $y\left(\frac{1}{3}\right) = 1.0315 , y\left(\frac{2}{3}\right) = 2.3222$
(38) $y_1 = -0.0461, y_2 = -0.0693, y_3 = 0.0584$
(39) $y_1 = 0.1736, y_2 = 0.5432, y_3 = 0.9961, y_4 = 1.4823$

Chapter 12   Numerical Solution of Partial Differential Equations

Objectives

- To know the concept of partial differential equation
- To know the difference between ordinary differential equation and partial differential equation
- To classify the given partial differential equation
- To know the concept of solving Laplace equation by finite differences
- To know the procedure of solving Laplace equation
- To know the procedure of solving Poisson's equation
- To know the procedure of solving parabolic equation
- To know the procedure of solving hyperbolic equation

Learning Outcomes

After reading this lesson students should be able to

- Know the concept of partial difference equations and classify them.
- Know the concept of solving Laplace equation by finite differences
- Apply Liebmann's iteration process and relaxation method to solve Laplace equation
- Solve Poisson's equation by finite difference method
- Solve parabolic equations by using Bender – Schmidt's and Crank-Nicolson's method
- Solve hyperbolic equations successfully

12.1 INTRODUCTION

Let us recall that a differential equation contains one or more terms involving derivatives of the dependent variable y with respect to the independent variable x. An ordinary differential equation, called an ODE, is an equation involving a function or functions of one independent variable and its ordinary derivative or derivatives. It is a special case of a partial differential equation but the behaviour of solutions is quite different in general. A partial differential equation(PDE) is a differential equation that involves two or more independent variables, an unknown function (dependent on those variables) and partial derivatives of the unknown functions with respect to the independent variables.

In many applications of applied mathematics, physics and engineering eg. in study of heat equation, diffusion equation, displacement of a vibrating string, wave equation, fluid dynamics, quantum mechanics, elasticity and electro–magnetic theory partial differential equations occur very frequently. In most of the cases, partial differential equations cannot be solved or very difficult to solve by analytical methods in closed form solution, we go in for sufficiently approximate solutions by numerical methods. Of all the numerical methods available for the solution of partial differential equations, the method of finite differences is most commonly used. In this, the derivatives appearing in the equation and the boundary conditions are replaced by their finite difference aproximations. Then this system of linear equations are solved by iterative procedures.

Partial derivatives are denoted by expressions such as

$$\frac{\partial u}{\partial x_1}, \quad \frac{\partial u}{\partial x_2}, \quad \frac{\partial^2 u}{\partial x_1 \partial x_1} = \frac{\partial^2 u}{\partial x_1^2}, \quad \frac{\partial^2 u}{\partial x_1 \partial x_2}$$

Some examples of partial differential equations are

$$\frac{\partial u}{\partial t} = \frac{\partial u}{\partial x_1} + \frac{\partial u}{\partial x_2}, \quad \frac{\partial^2 u}{\partial x_1^2} + \frac{\partial^2 u}{\partial x_2^2} + \frac{\partial^2 u}{\partial x_3^2} = 0 \text{ etc.}$$

Order of a PDE

The order of a PDE is determined by the highest derivative in the equation. For ex.

$$\frac{\partial u}{\partial x_1} - \frac{\partial u}{\partial x_2} = 0 \text{ is a first} - \text{order PDE}$$

$$\frac{\partial^2 u}{\partial x_1^2} + \frac{\partial^2 u}{\partial x_2^2} + \frac{\partial^2 u}{\partial x_3^2} = 0 \text{ is a second} - \text{order PDE}$$

$$\left(\frac{\partial u}{\partial x_1}\right)^4 + \frac{\partial u}{\partial x_2} + u^3 = 0 \text{ is a first} - \text{order PDE}$$

Linear and nonlinear PDEs

A linear PDE is of first degree in all of its field variables and partial derivatives. For example,

$$\frac{\partial u}{\partial x_1} + \frac{\partial u}{\partial x_2} = 0 \text{ is a linear function}$$

$$\frac{\partial u}{\partial x_1} + \left(\frac{\partial u}{\partial x_2}\right)^2 = 0 \text{ is nonlinear function}$$

$$\frac{\partial u}{\partial x_1} + \frac{\partial u}{\partial x_2} + u^3 = 0 \text{ is nonlinear function}$$

$$\frac{\partial^2 u}{\partial x_1^2} + \frac{\partial^2 u}{\partial x_2^2} = x_1 \text{ is a linear function}$$

In this chapter, we restrict ourselves to second order partial differential equations.

12.2   CLASSIFICATION OF SECOND ORDER PARTIAL DIFFERENTIAL EQUATIONS

The general second order linear partial differential equation in two independent variables is of the form

$$A\frac{\partial^2 u}{\partial x^2} + B\frac{\partial^2 u}{\partial x \partial y} + C\frac{\partial^2 u}{\partial y^2} + D\frac{\partial u}{\partial x} + E\frac{\partial u}{\partial y} + Fu = G \qquad \dots\dots\dots (12.2.1)$$

which can be written as

$$A\,u_{xx} + B u_{xy} + C u_{yy} + D u_x + E u_y + Fu = G$$

where A, B, C, D, E, F and G are functions of x and y.

An equation of the form

$$A\frac{\partial^2 u}{\partial x^2} + B\frac{\partial^2 u}{\partial x \partial y} + C\frac{\partial^2 u}{\partial y^2} + f\left(x, y, u, \frac{\partial u}{\partial x}, \frac{\partial u}{\partial y}\right) = 0 \qquad \dots\dots\dots (12.2.2)$$

in which the terms involving the second order partial derivatives alone are linear is known as a quasi-linear partial differential equation of the second order. The Equation (12.2.1) or (12.2.2) is classified as

(1)   elliptic at a point (x, y) in the plane if $B^2 - 4AC < 0$
(2)   parabolic at a point (x, y) in the plane if $B^2 - 4AC = 0$
(3)   hyperbolic at a point (x, y) in the plane if $B^2 - 4AC > 0$

Example 12.1   Classify the following equations:

(i) $x^2 \dfrac{\partial^2 u}{\partial x^2} + 4x\dfrac{\partial^2 u}{\partial x \partial y} + 4\dfrac{\partial^2 u}{\partial y^2} - \dfrac{\partial u}{\partial x} + 2\dfrac{\partial u}{\partial y} = 0$

(ii) $(3 + x^2)\dfrac{\partial^2 u}{\partial x^2} - (2x^2 + 5)\dfrac{\partial^2 u}{\partial x \partial y} + (2 + x^2)\dfrac{\partial^2 u}{\partial y^2} - 4u = 0$

(iii) $x^2 \dfrac{\partial^2 u}{\partial x^2} + (1 - y^2)\dfrac{\partial^2 u}{\partial y^2} = 0, \qquad -\infty < x < \infty, \qquad -1 < y < 1$

(iv) $\dfrac{\partial^2 u}{\partial x^2} + 4\dfrac{\partial^2 u}{\partial x \partial y} + (x^2 + 4y^2)\dfrac{\partial^2 u}{\partial y^2} = \sin(x + y),$

Solution:

(i)   Comparing this equation with Eq.(12.2.1) (or Eq.(12.2.2)), we get
$A = x^2, \qquad B = 4x, \qquad C = 4$
$B^2 - 4AC = (4x)^2 - 4(x^2)(4) = 16x^2 - 16x^2 = 0$, for all x and y
$\therefore$ The equation is parabolic at all points.

(ii)   Comparing this equation with Eq.(12.2.1) (or Eq.(12.2.2)), we get
$A = (3 + x^2), \qquad B = -(2x^2 + 5), \qquad C = (2 + x^2)$
$B^2 - 4AC = (-(2x^2 + 5))^2 - 4(3 + x^2)(2 + x^2)$
$= 4x^4 + 20x^2 + 25 - 4(6 + 5x^2 + x^4) = 1 > 0$, for all x and y
$\therefore$ The equation is hyperbolic at all points.

(iii)   Comparing this equation with Eq.(12.2.1) (or Eq.(12.2.2)), we get

$$A = x^2, \quad B = 0, \quad C = (1 - y^2)$$
$$B^2 - 4AC = (0)^2 - 4(x^2)(1 - y^2) = 4x^2(y^2 - 1),$$

Since for all x, $-\infty < x < \infty$, x^2 is positive

For all y, $-1 < y < 1$, $y^2 < 1$

$\therefore B^2 - 4AC < 0$

$\therefore$ The equation is elliptic at all points.

(iv)   Comparing this equation with Eq.(12.2.1) (or Eq.(12.2.2)), we get

$$A = 1, \quad B = 4, \quad C = (x^2 + 4y^2)$$
$$B^2 - 4AC = (4)^2 - 4(1)(x^2 + 4y^2) = 4(4 - x^2 - 4y^2)$$

$\therefore$ The equation is elliptic, if $4 - x^2 - 4y^2 < 0$

$$i.e \quad x^2 + 4y^2 > 4 \ \Rightarrow \ \frac{x^2}{4} + \frac{y^2}{1} > 1$$

$i.e$ outside the ellipse

The given equation is parabolic i.e. on the ellipse if $\frac{x^2}{4} + \frac{y^2}{1} = 1$

The given equation is hyperbolic i.e. inside the ellipse if $\frac{x^2}{4} + \frac{y^2}{1} < 1$

Some common examples of PDE are

(1) $\dfrac{\partial^2 u}{\partial x^2} + \dfrac{\partial^2 u}{\partial y^2} = 0$ *is a Laplace equation*

(2) $\dfrac{\partial^2 u}{\partial x^2} + \dfrac{\partial^2 u}{\partial y^2} = f(x, y)$ *is a Poisson equation*

Eqs. (1) and (2) are of the elliptic type.

(3) $\dfrac{\partial^2 u}{\partial x^2} = \dfrac{1}{\alpha^2} \dfrac{\partial u}{\partial t}$ *is a one dimensional heat flow equation*

Eq. (3) is of the parabolic type.

(4) $\dfrac{\partial^2 u}{\partial x^2} = \dfrac{1}{\alpha^2} \dfrac{\partial^2 u}{\partial t^2}$ *is a one dimensional wave equation*

Eq. (4) is of the hyperbolic type.

12.3   FINITE DIFFERENCE APPROXIMATIONS TO PARTIAL DERIVATIVES

Consider a rectangular region R in the xy plane. The xy plane is divided into a series of rectangles whose sides are parallel to the x and y axis such that $\Delta x = h$ and $\Delta y = k$ as shown in Figure 12.1. The points of intersection of the dividing lines are called *mesh, lattice, nodal* or *grid points*.

From the Figure 12.1 we have the following finite difference approximations for the partial derivatives.

$$\frac{\partial u}{\partial x} = \frac{u(x + h, y) - u(x, y)}{h} + O(h) \quad (forward\ difference)$$

$$= \frac{u(x,y) - u(x-h,y)}{h} + O(h) \quad (backward\ difference)$$

$$= \frac{u(x+h,y) - u(x-h,y)}{2h} + O(h^2)$$

$$\frac{\partial^2 u}{\partial x^2} = \frac{u(x-h,y) - 2u(x,y) + u(x+h,y)}{h^2} + O(h^2)$$

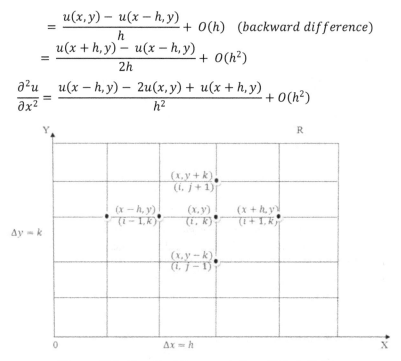

Figure 12.1 Graphical Representation of Mesh Points

The point (ih, jk) is called the mesh point (x,y) and is surrounded by the neighbouring grid points shown in the Figure 12.1. If u is a function of two independent variables (x,y), the value of $u(x,y)$ at the point (i,j) is denoted by u_{ij}. Using this notation, the above approximations become

$$u_x = \frac{u_{i+1,j} - u_{i,j}}{h} + O(h) = \frac{u_{i,j} - u_{i-1,j}}{h} + O(h)$$

$$= \frac{u_{i+1,j} - u_{i-1,j}}{h} + O(h^2)$$

$$u_{xx} = \frac{u_{i-1,j} - 2u_{i,j} + u_{i+1,j}}{h^2} + O(h^2)$$

12.4 ELLIPTIC EQUATIONS AND SOLUTION OF LAPLACE EQUATION BY FINITE DIFFERENCES

The Laplace equation

$$\frac{\partial^2 u}{\partial x^2} + \frac{\partial^2 u}{\partial y^2} = 0 \quad or \quad \nabla^2 u = 0 \quad or \quad u_{xx} + u_{yy} = 0 \quad \dots\dots..(12.4.1)$$

and the Poisson's equation

$$\frac{\partial^2 u}{\partial x^2} + \frac{\partial^2 u}{\partial y^2} = f(x,y) \quad or \quad \frac{\partial^2 u}{\partial x^2} + \frac{\partial^2 u}{\partial y^2} = -f(x,y) \quad \dots\dots..(12.4.2)$$

are known examples of elliptic partial differential equations.

Replacing the derivatives in Eq.(12.4.1) by finite difference approximations (based on central difference operator δ)

$$\frac{u_{i+1,j} - 2u_{i,j} + u_{i-1,j}}{h^2} + \frac{u_{i,j+1} - 2u_{i,j} + u_{i,j-1}}{k^2} = 0$$

We assume a square mesh by taking the step sizes for x and y as $h = k$ in the above equation

$$\frac{u_{i+1,j} - 2u_{i,j} + u_{i-1,j} + u_{i,j+1} - 2u_{i,j} + u_{i,j-1}}{h^2} = 0$$

$$\therefore \ 4u_{i,j} = u_{i-1,j} + u_{i+1,j} + u_{i,j-1} + u_{i,j+1}$$

$$\therefore \ u_{i,j} = \frac{1}{4}\left(u_{i-1,j} + u_{i+1,j} + u_{i,j-1} + u_{i,j+1}\right) \qquad \dots\dots(12.4.3)$$

Eq. (12.4.3) is the finite difference equation corresponding to Eq.(12.4.1).

The value of u at any interior point is the arithmetic mean of the values of u at the four lattice points. This is known as *standard five point formula (SFPF)*. See Figure 12.2

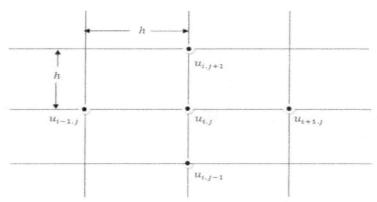

Figure 12.2 Standard Five Point Formula

Instead of Eq. (12.4.3), sometimes a similar formula is used which is given by

$$u_{i,j} = \frac{1}{4}\left(u_{i-1,j+1} + u_{i+1,j-1} + u_{i+1,j+1} + u_{i-1,j-1}\right) \qquad \dots\dots(12.4.4)$$

This formula shows that the value of $u_{i,j}$ is the average of its values at the four neighbouring diagonal grid or mesh points . Eq. (12.4.4) is called the *diagonal five point formula(DFPF)*. Diagramatically it can be shown in Figure 12.3

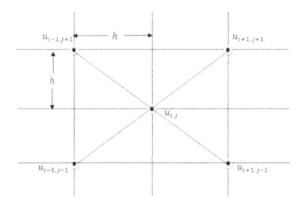

Figure 12.3 Diagonal Five Point Formula

This formula is valid since the Laplace equation remains invariant when the co-ordinate axes are rotated through 45^0 and coincide with the diagonals in the new position. However, the standard five point formula should be prefered over diagonal as the error in the diagonal formula is four times that in the standard formula.

12.4.1 Liebmann's Iteration Process for Solving Laplace Equation

We explain the Liebmaan's process to solve the Laplace equation $u_{xx} + u_{yy} = 0$ in a bounded region R with a boundary C where the values of u are known on boundary. Let the region R be divided into a network of small squares of size h as shown in Figure 12.4. Let the values of u on the boundary C be given by C_i , $i = 1,2,3, ..., n$ and the values of u at the interior lattice points be given by u_i , $i = 1,2,3, ..., n$. To start the iteration process, we find non – zero initial values as explained below in order to get the final values. First we find the crude approximation at interior points and then we improve by iterative process using standard five point formula.

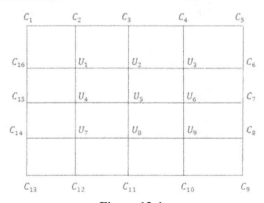

Figure 12.4

Initialize the iterative process by finding u_5 using standard five point formula.

$$u_5^{(0)} = \frac{1}{4} (C_3 + C_7 + C_{11} + C_{15})$$

Now, the values of u_1, u_3, u_7 and u_9 can be computed by using the diagonal five point formula (DFPF).

$$u_1^{(0)} = \frac{1}{4} (C_3 + C_{15} + C_1 + u_5^{(0)})$$

$$u_3^{(0)} = \frac{1}{4} (C_5 + u_5^{(0)} + C_3 + C_7)$$

$$u_7^{(0)} = \frac{1}{4} (u_5^{(0)} + C_{13} + C_{15} + C_{11})$$

$$u_9^{(0)} = \frac{1}{4} (C_7 + C_{11} + u_5^{(0)} + C_9)$$

Finally we compute u_2, u_4, u_6 and u_8 using the standard five point formula (SFPF).

$$u_2^{(0)} = \frac{1}{4} (u_1^{(0)} + u_3^{(0)} + C_3 + u_5^{(0)})$$

$$u_4^{(0)} = \frac{1}{4} (C_{15} + u_5^{(0)} + u_1^{(0)} + u_7^{(0)})$$

$$u_6^{(0)} = \frac{1}{4} (u_5^{(0)} + C_7 + u_3^{(0)} + u_9^{(0)})$$

$$u_8^{(0)} = \frac{1}{4} (u_7^{(0)} + u_9^{(0)} + u_5^{(0)} + C_{11})$$

Now we have all the boundary values and crude approximations of u at every grid point in the interior region of R. To improve the accuracy in u, we start with u_5 and compute u_i, $i = 1,2,...,9$ using the SFPF, by taking the latest available values of its four adjacent points. Thus, the iterative formula is given by

$$u_{i\,j}^{(n+1)} = \frac{1}{4} (u_{i-1\,j}^{(n+1)} + u_{i+1\,j}^{(n)} + u_{i\,j+1}^{(n+1)} + u_{i\,j-1}^{(n)}) \qquad \dots\dots(12.4.5)$$

Eq. (12.4.5) is known as the Liebmann iteration process. The iteration process is stopped when the values of u at each point are equal to the desired accuracy in two consecutive iterations.

Remark: In Eq. (12.4.5), the superscript of u denotes the iteration number. Liebmann's method is nothing but the modified version of Gauss – Seidel method.

Example 12.2 Solve the elliptic equation $u_{xx} + u_{yy} = 0$ for the following square mesh with boundary values as shown.

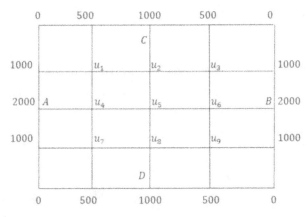

Figure 12.5

Solution: Let the values of u at the interior lattice points be given by u_i, $i =$ 1,2,3, ... , 9. Since, boundary values of u are symmetrical about AB, $u_1 = u_7$, $u_2 = u_8$, $u_3 = u_9$. Also, values of u are symmetrical about CD. Hence, $u_3 = u_1$, $u_6 = u_4$, $u_9 = u_7$.

Thus, we have $u_1 = u_3 = u_7 = u_9$, $u_2 = u_8$ and $u_4 = u_6$

Hence, it is enough to find u_1, u_2, u_4 and u_5 . Now, the initial values are given by

$$u_5^{(0)} = \frac{1}{4}(C_3 + C_7 + C_{11} + C_{15}) = \frac{1}{4}(1000 + 2000 + 1000 + 2000)$$
$$= 1500$$

$$u_1^{(0)} = \frac{1}{4}(C_3 + C_{15} + C_1 + u_5^{(0)}) = \frac{1}{4}(1000 + 2000 + 0 + 1500)$$
$$= 1125$$

$$u_2^{(0)} = \frac{1}{4}(u_1^{(0)} + u_3^{(0)} + C_3 + u_5^{(0)}) = \frac{1}{4}(1125 + 1125 + 1000 + 1500)$$
$$= 1188$$

$$u_4^{(0)} = \frac{1}{4}(C_{15} + u_5^{(0)} + u_1^{(0)} + u_7^{(0)}) = \frac{1}{4}(2000 + 1500 + 1125 + 1125)$$
$$= 1438$$

We continue the iteration procedure using the formulae:

$$u_1^{(n+1)} = \frac{1}{4}(1000 + u_2^{(n)} + 500 + u_4^{(n)})$$

$$u_2^{(n+1)} = \frac{1}{4}(u_1^{(n+1)} + u_1^{(n)} + 1000 + u_5^{(n)})$$

$$u_4^{(n+1)} = \frac{1}{4}(2000 + u_5^{(n)} + u_1^{(n+1)} + u_1^{(n)})$$

$$u_5^{(n+1)} = \frac{1}{4}(u_4^{(n+1)} + u_4^{(n)} + u_2^{(n+1)} + u_2^{(n)})$$

First Iteration: (for n = 0)

$$u_1^{(1)} = \frac{1}{4}\left(1000 + u_2^{(0)} + 500 + u_4^{(0)}\right) = \frac{1}{4}\left(1000 + 1188 + 500 + 1438\right)$$
$$= 1032$$

$$u_2^{(1)} = \frac{1}{4}\left(u_1^{(1)} + u_1^{(0)} + 1000 + u_5^{(0)}\right) = \frac{1}{4}\left(1032 + 1125 + 1000 + 1500\right)$$
$$= 1164$$

$$u_4^{(1)} = \frac{1}{4}\left(2000 + u_5^{(0)} + u_1^{(1)} + u_1^{(0)}\right) = \frac{1}{4}\left(2000 + 1500 + 1032 + 1125\right)$$
$$= 1414$$

$$u_5^{(1)} = \frac{1}{4}\left(u_4^{(1)} + u_4^{(0)} + u_2^{(1)} + u_2^{(0)}\right) = \frac{1}{4}\left(1414 + 1438 + 1164 + 1188\right)$$
$$= 1301$$

Second Iteration: (for n = 1)

$$u_1^{(2)} = \frac{1}{4}\left(1000 + u_2^{(1)} + 500 + u_4^{(1)}\right) = \frac{1}{4}\left(1000 + 1164 + 500 + 1414\right)$$
$$= 1020$$

$$u_2^{(2)} = \frac{1}{4}\left(u_1^{(2)} + u_1^{(1)} + 1000 + u_5^{(1)}\right) = \frac{1}{4}\left(1020 + 1032 + 1000 + 1301\right)$$
$$= 1088$$

$$u_4^{(2)} = \frac{1}{4}\left(2000 + u_5^{(1)} + u_1^{(2)} + u_1^{(1)}\right) = \frac{1}{4}\left(2000 + 1301 + 1020 + 1032\right)$$
$$= 1338$$

$$u_5^{(2)} = \frac{1}{4}\left(u_4^{(2)} + u_4^{(1)} + u_2^{(2)} + u_2^{(1)}\right) = \frac{1}{4}\left(1338 + 1414 + 1088 + 1164\right)$$
$$= 1251$$

Third Iteration: (for n = 2)

$$u_1^{(3)} = \frac{1}{4}\left(1000 + u_2^{(2)} + 500 + u_4^{(2)}\right) = \frac{1}{4}\left(1000 + 1088 + 500 + 1338\right)$$
$$= 982$$

$$u_2^{(3)} = \frac{1}{4}\left(u_1^{(3)} + u_1^{(2)} + 1000 + u_5^{(2)}\right) = \frac{1}{4}\left(982 + 1020 + 1000 + 1251\right)$$
$$= 1063$$

$$u_4^{(3)} = \frac{1}{4}\left(2000 + u_5^{(2)} + u_1^{(3)} + u_1^{(2)}\right) = \frac{1}{4}\left(2000 + 1251 + 982 + 1020\right)$$
$$= 1313$$

$$u_5^{(3)} = \frac{1}{4}\left(u_4^{(3)} + u_4^{(2)} + u_2^{(3)} + u_2^{(2)}\right) = \frac{1}{4}\left(1313 + 1338 + 1063 + 1088\right)$$
$$= 1201$$

Table 12.1 Remaining Iterations

Iteration	n	$u_1^{(n+1)}$	$u_2^{(n+1)}$	$u_4^{(n+1)}$	$u_5^{(n+1)}$
4	3	969	1038	1288	1176
5	4	957	1026	1276	1157
6	5	951	1016	1266	1146
7	6	946	1011	1260	1138
8	7	943	1007	1257	1134
9	8	941	1005	1255	1131
10	9	940	1003	1253	1129
11	10	939	1002	1252	1128
12	11	939	1001	1251	1126

Since the value of u at most of the grid points coincide in the 11th and 12th iterations, convergence has occurred. Hence, $u_1 = 939, u_2 = 1001, u_4 = 1251, u_5 = 1126$

Example 12.3 Given that $u(x, y)$ satisfies the equation $\nabla^2 u = 0$ and the boundary conditions $u(x, y) = 0, u(x, 4) = 8 + 2x, u(0, y) = \frac{1}{2} y^2$ and $u(4, y) = y^2$, find the values of $u(i, j), i = 1,2,3; j = 1,2,3$, correct to two places of decimals, by Liebmann's iteration method.

Solution:

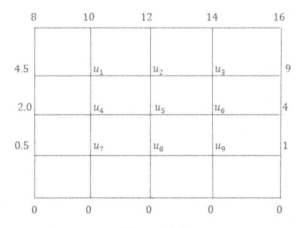

Figure 12.6

Let the values of u at the interior lattice points be given by u_i , $i = 1,2,3, \ldots\ldots, 9$. In this example, boundary values of u are not symmetrical about vertical as well as horizontal lines.

$$u_5^{(0)} = \frac{1}{4} (C_3 + C_7 + C_{11} + C_{15}) = \frac{1}{4} (12 + 4 + 0 + 2) = 4.5$$

$$u_1^{(0)} = \frac{1}{4} (C_3 + C_{15} + C_1 + u_5^{(0)}) = \frac{1}{4} (12 + 2 + 8 + 4.5) = 6.63$$

$$u_3^{(0)} = \frac{1}{4}\left(C_5 + u_5^{(0)} + C_3 + C_7\right) = \frac{1}{4}(16 + 4.5 + 12 + 4) = 9.13$$

$$u_7^{(0)} = \frac{1}{4}\left(u_5^{(0)} + C_{13} + C_{15} + C_{11}\right) = \frac{1}{4}(4.5 + 0 + 2 + 0) = 1.63$$

$$u_9^{(0)} = \frac{1}{4}\left(C_7 + C_{11} + u_5^{(0)} + C_9\right) = \frac{1}{4}(4 + 0 + 4.5 + 0) = 2.13$$

$$u_2^{(0)} = \frac{1}{4}\left(u_1^{(0)} + u_3^{(0)} + C_3 + u_5^{(0)}\right) = \frac{1}{4}(6.63 + 9.13 + 12 + 4.5) = 8.07$$

$$u_4^{(0)} = \frac{1}{4}\left(C_{15} + u_5^{(0)} + u_1^{(0)} + u_7^{(0)}\right) = \frac{1}{4}(2 + 4.5 + 6.63 + 1.63) = 3.69$$

$$u_6^{(0)} = \frac{1}{4}\left(u_5^{(0)} + C_7 + u_3^{(0)} + u_9^{(0)}\right) = \frac{1}{4}(4.5 + 4 + 9.13 + 2.13) = 4.94$$

$$u_8^{(0)} = \frac{1}{4}\left(u_7^{(0)} + u_9^{(0)} + u_5^{(0)} + C_{11}\right) = \frac{1}{4}(1.63 + 2.13 + 4.5 + 0) = 2.07$$

We continue the iteration procedure using the following formulae (from Eq. 12.4.5):

$$u_1^{(n+1)} = \frac{1}{4}\left(4.5 + u_2^{(n)} + 10 + u_4^{(n)}\right) \quad u_6^{(n+1)} = \frac{1}{4}\left(u_5^{(n+1)} + 4 + u_3^{(n+1)} + u_9^{(n)}\right)$$

$$u_2^{(n+1)} = \frac{1}{4}\left(u_1^{(n+1)} + u_3^{(n)} + 12 + u_5^{(n)}\right) \quad u_7^{(n+1)} = \frac{1}{4}\left(0.5 + u_8^{(n)} + u_4^{(n+1)} + 0\right)$$

$$u_3^{(n+1)} = \frac{1}{4}\left(u_2^{(n+1)} + 9 + 14 + u_6^{(n)}\right) \quad u_8^{(n+1)} = \frac{1}{4}\left(u_7^{(n+1)} + u_9^{(n)} + u_5^{(n+1)} + 0\right)$$

$$u_4^{(n+1)} = \frac{1}{4}\left(2 + u_5^{(n)} + u_1^{(n+1)} + u_7^{(n)}\right) \quad u_9^{(n+1)} = \frac{1}{4}\left(u_8^{(n+1)} + 1 + u_6^{(n+1)} + 0\right)$$

$$u_5^{(n+1)} = \frac{1}{4}\left(u_4^{(n+1)} + u_6^{(n)} + u_2^{(n+1)} + u_8^{(n)}\right)$$

First Iteration: (for n = 0)

$$u_1^{(1)} = \frac{1}{4}\left(4.5 + u_2^{(0)} + 10 + u_4^{(0)}\right) = \frac{1}{4}(4.5 + 8.07 + 10 + 3.69) = 6.57$$

$$u_2^{(1)} = \frac{1}{4}\left(u_1^{(1)} + u_3^{(0)} + 12 + u_5^{(0)}\right) = \frac{1}{4}(6.57 + 9.13 + 12 + 4.5) = 8.05$$

$$u_3^{(1)} = \frac{1}{4}\left(u_2^{(1)} + 9 + 14 + u_6^{(0)}\right) = \frac{1}{4}(8.05 + 9 + 14 + 4.94) = 9.00$$

$$u_4^{(1)} = \frac{1}{4}\left(2 + u_5^{(0)} + u_1^{(1)} + u_7^{(0)}\right) = \frac{1}{4}(2 + 4.5 + 6.57 + 1.63) = 3.68$$

$$u_5^{(1)} = \frac{1}{4}\left(u_4^{(1)} + u_6^{(0)} + u_2^{(1)} + u_8^{(0)}\right) = \frac{1}{4}(3.68 + 4.94 + 8.05 + 2.07)$$
$$= 4.69$$

$$u_6^{(1)} = \frac{1}{4}\left(u_5^{(1)} + 4 + u_3^{(1)} + u_9^{(0)}\right) = \frac{1}{4}(4.69 + 4 + 9.00 + 2.13) = 4.96$$

$$u_7^{(1)} = \frac{1}{4}\left(0.5 + u_8^{(0)} + u_4^{(1)} + 0\right) = \frac{1}{4}(0.5 + 2.07 + 3.68 + 0) = 1.56$$

$$u_8^{(1)} = \frac{1}{4}\left(u_7^{(1)} + u_9^{(0)} + u_5^{(1)} + 0\right) = \frac{1}{4}(1.56 + 2.13 + 4.69 + 0) = 2.10$$

$$u_9^{(1)} = \frac{1}{4}\left(u_8^{(1)} + 1 + u_6^{(1)} + 0\right) = \frac{1}{4}(2.10 + 1 + 4.96 + 0) = 2.02$$

Table 12.2 Remaining Iterations

It	n	$u_1^{(n+1)}$	$u_2^{(n+1)}$	$u_3^{(n+1)}$	$u_4^{(n+1)}$	$u_5^{(n+1)}$	$u_6^{(n+1)}$	$u_7^{(n+1)}$	$u_8^{(n+1)}$	$u_9^{(n+1)}$
2	1	6.56	8.06	9.01	3.70	4.71	4.94	1.58	2.08	2.01
3	2	6.57	8.07	9.00	3.72	4.70	4.93	1.58	2.07	2.00
4	3	6.57	8.07	9.00	3.71	4.70	4.93	1.57	2.07	2.00

Since the value of u at most of the grid points coincide in the 3rd and 4th iterations, convergence has occurred. Hence, $u_1 = 6.57, u_2 = 8.07$, $u_3 = 9.00, u_4 = 3.71, u_5 = 4.70, u_6 = 4.93, u_7 = 1.57, u_8 = 2.07, u_9 = 2.00$

12.4.2 Solution of Poisson Equation

As we have discussed earlier, an equation of the form

$$\frac{\partial^2 u}{\partial x^2} + \frac{\partial^2 u}{\partial y^2} = f(x, y) \qquad \qquad \dots \dots (12.4.6)$$

is called a Poisson equation. $f(x, y)$ is a function of x and y only. Since the method of solution is similar to that of the Laplace equation, if we replace derivatives in Eq.(12.4.6) by finite differences the standard five point formula takes the form

$$\frac{u_{i+1,j} - 2u_{i,j} + u_{i-1,j}}{h^2} + \frac{u_{i,j+1} - 2u_{i,j} + u_{i,j-1}}{h^2} = f(ih, jh)$$

where, $x = ih$, $y = jh$ as $h = k$ for square mesh

$$u_{i-1,j} + u_{i+1,j} + u_{i,j-1} + u_{i,j+1} - 4u_{i,j} = h^2 f(ih, jh)$$

$$u_{i,j} = \frac{1}{4}\left[u_{i-1,j} + u_{i+1,j} + u_{i,j-1} + u_{i,j+1} - h^2 f(ih, jh)\right] \qquad \dots \dots (12.4.7)$$

By applying Eq.(12.4.7) at each interior mesh point, we get a system of linear equations in the pivotal values $u_{i,j}$. These equations can be solved by Gauss – Seidal method.

Remark: The error in solving Laplace and Poisson's equations by finite difference method is of the order $O(h^2)$.

The difference equation corresponding to the Poisson equation $u_{xx} + u_{yy} = -f(x, y)$ is

$$u_{i,j} = \frac{1}{4}\left[u_{i-1,j} + u_{i+1,j} + u_{i,j-1} + u_{i,j+1} + h^2 f(ih, jh)\right]$$

Example 12.4 Solve the Poisson equation

$$\frac{\partial^2 u}{\partial x^2} + \frac{\partial^2 u}{\partial y^2} = -10(x^2 + y^2 + 10)$$

over the square mesh given in Figure 12.8 with sides $x = 0, y = 0, x = 3$ and $y = 3$ with $u = 0$ on the boundary and mesh length 1 unit, correct to one place of decimal.

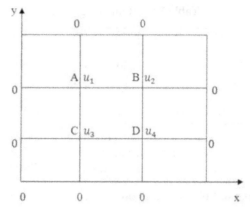

Figure 12.8

Solution: The standard five point formula corresponding to the Poisson equation $u_{xx} + u_{yy} = -f(x, y)$ is

$$u_{i,j} = \frac{1}{4}\left[u_{i-1,j} + u_{i+1,j} + u_{i,j-1} + u_{i,j+1} + h^2 f(ih, jh)\right]$$

i.e. $u_{i,j} = \frac{1}{4}\left[u_{i-1,j} + u_{i+1,j} + u_{i,j-1} + u_{i,j+1} + 10(i^2 + j^2 + 10)\right]\ldots(1)$

($\because$ Here, $h = 1$ and $f(ih, jh) = f(i, j) = 10\,(i^2 + j^2 + 10)$)

The co-ordinates of A, B, C and D are (1 ,2), (2, 2), (1, 1) and (2, 1) respectively. For A(1, 2) i.e. i = 1, j = 2, Eq. (1) gives

$$u_{1,2} = u_1 = \frac{1}{4}\left[u_{0,2} + u_{2,2} + u_{1,1} + u_{1,3} + 10(1^2 + 2^2 + 10)\right]$$

$$= \frac{1}{4}\,(0 + u_2 + u_3 + 0 + 150)$$

$$= \frac{1}{4}\,(u_2 + u_3 + 150) \hspace{4cm} \ldots\ldots(2)$$

For B(2, 2) i.e. i = 2, j = 2, Eq. (1) gives

$$u_{2,2} = u_2 = \frac{1}{4}\left[u_{1,2} + u_{3,2} + u_{2,1} + u_{2,3} + 10(2^2 + 2^2 + 10)\right]$$

$$= \frac{1}{4}\,(u_1 + 0 + 0 + 0 + 180)$$

$$= \frac{1}{4}(u_1 + u_4 + 180) \qquad\qquad \dots\dots\, (3)$$

For C(1, 1) i.e. $i = 1, j = 1$, Eq. (1) gives

$$u_{1,1} = u_3 = \frac{1}{4}\left[u_{0,1} + u_{2,1} + u_{1,0} + u_{1,2} + 10(1^2 + 1^2 + 10)\right]$$

$$= \frac{1}{4}(0 + u_4 + 0 + u_1 + 120)$$

$$= \frac{1}{4}(u_1 + u_4 + 120) \qquad\qquad \dots\dots\, (4)$$

For D(2, 1) i.e. $i = 2, j = 1$, Eq. (1) gives

$$u_{2,1} = u_4 = \frac{1}{4}\left[u_{1,1} + u_{3,1} + u_{2,0} + u_{2,2} + 10(2^2 + 1^2 + 10)\right]$$

$$= \frac{1}{4}(u_3 + 0 + u_2 + 150)$$

$$= \frac{1}{4}(u_2 + u_3 + 150) \qquad\qquad \dots\dots\, (5)$$

From Eq. (1) and (5) it is clear that $u_1 = u_4$. Therefore, above equations reduces to

$$u_1 = \frac{1}{4}(u_2 + u_3 + 150)$$

$$u_2 = \frac{1}{4}(u_1 + u_1 + 180) = \frac{1}{2}(u_1 + 90)$$

$$u_3 = \frac{1}{2}(u_1 + 60)$$

Now, solve these equations by Gauss – Seidal iteration method.

First Iteration: Let us assume that $u_2{}^{(0)} = u_3{}^{(0)} = 0$, we have

$$u_1{}^{(1)} = 37.5,\ u_2{}^{(1)} = \frac{1}{2}(37.5 + 90) = 63.8,\ u_3{}^{(1)} = \frac{1}{2}(37.5 + 60) = 48.8$$

Second Iteration:

$$u_1{}^{(2)} = \frac{1}{4}\left(u_2{}^{(1)} + u_3{}^{(1)} + 150\right) = \frac{1}{4}(63.8 + 48.8 + 150) = 65.7$$

$$u_2{}^{(2)} = \frac{1}{2}\left(u_1{}^{(2)} + 90\right) = \frac{1}{2}(65.7 + 90) = 77.9$$

$$u_3{}^{(2)} = \frac{1}{2}\left(u_1{}^{(2)} + 60\right) = \frac{1}{2}(65.7 + 60) = 62.9$$

Third Iteration:

$$u_1{}^{(3)} = \frac{1}{4}\left(u_2{}^{(2)} + u_3{}^{(2)} + 150\right) = \frac{1}{4}(77.9 + 62.9 + 150) = 72.7$$

$$u_2{}^{(3)} = \frac{1}{2}\left(u_1{}^{(3)} + 90\right) = \frac{1}{2}(72.7 + 90) = 81.4$$

$$u_3{}^{(3)} = \frac{1}{2}\left(u_1{}^{(3)} + 60\right) = \frac{1}{2}(72.7 + 60) = 66.4$$

Similarly,

$$u_1^{(4)} = 74.5, \qquad u_2^{(4)} = 82.3, \qquad u_3^{(4)} = 67.3$$
$$u_1^{(5)} = 74.9, \qquad u_2^{(5)} = 82.5, \qquad u_3^{(5)} = 67.5$$
$$u_1^{(6)} = 75.0, \qquad u_2^{(6)} = 82.5, \qquad u_3^{(6)} = 67.5$$
$$u_1^{(7)} = 75.0, \qquad u_2^{(7)} = 82.5, \qquad u_3^{(7)} = 67.5$$

Since these values are same in 6th and 7th iterations, we have $u_1 = 75.0, u_2 = 82.5$, $u_3 = 67.5$, $u_4 = 75.0$.

12.4.3   Solution of Laplace Equation by Relaxation Method

If we apply Eq.(12.4.7) at each interior mesh point, we get a system of linear equations in the pivotal values $u_{i,j}$ which can be solved by any method. The method of relaxation is particularly best suitable for such situation.

We have already discussed the solution of the Laplace equation (Eq. 12.4.3). Based on that the solution at the point u_1 (See Figure 12.10) is given by the relation

$$u_0 + u_5 + u_6 + u_7 - 4u_1 = 0 \qquad \dots \dots \dots (12.4.8)$$

by standard five – point formula. If R_1 is the residual at the mesh point u_1, then

$$R_1 = u_0 + u_5 + u_6 + u_7 - 4u_1 \qquad \dots \dots \dots (12.4.9)$$

The residual at the point u_0 is defined as $R_0 = u_3 + u_1 + u_2 + u_4 - 4u_0$. Similarly the residuals at all other mesh points are defined.

The main objective of the relaxation method is to reduce the residuals at all the interior mesh points to zero by making them as small as possible at each step.

If the exact values of u_0, u_5, u_6, u_7, u_1 are used in Eq. (12.4.8) (similarly, exact values of u_0, u_5, u_6, u_7, u_1 in Eq. 12.4.9 and so on) then R_1 will be almost zero. We, therefore, try to alter or relax the value of u at internal mesh points at each step.

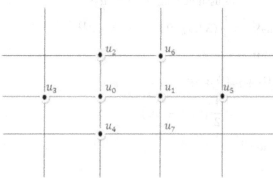

Figure 12.10

But when the value of u is changing at a mesh point, the value of the residuals at the neighbouring interior points will also be changed.

Let u_1 be altered by Δu_1 and ΔR_1 be the corresponding change in R_1. Then

$$R_1 + \Delta R_1 = u_0 + u_5 + u_6 + u_7 - 4(u_1 + \Delta u_1)$$

$$\therefore \ \Delta R_1 = -4 \, \Delta u_1 \qquad \text{(From Eq. 12.4.8)}$$

But when u_1 be altered by Δu_1, we have

$$R_0 + \Delta R_0 = u_3 + (u_1 + \Delta u_1) + u_2 + u_4 - 4u_0$$

$$\therefore \ \Delta R_0 = \Delta u_1$$

Thus, when the value of u at an interior mesh point is altered by some amount δ, the residual at that point gets altered by -4δ and the residuals at the adjacent interior mesh points get altered by δ. We can decide the mesh point and the amount of relaxation in the value of u at that point so as to liquidate the value of the numerically largest residual at any stage of the method.

Example 12.5 Solve by relaxation method, the Laplace equation $u_{xx} + u_{yy} = 0$, inside the square bounded by the lines $x = 0, x = 4, y = 0, y = 4$, given that $u = x^2 y^2$ on the boundary.

Solution: Here, h = 1 and $u = x^2 y^2$.

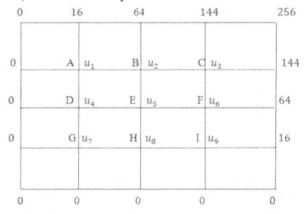

Figure 12.11

First the initial values of u at different mesh points are calculated by using the standard five point or diagonal five point formula (See Eq. 12.4.3 or Eq. 12.4.4). Therefore, the initial values of u at nine mesh points are estimated to be $u_5 = 32, \ u_1 = 24, \ u_3 = 104, \ u_7 = 8, \ u_9 = 24, \ u_2 = 56, \ u_4 = 16, \ u_6 = 56, \ u_8 = 16$. Then residuals at the 9 mesh points are calculated using the following formula.

$$R_{i,j} = u_{i-1,j} + u_{i+1,j} + u_{i,j-1} + u_{i,j+1} - 4 \, u_{i,j}$$

Residual at A = $R_1 = R_{1,3} = u_{0,3} + u_{2,3} + u_{1,2} + u_{1,4} - 4 \, u_{1,3}$

$$= 0 + 56 + 16 + 16 - 4(24) = -8$$

Similarly, $R_2 = 0, R_3 = -16, R_4 = 0, R_5 = 16, R_6 = 0, R_7 = 0, R_8 = 0, R_9 = -8$

The relaxation procedure is given in Table 12.4 in which there are three columns with headings $\Delta u_i, \ u_i \ and \ R_i$ for each point u_i.

Where,

Δu_i = increment given (if any) to u_i at any stage of relaxation

u_i = the current value of u_i after giving the increment

R_i = the current value of R_i after the relaxation

Here, $R_E = 16$ is numerically largest residual, which is to be first relaxed so as to make it either zero or near zero. Since $R_5 = -4\,\Delta u_5$, we choose

$$\Delta u_5 = \frac{R_5}{4} = \frac{16}{4} = 4$$

Due to this increment, u_5 gets revised as $32 + 4 = 36$ and R_5 gets revised as $16 - 4(4) = 0$. At the same time, the adjacent residuals, namely, R_2, R_4, R_6 and R_8 get altered each by Δu_5. Thus,

$R_2 = 0 + 4 = 4$, $R_4 = 0 + 4 = 4$, $R_6 = 0 + 4 = 4$, $R_8 = 0 + 4 = 4$ and so on.

Table 12.4

Trial	Δu_1	u_1	R_1	Δu_2	u_2	R_2	Δu_3	u_3	R_3	Δu_4	u_4	R_4	Δu_5	u_5	R_5
0		24	-8		56	0		104	-16		16	0		32	16
1						4						4	4	36	0
2						0	-4	100	0						
3	-2	22	0	-2								2			
4															
5															

Trial	Δu_6	u_6	R_6	Δu_7	u_7	R_7	Δu_8	u_8	R_8	Δu_9	u_9	R_9
0		56	0		8	0		16	0		24	-8
1			4						4			
2			0									
3												
4			-2						2	-2	22	0
5												

1. In the Table 12.4 we note down by trial. The first line in the table gives the initial values of u_i for all the interior mesh points and their corresponding R_i.

2. The second line shows the increment given to a particular u_i (corresponding to the numerically largest R_i), the revised values of u_i and only those residuals which get revised.

3. After effecting the changes due to the first trial of relaxation, we now relax the next numerically largest residual. The revised values after the second trial of relaxation are shown in the third line of the table and so on.

4. Stop the relaxation procedure when the current values of the residuals are quite small. The solution will be the current value of u at each of the nodes.

In our case, the numerically largest current residual being 2, we stop the relaxation process. Thus, the final values of u are $u_1 = 22$, $u_2 = 56$, $u_3 = 100$, $u_4 = 16$, $u_5 = 36$, $u_6 = 56$, $u_7 = 8$, $u_8 = 16$, $u_9 = 22$.

12.5 BENDER – SCHMIDT'S METHOD FOR SOLVING PARABOLIC EQUATION

$$\frac{\partial u}{\partial t} = \alpha^2 \frac{\partial^2 u}{\partial x^2}$$

One dimensional parabolic heat equation is

$$\frac{\partial u}{\partial t} = \alpha^2 \frac{\partial^2 u}{\partial x^2} \qquad \dots \dots (12.5.1)$$

where, $\alpha^2 = k/CP$, C is the heat of the material, P is the density and k is the thermal conductivity. Consider a rectangular mesh in the $x - t$ plane with spacing h along x direction and k along t direction.

$$x_i = x_0 + ih, \ t_j = t_0 + jk$$

and denoting a mesh point $(x, t) = (ih, jk)$ as i, j, then the finite difference approximation for the partial derivatives of $u(x, y)$ in Eq. (12.5.1) are given by

$$\frac{\partial u}{\partial t} = \frac{u_{i,j+1} - u_{i,j}}{h} \qquad \dots \dots (12.5.2)$$

and

$$\frac{\partial^2 u}{\partial x^2} = \frac{u_{i-1,j} - 2u_{i,j} + u_{i+1,j}}{h^2} \qquad \dots \dots (12.5.3)$$

Substituting Eq. (12.5.2) and (12.5.3) in Eq. (12.5.1), we have

$$u_{i,j+1} - u_{i,j} = \frac{k\alpha^2}{h^2} \left(u_{i-1,j} - 2u_{i,j} + u_{i+1,j} \right) \qquad \dots \dots (12.5.4)$$

Putting $k\alpha^2/h^2 = \lambda$, Eq. (12.5.4) becomes,

$$u_{i,j+1} = \lambda u_{i-1,j} + (1 - 2\lambda)u_{i,j} + \lambda u_{i+1,j} \qquad \dots \dots (12.5.5)$$

Eq. (12.5.5) helps us to determine the value of u at the point $t = t_{j+1}$ in terms of the values of u at $t = t_j$. Eq. (12.5.5) is called *Bender – Schmidt's equation.* This equation is also known as the *explicit formula.*

It gives a relation between the function values at the two time levels $j + 1$ and j. where $j + 1$ is the average of its values of the two adjacent points at the previous time j . Therefore, it is called a $2 - level \ formula.$ It is shown in Figure 12.13.

We simplify Eq. (12.5.5) for a chosen h and k such that co-efficient of $u_{i,j}$ vanishes. $i.e.\ 1 - 2\lambda = 0 \ \Rightarrow \lambda = 1/2$

$$\therefore \ \frac{1}{2} = \frac{k\,\alpha^2}{h^2} \quad \Rightarrow \quad k = \frac{h^2}{2\alpha^2}$$

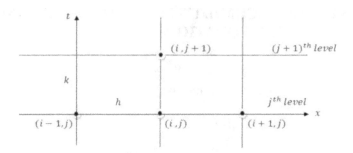

Figure 12.13

Hence, Eq. (12.5.5) reduces to,

$$u_{i,j+1} = \frac{1}{2}(u_{i-1,j} + u_{i+1,j}) \qquad \qquad \dots\dots\dots (12.5.6)$$

This is the simplest form of Bender- Schmidt's difference equation and is called *Bender- Schmidt's recurrence equation*. It reduces the computational work of solving Eq. (12.5.1). We should choose values of h and k such that $\lambda = ka^2/h^2 = 1/2$. If $\lambda \neq 1/2$, we should use Eq. (12.5.5). Hence, Eq. (12.5.5) is valid only for $0 < \lambda \leq 1/2$, it is not stable for $\lambda > 1/2$.

Example 12.6   Find the values of the function $u(x,t)$, satisfying the parabolic equation

$$\frac{\partial u}{\partial t} = 4\frac{\partial^2 u}{\partial x^2}$$

and the boundary conditions $u(0,t) = u(8,t) = 0$ and $u(x,0) = 4x - \frac{1}{2}x^2$ at the points $x = i, i = 0,1,2,3,4$ and $t = \frac{1}{8}j, \ j = 0, 1, 2, 3, 4$ and 5.

Solution: Here, $x = h = 1, \ t = k = 1/8$ and $a^2 = 4$

Hence,

$$\lambda = \frac{k\,a^2}{h^2} = \frac{\frac{1}{8} \times 4}{1} = \frac{1}{2}$$

Now, since the boundary conditions are $u(0,t) = u(8,t) = 0$. Therefore, $u_{0,j} = u_{8,j} = 0$ for all values of j i.e. the entries in the first and last columns are zero. Since,

$$u(x,0) = 4x - \frac{1}{2}x^2$$

$$u_{i,0} = 4i - \frac{1}{2}i^2; \quad i = 0,1,2,3, \dots\dots\dots, 8$$

The values of $u_{i,0}$ are computed and substitute in the table for the row $t = 0$, for $i = 0, 1,2,3, \dots\dots\dots, 8$. These values are 0, 3.5, 6, 7.5, 8, 7.5, 6, 3.5

The simplest form of Bender – Schmidt's difference equation

$$u_{i,j+1} = \frac{1}{2}(u_{i-1,j} + u_{i+1,j}) \qquad \ldots\ldots(1)$$

can be used to get other solutions.

Putting $j = 0$ in (1), we get

$$u_{i,\ 1} = \frac{1}{2}(u_{i-1,0} + u_{i+1,0}) \qquad \ldots\ldots(2)$$

Taking $i = 1, 2, 3, 4, \ldots\ldots, 7$ successively in (2), we get

$$u_{1,\ 1} = \frac{1}{2}(u_{0,0} + u_{2,0}) = \frac{1}{2}(0 + 6) = 3$$

$$u_{2,\ 1} = \frac{1}{2}(u_{1,0} + u_{3,0}) = \frac{1}{2}(3.5 + 7.5) = 5.5$$

$$u_{3,\ 1} = \frac{1}{2}(u_{2,0} + u_{4,0}) = \frac{1}{2}(6 + 8) = 7$$

$$u_{4,\ 1} = \frac{1}{2}(u_{3,0} + u_{5,0}) = \frac{1}{2}(7.5 + 7.5) = 7.5$$

Similarly, $u_{5,1} = 7, u_{6,1} = 5.5,\ u_{7,1} = 3$

These entries are substituted in the second row of the table.

Taking $j = 1$ in (1), we have $u_{i,\ 2} = \frac{1}{2}(u_{i-1,1} + u_{i+1,\ 1})\ for\ i =$ 1,2,3,4, \ldots\ldots, 7 \qquad \ldots\ldots(3)

Using (3), the values of $u_{1,\ 2}$, $u_{2,\ 2}$, $u_{3,\ 2}$ and $u_{4,\ 2}$ etc. are computed and put in the table. Similarly, putting $j = 2, 3, 4$ successively in (1), the entries of the fourth, fifth and sixth rows are obtained. Thus, the values of $u_{i,\ j}$ are given in the following table:

i / j	0	1	2	3	4	5	6	7	8
0	0	3.5	6	7.5	8	7.5	6	3.5	0
1	0	3	5.5	7	7.5	7	5.5	3	0
2	0	2.75	5	6.5	7	6.5	5	2.75	0
3	0	2.5	4.625	6	6.5	6	4.625	2.5	0
4	0	2.3125	4.25	5.5625	6	5.5625	4.25	2.3125	0
5	0	2.125	3.9375	5.125	5.5625	5.125	3.9375	2.125	0

Example 12.7 Solve $u_{xx} = 16\,u_t$, $0 \le x \le 4$, $t > 0$ with the conditions $u(0,t) = 0$, $u(4,t) = 8$ and $u(x,0) = 4x - \dfrac{1}{2}x^2$ taking $\Delta x = 1/2$ *and* $\Delta t = 1$, upto 5 time units.

Solution: Here, $\Delta x = h = 1/2$, $\Delta t = k = 1$ and $\alpha^2 = 1/16$

$$\lambda = \frac{k\,\alpha^2}{h^2} = \frac{1 \times \frac{1}{16}}{\frac{1}{4}} = \frac{1}{4}$$

so that the simplest form of Bender – Schmidt's reccurence equation cannot be used to get the solution.

$$\therefore \ k = \frac{h^2}{2\alpha^2} = \frac{1}{4} \qquad (as \ \alpha^2 = 2, h = 1)$$

Therefore, the general form of Bender – Schmidt's equation

$u_{i,j+1} = \lambda u_{i-1,j} + (1 - 2\lambda)u_{i,j} + \lambda u_{i+1,j}$ should be used with $\lambda = 1/4$

$$i.e. \quad u_{i,j+1} = \frac{1}{4}u_{i-1,j} + \frac{1}{2}u_{i,j} + \frac{1}{4}u_{i+1,j} \qquad \dots\dots(1)$$

Now, the boundary conditions $u(0,t) = 0$, $u(4,t) = 8$ and the initial values for $t = 0$ are first put in the table.

Then the values of u for $j = 1, 2, 3, 4, 5$ are computed by using Eq. (1) and put in the table.

i	0	1	2	3	4	5	6	7	8
	$(x=0)$	$\left(x=\frac{1}{2}\right)$	$(x=1)$	$\left(x=\frac{3}{2}\right)$	$(x=2)$	$\left(x=\frac{5}{2}\right)$	$(x=3)$	$\left(x=\frac{7}{2}\right)$	$(x=4)$
j									
0	0	1.875	3.5	4.875	6.0	6.875	7.5	7.875	8
1	0	1.8125	3.4375	4.8125	5.9375	6.8125	7.4375	7.8125	8
2	0	1.7656	3.3750	4.75	5.875	6.75	7.375	7.7656	8
3	0	1.7266	3.3164	4.6875	5.8125	6.6875	7.3164	7.7266	8
4	0	1.6924	3.2617	4.626	5.75	6.626	7.2617	7.6924	8
5	0	1.6616	3.2105	4.566	5.688	6.566	7.2105	7.6616	8

12.6   CRANK-NICOLSON'S METHOD FOR SOLVING PARABOLIC EQUATION

$$\frac{\partial u}{\partial t} = \alpha^2 \frac{\partial^2 u}{\partial x^2}$$

In Bender – Schmidt's method we require $0 < \lambda \le 1/2$ for convergent results. It is not stable for $\lambda > 1/2$. Though Bender – Schmidt's method is computationally very simple, we require small step size (i.e. h) for obtaining more accurate results. But this makes computations exceptionally lengthy as more time levels would be required to cover the region.

Crank and Nicolson proposed a method that does not restrict λ and also reduces the volume of calculations. In this method we replace

$$\left(\frac{\partial^2 u}{\partial x^2}\right) \text{ by } \frac{1}{2}\left\{\left(\frac{u_{i-1,j} - 2u_{i,j} + u_{i+1,j}}{h^2}\right) + \left(\frac{u_{i-1,j+1} - 2u_{i,j+1} + u_{i+1,j+1}}{h^2}\right)\right\}$$

and

$$\frac{\partial u}{\partial t} \text{ by } \left(\frac{u_{i,j+1} - u_{i,j}}{k}\right)$$

in parabolic equation

$$\frac{\partial u}{\partial t} = \alpha^2 \frac{\partial^2 u}{\partial x^2} \qquad \dots\dots\dots(12.6.1)$$

we get,

$$\frac{u_{i,j+1} - u_{i,j}}{k} = \frac{\alpha^2}{2}\left\{\left(\frac{u_{i-1,j} - 2u_{i,j} + u_{i+1,j}}{h^2}\right) + \left(\frac{u_{i-1,j+1} - 2u_{i,j+1} + u_{i+1,j+1}}{h^2}\right)\right\}$$

$i.e. \quad u_{i,j+1} - u_{i,j}$

$$= \frac{k\alpha^2}{2h^2}\left\{u_{i-1,j} - 2u_{i,j} + u_{i+1,j} + u_{i-1,j+1} - 2u_{i,j+1} + u_{i+1,j+1}\right\} \dots(12.6.2)$$

Taking $\frac{k\alpha^2}{h^2} = \lambda$ in Eq. (12.6.2), we get

$$2u_{i,j+1} - 2u_{i,j} = \lambda\left\{u_{i-1,j} - 2u_{i,j} + u_{i+1,j} + u_{i-1,j+1} - 2u_{i,j+1} + u_{i+1,j+1}\right\}$$

$i.e. \quad -\lambda u_{i-1,j+1} + (2 + 2\lambda)u_{i,j+1} - \lambda u_{i+1,j+1}$

$$= \lambda u_{i-1,j} + (2 - 2\lambda)u_{i,j} + \lambda u_{i+1,j} \qquad \dots\dots\dots(12.6.3)$$

Eq. (12.6.3) is known as *Crank – Nicolson's equation*. Also it is known as the *2 – level implicit formula* as the left side of Eq. (12.6.3) contains three values of u at $(j + 1)^{th}$ level while all the three values on the right side are known values at j^{th} level. Though it is convergent for any value of λ, we take $\lambda = 1$ in order to simplify the computation. It's computational model is given in Figure 12.14.

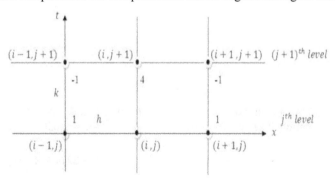

Figure 12.14

For $\lambda = 1$, the *Crank – Nicolson* difference equation takes the simplest form as

$$-u_{i-1,j+1} + 4u_{i,j+1} - u_{i+1,j+1} = u_{i-1,j} + u_{i+1,j} \qquad \dots\dots\dots(12.6.4)$$

The interpretation of Eq. (12.6.4) is that the weighted sum of three adjacent values of u on time level $(j + 1)$ equals the sum of the extreme values of u on time level j.

Example 12.8   Solve the equation

$$\frac{\partial u}{\partial t} = \frac{\partial^2 u}{\partial x^2}$$

subject to the conditions $u(x, 0) = \sin \pi x, 0 \le x \le 1; u(0, t) = u(1, t) = 0$ using Crank – Nicolson method. Carryout computations for two levels, taking $h = 1/3, k = 1/36$.

Solution: Here, $h = 1/3$, $k = 1/36$ and $\alpha^2 = 1$

$$\lambda = \frac{k\,\alpha^2}{h^2} = \frac{\frac{1}{36} \times 1}{\frac{1}{9}} = \frac{1}{4}, \qquad x = ih \Rightarrow x = i/3$$

Since $u(x, 0) = \sin \pi x = \sin \pi i/3$

$$u_{1,0} = \sin \frac{\pi}{3} = \frac{\sqrt{3}}{2}, \quad u_{2,0} = \sin \frac{2\pi}{3} = \frac{\sqrt{3}}{2}$$

and all boundary values are zero as shown *in Figure* 12.15.

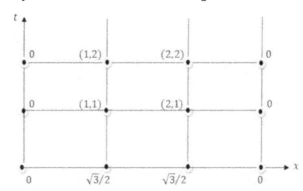

Figure 12.15

Since $\lambda = 1/4$, we can not use the simplest form of *Crank – Nicolson* difference equation. The general form of *Crank – Nicolson* equation (Eq. (12.6.3)) is

$$-\lambda\, u_{i-1,j+1} + (2 + 2\lambda)u_{i,j+1} - \lambda u_{i+1,j+1} = \lambda u_{i-1,j} + (2 - 2\lambda)u_{i,j} + \lambda\, u_{i+1,j}$$

$$\therefore \quad -\frac{1}{4}\, u_{i-1,j+1} + \frac{5}{2} u_{i,j+1} - \frac{1}{4} u_{i+1,j+1}$$

$$= \frac{1}{4} u_{i-1,j} + \frac{3}{2} u_{i,j} + \frac{1}{4} u_{i+1,j} \qquad \ldots\ldots (1)$$

Putting $i = 1, j = 0$ in Eq. (1), we get

$$-\frac{1}{4}u_{0,1} + \frac{5}{2}u_{1,1} - \frac{1}{4}u_{2,1} = \frac{1}{4}u_{0,0} + \frac{3}{2}u_{1,0} + \frac{1}{4}u_{2,0}$$

$$\therefore \quad -u_{0,1} + 10\,u_{1,1} - u_{2,1} = u_{0,0} + 6u_{1,0} + u_{2,0} \Rightarrow 10\,u_{1,1} - u_{2,1}$$

$$= \frac{7\sqrt{3}}{2} \qquad\qquad\qquad \dots\dots..(2)$$

$$(\because \text{From Figure 12.15}, \qquad u_{0,1} = u_{0,0} = 0)$$

Putting $i = 2, j = 0$ in Eq. (1), we get

$$-\frac{1}{4}u_{1,1} + \frac{5}{2}u_{2,1} - \frac{1}{4}u_{3,1} = \frac{1}{4}u_{1,0} + \frac{3}{2}u_{2,0} + \frac{1}{4}u_{3,0}$$

$$\therefore \quad -u_{1,1} + 10\,u_{2,1} - u_{3,1} = u_{1,0} + 6u_{2,0} + u_{3,0} \Rightarrow -u_{1,1} + 10\,u_{2,1}$$

$$= \frac{7\sqrt{3}}{2} \qquad\qquad\qquad \dots\dots..(3)$$

$$(\because \text{From Figure 12.15}, \qquad u_{3,1} = u_{3,0} = 0)$$

Solving Eq. (2) and (3), we get $\quad u_{1,1} = u_{2,1} = 0.673$

Similarly, putting $i = 1, j = 1$ in Eq. (1), we get

$$-\frac{1}{4}u_{0,2} + \frac{5}{2}u_{1,2} - \frac{1}{4}u_{2,1} = \frac{1}{4}u_{0,1} + \frac{3}{2}u_{1,1} + \frac{1}{4}u_{2,1}$$

$$\therefore \quad -u_{0,2} + 10\,u_{1,2} - u_{2,2} = u_{0,1} + 6u_{1,1} + u_{2,1} \Rightarrow 10\,u_{1,2} - u_{2,2}$$

$$= 4.711 \qquad\qquad\qquad \dots\dots..(4)$$

$$(\because \text{From Figure 12.15}, u_{0,2} = u_{0,1} = 0)$$

Putting $i = 2, j = 1$ in Eq. (1), we get

$$-\frac{1}{4}u_{1,2} + \frac{5}{2}u_{2,2} - \frac{1}{4}u_{3,2} = \frac{1}{4}u_{1,1} + \frac{3}{2}u_{2,1} + \frac{1}{4}u_{3,1}$$

$$\therefore \quad -u_{1,2} + 10\,u_{2,2} - u_{3,2} = u_{1,1} + 6u_{2,1} + u_{3,1} \Rightarrow -u_{1,2} + 10\,u_{2,2}$$

$$= 4.711 \qquad\qquad\qquad \dots\dots..(5)$$

$$(\because \text{From Figure 12.15}, \qquad u_{3,2} = u_{3,1} = 0)$$

Solving Eq. (4) and (5), we get $\quad u_{1,2} = u_{2,2} = 0.523$

Thus, we have $u_{1,1} = u_{2,1} = 0.673$ and $u_{1,2} = u_{2,2} = 0.523$.

Example 12.9 Given that $u_t = u_{xx}$, $u(0,t) = 0$, $u(4,t) = 0$ and $u(x,0) = \frac{x}{3}(16 - x^2)$, find $u(i,j)$, $i = 1,2,3$; $j = 1,2,3$, by Crank – Nicolson's method.

Solution: Here, $h = 1$, $k = 1$ and $\alpha^2 = 1$

$$\lambda = \frac{k\,\alpha^2}{h^2} = \frac{1 \times 1}{1} = 1$$

Hence, the simplest form of Crank – Nicolson's difference equation

$$-u_{i-1,j+1} + 4u_{i,j+1} - u_{i+1,j+1} = u_{i-1,j} + u_{i+1,j} \qquad \dots\dots(1)$$

can be used for solution. The boundary values on the lines $x = 0$ and $x = 4$ and the initial values on the line $t = 0$ are as shown in the Figure 12.16.

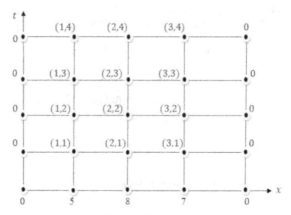

Figure 12.16

Putting $i = 1, j = 0$ in Eq. (1), we get

$$- u_{0,1} + 4u_{1,1} - u_{2,1} = u_{0,0} + u_{2,0} \Rightarrow 4 u_{1,1} - u_{2,1} = 8 \qquad \dots \dots . (2)$$

$$(\because \text{From Figure 12.16, } u_{0,1} = u_{0,0} = 0)$$

Putting $i = 2, j = 0$ in Eq. (1), we get

$$- u_{1,1} + 4u_{2,1} - u_{3,1} = u_{1,0} + u_{3,0} \Rightarrow - u_{1,1} + 4u_{2,1} - u_{3,1} = 12 \qquad \dots \dots . (3)$$

$$(\because \text{From Figure 12.16, } u_{0,1} = u_{0,0} = 0)$$

Similarly, putting $i = 3, j = 0$ in Eq. (1), we get

$$- u_{2,1} + 4 u_{3,1} - u_{4,1} = u_{2,0} + u_{4,0} \Rightarrow - u_{2,1} + 4 u_{3,1} = 8 \qquad \dots \dots . (4)$$

$$(\because \text{From Figure 12.16, } u_{4,1} = u_{4,0} = 0)$$

$$\begin{bmatrix} 4 & -1 & 0 \\ -1 & 4 & -1 \\ 0 & -1 & 4 \end{bmatrix} \begin{bmatrix} u_{1,1} \\ u_{2,1} \\ u_{3,1} \end{bmatrix} = \begin{bmatrix} 8 \\ 12 \\ 8 \end{bmatrix} \qquad \dots \dots . (5)$$

The set of equations (5) can be solved by using any of the mathematical methods. Here we have used matrix inversion method, as the same co-efficient matrix will occur in the equations for $u_{1,2}, u_{2,2}, u_{3,2}$ and also for $u_{1,3}, u_{2,3}, u_{3,3}$.

$$\begin{bmatrix} 4 & -1 & 0 \\ -1 & 4 & -1 \\ 0 & -1 & 4 \end{bmatrix}^{-1} = \frac{1}{56} \begin{bmatrix} 15 & 4 & 1 \\ 4 & 16 & 4 \\ 1 & 4 & 15 \end{bmatrix}$$

From (5), we have

$$\begin{bmatrix} u_{1,1} \\ u_{2,1} \\ u_{3,1} \end{bmatrix} = \frac{1}{56} \begin{bmatrix} 15 & 4 & 1 \\ 4 & 16 & 4 \\ 1 & 4 & 15 \end{bmatrix} \begin{bmatrix} 8 \\ 12 \\ 8 \end{bmatrix} = \begin{bmatrix} 3.1429 \\ 4.5714 \\ 3.1429 \end{bmatrix}$$

Put these values of $u_{1,1}, u_{2,1}$ and $u_{3,1}$ in the second row of the table given below. Putting $i = 1, 2, 3, j = 1$ in Eq. (1), we get

$$\begin{bmatrix} 4 & -1 & 0 \\ -1 & 4 & -1 \\ 0 & -1 & 4 \end{bmatrix} \begin{bmatrix} u_{1,2} \\ u_{2,2} \\ u_{3,2} \end{bmatrix} = \begin{bmatrix} 4.5714 \\ 6.2858 \\ 4.5714 \end{bmatrix}$$

$$\begin{bmatrix} u_{1,2} \\ u_{2,2} \\ u_{3,2} \end{bmatrix} = \frac{1}{56} \begin{bmatrix} 15 & 4 & 1 \\ 4 & 16 & 4 \\ 1 & 4 & 15 \end{bmatrix} \begin{bmatrix} 4.5714 \\ 6.2858 \\ 4.5714 \end{bmatrix} = \begin{bmatrix} 1.7551 \\ 2.4490 \\ 1.7551 \end{bmatrix}$$

Put these values of $u_{1,2}, u_{2,2}$ and $u_{3,2}$ in the third row of the table given below.
Similarly, putting $i = 1, 2, 3, j = 2$ in Eq. (1), we get

$$\begin{bmatrix} 4 & -1 & 0 \\ -1 & 4 & -1 \\ 0 & -1 & 4 \end{bmatrix} \begin{bmatrix} u_{1,3} \\ u_{2,3} \\ u_{3,3} \end{bmatrix} = \begin{bmatrix} 2.4490 \\ 3.5102 \\ 2.4490 \end{bmatrix}$$

$$\begin{bmatrix} u_{1,3} \\ u_{2,3} \\ u_{3,3} \end{bmatrix} = \frac{1}{56} \begin{bmatrix} 15 & 4 & 1 \\ 4 & 16 & 4 \\ 1 & 4 & 15 \end{bmatrix} \begin{bmatrix} 2.4490 \\ 3.5102 \\ 2.4490 \end{bmatrix} = \begin{bmatrix} 0.9504 \\ 1.3528 \\ 0.9504 \end{bmatrix}$$

Put these values of $u_{1,3}, u_{2,3}$ and $u_{3,3}$ in the fourth row of the table given below.

| i | 0 | 1 | 2 | 3 | 4 |
| | $(x = 0)$ | $(x = 1)$ | $(x = 2)$ | $(x = 3)$ | $(x = 4)$ |
j					
0	0	5	8	7	0
1	0	3.1429	4.5714	3.1429	0
2	0	1.7551	2.4490	1.7551	0
3	0	0.9504	1.3528	0.9504	0

12.7 DIFFERENCE EQUATION FOR SOLVING HYPERBOLIC EQUATION

$$\frac{\partial^2 u}{\partial t^2} = \alpha^2 \frac{\partial^2 u}{\partial x^2}$$

Consider the one dimensional wave equation

$$\frac{\partial^2 u}{\partial t^2} = \alpha^2 \frac{\partial^2 u}{\partial x^2} \qquad \dots\dots (12.7.1)$$

which is the simplest form of hyperbolic equation. To solve this equation subject to the initial conditions

$u(x, 0) = f(x)$, $u_t(x, 0) = g(x)$ $0 \le x \le 1$ at $t = 0$ $\dots\dots (12.7.2)$

and the boundary conditions $u(0, t) = \varphi(t)$, $u(1, t) = \Psi(t)$. $\dots\dots (12.7.3)$

We assume a spacing h for the variable x and k for t in the $x - t\,plane$ of the rectangular mesh such that $x_i = x_0 + ih$, $t_j = t_0 + jk$ and denoting a mesh point $(x, t) = (ih, jk)$ as i, j, then the finite difference approximation for the partial derivatives of $u(x, y)$ in Eq. (12.7.1) are given by

$$\frac{\partial^2 u}{\partial x^2} = \frac{u_{i-1,j} - 2u_{i,j} + u_{i+1,j}}{h^2} \qquad \ldots \ldots \ldots (12.7.4)$$

and
$$\frac{\partial^2 u}{\partial t^2} = \frac{u_{i,j-1} - 2u_{i,j} + u_{i,j+1}}{h^2} \qquad \ldots \ldots \ldots (12.7.5)$$

Using Eq. (12.7.4) and Eq. (12.7.5) in Eq. (12.7.1), we get

$$u_{i,j-1} - 2u_{i,j} + u_{i,j+1} = \frac{\alpha^2 k^2}{h^2} \left(u_{i-1,j} - 2u_{i,j} + u_{i+1,j} \right) \qquad \ldots \ldots \ldots (12.7.6)$$

Putting $\frac{\alpha^2 k^2}{h^2} = \lambda$ in Eq. (12.7.6), we have

$$u_{i,j+1} = \lambda \left(u_{i-1,j} + u_{i+1,j} \right) + (2 - 2\lambda)u_{i,j} - u_{i,j-1} \qquad \ldots \ldots \ldots (12.7.7)$$

This is the general form of the finite differential equation corresponding to Eq. (12.7.1). For given h, we choose k such that the co-efficient of $u_{i,j} = 0$

i.e.
$$2 - 2\lambda = 1 \Rightarrow \lambda = \frac{\alpha^2 k^2}{h^2} = 1$$

Replacing the derivatives in Eq. (12.7.2) by its finite difference approximation, we get

$$\frac{u_{i,j+1} - u_{i,j}}{k} = \frac{\partial u}{\partial t} = g(x)$$

$$u_{i,j+1} = u_{i,j} + kg(x) \quad at \ t = 0$$

i.e. $u_{i,1} = u_{i,0} + kg(x) \quad for \ j = 0 \qquad \ldots \ldots \ldots (12.7.8)$

Also, initial condition

$u = f(x) \quad at \ t = 0 \ becomes \ u_{i,0} = f(x) \qquad \ldots \ldots \ldots (12.7.9)$

From Eqs. (12.7.8) and (12.7.9), we have $u_{i,1} = f(x) + kg(x) \ldots\ldots (12.7.10)$
Also, from Eq. (12.7.3), $u_{0,j} = \varphi(j)$, $u_{1,j} = \Psi(j)$

The simplified form of Eq. (12.7.7) is

$$u_{i,j+1} = u_{i-1,j} + u_{i+1,j} - u_{i,j-1} \qquad \ldots \ldots \ldots (12.7.11)$$

Eq. (12.7.11) is an explicit formula as it gives the values of $u_{i,j+1}$ at the $(j + 1)th$ level when the nodal values at $(j - 1)th$ and jth levels are known.
It is to be noted that, if $\lambda > 1$, the solution of Eq. (12.7.7) is unstable and if $\lambda \leq 1$, the solution is stable but the accuracy of the solution is decreased with the decreasing value of λ. Eq. (12.7.11) is diagrammatically represented as shown in the Figure 12.17.

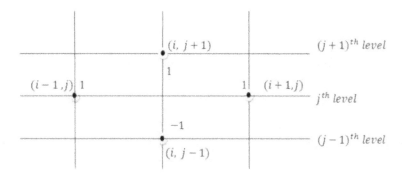

Figure 12.17

The interpretation of Eq. (12.7.11) is that the value of u on time level $(j + 1)$ equals the weighted sum of the adjacent values of u on time level j and time level $(j - 1)$.

Example 12.10   The transverse displacement u of a point at a distance x from one end and at any time t of a vibrating string satisfies the equation

$$\frac{\partial^2 u}{\partial t^2} = 4 \frac{\partial^2 u}{\partial x^2}, \qquad \text{with the boundary conditions}$$

$$u = 0 \text{ at } x = 0, \qquad t > 0$$
$$u = 0 \text{ at } x = 4, \qquad t > 0$$

and the initial conditions $u = x\,(4 - x)$ and $\partial u / \partial t = 0$ at $t = 0,\ 0 \leq x \leq 4$. Solve this equation numerically for $0 \leq t \leq 2$, taking $h = 1$ and $k = 0.5$.

Solution: Here, $\alpha^2 = 4,\ h = 1\ and\ k = 0.5$

$$\lambda = \frac{\alpha^2 k^2}{h^2} = \frac{4 \times 0.25}{1} = 1$$

We can use the simplest form of the difference equation $\dfrac{\partial^2 u}{\partial t^2} = 4 \dfrac{\partial^2 u}{\partial x^2}$ viz.

$$u_{i,j+1} = u_{i-1,j} + u_{i+1,j} - u_{i,j-1} \qquad \dots\dots(1)$$

We have to obtain the solution for $x = 0$ to 4, $t = 0$ to 2. Since $u(0,\ t) = u(4,\ t) = 0$. Therefore, $u_{0,j} = u_{4,j} = 0$ for all values of j. Hence, the entries in the first and last columns are zero. Since $u(x, 0) = x\,(4 - x)$

$$\therefore\ u(i, 0) = i\,(4 - i)\ = 3, 4, 3\ for\ i = 1, 2, 3\ at\ t = 0$$

These are the entries for the first row of the table.
Now, Eq. (1) cannot be used directly for $j = 0$, since it becomes

$$u_{i,1} = u_{i-1,0} + u_{i+1,0} - u_{i,-1} \qquad \dots\dots(2)$$

$u_{i,-1}$ has no meaning. We can get the interpretation for it by using the initial condition $u_t(x, 0) = 0$. The discrete form of this condition is

$$\left(\frac{u_{i,j+1} - u_{i,j}}{k}\right)_{(i,0)} = 0 \qquad as \ t = 0$$

i.e. $u_{i,1} - u_{i,0} = 0$ $\quad or \quad$ $u_{i,0} = u_{i,1}$ $\qquad \ldots \ldots (3)$

Thus, the entries of the second row are the same as those of the first row.

Putting $i = 1, 2, 3$ for $j = 1$ in Eq. (1), we get

$For \ i = 1,$ $\quad u_{1,2} = u_{0,1} + u_{2,1} - u_{1,0} = 0 + 4 - 3 = 1$

$For \ i = 2,$ $\quad u_{2,2} = u_{1,1} + u_{3,1} - u_{2,0} = 3 + 3 - 4 = 2$

$For \ i = 3,$ $\quad u_{3,2} = u_{2,1} + u_{4,1} - u_{3,0} = 4 + 0 - 3 = 1$

These are the entries of the third row.

Similalry, putting $j = 2, 3$ successsively in Eq.(1), the entries of the remaining third and fourth rows are obtained. Hence, the values of $u_{i,j}$ are as shown in the table below:

i / j	0 (x = 0)	1 (x = 1)	2 (x = 2)	3 (x = 3)	4 (x = 4)
0	0	3	4	3	0
1	0	3	4	3	0
2	0	1	2	1	0
3	0	-1	-2	-1	0
4	0	-3	-4	-3	0

12.8 PROGRAMS IN C

12.8.1 Program to find the solution of Laplace equation

```
//Solution of Laplace equation
#include<stdio.h>
#include <math.h>
#include<conio.h>
void main()
{
    float u[20][20], err, diff[20][20], it, utemp[20][20];
    int i,n,j;
    printf("\n\t\t\t SOLUTION OF LAPLACE EQUATION.....");
    printf("\n\t\t-----------------------------------------------------------");
    clrscr();
    printf("\nHow many subsquares you want to enter: \n");
    scanf("%d", &n);
```

```
printf("\nEnter the value of accuracy e: \n");
scanf("%f",&err);
printf("Enter the boundary values u(i,0)for all i\n");
for(i=0;i<=n;i++)
        scanf("%f", &u[i][0]);
printf("Enter the boundary values u(i,%d)for all i\n", n);
for(i=0;i<=n;i++)
        scanf("%f", &u[i][n]);
printf("Enter the boundary values u(0,j)for all j\n");
for(j=0;j<=n;j++)
        scanf("%f", &u[0][j]);
printf("Enter the boundary values u(%d,j)for all j\n", n);
for(j=0;j<=n;j++)
        scanf("%f", &u[n][j]);
for(i=1;i<n;i++)
{   for(j=1;j<n; j++)
    {    u[i][j]= 0.0;
         it = 0;
                          first:
                          it++;

    }
}
for(i=1;i<n;i++)
{   for(j=1;j<n;j++)
    {    utemp[i][j]= (u[i-1][j]+ u[i+1][j]+ u[i][j-1]+ u[i][j+1])/4;
                         diff[i][j]= fabs(u[i][j] - utemp[i][j]);
    }
}
for(i=1;i<n;i++)
{   for(j=1; j<n; j++)
    {    if(diff[i][j] > err)
             goto second;
         else
             goto final;
    }
}
second:
for(i=1;i<n;i++)
{   for(j=1;j<n;j++)
    {    u[i][j] = utemp[i][j];
    }
}
goto first;
```

```
final:
printf("\n");
printf("Solution of Laplace equation for interior mesh points\n");
for(j=1;j<n;j++)
{  for(i=1;i<n;i++)
    {    printf("u(%d,%d) = %f\t", i,j,u[i][j]);
    }
printf("\n");
}
printf("Convergence has occured after %4.0f iterations\n", it);
getch;  }
```

12.8.2   Program to find the solution of Parabolic equation

```
// Solution of Parabolic equation (Explicit Method)
#include<stdio.h>
#include <math.h>
#include<conio.h>
#define f(x)  0.1*x*(5-x)
void main()
{
     float u[20][20], h,k,a,c;
     int i,n,j,m;
printf("\n\t\t\t SOLUTION OF PARABOLIC EQUATION (EXPLICIT METHOD).....");
     printf("\n\t\t------------------------------------------------------------");
     clrscr();
     printf("\n Enter the values of h,k,a,n,m  : \n");
     scanf("%f %f %f %d %d", &h, &k,&a,&n,&m);
     for(j=0; j<=m; j++)
     {
         u[0][j] = 0;
         u[n][j]= 0;
     }
     for(i=1;i<n;i++)
         u[i][0] = f(i*h);
     c = ((a*k)/(h*h));
     for(j=0;j<m;j++)
     {  for(i=1;i<n;i++)
                 u[i][j+1] = c*(u[i-1][j] + u[i+1][j])+(1.0 - 2.0*c)*u[i][j];
     }
     printf("\n");
     printf("The solution of Parabolic Equation with u(x,0)=0.1x(5 - x)\n");
     printf("\n");
     printf("(i , j)\t");
```

```
for(i=1;i<n;i++)
            printf("u(%d, j)\t",i);
printf("\n");
for(j=0;j<=m;j++)
{          printf("(i, %d)\t", j);
              for(i=1;i<n;i++)
                            printf("%6.2f\t", u[i][j]);
              printf("\n");

}
getch();  }
```

12.8.3 Program to find the solution of Parabolic equation by Crank - Nicolson's Method

```
// Solution of Parabolic equation  (Crank - Nicolson's Method)
#include<stdio.h>
#include <math.h>
#include<conio.h>
#define f(x) (x/3)*(16-(x*x))
void main()
{
    float u[20][20], a[20][20], b[20][20],h;
    int i,n,j,m,k;
    printf("\n\t SOLUTION OF PARABOLIC EQUATION BY CRANK -
    NICOLSON'S METHOD.....");
    printf("\n\t----------------------------------------------------------------------");
    clrscr();
    printf("\n Enter the number of sub intervals on the x-axis: \n");
    scanf("%d", &n);
    printf("Enter the number of rows for which solution is required : \n");
    scanf("%d", &m);
    printf("Enter the step size h for x : \n");
    scanf("%f", &h);
    printf("\n");
    printf("j\t");
    for(i=1; i<n; i++)
                printf("u(%d,j)\t", i);
    printf("\n");
    for(j=0;j<=m;j++)
    {
                u[0][j]= 0;
                u[n][j]= 0;
    }
    for(i=1;i<n;i++)
```

```
                u[i][0] = f(i*h);
    for(i=1;i<n;i++)
    {   for(j=1;j<n;j++)
                    if(i==j-1 || i==j+1)
                            a[i][j] = -1;
                    else if(i==j)
                            a[i][j] = 4;
                    else
                            a[i][j] = 0;
    }
    for(i=1;i<n;i++)
    {
        for(j=1; j<n; j++)
        if(i==j)
                    a[i][n+j-1]=1;
        else
                    a[i][n+j-1]= 0;
    }
    for(k=1; k<n; k++)
    {   for(i=1;i<n;i++)
        if(i!=k)
                    for(j=k+1;j<(2*n-1); j++)
                            a[i][j] = a[i][j] - (a[i][k] / a[k][k])*a[k][j];
    }
    for(i=1;i<n;i++)
        for(j=n;j<2*n-1;j++)
                    b[i][j-n+1] = a[i][j]/a[i][i];
    for(j=1;j<=m;j++)
    {           printf("%d\t", j);
                for(i=1;i<n;i++)
                {   u[i][j] = 0;
                    for(k=1;k<n;k++)
                            u[i][j] = u[i][j] + b[i][k]* (u[k-1][j-1]+u[k+1][j-1]);
                            printf("%7.4f\t", u[i][j]);
                }
                printf("\n");
    }
    getch();  }
```

12.8.4   Program to find the solution of Hyperbolic equation

```c
// Solution of Hyperbolic equation
#include<stdio.h>
#include <math.h>
#include<conio.h>
#define f(x) (x/10)*(4-x)
#define g(x) (x/10)
void main()
{
    float u[20][20],h,k,a;
    int i,n,j,m;
    printf("\n\t\t SOLUTION OF HYPERBOLIC EQUATION.....");
    printf("\n\t----------------------------------------------");
    clrscr();
    printf("\n Enter the values of h,k,n,m  : \n");
    scanf("%f %f %d %d", &h,&k, &n, &m);
    for(j=0;j<=m;j++)
    {
            u[0][j]= 0;
            u[n][j]= 0;
    }
    for(i=1;i<n;i++)
            u[i][0] = f(i*h);
    for(i=1;i<n;i++)
            u[i][1] = (0.5)*(u[i-1][0]+u[i+1][0])+ k*g(i*h);
    printf("\n");
    for(j=1; j<m; j++)
        for(i=1; i<n; i++)
            u[i][j+1] = (u[i-1][j]+ u[i+1][j]-u[i][j-1]);
    printf("\n");
    printf("(i,j)\t");
    for(i=1; i<n; i++)
            printf("u(%d, j)\t", i);
    printf("\n");
    for(j=0; j<=m; j++)
    {
        printf("(i, %d)\t", j);
        for(i=1; i<n; i++)
            if(i==n-1)
                    printf("%5.3f", u[i][j]);
            else
                    printf("%5.3f\t", u[i][j]);
        printf("\n");
    }
    getch();   }
```

EXERCISES

1.   Multiple Choice Questions

(1)   If partial differential equation is given as $\frac{\partial u}{\partial x_1} + 5\left(\frac{\partial u}{\partial x_2}\right)^2 - 2u^2 = 0$ then
it is a
   (a)   First order PDE
   (b)   Second order PDE
   (c)   Third order PDE
   (d)   Can't decided
   (e)   None of these

(2)   If partial differential equation is given as $3\left(\frac{\partial u}{\partial x_1}\right)^4 - \left(\frac{\partial^2 u}{\partial x_2^2}\right)^2 + 11 = 0$
then it is a
   (a)   Linear PDE   (b)   Non – linear PDE   (c)   None of these

(3)   The partial differential equation
   $A\, u_{xx} + B u_{xy} + C u_{yy} + D u_x + E u_y + F u = G$ is hyperbolic if
   (a) $B^2 - 4AC < 0$
   (b) $B^2 - 4AC = 0$
   (c) $B^2 - 4AC > 0$
   (d) $B^2 - 4AC \neq 0$
   (e)   None of these

(4)   The partial differential equation $x^2 \frac{\partial^2 u}{\partial x^2} - 2xy \frac{\partial^2 u}{\partial x \partial y} + y^2 \frac{\partial^2 u}{\partial y^2} = 0$ is
   (a)   Elliptic
   (b)   Parabolic
   (c)   Hyperbolic
   (d)   Can't decided
   (e)   None of these

(5)   The error in solving Laplace and Poisson's equations by finite difference method is
   (a) $O(h^2)$ (b) $O(h)$ (c) $O(h^3)$ (d)   None of these

(6)   Which of the following method of solving partial differential equation is used to   reduce the residuals at all interior mesh points to zero by making them as small as possible at each step.
   (a)   Laplace   (b)   Poisson   (c)   Relaxation
   (d)   Bender – Schmidt   (e)   None of these

(7)   Bender – Schmidt's method is a stable method for all the values of λ.
   (a)   True   (b)   False

(8)   What is the stability condition in Bender – Schmidt's method?
   (a) $0 < \lambda \leq 1/2$ (b) $\lambda > 1/2$ (c) $0 < \lambda < 1$
   (d) $\lambda = 1/2$ (e)   None of these

(9) For what value of λ, Crank-Nicolson's method is convergent?
    (a) $0 < \lambda \leq 1/2$ (b) $\lambda > 1/2$ (c)   Any value of λ
    (d) $\lambda = 1/2$ (e)   None of these

(10) Which of the following is the hyperbolic equation?

    (a) $\dfrac{\partial^2 u}{\partial t^2} = \alpha^2 \dfrac{\partial^2 u}{\partial x^2}$

    (b) $\dfrac{\partial u}{\partial t} = \alpha^2 \dfrac{\partial^2 u}{\partial x^2}$

    (c) $\dfrac{\partial^2 u}{\partial x^2} + \dfrac{\partial^2 u}{\partial y^2} = 0$

    (d) $\dfrac{\partial^2 u}{\partial x^2} + \dfrac{\partial^2 u}{\partial y^2} = f(x,y)$

    (e) $\dfrac{\partial^2 u}{\partial x^2} + \dfrac{\partial^2 u}{\partial y^2} = -f(x,y)$

Answers: (1) (a) (2) (b) (3) (c) (4) (b) (5) (a) (6) (c) (7) (b) (8) (a)
             (9) (c) (10) (a)

2.   Problems

(1)   Solve $u_{xx} + u_{yy} = 0$ for the following square mesh with boundary values as shown in Figure 12.18. Iterate until the maximum difference between successive values at any grid point is less than 0.001.

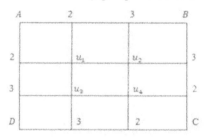

Figure 12.18

(2)   Find the values of $u(x,y)$ satisfying the Laplace's equation $\nabla^2 u = 0$, at the pivotal points of a square region, with boundary values as shown in the Figure 12.19.

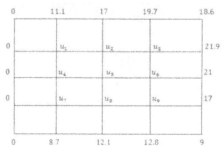

Figure 12.19

(3)   Using central difference approximation solve $\nabla^2 u = 0$ at the nodal points of the square grid of Figure 12.20 using the boundary values indicated.

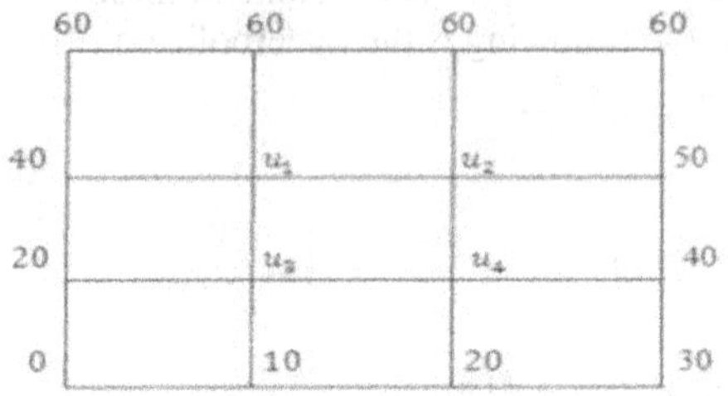

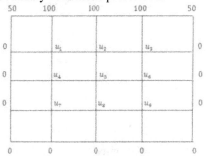

Figure 12.20

(4)   Apply Liebmann's method to approximate the solution of Laplace equation with $h = 1/3$ in a square with the vertices $A(0,0), B(0,1), C(1,1), D(1,0)$ given that the unknown function on the boundary is $u(x,y) = 9x^2y^2$.

(5)   Use Liebmann's iteration method to solve the Laplace equation $\dfrac{\partial^2 u}{\partial x^2} + \dfrac{\partial^2 u}{\partial y^2} = 0$ at the nodal points of the square grid given in the Figure 12.21 satisfying the boundary conditions prescribed.

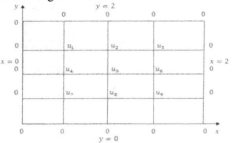

Figure 12.21

(6)   Solve the Poisson equation $\nabla^2 u = -160$ for the square mesh given in Figure 12.22, using the method of iteration, given that $u = 0$ on the boundaries and mesh length $= 0.5$ unit.

Figure 12.22

(7) Solve the Poisson equation $\nabla^2 u = -40$, over the square mesh with sides $x = 0, y = 0, x = 4$ and $y = 4$ with $u = 0$ on the boundary and mesh length 1 unit, correct to integers, using the method of relaxation.

(8) Solve the Poisson equation $\nabla^2 u = -4x^2 y^2$, over the square mesh with sides $x = 0, y = 0, x = 3$ and $y = 3$ with $u = 0$ on the boundary and mesh length 1 unit, correct to two places of decimals, using the method of relaxation.

(9) Given that $\frac{\partial^2 f}{\partial x^2} - \frac{\partial f}{\partial t} = 0; f(0, t) = f(5, t) = 0; f(x, 0) = x^2(25 - x^2)$, find the values of f upto 3 seconds, taking the step size for x as $h = 1$.

(10) Solve $u_{xx} = 32\, u_t$, taking $h = 0.25$, for $t > 0, 0 < x < 1$, and
$u(x, 0) = 0, u(0, t) = 0, u(1, t) = t$.

(11) Solve $u_{xx} = 2\, u_t$, given the boundary conditions $u(0, t) = u(5, t) = 0$ and $u(x, 0) = 100$, find the values of u upto 5 seconds, taking the step size for x as $h = 1$.
(**Hint:** In this example, boundary conditions are $u(0, t) = u(5, t) = 0$. So, $u(0, 0) = 0$ but as per the initial condition $u(x, 0) = 100$, we have $u(0, 0) = 100$ .Thus, u is discontinuous at $(0,0)$. So, we can assume that $u(0, 0) =$ the average of 0 and $100 = 50$ and then proceed.)

(12) Solve the equation $u_{xx} = 2\, u_t, 0 \le x \le 12; 0 \le t \le 12$ with the boundary conditions and initial conditions $u(0, t) = 0, u(12, t) = 9\ and\ u(x, 0) = (1/4)\, x\, (15 - x)$ using the (i) Bender – Schmidt difference equation and (ii) Crank – Nicolson's difference equation, taking h = 3 and k = 3.

(13) Solve, by Crank – Nicolson's method, the equation $\frac{\partial u}{\partial t} = 4 \frac{\partial^2 u}{\partial x^2}$, $0 < x < 4, t > 0$, satisfying the conditions $u(0, t) = 0, u(4, t) = 0$ and
$$u(x, 0) = \begin{cases} 20x, & for\ 0 \le x \le 2 \\ 20(4 - x), & for\ 2 \le x \le 4 \end{cases}$$
Compute u for two time – steps with $h = 1$ and a convenient value of k.

(14) Solve the heat equation $u_{xx} = u_t, 0 < x < 5, t > 0$ by Crank – Nicolson method satisfying the conditions $u(x, 0) = 20, u(0, t) = 0, u(5, t) = 100$ and taking $h = k = 1$.

(15) Solve, by Crank – Nicolson's method, the equation $\frac{\partial u}{\partial t} = \frac{\partial^2 u}{\partial x^2}$, $0 < x < 1, t > 0$, satisfying the conditions $u(0, t) = 0, u(1, t) = 0$ and $u(x, 0) = 100x(1 - x)$, taking $h = 0.25$ for one time step.

(16) Evaluate the pivotal values of the equation $25u_{xx} - u_{tt} = 0$ for one half period of vibration given $u(0, t) = 0, u(5, t) = 0$ and $u_t(x, 0) = 0$

$$u(x,0) = \begin{cases} 2x & for\ 0 \leq x \leq\leq 2.5 \\ 10 - 2x & for\ 2.5 \leq x \leq 5 \end{cases}$$

(17)   Solve the equation $u_{tt} = u_{xx}$, for $x = 0\ (0.2)1$ and $t = 0\ (0.2)1$, given that $u(0,t) = 0$, $u(1,t) = 0$, $u(x,0) = x(1-x)$ and $u_t(x,0) = 1$

Answers

(1) $u_1 = u_4 = 2.333,\ u_2 = u_3 = 2.667$

(2) $u_1 = 7.9, u_2 = 13.7, u_3 = 17.9, u_4 = 6.6, u_5 = 11.9, u_6 = 16.3, u_7 = 6.6, u_8 = 11.2,\ u_9 = 14.3$

(3) $u_1 = 26.66, u_2 = 33.33, u_3 = 43.33, u_4 = 46.66$

(4) $u_1 = u_4 = 80.999,\ u_2 = 202.499, u_3 = 40.999$

(5) $u_1 = u_3 = 42.86;\ u_2 = 52.68;\ u_4 = u_6 = 18.75;\ u_5 = 25.00;$ $u_7 = u_9 = 7.14;\ u_8 = 9.82$

(6) $u_1 = u_3 = u_7 = u_9 = 28, = u_2 u_4 = u_6 = u_8 = 35,\ u_5 = 45$

(7) $u_1 = u_3 = u_7 = u_9 = 28,\ u_2 = u_4 = u_6 = u_8 = 35,\ u_5 = 45$

(8) $u_1 = u_4 = 11.00,\ u_2 = 21.50,\ u_3 = 6.50$

(9)

i \ j	0 (x = 0)	1 (x = 1)	2 (x = 2)	3 (x = 3)	4 (x = 4)	5 (x = 5)
0	0	24	84	144	144	0
1	0	42	84	114	72	0
2	0	42	78	78	57	0
3	0	39	60	67.5	39	0
4	0	30	53.25	49.5	33.75	0
5	0	26.625	39.75	43.5	24.75	0
6	0	19.875	35.0625	32.25	21.75	0

(10)

i \ j	0 (x = 0)	1 (x = 1)	2 (x = 2)	3 (x = 3)	4 (x = 4)
0	0	0	0	0	0
1	0	0	0	0	1
2	0	0	0	0.5	2
3	0	0	0.25	1	3
4	0	0.125	0.5	1.625	4
5	0	0.25	0.875	2.25	5

(11)

i / j	0 (x = 0)	1 (x = 1)	2 (x = 2)	3 (x = 3)	4 (x = 4)	5 (x = 5)	6 (x = 6)
0	50	100	100	100	100	100	100
1	0	75	100	100	100	100	100
2	0	50	87.5	100	100	100	100
3	0	43.75	75	93.75	100	100	100
4	0	37.5	68.75	87.5	96.875	100	0
5	0	34.375	62.5	82.8125	93.75	96.875	0

(12)

i / j	1	2	3
1	8.25	12.75	12.75
2	7.625	12	12.125
3	7.083	11.292	11.583
4	6.604	10.639	11.104

i / j	1	2	3
1	8.3008	12.7113	12.1580
2	7.6858	11.8815	11.0838
3	7.1289	11.0652	10.1989
4	6.6174	10.2893	9.4531

(13)

x / t	1	2	3
1/4	14.2857	17.1429	14.2857
1/2	6.9388	10.6122	6.9388

(14)

0	20	20	20	20	100
0	9.80	20.19	30.72	59.92	100

(15)

x / t	0	0.25	0.5	0.75	1
0	0	18.75	25.00	18.75	0
1/16	0	9.82	14.29	9.82	0

(16)

i \ j	0	1	2	3	4	5
0	0	-2	4	4	2	0
1	0	2	3	3	2	0
2	0	1	1	1	1	0
3	0	-1	-1	-1	-1	0
4	0	-2	-3	-3	-2	0
5	0	-2	-4	-4	-2	0

(17)

i \ j	1 (x=0.2)	2 (x = 0.4)	3 (x = 0.6)	4 (x=0.8)
1 (t=0.2)	0.32	0.40	0.40	0.32
2 (t=0.4)	0.24	0.48	0.48	0.24
3 (t = 0.6)	0.16	0.32	0.32	0.16
4 (t = 0.8)	0.08	0	0	0.8
5 (t=1)	-0.16	-0.24	-0.24	-0.16

APPENDIX - I

Case Studies / Applications

We discuss here some applications on different disciplines like environmental science, engineeering etc. and try to solve few questions related to the study. We have also performed sensitivity analysis on these cases. The purpose of these case studies are to relate theoretical concepts with practical applications.

1. Application of System of Linear Equations and Gauss – Jordan method to Environmental Science

Problem: We start with the problem where there is one species of population and they are feeding on two species of insects. Our problem is to determine the average caloric value a fish is getting from a particular species of insect.

In a lake there are a lot of trout and they are feeding on moths and midges. We want to determine how much caloric value a trout is getting from moths and midges. This is really a difficult task as one can not measure that how many moths and midges they take daily on an average and secondly, it is really difficult to say that whether they eat insects other than moths and midges or not and in how much quantity. For making things easier, we will assume that all the trout in the lake only feeding on these two types of insects.

To initialize the process, we can catch some trout and examine the content in the stomach. We can also count the head of each moths and midges to determine how many moths and midges the trout had eaten. We will then use a calorimeter to measure the total caloric value of the stomach's content. Suppose we do this for two fish and get the following data:

Fish	Number of Moths	Number of Midges	Total caloric value of the stomach
A	12	18	660
B	8	14	480

Let's prepare a mathematical model from the above data.
Let x_1 represent the average caloric content of midges eaten and x_2 represent the average caloric content of moths eaten. Hence, the unit of x_1 is cal / midges and x_2 is cal / moths. Then the above data can be converted to the following two equations and two unknowns :

$$18x_1 + 12 x_2 = 660; \quad 14 x_1 + 8 x_2 = 480$$

If we solve these equations by any methods we get $x_1 = 20 \; cal/midges$ and $x_2 = 25 \; cal/moths$.

In previous scenario, we have included the measurements taken from only two fishes. If we take another two fishes, we might get a little different measurement and thus the values for x_1 and x_2 will also change. One way to remedy the situation is to find several possible values of x_1 and x_2 and then take the average. This average might be a good approximation of the actual answer. Let's say you caught four more trout and take the measurement and record this in the following table:

Fish	Number of Moths	Number of Midges	Total caloric value of the stomach
C	23	16	890
D	15	8	540
E	5	9	295
F	17	14	730

Sensitivity Analysis:

One reason that one could get different measurement for different fish has to do with different sizes of moths and midges. Some moths are bigger in size that the other moths. So the bigger moths will supply more caloric value than the smaller moths. Similar reason can apply for midges. In real life trout are not just feeding on moths and midges. They have other foods and this also contribute to the total caloric value in the stomach. But for simplicity, we assume our trout population only feed on moths and midges. When we calculate the total caloric value of the stomach by a calorimeter, this measurment is never exact. It is very hard to get a very accurate measurement of the caloric value. Hence, there is always a chance of errors in this measurment. So we are interested to know how sensitive our final answer is going to be on the potential errors of the measurement of the total caloric value.

We believe that there is a chance of 10% of error when we measure the caloric value. For fish A, the original measurement of total caloric value of the stomach's content is 660. But for a 10% error, we will incorporate $660 \pm 10\%$ of 660. Thus, the highest possible value is $660 + (0.1)(660) = 726$ and the lowest possible value is $660 - (0.1)(660) = 594$. Similarly the highest and lowest possible values for fish B are 528 and 432 respectively. We put all this information in the following table. We incorporate all four possibilities in the table.

Fish	Number of Moths	Number of Midges	Original Total caloric value of the stomach	A large B small	A small B small	A large B large	A small B large
A	12	18	660	726	594	726	594
B	8	14	480	432	432	528	528

The corresponding augmented matrix is

$$
\begin{array}{ccccccc}
12 & 18 & 660 & 726 & 594 & 726 & 594 \\
8 & 14 & 480 & 432 & 432 & 528 & 528
\end{array}
$$

One can perform Gauss – Jordan elimination using any tool and find the corresponding row reduced echelon form of the matrix.

Analysis:

From the previous problem, the five solutions for the five different output are given below:

x_1	20	-26	18	22	66
x_2	25	99.5	22.5	27.5	-49.5

One interesting note is that here we get some negative answer and the caloric value cannot be negative. So these are called errornous solutions. The main problem to this particular situation that there is no "*good way*" to determine or measure the average caloric value.

But let's analyze the solution further. It is clear from the table that 10% error cause the solution to differ dramatically. The value of x_1 range from 66 to -26 while the value of x_2 range from 99.5 to -49.5. This is an example of a linear system which is ill determined.

In real life we will probably end up with a bigger system of linear equations sometimes in the range of 100's of equations. In this case Gauss – Jordan elimination can be slow and time consuming and Gauss – Seidel method would be better.

This application is included here with the permission of the author.
Reference: Prince T. , Angulo N. (2015) Application of System of Linear Equations and Gauss – Jordan Elimination to Environmental Science. SOP Transactions on Applied Mathematics, 2 (1).

2. Application of Eigenvalues and Eigenvectors and Diagonalization to Environmental Science

Problem: Let's consider certain female population of a specific species of rabbits in the amazon rain forest. Let's say these species of rabbits only has four age groups as follows:

P_0 = age 0 = any rabbits that born on the current breeding season
P_1 = age 1 = any 0 age rabbits that is survived to the end of the year and move to the next stage
P_2 = age 2 = any 1 age rabbits that is survived to the end of the year and move to the next stage
P_3 = age 3 = any 2 age rabbits that is survived to the end of the year and move to the next stage

We will assume that the life cycle of this species of rabbits is ended in these four steps. That is any rabbit that survive in the age group 3 at the end of the year, all (or most of them) will die. The limited number that will survive will not affect the total number and can be ignored.

Now, each age group has certain mortality rate and certain reproduction rate. We will now describe this below:

P_0 = This group is too young. So this has no repreoduction rate
P_1 = Let say that this age group produce an average of 1.2 female rabbits which will survive
P_2 = This is the young generation and thus will have highest rate of reproduction. Let say that this age group produce an average of 1.5 female rabbits which will survive
P_3 = Since this is the oldest age, we may guess that this age group will have lowest rate of reproduction. Let say that this age group produce an average of 0.7 female rabbits which will survive

We will also make the following assumption about the surviving probability of each age group to the next age groups as follows:
50% of P_0 population survive from t to t + 1
35% of P_1 population survive from t to t + 1
15% of P_2 population survive from t to t + 1
0% of P_3 population survive from t to t + 1

In any given time, we will represent the total population as a vector:

$$P(t) = \begin{pmatrix} P_0(t) \\ P_1(t) \\ P_2(t) \\ P_3(t) \end{pmatrix}$$

This represent the population in time "t" of each of the age groups.

We want to find $\vec{P}(t+1)$ from $\vec{P}(t)$. This will be available by the following matrix multiplication.

$$\vec{P}(t+1) = \begin{pmatrix} P_0(t+1) \\ P_1(t+1) \\ P_2(t+1) \\ P_3(t+1) \end{pmatrix} = \begin{pmatrix} 0 & 1.2 & 1.5 & 0.7 \\ 0.5 & 0 & 0 & 0 \\ 0 & 0.35 & 0 & 0 \\ 0 & 0 & 0.15 & 0 \end{pmatrix} \begin{pmatrix} P_0(t) \\ P_1(t) \\ P_2(t) \\ P_3(t) \end{pmatrix}$$

This four by four matrix is known as the Leslie matrix. Since we only consider four age groups, we ended up with a four by four Leslie matrix. Let us assume the initial population is given by (in terms of thousand) and the time t is measured in years.

$$\vec{P}(t) = \begin{pmatrix} P_0(0) \\ P_1(0) \\ P_2(0) \\ P_3(0) \end{pmatrix} = \begin{pmatrix} 2 \\ 3 \\ 4 \\ 3 \end{pmatrix}$$

Use this initial population and the matrix equation to find the population after 1 year, after 2 year etc. From the above Leslie matrix we can easily find eigen values which , in our case, are *-0.430128 – 0.193858 i , -0.430128 + 0.193858 i , -0.087135 and 0.947391.*

Analysis:

We can analyze the long term behaviour of the Leslie matrix L (i.e. $\lim_{k \to \infty} L^k$) We can also calculate the power of matrix applied to a specific initial vector. That is, we will start with a given initial population and Leslie matrix and try to find the long term population where the initial population is approaching (if there is any). That means we can find the population after 10 , 15, after 20 years and after 50 years by taking different initial population. Given the Leslie matrix, we can compute its eigenvalues and eigenvectors correspond to population growth rate, stable age distribution and reproductive value. From the characteristic equation we can get several roots some of which may be real and some imaginary. The root with the largest absolute value is the *"dominant"* eigenvalue (refer [1]Lotka – Euler equation) and will determine population growth in the long run. The other eigenvalues will determine transient dynamics of the population. From the two sets of eigenvectors associated with the dominant eigenvalue, the right eigenvectors comprise the stable age distribution and left eigen vectors comprise the reproductive value.

---

[1]The Lotka – Euler equation has exactly one positive root. It is known as the dominate eigen value of Leslie matrix. This application is included here with the permission of the author.
Reference: Prince T. , Angulo N. (2014) Application of Eigenvalues and Eigenvectors and Diagonalization to Environmental Science. Applied Ecology and Environmental Sciences, 2(4), 106-109.

In this section, we give some references from where one can find more case studies / applications on different topics of numerical methods.

(1)   Adejumobi, I. A., & Adepoju, G. A. (2013). Iterative techniques for Load Flow Study: A Comparative Study for Nigeria 330 kV Grid System as a Case Study. *International Journal of Engineering Advanced Technology*, *3*, 153-157.

(2)   Islam, M. R., & Alias, N. (2010). A case study: 2D Vs 3D partial differential equation toward tumour cell visualisation on multicore parallel computing atmosphere. *International Journal for the Advancement of Science and Arts*, *10*(1), 25-35.

(3)   Thompson, C. A. (1992). A study of numerical integration techniques for use in the companion circuit method of transient circuit analysis. *ECE Technical Reports*, 297.

(4)   Maiden, Y., Jervis, B. W., Fouillat, P., & Lesage, S. (1999). Using artificial neural networks or Lagrange interpolation to characterize the faults in an analog circuit: An experimental study. *IEEE Transactions on Instrumentation and Measurement*, *48*(5), 932-938.

APPENDIX - II

Synthetic Division

Any polynomial of degree n can be written as

$$p(x) = a_0 x^n + a_1 x^{n-1} + a_2 x^{n-2} + \ldots\ldots\ldots + a_{n-1}x + a_n.$$

Hence, $p(x) = (x - x_i)q(x)$ where, x_i is a root of the polynomial $p(x)$ and $q(x)$ is the quotient polynomial of degree $n - 1$. We have to find an initial root x_i of the polynomial $p(x)$. Once a root is found, we divide the polynomial $p(x)$ by $(x - x_i)$ to obtain a lower degree polynomial $q(x)$.

This process of reducing the degree of a polynomial by dividing a polynomial by another polynomial (quotient polynomial) is known as synthetic division. The process of reducing the degree of a polynomial is known as *deflation*. Synthetic division is generally used for finding zeroes (or roots) of polynomials. The polynomial $q(x)$ is used to obtain other roots of polynomial $p(x)$, as the remaining roots of $p(x)$ are the roots of $q(x)$. When a root of $q(x)$ is found it is used for further deflation. The process is continued till the degree is reduced to one. Let's understand the process of synthetic division.

Let $p(x) = a_0 x^n + a_1 x^{n-1} + a_2 x^{n-2} + \ldots\ldots\ldots + a_{n-1}x + a_n$ and α is a root. Hence, $(x - \alpha)$ is one of the factors of $p(x)$.

α	a_0	a_1	a_2	....	a_{n-1}	a_n
	0	αb_0	αb_1	....	αb_{n-2}	αb_{n-1}
	a_0 $= b_0$	$a_1 + \alpha b_0$ $= b_1$	$a_2 + \alpha b_1$ $= b_2$	....	$a_{n-1} + \alpha b_{n-2}$ $= b_{n-1}$	$a_n + \alpha b_{n-1}$ $= R$

Therefore, quotient $= b_0 x^{n-1} + b_1 x^{n-2} + \ldots\ldots\ldots + b_{n-1}$ and remainder $= R$.
Here quotient polynomial $q(x)$ is obtained without performing actual division and hence this process is known as synthetic division (not actual division).

Similarly, the division of the polynomial $p(x)$ by the quadratic factor $x^2 - \alpha x - \beta$ is performed by synthetic division as follows:

	a_0	a_1	a_2	....	a_{n-1}	a_n
α	0	αb_0	αb_1	....	αb_{n-2}	αb_{n-1}
β			βb_0		βb_{n-3}	βb_{n-2}
	a_0 $= b_0$	$a_1 + \alpha b_0$ $= b_1$	$a_2 + \alpha b_1 + \beta b_0$ $= b_2$	....	$a_{n-1} + \alpha b_{n-2} +$ $\beta b_{n-3} = b_{n-1}$	$a_n + \alpha b_{n-1} + \beta b_{n-2}$ $= R$

Therefore, the quotient $= b_0 x^{n-2} + b_1 x^{n-3} + \ldots\ldots\ldots + b_{n-2}$ and remainder $=$ $b_{n-1}x + b_n$

Bibliography

1. Atkinson, L V, P J Harley and J D Hudson, Numerical Methods with *FORTRAN 77*, Addison – Wesley Publishing Company, 1989.
2. Balagurusamy, E, Numerical Methods, Tata McGraw – Hill Publishing Company, New Delhi, 1999.
3. Chapra, S. C. and R. P Canale, Numerical Methods for Engineers, Fifth Edition, McGraw – Hill Book Company, 2007.
4. Datta N, Computer Oriented Numerical Methods, Vikas Publishing House Pvt Ltd, New Delhi, 2004.
5. Gerald, C F and P O Wheatly, Applied Numerical Analysis, Fifth Edition, Addison – Wesley Publishing Company, 1994.
6. Jain M K, Numerical Solution of Differential Equations, Wiley Eastern Ltd., New Delhi, 1979
7. Jain M K, S. R. K. Iyengar and R. K. Jain, Numerical Methods for Scientific and Engineering Computation, New Age International Publishers, India, 2003.
8. Mathews, J H, Numerical Methods for Mathematics, Science and Engineering, Second Edition, Prentice – Hall of India, 1994.
9. Mollah S A, Numerical Analysis and Computational Procedures, Books and Allied Pvt. Ltd, 1996.
10. Sastry, S S, Introductory Methods of Numerical Analysis, Third Edition, Prentice – Hall of India, 2001.
11. Pal S, Numerical Methods Principles, Analyses and Algorithms, First Edition, Oxford University Press, 2009
12. Rao A. R. and P. Bhimasankaram, Linear Algebra, Tata McGraw – Hill, 1992.
13. Scarborough, J.B, Numerical Mathematical Analysis, Oxford & IBH Publishing Co., New Delhi, 1966.
14. Scheid, F., Theory and Problems of Numerical Analysis, McGraw-Hill, New York, 1968.
15. Veerarajan, T and T Ramachandran, Numerical Methods with Programs in C, Second Edition, Tata McGraw- Hill Publishing Company, New Delhi, 2006.

INDEX

www.ingramcontent.com/pod-product-compliance
Lightning Source LLC
Chambersburg PA
CBHW071353050326
40689CB00010B/1633